Wilderness *at the* Edge

Wilderness
at the Edge

A Citizen Proposal to Protect Utah's Canyons and Deserts.

Introduction by Wallace Stegner
Foreword by The Hon. Wayne Owens

The Utah Wilderness Coalition

Copyright ©1990 by The Foundation for the Utah Wilderness Coalition.
All rights reserved. Text excerpts and maps may be reproduced noncom-
mercially in critical reviews or to publicize UWC's wilderness proposals.
For other uses, call (801) 532-5959 or (801) 355-4742. Relief base map
layers ©1990 by Ray Wheeler [except West Desert and Book Cliffs relief
base map layers ©1961 by Merrill K. Ridd]. Used by permission.

Published by The Utah Wilderness Coalition,
P.O. Box 11446, Salt Lake City, UT 84147.
Distributed to the book trade by:
Gibbs Smith, Publisher
Peregrine Smith Books
P.O. Box 667
Layton, UT 84041

Design: Randall Smith Associates
Typesetting: Whipple/White Typographers
Printing: Publishers Press, Salt Lake City, Utah

Library of Congress Cataloging in Publication Data
Wilderness at the edge : a citizen proposal to protect Utah's canyons and
deserts / introduction by Wallace Stegner ; foreword by Wayne Owens.
     416 p.   30.5 cm.
     ISBN 0-87905-367-4 :
     Includes bibliographical references and index.

     1. Wilderness areas—Utah. 2. Nature conservation—Utah.
I. Stegner, Wallace Earle, 1909-   .
QH76.5.U8W55   1990
333.78'216'09792—dc20   90-47990

This page: Long Canyon in the proposed White
Canyon wilderness. *Opposite:* Factory Butte in
the proposed San Rafael wilderness. *Previous
pages:* The Book Cliffs proposed wilderness.

This page and opposite: Ray Wheeler; previous pages: Tom Till

Dedicated to Jim Catlin, whose 12 years of unstinting volunteer fieldwork, research, and advocacy have helped make this book possible, and to the many citizen advocates throughout the nation on whose work the future of Utah's wilderness depends.

The Utah Wilderness Coalition extends its appreciation to the Sierra Club Foundation, Patagonia, Inc., Recreational Equipment, Inc., the Wasatch Mountain Club, Perception Kayak, Inc., and numerous individual donors for underwriting the publication of this book.

Above: The Newfoundland Mountains loom out of the Basin and Range desert like a ship on the ocean. Although the BLM calls this range "perhaps the most isolated public lands administered by the Salt Lake District," the agency did not even study its wilderness potential. *Left:* The enormous western face of Notch Peak is the desert equivalent of Yosemite's El Capitan. Limestone escarpments also crop out in two additional wilderness units within the House Range. *Opposite:* Parunuweap Canyon in the proposed Greater Zion wilderness. Wilderness designation would help forestall a proposed dam and reservoir that would still the canyon's waters. *Below:* The benchlands surrounding many West Desert ranges are important habitat for pronghorn.

Above: John P. George; left and opposite: Tom Till; below: Utah Department of Wildlife Resources

Left: One of the most remote and least visited wild areas in the country, the Kaiparowits Plateau is a vast wedge extending south and west of the town of Escalante. The BLM is recommending against protecting most of this wilderness, including the Wahweap-Paradise Canyon unit shown here. *Below:* Sheep Creek, a tributary of the upper Paria River, dissects the sandstones below the rim of Bryce Canyon National Park. The entire Grand Staircase wilderness through which the Paria flows remains wild from top to bottom. *Right:* Lower Death Hollow in the Escalante Canyons wilderness is well-watered and inviting; upstream it closes to a challenging slot.

Left: Frandee and Dale Johnson; below: Brad Nelson; right: Bruce Hucko

Right: The Henry Mountains, with their forests of aspen and fir, seem out of place in the desert of south-central Utah. Mount Ellen, the northernmost sentinel of the Henrys, is accessible from roads and campgrounds on its eastern flank. *Below:* The Dirty Devil River trickles quietly on its 90-mile journey from Hanksville to Lake Powell. A candidate for wild and scenic designation, the river is surrounded by the most isolated of canyons.

Right: Jeff Garton; below: Ray Wheeler

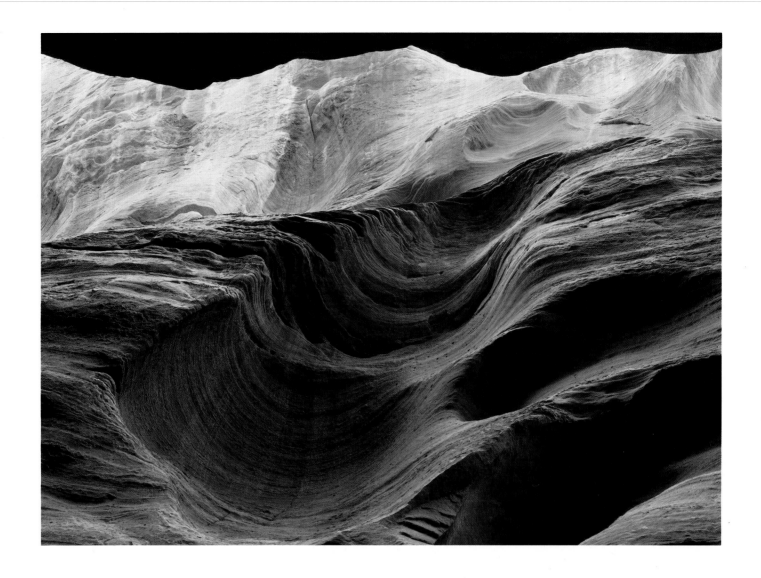

Above: Northwest of Natural Bridges National Monument, the Cedar Mesa Sandstone has been carved into the Black Hole of White Canyon—one of the most challenging hikes on the Colorado Plateau. *Right:* Southeastern Utah shelters some of the nation's best-preserved Anasazi ruins. These ruins are found in the proposed San Juan-Anasazi wilderness and probably owe their preservation to the lack of vehicle access.

Both: Bruce Hucko

Moab, Utah, owes its status as a tourist attraction to the red-rock wild lands surrounding it. South of Moab, Indian Creek canyon *(left)* offers easy hiking—until one reaches this pouroff near the Colorado River. The Fisher Towers *(top left)*, which rise above Highway 128 northeast of Moab, attract rock climbers from across the nation. West of Moab, Labyrinth Canyon *(above right)* is an elegant display of the power of a wild river cutting through the Navajo Sandstone. *Right:* The San Rafael River glides through the Little Grand Canyon below Sids Mountain—part of the proposed San Rafael Swell wilderness. *Far right:* A desert bighorn drinks from the Colorado River.

Left and right: Christopher Brown; top left: Ray Wheeler; above right and far right: Tom Till

One needn't be an expert canoeist or rafter to negotiate the White River *(top left and above)*. The river brings life and diversity to the desert landscape south of Vernal. Soloing the Green River in Desolation Canyon *(left)* calls for more skill. Or one can rent the services of one of the guiding companies that offer trips through Utah's largest roadless area.

Top left and left: Ray Wheeler; above: Will Durant

CONTENTS

FOREWORD

I N Wildness is the preservation of the world." When Henry David Thoreau expressed this belief in 1848, he could not have imagined how true his words would ring in the world of the 1990s. Today, faced with probable global warming, ozone depletion, acidic lakes, extinctions, desertification, and deforestation, we realize that our future quality of life—if not life itself—will in large part depend on the treatment we afford our natural environment.

A short time ago, I heard a moving story about the leader of one of the nation's largest environmental organizations. His daughter had been cured of a life-threatening illness more than a decade ago by a nearly miraculous drug found in a plant which grew only on the island of Madagascar. His daughter is now healthy, but the plant, like so many others, is now extinct.

Wilderness and the life dependent on it are fragile entities. They can be destroyed in a matter of years, if not days. Legislative protection is the surest way to maintain a wilderness reserve on our hungry and crowded planet. When wilderness is protected, watershed is protected. Biological diversity is protected. Game is protected. The proper functioning of a natural system is protected. Our quality of life is protected.

The scientific arguments for wilderness seem irrefutable. But will designation of large areas of wilderness in Utah, as I have proposed in H.R. 1500, harm the economy of the region? I honestly don't think it will. Everything I have read and researched indicates that few developable resources will be lost, while increased interest in the region will bring more visitors, money, and growth. But perhaps even more importantly, the quality of life that has drawn us to Utah will remain unimpaired.

I have had the privilege over the last few months of spending time with the residents of southern Utah who will be most affected by the passage of the wilderness bill I have proposed. Although the reception was always cordial, it was very clear that a great rift of opinion exists over Utah wilderness. I sometimes asked these residents if they would be willing to live in a place which was completely developed and exploited, without the quiet corners of natural beauty and solitude which make Utah so unique. The answer was invariably negative, so the real question becomes not whether to preserve significant portions of Utah's wilderness, but, simply, how much. I have proposed preserving over 5 million acres of wilderness in Utah in H.R. 1500. I admit that is an impressive number, but one of the most impressive areas on the planet deserves nothing less.

If we do not deliberately protect our remaining wilderness in Utah, I fear it will eventually disappear. It will not vanish through beneficial development, but will instead be lost through gradual attrition for no good reason at all. Having been born in southern Utah and having spent my youth in its unmatchable canyons and forests, I want to ensure that the same opportunity will be available for future generations. Fifty years ago, Utah had 18 million acres of wilderness land. Two-thirds of that is gone today and what remains is seriously at risk.

To paraphrase John Muir, anyone can destroy a wilderness. It has no natural defense. It cannot fight or run away. But only God can create a wilderness—and only wise government and wise laws can preserve it. What we now elect to save in Utah over the next few years of discussion will always remain. What we neglect to protect can never be recovered. This is a decision with lasting consequences for the future. I hope we will choose wisely and I look forward to participating in this exciting and essential process during the critical years to come.

Wayne Owens

U.S. HOUSE OF REPRESENTATIVES
SECOND DISTRICT, UTAH

INTRODUCTION

THE dispute over how much BLM land shall be set aside as wilderness in the state of Utah is one more round in the long disagreement between those who view the earth as made for man's domination, and wild land as a resource warehouse to be freely looted, and those who see wild nature as precious in itself—beautiful, quiet, spiritually refreshing, priceless as a genetic bank and laboratory, priceless either as relief or even as pure idea to those who suffer from the ugliness, noise, crowding, stress, and self-destructive greed of industrial life.

Between the extremes, between the interested and the disinterested, there is a large group of the confused, uncertain, and misled; but the conflicting parties are still the Birdwatchers and the Roughriders, the responsible stewards of the earth and those galvanized by the spirit that "won the West:" that reduced the beaver and bison to remnants, clear-cut the mountainsides, overgrazed and plowed up the grass, set the topsoil to blowing, pumped down the water table, dried up the springs, trampled the riparian zones of streams and silted up the gravelly spawning creeks, dammed and diverted the rivers, left its ghost towns in a hundred gulches and the outwash of its monitors at the mouths of a hundred canyons, and that in these days, as careless as ever, darkens and sours the air around Colstrip, Billings, Four Corners, Page, Huntington, Castle Dale, Lynndyl, and many another place.

Some of that damage was done in the rage to get rich quick, some in the defensible but often futile hope of creating homes and farms in unlikely country, some in the effort to fuel the industrial monster we have created. Some was done by individuals, some by corporations and governments; some in ignorance of consequences, some in reckless disregard of them. From one point of view, one that gains adherents steadily as the remaining wild country shrinks, the West was not won at all, but mainly lost.

In many parts of the arid interior West, the clean magnificence, the clean air and long views, the natural balances and interdependences that make its enduring flora and fauna object lessons in adaptation and survival, have been defaced or diminished by our efforts to make the country serve either our lust for quick wealth or our everyday needs. There are many places that are already dedicated to those purposes. But if the remaining wild country were put to its highest, most reasonable, most sustainable use, it would be asked to serve neither everyday needs nor get-rich-quick dreams. Except in well-watered areas such as the Wasatch Front in Utah and the apron of the Front Range in Colorado, no part of the West, and certainly none of the remaining wild parts, is ever going to support a large permanent population. If we surrender the wilderness areas to so-called

The Kaiparowits Plateau from near the Hole-In-The-Rock road in the Escalante country. Economic pressures to develop Kaiparowits coal and Escalante uranium will transform this wilderness unless it is given legal protection.

Stu Levy

"productive" uses, we will give up, for brief and ugly benefits, the highest values that wilderness provides.

Historically, every western boom has been followed by bust. The economics of liquidation—get in, get rich, get out, or, more commonly, go out, go broke, go back—has applied to fur, game, gold, timber, grass, oil, uranium. In the end it will prove to have applied to most irrigation agriculture as well. The Public Domain, which east of the 100th meridian was quickly disposed of, found few takers in the West except hit-and-run takers, and little by little the federal government began to assume responsibility for it. Since 1872, when Congress created Yellowstone National Park, large areas have been protected from exploitation by being set aside as national parks, national forests, wilderness areas, wildlife refuges, and wild rivers. The BLM lands are the left-overs. For generations they remained open, nearly empty, available to almost any use people chose to make of them.

What I mean to say is that the Public Domain started as an assumption, a sort of squatters' rights assumption, and quickly became a habit that remains long after it is no longer valid. It existed before law, and law was slow to protect it. The laws that grew up within it, such as most water law and the mining law, were essentially the justification of appropriation, which was itself essentially tolerated trespass.

Surrounded by open space, Westerners got to feeling that it was theirs, because they used it freely. Many still feel that way, and *de facto*, they are right. Even now, anybody can stake out a mining claim on BLM land wherever he finds color, and can remove without fee any minerals he finds. Permittees can run cattle or sheep at cheap subsidized rates on both BLM and National Forest land, and their privileges over the years have hardened into vested rights, to be bought and sold along with the home ranch. Anybody can hunt, camp, ride, hike, drive an ORV or a dirt bike, almost anywhere on BLM land, and many assume the right to pot-hunt in

Anasazi ruins and deface or steal whole panels of pictographs. If a local BLM man tries to keep livestock to the permitted numbers, or restrain pot-hunters and dirt bikers, he can be made very uncomfortable, can be harassed and threatened until the bureau transfers him to save him from violence, and replaces him with someone more willing to work with local interests.

It took a long time for even minimum acceptance of federal responsibility for these left-over lands. The first step came in 1934, the peak year of the Dust Bowl, when Congress passed the Taylor Grazing Act, eliminating the old General Land Office (and with it most of the land laws permitting the staking of agricultural claims), and creating the Grazing Service, which undertook not only to rescue the overgrazed range but to charge, finally, for the right to put stock on it. The West welcomed federal aid—it always does—and quietly sabotaged federal regulation by packing grazing district councils with local stockmen, foxes who knew what to do in a hen house. If the Grazing Service, which later became the BLM, caused trouble, congressional friends of the stockmen could always bring it to its senses by cutting its budget. The end result was a federal bureau manipulated by and subservient to local interests.

Then in 1976 Congress went a light-year beyond the Taylor Grazing Act, and passed the Federal Land Policy and Management Act (FLPMA), which gave the BLM both specific mandates and the teeth to enforce them. Suddenly it seemed that federal regulation was going to be a fact, not a fiction. Suddenly people were coming into local BLM offices with the intention of really enforcing the law and maintaining the resource. Also, it now appeared that FLPMA had ordered BLM to inventory all its potential wilderness areas. That meant that, if they were reported and certified and acted on by Congress, whole basins, whole systems of plateau and canyon, whole related playas and dry mountainsides and high snow-fed valleys, might be withdrawn from the traditional uses and abuses.

FLPMA instantly brought on the Sagebrush Rebellion, with its furious anti-Fed feelings, its threats of violence, its denial of both history and law in its assertion of states rights to lands that had never been anything but federal, that had been specifically renounced by every western state upon its admission to the Union. But the Sagebrush Rebellion ceased abruptly when Ronald Reagan was elected President and James Watt and Robert Burford occupied the Interior Building. With such friends in power, who needs a rebellion?

But FLPMA was still law, the wilderness inventory still had to be made. In some of the eleven public lands states, though it never identified and certified enough wilderness to satisfy environmentalists, the BLM did at least a token job. In Utah, as this book attests, it delayed, juggled boundaries, made recommendations on the basis of no more than a helicopter overflight, arbitrarily broke up or eliminated areas of bona fide wilderness because of real or hoped-for mineral resources or real or hoped-for power installations. It cut some areas because it already had plans to chain juniper-pinyon forests and plant crested wheat grass range that could then be leased at a fraction of its cost to local stockmen. If it moved reluctantly in much of the West, in Utah it appears to have done its best to evade its legal obligation, and at the same time to have exceeded its mandate. It had no mandate but to inventory its wilderness; as Ray Wheeler points out in this book, in Utah it came up with commercial and industrial zoning, usurping the function of Congress.

Why? Why in Utah, where there is more authentic wilderness than in almost any state except Alaska, and where much of the wilderness is unique, unmatched in any part of the world? Why Utah, where every tour-

If a local BLM man tries to keep livestock to the permitted numbers, or restrain pot-hunters and dirt bikers, he can be made very uncomfortable, can be harassed and threatened until the bureau transfers him to save him from violence, and replaces him with someone more willing to work with local interests.

ist turns into an awe-struck worshipper? Why Utah, where in the six Colorado Plateau counties most concerned with the wilderness inventory (an area slightly larger than Massachusetts, New Hampshire, and Vermont combined) there live barely 28,000 people, concentrated in a handful of oases where human habitation is feasible?

Well, Utahns were, and some still are, frontiersmen. They share states' rights assumptions and biases. Away from the Wasatch Front, the population is so thin and the wild land so extensive that they cannot conceive of its being damaged. Though many of them are hunters, they have not all made the connection between good hunting and good wildlife habitat; and though they all grew up in a country short of water, they have not all understood that a country short of water for agriculture is also short of water for industry or municipal use. No more than other Westerners do they like dictation or interference from outsiders, and they are as susceptible as other frontier Westerners to the temptation of violence. Many consider the wilderness inventory, and indeed all federal regulation, an unwarranted intrusion into land-use decisions that should properly be made by the people who live there.

But there are special, residual, half-lost reasons for Utah's intransigence. Utah is a desert state, drier than any other state except Nevada. It was settled by a God-guided, prophet-led, persecuted people who had good reason to hate and fear the United States, and who fled to Utah, then Mexican territory, thinking of it as the Canaan that the Lord had prepared for them. The Mexican War put them right back in the country they had fled from. Ten years after their arrival in Utah they were fighting a war against an invading American army, and in the 1870s and 1880s great-grandfathers of southern Utah's present generation were hiding out from U.S. Marshals bent on tracking down "cohabs." Many of those fugitives hid out in the fastnesses that the Utah BLM was told to inventory for wilderness designation a hundred years later. It is surely hard to think that country where so much of your intimate family and community and church history has taken place is not yours, and that strangers tell you what to do with it.

Moreover, the land that God and Brother Brigham brought the Mormons to turned out to be, in spite of truly heroic efforts, largely unfriendly to settlement. The Mormons quickly settled the Wasatch Front and the fertile Sanpete and Sevier valleys. They sent colonists across the desert to Genoa, on the eastern side of the Sierra, and down to Las Vegas and San Bernardino (Brigham's corridor to the sea), and up into the Salmon River country of Idaho, and down to Moab, on the Colorado, and to St. George, on the Virgin. In 1880 a belated wagon-train made an incredible journey down along the Kaiparowits Plateau, through the nearly vertical slot called Hole-in-the-Rock, across the Colorado in Glen Canyon, and across Wilson's Mesa to found the town of Bluff, on the San Juan.

But some of those extensions of Zion were overtaken by the expanding United States, and some, like the Lemhi Mission in Idaho, ran into trouble with the Indians, and some, like Bluff, almost as isolated as if they were on another planet, languished in their tiny pockets of fertility. Nowhere could the population expand except along the Wasatch Front from Brigham City to Nephi. Mormon families were big, and encouraged to be big. Now they are still big, but not so strenuously encouraged, for the land very early reached the limit of its capacity to support people. It is a distress to southern Utah's Mormons and to their friends, of whom I hope I am one, to watch generation after generation of young people take off for Salt Lake, Provo, Ogden, California, or "back east" in search of jobs by which to live. Some who manage to remain train as foresters or range managers and find jobs with the Park Service, Forest Service, or BLM; and some of them may never lose their inherited mind-sets, which may explain why the Utah BLM has been so sympathetic to local prejudices.

Residents of Loa, Panguitch, Blanding, Moab, for reasons that seem good to them and that are played on by mining and livestock interests, sometimes see wilderness advocates such as those who belong to the Utah Wilderness Coalition as people bent on killing the only chance their children have of getting a job close to home. Coal mines, uranium mines, oil wells, oil sands, oil shales, power plants, look like hope even when they are largely speculation, and even when their success would destroy the life these people have grown up in. Wilderness they could accept if it meant a lot of paved roads, motels and gas stations at every spring and stream, helicopter flights over wild eroded country, and all the rest of the tourist-resort syndrome. But wilderness that would *remain* wilderness seems to them a waste.

Sometimes the resentment against "outside interference" runs high. Thus the county supervisors of Grand County sent out their road crews to bulldoze a road up Negro Bill Canyon, a wilderness study area supposed to be protected until completion of the wilderness inventory. In effect, they were defying the United States to control its federal land. And thus local citizens threatened with death the dedicated people who discovered and exposed the shoddy nature of BLM's wilderness inventory. Thus, every now and then, they hang or burn in effigy people such as Clive Kincaid and Robert Redford, who work against the industrial development that some locals think so essential.

That violence is an expression of desperation, the frontier dying hard, the reaction of people pushed to the edge of their tolerance by forces they do not understand. I sympathize with their feelings; I also think they are profoundly wrong, or else that they are disguising some personal economic stake in the future that goes beyond use and into profit.

I think they fail to understand the nature and necessity of federal ownership and management in their arid, bony, nearly roadless country—that is, that they have not read their own history. I think they mistrust federal intervention because it is "outsider," and don't sufficiently mistrust the local mining and livestock interests most opposed to federal controls. I think that even in the area of tourism they expect too much, want too much—want not a sustaining economy but a boom; and I think that is pathetically western of them, because in the country they live in, booms are short, and are followed by busts, and an economy that can sustain itself is going to be far more modest than some motel-keeper's dream. I think they are wrong because, in their eagerness to find some way of family living and jobs for the children, they are too willing to sacrifice their air, their water, their views, their silence and peace, everything that makes their life, poor as it is, enviable. I think they are wrong because their Old Testament view of the earth conceives it to have been made for man's exploitation. What they have yet to come to is Aldo Leopold's view that earth is a community to which we belong, and to which, in consequence, we owe a duty.

I would urge upon the people of southern Utah, and upon the politicians who will be trying to give them what they want, that in their own long-range interest they look carefully at their options. One, represented by the BLM's meager 1.9 million acres of wilderness, would encourage maximum exploitation, maximum damage to the water table, wildlife habitat, scenery, and ultimately, tourist visitation. A second option, which would involve maximum roads and tourist development, would be every bit as damaging: take a look at Page or Wahweap now. A third, represented by the Utah Wilderness Coalition's 5.7 million acres of wilderness, would permit continued exploitation of coal and other mineral resources where the wilderness has already been invaded, and leave maximum wilderness intact for the future, guaranteeing Utah, America, and the planet something incomparable and increasingly precious.

Once, in the 1930s, Harold Ickes and others were proposing that almost all of southern Utah be made into one vast national park. That never came to pass; if it had, I suspect that the southern Utah economy would be stronger than it is now, and the wilderness would be more intact. But the 5.7-million-acre proposal of the Utah Wilderness Coalition is the closest thing still available. It is not a wish-list concocted by insatiable environmentalists. It is actually a true inventory of what is left, the precise thing that the BLM was instructed to prepare. With that inventory available, Congress can make the decisions that the BLM tried to take out of its hands.

The conflict in the Colorado Plateau and out in the Great Basin desert comes down to a conflict between the material and the spiritual. With only a minor and temporary sacrifice of material profit, the spiritual can be saved intact. But the attempt to generate maximum immediate profit to individuals or corporations will destroy the spiritual integrity of the wilderness.

Brigham Young told his people, made restless by the California Gold Rush, to forget about gold; gold was for paving streets. If he were alive now, he might tell them that uranium is for blowing up the world, not helping it; that coal is for increasing the greenhouse effect and poisoning the world's air; that electric power is for lighting the gaming rooms and whorehouses of Las Vegas. Wilderness is for something else.

The Utah deserts and plateaus and canyons are not a country of big returns, but a country of spiritual healing, incomparable for contemplation, meditation, solitude, quiet, awe, peace of mind and body. We were born of wilderness, and we respond to it more than we sometimes realize. We depend upon it increasingly for relief from the termite life we have created. Factories, power plants, resorts, we can make anywhere. Wilderness, once we have given it up, is beyond our reconstruction.

Wallace Stegner

WILDERNESS ISSUES

WILDERNESS and controversy are no strangers; the law that established the National Wilderness Preservation System in 1964 took eight years to pass Congress. Unfortunately, the basic questions that Congress attempted to settle with that legislation are still debated each time a new wilderness proposal is advanced. Far too often we hear the old myths that wilderness designation would halt livestock grazing; that untold mineral wealth would be locked up; that the state's school trust would suffer; that recreational access would be stifled; and that water rights would somehow be usurped. The following section addresses these issues in turn, and attempts to lay a factual foundation for the discussion of specific wilderness proposals.

WHAT IS A WILDERNESS AREA?

Beginning in 1872 with the creation of Yellowstone National Park, our nation has set aside tracts of undeveloped public land in order to preserve the unspoiled remnants of what was once a pristine continent. Formal standards for the designation and protection of Wilderness Areas were established in 1964, when Congress passed the Wilderness Act. In 1976, the Federal Land Policy and Management Act (FLPMA) directed the BLM to review the vast public lands under its management to determine which were suitable for designation by Congress as wilderness.

In 1984, while the BLM wilderness review proceeded, Congress designated two small BLM wilderness areas along the Utah-Arizona border: the Paria Canyon-Vermilion Cliffs and the Beaver Dam Mountains. Studies and debate continue over how much of Utah's remaining BLM wild lands should be protected.

The wilderness areas we propose in this book can be designated only by Act of Congress following extensive study by the managing agency, formal public hearings, and extensive written comment from citizens. Public debate over wilderness legislation ensures that Congressional leaders consider all the facts and varying viewpoints.

Wilderness is a key part of the multiple use idea, which does not mean—nor has it ever meant—*every* use on *every* acre. Beyond that, the uses of *wilderness* itself are multiple. Among those allowed in wilderness areas are:

Foot and horse travel; hunting and fishing; backcountry camping
Float boating and canoeing
Guiding and outfitting
Scientific study; educational programs
Livestock grazing, where previously established
Control of wildfires and insect and disease outbreaks

In order to assure that an increasing population, accompanied by expanding settlement and growing mechanization, does not occupy and modify all areas within the United States and its possessions, leaving no lands designated for preservation and protection in their natural condition, it is hereby declared to be the policy of the Congress to secure for the American people of present and future generations the benefits of an enduring resource of wilderness.

THE WILDERNESS ACT OF 1964

Mining on pre-existing mining claims

In order that natural forces can operate free from man's interference, and to preserve opportunities for solitude, certain uses are not allowed in wilderness areas:

Use of mechanized transport (except in emergencies, or such vehicles as wheelchairs)

Roadbuilding, logging, and similar commercial uses

Staking *new* mining claims or mineral leases

New reservoirs or powerlines, except where authorized by the President as being in the national interest.

When wilderness opponents claim that wilderness is "locked up" from multiple use without considering the views of local residents, look again. This myth dies hard. Logging, mining, and motorized vehicles, if not carefully regulated and limited, can monopolize the public's land for the benefit of the few. *These* are the real single-use lockups of public land, and they usually occur without much public debate.

The Question of Purity

We have carefully drawn the boundaries of our proposed wilderness areas to exclude maintained and traveled roads, heavily used vehicle ways or off-road vehicle routes, active mines, most developed livestock facilities, and developed recreation sites. But where the intrusions are crumbling back into the landscape, or could be restored to a near-natural condition, we have included them within our wilderness boundaries. As the BLM has, we have included a few old mining scars, little-used jeep tracks, and stock facilities such as fences, spring improvements, and gully check dams if they are located within an otherwise wild area and cannot reasonably be excluded by boundary adjustments. Existing commercial uses of stock facilities and mines would be allowed to continue within wilderness areas, subject to reasonable regulations designed to protect wilderness values.

Congress has made it clear that such intrusions do not disqualify an area from wilderness designation if they are "substantially unnoticeable" in the context of the whole area. This does not mean that such imprints must be *invisible*, only that the land retain an overall sense of wildness. Few desert lands are totally untouched by man. Too often, the BLM has allowed mineral exploration or off-road vehicle use to intrude into large wild regions. The agency often dropped those areas from its wilderness inventory. In many cases the roads were illegal in the first place, the mineral exploration proved fruitless, or the jeep trails served no important purpose. The legislative history of the Wilderness Act makes it clear that a few such imprints do not disqualify entire wild areas from protection.

Some people ask why, on the one hand, conservationists include jeep tracks and other human imprints in wilderness proposals, but, on the other hand, object to constructing such facilities within designated wilderness areas. The answer, quite simply, is that the primary goal is to prevent further damage to natural areas. Within limits, nature can heal old scars, but this cannot be used to justify further damage. Once an area is designated wilderness, it is the responsibility of the managing agency to prevent further impairment of the area's wild character.

Fire, Insect, and Disease Management

Wildfire is an important part of natural ecosystems. Fires remove debris, recycle soil nutrients, and encourage new plant growth. Fires caused by lightning within designated wilderness can be allowed to burn if there is no threat to life and property. Decisions related to wilderness fire management should conform to a fire management plan, adopted following comments from the public.

Fires are generally detected through the use of aircraft overflights and fire lookouts located outside the wilderness. If necessary, however, lookouts may be located within the wilderness. Fire suppression techniques must use minimum tools (e.g., avoid bulldozers where hand work is sufficient) and they must prevent unnecessary degradation of the land.

Prescribed burning may be permitted to restore and maintain the natural condition of a fire-dependent ecosystem. This can help perpetuate habitat for certain threatened and endangered plants or animals.

Insects and disease outbreaks, like fire, are normal events in natural ecosystems. Our use of the term "infestation" only shows how little we know of these natural processes. Still, insects and disease may be controlled within designated wilderness areas if not to do so would threaten endangered plant or animal species or other resources outside the wilderness.

Lawson LeGate

MINERAL RESOURCES AND WILDERNESS

Editor's Note: Would wilderness designations lock up vast quantities of minerals? And would employment in the mineral industries suffer as a result? Hard data on mineral potentials in candidate wilderness areas are scarce. But claimed mineral potential led the BLM to recommend against wilderness designation for many of its wilderness study areas (WSAs), as well as eliminate many WSAs from study. The Utah Wilderness Coalition asked Dr. W. Thomas Goerold, Chief Economist for Energy and Mineral Resources at The Wilderness Society, to make an independent assessment of the importance of the mineral industry to Utah's economy. His report is summarized below. A more detailed analysis can be found in *The Energy and Mineral Sector in Utah*, available from The Wilderness Society, 900 17th Street, N.W., Washington, D.C. 20006. Following his report is a brief analysis of specific minerals found within our proposed wilderness areas. This analysis is summarized from comments the Utah Wilderness Coalition submitted to the BLM on its 1986 draft wilderness EIS.

THE ENERGY AND MINERAL INDUSTRIES IN UTAH

Composition of Energy and Mineral Production in 1977 and 1987

Production of energy and mineral materials in Utah totalled $1.847 billion in 1977. [Totals reflect adjustments for inflation to 1989 dollars unless otherwise stated.] Slightly more than 50 percent of total energy and mineral revenues were obtained from energy commodities (oil, gas, coal, and uranium).

Copper production made up 25 percent of total energy and mineral production in 1977. Other metals produced in 1977 included minor amounts of silver, iron ore, zinc, magnesium, tungsten, zinc, and vanadium. Construction materials, commodities used primarily in the building industry such as limestone and sand and gravel, comprised about 13 percent of state output of total mineral materials.

In 1987, mineral firms in Utah produced approximately $1.982 billion worth of energy and mineral commodities, about 7 percent more than output in 1977. Approximately 62 percent of industry production in Utah was attributable to sales of energy commodities. The remaining 38 percent of minerals output was dominated by the "other" class, largely non-metallic materials not counted in the construction materials grouping and including gypsum, phosphate rock, potassium salts, sodium sulfate, and stone.

By 1986, natural resource extraction industries represented just over 3 percent of the Utah Gross State Product, a drop of approximately 75 percent over the quarter century. The oil and gas industry decreased its share of the Utah economic activity from 8 to less than 2 percent. Metals producers also showed a similar decline.

A comparison of mineral output in the two years shows the share of production from energy commodities increased from 53 to 62 percent in the 10-year period. Oil and gas and coal production values each expanded during this time. The large growth in energy prices since the mid-1970s resulted in greater exploration for energy commodities. Though energy prices have now decreased to near mid-1970s levels, energy deposits found in the last decade are still in production. In contrast to the increases in other energy commodity production shares, the uranium industry has struggled to maintain a 5 percent share of total commodity production values since 1977. Although the share claimed by the copper sector declined to just 5 percent in 1987, this was largely because of diminished production resulting from modernization of Utah's largest copper mine.

IMPACT OF THESE INDUSTRIES ON UTAH'S ECONOMY

A common index of economic impact, the contribution of the industry to the Utah Gross State Product, identifies the total amount of goods and services produced by industries. Gross State Product measures an entire state's industrial output and standard of living—analogous to Gross National Product. A second measure of the effect of the energy and mineral industries on the state is the employment impact.

Utah Gross State Product

The relative contribution of the energy and mineral sector to Utah's Gross State Product has continually declined over the past quarter century. Figure 1 shows the trend for this economic sector from 1963 to 1986.

In 1963, the share of Utah Gross State Product of all energy and mineral producers was approximately 13 percent. The oil and gas sector alone represented almost 8 percent of economic activity in Utah. Since 1963, even through the oil and mineral price escalation in the late 1970s and early 1980s, the relative contributions to the state economy by these commodities steadily declined. The almost total collapse of these markets in the early to mid-1980s aggravated this already negative trend.

By 1986, natural resource extraction industries represented just over 3 percent of the Utah Gross State Product, a drop of approximately 75 percent over the quarter century. The oil and gas industry decreased its share of Utah economic activity from 8 to less than 2 percent. Metals producers also showed a similar decline—from over 3 to under 1 percent of state economic activity.

In dollars, the cutback in the economic activity of the natural resource extraction sector was not as dramatic as the decrease in the share of the energy and mineral sector. From 1963 to 1986, the years available for analysis, the oil and gas and metals industries showed very large declines, but the non-metals and coal sectors grew faster than inflation. Though the coal and non-metals sectors indicated absolute dollar growth in state economic activity, the Utah economy as a whole grew faster than these sectors.

The services sector, one of the sectors exhibiting the most dramatic growth in the Utah economy, increased from about 9 to more than 13 percent of the Utah economy from 1963 to 1986. In dollars, this sector, covering a host of businesses including tourism and recreation, tripled during this period—from $1.11 to $3.33 billion. Most recent data show that services sector economic activity contributes approximately four times as much as the energy and mineral extraction industry to the Utah economy.

Employment in Utah

Another measure of the evolution of Utah's economy is found in employment trends. There was a near doubling of the number of jobs in

Figure 1 - Economic Impact of Utah's Energy and Mineral Sector.

The share of Utah State Product contributed by the energy and mineral industries to Utah's economy has fallen by more than 67 percent since 1963.

The oil and gas and metals industries have shown the largest decline.

Legend: OIL & GAS — METALS — NON-METALS — COAL

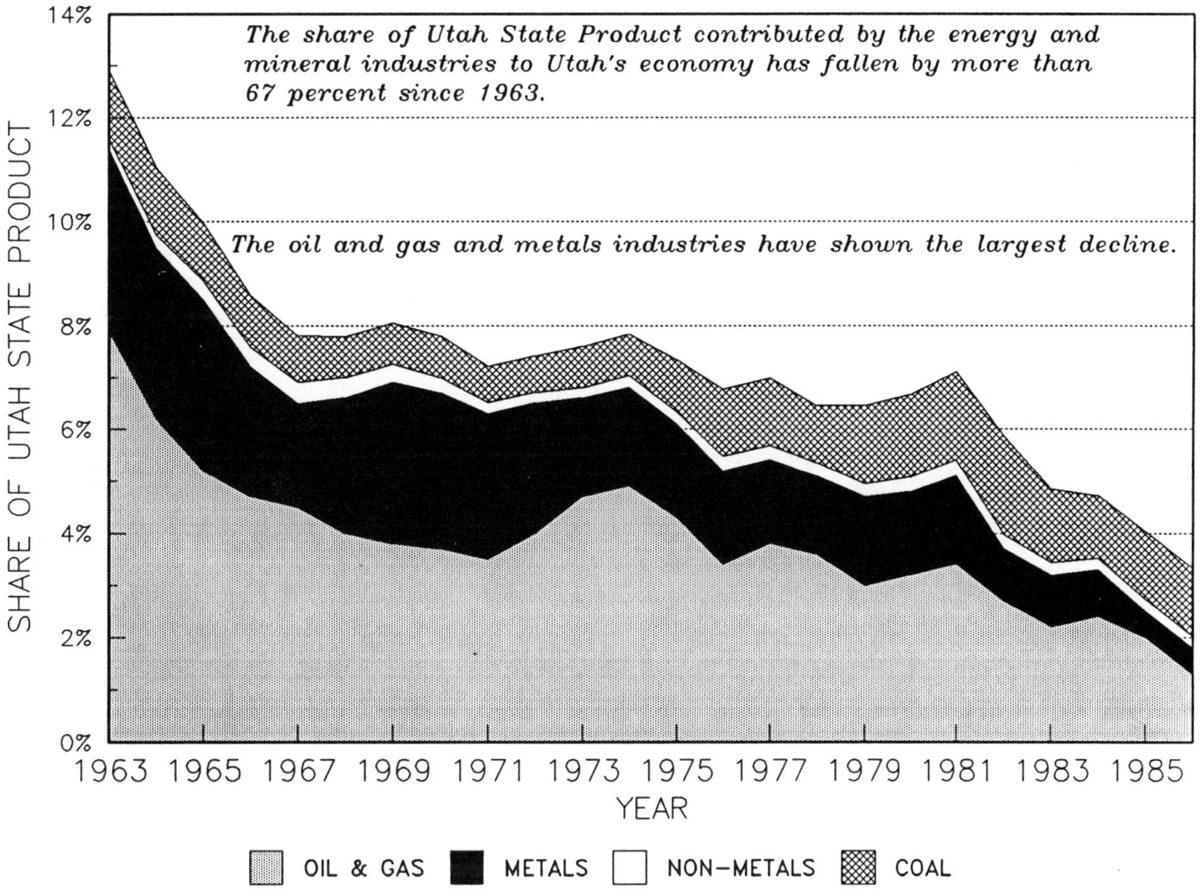

Source: U.S. Department of Commerce, 1988, Bureau of Economic Analysis.

Utah in the last 20 years, from about 430,000 in 1969 to slightly more than 800,000 in 1987. While total state employment has been increasing, the energy and mineral sector employment is actually lower now than in 1969.

The Bureau of Economic Analysis of the U.S. Department of Commerce shows that the mining industry employed approximately 13,000 people in 1969, but just under 9,000 workers collected paychecks from the industry in 1987. The share of total state employment attributed to energy and mineral firms declined 63 percent, from more than 3 to about 1 percent of total Utah employment. Simultaneously, total employment in the services sector increased by 180 percent—from 74,000 to 207,000 workers—representing a growth of from 17 to almost 26 percent of the Utah workforce.

The metals mining sector has experienced the largest job loss of any segment of Utah's mining industry during this interval. In 1969, metal mining firms employed almost 10,000 people, but by 1987 the employment in these firms totalled only about 3,000. Much of this decline can be attributed to the virtual extinction of the state's uranium industry, but some effects have also been caused by the cyclical market-related cutbacks in employment used in mining at Bingham Canyon's copper facilities.

CONCLUSIONS

Energy commodity production continues to dominate the mining industry in Utah. Oil, natural gas, and coal production contribute the largest

Current and future oil and gas operations in Utah are handicapped by very high drilling costs associated with petroleum operations in the state. Due to the high cost of producing petroleum in the state, even a large increase in the price of oil is unlikely to yield considerable additional reserves of petroleum.

revenues to this sector. Significant revenues are also generated by copper and gold mining operations in the state, with most of state production of these commodities coming from two sites in Utah.

The economic and employment trends for the energy and mineral sector show the effect of the long-term decline of the sector aggravated by the extreme recession of these markets during the early to mid-1980s. Since 1963, the share of Utah's economy contributed by the natural resource extraction industry has decreased by 67 percent—from 13 to 3.4 percent. Oil and gas and metals industries have borne the greatest losses, and the coal industry has shown a modest gain. Employment in the energy and mineral industries has also decreased, from 13,000 in 1969 to less than 8,000 in 1987. This translates to an aggregate employment share for the energy and mineral industries of approximately 1 percent of the total statewide labor force in 1987, compared with more than 3 percent in 1969.

In marked contrast to the declining trends seen in the energy and mineral sector, the Utah economy as a whole has generally shown healthy growth. The services industry in Utah has increased from 9 to 13 percent of the Utah Gross State Product and from 17 to almost 26 percent of Utah employment in the last 20 to 25 years.

All energy and mineral commodities produced in Utah have yet to match the sales obtained from production in the early to mid-1980s. Oil and gas production peaked in the mid 1980s and has declined dramatically since. Current and future oil and gas operations in Utah are handicapped by very high drilling costs associated with petroleum operations in the state. The average cost of drilling a well in Utah in 1986 was about $1.69 per barrel of production—approximately 2.5 times the national average and second highest in the conterminous United States. Utah ranks tenth and twelfth respectively among states in oil and natural gas reserves, containing about 1 percent of national totals. Due to the high cost of producing petroleum in the state, even a large increase in the price of oil is unlikely to yield considerable additional reserves of petroleum.

Although the tonnage of coal produced in Utah is at or near an all-time high, the value of coal production lies somewhat below levels seen in the early 1980s. The price paid for Utah coal has continually declined due, in part, to large quantities of lower cost production from Montana and Wyoming. Resources of Utah coal are abundant, but the high cost of extraction and huge reserves of less expensive coal in nearby states may hamper large scale expansion of coal mining in Utah. Nevertheless, most currently producing coal mines in the state contain enough reserves for a long period of continued production at current or even increased rates of output.

The continued production of uranium in Utah, and even the United States as a whole, is in doubt. After reaching a peak of more than $45 per pound in 1981, the uranium price now hovers near $9 per pound. One active mill remains in Utah, and most of the ore that is processed at this location comes from production obtained from the north rim of the Grand Canyon in Arizona. Reduced domestic demand for nuclear power combined with less costly foreign sources of uranium indicate that future production of this commodity from Utah mines is questionable.

Metal production in Utah is dominated by copper production from the Bingham Mine. Steel, gold, beryllium, and magnesium are also important commodities produced in the state. With a few notable exceptions, the pattern of production at metal mines in the state has followed the trend seen for the energy commodities—a production and price peak in the early to mid-1980s followed by a major collapse of the markets. Although copper production is likely to continue into the next century, barring any significant new finds, most of it probably will come from the Bingham

Mine. One mine, the Brush Wellman beryllium mine, contains strategic minerals of national importance. Many other mines, such as the Escalante silver mine and Burgin base metal mine, have closed or are scheduled to close due to depleted reserves and continued low mineral prices.

Using almost any economic measure, most sectors of the energy and mineral extraction industries in Utah have become less important during the last quarter century. Although oil, gas, coal, and copper producers (to name the most prominent industries) remain viable in the state, they no longer hold the economic or employment influence they wielded as recently as two decades ago.

W. Thomas Goerold, Ph.D.

MINERALS IN PROPOSED WILDERNESS AREAS

Some of Utah's wild lands contain deposits of coal, tar sands, oil and gas, uranium, and potash. The mineral industry opposes wilderness designation for lands containing such deposits. But few of these deposits are likely to be developed in the foreseeable future owing to economic, technological, and environmental problems not related to wilderness designation. With few exceptions, the lands within our proposal have remained wild because of the *lack* of economically feasible mineral deposits. Repeated investigations by exploration geologists have uncovered few real opportunities for mineral development. Further information is contained in the publications of the U.S. Geological Survey on individual BLM wilderness study areas.

Tar Sand

The BLM states in its draft wilderness EIS (1986) that tar sand development in Utah is unlikely, yet the BLM recommended against wilderness designation for parts of the North Escalante Canyons and Fiddler Butte units on the basis of possible tar sand development. Development of these areas is unlikely because of the low quality of the deposit, the lack of water, and limited access. The Circle Cliff deposit in the North Escalante canyons is ranked by the energy industry as very low on the list of developable resources in Utah and the United States. Wood and Ritzma, in a 1972 Utah Geological and Mineralogical Survey Special Study (#39), tested 12 Circle Cliffs deposits and found that "the tar sand is poorly saturated with oil, the oil is unusually heavy, and the oil contains a high percentage of sulfur."

In 1986, the BLM recommended that two parts of its Fiddler Butte and French Spring-Happy Canyon WSAs not be considered for wilderness designation in order to "avoid conflicts with potential tar sand development" (BLM, 1986, p. 12). This runs counter to the BLM's own analysis that the "probability of development is low due to topographic and economic constraints" (p. 20). Ritzma, in "Commercial Aspects of Utah's Oil-impregnated Sandstone Deposits" (1973) downgrades the Tar Sand Triangle deposits that underlie these two WSAs because "the area is exceedingly rugged and the deposit extends downdip beneath an intricately dissected plateau. Access to exposed areas is difficult." A Bureau of Mines report (Glassett and Glassett, Eyring Research Institute, 1976) concludes that "the deposit is quite lean," and states, "the relatively high sulfur content of the Tar Sand triangle bitumen may be a significant deterrent to . . . development of this huge deposit."

Though in-place resources of tar sand may be extensive, their commercial viability in the foreseeable future is nil, and no adverse effects on U. S.

Bulldozer track from uranium exploration in the Dirty Devil proposed wilderness area. As in so much of Utah's desert, the search for mineral wealth proved fruitless here. After more than a decade of disuse, the scars are now slowly being reclaimed by nature.

Ray Wheeler

hydrocarbon availability can be expected to result from their inclusion in wilderness areas.

Coal

Although Utah WSAs do contain large deposits of coal, these deposits generally are too remote from markets, too difficult to reach, and present such extreme problems of mining and reclamation that few are likely to be mined in the foreseeable future. Most WSAs with substantial coal deposits lie in the Kaiparowits, Book Cliffs, and Henry Mountains coal fields. Of these, only the Book Cliffs has significant current production, and only the southern tip of that field is within the Utah Wilderness Coalition proposal. That part of the field has up to 200 million tons of coal reserves, of which up to 70 million tons are minable (based on data in *Atlas of Utah*, 1981). In contrast, the remainder of Utah's producing coal fields (the rest of the Book Cliffs as well as the Wasatch Plateau and Salina Canyon fields) contain more than 3.3 billion tons of minable reserves. Current production could be sustained from these proven reserves for nearly two centuries.

Oil and Gas

Although the BLM states that 80 of its WSAs could contain oil and gas, it acknowledges that this is "very speculative for most WSAs" (BLM, 1986, vol. 1, p. 129). The BLM rated 19 of its WSAs as having a medium to high potential for oil and gas, based on ratings provided by its consultant, Science Applications, Inc. (SAI). But the BLM bases its resource estimates on only part of the SAI analysis—the "favorability" rating. That rating projects the size of any oil and gas reservoir that might be found beneath a WSA. This rating does not take into account the likelihood of finding such deposits, for which SAI assigns a separate "certainty" rating. Both ratings must be taken together to assess the likelihood of finding a resource of a certain size. For example, the Paria-Hackberry WSA was assumed to have a potential resource of 3-15 million barrels of oil. However, the *likelihood* of finding deposits of this size was rated as low.

We examined drilling records in the vicinity of three representative WSAs (Negro Bill Canyon, Mill Creek, and Behind the Rocks) to determine whether the SAI ratings themselves were reasonable. The lack of significant discoveries suggests that the favorability ratings for these areas are exaggerated, hence are suspect for other areas as well.

The BLM's DEIS states that "the potential for oil and gas within the [Behind the Rocks] WSA is believed to be moderate for Mississippian-aged rocks and lower for Pennsylvanian-aged rocks." (BLM, 1986, vol. V, Behind the Rocks analysis, p. 11; similar statements for Mill Creek and Negro Bill.) Over 70 wells have been drilled within a radius of about 15 miles of the center of the three areas. Nearly half of the wells tested Mississipian or older strata. Nine wells produced some oil, but only two were producing as of 1986. None of the 70-plus wells had significant shows in or produced from Mississipian-aged rock. The nearest wells with good shows or production are all 5 miles or more west or southwest of the Behind the Rocks WSA. Each of these wells produced from or had shows in Pennsylvanian-aged strata.

Recent exploration in southeastern Utah suggests the possibility that deeply buried Precambrian rocks may be a potential source of hydrocarbons. Oil and gas potential in Precambrian source rock is generally considered very low and is unlikely to ever generate meaningful quantities of oil. Even in the remote possibility of an occurrence, the depth of the deposit would exceed that of existing Utah oil fields; thus, extraction costs would be substantially greater. As is, Utah has the second-highest drilling cost per barrel for any state containing significant oil and gas reserves.

The BLM states in its DEIS (1986, vol. 1, p. 71) that "the projected amount of oil in Utah BLM WSAs (total estimated in-place resource) is less than four-tenths of one percent of the projected U.S. proven and indicated reserves and 12 percent of the estimated Utah proven and indicated reserves." Even this is an apples-and-oranges comparison, since the proven reserves in the WSAs are likely to be much less than the BLM "projected amount of oil."

Uranium

The BLM identified 22 WSAs as having potential uranium resources. Sixteen of those WSAs are either not recommended for wilderness or are only partially recommended. For example, 19,000 acres in the North Escalante Canyons/The Gulch WSA were left out of the BLM's wilderness recommendation presumably because of uranium deposits. Inferred and known uranium deposits in that WSA could be as much as a few hundred tons, but most of this material is currently not economic to extract.

The BLM estimates total reserves of uranium oxide in Utah WSAs as 70,343 tons (BLM, 1986, vol. 1, p. 75). However, this estimate was based on studies conducted for the Department of Energy in the 1970s. At that time there were considerably better prospects for uranium recovery in Utah at the then-current price of $30 per pound for uranium oxide. Demand has fallen considerably with the long term slackening of electric demand and the problems besetting the nuclear power industry. The current price of under $9 per pound has rendered many deposits uneconomic. Moreover, huge deposits of uranium ore have been opened in Australia and Canada. U.S. production is more likely to come from the lowest-cost uranium reserves in Wyoming, New Mexico, and northern Arizona, not from wilderness deposits in Utah.

Potash

Utah wild lands are unlikely to be significant producers of potash because of much larger known deposits closer to transportation and markets. The BLM's analysis of its Mill Creek WSA is illustrative. Mill Creek was assigned a moderately favorable rating for potash for both size of deposit and likelihood of occurrence. But the ratings do not take into account the depth of the potassium-bearing strata—at least 7,000 feet. Moreover, the deposit is likely to be small—1 to 10 tons. This may be why none of the WSA is currently under lease for potash. As the BLM states, "The likelihood of the area being explored or developed is remote due to more favorable areas elsewhere" (BLM, 1986, p. 22). Despite a favorable *geologic* rating, an *economic* analysis shows that no true resources are present.

Conclusion

A meaningful analysis of minerals in wilderness areas would distinguish between *deposits* of minerals, which may not be economic to mine, and mineral *reserves* that meet economic criteria. If a mineral deposit is unlikely to be developed because of basic economic or environmental constraints, it is dishonest to claim that wilderness designation would cause the loss of that resource. Mineral deposits on most of Utah's BLM wild lands are too remote from markets to be feasible to develop, or have other severe constraints on development such as lack of water, rugged topography, and difficult reclamation. Thus, wilderness designations will probably have much less effect on mineral availability than industry advocates claim.

GRAZING IN WILDERNESS

One of the little-understood provisions of the Wilderness Act of 1964 is that livestock grazing *is allowed* in designated wilderness areas. The Act's specific language (see sidebar) was further clarified by Congress in the Colorado Wilderness Act of 1980. The committee report accompanying that bill contains guidelines which the BLM has since incorporated into its wilderness management policy: "The legislative history of this language is very clear in its intent that livestock grazing, and activities and the necessary facilities to support a livestock grazing program, will be permitted to continue in National Forest wilderness areas, when such grazing was established prior to classification of an area as wilderness" (House Report 96-17).

This report specifies that wilderness designation cannot be used as an excuse to reduce or phase out grazing. Grazing levels may be allowed to increase if there would be "no adverse impact" on wilderness values. However, no new permits can be issued. New improvements such as fences and spring developments are permissible, but should be aimed at protecting resources, rather than increasing grazing levels. Livestock permittees cannot be compelled to use natural materials in the construction of facilities if doing so would impose "unreasonable" costs.

The Utah Wilderness Coalition's wilderness proposal would further minimize impacts to livestock permittees by "cherry-stemming" roads needed by ranchers for access to stock watering ponds and other range developments.

Wilderness designation can benefit a livestock operation by eliminating conflicts between off-road vehicles and livestock, including vandalism, open gates, and harassment and theft of livestock.

Livestock grazing, if improperly managed, can lead to soil erosion, competition for forage with wildlife species, the introduction of non-native plant species, the spread of disease to wildlife populations, damage to riparian areas, and deterioration of water quality. These problems must be dealt with regardless of whether an area is designated wilderness. To oppose wilderness because it might affect livestock operations shifts attention from the real issue—the desert's fragile soils and vegetation that must be protected at all costs.

Livestock Forage Values in BLM Wild Lands

Wilderness designation *would* limit the potential to increase grazing above current levels. In most cases grazing levels are already at or above the natural carrying capacity of the land; further increases would require significant range modifications such as new stock reservoirs, road access, chainings, and seedings. Such developments rarely bring returns commensurate with their cost because of the inherently poor forage values found on most arid lands.

Existing livestock grazing within our proposal would, of course, continue. But even this use is not a significant part of Utah's economy. As part of a landmark 1987 study of public attitudes toward wilderness protection in the state of Utah entitled *Non-Market Valuation of Wilderness Designation in Utah*, Dr. C. Arden Pope, Professor of Economics at Brigham Young University, established a relative value for livestock forage within the 3.2 million acres of WSAs to be about $500,000. And the sad state of the range itself precludes any significant increases. When the value of these wild lands for other uses is measured, livestock grazing appears even less significant. Dr. Pope's study showed that in terms of people's willingness to pay for recreation and other wilderness values, the BLM's WSAs alone would have a total relative value of $27 million to $47 million.

Manipulating the Range—The Chaining Boondoggle

One of the most objectionable practices still used on public lands is chaining. In this operation, two large bulldozers drag a ship-anchor chain through stands of trees and sagebrush, ripping them out. Chaining destroys stands of pinyon-juniper to encourage the growth of grass for livestock.

All too often, however, chaining destroys resources at tremendous cost to the taxpayer. Chainings eliminate thermal and hiding cover for big game. Undiscovered archeological resources are destroyed as the chain is dragged across the ground. Desert soils can take thousands of years to develop; chaining not only disturbs the topsoil, but permits erosion as water is allowed to run unimpeded across the newly barren ground.

The economics of chaining are also notoriously poor. Proposed range improvements in the Henry Mountains, for example, would cost $94,000 to increase forage by some 540 AUMs—a cost of $175 per AUM. Contrast the $1.81 per AUM fee paid in 1990 for public forage.

The abrupt, unnatural clearings created by chaining are similar to forest clearcutting, and just as esthetically offensive. In many instances, uprooted trees and shrubs are left in unsightly windrows to decay.

Much as with clearcutting, chaining proponents claim that the practice mimics natural processes such as wildfire that perpetuate grassland ecosystems by clearing off sagebrush and pinyon-juniper forests. But the shrubs and trees may simply be recolonizing their former habitat following severe grazing disturbance during the late 1800s. Chaining is a destructive way to create livestock forage, and is not permitted within Congressionally designated wilderness areas. A sound fire management policy, coupled with proper grazing management, can do more to perpetuate natural grassland ecosystems than intensive scarification practices such as chaining.

Lawson LeGate

OFF-ROAD VEHICLES

Off-road vehicles (ORVs), which include four-wheel-drive pickup trucks, three-and four-wheeled all-terrain vehicles, and trail bikes, are commonly used on BLM lands. State of Utah data from 1980, cited by the BLM (1986), indicate that off-road vehicle use was the 17th most popular recreation activity on all Utah lands, with a total of 2 million visits in 1976. (Hiking and backpacking was the 14th most popular with 2.3 million visits.) Utah has ample opportunities for vehicular recreation with thousands of miles of dirt roads outside of UWC's wilderness proposals.

Off-road vehicle users often ask why their form of recreation is not allowed within designated wilderness areas. Vehicles are essentially incompatible with wilderness and conflict with other users. When an ORV intrudes into a wild place, the solitude sought by the visitor on foot or horseback is lost as the natural silence is suddenly shattered.

Physical resource damage is another reason why ORVs are not permitted in wilderness areas. Such damage is apparent throughout Utah's desert lands. When operated off of established roads, ORVs can destroy fragile cryptogamic soils, break off delicate rock ledges, erode stream banks at stream crossings, and leave unsightly tire tracks.

The damage from vehicles is often irreparable. Cryptogam, the dark-brown or grey soil crusts formed by living organisms, is particularly susceptible to damage. Cryptogam evolves over many years to stabilize sandy desert soils. Once crushed by vehicles, it can take decades to become reestablished, if at all.

Before and after: These aerial photos of the Henry Mountains show the extent of recent forest chaining. The top photo was taken in 1955, the bottom photo in 1985. Unchained area at bottom right surrounds The Horn in the proposed Mt. Pennell wilderness unit.

U.S. Department of the Interior

All-terrain vehicle (ATV) tracks across cryptogam in the Fish and Owl Creek unit of the proposed San Juan-Anasazi wilderness west of Blanding. These tracks belong to one of four ATVs that entered the area as a group, sometimes riding two or three abreast and leaving scars that will last for decades.

Joseph Chiaretti

In 1977 the National Science Foundation and the Geological Society of America published a detailed analysis entitled *Impacts and Management of Off Road Vehicles*. This report found that ORVs disturb soils, increase erosion, damage water quality, destroy plants and adversely affect animals.

The analysis also raised concerns about long term effects of ORVs. In discussing impacts on plant communities, the study said: "Indeed, it seems certain that many delicate interdependencies between organisms and their habitats, having been obliterated by ORVs, can never be restored."

ORV use requires specific management by the BLM, especially in light of technological advances in the last few years. These newer vehicles have more power and better gear drives than their predecessors. With these advances comes an ability to generate more damage in less time on larger tracts of public land.

Some ORV users complain that they are willing to share their routes with hikers, so why can't hikers accept vehicles? The problem is that vehicles have an impact out of proportion to their numbers. One motorbike or ATV can destroy the desert's silence for miles around, interrupting the solitude for dozens of hikers. Yet that many foot travelers, properly dispersed, will not disturb each other.

Many ORV users desire easy access to scenic places. And Utah's desert lands have thousands of miles of highways, secondary roads, and backcountry jeep routes that will remain open even if our wilderness proposal is enacted. At no point in any of our proposed wilderness areas is one more than 7 miles from a road. Unless additional lands are placed off limits to vehicle use, the solitude, silence, and opportunity for physical challenge—so long a part of the American West—will become a thing of the past.

Rudy Lukez

STATE LANDS

Scattered evenly throughout the Utah Wilderness Coalitions's 5.7 million acres of proposed BLM wilderness are about 630,000 acres of land owned by the State of Utah. (State lands are not included in our acreage totals.) Every ninth square mile (four sections in every township) was given to the state by the federal government under the Statehood Act of 1894. Nearly half of the state's original holdings have been sold. But the state still holds sections 2, 16, 32, and 36 in every township of BLM land. (Much of its scattered holdings in national parks, national forests, Indian reservations, and military installations has been exchanged for large blocks of BLM land.) The state currently holds a total of 3.7 million acres.

The state was given the lands as a trust to help support the public schools. The Governor's Wilderness Subcommittee reports that the school trust lands generate about $12 million per year, which is only 2 percent of the uniform school fund. The Division of State Lands and Forestry (DSLF), which manages these lands, has tried to raise more money by emphasizing immediate economic return rather than sustained yield management.

The Public Trust For Sale

Tellingly, the state attempted to raise revenues by pressuring the National Park Service into exchanging the remaining scattered state sections in Capitol Reef National Park and Glen Canyon National Recreation Area (NRA) for prime development property on Lake Powell. The state planned to sell or lease these newly acquired lands—still within the NRA—to private developers for marinas, condominiums, and airports. Although these lands would be located within Glen Canyon NRA, the Park Service would have no control over their commercial use.

The Park Service, in fulfilling *its* trust obligations, could only answer with a resounding "no." Commercial development of such *newly created* inholdings would seriously compromise the Park Service's ability to manage the natural and recreational values of the NRA. Accordingly, it asked the DSLF to resume negotiations to exchange the inholdings for BLM lands outside of the parks as it had agreed to do in a 1987 memorandum of understanding. But instead the DSLF announced in mid-1989 that it would put the park inholdings up for sale to the highest bidder. This position has more to do with fulfilling the anti-park and anti-wilderness sentiments of some county commissioners than with protecting the school trust.

Strong protests by Utah citizens forced the DSLF to halt its land disposal plans, at least temporarily, but the state's willingness to make such a threat is disturbing, and does not bode well for BLM wild lands so long as they contain state inholdings. In addition to commercially developing the state sections themselves, the state may attempt to block wilderness protection by claiming a right to build roads to each section.

The deleterious effect of ORVs on native plants and animals is undeniable. Where their use is heavy, virtually all existing life is ultimately destroyed. As matters now stand, a form of play has joined with other destructive human activities in degrading the Earth's wild and unspoiled places.

IMPACTS AND MANAGEMENT OF OFF-ROAD VEHICLES
The Geological Society of America and National Science Foundation, Report EAR75-16285, May 1977, 8 p.

Minimal Returns

If state lands were retained within our proposed wilderness areas, what would be the effect on the school trust? The Governor's Wilderness Sub-committee found that the average annual rents for state sections within or adjacent to areas the BLM recommended for wilderness are $1 per acre. At this rate, the state lands within or adjacent to the Coalition proposal would generate about $630,000 per year. This is only one-tenth of one percent of the uniform school fund. Yet even these small returns would not be lost under wilderness designation. The DSLF would still rent the lands for grazing, and it could exchange its scattered sections for non-wilderness BLM lands (as the states of Arizona and Oregon have done with hundreds of thousands of acres in recent years).

Alternative Solutions

Given the DSLF's short-sighted, environmentally destructive management, the members of the Utah Wilderness Coalition are unwilling to see the state receive large blocks of public land with wilderness, scenic, or wildlife values. Any exchange program must include the safeguards contained in the Federal Land Policy and Management Act (FLPMA) to retain lands with significant public values in public ownership. More than 1.4 million acres of state land have been exchanged under FLPMA in other western states since 1983.

Another possible solution would be for the federal government to purchase some state inholdings within designated wilderness areas through the Land and Water Conservation Fund (LWCF), which was authorized in 1964 to use some of the revenues from offshore oil leasing to purchase lands for conservation and recreation purposes. Acquisitions through the LWCF have been limited, however, because of the failure of recent administrations to request full funding for the program.

Estimated values for recently proposed Utah BLM acquisitions through the LWCF range from $50 to $100 per acre for properties without high development potential to as much as $2,000 for prime recreation land in the St. George area. Because many state sections are isolated and have limited development potential, the lower figures are probably closer to the average. Even so, public purchase of the state inholdings in BLM wilderness lands could provide the school trust with more money than it would receive from grazing and mineral fees.

In other states, exchange and acquisition of state lands has been a part of the BLM's efforts to block up and improve management of its holdings. Management of both BLM and state lands would be simplified, and citizens could be assured that designated wilderness areas would be free of the pressure of inappropriate commercial uses.

Rodney Greeno

WILDERNESS WATER RIGHTS

Water is a critical component of desert ecosystems. If wilderness streams and wetlands were to dry up or diminish significantly due to their diversion and drainage, then water would not be available for wildlife, riparian plants, and recreation. Clearly, wilderness legislation must include a reserved water right if it is to include all the major elements of wild ecosystems in the protective umbrella.

The courts have consistently held that Congress intends to establish a federal reserved water right when it sets aside public land for special protective purposes. Thus, all federal reservations, such as Indian reservations, military reservations, national parks, and wilderness areas have federal reserved water rights. These federal water rights are administered by states and are determined on the basis of the principle, "First in time, first in right." This means that all water rights applicants line up behind all others whose rights have been previously established. A newly established wilderness area will have a recent priority date and be "junior" to all other existing water rights holders.

Most of the areas proposed for wilderness by the Utah Wilderness Coalition contain the middle or lower courses of the streams that flow through them. Though none of Zion National Park has been designated as wilderness, it stands as a good example of the need for a federal reserved water right for wilderness and parks. Few would argue against the proposition that the water of the Virgin River, which carved much of the spectacular scenery of Zion, is an essential component of the park and its ecosystem.

There are no serious proposals to locate water projects within the park. There are, however, designs to build a dam on the North Fork of the Virgin River *above* the park. The diversion of water from the reservoir behind such a dam would have obvious negative effects on the river downstream in the park. There would be less water to support riparian vegetation along the stream. Water diverted by the proposed project would not be available to support fish such as the endangered woundfin minnow, the Virgin River chub, or the Virgin River spinedace. In addition, less downstream water would detract from the experience of the thousands of park visitors every year who wade the Virgin River Narrows. Such damage could be avoided if the federal government were to claim a reserved water right for the park.

Courts have defined the quantity of a reserved water right for public land as the amount necessary to carry out the purposes for which the land was protected. Thus, a wilderness water right is the amount of water needed to ensure the integrity of wilderness values. The use of water in wilderness is nonconsumptive. Wilderness streams capture precipitation and contribute to groundwater recharge, and the primary users of water within wilderness are plants and animals. Water that flows into a wilderness flows out of a wilderness and is still available for downstream uses.

Due in part to unresolved legal battles on the issue of water rights, it is necessary for Congress to assert a reserved water right for each wilderness area it establishes. But some members of Congress from the West persist in their attempts to strip water rights from wilderness areas by attaching inappropriate language to wilderness bills under consideration by Congress. Moreover, an Interior Department Solicitor's opinion issued in the waning days of the Reagan administration officially denied the existence of wilderness water rights. Therefore the responsibility has fallen on Congress to assert such rights and Congress has done so repeatedly in recent years—with the Nevada wilderness bill in 1989, the El Malpais, New Mexico, legislation in 1988, and in the Arizona BLM wilderness bill in 1990. Each of these states is as arid as Utah and its citizens no less concerned about future economic growth.

In order to protect wilderness water resources for Utah BLM wilderness, legislation will need to follow these guidelines:

(1) An express reservation of water for the amount necessary to protect wilderness values . . .

(2) . . . with the priority date as the date of enactment.

(3) Wilderness water rights are subject to all valid existing water rights and . . .

(4) . . . are in addition to any other water rights already reserved by the United States.

(5) The federal government must promptly claim a wilderness water right for each of the areas designated as wilderness by the Utah BLM Wilderness Act.

Some federal land managers claim that they cannot be compelled by the courts to assert and defend wilderness water rights. Therefore, wilderness legislation should include a statement which ensures that the federal agency responsible for managing the new wilderness will not treat the assertion of a wilderness water right as discretionary and will enter without delay into the state's water rights adjudication process.

It would be difficult to find anyone who would seriously propose that after a wilderness is established, its forests could be clearcut, its most impressive geologic features stripped away, or its wildlife exterminated. Likewise, a wilderness would be greatly diminished with its water siphoned off. We must ensure, then, that legislation which establishes BLM wilderness in Utah includes measures necessary for the protection of wilderness water resources.

Maggie Fox and Lawson LeGate

WILDERNESS RESOURCES

I F it is clear from the preceding chapter what wilderness designations do *not* do, then what are the reasons *for* preserving wilderness? Protecting unspoiled scenery and opportunities for backcountry recreation are important, but in many cases other values are more important. Wilderness is also undisturbed watershed, habitat for wildlife, a hidden treasure of prehistoric cultural artifacts, and an immense natural laboratory for scientific research and education. Finally, there is a value to wilderness that may seem unrelated to our immediate needs and pleasures. A species that has altered so much of the Earth needs, out of humility if nothing else, to leave some land entirely undisturbed. Some call it respect for other forms of life; others call it an essential restraint upon our often self-destructive craftiness; still others identify a need to respect the original Creation. These values may have little currency in the marketplace, but in the end they may be more important than hiking trails and scenic viewpoints. Although one tends to lead to the other: a quiet walk in the desert, away from machines and material distractions, often engenders a healing peacefulness not easily found in our towns and cities.

This chapter, then, presents some of the fundamental reasons why our Utah BLM wilderness proposal should be enacted. This chapter also looks at Utah's national parks and their relation to BLM wilderness, and concludes with a plea for a reasonable balance between extractive uses of the land and its preservation.

PLANT COMMUNITIES

The natural vegetation that once covered Utah's desert lands is today found only in a few small, scattered localities, typically where cliffs or lack of water has limited livestock grazing and other human development. These "relict" plant communities are valuable as genetic reservoirs and as indicators of the desert's original vegetation. By showing the productive potential of undisturbed land, relict areas help scientists measure the effects of development activities (Tuhy and MacMahon, 1988).

State and federal agencies have active programs (such as the Utah Natural Heritage Program) for identifying and protecting relict plant areas. A goal of these programs is to ensure that representative samples of all vegetation types are protected from logging, mining, vehicles, grazing, and other disturbance. Federal agencies are also required to identify and protect the habitat of threatened and endangered plant species, as well as to identify candidates for potential addition to the list of protected species.

Wilderness designation can enhance these programs by limiting mechanized uses and development on tracts of federal lands. The wild lands in our BLM wilderness proposal harbor at least 2 endangered plant species, 2 threatened species, and 17 candidate species (see individual unit descriptions for details). More species would likely be found if thorough field inventories were performed, particularly in areas the BLM did not study for their wilderness potential. At least 13 relict plant communities and several near-relict areas have been identified within our wilderness proposals; notable examples are discussed under the Grand Staircase area (No Mans Mesa), Moquith Mountain, Glen Canyon (Mancos Mesa), and Canyonlands (Bridger Jack and Lavender Mesas).

Of all human activities, livestock grazing has had the most widespread effect on natural plant communities in the desert Southwest. Wilderness designation does not reduce existing levels of livestock grazing. But the restrictions that wilderness designation places on new road construction, mining, forest chaining, and off-road vehicle use provide an important additional overlay of protection to such areas. Wilderness complements administrative designations such as Research Natural Areas (which are often small areas surrounding particular plant communities) by placing further restrictions on human activities, restrictions that are not subject to administrative change.

Off-road vehicle use can have especially devastating effects on plant communities. Unlike large development projects such as mines and power plants, no site studies are conducted to identify rare plants before ORV riders blast off into the backcountry. Vehicle users tend to follow streamcourses and ridgetops that often are the specialized habitats of such plants. And tire tracks are death to cryptogamic soil crusts that anchor sandy desert soils and prevent erosion. Without wilderness designation, areas containing rare plants, such as the badlands surrounding North and South Caineville Mesas, are subject to severe ORV damage.

Wilderness visitors often seek spectacular views of canyons, rimrocks, and stone arches. But those who take a closer look at the land underfoot will notice a splendid community of life unlike that found on developed lands. Seeing the native grasses and shrubs of Utah's desert relict areas, uncontaminated with coarse, weedy species, is as much to be treasured as a golden desert sunset. And with proper protection, Utah's native plant communities need not simply fade away.

Fred Swanson

WILDLIFE

Native wildlife species are an integral and natural part of any wilderness area, as much a part of the ecosystem as trees and plants. The restoration of native wildlife populations dependent on natural habitats is one of the most important reasons for designating areas as wilderness.

Haven for Big Game

Wilderness designation will help those wildlife species that are sensitive to human intrusion and disturbance. Many types of birds and mammals found in wilderness cannot tolerate excessive human intrusion, especially during nesting, mating, birthing, and denning times. Wilderness provides a safe haven for large mammals such as the Rocky Mountain and desert bighorn sheep, elk, bison, mountain lion, and antelope, all of which are found within Utah's desert wilderness. With fewer mechanized intrusions, natural vegetation can grow and native wildlife can return to and thrive in its historic ranges. The Utah Department of Wildlife Resources (UDWR) has an active transplantation program for species such as desert bighorn. But such programs must emphasize the retention of natural conditions, not manipulation that favors some types of wildlife over others.

Rare Species

The desert lands proposed for wilderness are habitat for at least two dozen endangered or sensitive species that require specialized desert habitats. These range from the Gila monster, chuckawalla, and desert tortoise in the hot southwestern corner of Utah, to the bald eagle, peregrine falcon and endangered native fishes of the Colorado and Green Rivers. An unusually large number of endemic species (those found nowhere else) occur in the Colorado Plateau. This is a result of the region's diverse habitats including rivers, streams, and potholes; rocky cliffs and isolated mesas; and sand dunes, grasslands, upland forests, and alpine tundra. The Basin and Range mountains, isolated by salt flats and ancient glacial lakes, have also evolved endemic species such as the Bonneville cutthroat trout.

The large mammals found within Utah's desert wilderness include a majority of the big game species of the American West. Big game hunting is a major economic activity in Utah; backcountry hunts in the Book Cliffs or the Kaiparowits Plateau are as exciting as anywhere in the West. But nongame species are also important to Utahns. Mankind has to be the spokesman for all wildlife; animals cannot speak for themselves.

A Legacy of Wildlife

When all is said and done, the areas that would become wilderness will be those small islands of land where wildlife can survive mankind's relentless assault. Without man's help, the first casualty of today's society will be the wildlife. The chance to walk through wilderness areas and see the wildlife in their natural surroundings, where man is the visitor, is an important legacy for future generations. To insure our own survival and well-being, we must act now to prevent the loss of wilderness and the wildlife on which it depends; when they are in trouble, so are we.

Pat Sackett
Utah Wildlife Federation

A wilderness hunt, whether on foot or on horseback, takes one back to a more challenging and self-reliant life. This mule deer was taken in the proposed wilderness of the Kaiparowits Plateau, where big game thrive in the absence of roads and mechanized intrusions.

Kenley Brunsdale

ARCHEOLOGICAL RESOURCES

Introduction

The Coalition's proposed wilderness areas contain important archeological resources, including spectacular Anasazi pueblos in southeastern Utah and 10,000-year-old cave sites in the northwestern deserts. In between are Archaic foraging sites, Fremont villages, and dwellings of ancestors of modern Native Americans. People have lived in what is now called Utah for the past 11,000 or 12,000 years. The study areas contain portions of this record; their passage into wilderness will help ensure protection of our priceless heritage.

Utah prehistory is divided into four periods, each characterized by diet, dwelling style, and lifeway. The earliest is called Paleo-Indian, dated between 12,000 and 9,500 years ago. It represents the first great expansion of early populations in the New World. Paleo-Indians hunted large Ice-Age mammals, and were very mobile, living in small groups ranging over large areas in search of plant and animal food. They made beautifully flaked stone tools, including fluted projectile points.

With the extinction of large Ice-Age mammals about 10,000 years ago, human lifestyles underwent significant changes. Diet centered on smaller animals and a variety of wild plants. Populations were larger than in the Paleo-Indian period, but people still lived in small mobile groups. A survival strategy called foraging characterized this period, known as the Archaic. These people had remarkably stable relationships with their

Vandals attempted to make off with this petroglyph near Highway 12 in the Escalante River canyon. Wilderness designation can help preserve such sites by limiting vehicle access.

Elliot Bernshaw

environments, since their basic lifeway changed very little between 9,500 and about 2,000 years ago.

The period following the Archaic is characterized by corn horticulture, pottery and settled village life, traits shared by Anasazi and Fremont cultures in the region. It was thought that these traits came into the area around 1,300 years ago, but recent evidence has shown that horticulture began in Utah about 2,100 years ago. Settled lifeways began sometime later, and pottery was introduced into the region around 1,600 years ago. The spectacular Anasazi sites in southern Utah date to between 900 and 600 years ago, or between AD 1000 and 1300. Fremont sites, while less spectacular, are equally important. They are found throughout Utah, and in portions of Colorado, Wyoming, and Nevada.

The Anasazi left southwestern Utah around AD 1100; they remained in the southeast until AD 1300. Where did they go? Southward, to become the modern Hopi and other Pueblo peoples of Arizona and New Mexico. The Fremont left somewhat later, around AD 1350, but their movements are more of a mystery. Some suggest they lived in northwest Colorado until about AD 1500, then moved onto the Great Plains. Others claim they stayed in Utah, changed lifestyles and merged with ancestors of the Ute and Paiute.

The most recent period, beginning around AD 1300, is called the Late Prehistoric. It is characterized by a renewed foraging strategy throughout the state, practiced by ancestors of modern Navajo, Ute, and Paiute peoples. The ancestral Ute and Paiute, speaking a Numic language, entered the region around AD 1100. The ancestral Navajo, speaking an Athapaskan language, entered the region much later, possibly in historic times.

Archeological Resources

Proposed wilderness areas in the northwest part of Utah contain some of the oldest sites in the state. These include sites in the Silver Island, Fish Springs, and Deep Creek ranges dating to Archaic, Fremont, and Late Prehistoric times. Several are on the National Register of Historic Places (NRHP). All mountain ranges in this region were used throughout prehistory for hunting, fishing, and gathering seeds.

The Wah Wah Mountains and House Range contain similar evidence, with a broad range of known Archaic and Fremont sites. The Granite Peak area is one of the most important in Utah. It contains numerous obsidian quarries used from Paleo-Indian to Historic times. These have been heavily disturbed by casual collectors, so that virtually no large pieces of obsidian remain at most sites.

Moving southward, we enter the region of the Virgin Anasazi, centered around St. George and Kanab. Proposed wilderness here contains evidence of Anasazi and Late Prehistoric uses of landscapes around Zion National Park and the Vermilion Cliffs. These areas are little known, although some absolutely pristine cliff dwellings have been reported. They very much need protection.

The spectacular scenery in the Upper Paria, Kaiparowits, and Escalante areas is matched by remarkable Anasazi ruins. A little known Fremont component also exists in this area, but relations between the two are unclear, making preservation even more important. The areas are near Coombs Village (Anasazi State Park), an Anasazi site with interesting Fremont connections.

The Henry Mountains and Dirty Devil River areas contain diverse archeological resources. The Henrys contain evidence of Fremont foraging camps as high as 8,000 feet, and Fremont settlements have been studied on their northern slopes. The southern Henry Mountains contain early Anasazi storage and camp sites. The Dirty Devil and Labyrinth areas contain large Fremont habitation and rock art sites, as well as Cowboy Cave, with Ice-Age mammal, Archaic, and Anasazi cultural remains. The latter site yielded some of the earliest corn found in Utah.

The most spectacular Anasazi remains and rock art are found in the proposed White and Dark Canyon, Glen Canyon, and San Juan-Anasazi areas. White and Dark Canyon areas contain abundant early Anasazi high altitude camp and farming sites. These mostly date to the period between AD 1000 and 1150, when environmental conditions were more conducive to high altitude corn farming. The Glen Canyon area contains the relatively little-known Red Canyon cliff dwelling sites, as well as a wide range of farming sites on the mesa tops. Only a few Archaic and late Prehistoric sites are known from this region.

The San Juan-Anasazi area is the most popular region in the state for visiting Anasazi canyon sites. It contains some of the most important archeological sites in Utah, including those near Comb Ridge, in Fish and Owl Creek canyons, Arch and Mule Creek canyons, and, of course, Grand Gulch. The Bear's Ears, important in Navajo mythology, are landmarks visible from most mesa tops. A Paleo-Indian site was recently found near Bluff, and caves in the area contain remains of Ice-Age mammals.

The proposed Squaw and Cross Canyon area contains early Anasazi sites, as well as some of the latest, similar to Hovenweep sites on Cahone Mesa. Several rockshelter sites, as well as smaller Anasazi villages are known from the Canyonlands Basin area. This region is poorly known, but seems to have supported a large population between around AD 1000 to 1100. The general region near the Colorado River has produced several isolated Paleo-Indian artifacts, but no sites as yet.

Farther west, the Labyrinth area contains abundant rock art, mixing both Anasazi and Fremont styles. Few habitation sites of any period have been recorded in this area, partly because few studies have focused here. The opposite is true for the San Rafael area, where several important Fremont sites have been studied. Important rock art sites have also been recorded along the San Rafael River.

The areas around Moab and Arches National Monument are likely to contain small Anasazi sites, with some mixing in the area with Fremont. The Alice Hunt Site, Moonshine Cave, and the nearby Turner-Look Site in Colorado all show the presence of Archaic, Anasazi, and Fremont peoples in the region.

Northward, the proposed Desolation Canyon area contains a complex record of Archaic, Fremont, and Late Prehistoric habitation and travel. Large Fremont masonry sites are known from small canyons. Storage sites are found along the Green River, and the area contains abundant rock art. Historic Ute east-west travel routes through the area pass along the highlands of the Book Cliffs, where water was available. North-south routes followed the canyons.

The remaining areas, White River and the proposed Dinosaur Wilderness, contain Archaic and Fremont habitation and a few rock art sites. This region contains the latest Fremont habitation sites, which date well after the western regions were abandoned.

Conclusion

As the list illustrates, the most scenic areas in Utah are also some of the richest for important archeological sites. The proposed areas contain a great record of humanity.

The spectacular scenery in the Upper Paria, Kaiparowits, and Escalante areas is matched by remarkable Anasazi ruins. A little known Fremont component also exists in this area, but relations between the two are unclear, making preservation even more important.

Every site in Utah, however, is subject to destruction through vandalism, pothunting, and other criminal activities. At least three sites are destroyed by pothunters every weekend. Valuable information on others is destroyed by casual collectors every day. These are non-renewable resources! Other sites are destroyed by development, but most of these on public lands have been evaluated by professional archeologists. Inclusion in designated wilderness areas will help to protect many important sites for the enjoyment and study of future generations.

James D. Wilde, Ph.D.
Director, Office of Public Archaeology
Brigham Young University

RECREATION

Utah's BLM lands have a nationwide following, judging from the number of out-of-state license plates at desert trailheads. Most of this use, however, is concentrated in a few areas. Data from the BLM show that two-thirds of the recreational use of its 82 WSAs occurs in just 5 areas: Desolation Canyon, North Escalante Canyons, Phipps-Death Hollow, Grand Gulch, and Westwater Canyon.

The rest of Utah's BLM wild lands also provide surpassing beauty, are for the most part highly accessible, yet by and large are little known. Those with limited knowledge of this country can join a guided pack or float trip and have the adventure of a lifetime. More adventurous types can head into remote canyons and plateaus and find perfect solitude.

Only if we protect the full sweep of BLM wild lands will these diverse recreational opportunities be maintained. Designating wilderness in a handful of popular areas such as Grand Gulch and the Escalante canyons will only lead to permits and rationing as other wild areas become roaded and industrialized, and use is concentrated in a few areas.

Access for All

Hiking and backpacking is more popular in Utah than off-road vehicle use, according to 1980 State of Utah figures cited by the BLM (2.3 million visits versus 2 million). Furthermore, most vehicle use takes place on lands not being considered for wilderness designation, while most foot travel occurs in natural areas.

There is room for foot travelers *and* motorists in Utah's desert, but not in the same places. Some part of every wilderness area we propose may be viewed from a paved road, a car campground, or a roadside scenic stop. The Needles Overlook, for example, gives a superb view of our Canyonlands Basin wilderness; dizzying vistas lie right off Interstate 70 into Devils Canyon atop the San Rafael Swell; and Comb Ridge has a paved highway plowing right through it, just north of our proposed wilderness unit. Those with little time can find dozens of short hikes along gentle, sandy washes such as Calf Creek, Negro Bill Canyon, Beaver Dam Wash, and White Canyon.

Should more desert wilderness be roaded and developed to render it "accessible"? This approach would crowd incompatible recreational uses onto the same ground. Multiple use does not mean that hikers should have to listen to motorbikes, rafters should have to dodge motorboats, and backpackers should have to haul out trash hauled in on ORVs.

The fraction of Utah's landscape (about 15 percent at present) that is unroaded and undeveloped ought to be left to the voices of ravens and the occasional tromp of respectful feet.

Physically challenged people can enjoy wilderness adventures on trips organized by S'PLORE (Special Populations Learning Outdoor Experiences), a member of the Utah Wilderness Coalition. These rafters are launching into the Colorado River above the Fisher Towers, a proposed wilderness northwest of Moab.

Photo courtesy of S'PLORE

Recreation Economics

Designation of wilderness would increase recreation-based employment, both in outfitting and guiding and in expenditures for equipment and supplies. Moreover, by preserving its wilderness, Utah will enhance its image as a desirable place to live. Outdoor recreational opportunities rank high among the intangible benefits that companies offer potential employees. Because salaries in high-technology fields are higher in other regions of the country, Utah must compete for job talent with resources at hand—including its enviable natural environment.

Utah's BLM wild lands support a thriving small industry of guides and outfitters. The BLM notes that 47 outfitters use its WSAs. Such use could increase considerably if additional lands were designated wilderness. In Mancos Mesa alone, the annual income generated by commercial recreational use could increase to as much as $50,000, according to the BLM (1986, p. 26).

The Outdoor Classroom

At least 10 educational and outdoor adventure schools currently operate in Utah's desert lands. Their programs range from expeditions teaching desert survival skills to leisurely float trips. Participants include college students, retired persons, teachers, and business executives, spanning all levels of age, education, income, and fitness.

Several outdoor education programs make extensive use of Coalition-proposed wilderness areas. The Colorado Outward Bound School runs courses in the White Canyon, Dirty Devil, Labyrinth, and Behind the Rocks areas; the National Outdoor Leadership School uses the Canyonlands Basin, Dark Canyon, and San Juan-Anasazi areas; and the Canyonlands Field Institute runs about half of its programs in the Labyrinth, La Sal, and Westwater areas.

Studying plant and animal ecology, investigating archeology, and learning outdoor living skills are primary features of such programs. BLM lands offer the necessary pristine environment without the crowding and restrictions often found in national parks.

Whether one tests one's muscles against a difficult rapid, watches a canyon wren dart among the shadows of a sandstone boulder, or relaxes around a fragrant campfire while a wrangler tells tales of the Anasazi, desert wilderness has a reassuring sense of the real world. That function of the wilderness has proven useful in programs to rehabilitate alcoholics, drug users, welfare clients, and troubled youths. Wilderness is a powerful tonic for the troubled as well as for the healthy.

Restoring the Spirit

The opportunity to experience an elemental connection to primeval land is a basic right long treasured in this country. The need to restore the spirit in the wilderness was recognized by Utah's preeminent pioneer leader, Brigham Young, who exhorted his people to " . . . preserve the wild country. Keep it wild, and enjoy it as such. . . . The outdoor air is what people need for health, it is good for them to camp out." So long as we guard this birthright, using some lands to meet our needs, leaving other lands as the Creator made them, the earth will continue to sustain us.

Fred Swanson

It's important to have opportunities to be alone—to experience a sense of connection with the land . . . The paved trail and the visitor-center approach has its place—but it's a step removed from direct experience.

Karla VanderZanden
Director, Canyonlands Field Institute

WILDERNESS AND UTAH'S PARKS

How often have you thought, as you gazed across Utah's canyon country, that most of southern Utah could have been set aside as one huge national park? That in any other state, almost any chunk of this "ordinary" BLM land would probably *be* a national park?

A World Class Landscape

Southern Utah's canyon country is "world class:" a unique and unparalleled landscape. And while pieces of this superlative region have been preserved as national parks, crucial areas were excluded in drawing their boundaries. Those boundaries were all too often the result of political compromise, timid vision, and speculation about potential resource conflicts.

Other park boundaries were drawn narrowly to protect only specific scenic features—the pinnacles at Bryce, the Waterpocket Fold at Capitol Reef, the rock "bridges" at Natural Bridges National Monument. Too often those boundaries disregarded adjacent park-quality lands.

The BLM wilderness review gives us another chance to protect these areas before it is too late.

Key Wild Lands Adjacent to the Parks

Among the BLM wild lands adjacent to Utah's national parks are the following, all proposed for wilderness designation by the Utah Wilderness Coalition:

Parunuweap Canyon and Canaan Mountain south of Zion National Park, and many smaller parcels abutting the remainder of the park such as North Fork Virgin River. Reservoirs are proposed in Parunuweap and North Fork canyons upstream of Zion;

Box Canyon and Squaw and Willis Creek adjacent to Bryce Canyon National Park, as well as East of Bryce, which has many of the same erosional features as the park;

Fremont Gorge, Mt. Pennell, Red Desert, Colt Mesa and other units adjoining Capitol Reef National Park. A proposed dam in the Fremont River gorge would dewater a section of the river;

Bridger Jack Mesa, Indian Creek, Butler Wash, Labyrinth Canyon, Shafer Canyon and The Gooseneck next to Canyonlands National Park. Archeological values are noteworthy here;

Lost Spring Canyon, part of the view east from the Devils Garden area of Arches National Park;

The White Canyon wilderness surrounding Natural Bridges National Monument;

Bull Canyon, Daniels Canyon, and Moonshine Draw next to Dinosaur National Monument;

In addition, the proposed Labyrinth Canyon, Dirty Devil, Dark Canyon, Glen Canyon, Escalante, and Kaiparowits wilderness areas are adjacent to the Glen Canyon National Recreation Area.

Together these lands are the wild core of the canyon and plateau province, forming one of the Earth's last wild desert regions. To fragment these lands into arbitrary political jurisdictions runs the risk of losing regional integrity. Wild lands under Park Service and BLM management alike should be brought under the management principles of the Wilderness Act to ensure that the values people from all over the world come to see will remain unimpaired.

New Parks for Utah?

Proposals have been advanced by many groups and individuals to expand Utah's national parks or create new parks in areas such as the Escalante and the San Rafael Swell. There are many areas in southern Utah with superlative scenic, wilderness, and archeological values that deserve park protection. The increasing popularity of Utah's national parks also suggests that more parks are needed to meet public demand. Visitation to some Utah parks has increased as much as 20 percent in one year!

Some people promote the establishment of new national parks to increase tourism and promote local economic development. Long-term tourist benefits depend, however, on preserving the natural values parks are set aside to protect, and in preserving a visitor's opportunity to "get away from it all." Conservationists warn against overdeveloping and overcrowding our national parks. They recommend that new parks include wilderness designations, and that tourist facilities be built *outside* park boundaries, in nearby communities where existing businesses can benefit.

Creating new national parks in Utah offers one way to protect the outstanding natural values of the Colorado Plateau. So does Congressional designation of wilderness areas. What's most important is not that we choose to designate parks or wilderness areas or both, but that we choose to preserve Utah's natural wonders for generations to come.

Terri Martin

CONCLUSION—THE NEED FOR BALANCE

Utah currently has only 800,000 acres of designated wilderness—a mere 1.5 percent of the State's land area. Most of this is national forest wilderness in the High Uintas and the Wasatch Range. Only 149,000 acres of designated wilderness are located in southern Utah's canyon country, where some 3 million acres of wild lands lack even the temporary protection of BLM wilderness study areas or National Park Service wilderness recommendations.

More than eight out of ten Utah residents believe that it is important to preserve some wilderness in Utah, according to a survey conducted in 1987 at Brigham Young University (Pope and Jones, 1987). The study found "significantly high" support for additional wilderness designation for up to about 8-10 million acres—about 15 percent of the state. Allowing for about 3 million acres of protected National Park and National Forest lands leaves about 5 million acres for BLM wilderness, which is close to the UWC proposal. The study also found that 79 percent of the respondents would support legislation to designate additional wilderness in Utah.

The wild lands managed by the BLM offer Utah's greatest opportunities for wilderness designations, yet this agency has fallen far short of its mandate. The BLM administers 22 million acres in Utah, yet it only studied 3.2 million acres for its wilderness potential, and has recommended just under 2 million acres.

In contrast to the BLM, the Utah Wilderness Coalition has identified 5.7 million acres of BLM wild lands that qualify for wilderness designation. Our proposal, if enacted by Congress, would bring the percentage of the state's land area designated as wilderness to 11 percent. Add to this the lands already having some form of protection (chiefly recommended wilderness within units of the National Park System), and a mere 16 percent of the State's land area would be protected from degradation. In a state renowned for its scenic beauty, this is an eminently reasonable proposal, befitting the great desert landscape of Utah.

THE BLM WILDERNESS REVIEW

AFTER 200 years of agricultural, industrial, and urban development, very little remains of the American wilderness. Today, less than eight percent of the land area of the lower 48 states remains wild. Most Americans understand how much has been lost. And as opinion polls show, most want to preserve what little remains of the American frontier.

Born of national pride in the natural splendor of America, the Wilderness Act of 1964 was an event of profound historic significance. Never before had a nation taken such deliberate measures to protect its wilderness heritage. The Act created a National Wilderness Preservation System and mandated a nationwide inventory of roadless national forest and national park lands which might qualify for inclusion.

In 1976 the Federal Land Policy and Management Act (FLPMA) directed the BLM to conduct a nationwide inventory of all BLM-managed roadless areas and assess their potential for wilderness designation. While the inventory was under way, the law required the BLM to prohibit new development on all lands under review. Once the inventory was complete, the moratorium on development would end for all lands which failed to meet the BLM's criteria for further study. Qualifying lands were to be identified as Wilderness Study Areas (WSAs) and would remain closed to new development until the Congress could determine their fate by means of wilderness legislation.

In Utah, where BLM lands comprise over 40 percent of the state, the BLM wilderness inventory was an opportunity to protect some of the largest remaining tracts of roadless land in the southwestern United States. Yet despite the superb character of Utah's roadless lands, the BLM's wilderness review went seriously astray from the policies established by Congress. Huge blocks of wild land were "inventoried" by helicopter without adequate field-checking on the ground. Remote and beautiful expanses of slickrock and sagebrush were excluded from wilderness study for the most spurious reasons. And in direct violation of its own policy, the BLM repeatedly dropped from its wilderness inventory those lands with potential— real or imagined— for mineral development.

To understand what went wrong with the BLM wilderness review in Utah, we focus on Mancos Mesa, where only through the diligent efforts of conservationists was a wilderness study ever conducted at all.

The Case of Mancos Mesa

To watch dawn unfold over Mancos Mesa is to experience the silence, the clarity, the sense of infinite distance that can be found in few other places in America. Rising to elevations of between 5,000 and 6,000 feet, Mancos Mesa is an island in the sky, cut off from the outside world by canyons and cliffs. The top of the mesa is a mosaic of bare rock, sand, and sage. Its surface is incised with more than 200 miles of winding canyons. Mancos Mesa is not easy to reach by foot. Once there, you want to linger.

For more than a decade, Mancos Mesa had been one of the BLM's top candidates for primitive area designation. "The intrigue and adventure of this totally isolated area, coupled with its history, offers an unusual opportunity for man to participate among the true essences of nature," concluded a 1970 BLM staff report. "... an 'ecological island' such as Mancos is a rare find." In December, 1970, the BLM held public meetings in nearby Monticello, Utah, to unveil its primitive area proposal for Mancos Mesa. But when powerful mining and livestock interests attacked the proposal, the agency quietly abandoned it.

The One-Day Inventory

On the morning of June 12, 1979, the BLM wilderness inventory team arrived at remote Mancos Mesa—in a Bell jet helicopter. "We wanted to backpack into the area, but upper management decided we couldn't do that," recalls team member Janet Ross. Instead, the team was given just one day to assess the wilderness character of the 110,000-acre Mancos Mesa roadless area from the air.

The helicopter dropped the three inventory crew members at two different locations on Mancos Mesa. "We took pictures for five or ten minutes at each location," recalls Ross. "That was the entire inventory." Almost. After making its first drops, the helicopter circled—and circled again. Something had gone wrong. In the rugged vastness of Mancos Mesa, the helicopter pilot could not *find* two of the three inventory team members. "We couldn't get them on the radio, and we were running out of gas," recalls Ross. After refuelling, the pilot searched for another hour before finding his lost crew. Tormented by swarming gnats, they had pulled their flight jackets over their heads and zipped them shut, thus accomplishing nothing in the way of inventory.

Several weeks later, the inventory crew filed its report on the wilderness character of Mancos Mesa. To qualify for wilderness study, a roadless area must meet three basic criteria. First, it must be undeveloped—in the words of the Wilderness Act, "primarily affected by the forces of nature, with the evidence of human activity substantially unnoticeable." Second, it must be at least 5,000 acres in size. Third, it must offer outstanding opportunities either for solitude or for primitive recreation.

In the unanimous opinion of the inventory field team, the Mancos Mesa roadless area met all three criteria. "As nearly as I could tell, from my ten minutes on the ground, there were quite outstanding opportunities for solitude," recalls Janet Ross. "Those canyons and mesas are just as spectacular as anything in southeastern Utah." Yet in November, 1980, when the BLM announced its final wilderness inventory decisions, Mancos Mesa was missing from the list of new wilderness study areas. While the mesa met size and naturalness requirements, the BLM ruled that it failed to provide "outstanding opportunities" for solitude or recreation. "The canyons have sparse vegetation, and are fairly open in character," the BLM explained. "Opportunities here for solitude are present, but not outstanding."

The recommendation of the BLM's field inventory team had been quietly reversed by the Utah BLM state director.

BLM Overrides Staff, Rewrites Documents

On Mancos Mesa, and throughout Utah, the BLM conducted its wilderness inventory with reckless haste. Though FLPMA had allowed 15 years for the BLM to complete its wilderness review, the Utah state BLM

The helicopter dropped each of three inventory crew members at two different locations on Mancos Mesa. "We took pictures for five or ten minutes at each location," recalls Janet Ross. "That was the entire inventory."

"What the BLM was trying to do was totally absurd," recalls Terry Sopher. Flying over Labyrinth Canyon, he remembers, "you were looking down on the ground, and one side of the river was said to have outstanding characteristics, and the other side was said not to have, and they both looked identical."

office had allocated just 2 years to evaluate nearly 900 individual roadless units and 22 million acres of land. Lack of time, inadequate resources and poor organization, recalls Janet Ross, made the inventory "heavily dependent upon vehicular and aerial reconnaissance which, given the very nature of wilderness, are extremely unreliable ways to assess wilderness characteristics."

The case of Mancos Mesa was far from unique. Throughout Utah, the BLM cut millions of acres of pristine mountain, desert, and canyon wilderness from the inventory.

In numerous cases, the final decision reversed a favorable recommendation from inventory field crews. "Most of the input came from the line management, not the wilderness staff," recalls former Moab district wilderness specialist Peter Viavant. "There were many times when a decision would be changed after a recommendation was written, and one would just go back and rewrite it again. I mean, you'd write, 'The canyons are 500 feet deep, providing great solitude . . . ' And then they'd change their mind and decide it should be out of the wilderness inventory, and you'd come back and write "there's only 500 feet of relief and this does not provide very good solitude."

In the case of Mancos Mesa, managers instructed inventory team leader Paul Happel to alter the recommendation of his own field crew. The alteration was discovered by Interior Board of Land Appeals judge Bruce Harris. "Close inspection," he wrote in a 1983 court decision, "indicates that a mark in the "Yes" box is whited out . . . . An "X" is typewritten in front of the statement 'Unit does not qualify for wilderness study.'"

Along with Mancos Mesa, the BLM had eliminated more than 90 percent of all lands originally under study. By November 1980, the BLM had cut from the inventory 89 roadless areas with outstanding wilderness character. An additional 32 roadless areas were arbitrarily cut up into smaller units or radically reduced in size. On the southern perimeter of the San Rafael Swell, for example, the BLM eliminated 80,000 acres of wild lands from the Muddy Creek wilderness inventory unit by adopting a BLM district line as the roadless area boundary. In Labyrinth Canyon, the BLM drew a roadless area boundary down the center of the Green River, identifying the west half of Labyrinth Canyon as a WSA while eliminating 57,000 acres along the east side of the canyon from wilderness study. In Arch Canyon, the BLM concluded that a 27,000-acre roadless area was "too small" to be wilderness because half of it lay on lands managed by the U.S. Forest Service.

Violations of Policy

Many inventory decisions directly violated the BLM's own wilderness inventory policy. That policy stated, for example, that roadless areas should not be eliminated from the inventory because of minor human impacts located around the periphery, where those impacts could be eliminated by means of a boundary adjustment. Yet the BLM dropped dozens of roadless areas because of impacts which could easily have been excluded by minor adjustments in the boundary. The Harts Point roadless area was a typical case. The unit featured an 800-foot-deep canyon system, at least three huge natural bridges, pools, waterfalls, and abundant wildlife. The BLM cut the entire unit from wilderness study, claiming that human impacts had ruined wilderness character throughout the unit. Yet simple boundary adjustments could have eliminated all significant human impacts, leaving a wild area of more than 68,000 acres.

"The boundary of a unit is to be determined based on evaluation of the imprints of man," read the policy, " . . . and should *not* be further constricted on the basis of opportunity for solitude and primitive and unconfined recreation." Yet more than 300,000 acres of lands were trimmed from a dozen WSAs when the Utah BLM state director determined that "portions of these units contain outstanding opportunities, while other parts clearly do not."

"It is erroneous," read the BLM's inventory guidelines, "to assume that simply because a unit or a portion of a unit is flat and/or unvegetated, it automatically lacks an outstanding opportunity for solitude." Yet in Utah the BLM cut millions of acres of wilderness from the inventory for the sole reason that *portions* of roadless areas were flat or sparsely vegetated. The entire 140,000-acre Wahweap roadless area, for example, was cut from the wilderness inventory after the BLM concluded that "on the flat upper bench areas . . . the opportunity for solitude is limited because of the flatness of the terrain."

Such procedural violations were so numerous that in August, 1980, just prior to the BLM's final inventory decision, the national director of the BLM wilderness program, Terry Sopher, came to Utah to investigate. A single overflight, recalls Sopher, convinced him that "what the BLM was trying to do was totally absurd." Flying over Labyrinth Canyon, he remembers, "you were looking down on the ground, and one side of the river was said to have outstanding characteristics, and the other side was said not to have, and they both looked identical . . . . Based on what we had seen, there was an egregious violation of the policies."

Sopher immediately returned to Washington, D.C., where he met with BLM national director Frank Gregg to report the problems in Utah. "I recommended," recalls Sopher, "that the director should intervene and take steps to stop the current direction of the inventory, and require it to be done over." But before Gregg could take action, all Interior Department appointees were swept out of office with the defeat of President Jimmy Carter.

Appeals Board Reverses State BLM Office

Meanwhile Utah conservation groups tried to reinstate lands cut from the inventory. After the BLM denied their formal protests, conservationists filed a series of appeals with the Interior Board of Land Appeals (IBLA). One such appeal was 2,000 pages long, containing 300 photographs and 120 affidavits. Covering 925,000 acres on 29 roadless areas, it was the largest appeal of its kind in the history of the IBLA. In 1983, the IBLA responded with a stunning indictment of the BLM inventory. Utah BLM inventory decisions had been in error, the Board ruled, on 90 percent of the lands under appeal.

But appeals could not correct the deficiencies of the Utah BLM wilderness inventory. Upon reconsideration, the BLM ultimately reinstated less than half of all lands under appeal. More important, many key inventory omissions were never appealed.

"Conservationists' resources were stretched to the breaking point in order to appeal more than 1.4 million acres," recalls Sierra Club activist Jim Catlin. "If we had more time, money, and people, we might have appealed up to 2.9 million acres in 122 inventory units."

"You only have 30 days to file an appeal," explains Terry Sopher. "It was damn near impossible for citizens to appeal every area that deserved an appeal."

Yet publicity surrounding the appeals had begun to expose the true magnitude of the BLM wilderness inventory omissions. "The work of the Bureau has been too hasty and too piecemeal . . . " editorialized the *Deseret News* in August, 1982. " . . . there was much Utah land that should have

The Green River in Labyrinth Canyon, looking south toward Tenmile Canyon (entering from left).

Tom Miller

been considered for possible designation as wilderness, but the BLM did not study it."

In 1983, charges of mismanagement in the Utah BLM wilderness inventory brought House Public Lands Subcommittee chairman John Seiberling on a fact finding mission to Utah. Seiberling returned to Washington convinced that the BLM had indeed mismanaged the inventory. "They've left out areas that obviously qualify for wilderness—and I've seen a lot of them," he told reporters. "I mean, their position is absolutely absurd, where they've said that they dropped a particular area because it didn't give opportunities for solitude."

Congressional Testimony Underscores Inventory Abuses

In 1984 and 1985, Seiberling held a series of oversight hearings to investigate the problems of the BLM wilderness inventory. As the hearings progressed, the story of the Utah wilderness inventory gradually unfolded. Key witnesses included former BLM wilderness inventory staff.

"The American public, you and I, have suffered a great tragedy in Utah," testified former BLM wilderness coordinator Clive Kincaid. "We have been the victims of ineptitude or deception, and the price has been a heavy one."

Kincaid had earned two outstanding achievement citations for directing one of the Bureau's first complete district-wide wilderness inventories, in Arizona. After resigning his job with the Bureau, he spent a full year investigating BLM wilderness inventory violations in Utah. Kincaid summarized his findings for the subcommittee by presenting five case studies, including that of Mancos Mesa. In each case, Kincaid's research suggested that the BLM had cut land from the inventory because of its potential for mining, grazing, or industrial development.

"It's rather interesting," said Rep. Seiberling, "that in many cases those areas which they dropped happened to coincide with things like tar sands, or coal fields." In the Henry Mountains, for example, the BLM trimmed nearly 200,000 acres of rugged badlands from the Mt. Ellen and Mt. Pennell WSAs—neatly excluding 100 percent of the known recoverable coal in the two roadless areas. North of Canyonlands National Park, the BLM omitted 57,000 acres of wild lands bordering the site of a proposed potash solution mining complex. Sixty-five thousand acres of spectacular slot canyons surrounding Natural Bridges National Monument were dropped from the inventory while under siege by oil and uranium exploration companies. Eighty-eight thousand acres of wilderness adjacent to Canyonlands Park vanished from the BLM wilderness inventory after the area was identified as a candidate site for a nuclear waste repository and its railroad. In the San Rafael Swell, the BLM cut 350,000 acres of wild lands surrounding the proposed Intermountain Power Project's transmission line, rail corridor, and power plant sites. And on the Kaiparowits Plateau the BLM cut nearly 400,000 acres underlain by coal.

For Utah, the BLM wilderness inventory had been precisely the reverse of what Congress had requested. Congress had asked for a thorough inventory of the nation's last unprotected wild lands. What it got, instead, was commercial and industrial zoning. Instead of letting Congress strike a balance between commercial uses and wilderness protection, the BLM quietly dropped any lands having mining claims or other mineral potential.

"Congress told us to identify every acre of land that had wilderness characteristics," said Terry Sopher. "BLM was directed simply to identify the areas that had wilderness qualities and let Congress decide which ones were outstanding. Yet it is now apparent that there was egregious violation of that mandate of the law."

"We tried to make the decision for somebody else, that we had no right to make," recalls a BLM inventory team member, who risked his career to protest mismanagement of the Utah BLM inventory. "We cut the pie the first time. If Congress never sees the whole pie, then they don't make decisions on it, do they? And that's exactly what happened."

In many cases the BLM altered WSA boundaries to promote industrial development which would never take place. The Intermountain Power Project was finally located on a different site 100 miles west of the San Rafael Swell. Between 1979 and 1983, worldwide uranium and oil prices plummeted, and energy exploration in Utah virtually ceased. A stagnant energy market killed the Kaiparowits Power Project, and Kaiparowits coal was never developed. The potash market slumped, and Buttes Oil and Gas abandoned its proposed solution mine north of Canyonlands National Park. And in 1984, the Department of Energy eliminated Davis Canyon as a candidate site for the nation's first nuclear waste dump.

Administration Lets Violations Stand

In a July, 1985, BLM oversight hearing Rep. Seiberling specifically requested Interior Secretary Donald Hodel to "take a final look at the inventory, especially in Utah . . . to assure that they have not overlooked deserving lands." In December 1985, Seiberling repeated the request in writing, identifying 18 Utah roadless areas where critical inventory omissions had occurred. The Department of the Interior responded in February, 1986. The reply was terse. The BLM flatly refused to add lands to the wilderness inventory. "We believe the inventory in Utah was as accurate and consistent as possible," explained deputy assistant secretary James Cason. "The time for initiating such an appeal has long since expired. Failure to raise these allegations at the appropriate time in the formal appeal period does not constitute sufficient reason to disrupt the systematic review process."

The Utah Wilderness Coalition

By the spring of 1985, it was clear that the Utah BLM wilderness review had been a failure. The BLM had arbitrarily cut more than 2 million acres of wild lands from its inventory, removing interim management protection and throwing the lands open for development. An additional 1.1 million acres would ultimately be omitted from the agency's draft wilderness recommendation to Congress, announced in February 1986. A final version of that proposal, due to be released in 1990, is expected to increase that recommendation by only some 80,000 acres—adding some areas, dropping others.

On the Colorado Plateau—the canyon country of southern Utah—the BLM's piecemeal, development-oriented wilderness recommendations would transform one of the nation's last great blocks of high desert wilderness into islands of protected land in a sea of industrial development.

Utah conservationists were convinced that the BLM wilderness review had fallen short of its congressional mandate. To take their case to the public, they formed the Utah Wilderness Coalition, which has grown to include 35 local and national conservation groups.

In February 1985, coalition members convened the first of nine conferences to hammer out a citizen's BLM wilderness proposal for Utah. Where BLM inventory work was inadequate, the coalition sent volunteers into the field to map the true extent of Utah's BLM wild lands. "Our members have walked and flown extensively over the lands in our proposal," says Utah Wilderness Coalition spokesman Darrell Knuffke. "We know

For Utah, the BLM wilderness inventory had been precisely the reverse of what Congress had requested. Congress had asked for a thorough inventory of the nation's last unprotected wild lands. What it got, instead, was commercial and industrial zoning.

The Coalition's objective is to do what the BLM failed to do during the Utah wilderness inventory: to fully document the wilderness resources of some of the largest blocks of undeveloped land in the nation.

what's out there. It's wilderness. And we intend to do everything in our power to keep it that way."

Developing a Citizen Proposal

On July 16, 1985, the newly formed Utah Wilderness Coalition announced a 5.1-million-acre BLM wilderness proposal for Utah. During the five-year interval between that announcement and the publication of this book, UWC staff and volunteers have spent thousands of additional hours in the field, documenting wilderness character and accurately mapping the boundaries of proposed areas. We have added wild lands to our proposal where human impacts had previously been overestimated, or where erosion and vegetation growth had further obscured faint, unused vehicle tracks. These additions, along with more accurate, computer-generated acreage calculations, have increased the UWC proposal to 5.7 million acres.

This book presents the combined knowledge of hundreds of Utah conservation activists. Its goal is to do what the Bureau of Land Management failed to do during the Utah wilderness inventory: to fully document the wilderness resources of some of the largest blocks of undeveloped land in the nation.

The BLM took a piecemeal approach to the wilderness inventory, dividing huge roadless areas into numerous smaller units, and omitting large blocks of land. By contrast, the Coalition identified 42 integral wilderness areas, many of which are contiguous to national park or national forest wild lands. While each proposed wilderness *area* may contain separate individual roadless *units* that are separated by narrow road corridors, each should be viewed as one wilderness, with a physical, geological, and biological character all its own.

Our proposal will protect the visual integrity of the entire Canyonlands Basin—the million-acre labyrinth at the heart of the Colorado Plateau. It will protect the viewsheds of Capitol Reef and Bryce Canyon national parks by precluding strip mining and chaining on adjacent BLM wild lands. It will protect the scenic and recreational resources of the entire San Rafael Swell, not just a narrow band around the Swell's perimeter. It will protect the biological integrity of the Book Cliffs, the Escalante canyon country, and the Henry and La Sal Mountains, by preserving habitat size and diversity, wildlife migratory routes, and numerous endangered species. It will preserve the inspiring solitude of the Kaiparowits Plateau, the cliffs and mesas of the Grand Staircase, and parts of the Great Basin desert. It will protect the archeological treasures of Cedar Mesa and the San Juan River Basin by prohibiting new road development and vehicle access to remote archeological sites. And it will preserve, for our children and their children, the opportunity to experience wilderness on a scale such as that of the original American frontier.

The silence, solitude, and sheer beauty of Utah's high desert wild lands are among America's scarcest and most valuable natural resources. It is a landscape so diverse, so intricate, that it requires much more than the cursory inventory given it by the BLM. The Utah Wilderness Coalition proposal is our effort to redress that inventory's failings and present a full picture of Utah's desert wild lands to the American public.

Ray Wheeler

THE COALITION PROPOSAL

THE 42 proposed wilderness areas described in the following pages encompass the wild heart of Utah's Basin and Range and Colorado Plateau regions. Twenty-one of these areas are divided into subunits separated by narrow road corridors. (Precedent for this clustering is found in wilderness legislation enacted previously by Congress.) Narrative overviews of each area discuss its ecological significance and management history. Each unit has a more detailed listing of its physical and biological features and the BLM and Utah Wilderness Coalition proposals.

This book does not attempt to be a hiker's or floater's guide (many published guides are available), but the maps, photos, and text ought to suggest a great many places to explore. We have made every effort to ensure the accuracy of our wilderness proposals by field-checking boundaries and researching BLM files. However, further incursions into some wild areas have occurred since our most recent field visits. The BLM does not notify citizens of new road construction or other development activities outside of its own wilderness study areas. Thus, minor boundary modifications (or, to the extent possible, restoration work) may be necessary where recent development has occurred within our proposal. Such intrusions only demonstrate the need for legal protection of wild areas under the Wilderness Act.

Although we fault the BLM's leadership for succumbing to industry's pressure to minimize wilderness recommendations, the BLM's field staff collected a great deal of basic information that we used in our analysis. Often the BLM's field data support conclusions opposite from those reached by the agency's leaders. Frequent reference is thus made to the seven-volume, 2,700-page draft environmental impact statement the BLM published in 1986. The final version of that document is expected to be published sometime in 1990. We have added advance information on the BLM's final proposal to the text.

Despite a decade of fieldwork—our own and the BLM's—there is still a great deal waiting to be discovered about the lands in our proposal. Which contain rare plants that could offer medicinal uses or new scientific knowledge? Which shelter prehistoric artifacts not yet wrecked by vandals? Which areas are critical wildlife habitat, and which are essential for the health of whole ecosystems? If we preserve the wilderness, we preserve more than outstanding scenery and backcountry recreation. We preserve the answers to those fundamental ecological questions.

Indeed, our own fieldwork since 1985 (when we first presented our proposal to the public) has indicated that there are additional BLM wild lands in Utah that deserve to be protected. We have added undeveloped lands at the edges of many units where our recent fieldwork indicated that human intrusions were minor. We have also added two small units (Nipple Bench in the Kaiparowits Plateau and Wild Mountain on the Colorado-Utah border near Dinosaur National Monument.) As Ray Wheeler explains in the preceding section, these additions, along with more accurate computer-generated acreage calculations, bring our total Utah BLM wilderness proposal to 5.7 million acres, up from 5.1 million acres in 1985. (Like the BLM, we do not include State lands in our acreage totals, although many State sections should eventually be incorporated into these wilderness areas.)

There has been much debate in Utah about how many acres of BLM wilderness should be protected. For too long this debate has focused on numbers instead of on the land. Acreage tallies—whether the BLM's or ours—only obscure the qualities of individual wild areas. You will find in the pages that follow an emphasis on the land itself, not on acreages.

Edward Abbey once wrote that "the idea of wilderness needs no defense. It only needs more defenders." Increasingly, however, it needs both. We hope that our descriptions of these wild lands will help you come to their defense with knowledge and with enthusiasm.

Fred Swanson

THE BASIN AND RANGE REGION

TO a driver hurtling through Utah's West Desert along Interstate 80 at a cool 65 or better, the country seems a lonely succession of pale and brown, basin after range after basin. It is rugged country, a vast and mostly unpeopled landscape. The climate is harsh, with summer temperatures regularly topping 100 degrees, frigid, still winters, and year-round drought. Yet the loftier mountains draw enough moisture from the air to support perennial streams (even a few trout streams), alpine meadows, and forests of pine, fir, and aspen.

As Mary Austin wrote in *The Land of Little Rain* (1903), it is "a land one doesn't love instinctually but one that takes hold of the soul." The Utah Wilderness Coalition's proposal for Utah's Basin and Range region would maintain the wildness of 17 mountain and desert areas in western Utah.

At War with the Land

During the latter half of the nineteenth century, thousands of travelers, many caught up in the California gold rush, crossed this desert's waterless stretches in withering summer heat. The Donner Party, taking the untested Hastings Cutoff through the Cedar Mountains and across the salt flats towards California in 1846, was so delayed and weakened by its desert crossing that it was trapped in the lethal winter snows of the Sierra Nevada. During 1860 and 1861 the Pony Express mail route crossed the West Desert, the lean riders hastening from waterhole to waterhole, opening the route for later road travel.

But ever since the passage of explorer Jedediah Smith in 1827, Americans have tried to tame, manipulate, and transform the desert into something more to their liking. Failing consistently to civilize it, we call it wasteland. Nowhere has this attitude led to more destruction than in the northern portion of the West Desert where our military practices war.

For many years the West Desert has been a patchwork of bombing and gunnery ranges and closed airspace where fighter jets run strafing missions. The MX nuclear missile system was originally proposed for the West Desert. Nearly 100 square miles of public land beside the Cedar Mountains are set aside as a special hazardous waste incineration zone. Close by, the AMAX magnesium plant spews more than 68 million pounds of chlorine and other toxic compounds into the air each year, making this the nation's largest single source of toxic air pollutants. Hazardous materials and nuclear wastes are buried in the vicinity.

At the Tooele Army Depot 42 percent of the nation's nerve gas is stored in containers underground; unofficial reports of leaking containers and classified accidents are legion. In 1988, the largest non-war troop mobilization ever held, called Project Firex, took place in the Onaqui Mountains, leaving behind several thousand acres of burned-over

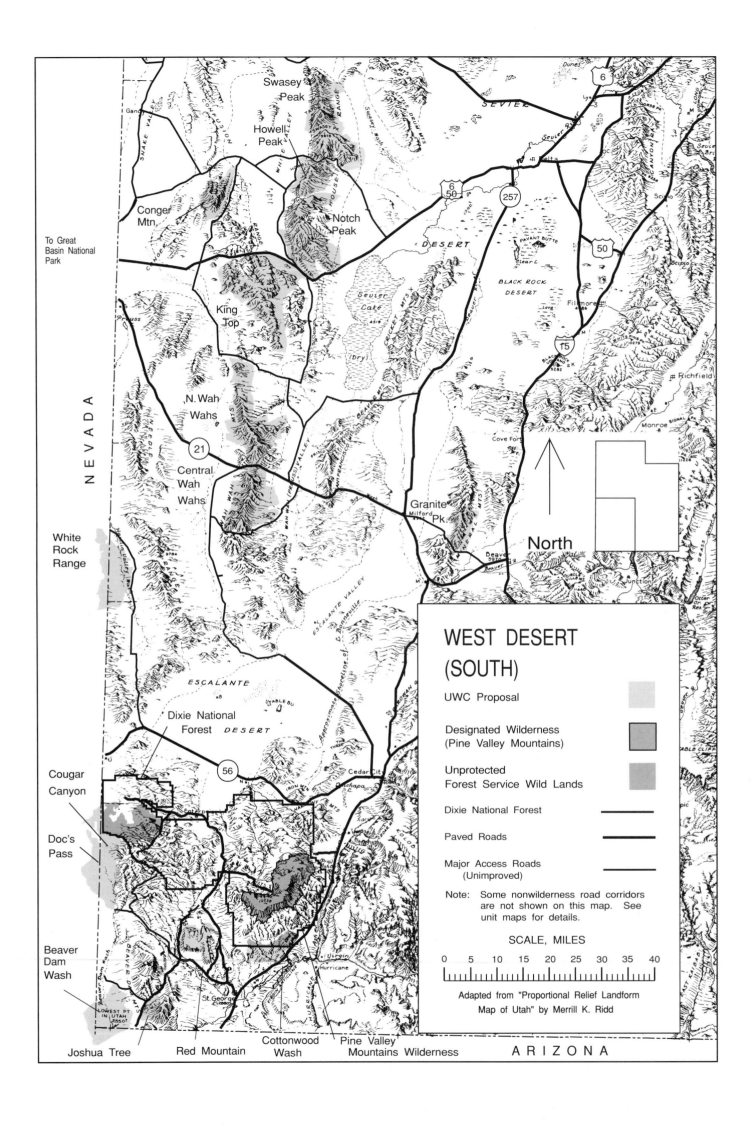

Swasey
Peak

Howell
Peak

Conger
Mtn.

Notch
Peak

To Great
Basin National
Park

King
Top

NEVADA

N. Wah
Wahs

White
Rock
Range

Central
Wah
Wahs

Granite
Pk.

DESERT

PAVANT BUTTE

BLACK ROCK
DESERT

Fillmore

Richfield

Monroe

Cove Fort

North

ESCALANTE

Dixie National
Forest DESERT

Cougar
Canyon

Doc's
Pass

Cedar City

WEST DESERT
(SOUTH)

UWC Proposal

Designated Wilderness
(Pine Valley Mountains)

Unprotected
Forest Service Wild Lands

Dixie National Forest ————

Paved Roads ————

Major Access Roads
(Unimproved) ————

Note: Some nonwilderness road corridors
       are not shown on this map. See
       unit maps for details.

SCALE, MILES

0   5   10   15   20   25   30   35   40

Beaver
Dam
Wash

St. George

LOWEST PT
IN UTAH
2550'

Joshua Tree   Red Mountain   Cottonwood   Pine Valley   A R I Z O N A
                                     Wash   Mountains Wilderness

Adapted from "Proportional Relief Landform
Map of Utah" by Merrill K. Ridd

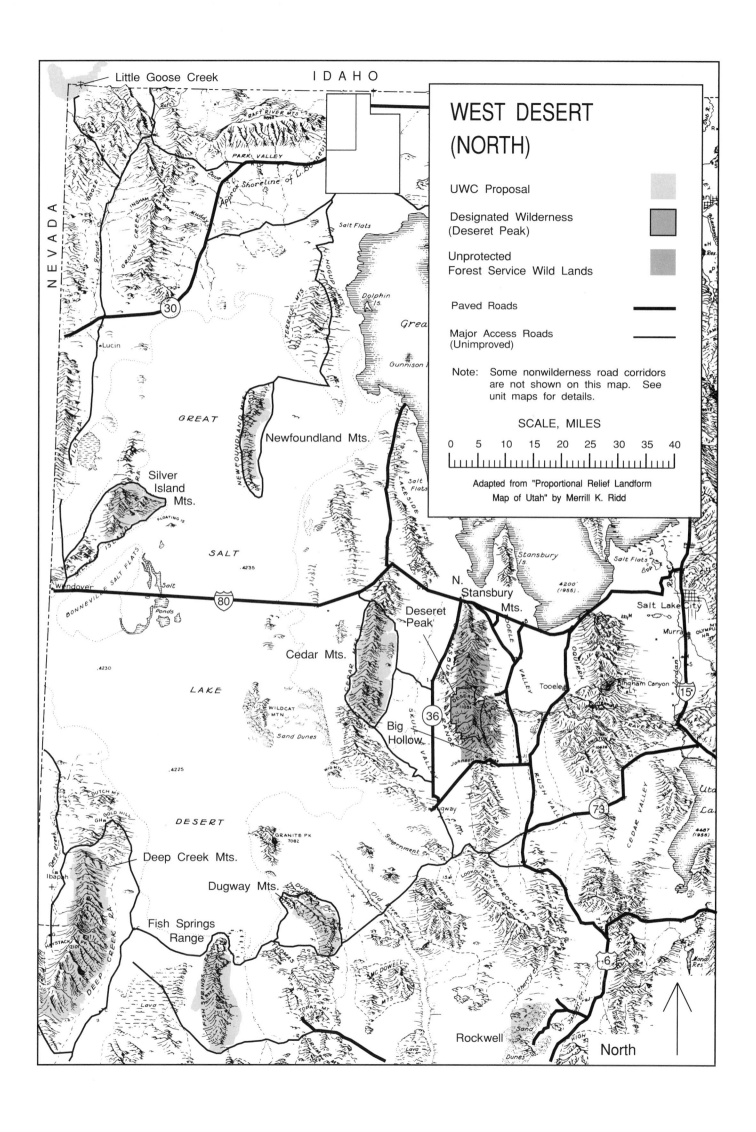

Little Goose Creek

IDAHO

NEVADA

WEST DESERT
(NORTH)

UWC Proposal

Designated Wilderness
(Deseret Peak)

Unprotected
Forest Service Wild Lands

Paved Roads

Major Access Roads
(Unimproved)

Note: Some nonwilderness road corridors
are not shown on this map. See
unit maps for details.

SCALE, MILES

0   5   10   15   20   25   30   35   40

Adapted from "Proportional Relief Landform
Map of Utah" by Merrill K. Ridd

RAFT RIVER MTS

PARK VALLEY

Approx Shoreline of L. Bonneville

Salt Flats

30

Lucin

Dolphin Is.

Great

Gunnison I.

GREAT

Newfoundland Mts.

Silver
Island
Mts.

FLOATING IS

SALT

.4235

Stansbury Is.

Salt Flats

4200' (1955)

N.
Stansbury
Mts.

Salt Lake City

Wendover

BONNEVILLE SALT FLATS

Salt

Ponds

80

.4230

LAKE

WILDCAT MTN

Sand Dunes

.4225

Cedar Mts.

Deseret
Peak

Big
Hollow

36

Tooele

Murray

Bingham Canyon

15

DUTCH MT

GOLD HILL

DESERT

GRANITE PK
7082

Deep Creek Mts.

Ibapah

Dugway Mts.

Fish Springs
Range

HAYSTACK PK

DEEP CREEK RA

Lava

Dugway

73

CEDAR VALLEY

4467
(1958)

Utah
La

6

Rockwell

Sand
Dunes

Lava

North

None other than this long brown land lays such a hold on the affections. The rainbow hills, the tender bluish mists, the luminous radiance of the spring, have the lotus charm. They trick the sense of time so that once inhabiting there you always mean to go away without quite realizing that you have not done it.

Mary Austin

THE LAND OF LITTLE RAIN (1903)

countryside. The Air Force has proposed a permanent electronic battlefield and the Army a biological warfare testing center.

While these wars may be only practice, the desert knows no such distinction. Bombs, bullets, fires, poisonous gasses, deadly bacteria: the weapons of destruction are real. Adding insult to injury, these public lands are off limits to the public. None of these restricted lands is in our wilderness proposal; their existence, however, emphasizes the need to protect the unspoiled remainder. Each of these developments has effects over a large area, and the population growth associated with West Desert development brings with it off-road vehicles and their widespread damage.

Basin and Range Geology

The powerful block faulting that gave birth to these mountains is nowhere more graphically displayed than on the west face of the House Range, a long, twisted wall of laminated gray and white limestone. The range culminates at Notch Peak, which appears freshly torn from the earth, its scarp looming 2,700 feet skyward.

About 20 million years ago the opposite motion of enormous plates of the earth's crust began forming the Great Basin. Land east of California's San Andreas Fault, where the plates meet, has since been stretched, creased, and wrenched into shape like so much soft clay, forming the Sierra Nevada and the hundreds of ranges east to Utah's Wasatch Mountains. Throughout the Great Basin, massive walls of rock rise abruptly, lifted at an angle approaching 60 degrees. The landscape is young geologically, and in the profound silence of the desert one may easily imagine that these mountains are still growing, which is precisely the case.

Biological Diversity—An Unexpected Bonanza

Two treelines, an upper and lower, define three life zones in the higher mountains of the Basin and Range. Above treeline in the Deep Creek Mountains, for instance, flowered meadows sprawl among the granitic peaks and glacial cirques. On the limestone soils of high ridges in the Wah Wah Mountains, House Range, and Deep Creek Mountains grow bristlecone pine trees, gnarled and tenacious, among the earth's oldest living things. In sheltered slopes and valleys are clusters of spruce, subalpine and Douglas fir, limber pine, and aspen.

At lower elevations, where available moisture diminishes, is a broad belt of pinyon pine and juniper woodlands, interspersed with patches of wiry mountain mahogany and sagebrush. Below this woodland are hills covered with sage, grasses, and shadscale. Saltbush and greasewood dominate the benchlands, though in places spring-watered marshlands contrast with the arid surroundings. Finally there is the enormous solitude of wide salt flats, their white alkali crusts and brackish water seeming to lead downhill only because of the earth's curvature.

Each of the mountain ranges in Utah's Basin and Range Province is an isolated ecosystem, a biological island surrounded by desert playas, where many unique species have evolved or survive as relicts after separation from a larger historic range. Several of these montane islands have been the subject of ecological studies.

Many native plants and animals, while adapted to the dry climate of the Basin and Range region, still cling tenuously to existence, unable to endure more than the lightest human touch.

The Deep Creek Mountains support two species of plants found nowhere else on earth, and 10 that are exceedingly rare; the proposed Rockwell wilderness supports a rare species of desert shrub that once covered large parts of the western United States. Due to extensive over-

grazing by domestic livestock and a reduction in natural range fires for the past 100 years, there has been a widespread change in native plant communities throughout the Basin and Range country (Rogers, 1982). According to Rogers, basic research and planning are necessary to head off further loss of native vegetation. Wilderness designation can help protect these vulnerable native plant communities.

Six of the proposed wilderness areas in the West Desert encompass habitat for the endangered peregrine falcon. Eagles and many other uncommon birds also winter there. Trout Creek and Birch Creek in the Deep Creek Mountains support the rare Bonneville cutthroat trout. The desert tortoise, already federally listed as an endangered species, lives in the proposed Beaver Dam Slopes wilderness and needs greater protection of its habitat to ensure its survival.

The Utah Wilderness Coalition's proposal would protect the rugged mountain habitat of both the desert and Rocky Mountain bighorn sheep and, along the periphery of the mountains, important antelope habitat. Both bighorn and antelope, native to the Basin and Range country, were nearly extirpated from the region by overgrazing by livestock, poaching, predation, and habitat destruction (BLM, 1988; Durrant, 1952). Wilderness designation will help the BLM to manage for the needs of native wildlife and protect vulnerable species.

Ten Thousand Years of Human History

Several rich and well-documented habitation sites in Utah's West Desert indicate human occupation by Desert Archaic and Fremont Indian cultures in the region for at least 10,000 years (Madsen, 1986; Jennings, 1973). The most important cultural sites are caves, which were apparently

In the Wah Wah Mountains, as throughout the Great Basin, massive walls of rock have been lifted at an angle approaching 60 degrees. The land has been wrenched into shape like so much soft clay.

Tom Miller

created by the wave action of Lake Bonneville during the Pleistocene Epoch, and rock shelters. Danger Cave near Wendover, Hogup Cave just west of the Great Salt Lake, Scribble Shelter in the Deep Creek Mountains, and Fish Springs Caves at the north end of the Fish Springs Mountains are well-known and important sites.

Major cultural sites have been identified in the Deep Creek, Fish Springs, and Silver Island Mountains, and near Granite Peak, but all of the ranges within the Utah Wilderness Coalition's proposal have been only lightly inventoried, and it is probable that important finds await discovery. Other known archeological sites remain unpublicized to protect them from vandalism, although the artifacts being recovered in the West Desert are generally of little commercial value.

Recreation: Solitude and Challenge

World-class rock climbing and cave exploring are available in the House Range. Fossil Mountain in the King Top area affords rockhounds and scientists superb specimens of long-extinct plants and animals preserved in stone. Bird watching is especially good during spring in the Joshua Tree forest and riparian habitats of the Beaver Dam Slopes where the Upper Sonoran, Great Basin, and Colorado Plateau provinces overlap. Eighteen bird species found nowhere else in Utah are seasonal or permanent residents of the Beaver Dam Slopes (Hedges, 1985). Wild horses and antelope roam the Conger and Cedar Mountain areas, and a fortunate visitor may see these spirited animals galloping across grassy hillsides.

Several guidebooks describe hikes in the Wah Wah, House, and Deep Creek ranges, but some of the lesser known areas offer equally interesting hikes. The Granite Peak area, with its odd, Stonehenge-like natural rock slabs and rocky canyons, is well worth a visit. Hikes into the Silver Island and Newfoundland Mountains will provide solitude with spectacular views of the surrounding Basin and Range country.

Hunters will find upland game birds and deer throughout the West Desert ranges, but the Little Goose Creek, Stansbury, Deep Creek, and White Rock ranges are most promising. Special permits are available to hunt antelope, bighorn sheep, and elk in some areas, and anglers can fish for Bonneville cutthroat in the Deeps.

Threats to the Basin and Range Wilderness

During its wilderness review the BLM omitted over 250,000 acres in Utah's Basin and Range region that are included in the Utah Wilderness Coalition proposal. The BLM eliminated nine entire units considered by the Utah Wilderness Coalition: the Newfoundland Mountains, Silver Island Mountains, Big Hollow, Dugway Mountains, Little Goose Creek, Central Wah Wah Mountains, Granite Peak, Beaver Dam Wash, and Joshua Tree. In addition to whole areas, the BLM lopped off thousands of acres from wild areas it did identify as wilderness study areas. The agency eliminated much of this land for specious reasons, stating that there were no "outstanding opportunities for solitude" nor any chance for "primitive or unconfined recreation." After checking boundaries, visiting areas, and researching the issues, we strongly disagree with the agency about these areas. They are wild and deserve wilderness designation.

In a few areas of the Basin and Range Province, the damage from old mining has forced us to draw a boundary to exclude mine sites or access roads. Elsewhere, old two-rut tracks which receive little use have been included within our proposed wilderness boundaries. These tracks have evolved by use, whether by hikers, horses, or off-road vehicles, but have never been legally constructed or maintained as roads. Nature, given half a chance, will reclaim them. Unfortunately, opponents of wilderness designation encourage vehicle use on some of these tracks, sometimes with BLM acquiescence, to destroy the wilderness qualities of an area before Congress acts to protect it.

The vast majority of West Desert lands that are not under military restriction are open to grazing, mining, and off-road vehicles. Of these, only vehicle use would be precluded by wilderness designation. If every acre of land we propose for wilderness in the West Desert were designated, many hundreds of square miles of non-wilderness land in the region would still remain open to ORV use.

While the location of mining claims would be allowed for a period of time within designated wilderness, access to new mines could be limited to means that are compatible with protecting the integrity of the wilderness. Fortunately, according to recent USGS mineral reports, there are few areas in our proposal that show promise of yielding valuable mineral deposits. However, statements have been made by Utah miners that a fortune in gold and silver may be found in the proposed King Top wilderness. Mining this area would require environmentally destructive open-pit mining and cyanide heap-leaching methods.

While the mineral claims are speculative, the wilderness values of this and other areas in the West Desert are certain; the value of wilderness does not fluctuate with the price of gold and should not be sacrificed. It is most likely, however, that the gold fever will yield nothing more than tall talk and a litter of plastic mining claim markers in Utah's deserts.

Toward a Desert Ethic

The challenge of protecting wilderness is really one of restraint. The inherent natural value of the places in our wilderness proposal exceeds their mineral potential. As a society, we can afford to protect these wild lands from all forms of degradation for all time.

Included in the Utah Wilderness Coalition's wilderness proposal are 17 mountain ranges covering 754,300 acres within Utah—about 1.4 percent of the state. We offer a vision of the desert as it is, not as a utilitarian thing to be molded in the shape of our ambitions or as a vast carpet under which to sweep our most odious wastes, but as a place of inherent value, dignity, and beauty, worthy of protection.

Mike Medberry

THE LITTLE GOOSE CREEK WILDERNESS

Located in the extreme northwest corner of Utah, Little Goose Creek is 1,300 acres of rolling desert hills, sagebrush flats, and small, abrupt anticlines. An additional 12,000 acres extend into Idaho and Nevada. Desert wildlife thrives in and around the area, making it popular with hunters. Grouse are particularly abundant. Little Goose Creek is seldom visited during most of the year and offers a place to hike, camp, and ride horses, as well as photograph and study the biota and geology. Two rare birds, the ferruginous hawk and western burrowing owl, are found in the area. Designating Little Goose Creek would help diversify the National Wilderness Preservation System, which currently has few areas of topographically gentle desert grasslands.

To visit Little Goose Creek, a traveler from the northern Wasatch Front should head west on Utah Highway 30 from the Interstate 15 Park Valley exit near Snowville. It is a two-hour drive to the Grouse Creek road turnoff. If you are traveling from the Salt Lake City area or farther south, take Interstate 80 west to Oasis, Nevada, and follow the paved highway

IN BRIEF

Index Map: Area No. 16

Highlights: Located at the transition between the Great Basin and the Snake River Plain, this area is a haven for hawks and owls. Hunters, horseback riders, and hikers can find solitude here amid rolling desert hills.

Maps: USGS 1:100,000 Grouse Creek

Area of wilderness proposals in acres (Utah):

Area	UWC	BLM
Little Goose Creek	1,300	0

Adjacent wild lands: Idaho, Nevada BLM

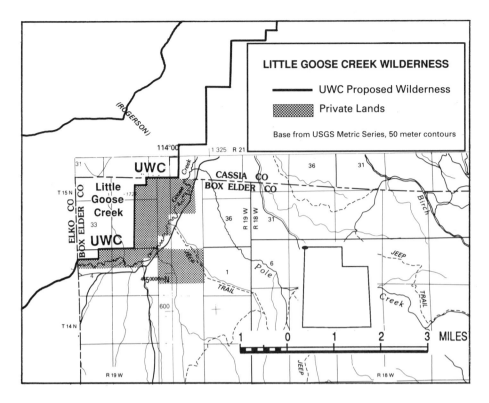

(Route 233) north for one hour to the turnoff. From there head north through the town of Grouse Creek on a secondary graveled road and travel about 26 miles to a major "Y" intersection; take the western road to the Nevada-Utah border and park near the state line. The area boundary is a few hundred yards north of the road. This is the best access point, and there is plenty of space nearby for car camping.

Another good access point is about seven miles north of the "Y" intersection. A few miles north of the Utah-Idaho border, the proposed wilderness boundary touches the road at a gated entrance. Park near the gate and walk the short distance to the creek. Since Little Goose Creek is in the heart of the cleanest airshed in the nation (according to Park Service studies) the views from the tops of ridges can extend nearly 180 miles. Vistas include the Pilot Range and Jarbidge Wilderness in Nevada.

Open, Spare Country

Since it is so remote, visitors to the proposed Little Goose Creek wilderness seldom see or hear any outside activities. Numerous small valleys enhance the feeling of solitude and there is little sign of human intrusion. The undulating sagebrush hills are especially dramatic in changing weather. In summer, thunderclouds cast great shadows across the spare desert landscape.

Sagebrush, cacti, pinyon pine, juniper, and a variety of desert grasses are the predominant vegetation. The range appears to be in good condition. Western burrowing owls and ferruginous hawks, both sensitive species, do well here because of the undisturbed terrain and the abundance of prey. Little Goose Creek also provides important winter deer habitat and good habitat for grouse, other birds, and small mammals. The northwest corner of Utah is a transition zone between the Great Basin and Snake River Plain ecosystems and is of interest to ecologists studying the biology of these two regions. Wilderness designation would help preserve an unspoiled example of this zone.

On the Idaho side, the rolling hills end in 100-foot-high shale bluffs that overlook the wilderness drainage. Near the tri-state border a hiker will find an excellent example of a little-grazed grassland.

The Utah Wilderness Coalition Proposal

We propose that the entire Little Goose Creek area, with 1,300 acres in Utah, be designated as wilderness. During the BLM's wilderness inventory, the agency ignored the nearly unspoiled naturalness of the Little Goose Creek area; no mention was made of the continuous rolling hills that provide excellent watershed and wildlife habitat. There are no known developments planned for the area, and overall, the area has little mineral potential.

Rudy Lukez

NEWFOUNDLAND MOUNTAINS WILDERNESS

Rising abruptly 2,000 feet above seemingly endless salt flats, the New-foundland Mountains loom out of the Great Salt Lake desert like a ship on the ocean. Although these mountains are separated from biological systems on neighboring mountain islands, there is enough water here to support diverse populations of wild plants and animals. Golden eagles, red-tailed hawks, prairie falcons, and other raptors nest in the high rocky cliffs; on the benchlands are the nests of burrowing owls and ferruginous hawks. The BLM and UDWR plan to reintroduce desert bighorn sheep to the Newfoundland Mountains in the near future. Vistas across the snow-white Bonneville Salt Flats to the Pilot Range, Promontory Mountains, and a dozen other ranges, give one a powerful sense of solitude. We propose a 23,300-acre wilderness for the Newfoundland Mountains; the BLM failed even to designate this rough and unspoiled mountain range as a WSA.

To visit the Newfoundland Mountains, take Interstate 80 west from Salt Lake City. Turn north about five miles past Delle to the small railroad workers' town of Lakeside; from here follow the railroad tracks past the mothballed West Desert Pumps to the northern tip of the mountains. Cross the tracks where an unmarked dirt road leads in a southerly direction toward the Newfoundland Mountains. This road loops around the mountain range, but the military has closed it at the south end of the mountains. Hikes up any number of canyons or up Desert Peak from either side of the range present glorious views and wild country.

Recognized Wilderness Values

The Newfoundland Mountains offer a view of nature operating essentially unaffected by human actions. The BLM's wilderness inventory found " . . . an abundance of [raptor] aeries and potential aerie sites. Vertical cliffs, promontories and outcrops offer shelter and safety to nesting pairs and their brood . . . . Ecologic, geographic and scenic values are obvious . . . . Scenic vistas from the unit extend over many miles in every direction and are of high quality." With 4 perennial springs and 12 that run seasonally, these mountains support a remarkable variety of wildlife species. Deer, badger, fox, coyote, and many bird species and small mammals live in the Newfoundlands. Desert bighorn probably inhabited these mountains before the introduction of domestic sheep.

Historic evidence of mining for precious and base metals exists in the northern part of the mountains. A cablecar ore shuttle system up Dells Canyon is of historic interest, but in most places the effects of past mining are not noticeable. While little archeological survey work has been done in the Newfoundlands, the many springs in these mountains would likely have been used by prehistoric cultures, suggesting a high probability of significant finds in the future.

IN BRIEF

Index Map: Area No. 17

Highlights: Isolated by salt flats, this ecological island supports abundant raptor populations and diverse other wildlife. Expansive views across the Great Salt Lake Desert reward the hiker.

Maps: USGS 1:100,000 Newfoundland Mountains

Area of wilderness proposals in acres:

Area	UWC	BLM
Newfoundland Mtns.	23,300	0

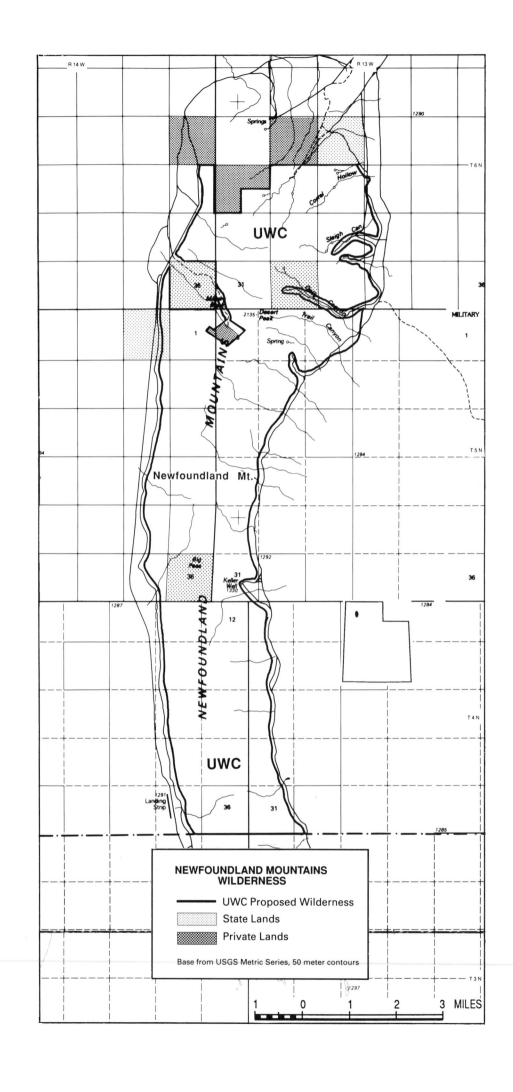

R 14 W

R 13 W

1290

T 6 N

Springs

Hollow

UWC

Sleigh Can

Corral

Can

36

MILITARY

1

31

2135

Desert
Peak

Trail

Spring

Canyon

1284

T 5 N

Newfoundland   Mt.

1292

Big
Peak
36

31
Keller
Well
1330

36

12

1284

1287

T 4 N

UWC

1291
Landing
Strip

36

31

1285

**NEWFOUNDLAND MOUNTAINS
WILDERNESS**

—————— UWC Proposed Wilderness

State Lands

Private Lands

Base from USGS Metric Series, 50 meter contours

T 3 N

1297

1   0   1   2   3   MILES

We recommend a 23,300-acre wilderness to protect the area's outstanding opportunities for hiking, camping, solitude, and nature study. The BLM dropped the Newfoundland Mountains from its initial inventory despite recognizing its substantial wilderness values. Conservationists appealed that decision to the Interior Board of Land Appeals and gained for the area a reassessment of its values. The agency again dropped the area based on the intrusion of military airplane overflights. But Congress specifically excludes outside sights and sounds when considering wilderness designation; the area has fewer overflights than the Lone Peak Wilderness near Salt Lake City.

Mike Medberry

SILVER ISLAND MOUNTAINS WILDERNESS

During the Pleistocene Epoch the Silver Island Mountains were an island in vast Lake Bonneville. Today, as one looks across the Great Salt Lake Desert from Interstate 80 in the heat of summer, the entire range seems to float on a shimmering mirage, giving currency to its name. We propose that 27,200 acres of the Silver Island Mountains, the part of the range least influenced by human actions, be designated wilderness. The BLM has recommended against any wilderness designation in these mountains.

The Silver Island Mountains are most accessible from Interstate 80 near Wendover, Utah. A rough dirt road leads northeast from Wendover and splits near Danger Cave State Park to encircle the mountain range. Follow the right-hand branch, which parallels the southeastern side of the mountains. Four-wheel-drive tracks depart from the loop road and lead into Jenkins, Cave, Silver Island, and Donner canyons. A hike up trailless ridges to the main peaks may depart from any of these spur roads.

Views of Distant Ranges

Vistas from the mountain tops out over the desert are superb, taking in the enormous expanse of salt flats and range upon range of Great Basin topography, including the Deep Creek, Pilot, and Newfoundland Mountains. Hiking, hunting, camping, rock collecting, photography, sightseeing, and horseback riding are all possible in the primitive setting of these mountains.

Danger Cave, a major archeological site just northeast of Wendover and close to the Silver Island Mountains, has given researchers a great deal of information about human culture spanning more than 9,000 years. Most of the known cultural sites in the region were found along the ancient shoreline of Lake Bonneville, but a few also occur in upland areas (Aikens and Madsen, 1986). The Silver Island Mountains have never been thoroughly inventoried for cultural resources, but because of their proximity to known sites and the favorable environmental conditions, it is likely that cultural sites exist within the proposed wilderness. The cultural resources in this region have no commercial value but are of scientific interest.

There are also significant biological, geological, and historical values in the Silver Island Mountains. The wave-cut terraces and accompanying deposits of tufa (an evaporite mineral) at the northeast corner of the unit are of special interest to geologists and rockhounds. The path of the Donner Party skirts the northern boundary and is still visible in some locations.

IN BRIEF

Index Map: Area No. 18

Highlights: Undiscovered archeological sites probably occur in this 7,500-foot-high range at the edge of the Great Salt Lake Desert. Wave-cut terraces from Lake Bonneville, and evaporite deposits are of geological interest.

Maps: USGS 1:100,000 Bonneville Salt Flats, Newfoundland Mountains

Area of wilderness proposals in acres:

Area	UWC	BLM
Silver Island Mtns.	27,200	0

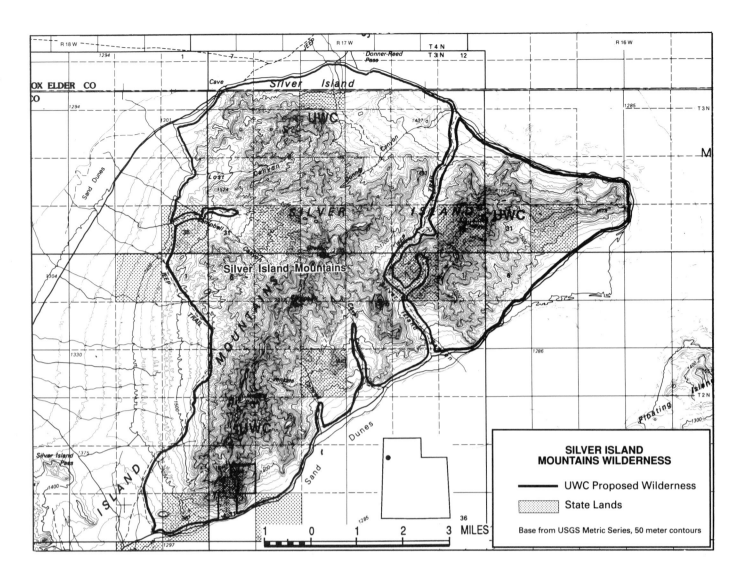

Studies Needed

Rising to an elevation of 7,500 feet, the Silvers are not high enough to wrest much moisture from the parched desert air. Consequently, the mountain slopes and canyons are dry and their streams ephemeral; they are dominated by heat- and drought-resistant vegetation. Small mammals are present as well as some deer, coyotes, and an occasional cougar. Thorough biological inventories of sensitive, threatened, or endangered species have not been done. However, a variety of raptors nest in the area or migrate through, including hawks, falcons, and eagles.

The Utah Wilderness Coalition Proposal

We recommend that Congress designate 27,200 acres in the northern portion of the Silver Island Mountains as wilderness. This excludes abandoned mines on the south end of the area. The easternmost part of the range, divided from the main part by a well used jeep trail, is included in our proposal. No intrusions whatsoever occur in the part of this unit which lie above an elevation of 5,200 feet.

The BLM dropped the entire Silver Island range from further study during its intensive inventory, claiming that daily Air Force overflights significantly interrupt solitude and that vegetative and topographic screening is inadequate. The BLM's "screening" argument is specious; the area is unlikely to attract so many visitors that they could not easily find solitude. And as explained above, Congress specifically prohibited the agency from disqualifying wilderness on the basis of outside sights and sounds.

The view from this cave near the top of the Silver Island Mountains takes in the enormous expanse of salt flats and range upon range of Great Basin topography.

Jim Catlin

Although airplane flights over wilderness areas need to be regulated, Congress designated several wilderness areas just east of Salt Lake City that receive a higher number of overflights.

The "overflights" argument hides an issue more directly concerned with land use: the military's proposed placement of electronic facilities throughout the West Desert. Ample lands outside of the UWC proposal are available for such facilities.

The BLM's inventory decision recognizes that existing vehicle ways do not detract significantly from wilderness values, but asserts that "ORV play has left its impression." Of the eight vehicle ways in the area, seven show no evidence of regular use and no evidence of construction or maintenance. All of these ways are two-wheel ruts with vegetation between them. Those in North Campbell and Lost canyons and those east of Jenkins Peak and west of Lambs Peak are largely revegetated. Their overall impression on the wildness of the area is negligible.

Mike Medberry

THE CEDAR MOUNTAINS WILDERNESS

Located only an hour's drive east of Salt Lake City, the proposed Cedar Mountains wilderness offers hiking, horseback riding, photography, and nature study amid rolling hills, juniper woodlands, and rugged limestone outcrops. On the east side of the mountains the main ridge breaks into sheer cliffs. In addition to supporting about 300 deer, the Cedars support about 200 wild horses, upland game birds, both American eagles, prairie falcons, and an occasional mountain lion; the benchlands on the west side provide year-round habitat for antelope. Surrounded by desert playas, these mountains rise to 7,700 feet and offer outstanding views across the Great Basin, the Great Salt Lake, and toward the high peaks of the Wasatch Mountains.

Access to the Cedar Mountains from Salt Lake City is quickest by travelling west on Interstate 80 to the Delle exit. From Delle, a dirt road parallels the freeway on its south side for a little more than a mile, then cuts southwest, away from the freeway, and leads about nine miles to Hastings Pass. A hike along the trailless ridgelines south of here will take you into the proposed wilderness. Access to the western side of the mountains is also possible off Interstate 80.

Bands of Wild Horses

Exceptional views across Skull Valley toward the Stansbury, Lakeside, and Wasatch Mountains may be had looking east from the Cedar Mountains. To the west may be seen the Deep Creek Mountains, the Pilot Range, the Silver Island Mountains, and miles of open country. To the south are the House Range, Confusion Range, and Wah Wah Mountains. The landscape is vast and isolating.

Blonde grasslands at lower elevations in the Cedars are broken by many interesting outcroppings of limestone. The limestone occurs in colorful layers, an iron-gray stone alternating with rusty brown hues. An eagle nesting site was recently identified on one of these outcrops, and many raptors are known to winter in the area. At higher elevations the mountainsides are steep and peppered with junipers, which, because they resemble cedar trees, gave this range its name. Tabbys Peak is a colorful volcanic peak at the southern end of the unit.

The Cedar Mountains wild horse herd fluctuates from about 125 to 200 animals, according to the BLM's Pony Express Resource Management Plan and EIS (BLM, 1988, p. 26), while the resident deer herd is more

IN BRIEF

Index Map: Area No. 19

Highlights: Located west of Skull Valley and the Stansbury Mountains, this area has one of the state's most important wild horse herds, as well as habitat for antelope, deer, and raptors. Low-elevation, relatively gentle terrain makes for good early season hiking.

Maps: USGS 1:100,000 Tooele, Rush Valley, Bonneville Salt Flats, and Wildcat Mountain

Area of wilderness proposals in acres:

Area	UWC	BLM
Cedar Mountains	62,100	0

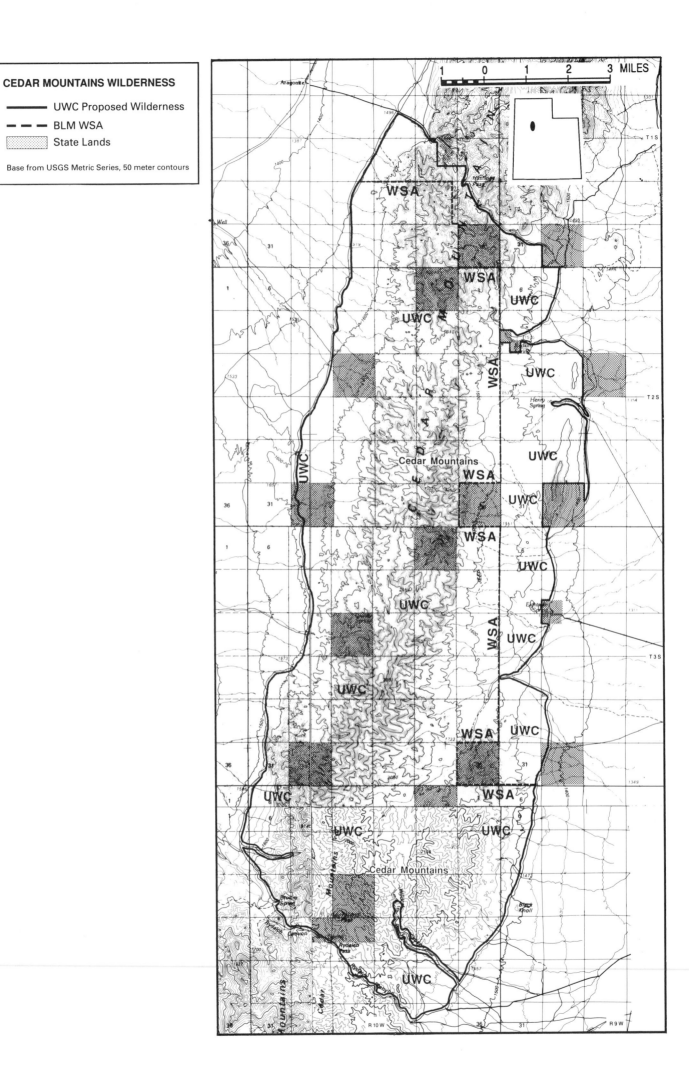

CEDAR MOUNTAINS WILDERNESS

——— UWC Proposed Wilderness

– – – BLM WSA

State Lands

Base from USGS Metric Series, 50 meter contours

stable at 300 animals. The Cedars also support a variety of smaller animals including coyotes, bobcat, and badger.

Seventeen archeological sites have been identified in the northern portion of the mountains, but the central and southern portions have not been inventoried. Most of the inventoried sites are lithic scatters, although one pictograph has been found. The historic Donner-Reed Party in 1846 passed through Hastings Pass on its way to California; and the explorer John C. Fremont used the route a year before.

Hazardous Wastes and Military Operations

Just west of the Cedar Mountains, Tooele County has defined a "West Desert Hazardous Industry Area" where several hazardous waste incinerators are being proposed. Although an improperly operated hazardous waste incinerator could also harm wildlife, vegetation, and existing high-quality air in the region, designation of our proposed wilderness would not prohibit the siting of the facility.

Phosphate rock occurs in the area but is probably economically infeasible to develop. Military electronic sites are proposed for high ground in the vicinity, but sites are available outside the proposed wilderness.

The Utah Wilderness Coalition Proposal

We propose a 62,100-acre wilderness in the Cedar Mountains; the BLM recommended none of its 50,500-acre WSA. The eastern boundary of the WSA is a nonsensical straight line. Our boundary follows topography and existing impacts more faithfully, as well as including important wildlife habitat on the benchlands. There are 11 privately owned sections in this area, and the BLM is attempting with the support of the landowner to acquire 7 of them through an exchange.

Mike Medberry

THE STANSBURY MOUNTAINS WILDERNESS

In 1984 Congress established the 25,500-acre Deseret Peak Wilderness on National Forest lands in the center of the Stansbury Mountains. The entire range deserves to be designated and managed as wilderness, however, since it is a single ecological unit that remains essentially wild. The range provides diverse habitat for deer, cougar, bobcat, birds, and reptiles; it also offers exceptional views of the West Desert, the Wasatch Mountains, and the Great Salt Lake from many ridgetop vantage points. The Utah Department of Wildlife Resources plans to re-introduce Rocky Mountain bighorn sheep here and is considering introducing elk. The Stansbury Mountains are jointly managed by the U.S. Forest Service and the BLM. Unfortunately, artificial federal agency boundaries cross the mountains and create unnecessary land management difficulties.

Away from the Crowds

The existing Deseret Peak Wilderness is a popular destination for backpackers, day-hikers, and hunters from the populous Wasatch Front. Immediately north and south of the designated wilderness is land managed by the Forest Service that qualifies for eventual wilderness designation but that was not protected by the 1984 legislation. The proposed BLM wilderness units are at the extreme ends of the range: North Stansbury (18,300 acres) on the north and Big Hollow (4,200 acres) on the south.

In 1982 the Department of Interior released from further study 18 WSAs around the West that are adjacent to Forest Service roadless areas. These 18 areas were considered for but not designated as wilderness

IN BRIEF

Index Map: Area No. 20

Highlights: A logical extension of the existing Deseret Peak wilderness and adjacent national forest roadless land, the Stansburys offer hikes along flower-covered mountainsides, good hunting for deer and game birds, and fine views of the Great Salt Lake.

Guidebooks: Hall (1982), Kelsey (1986)

Maps: USGS 1:100,000 Tooele, Rush Valley

Area of wilderness proposals in acres:

Unit	UWC	BLM
Big Hollow	4,200	0
North Stansbury	18,300	10,480
TOTAL	22,500	10,480

Adjacent wilderness area: Deseret Peak (USFS)

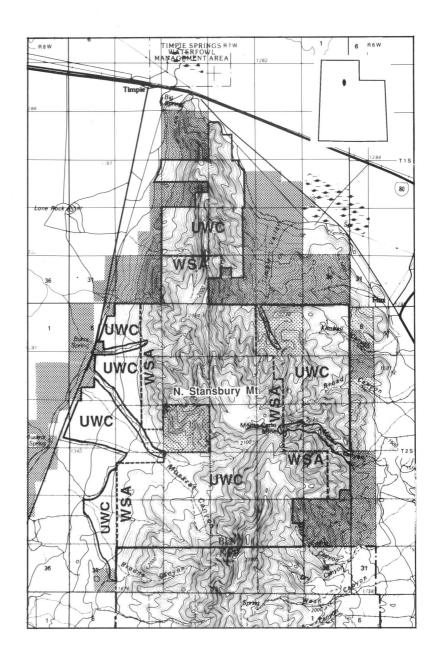

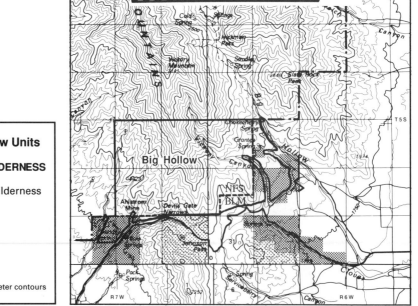

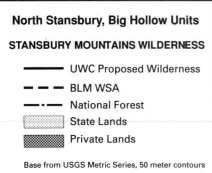

North Stansbury, Big Hollow Units

STANSBURY MOUNTAINS WILDERNESS

—————— UWC Proposed Wilderness

– – – – BLM WSA

–·–·– National Forest

State Lands

Private Lands

Base from USGS Metric Series, 50 meter contours

under the RARE II process. According to the Department of the Interior, they were of insufficient size to be managed as wilderness independent of the adjacent USFS areas. Since the 1984 Utah Wilderness Act released land between the Deseret Peak Wilderness and the BLM-managed Big Hollow WSA, the latter was dropped from wilderness review. The North Stansbury WSA escaped such treatment because the BLM considered it to be more easily managed as wilderness independent of the USFS land.

One Wilderness

This piecemeal approach to wilderness on the part of the Departments of Interior and Agriculture fails to respond to the need to protect natural ecosystem boundaries, and shows an unwelcome deference to political rather than resource-based decision making. Both departments missed the point that these lands are integral parts of a single mountain ecosystem surrounded by desert flats. One county official admitted at a public hearing that the national forest wilderness boundary had been shrunk six miles back on the north and one and a half miles on the south to prevent future designation of BLM wilderness. The deleted lands included three major mountain peaks and 13 drainages.

The Utah Wilderness Coalition Proposal

Instead of dropping the Big Hollow unit from further study, the BLM and the USFS should collaborate in evaluating the entire mountain range as a single wilderness area. Congressional designation is needed to ensure that these wild lands are not compromised by agency politics.

Mike Medberry

NORTH STANSBURY UNIT

Highlights—The northern 18,300 acres of the Stansbury Mountains are a logical part of the proposed Stansbury wilderness. Expansive views of the Great Salt Lake, the West Desert, and the Wasatch Mountains are but one mark of excellence for this unit; it also contains crucial summer mule deer habitat and is home for cougar, bobcat, golden and bald eagles, and a wide variety of other species. The UDWR has identified the area for reintroduction of bighorn sheep. Vegetative cover includes fir, aspen, pine, and juniper. There are no substantive conflicts standing against wilderness designation. Vehicle access to the North Stansbury Mountains is easiest from Interstate 80 heading west out of Salt Lake City. Take the Rowley Junction-Timpie Springs exit six miles east of Delle and follow the road six miles south to a dirt road that heads up Muskrat Canyon. After about a mile the road degenerates, and good hiking begins. The central and southern portions of the Stansbury Mountains are more easily reached from the east side of the range, south and west of Grantsville.

Geology and landforms—The ridgeline of the North Stansburys is steep, grassy, and cut by rugged canyons. Views across the West Desert from the many ridgetops in the North Stansburys are outstanding.

Plant communities—At elevations below 7,500 feet juniper forests dominate, while the higher ridges and mountain tops are dominated by shrubs, mountain mahogany, and grasses. Cottonwood, chokecherry, and aspen are commonly found in the drainages; the northern exposures of the unit are forested with conifer and aspen. During spring the mountainsides are aglow with early wildflowers, and the entire area is surprisingly lush.

Wildlife—According to the BLM, there are approximately 180 species of wildlife in the unit: 114 are bird species, 51 are mammals, and 15 are reptiles. The game species include deer, grouse, chukar, and cottontails.

Mountain lion, bobcat, and 17 species of raptors frequent the area. Both golden eagle and bald eagle are commonly found. The area contains superb habitat for Rocky Mountain bighorn sheep, and the UDWR plans reintroduction of these animals in the near future.

Recreation—The area is used extensively by hunters during deer and upland game bird seasons and by hikers and sightseers at other times of the year. The North Stansburys offer an excellent opportunity to escape the crowds while remaining within easy reach of the Salt Lake area.

BLM recommendation—The BLM in 1986 recommended that 10,000 acres of its 10,480-acre WSA be designated; it claimed that 480 acres contain potential for recovery of copper and disseminated gold. There are no data to support the occurrence of either mineral within the WSA (BLM, 1986, p. 17). The BLM's final recommendation is expected to reinstate the missing acreage. According to the BLM's intensive wilderness inventory, the WSA is essentially pristine. The BLM found an old mining road, an adit shaft, and two miles of ways to be "substantially unnoticeable."

Coalition proposal—We propose that 18,300 acres of the North Stansbury Mountains be designated wilderness. Our proposal includes benchlands west of the BLM's WSA and the steep lower mountainsides north and east of the WSA.

BIG HOLLOW UNIT

Highlights—Located at the southern tip of the Stansbury Mountains, the 4,200-acre Big Hollow unit completes the proposed Stansbury Mountains wilderness. The unit is bounded on the south by Utah 199 where it passes near Johnson Pass. Travelling south of Tooele on Utah 36, take Utah 199 west towards Clover and Dugway. About a mile and a half east of the pass, a narrow dirt road cuts north for just over a mile to Vickory Canyon, where visitors may begin an uphill walk into the foothills and on into the higher mountains of the Stansburys.

Plant communities—With more than 3,000 feet of vertical relief, this unit embraces the transition zone from alpine vegetation to a drier pinyon pine and juniper woodland habitat. Above 6,500 feet aspen and Douglas fir grow in the shaded valleys.

Wildlife—Mountain lions find their way down from the more rugged peaks of the Stansbury Mountains, following deer to gentler winter habitat in the Big Hollow unit. Many smaller mammals are year-round residents, and serve as prey for hawks and both types of eagles.

Recreation—Deer hunting, hiking, and horseback riding are the main recreational uses of Big Hollow.

BLM recommendation—The BLM initially recommended the unit for wilderness study because it makes a logical component of a larger adjacent national forest roadless area. But the agency later dropped the unit from further study. The BLM acted outside its legal authority; Congress reserves the right to determine the wilderness suitability of BLM lands.

Coalition proposal—Our boundary takes in fewer than three miles of vehicle ways that occur in the unit, and these are largely reclaimed and unused. Mineral conflicts are minor, and there are no other known conflicts with wilderness designation.

THE DEEP CREEK MOUNTAINS WILDERNESS

Summary

Rising from the desert floor at an elevation of 4,800 feet to peaks over 12,000 feet high, the Deep Creek Mountains are indisputably Utah's most spectacular West Desert range. The contrast between the white granite of Ibapah and Haystack peaks and the colorful talus slopes of Red Mountain make the range both scenic and geologically unique. These steep, rocky, glacially scoured peaks often hold snow well into summer. For all their ruggedness, the Deeps also contain verdant alpine meadows and forested canyons that are an unexpected delight to desert travelers.

The enormous vertical relief—greater than that of the Teton Range from Jackson Hole—creates a variety of ecological conditions that foster biological diversity unmatched in Utah's desert mountains. Eight perennial streams flow from the rough-hewn canyons, allowing deer, elk, bighorn sheep, cougar, bobcat, coyote, and other wildlife to flourish. Antelope roam in small bands along the benchlands surrounding the mountains. Due to their isolation from other similar environments, the Deeps also support a dozen plant and animal species found nowhere else.

Recreational opportunities in the Deeps are excellent, with many rugged and remote canyons. Scientific and educational values are high, including opportunities to study endemic, threatened, or endangered species, archeology, geology, and desert ecology. The rare Bonneville cutthroat trout and ancient bristlecone pine trees are of special interest.

Past mineral conflicts have mostly been resolved; water development occurs at the fringe of the proposed wilderness but has little impact within it. We propose a 90,200-acre wilderness, while the BLM is expected to recommend 57,384 acres in its final EIS. The Goshute Indian Reservation adjoins the proposed wilderness on the west; wilderness designation is consistent with the management of the reservation.

Walking in Beauty

The easiest approach to the Deep Creek Mountains is by way of Interstate 80 to Wendover, then south on Utah Highway 93. Turn southeast off Highway 93 toward the town of Callao and continue south along the eastern side of the range. Dirt roads branch west into Granite Creek, Trout Creek, and Birch Creek canyons. A hike up any of these canyons or up Basin Creek is rewarding. The steep route up Granite Creek to the top of Ibapah Peak leads through stands of cottonwood into evergreen forest, aspen groves, alpine meadow, and bare granite, affording spectacular views all along the way. Hikes up Basin Creek, Trout Creek, Goshute, Red Cedar, or Indian Creek canyons are rugged and rewarding. Upland game

IN BRIEF

Index Map: Area No. 21

Highlights: Utah's third-highest mountain range has eight perennial streams, abundant wildlife (including elk, deer, bighorn sheep, antelope, and a rare trout species), and lovely forests, meadows, and alpine tundra.

Guidebooks: Hall (1982), Hart (1981), Kelsey (1983)

Maps: USGS 1:100,000 Fish Springs, Wildcat Mountain

Area of wilderness proposals in acres:

Area	UWC	BLM
Deep Creek Mtns.	90,200	57,384

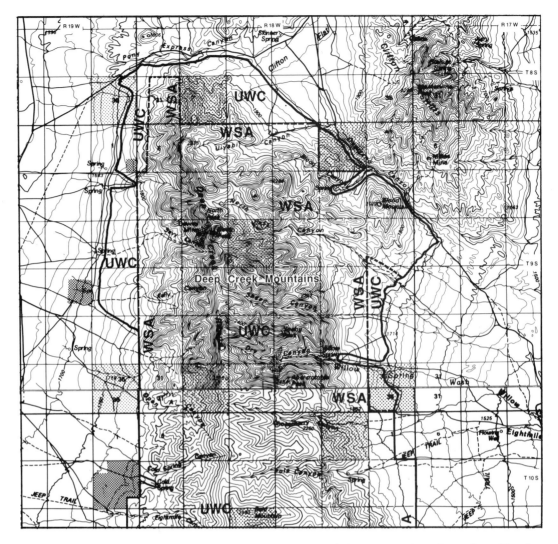

birds, many non-game birds, deer, elk, bighorn sheep, and antelope live in the proposed wilderness, and anglers may fish for native cutthroat in several streams. The Deeps also offer outstanding opportunities for mountaineering, rock climbing, photography, rock collecting, and geologic study. The BLM estimates annual use at 3,500 hunter days, 3,000 backcountry days, and 1,500 angling days.

Four-wheel-drive vehicles have left their mark in a few canyons where they clearly don't belong, but the scars will not be long in healing after roads are posted as being closed. The BLM has left open many miles of vehicle ways on steep, erosive slopes that should be closed to vehicles.

Birch and Trout Creeks, from their sources to their junction, are listed as Nationwide Rivers Inventory segments and are eligible for addition to the Wild and Scenic Rivers System. The BLM (1986) notes that "these segments possess excellent primitive recreation opportunities, unique geological features relating to ancient Lake Bonneville, a vertical granite canyon, Utah cutthroat trout, and bristlecone pine."

Deeps Ecology: Unmatched Biological Diversity

Since the Deep Creek Mountains are isolated in a sea of desert and present such a wide range of habitats, a unique assortment of plant and animal species has evolved here. Botanists divide the mountains into four plant areas: desert type (sagebrush and shadscale), xeric forests (juniper and pinyon pine woodland), mesic forests (coniferous forest), and alpine tundra (low-growing shrubs, herbs, and wildflowers). Sixty families of plants, including at least 431 species, live in the Deeps (McMillan, 1948).

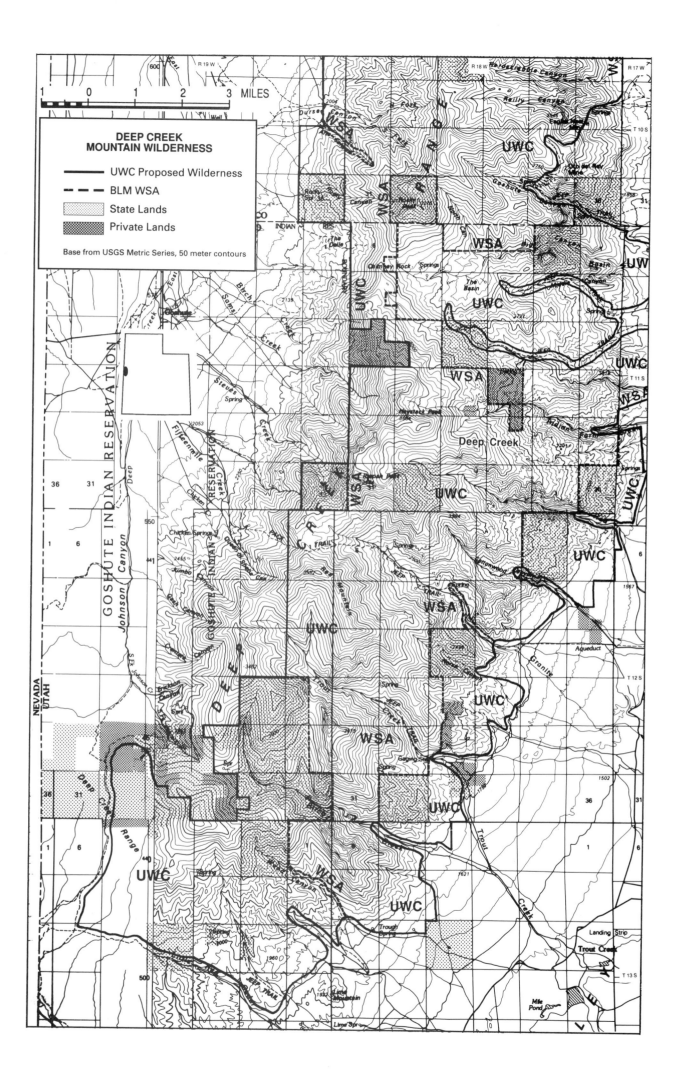

DEEP CREEK MOUNTAIN WILDERNESS

—————— UWC Proposed Wilderness

– – – – – BLM WSA

State Lands

Private Lands

Base from USGS Metric Series, 50 meter contours

Although the BLM fails to mention it in the DEIS, the agency elsewhere identified at least 12 of these plants as endemic (found nowhere else); they include several varieties of wildflower and cactus.

In addition, the bristlecone pine trees found on high-elevation limestone soils in the Deeps "approach the size and appearance of the (bristlecone pine) trees in California's Methuselah Grove, home of the world's oldest living trees. There are also significant stands of young bristlecone pine that provide the WSA with a self-perpetuating community of significant ecological interest." (BLM, 1986).

The proposed wilderness provides crucial habitat for a herd of Rocky Mountain bighorn sheep, critical summer and winter range for mule deer, and important year-round habitat for elk and pronghorn antelope. Cougar are relatively abundant in the Deeps, especially in areas such as Granite Creek Canyon where water is abundant and caves common. The mountains also support lynx, bobcat, coyote, fox, badger, porcupine, rabbit, and other small mammals (Durrant, 1952).

Rocky Mountain bighorn sheep were reintroduced to the Deeps in 1984 by the Utah Division of Wildlife Resources (UDWR). At about the same time, the animals had begun to recolonize the Deeps from a population in Nevada's Snake Range. In January of 1989, the UDWR supplemented the 22-member Deep Creek Mountains population with 17 more bighorns. Elk, a species not native to the Deeps, were introduced to the mountains by the Goshute Indians in 1988 and are expected to do well.

One-hundred eighty-five species of birds live in or migrate through the Deeps, according to the BLM (1986, p. 21), including the endangered bald eagle and peregrine falcon, and a rare variety of blue grouse. The proposed wilderness is crucial yearlong habitat for the golden eagle.

The Bonneville cutthroat trout, which has been nominated for protection under the Endangered Species Act, is found in Birch Creek and Trout Creek. This fish, once common in streams of the Great Basin, has been eliminated from most of its historic range by habitat destruction and hybridization with rainbow trout. A private developer, BMB Enterprises Inc., has received a license from the Federal Energy Regulatory Commission to build a small hydroelectric project near the proposed wilderness. While this project will not affect the wilderness, it will dry up 3,200 feet of Birch Creek, habitat for the Bonneville cutthroat.

Also found in several streams in the Deep Creek Mountains is a rare insect, the giant stonefly, which is only found elsewhere in watercourses flowing to the Pacific Ocean. Some cite the presence of this insect in the Deeps as proof that streams on the west side of the mountains once drained into the Columbia River.

8,500 Years of Human History

A 1977 archeological survey of the southeastern portion of the Deeps identified 28 archeological sites, including cave and rock shelters, pictographs, campsites, and open lithic scatters. The variety of artifacts found suggests semi-permanent occupation by Archaic, Sevier, and Paiute-Shoshone Indian populations for more than 8,500 years (Lindsay and Sargent, 1977). The likelihood of other archeological finds in the proposed wilderness is high, but no other inventory work has been done.

Jedediah Smith, the first white explorer to come across the Deep Creek Mountains, did so in the spring of 1827. He and later travellers used the Deeps as a landmark and source of water. The Pony Express route skirts the northern end of the mountains.

The summit of Haystack Peak in the Deep Creek Mountains is more than 7,000 feet above the desert floor—a vertical rise greater than that of the Teton Range. Ibapah Peak is in the background.

Fred Swanson

Mining Conflicts

Although there has been a great deal of mineral exploration within the proposed Deep Creek Mountains wilderness, little production has resulted. According to Stokes (1986, p. 181-2), "The Deep Creek Range is a potential producer of gold, silver, copper tungsten, beryllium, and mercury. There has been a great deal of prospecting and exploration in the area, but to date production has been minor." Mines near the Deep Creek Mountains have produced a variety of both precious (gold and silver) and base metals (copper, mercury, lead, and iron), but due to the remoteness of the tracts and probable small size of deposits, further mineral production is unlikely. Extensive exploration for uranium in the Deeps during the 1970s stirred controversy but turned up no minerals of value.

The BLM is acquiring two patented but unproductive mining claims at the north end of the mountains. Acquisition of these properties, the Dewey and Roy mines, would diminish perceived mineral conflicts and allow the agency to expand its wilderness recommendations to the northern boundary of the WSA. The Dewey and Roy lands are little more than prospects that didn't pan out, and our proposal already includes this land. Both the BLM and our proposals exclude the Oro Del Ray mine and its access road up Goshute Canyon from the wilderness. Exploration for gold during the summer of 1988 near the mouth of Horse and Granite canyons disturbed about four acres and showed no development potential; reclamation of the land, we are promised, will be more successful.

There are currently 46 unpatented mining claims within or overlapping the Deep Creek Mountains WSA, 32 of which were filed after the passage of FLPMA in 1976. Validity determinations will be made on all of these claims if the area is designated as wilderness. Due to the intrusive granitic stock, the likelihood of oil and gas discoveries in the Deep Creek Mountains is low, and no pre-FLPMA leases exist in the area.

The presence of any minerals in economic quality or quantity within the proposed wilderness is unlikely. Regardless of mineral values, however, the proposed Deep Creek Mountains wilderness is a perfect example of an area where preservation of unique natural values and solitude outweighs the value of potential mineral development.

The Utah Wilderness Coalition Proposal

Our proposal includes the entire WSA and adds additional undisturbed wild land for a total of 90,200 acres. The Coalition proposal extends north to the road through Pony Express and Overland canyons and also adds wild land on the east and south sides of the range to include unroaded antelope habitat. We've added 3,200 acres in The Basin that The Nature Conservancy purchased and deeded to the BLM. In addition, we include mixed-jurisdiction roadless land on the southwest side of the range to protect rugged mountainsides adjacent to the Goshute Indian Reservation and the lovely upper reaches of Birch Creek with its alpine meadows and aspen groves.

The BLM initially recommended only 51,000 acres of its WSA for wilderness designation, leaving off undeveloped lands in the northern and eastern parts of the range. (The agency's final recommendation is expected to be 6,400 acres larger.) The agency claimed that the omitted lands had less outstanding wilderness values and higher potential mineral values. We believe these lands are an integral part of the wilderness and that the entire range should be protected rather than only those parts that lack commercial uses. Our boundary excludes recent mining activities, although they have not shown economic deposits.

Our proposal cherrystems the road up Granite Creek to the stream crossing where there is room to park a few cars. The developed spring is easily accessible from here on foot or horseback and should be maintained without mechanized equipment. Access roads to the Dewey and Roy mines are unnecessary, as are roads up Basin Creek, Art's Canyon, and Blood Canyon to the spring. The road up Birch Creek extends only to the spring development and is a primitive way beyond there; this should be closed to all vehicles.

Mike Medberry

THE FISH SPRINGS RANGE WILDERNESS

IN BRIEF

Index Map: Area No. 22

Highlights: This rugged range is habitat for peregrine falcon, bald eagle, and many other bird species that use the adjacent Fish Springs National Wildlife Refuge. Significant archeological sites and good big game habitat round out the area's high wilderness values.

Maps: USGS 1:100,000 Fish Springs

Area of wilderness proposals in acres:

Area	UWC	BLM
Fish Springs Range	55,200	33,840

The Fish Springs Range rises like an enormous dorsal fin out of the flat desert. Steep, dry, craggy, and remote, bisected by rugged canyons, the range offers solitude just a short distance from good roads. The Utah Wilderness Coalition is proposing that 55,200 acres be designated wilderness. Such designation would protect roughly four-fifths of the range, which measures 6 miles wide by 16 miles long.

The Fish Springs Range is best reached by good dirt and gravel roads leading southwest from Salt Lake City or southeast from Wendover. From Salt Lake City take Interstate 80 west to the Tooele exit. At Faust Junction, 28 miles south of Tooele, turn west off the pavement onto the Old Pony Express and Stage Route. This road takes you to the Fish Springs National Wildlife Refuge, which lies at the base of the range, and continues around the northern end of the range toward Callao and on to Wendover.

About two miles before the refuge, a dirt road leaves the Pony Express road and travels south along the eastern edge of the mountains, providing hiker access. A hike to the top of the main ridgeline, 3,000 feet above the desert floor, gives unsurpassed views: range after range recedes into the distance, clear to the Wasatch Mountains.

Wildlife and Cultural Resources

The Fish Springs Mountains offer opportunities for hiking, backpacking, hunting, rock collecting, photography, and rock climbing in a primitive setting. Solitude is easily found and seldom interrupted even a short distance from access roads.

Because it is adjacent to plentiful water in the Fish Springs National Wildlife Refuge, the proposed wilderness is an excellent area in which to find wildlife. Two endangered species live here: the peregrine falcon and the bald eagle. The entire area is crucial yearlong habitat for golden eagle. Also present are deer, pronghorn antelope, cougar, coyote, badger, bobcat, and many bird species. More than 800 acres are identified as crucial deer summer range. Although desert bighorn sheep were long ago extirpated from the Fish Springs Mountains, good habitat exists, and the UDWR is contemplating reintroducing them.

The range is dominated by shrubs and grasses at lower elevations and pinyon pine and juniper trees higher up. At the highest elevations the juniper trees grow to an uncommonly large size, some with trunks exceeding eight feet in circumference.

Several limestone caves on the northern tip of the Fish Springs Range were surveyed for archeological resources in 1978 and found to have been occupied by Archaic and Fremont/Sevier peoples for nearly 5,000 years. Artifacts included textiles, projectile points, bone tools, and pottery; a burial site was also found. These sites have provided important information about the lifestyle of ancient humans in the Great Basin (Madsen, 1979).

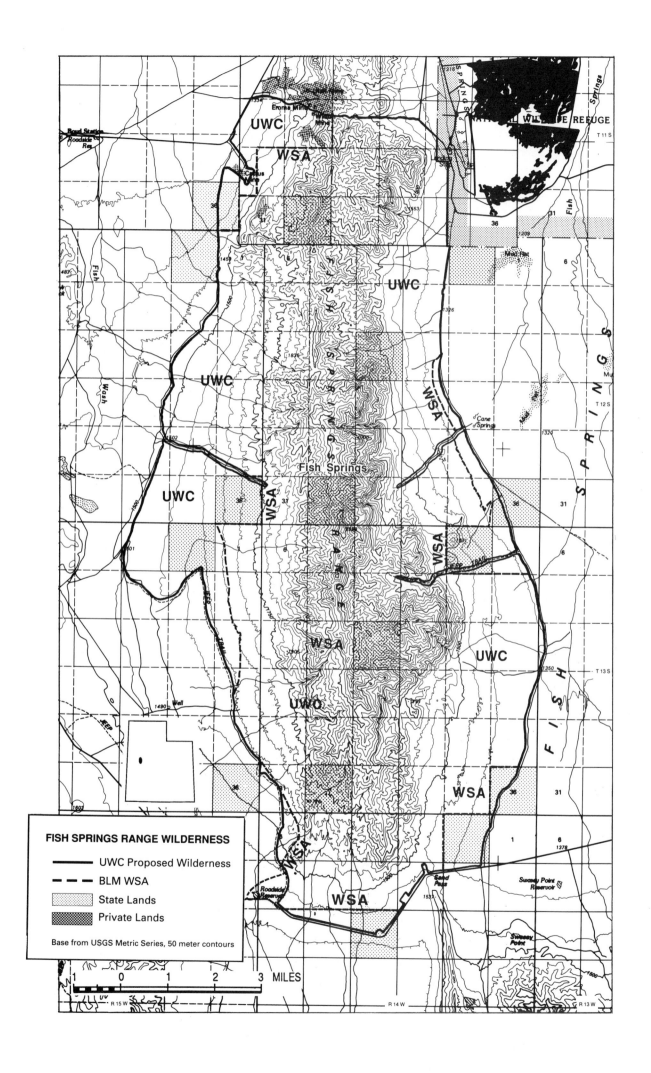

FISH SPRINGS RANGE WILDERNESS

— UWC Proposed Wilderness

- - - BLM WSA

State Lands

Private Lands

Base from USGS Metric Series, 50 meter contours

1 0 1 2 3 MILES

While the caves are outside the proposed wilderness, it is likely that there are other archeological sites within the area. Thorough inventories of cultural resources and threatened and endangered species are needed.

The Utah Wilderness Coalition Proposal

We propose that 55,200 acres of the Fish Springs Mountains be designated as wilderness, in contrast to 33,840 acres proposed by the BLM. The agency's analysis speaks for itself: "The main portion of the Fish Springs Range is in a completely natural condition with no human intrusions. Lower slopes on the margin of the 52,500-acre WSA have a variety of vehicular ways in various stages of rehabilitation by natural processes. These are substantially unnoticeable in the area as a whole" (BLM, 1986, p. 15).

The BLM's use of the term "substantially unnoticeable" is telling; that is precisely the criterion Congress stipulated in the Wilderness Act to determine the suitability of land for wilderness designation. The lower slopes should be included to give integrity to the entire area rather than allowing them to be further scarred by encroaching roads and ways. Moreover, the benchlands on the lower slopes provide important habitat for such animals as pronghorn antelope and badger.

Livestock are limited by rugged terrain to the lower lying and more gentle benchlands. Competition between wildlife and livestock for scarce forage is currently a problem but will be unaffected by wilderness designation. Local ranchers occasionally use some of the existing ways to herd and feed their animals but could continue to do so by horse.

Other conflicts with wilderness designation are minimal. Few off-road vehicles use the area. No leasable or locatable minerals are known to occur in commercial quantities. There are hard-rock mining claims and mineral leases (both pre- and post-FLPMA) within the area, but none has produced commercially. The northern tip of the range, outside of our proposal, contains proposed sites for electronic facilities for law enforcement and military use.

Mike Medberry

THE DUGWAY MOUNTAINS WILDERNESS

IN BRIEF

Index Map: Area No. 23

Highlights: Canyons, peaks, and bluffs ensure solitude in this dry range, sandwiched between the Pony Express Trail and the Dugway Proving Grounds. Mining has scarred the northern part of the range outside the proposed wilderness.

Maps: USGS 1:100,000 Fish Springs

Area of wilderness proposals in acres:

Area	UWC	BLM
Dugway Mtns.	23,100	0

A dry, corrugated range, the Dugway Mountains are a single curved ridgeline gouged by canyons trending east and west. At the north end of the ridge, Castle Mountain rises to 6,700 feet and is the highest peak in the range. Scenic and seldom visited, this 23,100-acre area provides interesting day hikes where a visitor is unlikely to see another person.

Access to the Dugway Mountains is provided by the graveled Pony Express Road, which passes along the south boundary of the area. Two little-used dirt roads leave the Pony Express road at points about 14 and 20 miles east of the Fish Springs National Wildlife Refuge boundary. These roads form a loop around the Dugway Mountains.

Panoramic Views

The rugged Dugway crestline offers panoramic views of the Great Salt Lake Desert and mountain ranges stretching into the distance in every direction. At the highest elevations the Dugways are covered mostly with juniper and sage, while the lower hillsides are speckled with blackbrush, shadscale, winterfat, and greasewood. There are small mammals and upland game birds here as well as migrating raptors and an occasional deer.

North of the area proposed for wilderness there is heavy mining damage. In its intensive wilderness inventory, the BLM was uncharacteristically forceful in describe those impacts: "Mining remnants saturate the

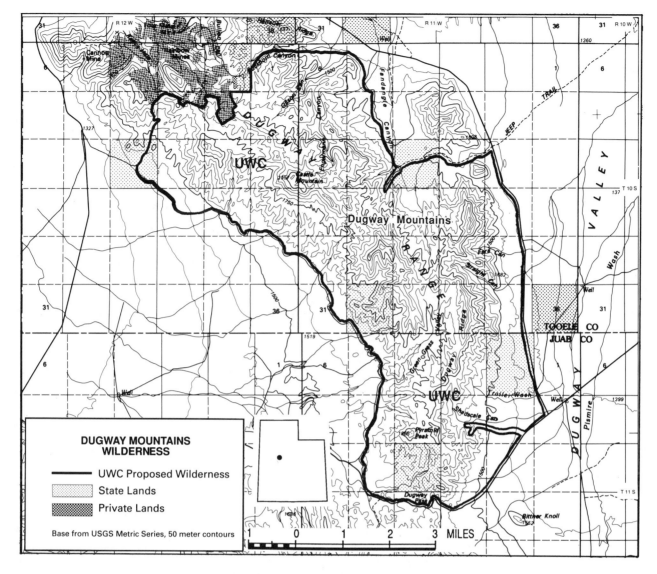

**DUGWAY MOUNTAINS
WILDERNESS**

——— UWC Proposed Wilderness

State Lands

Private Lands

Base from USGS Metric Series, 50 meter contours

1   0   1   2   3   MILES

landscape; tunnels, adits, pits, shafts and dumps lie scattered as bones after the feast; unsteady buildings and newly posted claim markers remind that perhaps the banquet is not yet over." These impacts stop at the edge of the extent of the mineral deposits, which is also our proposed wilderness boundary.

The Utah Wilderness Coalition Proposal

The BLM invoked its own esoteric definitions of "outstanding solitude" and "primitive and unconfined recreation" to eliminate the Dugway Mountains from administrative consideration for wilderness designation. Yet a trip to the Dugway Range will show a visitor virtually nothing *but* primitive country and solitude. While low-level military overflights are frequent in the area, they do not disqualify these mountains from deserving wilderness designation (see Newfoundland Mountains). We propose an 23,100-acre wilderness. Fourteen miles of ways extend into the area but are seldom used and are insignificant intrusions upon the land.

Mike Medberry

THE ROCKWELL WILDERNESS

The proposed Rockwell wilderness is 13,400 acres of shifting sand dunes interspersed with juniper and pinyon pine trees on the more stable sand ridges and sagebrush or grass on the flats. The area is a graben valley, a downthrust block surrounded by higher ground, covered with alluvium

Index Map: Area No. 24

Highlights: The northwest corner of the popular Little Sahara Recreation Area offers hiking and solitude in the shifting sand dunes, away from vehicle noise. A rare plant species, the fourwing saltbush, grows in this undisturbed area.

Maps: USGS 1:100,000 Delta

Area of wilderness proposals in acres:

Area	UWC	BLM
Rockwell	13,400	0

and sand. The free-moving sand dunes are a special treat for visitors here, offering changing displays of color and form. Rockwell also supports a surprising array of wildlife and is home for a unique four-wing saltbush, *Atriplex canescens*, which is found nowhere else.

Access to the proposed Rockwell wilderness is from Utah Highway 6, 32 miles north of Delta. Turn west then, in three miles, southwest into the Little Sahara Recreation Area. Rockwell is the northwest corner of the BLM-administered Recreation Area and is easily reached from the White Sands Campground.

Sand Dunes and Scientific Values

The Rockwell portion of the Little Sahara Recreation Area is mostly used for nature study, photography, day hiking, camping, sightseeing, horseback riding, hunting, and rock climbing. While the unit is relatively small, it provides ample room for visitors to find solitude among the dunes and rolling hills. Large juniper trees and gnarled snags in the Rockwell area make good photographic studies. As the BLM has stated (1986), "These picturesque trees, the unusual *Atriplex* species, and other forms of plant and animal life existing in a natural state in the sand dune environment combine to provide outstanding opportunities for scientific, educational, and recreational uses." The agency further states that "Nature study and photography opportunities are very good, primarily due to the presence of unique sand dunes and the accompanying wildlife and vegetation ecosystem."

The Rockwell area provides habitat for 115 bird species, 48 mammal species, 15 reptile species, and 1 amphibian, according to the BLM. The endemic four-wing saltbush, *Atriplex canescens*, grows as tall as 12 feet and

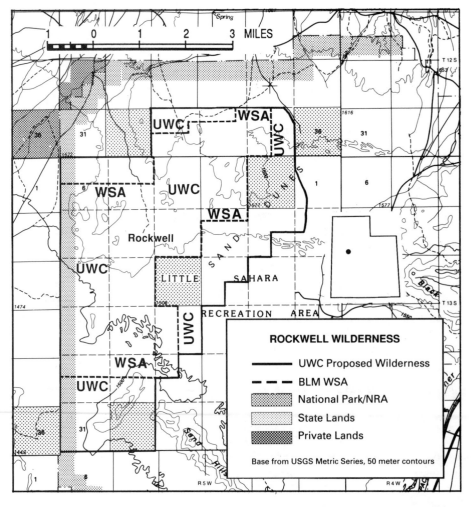

is thought to have been widespread at one time. However, apparently due to heavy grazing throughout the West, it has retreated to this single isolated spot. While not currently listed as a threatened or endangered plant, this giant saltbush is a likely candidate for eventual listing. The relict plant community in this area also includes ancient junipers, big sagebrush, and other sand dune species, all in a natural condition and unaffected by human intrusion. Because this community is a remnant of the vegetation that once covered much of the western deserts, it is of special interest to botanists.

The Utah Wilderness Coalition Proposal

Almost all of our proposed 13,400-acre wilderness is a designated BLM Natural Area that is closed to motor vehicles. Our proposal also includes the natural part of the sand dunes south of this area. These dunes are seldom used by ORVs and are a logical part of the wilderness. There is only a single, one-mile-long vehicle way intruding into the proposed Rockwell wilderness, and it was declared by the BLM to be "substantially unnoticeable." Thus, the entire area is in a natural condition.

The proposed wilderness is bordered by the 60,000-acre Little Sahara Recreation Area, two-thirds of which is available for ORV use and would remain open even if the Rockwell area were designated wilderness. The BLM has not proposed wilderness protection for any of the Rockwell area,

The shifting sand dunes of the proposed Rockwell–Little Sahara wilderness offer constantly changing displays of color and form.

John P. George

yet is applying restrictions on ORVs within its natural area that are similar to those for wilderness areas.

The BLM (1986) cites a "low likelihood of recovery" of locatable minerals and a "low favorability" for oil and gas. In the absence of mineral and ORV conflicts, the Rockwell area should be designated as wilderness, thus conferring a greater degree of protection than the current administrative designation.

Mike Medberry

THE HOUSE RANGE WILDERNESS

IN BRIEF

Index Map: Area No. 25

Highlights: Fossil beds, big game and raptor habitat, and excellent mountain hiking are found in this major West Desert range. The enormous sheer west face of Notch Peak is a spectacular culmination to a hike up the gentler east side.

Guidebooks: Hall (1982), Hart (1981), Kelsey (1983)

Maps: USGS 1:100,000 Tule Valley

Area of wilderness proposals in acres:

Unit	UWC	BLM
Howell Peak	25,000	14,800
Notch Peak	57,400	28,000
Swasey Mountain	57,000	34,376
TOTAL	139,400	77,176

Parched and rugged, the House Range extends nearly 40 miles from north to south and averages 5 to 7 miles wide. Its western edge is a winding and nearly vertical limestone escarpment that culminates in the imposing cliff of Notch Peak. The House Range is renowned for its extensive fossil beds and biological diversity. The oldest known animal fossils from Utah, 500-million-year-old trilobites, were collected in the House Range. While the heavily explored fossil beds at Antelope Springs lie outside our proposed wilderness, fossils are abundant within portions of the Swasey Mountain and Howell Peak units. The mountains provide year-round habitat for antelope, mule deer, golden eagles, prairie falcons, red-tailed hawks, marsh hawks, and chukar; winter residents include ferruginous hawks, bald eagles, and rough-legged hawks. At least four rare plants live in the House Range, and on the highest ridges are bristlecone pine trees, which are among the earth's oldest living things. Hikers, climbers, spelunkers, rockhounds, and hunters are especially drawn to the House Range for its solitude, wildlife, fossil records, and the grandeur of its peaks.

Extensive exploration has shown little promise for any mineral development within the proposed House Range wilderness, and off-road vehicle conflicts are few. While our proposal is similar in size to that of the BLM, we have eliminated some areas of conflict and added important antelope habitat in the scenic benchlands on the west. Our boundary carefully excludes vehicle access routes to currently used livestock corrals, developed springs, and other facilities.

The 139,400-acre House Range wilderness includes three units along the spine of the mountains. The most northerly unit is Swasey Mountain (57,000 acres). Immediately south is Howell Peak (25,000 acres) followed by Notch Peak (57,400 acres). The adjacent units are separated only by a dirt road, and remain part of a single ecosystem.

Mike Medberry

SWASEY MOUNTAIN UNIT

Highlights—At over 9,600 feet, Swasey Mountain is the highest peak in the House Range and a prominent West Desert landmark. Our 57,000-acre Swasey Mountain unit is also the largest of three components of the proposed House Range wilderness. There are four limestone caves in the area as well as a nationally significant fossil collecting site. Mule deer, wild horses, and antelope are plentiful, hiking and scenery are excellent, and potable water is available at several springs. Swasey Mountain may be reached by travelling the Tule Valley road north from old Highway 50, which branches west from Utah Highway 6-50 10 miles west of Delta. Alternatively, from Highway 6 about 10 miles northeast of Delta, the Topaz Mountain road turns west; follow road signs to Sand Pass, which is at the northern tip of Swasey Mountain. Low-grade dirt roads parallel the range on either side, providing access to the ridges and canyons.

Swasey Mountain is the north-ernmost unit of the proposed House Range wilderness. Beyond lies the Fish Springs Range.

Tom Miller

Geology and landforms—The range's rough-hewn ridgelines offer a spectacular panorama of desert ranges and wide flatlands that define the horizon. According to a Smithsonian Institution report, the Antelope Springs Trilobite Beds on the southwestern side of the WSA are "the most outstanding field for gathering fossils of the Cambrian geologic era in Utah and one of the most outstanding fields in the United States" (BLM, 1986). Forty species have been found. While much of the fossil collection takes place outside the proposed wilderness, more specimens occur within it. Protection of the fossil beds from further commercial exploitation is needed.

Plant communities—Vegetative cover is widely varied and includes Douglas fir, white fir, limber pine, ponderosa pine, and bristlecone pine in the highlands; pinyon pine, juniper, shrubs, and grasses grow lower down. Of special interest to botanists is a forest of mountain mahogany.

Wildlife—Swasey Mountain contains important habitat for the estimated 100 antelope and 1,000 mule deer in the area. Bald and golden eagles, peregrine and prairie falcons, and other raptors live along Swasey Mountain or migrate through. The BLM considers all of the area to be crucial yearlong golden eagle habitat.

Recreation—Swasey Mountain offers high-quality primitive recreational activities, including rock collecting, hiking, hunting, and horseback riding. The road leading west from Antelope Spring provides access to hiking routes up the southern and western sides of Swasey Peak, the highest point in the area. The area is also a prime destination for those who enjoy cave exploration. There are seven undisturbed caves within the proposed wilderness (three on a state-owned section), and there are probably others nearby awaiting discovery.

BLM recommendation—The BLM recommended 34,500 acres in 1986. Its final recommendation is expected to delete lands in the northern part of the area for a speculative gold mine, and add important natural areas in the southern and eastern parts, for a net reduction of 124 acres. Eleven miles of vehicle ways on the east side of the unit were considered substantially unnoticeable by the BLM.

Coalition proposal—We propose 57,000 acres of Swasey Mountain for wilderness designation. We cherrystemmed the Antelope Springs road to its end just southwest of Swasey Peak proper. Some of the benchlands on either side of the range should be designated as wilderness in order to protect important wildlife habitat from future ORV damage. In addition,

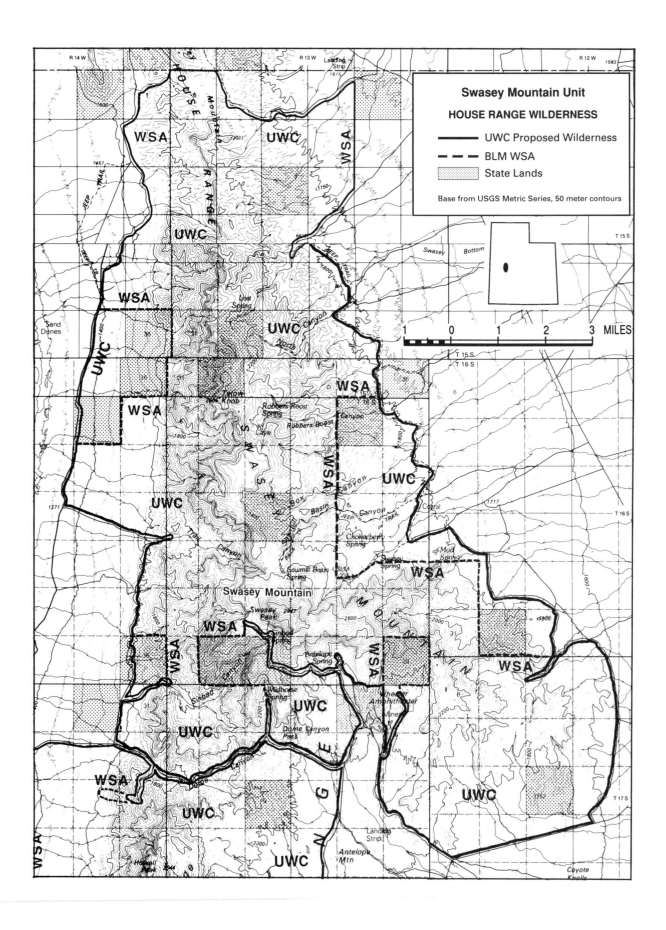

Swasey Mountain Unit

HOUSE RANGE WILDERNESS

———— UWC Proposed Wilderness

– – – – BLM WSA

State Lands

Base from USGS Metric Series, 50 meter contours

1 0 1 2 3 MILES

shadscale-greasewood communities on this lower-lying land would add diversity to the Wilderness Preservation System. Mineral values and conflicts are low.

NOTCH PEAK UNIT

Highlights—The 57,400-acre Notch Peak unit is the most dramatic and diverse of the three units that make up the House Range proposed wilderness. In addition to the scenic grandeur it provides, the area also supports rare plants, a stand of ancient bristlecone pines, and an abundance of birds of prey. A hiking route up Sawtooth Canyon to the summit of Notch Peak offers spectacular views of the surrounding desert. While this area is circumscribed by two-wheel-drive roads, it retains its wild character. Access is by dirt roads that turn north off Highway 6-50. The first road turns off the highway about 50 miles west of Delta, Utah, at Skull Rock Pass, and leads into Sawtooth Cove at the south end of the mountain. About four miles beyond the pass a second road proceeds north from the highway, paralleling the mountains on their western side.

Geology and landforms—The enormous western face of Notch Peak is the desert equivalent of Yosemite's El Capitan. According to William Lee Stokes in his *Geology of Utah* (1988), Notch Peak "rises vertically almost 4,450 feet and is one of the highest cliffs in North America." Rock climbers consider the face one of the finest and most challenging climbs in Utah. Striking bands of gray and white limestone decorate the sheer rock face, and twisting canyons give it dimension.

Plant communities—While much of the Notch Peak unit is dominated by pinyon pine-juniper or sagebrush-shadscale communities, aspen and conifers grow at higher elevations. In addition, the highest ridges support a healthy population of ancient bristlecone pine. According to the BLM, the Notch Peak unit contains three sensitive plant species: two species of wild buckwheat, *Eriogonum ammophilum* and *Eriogonum nummulare*, and a milkvetch, *Astragalus callithrix*, which are candidates for listing by the Fish and Wildlife Service as threatened or endangered; a rare plant known as *Primula domensis* is also found here.

Wildlife—Wildlife in the Notch Peak area includes mule deer, antelope, cougar, coyote, badger, chukar, and a variety of raptors. The area provides crucial habitat for golden eagles and for the endangered bald eagle and peregrine falcon.

Recreation—This southern end of the House Range offers excellent opportunities to hike, rock climb, study nature or geology, sightsee, ride horses, and take pictures. Year-round water is available from springs in scattered locations. As forbidding as Notch Peak may appear, there are several hikes that open up stunning scenery in return for a modest expenditure of time and energy. Hikes up Hell'n Maria Canyon from the west side, Sawtooth Cove from the south, or Sawtooth Canyon from a road on the east side toward Notch Peak are all rewarding. Solitude is easily found, even just off the road; what few two-lane ways exist are of little consequence and seldom travelled. The Notch Peak massif is cut by several deep and narrow canyons; the most commonly hiked are Hell'n Maria and Sawtooth canyons. Military overflights do not detract significantly from the area's solitude.

BLM recommendation—In its Resource Management Plan for the Warm Springs Resource Area, the BLM nominated 9,000 acres of Notch Peak as a National Natural Landmark and an ACEC (Area of Critical Environmental Concern). These designations would include closure to ORV use and withdrawal from mineral claims. BLM management objectives would entail protecting "the area's outstanding examples of ecologic and geologic

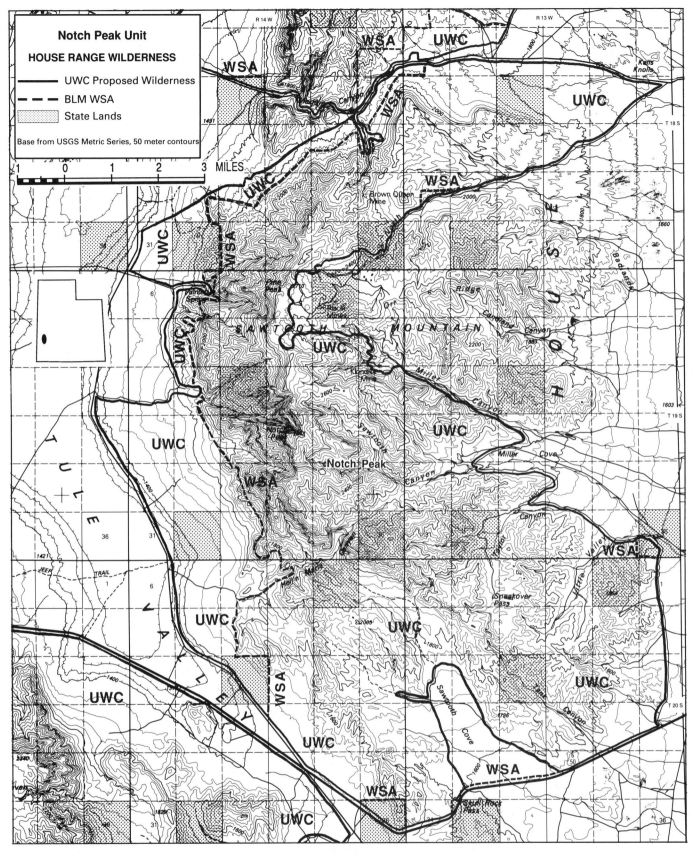

features and other natural values for educational, recreational, and inspirational benefit" (BLM, 1987, p. 43). Although the agency views these designations as an alternative to wilderness management for the area, we seek more permanent concurrent designation as wilderness. The BLM identified 20 miles of ways in the southern and eastern portions of the WSA but considered these "substantially unnoticeable." The BLM's wilderness recommendation (28,000 acres) would unnecessarily cut wild land in the southern section of the WSA on the assumption that this land lacks outstanding wilderness characteristics. The southern third of the WSA, with the exception of Sawtooth Cove, is much like other parts of the WSA that the BLM supports for wilderness designation. All of the Notch Peak unit is isolated and the topography varied; it most certainly offers outstanding opportunities for solitude.

Coalition proposal—Our 57,400-acre proposed wilderness unit incorporates the wildest country in and around the BLM WSA and eliminates significant resource conflicts. Compared to the WSA, our proposal excludes roads in Sawtooth Cove at the south end of the unit and adds the benchland on the western side, which is excellent antelope habitat. We include unimpaired benchlands on the north by moving the boundary out to the edge of a powerline corridor. We recommend cherrystemming about half a mile of the mine access road to the Brown Queen mine on the south side of Marjum Canyon. The mouth of Hell'n Maria Canyon is included in our wilderness proposal but is outside the WSA.

HOWELL PEAK UNIT

Highlights—This unit at the mid-section of the House Range is little known and offers cave exploration and hiking in solitude. Mule deer browse the highlands and canyons, while antelope graze the lower, flatter margin of the unit. Howell Peak may be reached from old Highway 50, which leaves the new highway 10 miles west of Delta, Utah. This dirt road leads through dramatic Marjum Canyon between the Howell Peak and Notch Peak units. The Antelope Mountain road departs from old Highway 50 about four miles east of Marjum Pass; it aims north, forming the WSA's eastern boundary. West of Marjum Pass the Tule Valley Road turns north from old Highway 50 and follows the mountain range along its western flank.

Geology and landforms—The unit takes in seven miles of the 3,000-foot-high striated limestone escarpment that culminates in 8,348-foot Howell Peak. The area contains about 10 acres of fossil trilobite beds and is full of caves, including Council Cave near Antelope Mountain.

Plant communities—Vegetation includes sagebrush and shadscale at lower elevations, with pinyon pine and juniper trees dominating the higher slopes.

Wildlife—Antelope frequent the sagebrush and grassy flatlands below the House Range escarpment as well as the gentler countryside to the east. While the animals commonly live in the playas between mountain ranges, little of this habitat is currently protected from mining, ORV use, road construction, and the increased hunting pressure that accompanies human use. As use increases, protection of antelope habitat will become increasingly important. Wild horses, deer, cougar, coyote, both American eagles, and the peregrine falcon are also among the inhabitants of the Howell Peak unit.

Recreation—Spelunking, fossil collecting, hiking, and hunting are the most significant recreational uses of this area. Since the area is not heavily used (even the roads around it are not often travelled), this middle portion of the House Range offers plenty of solitude. Military overflights are infrequent. Access into the Howell Peak area is possible from Marjum Canyon or from the roads on either side of the range.

BLM recommendation—The BLM claimed that 9,920 acres of its 24,800-acre WSA—the benchlands on the east and west sides—do not have outstanding opportunities for solitude due to their flat, sparsely vegetated terrain. But the BLM's wilderness study regulations do not allow the agency to drop areas because they lack one characteristic of wilderness. Fur-

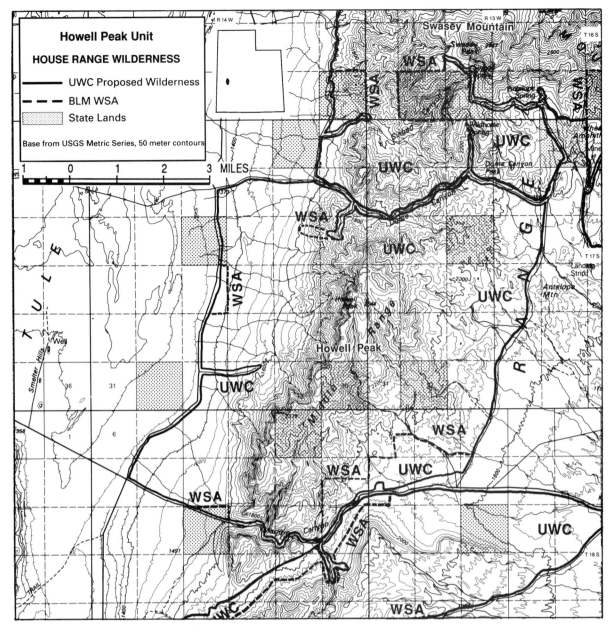

Howell Peak Unit

HOUSE RANGE WILDERNESS

— UWC Proposed Wilderness

– – – BLM WSA

State Lands

Base from USGS Metric Series, 50 meter contours

1   0   1   2   3   MILES

thermore, the BLM's claim neglects the importance of protecting wildlife habitat as a component of wilderness management and advances the prejudice that flat or gently rolling land cannot be wild. These nearly 10,000 acres are appropriately part of the House Range wilderness, adding a poorly represented biotype to the National Wilderness Preservation System and protecting important antelope habitat from ORV damage. The BLM has identified five additional miles of ways that it determined to be "substantially unnoticeable."

Coalition proposal—We propose 25,000 acres for wilderness designation. Our wilderness boundary includes natural benchlands that were excluded from the WSA. Our boundary also cherrystems the mine access road in the northern portion of the WSA pending a minerals validity examination. This examination should occur if Howell Peak is designated wilderness, and the road should be closed if the claim is invalidated. The mineral potential of the area is rated by the USGS (1989) as "moderate" for several base metals and gold. High mineral values have been asserted for an old digging in the southwest corner of the WSA, but a 1989 Bureau of Mines investigation showed no significant mineral occurrence in the area. There are few other conflicts with wilderness designation for the unit.

THE CONGER MOUNTAIN WILDERNESS

The Conger and Confusion Ranges are an odd jumble of hills, mountains, and rugged cliffs that culminate in the 8,000-foot summit of Conger Mountain. Creased ridgelines leading to a forested peak mark the view of Conger Mountain from the west, while the eastern side is sheer and rocky; more than a dozen canyons slice into the area. The Utah Wilderness Coalition is proposing a 20,400-acre wilderness area that embraces important habitat for antelope, deer, and wild horses.

Conger Mountain is remote and little known, but can be easily visited by travelling north on a dirt road that turns off Utah Highway 6-50 about 10 miles west of Kings Canyon (west of Delta). The road branches several times (a good road map is important) and continues almost straight north toward the southern end of Conger Mountain. From the south and east the mountain looks like the stern of a many-decked steamboat. Hike north from a developed spring below the mountain onto the dry, rugged ridgetop.

Little-Known Wilds

Solitude is easily found here, and primitive recreational activities include hunting, wildlife observation, hiking, horseback riding, photography,

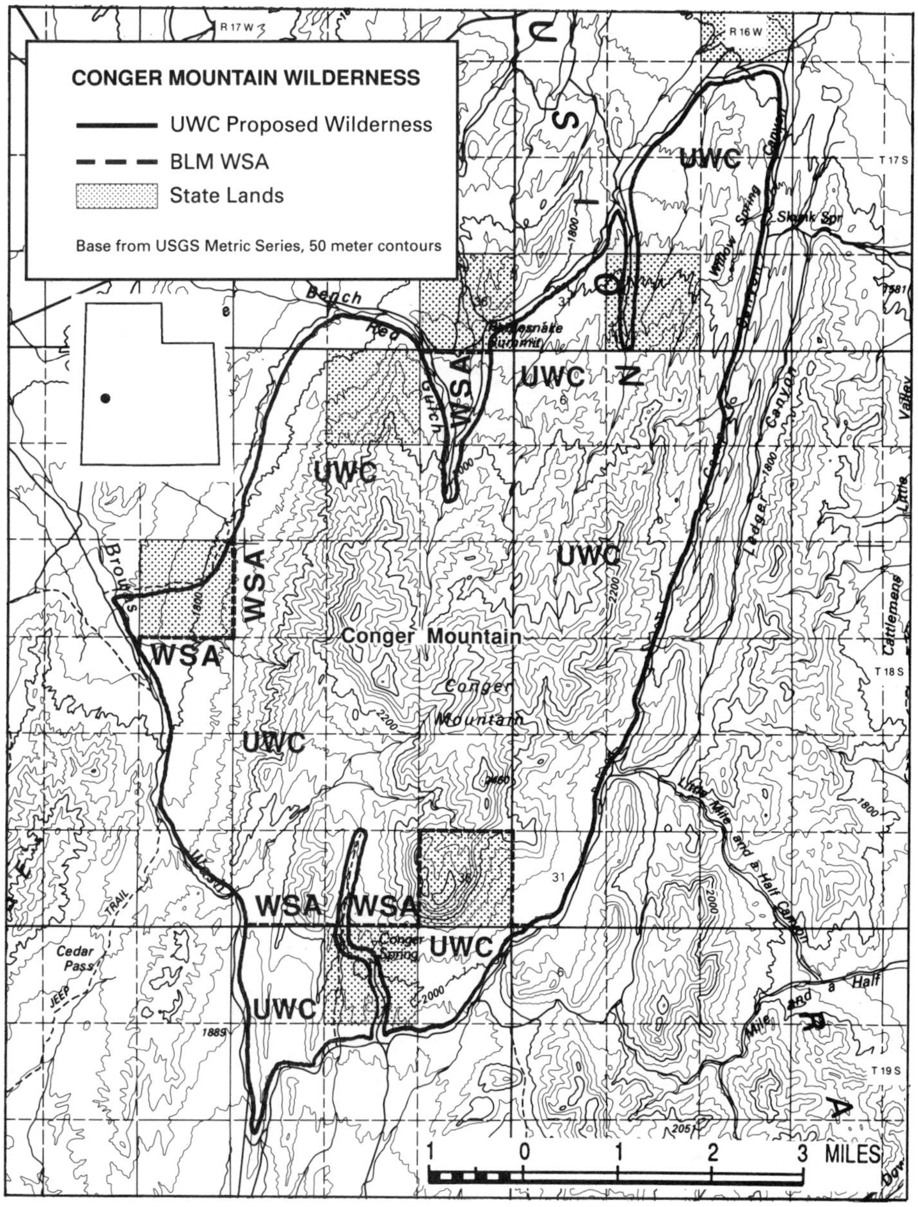

IN BRIEF

Index Map: Area No. 26

Highlights: Wild horses, mule deer, and antelope roam the benches and hills of this isolated range. Golden and bald eagles and other raptors also find refuge here.

Maps: USGS 1:100,000 Tule Valley

Area of wilderness proposals in acres:

Area	UWC	BLM
Conger Mtn.	20,400	0

CONGER MOUNTAIN WILDERNESS

——— UWC Proposed Wilderness

– – – BLM WSA

State Lands

Base from USGS Metric Series, 50 meter contours

rock climbing, and fossil collecting. Shadscale and sagebrush dominate the vegetation at elevations below 7,000 feet, while juniper trees are found above that level. One sensitive species, *Astragalus callithrix*, a milkvetch, is found in the northern portion of the proposed wilderness (BLM, 1986).

A herd of 70 wild horses roams Conger Mountain, and the animals are often seen by visitors to the area. Conger Mountain also includes 16,000 acres of high-priority winter range for mule deer and 1,800 acres of high-priority yearlong habitat for antelope (BLM, 1986). The BLM recently developed a spring up Willow Spring Canyon inside the proposed wilderness for use by wildlife. Most of Conger Mountain is crucial yearlong habitat for the golden eagle; the bald eagle, an endangered species, also uses Conger Mountain. Ferruginous hawk, Swainson's hawk, and mountain bluebird, which are considered sensitive species by the BLM, also live in the area, as do red-tailed hawks, prairie falcons, kit foxes, badgers, and chukar.

The Utah Wilderness Coalition Proposal

We propose that 20,400 acres of Conger Mountain be designated wilderness. This area includes five miles of vehicle ways, four in the northern end and one in the southern end, which the BLM found to be "substantially unnoticeable" in its intensive inventory. But even this is misleading, as all of Conger Mountain offer outstanding opportunities for solitude because of the remote, rugged, and untrammelled terrain. The BLM recommends that none of the area be designated wilderness, despite Conger Mountain's naturalness and the absence of significant mineral or livestock grazing conflicts.

Mike Medberry

IN BRIEF

Index Map: Area No. 27

Highlights: The largest remaining wild area in Utah's Basin and Range, King Top's high, remote plateau and surrounding benchlands are home to eagles, falcons, and a wide variety of wildlife. Backcountry deer hunting is good here, as is fossil collecting.

Maps: USGS 1:100,000 Wah Wah Mountains North, Tule Valley

Area of wilderness proposals in acres:

Area	UWC	BLM
King Top	78,800	0

THE KING TOP WILDERNESS

The Utah Wilderness Coalition is proposing an 78,800-acre wilderness in the King Top area of the Confusion Range, the largest of our proposed Basin and Range wilderness areas. Fossil Mountain, in the southern portion of the WSA, contains unique Ordovician fossils, which have special scientific and educational value. King Top Mountain, with an elevation between 5,000 and 8,000 feet, supports wild horses and antelope and is well used during autumn by deer hunters. Much of the area is a high plateau, rugged and sere, remote from human intrusion.

The King Top proposed wilderness is 50 road miles southwest of Delta, Utah, just south of Highway 6-50. Several minor dirt roads leave the highway near Kings Canyon and head south for a short distance to the northern boundary of the WSA. We recommend hikes in Cat Canyon, Little Horse Heaven, King Top Mountain, and Fossil Mountain.

Fossils and Solitude

The King Top area provides ample opportunity to hike, ride horses, hunt, observe wildlife, and backpack in an exceptionally primitive and seldom-visited region. Excellent rock collecting and fossil collecting opportunities are available on the 1,920 acres of Fossil Mountain the BLM identified as one of the world's most important collection sites for Lower Ordovician fossils.

Antelope, mule deer, wild horses, and chukar partridge live in the area. Two endangered species, the peregrine falcon and the bald eagle, also live here, as does the golden eagle, a sensitive species. The area accommodates a wide variety of indigenous animals but few in abundance because of the harsh climate. King Top is dominated by desert shrubs like

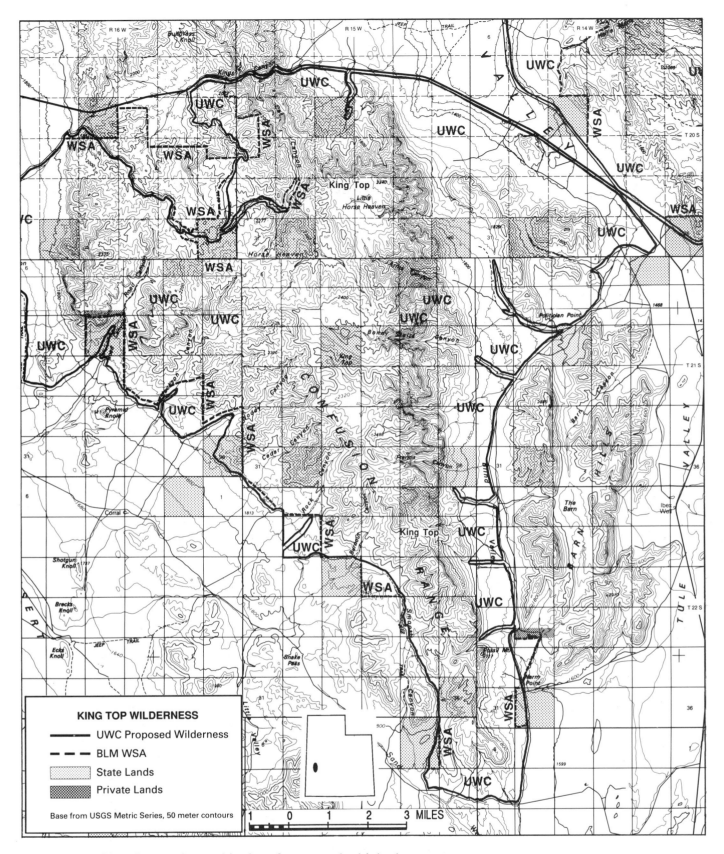

KING TOP WILDERNESS

—— UWC Proposed Wilderness
- - - BLM WSA
░░ State Lands
▓▓ Private Lands

Base from USGS Metric Series, 50 meter contours

1   0   1   2   3 MILES

shadscale, and by pinyon pine and juniper forest; on the high plateau
Douglas fir is also present.

Although the area is well known for its fossils, little archeological survey work has been done to uncover cultural sites. The Fremont and
Paiute-Shoshone Indians passed through or lived in the area for several
thousand years, so the potential for significant finds is high.

The Utah Wilderness Coalition Proposal

We propose that 78,800 acres of the 84,770-acre WSA be designated as wilderness. The area is wild, desolate, and diverse, offering solitude to match anyone's desire. The BLM's consultant rated the potential for mineral, oil, and gas resources low (BLM, 1986). Nonetheless, the BLM did not recommend any of the area for wilderness designation. The rationale for the agency's proposal is unclear even in its own documents.

Of the 30 miles of vehicle ways within the WSA (which the BLM judged to be "substantially unnoticeable"), our proposal excludes 10 miles. Many of these ways are in the bottoms of dry washes that are occasionally scoured clean by summer thunderstorms. Our proposal deletes an area on the northern part of the WSA that is separated by a well-used road. There are no permanent intrusions within our proposed wilderness.

Given the area's size, remoteness, unique recreational and scientific resources, and the absence of permanent intrusions or other serious conflicts, the BLM's no-wilderness recommendation seems inexplicable. Recent assertions by prospectors that large deposits of disseminated gold lie within the WSA are, as yet, unproven. Regardless of mineral values, designation of a King Top Wilderness would serve the public interest well.

Mike Medberry

THE WAH WAH MOUNTAINS WILDERNESS

From Crystal Mountain at the northern end of the proposed wilderness to 9,400-foot Wah Wah Peak at the south are 32 miles of rugged coves and canyons. The western escarpment of these mountains is a dramatic example of the blockfaulting that created most of the Great Basin mountain ranges. Standing out against the gray limestone, pure white Crystal Mountain is of particular interest to geologists because it is the last remnant of volcanoes that preceded basin-and-range faulting in this region. The Wah Wah Mountains also contain the only known Jurassic rock within the Great Basin (Stokes, 1986, p. 119).

Climbing and hiking in the Wah Wahs are excellent. While there are no trails, there is plenty of country to explore. Kelsey includes a hike up Wah Wah Peak in his *Utah Mountaineering Guide* (1986). He mentions stands of bristlecone pines along the main ridgeline and running water in a drainage or two. Deer are found in the brushy uplands and antelope on the benchlands. There are no serious mineral or ORV conflicts with wilderness designation.

The 109,700-acre proposed wilderness is divided into two units by Utah Highway 21 but retains an ecological integrity. The 60,500-acre North Wah Wahs unit includes a 42,140-acre BLM WSA. By contrast, the Central Wah Wahs unit contains 49,200 acres of roadless land that the BLM failed even to recognize as having wilderness qualities. Together these two units include the bulk of wild lands in the Wah Wah Mountains.

Mike Medberry

NORTH WAH WAHS UNIT

Highlights—The 60,500-acre North Wah Wah Mountains unit is extremely rugged, with rough-hewn, rocky slopes on the eastern side and steep cliffs on the west. At the northern end of the mountains, cool white Crystal Peak contrasts sharply with the surrounding land, a distinctive landmark in the West Desert. These mountains are frequented by many birds of prey and support cougar, deer, and antelope as well as a variety of smaller mammals. Two rare plants and a stand of ancient bristlecone pine

IN BRIEF

Index Map: Area No. 28

Highlights: A dramatic example of Basin and Range block-faulting, the Wah Wahs offer remote hiking along a 32-mile-long mountain spine. Bristlecone pine, deer, cougar, and antelope are among the area's attractions; Crystal Peak stands out in the northern part of the range.

Guidebooks: Kelsey (1986)

Maps: USGS 1:100,000 Wah Wah Mountains North, Wah Wah Mountains South

Area of wilderness proposals in acres:

Unit	UWC	BLM
North Wah Wahs	60,500	36,382
Central Wah Wahs	49,200	0
TOTAL	109,700	36,382

are found in the unit, as are significant archeological sites and collectable fossils. From Crystal Peak, the unit extends south nearly 20 miles to Highway 21. This northern unit is the larger of the two that make up the Wah Wah Mountains proposed wilderness. The BLM (1986) stated that its Wah Wah Mountains WSA, which is included within the Utah Wilderness Coalition's proposal, is "one of the most remote, untouched mountain ranges in the West Desert."

Geology and landforms—Unlike the surrounding mountains, Crystal Peak is white volcanic rock. It is a relic from the distant past, a reminder of the string of volcanoes that predate the block faulting responsible for most of Utah's present basin-and-range topography. Crystal Peak gives the Wah Wah Mountains an especially scenic character and is of interest to geologists. Fossils are found in the unit's sedimentary rocks.

Plant communities—The BLM recognizes that "the central portion of the range contains an important undisturbed biotic community representing a typical example of a desert mountain ecosystem" (BLM, 1987a).

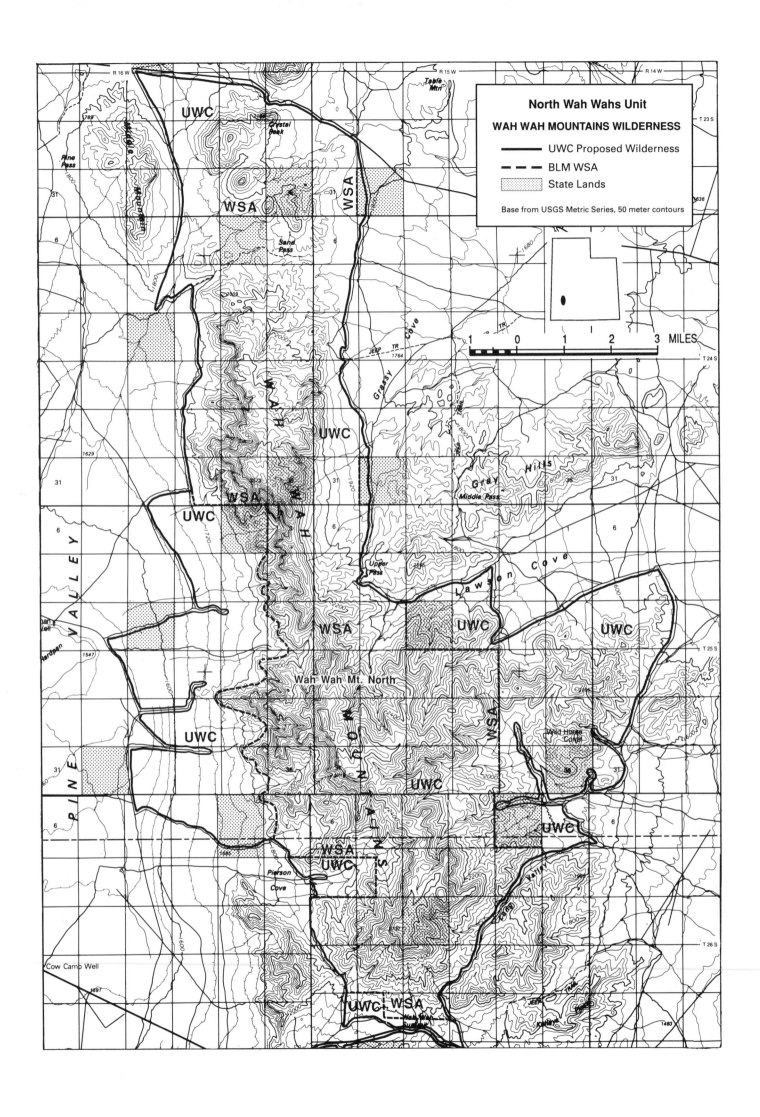

North Wah Wahs Unit

WAH WAH MOUNTAINS WILDERNESS

——— UWC Proposed Wilderness

– – – BLM WSA

State Lands

Base from USGS Metric Series, 50 meter contours

1 0 1 2 3 MILES

Exceptionally large bristlecone pines, some over 50 feet tall and more than 4,000 years old, grow on about 200 acres of the main ridge. Pinyon pine-and-juniper woodland is the most common vegetation type in the Wah Wahs, but mixed stands of ponderosa pine, white fir, and mountain mahogany also occur, as do small groves of aspen. Two sensitive plant species, the beardtongue *Penstemon nanus* and the globemallow *Sphaeralcea caespitosa*, may also grow in the area (BLM, 1986).

Wildlife—Cougar, antelope, deer, chukar, and raptors such as the endangered peregrine falcon and bald eagle live in the unit. The benchlands skirting the mountains are critical habitat for antelope. The unit provides crucial yearlong habitat for golden eagles and prairie falcons. Good deer hunting is possible in the northern Wah Wahs.

Archeology and history—According to the BLM, two archeological sites have been found near Crystal Peak, and the existence of additional sites is likely.

Recreation—The sheer limestone cliffs and rough, secluded canyons of the Wah Wah Mountains provide challenging hiking, climbing, and sightseeing. Impressive views from the central ridgeline of the mountains give one a sense of the region's vastness and of the desert's profound solitude.

BLM recommendation—The BLM (1986) recommended 36,382 acres of its 42,140-acre WSA. Although there are five miles of vehicle ways within the WSA boundary, the BLM judged these "substantially unnoticeable" during its intensive inventory. The BLM also noted that Crystal Peak is "an area of exceptional scenic splendor and is a unique undisturbed geologic landmark." Recognizing these values, the agency has nominated 640 acres of Crystal Peak as an Outstanding Natural Area and ACEC (Area of Critical Environmental Concern) and 5,970 acres in the southeast portion of the WSA as a Research Natural Area and ACEC. Both areas would be closed to ORV use and withdrawn from mineral entry if they were so designated.

Coalition proposal—Our boundary follows topographic contours more faithfully than does the WSA boundary and is expanded on the southeast side to include the roadless land north and east of Wild Horse Corral. Mineral development conflicts are minor. The BLM states that there are no known deposits of leasable minerals in the WSA. The same is true for locatable minerals with the possible exception of clay and silica deposits. These commonly occurring deposits are of uneven quality in this region and there is little current demand for them.

CENTRAL WAH WAHS UNIT

Highlights—Looming above the desert flats, the Central Wah Wah Mountains consist of a primarily north-south running ridgeline with weatherbeaten sidecanyons falling off to the east and west. This 49,200-acre unit completes the proposed Wah Wah Mountains wilderness; it contains deer, cougar, and antelope habitat and offers a variety of recreational opportunities. As an ecological unit embracing important plant and wildlife habitat, the Wah Wah Mountains wilderness would be incomplete without both the northern and central portions of the range. The Central Wah Wahs are most easily accessible by travelling west from Milford on Utah Highway 21. One-and-a-half miles east of Wah Wah Pass, a short dirt road leads southwest to the northern boundary of the proposed wilderness.

Geology and landforms—The main ridge has 15 separate peaks along its 12-mile length, creating a rough and diverse topography. Perennial streams flow in a few drainages. Some of the sidecanyons are rocky, steep, and boxlike, while others are wider.

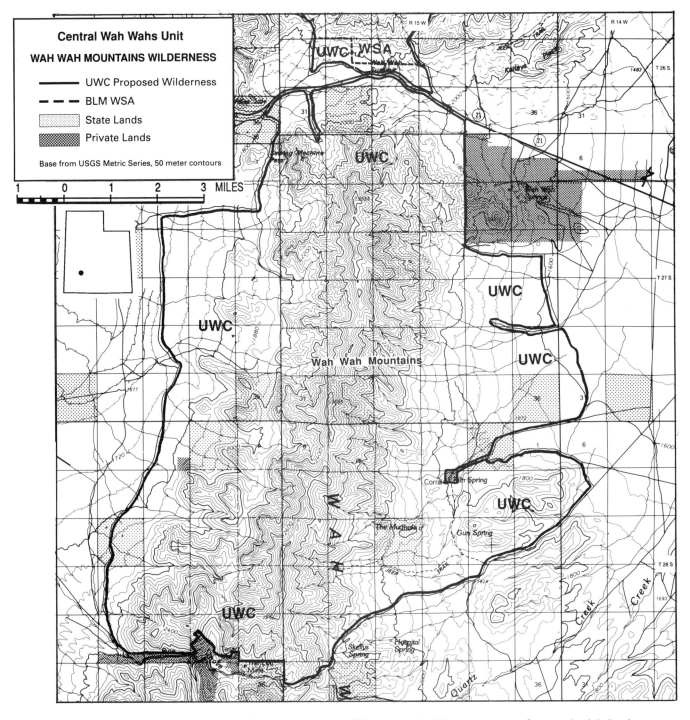

Central Wah Wahs Unit

WAH WAH MOUNTAINS WILDERNESS

— UWC Proposed Wilderness
--- BLM WSA
State Lands
Private Lands

Base from USGS Metric Series, 50 meter contours

1 0 1 2 3 MILES

Plant communities—The rugged sidecanyons are forested with juniper, pinyon pine, ponderosa pine, and fir. Bristlecone pine grow on the highest ridges.

Wildlife—Among the wildlife found here are deer, cougar, chukar, and, on the flatter land, antelope. Bald and golden eagles have been sighted in the proposed wilderness, and the threatened Utah prairie dog lives on the flats west of the main ridge.

Archeology and history—No thorough surveys of cultural resources have been done in the area.

Recreation—Recreational activities in the central Wah Wahs include hiking, photography, birdwatching, backpacking, rock climbing, sightseeing, and hunting for chukar and deer. Solitude is easily found in the topographic relief and vegetative cover of the central Wah Wahs. Hikes along the main ridge may start from points along the dirt road leading southwest from near Wah Wah Pass. High peaks along the ridge rise to well over 9,000 feet and present long views of the surrounding desert to climbers who reach the top. From any of the ridgetops a visitor has a commanding view of the Great Basin Desert and feels the isolation of these remote mountains.

BLM recommendation—During its intensive inventory, the BLM concluded that the Central Wah Wah Mountains lacked "an outstanding opportunity for solitude" and offered no "outstanding opportunities for primitive and unconfined types of recreation." The agency claimed that "the opportunity for avoiding the sights, sounds, or evidence of other people on the ridgetop or slopes within the unit is limited and considerably less than outstanding." Conservationists twice appealed this determination to the Interior Board of Land Appeals, stating that there is indeed abundant solitude to be had in the central Wah Wahs and that the area deserves designation as wilderness. The unit is undeniably rugged and remote with plenty of room to find solitude. The IBLA, however, supported the BLM's final opinion. Today the central Wah Wahs are not protected by WSA status and are therefore vulnerable to development.

Coalition proposal—The Central Wah Wah Mountains unit includes 49,200 acres of the two-parcel, 109,700-acre proposed Wah Wah Mountains wilderness. Just south of the proposed wilderness is the Tasso Mine, an area scarred by roads and mining. These intrusions are the only major disturbance in the central Wah Wahs and are outside the proposed wilderness. About six miles of vehicle ways run into the proposed wilderness. We agree with the BLM that their impact on the naturalness of the area is insignificant.

THE GRANITE PEAK WILDERNESS

Alabaster-white Granite Peak stands out dramatically from the surrounding brown-and-olive slopes of the Mineral Mountains. The scenery behind the main ridge's jagged exfoliated granite slabs and enormous standing rocks is spectacular, too. Located between Milford and Beaver, Utah, the 16,000-acre Granite Peak area is readily accessible from those towns or from Interstate 15 and provides a scenic, natural area for backcountry recreationists. The proposed wilderness also contains important archeological sites, obsidian quarries that were used from Paleo-Indian to historic times.

Access is easiest from Beaver, Utah. From town, travel west towards Minersville Lake. Turn right onto a dirt road about five miles out of Beaver and right again after a mile. Old mining roads parallel the mountain on either side, but the most interesting views and hikes are from the western flank, on the far side of Soldier Pass from Beaver.

Granitic Walls and Gothic Spires

The Mineral Mountains, of which Granite Peak is the most notable feature, have been studied intensively by scientists from the University of Utah in connection with geothermal and volcanic activity in the Great Basin. The striking white rock of Granite Peak is 11-million-year-old quartz monzonite, while the darker rhyolite extrusions in the area are young by comparison at 400,000 years (Stokes, 1986).

The igneous rocks of the Mineral Mountains are the source of heat for several nearby springs, such as Roosevelt Hot Springs. Development of the springs for power generation is a possibility, but the proposed wilderness would remain unaffected. Although extensively explored for minerals, Granite Peak supports no active mines and offers little promise of doing so in the foreseeable future. Most of the highlands are too rugged

IN BRIEF

Index Map: Area No. 29

Highlights: A popular day hike located just west of the town of Beaver, Granite Peak's cliffs offer rock climbing and unusual desert scenery. Prehistoric visitors chipped obsidian from volcanic outcrops in the area.

Maps: USGS 1:100,000 Beaver

Area of wilderness proposals in acres:

Area	UWC	BLM
Granite Peak	16,000	0

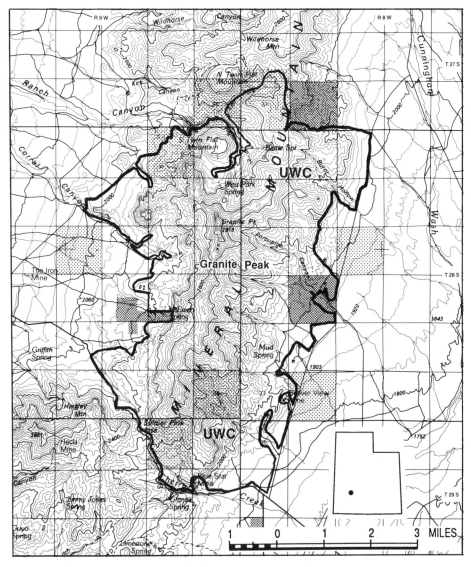

GRANITE PEAK WILDERNESS

▬▬▬	UWC Proposed Wilderness
▨	State Lands
▩	Private Lands

Base from USGS Metric Series, 50 meter contours

for livestock grazing; the BLM has instituted grazing reductions on the lower slopes (independent of wilderness reviews) to rehabilitate damaged range.

Residents of Milford and Beaver commonly use the Rock Corral Recreation Site on the flats west of Granite Peak for picnics and day hikes. An overnight trip from the picnic area into the rugged uplands of Granite Peak is likely a trip into solitude. Hunters may find deer and blue grouse in the pinyon pine and juniper woodlands, while wildlife watchers may see a variety of birds and small mammals. The granitic walls and spires offer challenging rock climbing.

During its intensive inventory, the BLM eliminated the wilderness core of the Granite Peak area because of old mining impacts on its periphery. Had the BLM made a small boundary change for its inventory area, it could have proposed Granite Peak as a WSA.

The Utah Wilderness Coalition Proposal

There are 16,000 acres of unroaded land around Granite Peak that should be designated as wilderness. The major attraction for most visitors is its handsome scenery and rugged terrain. Wilderness designation would also protect archeological sites of major significance, maintain high-quality wildlife habitat, and ensure that this wild land remains undiminished in the future.

Mike Medberry

THE WHITE ROCK RANGE WILDERNESS

Straddling the Utah-Nevada border west of Milford, the proposed White Rock Range wilderness includes 3,900 acres in Utah and 24,065 acres in Nevada. These pristine mountains are bordered by steep fault scarps on the east and west; the summit plateau stands 2,500 feet above the pinyon-covered lowlands. The crest of the range offers excellent views of Wheeler Peak in Great Basin National Park and of the serrate ridges of many distant ranges. The many mid-elevation springs make the area a haven for wildlife. Almost all of the area is recommended for wilderness by the Nevada BLM.

Access to the area is from Modena, Utah, which is 45 miles west of Cedar City. Travel the Hamblin Valley dirt road 30 miles north to the edge of the White Rock Range. From here, we recommend a hike to the ridgetop by way of White Rock Cabin Springs.

In the Company of Deer and Elk

The White Rock Range is as isolated from human activity as any place in Utah. As a Coalition field researcher put it, "the upper plateau gives a feeling of spaciousness where my only company were deer, elk, hawks, and wind through the scattered trees." The Nevada BLM concurred, stating in its 1987 Schell Wilderness Recommendations final EIS: "The impact of designation of the WSA as wilderness would be to preserve the excellent opportunities for solitude, important scenic values, elk habitat, and the pristine character of the unit."

Hunters favor the White Rock Range for deer and elk and the wilderness hunting experience available in the area. The UDWR has identified the northern half of the unit as critical summer range for deer, and the BLM manages 18,200 acres of the WSA as crucial deer summer range. Cougar, bobcat, badger, jackrabbit, and other furbearers are found in the area, as are a variety of birds of prey and desert reptiles.

The main ridgeline of the White Rock Range rises from about 6,200 feet to over 9,000 feet. The gently mountainous terrain is mostly covered with pinyon pine and juniper woodland, but also supports ponderosa pine and white fir. There are several springs and meadows and two seasonal mountain lakes.

There has been no mining in the White Rock Range and, according to the BLM, none is expected. The Nevada BLM rated the oil and gas potential for the White Rock Range as low.

The Utah Wilderness Coalition Proposal

We agree with the Nevada BLM's judgment that its entire WSA should be designated wilderness. The BLM, however, excluded White Rock Mountain itself by truncating the WSA on the north along an imaginary line crossing cliffs and ridges. The line connects two rough jeep tracks between White Rock Springs and Ripgut Springs. Our proposal includes this area for a total of 3,900 acres in Utah, compared to the BLM's 2,900 acres. The BLM recommends that about a mile of jeep trail just south of Log Cabin Spring, in Utah, be cherrystemmed out of the wilderness proposal. We recommend that this and four other short ways (each less than a mile long) on the Nevada portion of the WSA be closed to motorized vehicles and included within the wilderness. We also note that the proposed spring and trough developments and 2,500 acres of chaining and burning on the western side of the area are unnecessary and incompatible with wilderness management.

Mike Medberry

IN BRIEF

Index Map: Area No. 30

Highlights: A dense pinyon-juniper forest creates good deer summer range; scattered pines also grow here. Ridgetop hikes across this remote area will be in certain solitude.

Maps: USGS 1:100,000 Wilson Creek Range

Area of wilderness proposals in acres (Utah):

Area	UWC	BLM
White Rock Range	3,900	2,900

Adjacent wild land: Nevada BLM

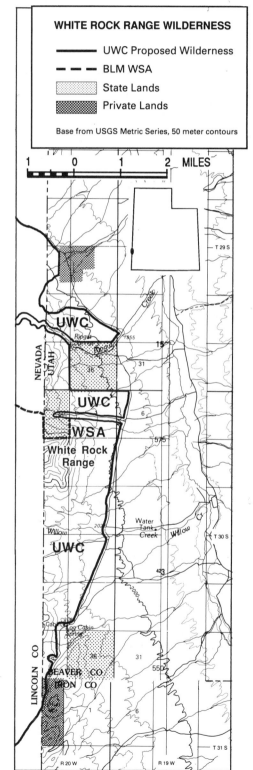

WHITE ROCK RANGE WILDERNESS

——— UWC Proposed Wilderness
– – – BLM WSA
State Lands
Private Lands

Base from USGS Metric Series, 50 meter contours

COUGAR CANYON-DOCS PASS WILDERNESS

Remote and rugged, Cougar Canyon is lined with lava and outcrops of granite. After rejecting this area in 1986, the BLM appears likely to respond to public concerns and include part of this area in its final wilderness recommendations.

Ray Wheeler

The proposed Cougar Canyon-Docs Pass wilderness (29,400 acres) includes twisted, narrow drainages lined with lava and granite, and peaks densely forested with pinyon pine and juniper. This remote and rugged area offers outstanding opportunities for hiking, rock climbing, deer hunting, and trout fishing. The area, as one might expect from its name, also supports a healthy population of mountain lion. It is surrounded by wild country in Nevada's Beaver Dam State Park and by a 3,000-acre national forest roadless area in Utah's Split Pine Hollow, Pine Canyon, and Barn Pole Hollow. Beaver Dam Wash runs through the area and provides important wildlife habitat.

Access to the area is difficult by any route. Perhaps the easiest way is to drive northwest from St. George through Santa Clara and Shivwits to Motoqua. Proceed north up Slaughter Creek to the southern end of the roadless area.

Hunting and Fishing in Rugged Country

In its upper drainage within this proposed wilderness, Beaver Dam Wash is a cool stream slicing through granite and lava rock. The stream is flanked by riparian vegetation, and even in this reach of swift turns and twists, it forms emerald pools that are an invitation to swim or fish. Much of the area is covered with pinyon pine and juniper, although there are places where sagebrush and grasses dominate. The most diverse wildlife cover is found in the wash where thick brush, willows, and cottonwood trees flourish. A small herb, *Epilobium nevadensis*, which is a candidate for listing under the Endangered Species Act, also grows in the area (BLM, 1986).

Deer hunting is especially good here, and trout fishing can be excellent. Campsites, mostly remnants of autumn hunting camps, are plentiful, and adventurous hikers will be tempted to investigate the rugged interior of this proposed wilderness. The upper stretch of Beaver Dam Wash provides the only native trout fishery in the area. The creek may also support the Virgin spinedace, a fish that is a candidate for protection under the Endangered Species Act (BLM, 1986). Archeological values in the unit are uncertain since little inventory work has been done.

The Utah Wilderness Coalition Proposal

We seek 29,400 acres of wilderness designation for Cougar Canyon-Docs Pass in two units. The area is remote from the sights and sounds of human activity, is entirely natural, contains significant wildlife habitat, and offers solitude to any who wish to find it. According to the BLM's DEIS (1986), "The only human intrusions in the WSA are from approximately 6 miles of range fences, a tree and shrub planting, and a study exclosure. Imprints are substantially unnoticeable and the 15,968-acre area is natural." Despite this, the BLM initially recommended none of the area for wilderness designation.

Elsewhere in its 1986 DEIS, the BLM makes the mystifying statement that " . . . the WSA cannot meet the scenic quality standard of section 2(c) of The Wilderness Act because such scenery is not unusual to southern Utah and Nevada . . ." Besides misinterpreting the Wilderness Act, which states that wilderness areas *may* (not must) contain scenic features, the BLM sets up a specious comparison to a region that is scenic throughout.

In response to public opinion, however, it is likely that the BLM will recommend 6,400 acres of the WSA for wilderness designation in its final

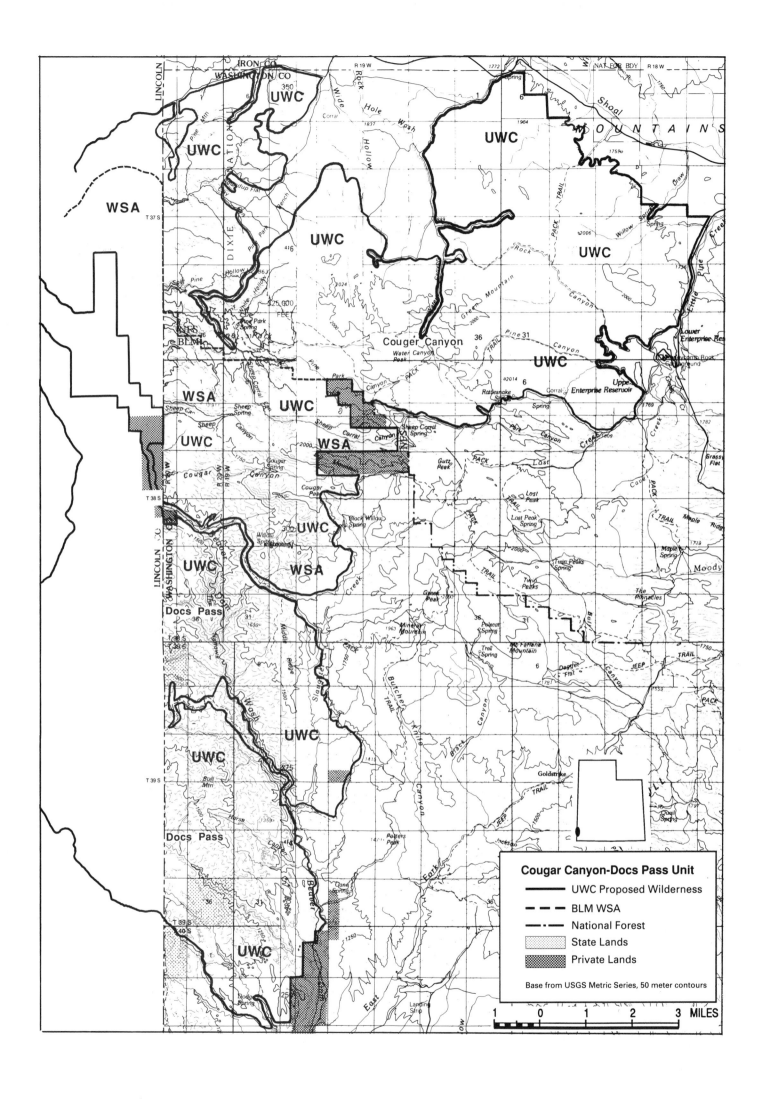

Cougar Canyon-Docs Pass Unit

——— UWC Proposed Wilderness

– – – BLM WSA

–·–·– National Forest

State Lands

Private Lands

Base from USGS Metric Series, 50 meter contours

1   0   1   2   3   MILES

report to the President. Even so, this recommendation fails to protect this important watershed.

The unit shows no potential for development of either leasable or locatable minerals. In fact, according to the BLM's DEIS (1986), there are no mining claims in the entire WSA. There are no known conflicts with off-road vehicle users in this area because of the rugged terrain and lack of vehicle ways. Our proposal abuts a National Forest roadless area surrounding Pine Park. The country here is wild and unspoiled; with no apparent conflicts and very high wilderness values, Cougar Canyon is a prime candidate for wilderness designation.

Mike Medberry

THE BEAVER DAM SLOPES WILDERNESS

Although the 1984 Arizona Strip Wilderness Act designated 19,600 acres of the Beaver Dam Mountains as wilderness, including 2,597 acres in Utah, it did not fully protect Utah's Beaver Dam Slopes. Our 38,400-acre Beaver Dam Slopes wilderness proposal completes what Congress began with the Arizona legislation. Our proposal includes two units: Beaver Dam Wash (24,900 acres) and Joshua Tree (13,500 acres), which is divided from the designated wilderness by a powerline.

The entire southwestern slope of the Beaver Dam Mountains is an integrated biological community embracing a portion of three life zones: the Great Basin, the Colorado Plateau, and the Mojave or Sonoran Desert Provinces. With its diverse, low-elevation habitat, this area is unlike any other in Utah. Although the area offers excellent early-season hiking and camping, it is relatively obscure and shows few signs of human intrusion. When the rest of Utah is still in winter, the willows, grasses, and cottonwoods along Beaver Dam Wash are beginning to green up and attract migratory songbirds, and the higher slopes of Joshua Tree are warming to the afternoon sun.

The desert tortoise, in jeopardy of extinction in Utah, inhabits much of this proposed wilderness. A respiratory disease is believed to contribute to tortoise mortality, although competition with cattle for forage and natural predation may also be factors. Nor can the tortoise escape habitat destruction caused by urban sprawl around the city of St. George and its outskirts, or from people who—usually innocently—collect tortoises as pets or destroy habitat with off-road vehicles. The continued decline of the tortoise population has prompted the U.S. Fish and Wildlife Service to seek emergency listing of the tortoise as an endangered species.

The proposed wilderness is home to the endangered peregrine falcon as well as to a variety of birds that live nowhere else in Utah. Several rare lizards are also found here: the Gila monster (a candidate for protection under the Endangered Species Act), the Mojave and speckled rattlesnakes, the desert iguana, and the desert night lizard. Designated wilderness is an important refuge for these species which cannot tolerate human intrusions. Wilderness designation would force the BLM to prohibit vehicle access, thereby protecting sensitive species and their habitat.

Mike Medberry

JOSHUA TREE UNIT

Highlights—The Joshua Tree unit (13,500 acres) is located in the southwest corner of Utah on the southwestern slope of the Beaver Dam Mountains, which drain into Beaver Dam Wash. Like Beaver Dam Wash, this unit contains some of the only Mojave desert vegetation found in Utah, in-

IN BRIEF

Index Map: Area No. 32

Highlights: Critical habitat for the desert tortoise, this area's Joshua tree forest also supports wildlife found in the Mojave Desert. Low elevation makes it a good place to hike during winter and early spring.

Maps: USGS 1:100,000 Clover Mountains, St. George, Overton, Littlefield

Area of wilderness proposals in acres (Utah):

Unit	UWC	BLM
Joshua Tree	13,500	0
Beaver Dam Wash	24,900	0
TOTAL	38,400	0

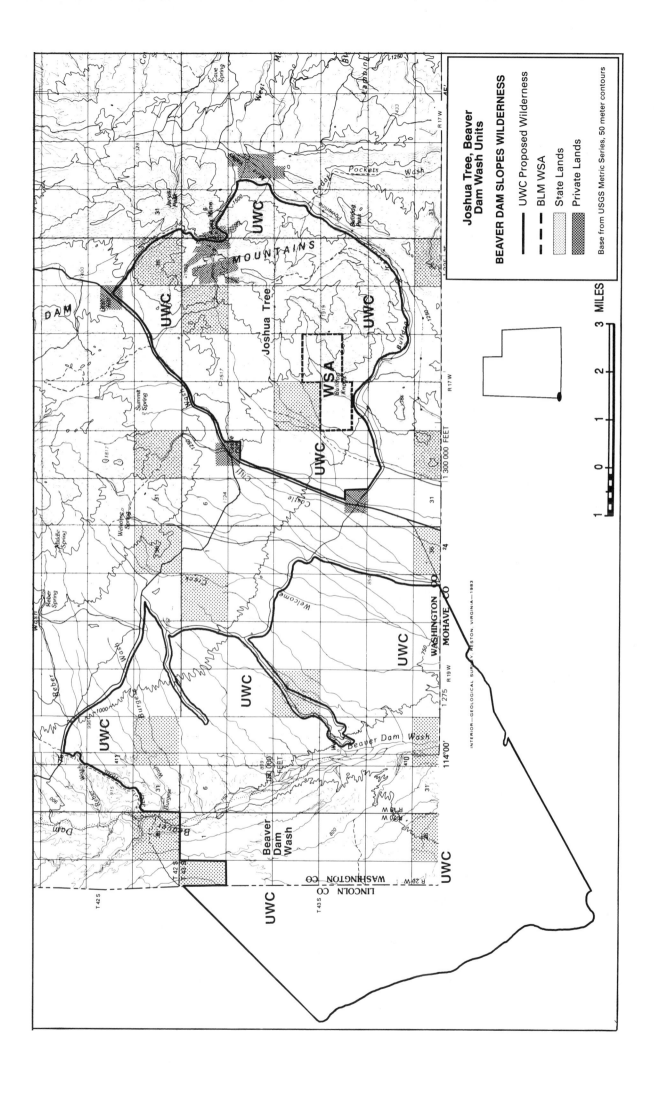

Joshua Tree, Beaver
Dam Wash Units

BEAVER DAM SLOPES WILDERNESS

UWC Proposed Wilderness

BLM WSA

State Lands

Private Lands

Base from USGS Metric Series, 50 meter contours

MILES

INTERIOR—GEOLOGICAL SURVEY, RESTON, VIRGINIA—1983

cluding Joshua trees, creosote bush, cholla, barrel, hedgehog, and prickly pear cactus, agave, and Spanish bayonet. The Joshua tree forest is also home for the desert tortoise, the Gila monster, the Mojave rattlesnake, and a large population of mourning doves. Old U.S. Route 91, once the only highway from St. George to Las Vegas, provides the primary access to the area. A gravel road leads east off Route 91 to the Joshua Tree Natural Area and continues in a loop that returns hardy drivers to Highway 91 at the Shivwits Reservation to the north or at Bloomington to the east.

Plant communities—The Joshua Tree Natural Area, a 1,040-acre island within the larger stand of Joshua trees, was designated over 20 years ago by the BLM in recognition of its unique ecological character. The Joshua tree forest with its accompanying desert vegetation is an outstanding undisturbed example of the Mojave vegetative community. Additionally, plant and animal communities in the Joshua Tree unit span three life zones, from Great Basin and Colorado Plateau in the uplands to hot desert flora and fauna nearer the Beaver Dam Wash. This habitat variety makes the area especially significant and interesting to naturalists. The Woodbury Desert Study Area, which is included within the unit, is a 3,040-acre community of creosote bush, Joshua trees, bursage, and pinyon-juniper that has been closed to grazing and is returning to its natural state. Near-relict communities such as this are important for scientific study and for their intrinsic value.

Wildlife—The desert tortoise, the Gila monster, the Mojave rattlesnake, and a significant raptor community, including the peregrine falcon and the golden eagle, live in the unit.

Archeology and history—The unit is historically significant as the route of the Old Spanish Trail, the first pack train trail between Santa Fe and the Los Angeles basin, which saw its greatest use in the 1820s. The road to Bloomington was used by Mormon settlers crossing from the Nevada and Arizona settlements to St. George.

Recreation—The highlands offer excellent hiking and camping, while the lower country offers scenic walking, hiking, and horseback riding. The entire unit offers solitude only a short distance from the highway.

BLM recommendation—The BLM recommended against wilderness designation for the Joshua Tree Natural Area and, in violation of its own rules, dropped the surrounding 12,000 acres of roadless land during its initial inventory. Damage from the Apex mine and other small intrusions, given as reasons for the BLM's decision, are excluded from our proposal. Lack of screening (requiring dense vegetation, deep canyons, etc.) was also inappropriately used by the BLM to drop the unit. Such a prejudice against the Mojave Desert terrain is unwarranted.

Coalition proposal—Stronger protection for the tortoise and the entire Joshua tree community is needed; hence our 13,500-acre wilderness proposal. We exclude about 400 acres of old mining activities in the northeastern portion of the unit. The inclusion of the Joshua Tree unit in the National Wilderness Preservation System would add unique "hot desert" flora and fauna to the system and protect the habitat of several sensitive species, among them the endangered desert tortoise and peregrine falcon.

BEAVER DAM WASH UNIT

Highlights—Like Joshua Tree, the 24,900-acre Beaver Dam Wash unit is exceptional for its biological and scenic diversity. The unit provides critical habitat for the desert tortoise and other uncommon reptiles including the sidewinder rattlesnake and the Gila monster. Many species of birds and large and small mammals are also found here. Beaver Dam Wash is west of St. George in the extreme southwest corner of Utah. From St.

George, drive northwest through Santa Clara and Shivwits, turning south onto old Highway 91 toward Littlefield. Drive about 10 miles to the dirt road that takes off to the west, opposite Castle Cliff. This road heads toward Lytle Ranch in the Beaver Dam Wash.

Geology and landforms—Beaver Dam Wash, at an elevation of 2,200 feet, is the lowest point in Utah. It is also some of the driest land in the state and is particularly inhospitable during summer, when temperatures regularly top 100 degrees. It is a rugged landscape with deeply incised arroyos, stark rock outcroppings, and corrugated outwash from the Beaver Dam Mountains. Beyond the wash loom the stark and angular Beaver Dam Mountains. This country's harshness makes the presence of intermittent water all the more impressive, and all the more important to wildlife.

Plant communities—Beaver Dam Wash itself is an intermittent stream with occasional pools and riparian vegetation. Nearby hillsides support dryland forests of Joshua trees and creosote bush. Due to the diversity of habitat types, the Beaver Dam Wash unit attracts both scientific research and recreational use.

Wildlife—Beaver Dam Wash is renowned for the variety of birds it attracts, from the showy lazuli bunting, phainopepla, and Crissal thrasher to seldom-seen cactus wrens and Says phoebe. More than 180 bird species, many occurring nowhere else in Utah, have been identified at the Lytle Ranch research station just north of the unit. Diligent observers may also see a roadrunner scurrying across the landscape or a prairie falcon diving at high speed after an unwary rodent. Many of these birds migrate along a route leading from the lower Colorado River into the Great Basin along the Virgin River and up Beaver Dam Wash (Hedges, 1985). According to Hedges, "The Beaver Dam Mountains appear to be a migration barrier to

A young naturalist "captures" a desert tortoise in the Joshua Tree unit of the proposed Beaver Dam Slopes wilderness. The tortoise was recently listed as endangered to protect it from habitat loss and illegal collecting. Designation of its disappearing habitat as wilderness would aid the species' recovery.

Elliot Bernshaw

several species that occur in Utah only or primarily in Beaver Dam Wash: white-winged dove, vermillion flycatcher, brown-crested flycatcher, verdin, black-tailed gnatcatcher, and hooded oriole." In recognition of the special value of the area, Brigham Young University recently acquired the Lytle Ranch in the Beaver Dam Wash upstream of the proposed wilderness for scientific study and the preservation of unique riparian and upland habitat. The BLM portion of the wash contains habitat of similar value, although the spring-fed wash becomes intermittent below the research station. Reptiles that occur only in this area of Utah include the desert iguana, the desert night lizard, the Mojave rattlesnake, and the speckled rattlesnake (Hedges, 1985), in addition to the desert tortoise, the sidewinder rattlesnake, and the Gila monster. The unit also supports beavers, which give the wash its name, bobcats, deer, foxes, porcupines, eagles, owls, and small mammals such as rabbits and kangaroo rats.

Recreation—During the cooler months hiking and camping are pleasant and, in the spring, colorful wildflowers, yucca, and cactus flowers are abundant. Hikes downstream of the Lytle Ranch research station will take you into the heart of this proposed wilderness.

BLM recommendation—The BLM eliminated the entire unit from wilderness consideration in 1979 during an accelerated inventory inspired by a proposal to construct the Intermountain Power Plant. The powerline eventually built for this project lies outside of our proposal.

Coalition proposal—We propose a 24,900-acre wilderness unit. An additional 13,300 acres of adjacent BLM wild land lie in Nevada and Arizona. Our fieldwork shows that there are two constructed roads that enter the unit and lead to regularly used stock-watering facilities. These vehicle routes total 8 miles and affect 14 acres of land. We have cherrystemmed these roads from the proposed wilderness. A third road that shows regular use enters the unit from the west and should also be cherrystemmed as shown on the map. Other range improvements in the unit do not affect the area's wilderness qualities. Our proposal excludes areas which the BLM claimed were not natural.

THE COLORADO PLATEAU REGION

FROM Bowns Point, at the southeastern rim of the 11,000-foot-high Aquarius Plateau, you can see out over the landscape of southern Utah with the perspective of an Olympian god. In every direction the land falls away in thousand-foot leaps, dropping a vertical mile before finally losing itself in a chaos of mesas, buttes, cliff-walls, terraces, domes, amphitheaters, hogbacks, and canyons. Gigantic landforms rise off that desert floor. To the south, a cliff-wall 2,000 feet high and 50 miles long— the northern edge of the Kaiparowits Plateau—points like a semaphore at 10,000-foot-high Navajo Mountain. To the east, the purple domes of the Henry Mountains hover above the mesas and badlands which surround them. A 1,000-foot-high hogback called the Waterpocket Fold shoots across the field of view from south to north, its jagged crestline running straight as an arrow for nearly 100 miles. Forty miles away to the northeast, you can see the 35-mile-wide dome called the San Rafael Swell. Closer at hand lies a 100,000-acre amphitheater ringed by the thousand-foot-high Circle Cliffs. Still closer, to the south and southeast, lies the labyrinthine canyon system of the Escalante River.

A Landscape in Equilibrium

The Colorado Plateau is a physiographic "province," a region distinct from other parts of the West. Originally named the "Colorado Plateaus" by explorer John Wesley Powell, the "Plateau" is in fact a huge basin ringed by highlands and *filled* with plateaus. Sprawling across southeastern Utah, northern Arizona, northwestern New Mexico, and western Colorado, the Colorado Plateau province covers a land area of 130,000 square miles. Of America's 50 states, only Alaska, Texas, California, and Montana are larger.

Geologically, the Colorado Plateau is perhaps best defined by what did *not* happen to it. While the Rocky Mountains to the east and the basin and range country to the west were being thrust, stretched, and fractured into existence, the Colorado Plateau remained structurally intact.

"The Colorado Plateau is extremely ancient," says author F.A. Barnes, an expert on the region's geology. "As a distinct mass of continental crust, it is at least 500 million years old—probably a lot older." Such longevity is especially impressive when one considers the globetrotting adventures of the North American continent from the perspective of continental drift theory. Over a period of 300 to 400 million years, while the North American continent inched northward from the South Pole, gradually disengaging itself from Africa, Asia, and South America, the Colorado Plateau region drifted along comfortably on its western edge. Now shoreline, now inundated by rising seas, the entire region accumulated huge quantities of sediment, gradually sinking under its own weight until heat and pressure hardened the deposits into a mantle of sedimentary rock several miles thick. Even when the entire western United States began to rise some 10 million years ago, eventually climbing to elevations as much as three miles above sea level, the Colorado Plateau region remained stable—perhaps "floating" on a cushion of molten rock.

Though volcanic eruptions ring its perimeter, few have penetrated the interior of the Colorado Plateau. Blocked by massive layers of sedimentary rock, rising magma could do no more than bulge its thick roof into domes—the "laccolithic" Henry, La Sal, and Abajo mountain ranges—before cooling and hardening in place. The tremendous tectonic forces which formed the Sierra Nevada and Rocky Mountains had far less effect on the Colorado Plateau. Shielded or cushioned by something deep in the earth, the Plateau mirrored those forces but dimly—as broad, dome-shaped uplifts, shallow basins, and long folds or "reefs."

As provinces go, the Colorado Plateau is therefore a rugged individualist. While its neighbors have succumbed either to uplift or erosion, the Plateau held those forces in equilibrium. Even as its landscape continues to rise with the thrust of the continent, erosion is simultaneously wearing it down.

The Vast and the Intimate

Riddle, paradox, and anomaly are the Plateau's stock-in-trade. A structural and topographic depression, the entire region has been uplifted more than a mile. A desert, it contains two of the continent's largest rivers, and channels enough water to supply millions of people in four western states. Its landscape is a conjugation of the vertical and the horizontal; its landforms, a debate between hard and soft rock. It is a world of sudden displacements and bizarre juxtapositions. Separated only by cliff-walls, subarctic tundra and Sonoran desert are neighbors on the Colorado Plateau. Snow-capped mountains rise improbably off the desert floor, each carrying its arctic-alpine biota like the cargo of an ark. Among petrified sand dunes are deep pools of water; on burning cliff-faces, luxurious flower gardens hide in alcoves, watered by springs.

Perpetually carved by erosion, the canyon lands of the Colorado Plateau are one of the most intricate landscapes on earth. Consider a single canyon system—that of the Escalante River and its sidecanyons—which comprise a network of nearly *one thousand miles*. Yet the Escalante is itself but a sidecanyon—one of 50 major sidecanyon systems tributary to the Colorado and Green rivers. To borrow a term recently coined by mathematicians, the landscape is "fractal;" no matter how closely you examine or how thoroughly you explore it, its complexity remains infinite. You could spend a lifetime in the Escalante without fully exploring it; yet a single week there can exhaust the mind with its diversity, its fusion of the vast and the intimate.

Bowl, basin, canyon, alcove. Everywhere the land is concave. Hidden within this huge river basin are bowls within bowls: the Canyonlands Basin, the interior of the San Rafael Swell, the Circle Cliffs amphitheater, the Escalante River basin, the paradoxical salt valleys near Moab. From nearly any vantage point the land drops away only to rise again far in the distance. This concave structure, coupled with the lack of screening vegetation, the gigantic scale of the landforms, and the clarity of the air, makes for vistas of breathtaking hugeness. Yet the same features create intimacy as well. There is always a feeling of being enclosed, surrounded, sheltered. Magnified in the crystalline air, distant objects seem deceptively close—a compression of space neatly balanced by an equal and opposite expansion of time. That butte may *seem* close enough to hit with a stone—but if it

lies on the opposite side of a sheer-walled canyon, it could take you days to reach it on foot.

Suspended in Time

The Plateau is the world's foremost museum of earth history. To descend into its canyons is to experience history in reverse. Each layer of rock represents an earlier epoch on the calendar of geological time. Scattered through these layers one can find fossil life-forms that span the history of evolution between single-celled life and the dinosaur. At a single quarry, in Dinosaur National Monument, scientists have uncovered the bones of 300 dinosaurs representing 10 different species. More recent relics lie hidden in time-pockets such as Cowboy Cave, where scientists have found the dung of extinct camel, mammoth, and sloth, all buried beneath human artifacts nearly 7,000 years old.

Even living creatures in this strange landscape may hang suspended in time. Cryptobiotic life forms—half alive and half dead—can lie dormant in dry potholes for as long as 25 years, patiently waiting for rain. There are juniper trees 1,000 years old, and bristlecone pines that were 1,000 years old at the dawn of the Christian era. Hidden in basins and canyons, cut off by cliffs and desert, the biota of the Colorado Plateau is as diverse as the landscape itself. Nearly 80 species of fish and 340 species of plants are endemic, and the region hosts more than 80 plants listed or recommended for protection as threatened or endangered species.

The Colorado Plateau region has vistas of breathtaking hugeness yet is also an intimate landscape. Nowhere is this paradox more evident than in the proposed Escalante Canyons wilderness, seen here in the Little Egypt unit.

Tom Miller

Asked by the National Park Service to identify potential "Natural Landmarks" on the Colorado Plateau, two teams of geologists returned with a list of no fewer than 110 sites which deserve national recognition as classic displays of geologic phenomena.

Here too, also frozen in time, lie the remains of 12,000 years of human occupation, spanning the entire temporal range of human prehistoric development from the Paleo-Indian culture to the modern Pueblo Indians. The civilization of the Anasazi, which mysteriously disappeared around 1300 AD, left behind one of the richest archeological treasure-troves on the planet. Scattered throughout the canyons and mesas of the Colorado Plateau are thousands of prehistoric stone structures—granaries, pithouses, cliffhouses, kivas, watchtowers—entire cities of stone. In parts of southeastern Utah the archeological site density is as high as 80 sites per square mile. In San Juan County alone, there are 15,000 known archeological sites, a mere 10 percent of the estimated total number.

A Textbook of Geomorphology

The landscape itself holds history frozen in stone. There are petrified sand dunes and ripple marks, inverted valleys, entrenched river meanders, and whole forests of petrified trees. Asked by the National Park Service to identify potential "Natural Landmarks" on the Colorado Plateau, two teams of geologists returned with a list of no fewer than 110 sites which deserve national recognition as classic displays of geologic phenomena. "In no other province in America," they explained, "are the relationships between morphology and geology more clearly or graphically revealed."

Consider, for example, the work of erosion. There are thousands of miles of canyons on the Colorado Plateau, and every one of those miles is a hoard of erosional sculptures. There are alcoves, grottoes, potholes, pouroffs, plunge basins, and rincons. There are windows and towers, cliff-walls riddled with honeycombing or pitted with conchoidal fractures. Above the rims of the canyons one finds retreating cliff-walls hundreds of miles long, each leaving behind it a landscape strewn with gigantic erosional remnants. There are at least 25 major plateaus, hundreds of mesas, thousands of buttes, domes, towers, monuments, temples, spires. There are whole valleys filled with stone hoodoos and goblins. Far out in the desert, one can find solitary monoliths and preposterous balanced rocks.

There are thousands of natural stone arches and bridges on the Colorado Plateau, at least five with spans of more than 200 feet.

The Colorado Plateau harbors some of the world's most spectacular volcanic formations, including laccolithic mountain ranges, arrow-straight dikes, and expanses strewn with obsidian and volcanic bombs.

There are badlands, sand dunes, painted deserts . . .

All this, and one thing more.

The Colorado Plateau is wilderness. It is a remnant of the American frontier, a place where even contemporary human history hangs suspended in time. Just 50 years ago Wilderness Society founder Robert Marshall identified the region surrounding the Colorado River canyons in southeastern Utah as the single largest roadless area in the coterminous United States. In all, Marshall found 20 million acres in six huge roadless areas on the Plateau. And though mineral exploration has reduced the size of those roadless areas, the region still remains one of the largest blocks of undeveloped land in the West.

Parks and Wilderness

Americans love this strange landscape of stone. Since the turn of the century they have travelled from every corner of the nation to visit it. Between 1900 and 1972, the federal government created 23 national parks, national monuments, national recreation areas, and national landmarks on the Colorado Plateau. Today those parks are among the most popular in America. In 1988, the Park Service recorded 24 million visits to national parks on the Colorado Plateau, and in recent years visitation to the Plateau's national park lands has been increasing at a rate of nine percent per year—a rate 36 times greater than that of all national parks.

Unfortunately, the National Park System protects only 5 million acres—barely seven percent of the land area of the Colorado Plateau. The Plateau's national parks are islands of protected land surrounded by publicly owned wild lands which remain open to development. There are several large Indian reservations and small holdings of state and private lands at the wild core of the Colorado Plateau. But most of the lands which surround the Plateau's national parks are controlled by the Bureau of Land Management.

No one knows exactly how much land remains wild on the Plateau. Definitions of wilderness vary, and the nationwide wilderness inventories by federal agencies are far from complete. But recent studies by environmental groups suggest that there are at least 10 million acres of BLM, Park Service, and Forest Service lands which meet the criteria for inclusion in the National Wilderness Preservation System.

Park Plans

Roads, jeep trails, and seismic lines can be found within this wilderness core. Yet most such impacts are trivial in comparison to the huge tracts of roadless land which surround them. Many roadless areas at the heart of the Plateau are contiguous with the national parks or with other roadless areas, separated from one another by no more than a single dirt road. Thus the core of the Colorado Plateau Province today remains one wilderness. And for at least half of this century, Americans have been fighting to keep it that way.

The first such initiative came in 1936, when the National Park Service announced a proposal to create a new national monument of 4.5 million acres in southeastern Utah. The proposal won enthusiastic support from Secretary of the Interior Harold Ickes and the endorsement of Utah State Planning Board Chairman Ray West, but it was defeated by politicians who favored development. Between 1935 and 1961, a fleet of ambitious protection plans foundered against the same opposition. The proposals included a Wayne County National Park of 365,000 acres, a Four Corners National Monument, a Rainbow Plateau or Navajo Plateau National Monument, an Arch Canyon National Monument, and an original Canyonlands National Park proposal of over 1,000 square miles.

The Grand Plan

By the mid 1960s, however, the developers were formulating a Colorado Plateau master plan of their own. Conceived by a coalition of 21 utility companies, it quickly became known as "the Grand Plan" (Gottlieb and Wiley, 1982, p. 42). The idea was simple and powerful. To supply the water and energy needs of the great cities that ring the Intermountain West, the Colorado Plateau would become their natural resource colony and waste dump. Coal mined on the plateau would be burned in huge new coal-fired power plants whose polluting emissions could be expelled across the uninhabited wilderness at the heart of the Plateau. A string of hydroelectric dams on the Colorado and Green rivers would supply water and power to Denver, Salt Lake City, Phoenix, and Los Angeles.

The oil embargo and energy crisis of the 1970s pushed the Grand Plan into overdrive. Additional electricity would be generated in nuclear power plants located along the Green River. Oil, natural gas, tar sand, and oil shale would be developed throughout the Colorado Plateau. Uranium, mined and milled on the Plateau, would supply nuclear power plants

The vast tourist potential of the Colorado Plateau is largely unrealized because reliance on the traditional industries of the region—energy, cattle, forest products, mining and agriculture—has obscured in large measure the potential of the Plateau as a world-class tourist destination.

Kent Briggs
THE HIGH FRONTIER [1976]

To supply the water and energy needs of the great cities that ring the Intermountain west, the Colorado Plateau would become their natural resource colony and waste dump. Coal mined on the plateau would be burned in huge new coal-fired power plants whose polluting emissions could be expelled across the uninhabited wilderness at the heart of the Plateau. A string of hydro-electric dams on the Colorado and Green rivers would supply water and power to Denver, Salt Lake City, Phoenix, and Los Angeles.

throughout the nation, after which it would return to the Plateau for permanent storage in a high-level nuclear waste repository. For developers, as for conservationists, the Colorado Plateau had become the final frontier.

Nationwide Issue

There have been at least 10 major confrontations between developers and conservationists on the Colorado Plateau. The first came in 1956, when conservationists waged a successful nationwide campaign to prevent the construction of a dam within Dinosaur National Monument.

Conservationists lost their second round with the Grand Plan, when in 1963, water began rising behind Glen Canyon Dam, inundating 183 miles of stunningly beautiful canyons at the heart of the Colorado Plateau. Unlike Dinosaur National Monument, Glen Canyon had little national recognition; it was "The Place No One Knew." For conservationists the lesson was clear. Only a nationwide campaign could protect the scenic wonders of the Colorado Plateau from destructive development.

The damming of Glen Canyon proved the exception to the rule. For the following 20 years—straight through the energy crisis and the mining booms of the late 1960s and 1970s—environmentalists won battle after battle on the Colorado Plateau, and public outcry stymied development. In 1966, conservationists prevented the construction of two dams in the Grand Canyon. In 1976 they prevailed against a proposed coal mine and power plant on the Kaiparowits Plateau. In 1979 they forced the relocation of the proposed Intermountain Power Project to a site off the Plateau. They defeated the proposed Trans-Escalante highway in 1979, the proposed Warner Valley power plant near Zion National Park and the proposed Alton coal strip mine in 1980. In 1984, backed by Utah Governor Scott Matheson and two-to-one support in statewide opinion polls, Utah conservationists defeated a proposal to build a nuclear waste dump next to Canyonlands National Park. Asked to choose between development and preservation, Americans, the federal government, and Utahns themselves repeatedly chose preservation for the Plateau.

At the publication of this book, mineral exploration and production have virtually ceased on the Colorado Plateau—a clear indication that the Plateau's mineral resources are of marginal value to the nation and the world. For the next few years, perhaps even longer, there may be a reprieve from the "Grand Plan."

New technologies, both in energy production and conservation, will one day replace the use of fossil fuels. But when? Energy prices are again on the rise, and will probably continue to rise for the foreseeable future. At today's prices energy development is not economically viable on the Colorado Plateau. At tomorrow's prices, it may once again boom.

That is but one reason (and there are many others) why the scenic wonders of the Colorado Plateau, without formal protection, will be greatly at risk in the future. Recognizing that risk, Utahns have in recent years redoubled their efforts to achieve national recognition for the Plateau.

Protecting a Region

In the early 1970s, Utah writer Ward Roylance launched a campaign to develop a preservation plan for the entire Colorado Plateau. A former Utah Travel Council employee and author of the popular guidebook, *Utah, A Guide to the State*, Roylance had spent a lifetime exploring the wild lands of southern Utah. The entire region, he declared, was an "Enchanted Wilderness" whose public domain lands should be managed "not as a shattered entity broken up into political subdivisions, but rather as an integral, homogeneous wilderness." Recreation and "controlled travel," Roylance wrote, were the "highest uses" of this land, and "a few dozen national parks and monuments . . . will not suffice in this region for the future." What *was* needed, he wrote, was a "major campaign . . . to save the entire region through formal planning and zoning."

By 1985, Roylance's visionary ideas had percolated up to the highest levels of Utah State government. In January, 1985, Utah Governor Scott Matheson announced a proposal to request World Heritage List designation for key sites on the Colorado Plateau. A 167-page report, published in June, 1986, detailed the governor's proposal. "Because of the tremendous variety of land forms and ecosystems," the report explained, "no one park or wilderness area can effectively represent the Colorado Plateau." The study recommended World Heritage List designation for 67 national and state parks, monuments, and recreation areas.

"Utah's five national parks are part of a much larger whole," explains Rod Millar, co-author of the report. "The parks are islands in a sea of land down there—but they're not separate, isolated entities. They are part of a larger whole, and what connects them is the land which surrounds them. Maybe our geopolitical systems won't allow for a complete integration of these isolated entities, but World Heritage List nomination is a step in that direction."

If Millar is correct, and our "geopolitical systems" won't allow for "complete integration," then perhaps we should *change* our systems—or our thinking. That radical notion comes not from environmentalists, but from Dr. Phillip Burgess, president of a Denver think-tank called the Center for the New West. The Center was established in 1989 with joint sponsorship from U.S. West Communications and the Western Governor's Association.

Tourism Potential

In 1987 Burgess and Kent Briggs, a former aide to Matheson, co-authored a study of the economic future of the Colorado Plateau. While the purpose of the study was to promote economic development, its recommendations were far closer to Roylance's "Enchanted Wilderness" than to the "Grand Plan." Prosperity for the region, argued the authors, will not come from mining or energy development but from tourism.

"The rich raw materials of the plateau have not produced a stable economic base," explains Burgess. "The depressed markets for energy, minerals, food and fiber have resulted in high unemployment and the emptying out of an area that already has less than two people per square mile." By contrast, says Briggs, "the vast tourism potential of this region offers the promise of a stable, long term growth industry."

Central to this vision is the notion that a tourism-centered economy would "rearrange the hierarchy of desired development."

"Each development would have to be evaluated on a case-by-case basis depending on how it affected the tourism resource," says Burgess. "Certainly the high level nuclear waste repository that was once proposed for siting near Canyonlands Park would be a classic example of a 'non-conforming use.'"

Secretary of the Interior Stewart Udall advanced a similar idea in the 1960s. He envisioned a "Golden Circle" of national parks in Utah, Colorado, and Arizona, linked by paved highways. The unspoiled scenery inside the circle would be left alone—to attract tourists to the existing communities, where development would be concentrated.

In essence, the proposal by Burgess and Briggs is but the latest reiteration of what Utah conservationists have been saying for at least 50 years. The natural wonders of the Colorado Plateau are a priceless asset, and their protection will require a region-wide protection plan for the entire Colorado Plateau.

The Role of Wilderness Designation

"Utah's natural beauty is its most important economic asset," says Utah Congressman Wayne Owens. To protect that asset—and to protect the region's beauty for its own sake—Owens has vigorously supported wilderness designation for the BLM wild lands that surround Utah's national parks. "There is substantial evidence," Owens explains, "that progressive federal wilderness designations may indeed be the single most important economic opportunity available to Southern Utah."

In March 1989, with the introduction of H.R. 1500, Congressman Owens endorsed the principle underlying the Utah Wilderness Coalition's proposal: the preservation of the BLM wild lands which lie between—and connect—the national parks at the heart of the Colorado Plateau.

Economic benefit, large though it is, will not in the end be the highest reason for preserving the wild lands of the Colorado Plateau. Silence, beauty, vastness, solitude, challenge, wonder, mystery, unspoiled natural systems—a link with our past which spirals through eons of geologic time to the beginning of life on earth. Those are the real treasures of the Colorado Plateau, and it is those treasures, far more than economics, which must inspire the hope that the Plateau Province will remain in the future what it has been for 500 million years—serenely and splendidly intact.

Ray Wheeler

THE RED MOUNTAIN WILDERNESS

Summary

The vivid sandstones of the Colorado Plateau meet the block-faulted rocks of the Basin and Range province at Red Mountain, located six miles northwest of St. George. Plants of the warm Mojave Desert and the cooler Great Basin Desert mingle in this transition area. Red Mountain's 1,400-foot cliffs are a spectacular backdrop for the rapidly growing towns of Santa Clara and Ivins to the south and the adjacent Snow Canyon State Park to the east. Hiking and sightseeing opportunities extend from the state park into the proposed wilderness. We propose an 18,500-acre wilderness; the BLM initially recommended 17,450 acres of its 18,250-acre WSA, but is expected to reduce its final recommendation to 12,842 acres.

Bordering Two Regions

Red Mountain is a great block of Navajo Sandstone bounded by the Gunlock Fault on the west, and by the Santa Clara River valley and Snow Canyon on the south and east. The top of the mountain is a dramatic expanse of rugged sandstone, which supports pinyon-juniper and sagebrush plant communities. The mixing of species from the Mojave and Great Basin deserts makes for unusually diverse vegetation, including (according to the BLM) ponderosa pine, yucca, agave, and Gambel oak. Mule deer, mountain lion, peregrine falcon, and bald eagles inhabit the area.

Prehistoric use by the Southern Paiute Indians has been documented at seven sites in the area, and the BLM (1986, p. 16) estimates archeological site densities between 4 and 40 per square mile.

For modern-day visitors, an old vehicle route leads to the slickrock summit of Red Mountain. Hikers and backpackers will have outstanding vistas across the area and into Snow Canyon. A sidecanyon heading east from Snow Canyon into the area can be explored from the state park.

IN BRIEF

Index Map: Area No. 33

Highlights: Sandwiched between Snow Canyon State Park and Gunlock State Beach, Red Mountain offers hunting, backpacking, and horseback riding for the St. George area. Unusually diverse vegetation grows here where basin meets plateau.

Maps: USGS 1:100,000 St. George

Area of wilderness proposals in acres

Area	UWC	BLM
Red Mountain	18,500	12,842

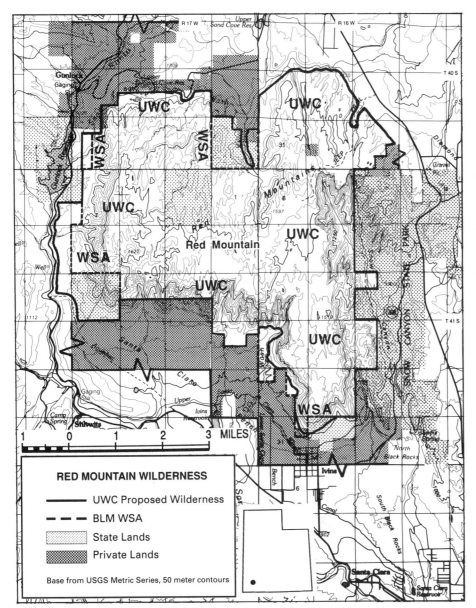

Red Mountain's rugged sandstone outcrops are one of the westernmost extensions of the Colorado Plateau. Hellhole Canyon, shown here, dissects the mountaintop just above Santa Clara Bench.

Lin Alder

The Utah Wilderness Coalition Proposal

Our 18,500-acre wilderness proposal is similar to the BLM's 17,450-acre draft wilderness recommendation. The agency excluded 800 acres on the Santa Clara Bench from its 18,250-acre WSA, saying it would be "difficult to manage . . . because of indiscriminate uses stemming from adjacent residential areas" (BLM, 1986, p. 1). We also exclude this area from our proposal, but we add 250 acres to the WSA by drawing the wilderness boundary to the edge of the physical disturbances, including some cliffs above the bench. (The BLM boundary was drawn along section lines.) Unfortunately, the final BLM recommendation apparently will omit an additional 4,600 acres from its draft recommendation.

As the towns of the Santa Clara valley continue to expand, attracting retirees and recreationists, it becomes important to protect the scenic backdrop and recreational opportunities that make these communities attractive places to live. Civilization and wildness can coexist in proximity here, but only if steps are taken now to set aside the key wild lands such as Red Mountain.

Lissa Leege and Rodney Greeno

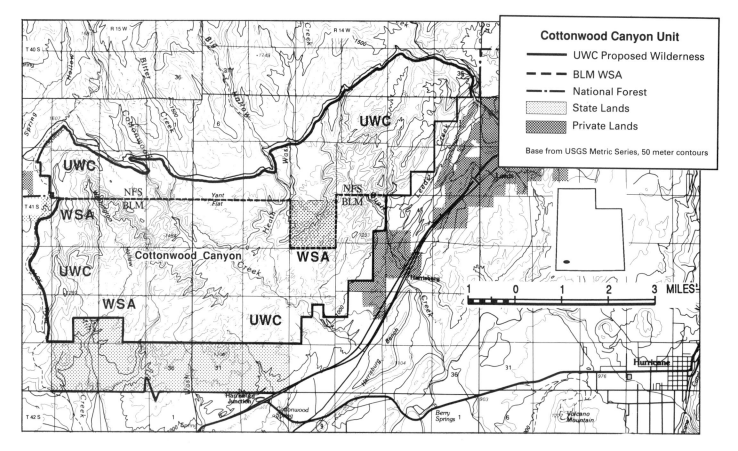

THE COTTONWOOD CANYON WILDERNESS

Summary

A transition zone between the canyons and plateaus to the east and the Mojave Desert to the west, Cottonwood Canyon offers diverse wildlife, rugged topography, and fine early-season hiking. The area is a scenic backdrop to Interstate 15, its red sandstone contrasting with the forested Pine Valley Mountains. Its easy access from the Red Cliffs Recreation Area and its proximity to St. George have made it one of the most visited wild areas in southwestern Utah.

We recommend 11,500 acres for wilderness designation. Additional national forest lands immediately to the north should also be designated. State lands bordering the area on the south should be placed under BLM wilderness management.

Bordering Plateau and Desert

Numerous small canyons cut across a series of sculpted sandstone ridges, forming a rugged, exposed, intimate landscape. The intricately carved, reddish-colored Navajo Sandstone contrasts beautifully with the dark green Pine Valley Mountains in the background.

Although the area geologically is part of the Colorado Plateau, ecologically it resembles the hot, dry Mojave Desert region. Vegetation includes pockets of desert shrubs between the stony ridges, including yucca, cholla, and mesquite; lovely riparian vegetation, including the shade-giving Fremont cottonwood, grows along several intermittent streams. Higher up toward the Pine Valley Mountains are pinyon pine and juniper. The endangered purple-spined hedgehog cactus (*Echinocereus engelmannii* var. *purpureus*) may occur in the area, according to the BLM.

The transition zone supports diverse wildlife. Mule deer, mountain lion, bobcat, and kit fox live here as do they farther east on the Colorado Plateau. You'll also find the Gila monster and the chuckawalla—the fat,

IN BRIEF

Index Map: Area No. 34

Highlights: Navajo Sandstone canyons are exposed on the south slopes of the Pine Valley Mountains northeast of St. George. Wilderness designation would protect sensitive wildlife species in this ecological transition zone.

Maps: USGS 1:100,000 St. George

Area of wilderness proposals in acres:

Area	UWC	BLM
Cottonwood Canyon	11,500	9,583

Adjacent wild lands: Dixie National Forest, State of Utah

ponderous desert lizards so unlike the tiny scurrying ones of the canyons. Both of these species are on the State of Utah's list of sensitive species; their habitat is shrinking as desert lands become subdivisions. Gambel's quail and mourning dove, popular game birds, live here. The BLM also lists the prairie falcon and golden eagle, the endangered bald eagle and peregrine falcon, and the more common red-tailed, Cooper's, and sharp-shinned hawks. The UDWR has identified a peregrine falcon use area in both the western and eastern thirds of the area.

Desert Exploration Just Off the Freeway

The lower elevations and southern exposures in the area make for early-season hiking, riding and camping. Access is convenient from Interstate 15 via the Red Cliffs BLM recreation area located between Leeds and Harrisburg. BLM data indicate that more than 2,000 people use the WSA annually, mostly within Quail Creek canyon.

Hunters can find quail, mourning dove, and mule deer here. Hikes begin in the Red Cliffs campground and wind over slickrock domes. The broken, dissected topography provides outstanding solitude. But the area's proximity to civilization has its drawbacks: two archeological sites have been heavily vandalized, according to the BLM. (Others may exist but are not inventoried.)

Stinting on Wilderness

The area's diversity, recreational opportunities, and proximity to a growing urban area give Cottonwood Canyon high value as wilderness. The BLM, however, has arrived at a compromised wilderness recommendation. In fact, it took extensive public comments during the wilderness inventory to get the BLM to reverse an initial recommendation against wilderness recommendation. The agency proposes 9,853 acres of its 11,330-acre WSA as wilderness. Several hundred acres on the southeast side of the area are excluded due to potential conflicts with ORVs; two parcels are also excluded on the southwest side where the city of St. George has filed for water from a Navajo Sandstone aquifer.

Rather than pump ground water from within the wilderness, the BLM should explore the alternative of drilling wells just south of the area. Moreover, it is questionable whether the St. George area can continue to expand indefinitely without eventually having to adopt conservation measures appropriate to life in the desert. Such measures, if pursued now, could forestall the need to draw ever-increasing amounts of water from limited sources.

The Cottonwood Canyon area has a low potential for minerals other than uranium, according to BLM data. The area is located within a larger region believed to contain deposits of uranium, according to the BLM's consultant, but the occurrence of such resources within the proposed wilderness is purely speculative. Depressed uranium prices make development unlikely (see Minerals section).

The Utah Wilderness Coalition Proposal

We propose an 11,500-acre wilderness, taking in all of the BLM's 11,330-acre WSA. About 6,700 acres of national forest roadless lands to the north should also be designated as wilderness; about 4,200 acres of State lands, chiefly to the south of the proposed wilderness, should be consolidated with BLM lands in the wilderness.

Lissa Leege and Jan Holt

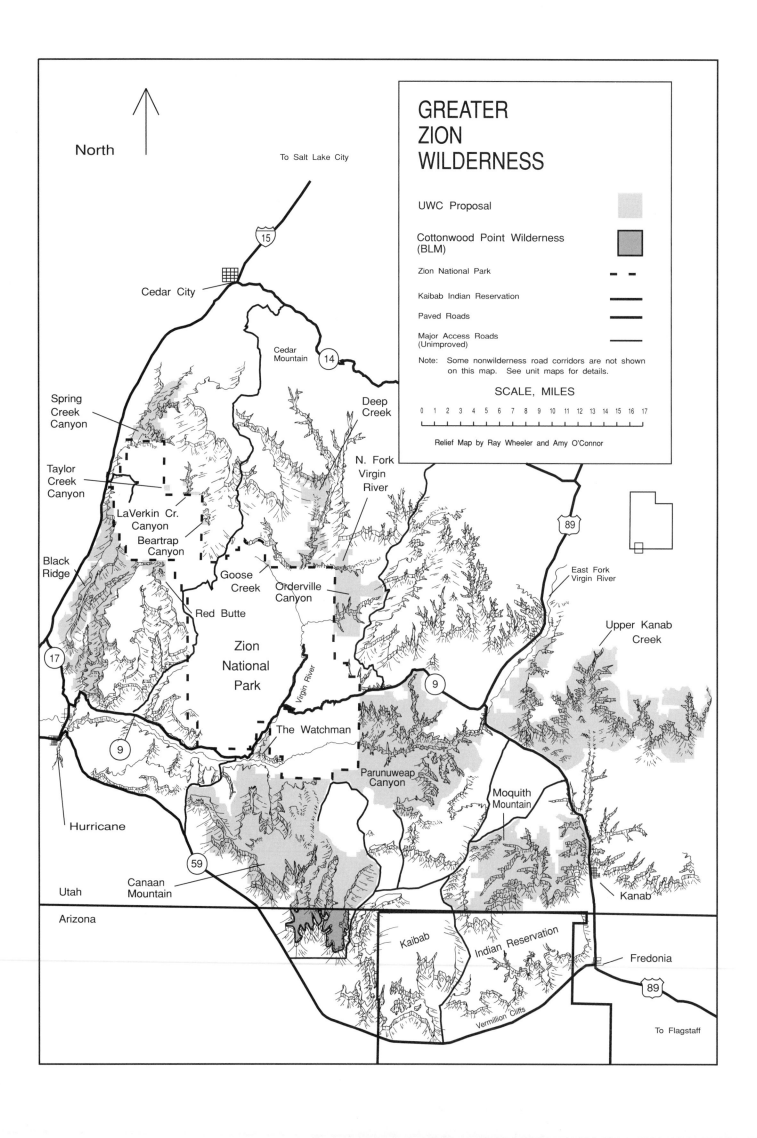

North

To Salt Lake City

**GREATER
ZION
WILDERNESS**

UWC Proposal

Cottonwood Point Wilderness
(BLM)

Zion National Park

Kaibab Indian Reservation

Paved Roads

Major Access Roads
(Unimproved)

Note: Some nonwilderness road corridors are not shown
        on this map. See unit maps for details.

SCALE, MILES

0 1 2 3 4 5 6 7 8 9 10 11 12 13 14 15 16 17

Relief Map by Ray Wheeler and Amy O'Connor

Cedar City

15

14

Cedar
Mountain

Deep
Creek

Spring
Creek
Canyon

Taylor
Creek
Canyon

LaVerkin Cr.
Canyon

Beartrap
Canyon

Black
Ridge

Goose
Creek

Red Butte

Zion
National
Park

Orderville
Canyon

N. Fork
Virgin
River

89

East Fork
Virgin River

Upper Kanab
Creek

Virgin River

17

9

9

The Watchman

Parunuweap
Canyon

Moquith
Mountain

Hurricane

59

Canaan
Mountain

Utah

Arizona

Kaibab

Indian Reservation

Moquith
Mountain

Kanab

Fredonia

89

Vermillion Cliffs

To Flagstaff

THE GREATER ZION WILDERNESS

Zion National Park's world-famous landscape of soaring cliff walls, forested plateaus, and deep, narrow gorges extends well beyond the boundaries of the park onto surrounding BLM lands. In these as yet unprotected lands, clear mountain streams descend from the juniper-dotted uplands into a network of canyons. On the highest plateaus, islands of ponderosa pine forest are surrounded by cream-colored slickrock. Seeps in the canyon walls provide water for bouquets of maidenhair fern, scarlet monkeyflower, and columbine. Hawks, falcons, and eagles nest along the sandstone walls, while ringtailed cats, deer, cougar, and bear live in the canyon bottoms.

Water is everything here. It is the architect of natural stone temples and slot canyons of the Greater Zion wilderness; it is life to the area's many plants and animals, sustenance to the nearby human population. Yet it is a capricious provider—sometimes coming not at all for months, sometimes swelling the canyons with floodwater.

In the West it is said that water flows towards money. And in southwestern Utah the money is in the city of St. George, where the population has more than quadrupled since 1970. With Washington County, which surrounds St. George, becoming a magnet for retirees, this trend is likely to continue. Burgeoning population has put escalating demands on all of the area's resources, but none is more affected than the supply of water. The Virgin River and its tributaries—Deep Creek, the North Fork, South Creek, North Creek, the East Fork, Orderville Creek, LaVerkin Creek, Goose Creek—not only provide water for the natural functioning of the national park and surrounding BLM wild lands, but are also being asked to satisfy the agricultural and residential demands of Washington County.

Damming the Virgin

Among the schemes driven by this demand for water is a proposed dam on the East Fork of the Virgin River. The Washington County Water Conservancy District wants to build a dam in the proposed Parunuweap Canyon wilderness unit immediately upstream from Zion National Park. The Conservancy District also hopes to construct a dam across the North Fork of the Virgin not far above the tightest portions of the Zion Narrows. This dam would flood a proposed BLM wilderness unit. Already, plans are in motion to site another impoundment just downstream of the national park on North Creek. Gunlock and Kolob Reservoirs are already in place. If the Conservancy District had its way, the entire Virgin River drainage would become little more than a plumbing system for the city of St. George.

All of this proposed water diversion would only encourage further development in a desert where profligate water use is an old habit, water conservation an obscure notion, and growth control pure blasphemy. Washington County proposes to construct all of the dams it possibly can on the Virgin River before instituting any meaningful water conservation measures. Such a strategy would maximize the raw volume of water available for eventual residential growth, but would simultaneously minimize the amount available to the national park, wildlife, and fish. In addition to obliterating major portions of wild canyons, the proposed reservoirs would diminish habitat for the endangered woundfin minnow, threatened Virgin roundtail chub, endemic Zion snail, and rare Virgin spinedace, and radically alter the natural functions of the river. Water flows through Zion National Park would be subverted, and the park's famous hanging gardens adversely affected.

IN BRIEF

Index Map: Area No. 35

Highlights: With classic "wet narrows" hikes, views across sculpted sandstone plateaus, and imposing red-rock monoliths, the BLM wild lands surrounding Zion National Park are part of a whole that deserves protection as wilderness.

Guidebooks: Brereton and Dunaway (1988), Kelsey (1986a), Hall (1982)

Maps: USGS 1:100,000 St. George, Kanab

Area of wilderness proposals in acres:

Unit	UWC	BLM
Beartrap Canyon	40	40
Black Ridge	21,800	0
Canaan Mountain	52,100	33,800
Deep Creek	7,100	3,320
Goose Creek	89	89
LaVerkin Creek	567	567
North Fork Virgin River	1,040	1,040
Orderville Canyon	6,500	1,750
Parunuweap Canyon	37,700	17,888
Red Butte	804	804
Spring Creek Canyon	4,400	1,607
Taylor Creek Canyon	35	35
The Watchman	600	600
TOTAL	132,775	61,540

Adjacent wild lands: Zion National Park

According to biology professor James Deacon (1988), the Virgin River "supports one of the few remaining native fish assemblages in the American Southwest." This assemblage includes, in addition to those previously mentioned, the speckled dace, desert sucker, and flannelmouth sucker. While the woundfin and Virgin chub occur downstream from Zion National Park, their habitat would suffer from upstream water manipulations. These federally protected fish are becoming increasingly scarce despite measures taken to enhance their chances for survival. Fish in the Virgin River drainage have evolved to thrive in flash flood conditions; a change in flow regimes could seriously affect their numbers by changing water temperatures and decreasing nutrient availability. Water conservation and realistic limits to residential growth are good planning and are essential to preserving the Zion wilderness as a living resource.

World Class Hiking

Some of the most challenging and delightful canyon hikes to be found anywhere are available in the Greater Zion wilderness. Consequently, the area receives some of the heaviest recreational use of any area in our wilderness proposal. North Fork Virgin River, Orderville, and Deep Creek canyons provide alternative access routes to the popular Zion Narrows hiking route across BLM and Park Service land. The Canaan Mountain and Black Ridge proposed wilderness units, while lesser known than the other areas adjacent to the park, offer equally outstanding hiking and superlative views of the surrounding country.

The National Park Service estimates that nearly 5,000 people annually hike the Narrows from Chamberlain Ranch. This primary access route into the Narrows leads through the North Fork Virgin River WSA. Every year about 2,000 visitors hike the Narrows by way of Deep Creek and Orderville Canyon WSAs, and about 1,000 people walk through the Parunuweap Canyon WSA (BLM, 1986). The proposed dams would eliminate hiking in the upper portions of the Narrows and Parunuweap Canyon.

The Utah Wilderness Coalition Proposal

In 1974 the National Park Service recommended 120,620 acres of Zion National Park backcountry as wilderness. Since each of the Greater Zion wilderness units is adjacent to park backcountry, they would make sensible and manageable wilderness units. However, in 1982, the BLM (with James Watt as Interior Secretary) dropped all WSAs smaller than 5,000 acres from further study. Conservationists went to court and won a decision forcing reinstatement of these areas as WSAs. Later, legislation was twice introduced to add the adjacent BLM WSAs to Zion National Park. The current wilderness debate may again raise the question of whether NPS or BLM jurisdiction is best for these WSAs adjacent to Zion National Park. Regardless of which agency eventually manages these units, however, the critical point is that they be designated and managed as wilderness rather than opened to development.

While the BLM eventually studied 90,648 acres of the Greater Zion wilderness for wilderness designation, the agency recommended only 59,578 acres as suitable in its DEIS. The final recommendation is expected to be only about 2,000 acres larger. We recommend wilderness designation for 132,775 acres of BLM land adjacent to Zion National Park. The Coalition proposal embraces the entire BLM recommendation and would protect additional land declared unsuitable by the agency, including acreage in Parunuweap Canyon, Deep Creek Canyon, Black Ridge, and Canaan Mountain.

Mike Medberry

Opposite: the North Fork of the Virgin River is one of the most delightful canyon hikes in the Colorado Plateau. Many hikers, however, are unaware of the ruler-straight boundary that divides this proposed BLM wilderness from Zion National Park, and believe they are walking in protected park lands throughout the canyon.

Alexis Kelner

CANAAN MOUNTAIN UNIT

Highlights—For enthusiasts of slickrock and wilderness, Canaan Mountain is a promised land: an eight-by-ten mile block of Navajo Sandstone bounded by 2,000-foot-high cliffs with groves of ponderosa pine scattered across the sculpted surface of solid rock. Adjacent to the southeast boundary of Zion National Park, Canaan Mountain is a glorious variation on the topographic and ecologic themes found in the park, with emphasis on plateau more than canyon. The BLM included the top of Canaan Mountain in its wilderness recommendation, but left the approaches to the mountain unprotected. We propose 52,100 acres for wilderness, including Water and Squirrel canyons on the south, South Creek and the Eagle Crags Trail on the north, and less steep approaches on the east. The Arizona portion of the Canaan Mountain WSA was designated as the Cottonwood Point Wilderness in 1984.

Geology and landforms—Canaan Mountain is a great promontory surrounded on three sides by the 2,000-foot-high White Cliffs composed of Navajo Sandstone. The 500-foot-high Vermilion Cliffs, composed of the Moenave Formation, lie at the base of the White Cliffs; the two formations are separated by a wide bench of the Kayenta Formation's soft mudstones. The Navajo Sandstone surface of Canaan Mountain has been carved into bold ridges, hummocks, hollows, and passageways. Canaan Mountain, Smithsonian Butte, and the Eagle Crags are scenic attractions for visitors entering Zion National Park from the south; El Capitan and the Vermilion Cliffs rise north of Highway 89 near Colorado City, Arizona.

Plant communities—Most of the unit is dominated by ponderosa pine and Douglas fir scattered among large areas of barren slickrock. Pinyon pine, manzanita, Gambel oak, and Indian ricegrass are found on the pockets of soil amid the slickrock. The lower slopes on the eastern side of the unit and at the base of the White Cliffs support pinyon-juniper with serviceberry, manzanita, and grasses. Riparian areas are found along South Creek, Water Canyon Creek, Squirrel Creek and several other drainages; maidenhair fern, shooting star, scarlet monkeyflower, and columbine grow in hanging gardens by cliff-side springs and seeps (BLM, 1986, p. 13).

Wildlife—The western half of the unit is a peregrine falcon use area; South Creek and the northwest side are critical winter range for mule deer, according to the UDWR. The northern side of Canaan Mountain is "highly suitable potential habitat for desert bighorn sheep" according to the BLM and the UDWR (BLM, 1986, p. 16). Bighorn sheep were reintroduced nearby in Zion National Park in 1977 and have made "light use" of part of this unit since. Other animals include mountain lion, coyote, bobcat, Gambel's quail, mourning dove, several species of nesting raptors, and "a number of sensitive animals including the desert shrew, spotted bat, Lewis's woodpecker, and golden eagle" (BLM, 1986, p. 16).

Archeology and history—Hunting camps of the Virgin River Anasazi and Southern Paiutes are likely to be present, according to the BLM, but are as yet unidentified. A pulley system and collapsed buildings are remnants of logging on Canaan Mountain between 1915 and 1928.

Recreation—Though often overlooked by visitors to Zion National Park, Canaan Mountain offers excellent day hikes and short backpack trips on its convoluted sandstone plateau. Trailheads on the mesa south of Rockville and at Squirrel and Water canyons north of Colorado City, Arizona, allow access to the plateau (see Hall, 1982). Once on top, water is available from potholes following rainstorms and a few scattered springs.

BLM recommendation—The BLM initially recommended only 32,800 acres of its 47,170-acre Canaan Mountain WSA, omitting many of the slopes beneath the main cliff walls, several sections of state lands, and

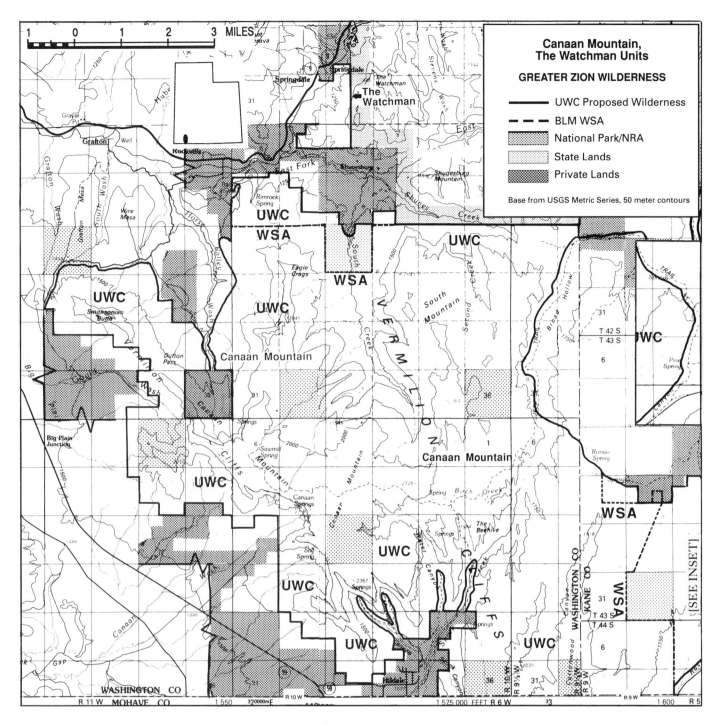

lands along the eastern fringe of the unit. The final recommendation is expected to be 1,000 acres larger. Small areas of human impact exist on the eastern and western edges, but instead of making wholesale deletions, these lands should be reclaimed. Lands deleted north of the Eagle Crags more closely follow Exxon's uranium claims than a natural wilderness boundary. A large natural area south of Rockville was deleted; this area includes a constructed BLM hiking trail which is the main hiking route to the top of Canaan Mountain from the north. In the eastern part of the WSA the BLM deleted about 11,000 acres of natural, rugged mesa tops and canyons. The agency plans range manipulation projects here which would remove the pinyon-juniper forest (BLM, 1986).

Coalition proposal—We propose to designate as wilderness the entire WSA and the scenic foothills of the Eagle Crags. Our boundary excludes a few small impacted areas, including a short vehicle way on the east and an area above Hilldale necessary for the town water supply. We include lands in Broad Hollow on the northeast side of the unit which the BLM acquired in 1988 through exchange. The Shunesburg unit south of The Watchman is no longer in public ownership and is not included.

PARUNUWEAP CANYON UNIT

Highlights—Named by John Wesley Powell in 1872 after a Paiute Indian word meaning "roaring water canyon," Parunuweap Canyon on the East Fork of the Virgin River is one of the West's finest examples of a flash flood canyon. Its spectacular narrows, twisting sidecanyons (with such descriptive names as Fat Man's Misery), significant archeological finds, showy rock formations, and hanging gardens all qualify Parunuweap for wilderness designation. However, due to plans by the Washington County Water Conservancy District to put a dam across the canyon, wilderness designation for the Parunuweap is embroiled in controversy. We recommend 37,700 acres for wilderness designation.

Geology and landforms—The East Fork of the Virgin River, where it gouges deeply into Navajo Sandstone, forms the most dramatic features of this unit. Carved over millions of years and scoured annually, Parunuweap Canyon funnels water from an enormous drainage into a chute that is several hundred feet deep but only a dozen feet wide in places. Hikers report seeing large tree trunks wedged 40 feet above the canyon floor. The uplands, which span the Carmel Formation and Navajo Sandstone and include the White Cliffs, the Black Mesas, and Poverty Flat, also contain a variety of scenic landforms and colorful rock formations.

Plant communities—In the lower reaches of this unit the vegetation is characteristic of the Lower Sonoran Zone with blackbrush, sage, and saltbush predominating. The higher country supports abundant stands of pinyon pine, juniper, Gambel oak, and mountain mahogany; two types of yucca are common. Since the canyons are cooler and wetter than surrounding lands, the vegetation differs from the higher or more open country. Here one finds willows and cottonwoods in the riparian areas, grass along the streamsides, and a few ponderosa pines above the flood level. Where springs issue from cracks in the canyon walls ferns and flower gardens grow. These hanging gardens harbor a wildflower bouquet of brilliant yellow and scarlet monkeyflowers, columbine, shooting star, red penstemon, and Hellebore orchid, arranged by nature against a background of maidenhair fern. The Zion tansy, a sensitive species, grows in the unit.

Wildlife—This unit contains four major habitat types for wildlife: pinyon pine and juniper country, riparian habitat, open sage lands, and cliffsides. Mammals found in the unit include mule deer, cougar, cottontail rabbit, and ringtail cat. A variety of birds also live in the area including mourning doves, bandtailed pigeons, canyon wren, and several species of raptors, perhaps including the endangered peregrine falcon which nests along cliffs.

Archeology and history—Archeological sites are identified within the canyon portion of this unit, and it is very likely that many others exist on the mesa. Within the Zion National Park section of Parunuweap Canyon are 88 identified archeological sites. One of these, a village site, is of such significance that it is the focus of a major display in the visitor center. A plaque at the boundary of the national park and BLM WSA memorializes the trip Major John Wesley Powell took through Parunuweap Canyon in 1872. The Foote Ranch Road at the edge of the proposed wilderness is believed to follow the pioneer road from Pipe Spring, Arizona, to Long Valley, Utah.

Recreation—The hike through Parunuweap Canyon is a wilderness hike *par excellence* offering challenge, solitude, and beauty. While similar to

the more famous hike through the Zion Narrows, a hike along Parunuweap is likely to be done without uninvited company.

BLM recommendation—In 1986, the BLM recommended 14,100 acres
of its 30,800-acre WSA for wilderness. This includes the canyon bottom
and walls, but excluded important wildlife habitat on the uplands. (The
final recommendation is expected to be 17,888 acres.) In its draft proposal
the BLM cherrystemmed from the unit a 4.5-mile-long trail from Ele-
phant Cove to the Foote Ranch. The BLM also allowed illegal road construction and damsite exploration and drilling to occur within the WSA
without prosecuting the lawbreakers. The scars of these activities are now
recovering, but the BLM nonetheless dropped parts of the affected area
from its draft wilderness recommendations. Mineral potential in the unit is
low. The National Park Service recognizes the wilderness values of
Parunuweap Canyon, and recommends park land adjacent to the WSA for
wilderness designation.

Coalition proposal—Parunuweap Canyon is intensely loved by those
who have been there and is hailed by hikers and canyoneers as one of the
most inspirational canyons on the Colorado Plateau. Wilderness designation of the entire 37,700-acre unit is needed to prevent dam construction
in the canyon and loss of the wild upland country.

THE WATCHMAN UNIT

Highlights—Just east of Springdale, Utah, and contiguous to Zion National Park, the massive buttress of the Watchman attracts visitors' attention as they enter and leave the park. The lower southwestern slopes of
this mountain lie on BLM lands outside of the park in the 600-acre Watchman unit, which should be protected as part of the area's impressive scenic
backdrop.

Geology and landforms—Johnson and Watchman Mountains rise above
the north and east forks of the Virgin River. The bases of these impressive
monoliths are composed of the Chinle Formation at elevations of 3,700
feet to 5,200 feet.

Plant communities—The sunny west- and south-facing slopes below the
cliffs support plants that are well adapted to heat; herbaceous vegetation
covers the higher altitudes and north facing slopes where the climate is
slightly cooler and more hospitable.

Wildlife—A number of raptors nest on the sheer canyon walls, including the bald eagle, golden eagle, peregrine falcon, prairie falcon, American
kestrel, red-tailed hawk, and Cooper's hawk. The unit also provides summer feeding grounds for desert bighorn sheep en route to Parunuweap
Canyon, according to the BLM. Mule deer and, occasionally, mountain
lion inhabit the unit as well.

Recreation—Spectacular hikes into the abutting national park begin at
the Watchman Campground and lead south through this unit. Nature
study and geologic observation are excellent.

BLM recommendation—The 600-acre WSA was dropped from study by
Interior Secretary James Watt, but was reinstated after a conservationist
lawsuit. The BLM now recommends wilderness designation.

Coalition proposal—We also propose wilderness designation for the
Watchman unit (see map, Canaan Mountain unit). No significant wilderness conflicts exist, and the unit is in a natural state. A logical extension of
the proposed wilderness in Zion National Park, the Watchman unit en-
hances that wild land and deserves protection.

*The canyon is steadily becoming
deeper and in many places very narrow—only 20 or 30 feet wide
below, and in some places no wider,
and even narrower, for hundreds of
feet overhead . . . . Everywhere this
deep passage is dark and gloomy
and resounds with the noise of
rapid waters . . . . The Indian
name of the canyon is
Paru'nuweap, or Roaring Water
Canyon.*

John Wesley Powell
EXPLORATION OF THE COLORADO RIVER
AND ITS CANYONS (1895)

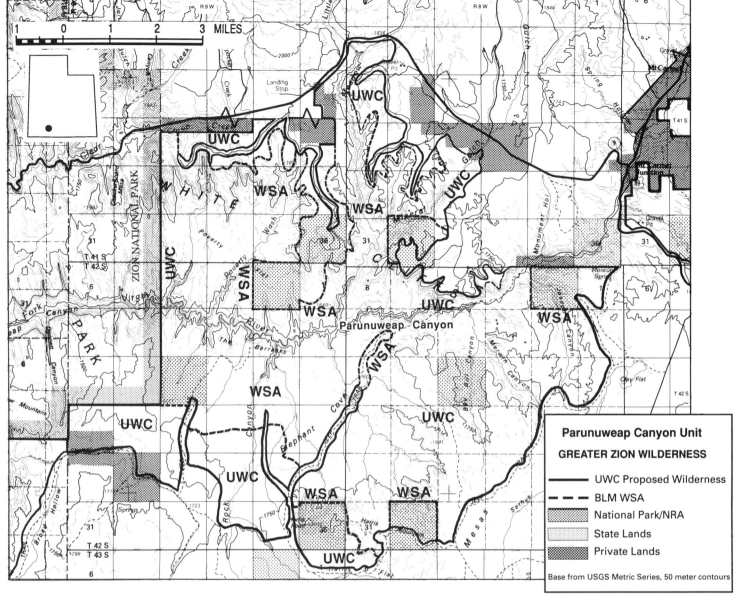

Parunuweap Canyon Unit

GREATER ZION WILDERNESS

——— UWC Proposed Wilderness

- - - - BLM WSA

National Park/NRA

State Lands

Private Lands

Base from USGS Metric Series, 50 meter contours

ZION ADJACENT UNITS

(North Fork Virgin River, Orderville Canyon, Deep Creek, and Goose Creek)

Highlights—The North Fork of the Virgin River and its tributaries carved the principal scenery of Zion National Park. Their canyons also extend onto BLM lands which, together with their surrounding uplands, compose four wilderness units. Geologically and scenically, these lands are a part of the park's canyon system. Orderville Canyon and the North Fork Virgin River are reached by a gravel county road intersecting Utah Highway 15 just east of the park. Access to upper Goose Creek is from Horse Pasture Plateau to its west; this unit is the starting point for many backpack and horseback trips. Deep Creek is reached by an unpaved road leading south from Highway 14, 15 miles east of Cedar City.

Geology and landforms—Sheer canyon walls of red Navajo Sandstone are capped by rims of the Carmel Formation. Canyons in all four units are deeply entrenched, serpentine, and narrow.

Plant communities—Pinyon-juniper woodlands with scattered ponderosa pine and mountain shrubs such as Gambel oak dominate the upland benches above the incised streams. Goose Creek and parts of Deep Creek are in a transition zone and support Douglas fir, white fir, aspen, and some ponderosa and juniper. Within the canyons is a lining of riparian habitat. Colorful hanging gardens grow in seeps along the canyon walls.

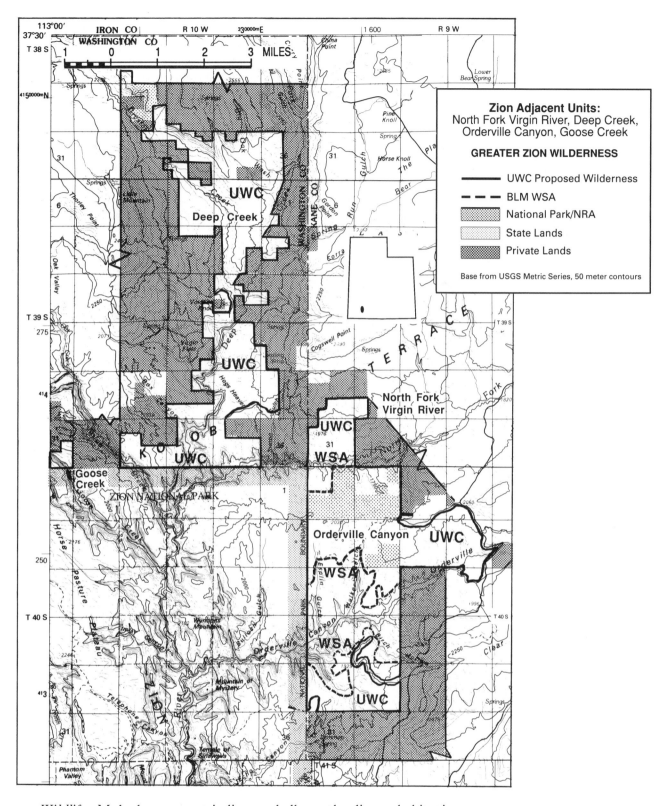

Wildlife—Mule deer, mountain lion, and elk use the diverse habitat in these units. The northern half of Deep Creek is a critical elk calving area, according to the UDWR; the agency identified all four units as endangered peregrine falcon use areas. The endangered bald eagle is sighted occasionally. A number of other raptors, including prairie falcon, American kestrel, red-tailed hawk, Cooper's hawk, and golden eagle inhabit the units as well, according to the BLM. According to the Nationwide Rivers Inventory (National Park Service, 1982), the perennial waters of the North Fork Virgin River unit provide potential habitat for the endangered woundfin minnow, the Virgin River chub, and the sensitive Virgin River spinedace.

The Zion snail (*Physa zionis*) is endemic to hanging gardens of Zion and Orderville canyons.

Archeology and history—No official inventory of this group of units has been completed. According to the BLM, the trail leading from Virgin Flats into Deep Creek was probably used for hunting and water access.

Recreation—The North Fork and Orderville units are the beginning sections of popular one-way hikes and backpacks into the "Narrows," the heart of the northern part of Zion National Park. These hikes presently provide 4,000 visitor days of primitive recreation annually, according to the BLM. Access to the Narrows is also possible through the Goose Creek and Deep Creek units. Their sheer canyon walls are a prelude to the Zion Narrows further downstream in the park. (See Brereton and Dunaway, 1988, for detailed hiking information.)

BLM recommendation—The BLM recommends wilderness for all of three units (1,750 acres in Orderville Canyon, 1,040 acres in the North Fork Virgin River, and 89 acres in Goose Creek) and part of Deep Creek (3,320 acres). No significant conflicts exist within these units. The Bureau is making a commendable effort to obtain private lands abutting North Fork Virgin River to augment natural resource protection.

Coalition proposal—We support the BLM recommendations with two exceptions. In Deep Creek the BLM claimed that a vehicle way divided the unit and it dropped the northern half. This way did not cross the unit, but one has reportedly since been bladed across the canyon. In Orderville Canyon we add undisturbed canyon walls and rims that the BLM excluded. All of these lands are natural continuations of the national park and deserve protection as well in an effort to conserve a more complete ecosystem. Accordingly, we propose 7,100 acres in Deep Creek and 6,500 acres in Orderville Canyon.

KOLOB ADJACENT UNITS

(Red Butte, LaVerkin Creek Canyon, Spring Creek Canyon, Taylor Creek Canyon, Beartrap Canyon, and Black Ridge)

Highlights—These six units are logical extensions of proposed wilderness in the Kolob Terrace section of Zion National Park. They are part of the integrated watershed, wildlife habitat, and scenic terrain of the park, and are among "the most pristine, spectacular, and ecologically significant BLM-administered wild lands in Utah" (Aitchison, 1987). Red Butte rises 1,800 feet above the Kolob Reservoir road about 10 miles north of the Virgin River. Access to the 804-acre unit is from the end of the Lamareau Tank service road to the southeast and from the west from a jeep trail that heads north from Rock Spring. LaVerkin Creek Canyon (567 acres) emerges south of Kolob Arch. Its deep canyons topped by conifer forests are a logical extension of the Kolob section of the park. Immediately east of Kolob Arch and two miles west of Kolob Reservoir, the 40-acre Beartrap unit contains the headwater areas for tributaries that flow through the Beartrap Canyon of the Kolob Terrace. The Middle Fork of Taylor Creek Canyon (35 acres) lies immediately east of the Taylor Creek Road and the park's west entrance and is a headwaters for the park. Its sheer-walled canyons are natural extensions of the park. Spring Creek Canyon (4,400 acres) is adjacent to the northern edge of the Kolob section of the park, directly east of Kanarraville. Black Ridge, at 21,800 acres the largest of the six units, includes the drainage of LaVerkin Creek as it exits the park, as well as the ridgeline west of Interstate 15 north of the Highway 17 junction.

Geology and landforms—These units are composed of rugged sedimentary cliffs formed among the Grand Staircase plateaus. The canyons in these units have cut up to 1,000-foot-deep sheer walls of red Navajo Sand-

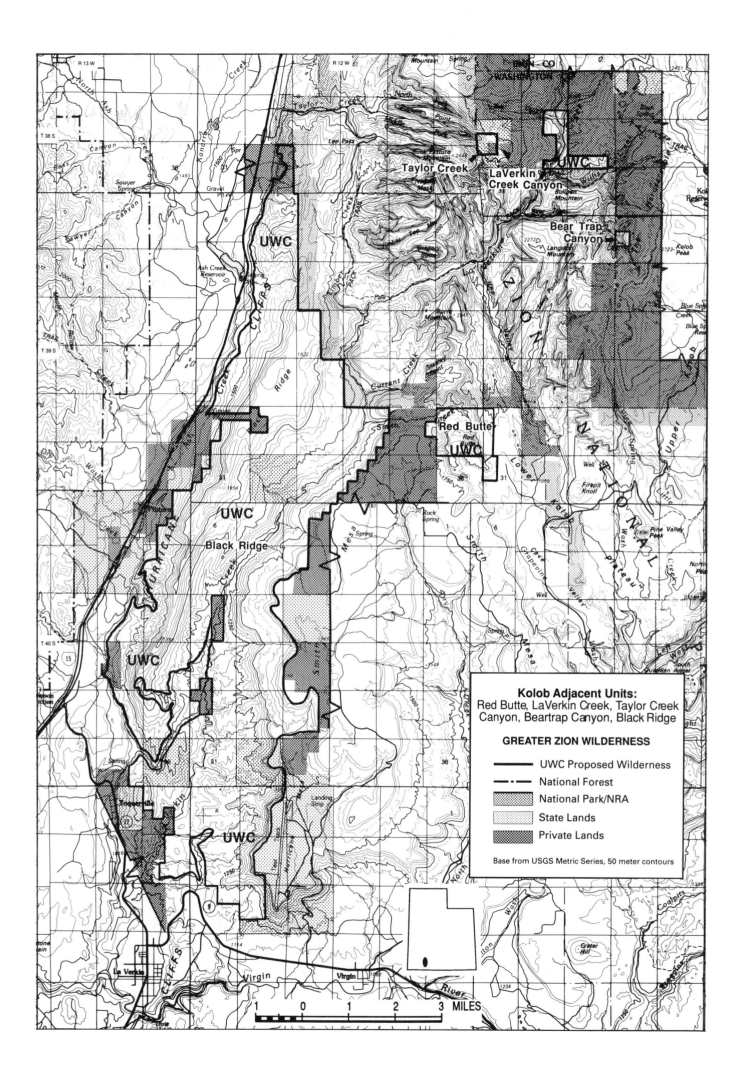

Kolob Adjacent Units:
Red Butte, LaVerkin Creek, Taylor Creek
Canyon, Beartrap Canyon, Black Ridge

GREATER ZION WILDERNESS

—— UWC Proposed Wilderness

—·— National Forest

National Park/NRA

State Lands

Private Lands

Base from USGS Metric Series, 50 meter contours

1   0   1   2   3   MILES

LaVerkin Creek flows out of the Kolob section of Zion National Park through BLM lands in our proposed Black Ridge wilderness unit. The BLM recommended against preserving this unit despite its scenic features, wildlife habitat, and recreational possibilities.

Tom Miller

stone capped by the Carmel Formation. The rugged topography of these units makes them important scenic viewpoints. Rising almost 1,800 feet in less than a mile, Red Butte stands out when viewed from the Kolob Reservoir road. Black Ridge, formed by the Hurricane Fault, is a major geologic feature and provides outstanding views into Zion National Park, over into Canaan Mountain, and west to the Pine Valley Mountains.

Plant communities—These units vary in elevation from 7,700 feet on the ridge above Taylor Creek Canyon to 4,000 feet in the LaVerkin Creek canyon bottom. Consequently, vegetation is of several different zones. According to the BLM (1982), the upper elevations and north- and east-facing slopes are populated with ponderosa pine, Douglas fir, white fir, aspen, and Rocky Mountain juniper. The middle elevations are predominately shrub woodlands supporting oak, pygmy pinyon-juniper, yucca, serviceberry, littleleaf mountain mahogany, and princess plume. Below 4,500 feet is the American Desert zone with blackbrush, salt bush, and creosote bush, which are adapted to drier conditions. Riparian habitat also occurs along streambeds, and hanging gardens grow in seeps and drips on canyon walls. Maidenhair fern, pink-flowered shooting star, and scarlet monkeyflower inhabit these verdant areas.

Wildlife—Mule deer winter on the sunny slopes of Red Butte and the foothills of Spring Creek Canyon. They spend their summers along with elk in LaVerkin Creek and other nearby units. Mountain lions prey on the deer throughout the area, according to the BLM, and in places are relatively numerous. Seven different species of raptors inhabit the area and often nest in the steep cliff walls. These include the bald eagle and peregrine falcon, the golden eagle, prairie falcon, American kestrel, red-tailed hawk, and Cooper's hawk. Peregrine falcons use much of the area, according to the UDWR, and bald eagles are known to winter in the Virgin River drainage south of the WSAs, according to the BLM. Turkey, blue grouse, and band-tailed pigeons inhabit LaVerkin Creek and Taylor Creek canyons.

Recreation—Hiking and backpacking are outstanding in all six units as extensions of the national park. Scenic and photographic values are obvious and some fishing and rock climbing occur in LaVerkin Creek Canyon. Technical and non-technical climbing opportunities are found on Red Butte and on cliff walls in the other units.

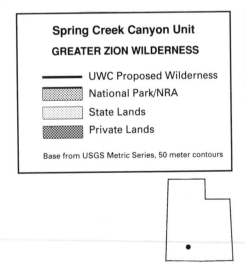

Spring Creek Canyon Unit

GREATER ZION WILDERNESS

——— UWC Proposed Wilderness

National Park/NRA

State Lands

Private Lands

Base from USGS Metric Series, 50 meter contours

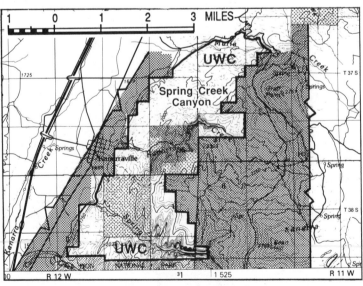

BLM recommendation—In 1986, the BLM recommended that all of these units except Black Ridge be designated wilderness. Its final recommendation is expected to omit 2,800 acres in Spring Creek Canyon. The BLM dropped Black Ridge from its wilderness inventory after subdividing the unit into three pieces and then finding two of them too small for wilderness designation. The remainder of this unit was dropped, improperly, due to exaggerated claims of outside sights and sounds.

Coalition proposal—We applaud the BLM's recommendation to preserve four of these units as wilderness. Black Ridge and all of Spring Creek Canyon, however, should be designated along with the others. Black Ridge, like the others, is essentially pristine, and the vehicle ways cited by the BLM are returning to a natural condition. Spring Creek Canyon has two short vehicle ways in the mouths of Spring Creek and Kanarra canyons. These unmaintained and almost unnoticeable trails, and a half-mile of water pipeline in Kanarra Canyon, are insignificant intrusions into this unit.

THE MOQUITH MOUNTAIN WILDERNESS

Tucked between Coral Pink Sand Dunes State Park and the town of Kanab is Moquith Mountain, an ecologically diverse extension of the Vermilion Cliffs that is easily accessible off of U.S. Highway 89. Here, slickrock plateaus sprout pinyon and juniper, while vegetation carpets the edges of flowing streams. Aspen groves flourish at the heads of two canyons and hanging gardens cling to the cliff bases. But the area's most surprising feature is its active sand dunes dotted with groves of ponderosa pine. The BLM recommended against wilderness, probably because of ORV use in the adjacent state park; the Coalition believes that a 26,500-acre wilderness is needed to prevent degradation of the dunes.

Extraordinary Habitats

Moquith Mountain is a small plateau reaching about 7,000 feet and covered with thick stands of ponderosa pine mixed with Gambel oak and isolated stands of aspen. From its heights are expansive vistas across the vivid pinks of the Coral Pink Sand Dunes, dotted with rich green islands of isolated ponderosa pine groves, to the equally stunning colors of the White and the Pink Cliffs to the north. To the east are views into the cliffs and canyons of the area, covered with pinyon and juniper, and beyond to distant mesas and cliffs. The canyon rims offer vertiginous views of sheer, desert-varnish-streaked walls which line narrow, rushing streamcourses.

Along the rims, the brilliant green of manzanita stands out against the vivid redrock, which is dotted with the blue-grey of the banana yucca and the dark, rounded forms of blackbrush. Many of the signature plants of the Upper Sonoran zone are represented along the rims and in the canyons: rabbitbrush, cliffrose, littleleaf mountain mahogany, Apache-plume, etc. Boxelder and cottonwood grow along the eight miles of perennial streams in the canyons. The South Fork of Indian Canyon houses a magical hanging garden, the heads of two unnamed canyons harbor mysterious quaking aspen groves, and in Water Canyon, Douglas fir groves perch on north-facing ledges—remnants of a colder and moister period.

Accessible only with ropes and rappelling skills, the 225 acres in Water Canyon and South Fork Indian Canyon represent two of the last relict riparian areas in the state. Tall rushes and grasses, including a number of unfamiliar species, grow in the stream itself. Hanging gardens, oak, maple, and Douglas fir thrive in this completely natural area.

IN BRIEF

Index Map: Area No. 36

Highlights: Noted for ponderosa pine growing out of pink sand dunes, Moquith's relict plant community is threatened by ORVs from the adjacent Coral Pink Sand Dunes State Park. Several deep canyons incise the Vermilion Cliffs and offer hanging gardens and archeological sites.

Maps: USGS 1:100,000 Kanab

Area of wilderness proposals in acres:

Area	UWC	BLM
Moquith Mountain	26,500	0

The area contains *Erigeron religiosus* (a rare fleabane daisy of the Zion area), *Asclepias welshii* (a threatened milkweed), and *Astragalus striatifious* (a rare milkvetch). Wildlife includes the resident mule deer and cougar, cottontail rabbit, raven, mourning dove, and coyote. Three sensitive species live here: roadrunner, Lewis's woodpecker, and fox sparrow. Two endangered species, bald eagle and peregrine falcon, visit the area. The varied terrain provides an abundance of habitats that remain uninventoried even for a definitive species checklist, let alone for rare and endangered species.

Archeological surveys performed for the Southern Utah Coal Project revealed densities of over 50 sites per 23,000 acres. A thorough inventory of archeological sites would likely disclose many. The mysterious faces and figures of the South Fork Indian Canyon pictographs are the best-known evidence of prehistoric rock art in the area.

A Silent World

Two developed campgrounds and several undeveloped campgrounds bordering the area provide good starting points for day hikes and backpacks into the area. The top of Moquith Mountain and the South Fork Indian Creek-Water Canyon area are favored destinations. One does not have to venture far to find oneself in a silent and pristine world, broken only by the croak of a raven or the rush of wind in the pinetops. The area is part of the BLM's 50,632-acre Moquith Mountain Special Recreation Management Area. The agency states that "educational values are particularly significant because they are diverse, conveniently concentrated in a small area and accessible."

Machines Over Wilderness?

The BLM recommended against wilderness for its 14,830-acre Moquith Mountain WSA. No rationale was given, although off-road vehicle use is permitted in three-fourths of the area. A sandy way leads to the top of Moquith Mountain and another to the South Fork of Indian Canyon. Vehicles branching off these routes have created ruts and scars in the

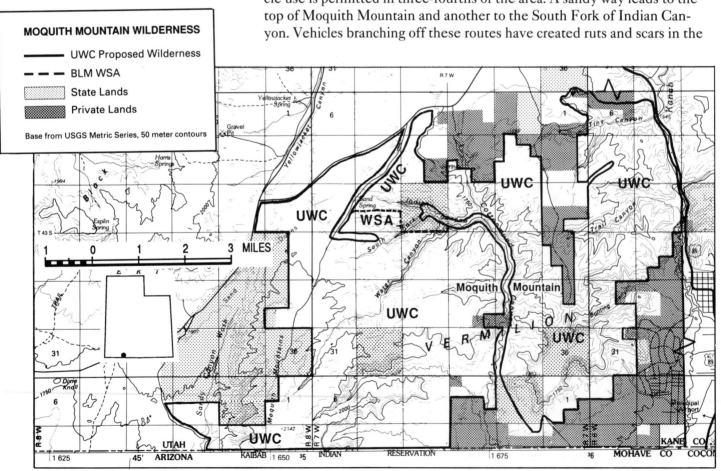

MOQUITH MOUNTAIN WILDERNESS

——— UWC Proposed Wilderness

– – – BLM WSA

State Lands

Private Lands

Base from USGS Metric Series, 50 meter contours

sand dune areas, but these are slowly being reclaimed by cryptogamic soil and grasses. These vehicles, however, continue to run across the small population of the threatened milkvetch identified in the area.

Few other conflicts exist. The BLM cites an antique corral, nine miles of fence, three spring developments, one windmill, and some stumps and logs here and there, but these are substantially unnoticeable or are on the edge of the unit. The trend, however, appears to be towards further degradation of this outstanding ecosystem through continued ORV use and woodcutting—activities readily available in surrounding developed areas.

The Utah Wilderness Coalition Proposal

We recommend wilderness designation for a 26,500-acre area, including additions to the BLM's WSA in the Cottonwood Creek drainage and to the northeast of the WSA. In Cottonwood Canyon we cherrystem a road and pipe to the BLM's boundary, including in our proposal the east side of the canyon. Although ORV use in the area is currently small, its use as a motorized playground will lead to the area's degradation. Wilderness status would protect fragile sand dune and cryptogamic soil areas from damage (the BLM notes that 56 percent of soils in its WSA fall into the severe or critical erosion class). Since ORV users have free access to the adjacent state park, it is reasonable to reserve the Moquith Mountain area for those who want to enjoy its superb scenery and unique life forms in peace.

Dave Hamilton

THE UPPER KANAB CREEK WILDERNESS

The White Cliffs in the proposed Kanab Creek wilderness are a spectacular backdrop for U.S. Highway 89—the route used by travellers between three national parks (Zion, Bryce Canyon, and the North Rim of Grand Canyon). The quality of the scenery, the presence of a stream with riparian vegetation, and the diverse character of the area, varying from lava flows and sand dunes to dense ponderosa pine forests as well as vertical cliffs, make this an attractive, easily accessible area for backcountry recreation. Although the BLM found this area to be natural and "highly scenic and colorful," the agency denied it WSA status and released it from further wilderness review. We propose a 42,200-acre wilderness area reaching from Mount Carmel Junction on the west to Johnson Canyon on the east.

IN BRIEF

Index Map: Area No. 37

Highlights: North of Kanab, Utah, the White Cliffs wrap around the headwaters of Kanab Creek. Several deep canyons with clear streams offer hikes with a spectacular white Navajo Sandstone backdrop.

Maps: USGS 1:100,000 Kanab

Area of wilderness proposals in acres:

Area	UWC	BLM
Upper Kanab Creek	42,200	0

The white Navajo Sandstone cliffs that rise above upper Kanab Creek are the spectacular backdrop east of U.S. Highway 89 near Mt. Carmel Junction. Through contorted argument, the BLM dropped this area from its wilderness review.

Ray Wheeler

Imposing White Cliffs

The thousand-foot-high White Cliffs, composed of Navajo Sandstone, run the 10-mile length of the area from east to west. Kanab Creek cuts through the center of the area, flowing seven miles from north to south. Lava flows from craters to the north fill the bottom of Kanab Creek's canyon and sand dunes have formed on the bench below the cliffs. Pinyon and juniper trees cover most of the bench area and a ponderosa forest caps the benches above the White Cliffs. Cottonwood trees and other riparian vegetation line the entire length of Kanab Creek. According to the U.S. Fish and Wildlife Service, the threatened milkweed *Asclepias welshii* may occur in the area.

The Kanab Creek area offers outstanding opportunities for hiking, backpacking, photography, and rock climbing. Access is convenient off of U.S. 89 south of Mt. Carmel Junction. The undeveloped Diana's Throne campground is on the southwest boundary of the area, and a road follows Kanab Creek itself through private lands to the southern boundary.

Lost from Sight

The BLM found two-thirds of its 61,430-acre inventory unit to be in a natural condition; however, in a contorted and illogical argument, the agency did not find outstanding opportunities for solitude or primitive recreation and thus did not designate a WSA. In its decision the BLM cited "flat terrain and open vegetation cover" as reasons for lack of outstanding solitude. But the sand dunes on the lower bench are capped with brush taller than a person; one is lost from sight when one is less than 100 yards over the first dune. Most of the bench area is a dense pinyon-juniper forest with closely spaced trees 15 feet high.

The several canyons also offer outstanding solitude and are not "open." They have a variety of smaller benches in them, dense pinyon-juniper forest, and thick vegetation taller than a person along the stream. Clearly, an area as large as this (7 by 17 miles) does offer outstanding solitude.

Beauty Contest

In a 1981 response to conservationists' protest of the BLM's decision to drop the area from study, the agency stated that "Pinyon and juniper tree vegetative screening does not inherently offer *outstanding* opportunities for solitude. Pinyon-juniper forests are common in the area of this unit and the protest does not indicate that the unit's forest cover is superior in density or other screening factors to the other pinyon-juniper forests of the area." Thus the BLM raised a standard often repeated in its wilderness inventory: a wild area had to be better than its neighbor to qualify for study. The mere fact of being splendidly typical in a region of splendid terrain was enough to disqualify an area, in the BLM's view.

This "beauty contest" approach to wilderness was ridiculously subjective and a transparent excuse for excluding lands the BLM wanted to leave open for development. The Kanab Creek wilderness was but one victim of this unwritten policy.

The BLM concocted these arguments and dropped the area from wilderness review in order to facilitate a coal slurry line for the now-defunct Allen-Warner Valley Energy System. Changes in energy demand, and environmental problems with mining the Alton coal field to the north—which would have supplied Allen-Warner Valley— have rendered the slurry line at least temporarily defunct.

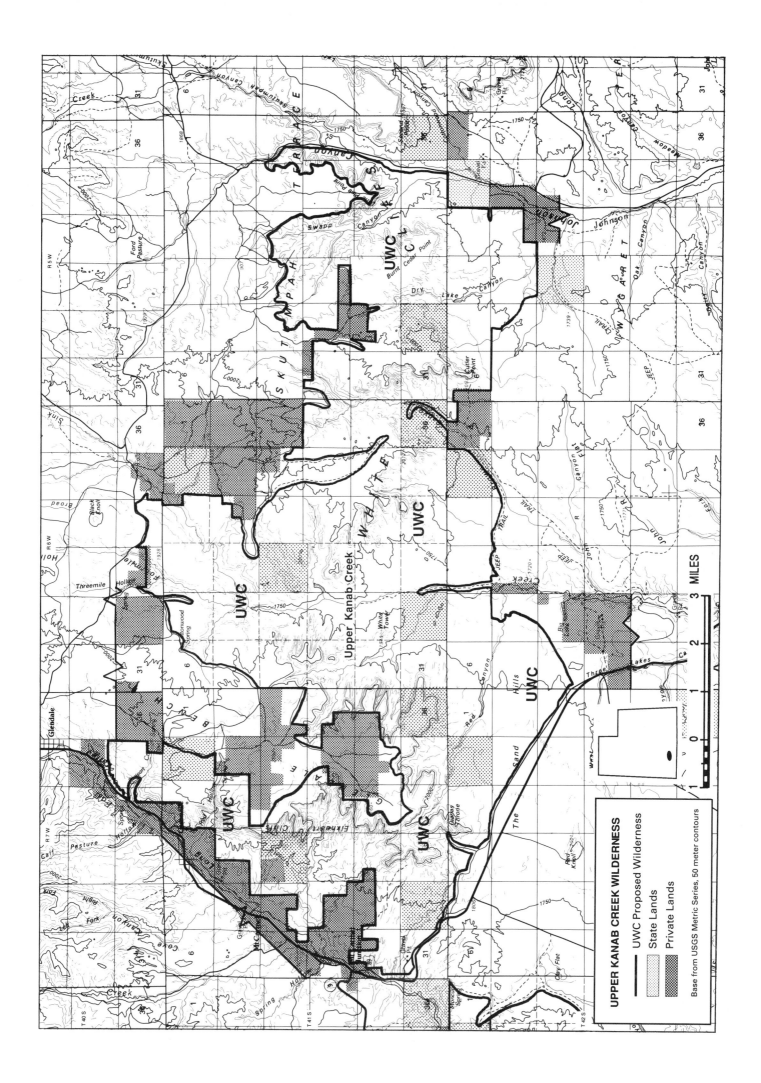

UPPER KANAB CREEK WILDERNESS

UWC Proposed Wilderness

State Lands

Private Lands

Base from USGS Metric Series, 50 meter contours

MILES

The Utah Wilderness Coalition Proposal

The Utah Wilderness Coalition Proposal

Without wilderness designation Kanab Creek will remain at risk from energy development and other commercial schemes. Our 42,200-acre proposal encompasses the most natural part of the BLM's inventory unit. A short cherrystem excludes the undeveloped campground at Diana's Throne. A frequently used vehicle way along Kanab Creek itself is also excluded. Where vehicle ways crossed sand and did not appear to have frequent use, we included them in our proposal.

Rodney Greeno

THE GRAND STAIRCASE WILDERNESS

IN BRIEF

Index Map: Area No. 38

Highlights: The upper Paria River and its tributaries have carved a rugged landscape through the stair-stepped Pink, White, and Vermilion Cliffs, forming a wilderness corridor stretching from the high cliffs of Bryce to the Grand Canyon.

Guidebooks: Hall (1982), Kelsey (1986a, 1987b)

Maps: USGS 1:100,000 Panguitch, Kanab, Escalante, Smoky Mountain

Area of wilderness proposals in acres:

Unit	UWC	BLM
Box Canyon	2,300	0
East of Bryce	900	0
Mud Spring Canyon	55,100	0
Paria-Hackberry	158,700	95,042
Squaw & Willis Creeks	22,300	0
The Blues-Table Cliff	18,700	0
The Cockscomb	10,300	5,100
TOTAL	268,300	100,142

Adjacent wild lands: Dixie National Forest (Table Cliff Plateau)

Between the floor of the Grand Canyon and the rim of Bryce Canyon, the land rises 7,000 feet in a series of great cliffs and plateaus. This is the "Grand Staircase," a masterpiece of geologic and biological innovation, a world where time itself lies suspended in horizontal and vertical planes. Its huge stairway spans six major life zones, from Lower Sonoran desert to Arctic-Alpine forest. Its colorful rock formations contain some four billion years of geologic history, and its fossils are a biography of life on Earth.

The Grand Staircase forms a nearly continuous wall winding 100 miles across southern Utah, from Zion National Park to Glen Canyon National Recreation Area. Yet only one section of the Staircase—the rugged canyon country of the Paria River basin—remains wild from top to bottom. Here lies our best opportunity to preserve, unaltered by man, a complete vertical cross-section of this remarkable landform. Yet the BLM's fragmented wilderness recommendations would leave unprotected 168,000 acres throughout the Paria River basin, permitting a host of developments including coal mines, oil fields, truck haul roads, a railroad corridor, a dam and reservoir on the Paria River, off-road vehicle corridors, and thousands of acres of forest chainings.

By contrast, the Utah Wilderness Coalition seeks wilderness designation for 268,300 acres, encompassing all five BLM roadless units lying between Bryce Canyon National Park and the newly designated Paria Canyon Wilderness. From its headwaters to its mouth, the Paria watershed is one wilderness. Only by protecting *all* of the wild country surrounding the Paria River, can we hope to keep it that way.

No Mans Mesa—An Ecological Wonder

On a warm, hazy, golden afternoon in November of 1985, two National Park Service employees entered a clearing in the pinyon-juniper forest on top of No Mans Mesa. At the center of the clearing Norman Henderson, a grazing specialist at Capitol Reef National Park, dropped to one knee. Noel Poe, the park's chief ranger, peered over Henderson's shoulder. Smiling with satisfaction, Henderson examined the flora surrounding him, fingering leaves, stroking seed pods, and softly naming each plant. "Manzanita," he muttered. "Aster. Muhley grass. Poa, buckwheat, dropseed, ricegrass . . ."

For a plant ecologist, the top of No Mans Mesa is a natural wonder. Lost in a maze of sidecanyons at the headwaters of the Paria River, the mesa is solitary and remote, a 2,000-acre island ringed by 1,000-foot-high cliffs. The mesa has never been grazed by cattle nor disturbed by agriculture or mining; its occasional small wildfires have been allowed to burn, creating grassy parklands amid the pinyon-juniper forest. It is, in sum, a classic "relict plant area"—a rare example of a pristine plant ecosystem.

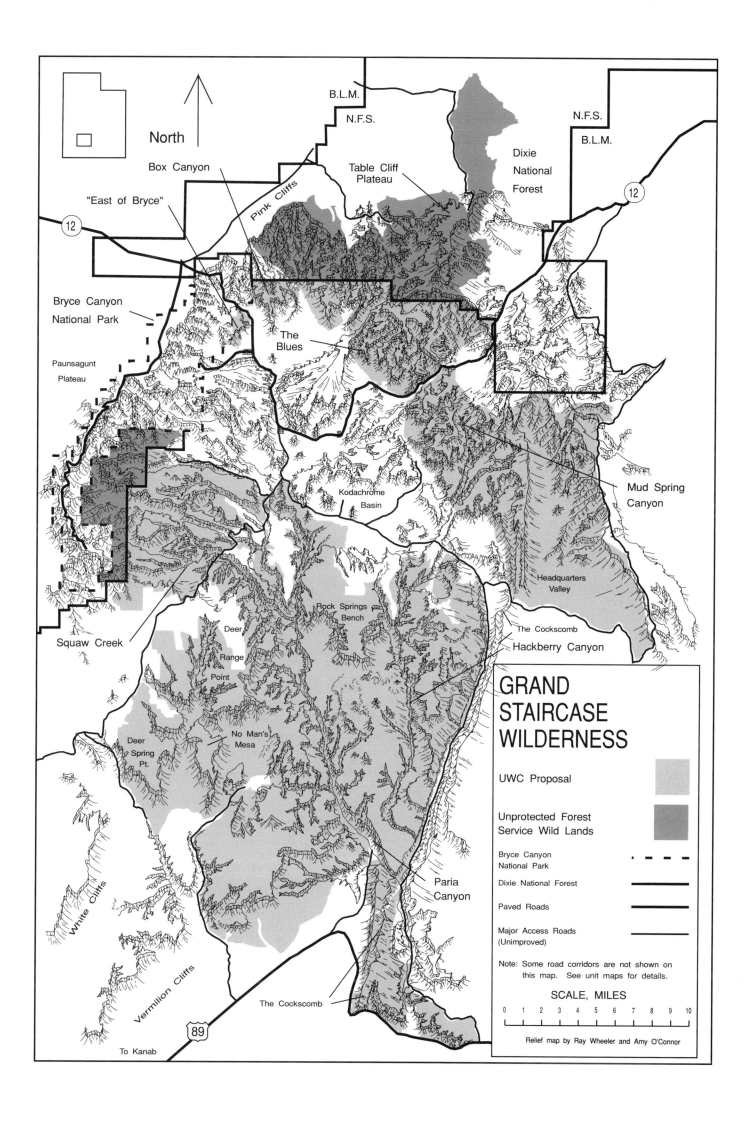

North

"East of Bryce"

Box Canyon

Pink Cliffs

B.L.M.

N.F.S.

Table Cliff
Plateau

Dixie
National
Forest

N.F.S.

B.L.M.

12

12

Bryce Canyon
National Park

Paunsagunt
Plateau

The
Blues

Mud Spring
Canyon

Kodachrome
Basin

Headquarters
Valley

Squaw Creek

Rock Springs
Bench

The Cockscomb

Hackberry Canyon

Deer
Range
Point

No Man's
Mesa

Deer
Spring
Pt.

White Cliffs

Vermilion Cliffs

89

To Kanab

The Cockscomb

Paria
Canyon

GRAND
STAIRCASE
WILDERNESS

UWC Proposal

Unprotected Forest
Service Wild Lands

Bryce Canyon
National Park

Dixie National Forest

Paved Roads

Major Access Roads
(Unimproved)

Note: Some road corridors are not shown on
this map. See unit maps for details.

SCALE, MILES

0 1 2 3 4 5 6 7 8 9 10

Relief map by Ray Wheeler and Amy O'Connor

For Henderson and Poe, the 150-mile journey from Capitol Reef National Park to No Mans Mesa had been a professional pilgrimage. Henderson was conducting a major study of the effects of livestock grazing within Capitol Reef National Park. He had come to No Mans Mesa in search of a relict plant area to serve as a baseline for the study. Sadly, no such area could be found within Capitol Reef National Park.

Islands of Biological Diversity

It is indeed ironic that undisturbed plant communities cannot be found within a national park. But recent studies suggest that animal species are also vanishing from our national parks. A 1987 study by ecologist William D. Newmark, for example, cited 42 cases of extirpation of mammal species in 14 North American parks. Many of our national parks, Newmark concluded, are islands of biological diversity surrounded by a sea of developed land. Like the land-bridge islands of the Aleutian archipelago, these protected areas are simply too small to support species of wildlife once common to them.

One of the parks Newmark studied was Bryce Canyon, just 10 miles northwest of No Mans Mesa on the eastern flank of the Paunsaugunt Plateau. For all its natural splendor, Bryce Canyon has been slowly losing its wildlife. The red fox has not been seen there for 28 years. The pronghorn antelope, the beaver, and the northern flying squirrel have all vanished since the park was established in 1924.

In lands bordering the park, livestock forage competition and hunting pressure has reduced or eliminated the populations of certain large mammal species. "Bears, once common on the Paunsaugunt Plateau, seem to have been exterminated," wrote geologist Herbert Gregory in 1951. "No grizzly bear has been reported during the last half century, and only three brown [black] bears are known to have visited the region since 1920. Wolves and coyotes, the bane of the stockman, have been so reduced in numbers as to be no longer a serious menace. Beavers, formerly abundant, have been exterminated by trappers. Of the 'great herds' of elk, antelope, and deer that provided food and raiment for the Indians and the Mormon pioneers, only the mule deer remains . . . ."

Wilderness—the Best Ecological Medicine

This steady decline of wildlife species is not inevitable. In recent years, better management practices have begun to curb overgrazing and overhunting, and the Utah Department of Wildlife Resources has been systematically reintroducing native wildlife species throughout Utah. The Department has recently established an elk herd just north of Bryce, and antelope to the south. But the success of such programs is directly dependent upon the amount of undisturbed wildlife habitat. As the Newmark study suggests, to survive, many wildlife populations need habitat *of sufficient size and diversity.*

That is precisely what the Grand Staircase wilderness provides in abundance: size and diversity. The entire region contains more than 300,000 acres of Park Service, Forest Service, and BLM-managed wild lands. For seasonally migratory species such as deer and elk, it provides a wilderness corridor linking summer range at the summit of the Paunsaugunt Plateau and critical winter range among the mesas, valleys, and canyons of the upper Paria watershed. For antelope, it provides critical fawning habitat along the Paria River. And for many other species of plants and animals, it provides undisturbed habitat of sufficient size to ensure long-term survival.

For humans, too, the Grand Staircase wilderness provides exceptional habitat. Its scenic and recreational opportunities are superb, and its cliffs and canyons are a museum of earth history. The region has recently inspired several books, including a hiking guidebook which features more than 300 miles of backcountry routes in the Paria wilderness. As National Geographic editor Ralph Grey observed (in Geerlings, 1980), a journey down the Grand Staircase—descending from arctic-alpine to Sonoran desert habitat—is a reenactment of human as well as geologic history. "Travel the mere 90 miles to the depths of Grand Canyon from the lofty plateaus of Bryce," he wrote, "and you are experiencing in compressed space and time the migration of the Ice Age people—the first Americans—from the Alaska land bridge to the tropics."

The bottom and the top "stairs" of the Grand Staircase wilderness are already protected within Bryce Canyon National Park and the newly established Paria Canyon Wilderness Area. But the heart of this region—the upper Paria canyon system—remains unprotected. Wilderness designation for this vital "missing link" is the key to the scenic, recreational, and biological integrity of the entire Grand Staircase wilderness.

Strip Mines, Power Lines, and Railroads

Unfortunately, the BLM's wilderness recommendations would shatter the integrity of the Grand Staircase wilderness. Of 268,000 acres of BLM wild lands in six roadless units, the BLM is likely to recommend wilderness for only 100,000 acres—leaving most of Paria basin wild lands wide open for development.

To understand why the BLM has recommended against wilderness protection for more than half of the Grand Staircase wilderness, one must turn the clock back to the mid-1970s. In 1976, during the energy crisis brought on by the Arab oil embargo, four giant utility and energy companies launched a proposal to strip mine coal on 25,000 acres of land south and west of Bryce Canyon National Park. Still more coal development was proposed for the northern rim of the Paria River basin, and for the Kaiparowits Plateau to the east. To transport coal, mine equipment, electrical power, and personnel, the developers drew plans for a network of slurry pipelines, truck haul routes, railroads, and transmission lines crisscrossing the entire region. A 1980 BLM study (ERT, 1980) identified six potential coal transportation corridors linking the Alton, South Kaiparowits, and North Kaiparowits coal fields. Four of the six corridors crossed parts of the Paria River basin.

Meanwhile BLM range specialists were developing ambitious proposals for "vegetation treatments," such as chaining, burning, spraying, plowing, and seeding, on up to 100,000 acres of land within the Paria River watershed (BLM, 1980). With local rangelands seriously depleted by overgrazing—and the expected loss of more than 8,000 acres of rangelands to strip mining—the agency was searching for ways to increase livestock forage. Its solution was to remove thousands of acres of natural vegetation so as to create new artificial pastures for cattle.

By 1980 both the Alton and Kaiparowits coal mine projects had been shelved. The Kaiparowits project was abandoned in 1976, when developers discovered that demand for electrical power was falling far short of projections. And in December of 1980, Interior Secretary Cecil Andrus declared lands adjacent to Bryce Canyon National Park unsuitable for strip mining. But despite such setbacks and the staggering economic and environmental costs, the BLM has never abandoned its commitment to developing the region's coal. In 1986, the strength of that commitment became apparent when the agency released its draft wilderness recommenda-

But the eastern and northeastern view is one which the beholder will not easily forget. It is the great amphitheater of the Paria . . . . An almost semicircular area, with a chord 30 miles in length, has been excavated into a valley by numberless creeks and brooks, which unite into one stream named the Paria.

Clarence Dutton

REPORT ON THE GEOLOGY OF THE HIGH PLATEAUS OF UTAH (1880)

Long Valley Draw in the Paria-Hackberry unit of the proposed Grand Staircase wilderness.

Bruce Barnbaum

tion for Utah. At the headwaters of the Paria River, the BLM recommended against wilderness designation for two wilderness study areas totalling nearly 60,000 acres. The Mud Springs WSA was unsuitable for wilderness designation, the BLM claimed, because "The WSA's potential for coal, oil, and gas development outweighs its value for wilderness." Likewise, the "Blues" WSA was rejected because, in the BLM's view, "only seven percent of the unit contains high quality wilderness values while 75 to 100 million tons of coal underlie the unit."

The BLM's campaign to increase livestock forage has had a similar effect upon the wilderness inventory. So determined was the agency to press forward with proposed range treatment projects, that in 1980 the Utah state director requested special permission to eliminate 40,000 acres proposed for vegetation treatments from the Paria-Hackberry and Mud Springs WSAs. On Calf Pasture Point, for example—a cliff-walled peninsula of forested land directly north of No Mans Mesa—the BLM leveled 1,000 acres of pinyon-juniper forest within weeks after the land was officially eliminated from the Paria-Hackberry WSA.

In all, at least 60,000 acres of land in the Paria basin were ejected from the wilderness inventory because of their potential for "range improvement" projects. Many thousands of acres of proposed range treatment projects lie directly below Bryce Canyon National Park. If the projects are ever completed, their effect on the park's vistas will be devastating. The patchwork of scars left by pinyon-juniper chainings could take half a century to heal—and perhaps much longer.

The economics of range treatment are notoriously bad. According to the BLM's wilderness DEIS, for example, 12,300 acres of proposed range treatments within the Paria-Hackberry WSA will increase ranching revenues by $3,240 and federal grazing permit revenues by $1,722 annually—a net annual benefit of about $5,000 at a potential cost of $400,000. Interest and inflation will make the net loss on such projects even worse.

Vehicle Corridor—or Wilderness Refuge?

Nowhere on the Colorado Plateau do the BLM's wilderness recommendations and the Utah Wilderness Coalition proposal stand in starker contrast. The BLM proposal envisions coal mines, oil and gas fields, railroads, transmission lines, new roads, a reservoir, and many thousands of acres of vegetation manipulation throughout the Grand Staircase wilderness. To facilitate such development, the BLM dropped numerous key features of the Grand Staircase from its draft recommendation—even No Mans Mesa, with its rare relict plant communities. Perhaps most disturbing of all, the BLM's draft recommendation would have created a non-wilderness corridor—open to off-road vehicle use—straight up the bed of the Paria River through the center of the Paria-Hackberry WSA. The final BLM proposal may, however, include these key lands dropped in the draft recommendation.

The Paria River basin's coal has never been crucial to the nation's energy supplies. The entire region contains less than one-tenth of one percent of U.S. proven recoverable coal reserves (from Doelling and Graham, 1972). The wilderness values of the entire Grand Staircase, however, are of national and international importance. The Utah Wilderness Coalition's proposal would protect the vital middle "stair" of the Grand Staircase, preserving the scenic, recreational, and biological integrity of the entire Paria basin wilderness.

Ray Wheeler

PARIA-HACKBERRY UNIT

Highlights—One of the largest roadless areas in Utah, this complex and colorful landscape is dominated by the thousand-foot-high White Cliffs, which divide high, forested benches from slickrock canyons and banded badlands. Located north of Highway 89 east of Kanab, Utah, and south of Henrieville on Highway 12, Paria-Hackberry links the High Plateaus with the designated Paria Canyon-Vermilion Cliffs Wilderness near the Colorado River. Together these areas form a wilderness travel corridor extending from Bryce Canyon National Park to Grand Canyon National Park, encompassing a complete vertical cross-section of the Grand Staircase.

Geology and landforms—Two steps of the Grand Staircase are in this unit. The Vermilion Cliffs of deep-red Moenave Sandstone, with banded red, grey, and white Chinle badlands at their base, line the southern boundary and the lower eight miles of the Paria River. The remainder is in the White Cliffs of the Navajo Sandstone, except for the high mesas on the north and west boundaries, which are capped by the Carmel Formation. Some 25 miles of the shallow, silty Paria River cut through these cliffs and benches. Clear water flows in Sheep Creek, Hackberry Canyon, and several other perennial streams. These canyons are more than 1,000 feet deep in places and have sections of fine narrows. The unit is bounded on the east by Cottonwood Creek and The Cockscomb.

The bottom and the top "stairs" of the Grand Staircase wilderness are already protected within Bryce Canyon National Park and the newly established Paria Canyon Wilderness Area. But the heart of this region— the upper Paria canyon system— remains unprotected. Wilderness designation for this vital "missing link" is the key to the scenic, recreational, and biological integrity of the entire Grand Staircase wilderness.

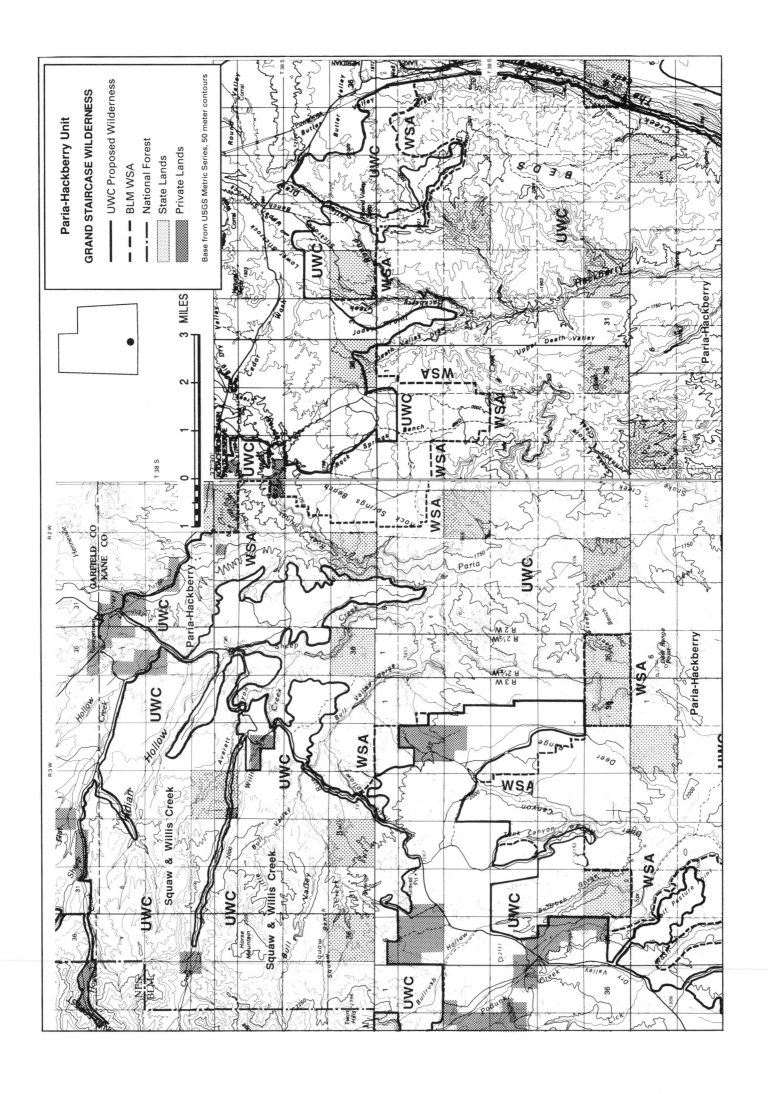

Paria-Hackberry Unit

GRAND STAIRCASE WILDERNESS

UWC Proposed Wilderness

BLM WSA

National Forest

State Lands

Private Lands

Base from USGS Metric Series, 50 meter contours

0   1   2   3   MILES

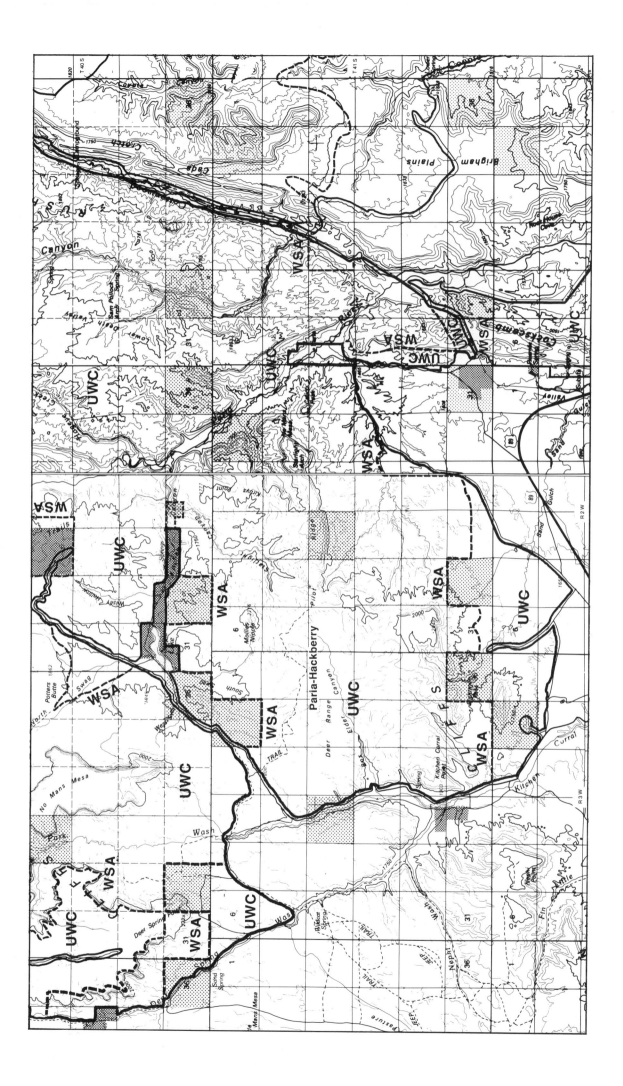

Plant communities—The benchlands of Paria-Hackberry are covered with a pinyon-juniper forest, with areas of shrubs, sand dunes, and important relict grasslands on No Mans and Little No Mans mesas. Some ponderosa pine is found in higher areas, and cottonwood trees and associated riparian species grow along the more than 50 miles of streamcourses. The BLM notes the presence of *Psoralea pariensis* (Paria scurfpea), under review for possible threatened or endangered status. The unique relict plant community of pinyon-juniper and sagebrush-grass park vegetation on No Mans Mesa is accessible only by a steep, almost impassible trail. This mesa was grazed by goats for two years in the early 1900s, and is one of the few remaining unaltered plant communities in the state. The waist-high perennial grasses and thick cryptogam found here represent the natural, pre-grazing vegetative cover of much of Utah.

Wildlife—Mountain lion and mule deer inhabit the unit, and the UDWR identified the southeast half of the unit as a peregrine falcon use area (see also area overview).

Archeology and history—Pictograph and petroglyph panels are known in the unit, and there is a potential for significant cultural resources based on known sites elsewhere in the Grand Staircase area, according to the BLM.

Recreation—The Paria River, Hackberry Canyon, Sheep Creek, and Bull Valley Gorge are prime hiking routes (Kelsey, 1987; Hall, 1982). Loop trips can be made from one drainage to another by crossing the intervening benchlands. The Round Valley Draw, Stone Donkey Canyon, and Sam Pollock Arch are notable attractions, and the presence of perennial streams makes hiking relatively easy and accessible. This segment of the Paria River is not nearly so well known as the Paria Canyon narrows farther downstream, so solitude is easy to find. Cottonwood Creek and the ghost town of Old Paria are enjoyable destinations accessible by road just outside the proposed wilderness and offer spectacular views into the wilderness. The National Park Service has identified the Paria River as a potential wild and scenic river.

BLM recommendation—Of its 135,822-acre WSA, the BLM initially recommended wilderness designation for only 59,270 acres, split into two separate units. The agency excluded 10,200 acres from its WSA claiming they lacked naturalness, and another 12,700 acres for supposed lack of solitude or primitive recreation opportunities. The excluded lands are in several separate parcels along the southern, western, and northern boundaries. Following public review of its draft recommendation, the BLM has indicated that it will add some 35,700 acres to its recommendation for a total of 95,042 acres. Much of the area excluded from the WSA, as well as WSA lands omitted from the final recommendation, are targeted for chaining and ORV use. Most of the excluded lands have "low potential" for oil and gas, and under the BLM's all-wilderness alternative, "the loss of development opportunity for uranium would not be significant" (BLM, 1986, p. 14). The BLM's final recommendation would split the unit in two along the Paria River, leaving the river canyon open to ORV use.

The Paria Box, the spectacular lower canyon of the Paria River through the Cockscomb, was excluded to allow for a potential coal haul railroad (BLM, 1986, p. 10 and 22). The Paria River bed *through* the proposed wilderness was excluded from the draft recommendation to allow ORV use, even though current use is low and closure "would not be a significant impact" (BLM, 1986, p. 29 and 32). Although the BLM claimed that "the aggregate area of scenic values in its WSA is about 59,300 acres" (the area it initially recommended for designation), it rates 97,800 acres as Class A scenery (BLM, 1986, p. 19 and 22).

Coalition proposal—We recommend a single 158,700-acre Paria-Hackberry wilderness unit which will protect the most important natural features of this area, including the Paria River and its tributary canyons, the forested benchlands above the White Cliffs, and the ecologically significant No Mans Mesa.

BRYCE ADJACENT UNITS

(Squaw and Willis Creek, East of Bryce, and Box Canyon)

Highlights—Bryce Canyon National Park is renowned for its expansive vistas across the canyons and mesas of the Grand Staircase. Three BLM wild land units—Squaw and Willis Creek, East of Bryce, and Box Canyon—lie below Bryce's cliffs and form part of the scenic foreground of the national park. The BLM, however, dropped each of these units from wilderness study. Every other component of the Grand Staircase is at least partly protected in wilderness study areas. Wilderness designation would protect an important part of the view from the national park, hiking and horseback riding routes leading up into the park and adjacent national forest land, and important habitat for big game and songbirds. A dirt road leading from Cannonville to Alton separates the Squaw and Willis Creek unit from the Paria-Hackberry unit.

Geology and landforms—Squaw and Willis creeks dissect benchlands lying at about 7,000 feet to the east of the cliffs of Bryce Canyon. (A narrow strip of Dixie National Forest land separates the BLM unit from the national park.) Squaw Creek eventually flows into Bull Valley Gorge in the Paria-Hackberry unit. Willis Creek, a major drainage bisecting the unit from Bryce Canyon to Sheep Creek, also flows into the Paria-Hackberry unit. The red beds of the Carmel Formation cover most of the unit with an exposure of Navajo Sandstone in upper Bull Valley Gorge at the eastern boundary of the unit. Farther north, the East of Bryce and Box Canyon units directly adjoin the national park, and consist of steep-walled canyons and cliffs as high as 500 feet. Outcrops of shale give a badlands appearance to the lower slopes. Views from each of these units toward Kodachrome State Park, Table Cliff Plateau, and the Paria River canyons are outstanding. Within the national park, Box Canyon and East of Bryce can be seen from Shakespear Point north of Highway 12; Squaw and Willis Creek can be seen from "The Promontory" located east of Rainbow and Yovimpa Points.

Plant communities—A dense pinyon-juniper forest covers the higher benchlands. The wider valleys and washes contain scrub-oak thickets, serviceberry bushes, and ponderosa pine groves.

Wildlife—These units provide important habitat for mule deer, black bear, and a variety of songbirds. Wildlife such as bear use the area to travel between the high plateau of Bryce to the warmer Paria River country below.

Recreation—Hikes along the canyon bottoms lead up from the lower benches into the high country of Bryce Canyon. Opportunities here vary from strenuous cross-country travel in steep terrain to easy day hikes and horseback rides along game trails and old vehicle ways. East of Bryce and Box Canyon are easily accessible from Utah Highway 12 north of the town of Tropic. Squaw and Willis Creek can be reached from the national park (through national forest lands) below the southernmost cliffs of Bryce. A jeep trail down Willis Creek is no longer passable to vehicles. The Alton-Cannonville road provides access to the lower part of this unit.

BLM recommendation—The BLM dropped Box Canyon and East of Bryce from wilderness study in its 1979 initial inventory. Squaw and Willis Creek was dropped from the 1980 final wilderness inventory. The agency claimed that a few impacted areas affected the whole unit, and that recreational opportunities and solitude were lacking. Most puzzling, the BLM claimed that these units were not logical extensions of the wild lands in Bryce Canyon National Park that are recommended for wilderness designation by the Department of the Interior. Instead of considering the

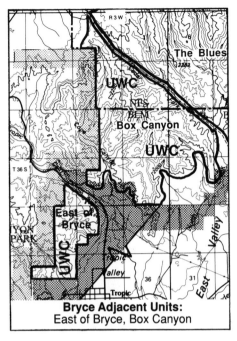

Bryce Adjacent Units:
East of Bryce, Box Canyon

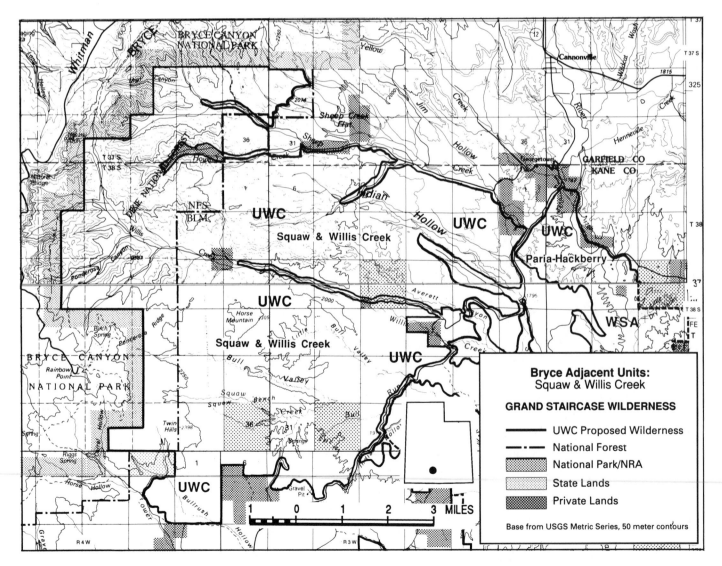

Bryce Adjacent Units:
Squaw & Willis Creek

GRAND STAIRCASE WILDERNESS

———	UWC Proposed Wilderness
—·—·—	National Forest
▨	National Park/NRA
░	State Lands
▦	Private Lands

Base from USGS Metric Series, 50 meter contours

proximity of Bryce Canyon as an asset to wilderness values, the BLM downrated its lands, saying that hiking opportunities were not "superior" to those found in the park.

Coalition proposal—Designation of each of these three units (Squaw and Willis Creek, 22,300 acres; East of Bryce, 900 acres; and Box Canyon, 2,300 acres) would complement the adjacent national park and national forest wild lands, and would provide an ecological link with the Paria-Hackberry unit to the southeast. Our boundaries exclude the major impacted areas, including (in Squaw and Willis Creek) the jeep road up Willis Creek as far as Iron Spring Ranch, a pipeline on the southern edge, and some forest chainings on the northern edge. The remainder of the jeep road up Willis Creek has not been used for years and is no longer passable; a locked gate limits vehicle access at the Iron Spring Ranch. Sections of private and state lands are also excluded, and two short cherrystems exclude jeep trails in the southern part of the unit. A road and private lands along Howard Creek form the northern boundary of this unit. A power line and jeep road form the northern boundary of the Box Canyon unit (see map, The Blues unit). Other impacts, such as fences, are minor intrusions on the landscape and would be allowed within the wilderness. Protection of the visual resource should be a primary goal for management of these park, forest, and BLM lands. Wilderness designation would further this management goal, and would help preserve the splendid views from Bryce Canyon National Park.

THE BLUES UNIT

Highlights—Northeast of Bryce Canyon National Park, and north of Highway 12, an area of blue-grey badlands crops out beneath the prominent summit of Powell Point on the Table Cliff Plateau. These richly colored badlands, together with canyons eroded into sandstone immediately to the west, form a scenic 18,700-acre wilderness unit that adjoins a national forest roadless area of equal size.

Geology and landforms—The Blues, a Cretaceous shale badlands in the eastern part of the unit, contrasts with the pink cliffs below 10,000-foot-high Powell Point. The 3,000 feet of vertical relief from Highway 12 to the top of the Table Cliff Plateau makes this unit, along with the adjacent forest land, a scenic attraction to highway travelers and a significant part of the vista from Bryce Canyon National Park. More than half of the soils in the unit are in a "critical" erosion condition, according to the BLM (1986, p. 8), and would have limited development potential.

Plant communities—Pinyon and juniper cover most of the unit, except for the barren shale outcrops. The BLM's intensive inventory documents (1980) note that the rare aster *Xylorhiza confertifolia* has been found in similar geologic formations elsewhere in the region.

Wildlife—The BLM (1986, p. 12) notes that mule deer, black bear, cougar, Gambel's quail, and band-tail pigeons live in the unit. The topographic diversity of the unit creates diverse habitat conditions, including some riparian habitat along Henrieville Creek at the southeastern edge of the unit.

Archeology and history—The BLM's inventory documents (1980) note that The Blues contain known paleontological resources.

Recreation—The badlands topography of The Blues makes for interesting and varied hiking, although few people visit the area at present. The BLM has considered placing an interpretive sign along Highway 12 below this feature. Hikes could also be taken up Henderson Canyon to the Table Cliff Plateau; the steep climb may be undertaken on either side of

Box Canyon is part of the scenic foreground of Bryce Canyon National Park. Its steep-walled cliffs continue into The Blues unit located to the east (right of photo). The BLM dropped Box Canyon from its wilderness inventory despite the solitude to be found there.

Tom Miller

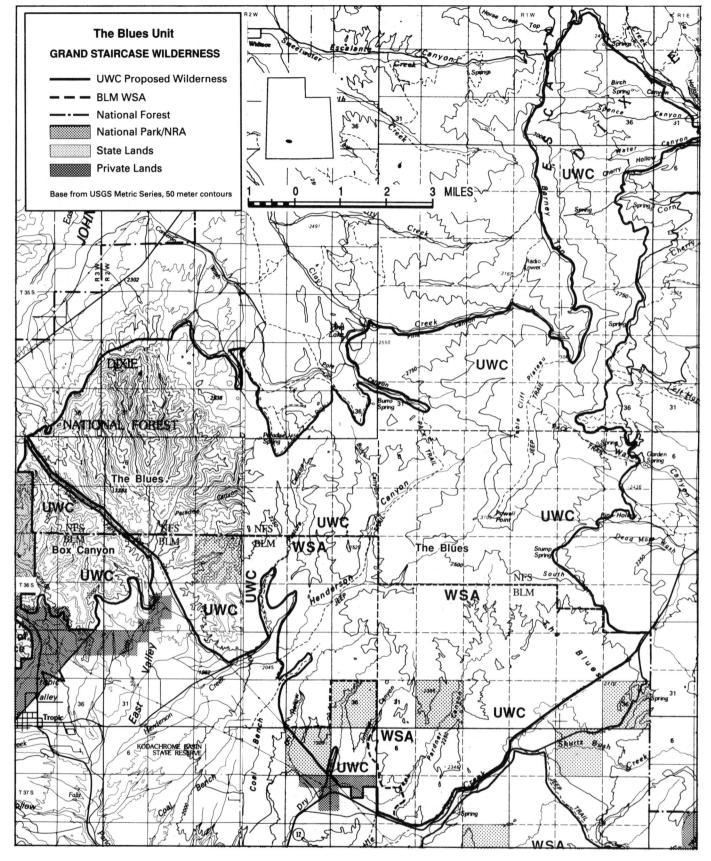

Powell Point on national forest land, and yields one of the best panoramas in southern Utah.

BLM recommendation—None of the 19,000-acre WSA was recommended for wilderness in 1986. Potential coal development is the likely reason, although actual development is probably not feasible. The agency downgraded the opportunity for solitude in the badlands area, although that portion of the area would probably be lightly used, thus ensuring solitude even in relatively open terrain.

Coalition proposal—We propose a 18,700-acre wilderness unit, including the entire WSA and additional lands in Pasture Canyon and elsewhere along the edge of the WSA. Rights-of-way for two electric transmission lines, a telephone line, and a pipeline are located just outside the boundary of the unit; these were intended primarily for the now-defunct Kaiparowits power project. Proposed chaining of the pinyon-juniper forests found in the higher elevations of the unit would occur on soil unsuitable for this activity. Our boundary cherrystems a jeep trail part way up Pasture Canyon, and includes substantially unnoticeable ways in the Henderson Canyon area. The entire roadless unit should be designated as wilderness, along with the adjacent Table Cliff Plateau-Henderson Canyon national forest roadless area, for its scenery and outstanding opportunities for solitude and primitive recreation.

MUD SPRING CANYON UNIT

Highlights—This diverse unit ranges from rugged badlands of blue-gray shale to the Cockscomb with its sharp rows of vertical fins. An expansive juniper forest covering most of the unit is dotted with pine groves on the mountain tops. We propose a 55,100-acre wilderness unit as a link between the Grand Staircase and Kaiparowits wilderness areas. The BLM pared down its initial wilderness inventory unit to a 38,000-acre WSA and then recommended against designating that remnant.

Geology and landforms—The unit varies from exposed bedrock and rugged badlands of blue-gray shale in the south to mountainous terrain reaching 8,000 feet in the north near Canaan Peak. The spectacular Cockscomb, a double row of jagged, steeply tilted fins, rises in the middle of the unit and continues south almost to the Arizona border. Wahweap Creek heads in the unit and flows south into an adjacent wilderness unit; Round Valley Draw also begins here and flows into the Paria-Hackberry unit. Mud Spring Canyon itself is a moderately incised canyon in the northwestern part of the unit.

Plant communities—A pinyon-juniper forest covers most of the higher elevations, grading into desert shrubs in the lower, southeastern part. Near Canaan Peak, ponderosa pine, Douglas fir, and spruce grow, adding diversity to the higher-elevation forest. Limited riparian areas occur in the major washes. A relict plant community in the upper part of Dry Valley "probably possesses important scientific values," according to the BLM (1986, p. 15).

Wildlife—The BLM (1986, p. 13) notes that the diverse habitats within its WSA support mule deer, black bear, cougar, cottontail rabbits, blue grouse, Gambel's quail, mourning doves, and band-tailed pigeons.

Archeology and history—The unit has not been surveyed for cultural resources.

Recreation—The unit receives little use at present; hunting is the major activity. The BLM (1986, p. 14) describes big game hunting as "among the best" in the area. The large size and solitude available in the unit would attract those who prefer to get off the roads and jeep trails and explore the canyons and broken terrain.

BLM recommendation—In 1980, the BLM excised about 27,000 acres from its 65,000-acre wilderness inventory unit. Some of the deletions made sense, such as in Round Valley where a twin high-voltage powerline cuts northwest from Cottonwood Creek. But the agency also deleted a larger area in the southeastern part of the unit, claiming that it lacked outstanding opportunities for solitude and primitive recreation owing to the

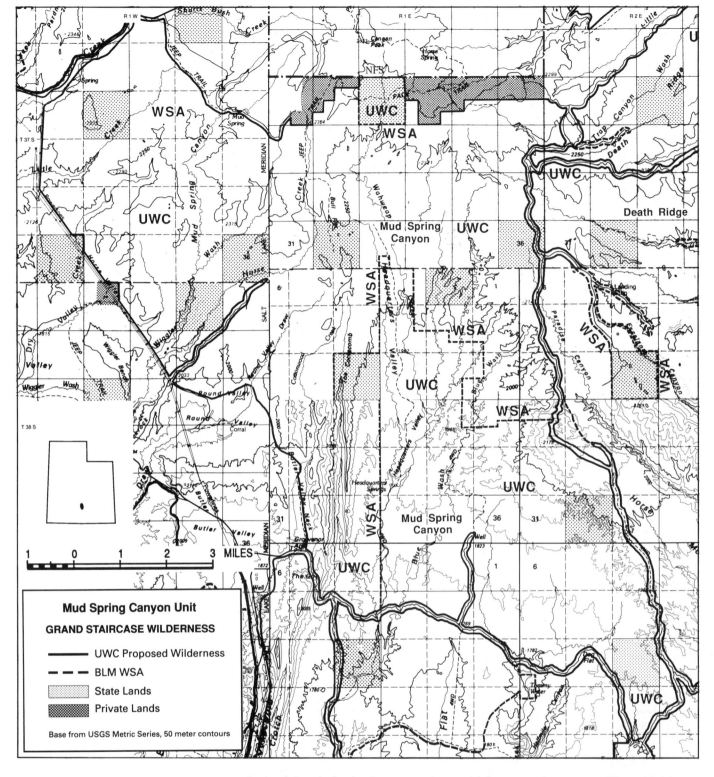

Mud Spring Canyon Unit

GRAND STAIRCASE WILDERNESS

——————— UWC Proposed Wilderness

– – – – – BLM WSA

State Lands

Private Lands

Base from USGS Metric Series, 50 meter contours

lack of deeply incised topography or thick vegetative cover. (Even if this criterion were suitable to the desert, the lands the BLM dropped are not exactly smooth, and the pinyon-juniper cover affords excellent solitude.) The BLM gave the resulting 38,000-acre WSA high marks for naturalness, solitude, and primitive recreation opportunities, but it recommended against any wilderness, giving no explicit reason. The presence of coal in the unit, as well as a potential coal haul right-of-way across The Gap, is probably the impetus. Other mineral values are rated low, including oil and gas which are assigned the lowest rating for "certainty of occurrence" (BLM, 1986, p. 10). A rail corridor to haul coal, identified during the Kaiparowits coal studies, blankets the entire unit, but a much narrower corridor could probably be found along Cottonwood Creek outside the unit. The 9-to 15-mile-wide corridor identified in the Kaiparowits study is excessive, and the viability of Kaiparowits coal in this arid, remote region is questionable (see area overview).

Coalition proposal—We propose a 55,100-acre wilderness unit, restoring the wild lands the BLM deleted in the southeastern part of the unit but leaving out the Cottonwood Creek powerline and nearby impacted lands. A vehicle route up Horse Creek is cherrystemmed; primitive ways up Headquarters Valley and to an abandoned well in the southeastern part of the unit are substantially unnoticeable. This part of the unit is needed to protect habitat for wildlife and scenic badland areas. The entire unit is valuable as a link between the rest of the proposed Grand Staircase wilderness and the Wahweap-Paradise Canyon unit of the proposed Kaiparowits wilderness. Tenneco, Inc., drilled an exploratory oil well just inside the northeastern boundary of the unit; the BLM's analysis indicates that this is probably the upper limit to the Upper Valley oil field that lies north of the unit. The well did not produce and has been reclaimed. Wilderness designation would prevent 8,330 acres of chaining and burning of pinyon-juniper forest. Watershed protection needs and erosion control standards render this land unsuitable for such activities.

THE COCKSCOMB UNIT

Highlights—The upthrust ridge of The Cockscomb, one of the region's most startling geologic features, is the major landmark along U.S. 89 between Lake Powell and Kanab. Located north of the highway and southwest of the Cottonwood Wash road, this 10,300-acre unit contains three miles of the Paria River and is a logical southern continuation of the Paria-Hackberry unit.

Geology and landforms—The Paria River cuts through the center of the unit. West of the river is the sawtooth ridge of The Cockscomb, a northern continuation of the East Kaibab Monocline. East of the river are plateaus and benches (called The Rimrocks) cut by small side drainages to the Paria.

Plant communities—A few pinyon pine and juniper cling to the rocky spine of The Cockscomb, while areas of shadscale, blackbrush, sagebrush, and other desert shrubs cover the remainder of the unit. Tamarisk grow along the Paria but the variable course of the river and its high mineral content limits the number of riparian species. According to the BLM, the milkvetch *Astragalus ampullarius*, a candidate for threatened and endangered listing, may occur in the unit.

Wildlife—The BLM has identified habitat for mule deer, antelope, cougar, cottontail rabbits, chukar, quail, and mourning doves in the unit. Critical antelope fawning areas are found along the river. Peregrine falcon and bald eagle pass through the area; other sensitive species include Lewis's woodpecker and the western and mountain bluebirds.

Archeology and history—The Hattie Green mine, an early copper working located on the crest of the Cockscomb, is of historic interest.

Recreation—Hikes or horseback rides along the Paria River north of Highway 89 pass through the unit and continue up to and along the Cottonwood Wash road. As in the Paria-Hackberry and Wahweap units to the north, both the river and the Cockscomb itself offer hikes and horseback rides in a wilderness setting.

BLM recommendation—The agency recommended only 5,100 acres of its 10,080-acre WSA, omitting the rimrocks in the southeastern corner of the unit. It described more than half of the unit as having less than outstanding opportunities for solitude and primitive recreation, and notes that

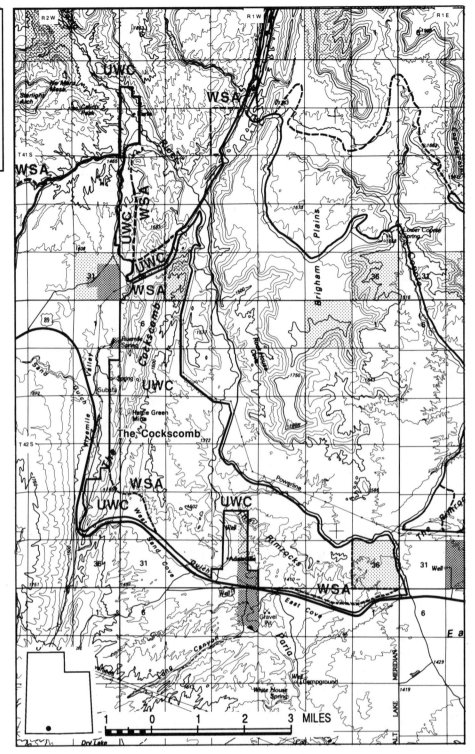

The Cockscomb Unit

GRAND STAIRCASE WILDERNESS

——— UWC Proposed Wilderness

– – – BLM WSA

State Lands

Private Lands

Base from USGS Metric Series, 50 meter contours

1 0 1 2 3 MILES

mineral and water development could occur in the lands it omitted from its recommendation.

Coalition proposal—We recommend that all of the WSA be designated plus a few hundred acres on the fringes of the WSA. The presence of a spectacular geologic feature in the western half of the unit should not be reason for downplaying the remainder by comparison. This unit is easily accessible by road and should remain wild to allow continued backcountry uses. Our proposal includes the scenic badlands south of the Paria townsite and important scenery and antelope habitat in the southeastern corner of the unit. It also more accurately follows the powerline corridor along the northern boundary.

THE KAIPAROWITS PLATEAU WILDERNESS

Summary

Surrounded by the canyons of the Paria, Escalante, and Colorado Rivers, the Kaiparowits Plateau is one of the most remote and least visited wild areas in the southwestern United States. Rugged landscape, isolation, and sheer size have made the Kaiparowits a refuge for a remarkable variety of plants and animals. The Plateau features a climax forest of thousand-year-old juniper and pinyon trees, an exceptionally large and diverse population of raptors, spectacular displays of metamorphosed rock created by natural coal fires, and some 300 recorded archeological sites. But the Plateau's most valuable commodities are those most difficult to measure: wind, space, distance, silence, and solitude.

The Kaiparowits Plateau also harbors an estimated 5 to 7 billion tons of recoverable coal. But to amortize the enormous cost of transporting the coal, development on a huge scale would be required, which would destroy the Plateau's wild character.

The BLM's wilderness recommendation for the Kaiparowits is predicated upon just such a future, for it systematically excludes all lands identified as potential sites for power plants, coal mines, oil exploration, or coal transportation corridors. By contrast, the Utah Wilderness Coalition's proposal would preserve one of the largest remaining blocks of undeveloped public land in the nation.

No Trails, No Guidebooks

From the northern rim of the Kaiparowits Plateau, at evening, the shadow of the Straight Cliffs reaches eastward toward the intricate canyon system of the Escalante River. Directly below is Coyote Gulch, one of the most beautiful—and popular—hiking areas in the state. The contrast between the Kaiparowits and Escalante areas is as great as the cliffline separating them. For there are no smooth, well-watered canyon bottoms to follow on the Kaiparowits as there are in the Escalante, nor any published hiking guides. Routes are pencil lines on a topographic map. If the Escalante offers splendid wilderness trips for the novice, the Kaiparowits challenges the most experienced.

In the spring of 1988 this writer began a cross-Plateau trip by climbing the 1,500-foot-high wall called "The Cockscomb," carrying gallons of water in a heavy pack. I needed two days to cross Wahweap Canyon; in places I had to let my pack down with ropes, using finger- and toe-holds to descend canyon walls. Crossing Fourmile Bench, I got lost, dropped into the wrong sidecanyon and ended the day without water, miles from the nearest spring. Lack of potable water was a perpetual worry; in places I had to dig for it in the mud.

Only after seven days of exploration, camped at the brink of a huge amphitheater, did I see the first evidence of 20th-century man. Far away to the south, surrounded by stone monoliths, lay the glittering lights of Glen Canyon Dam.

In the annals of southern Utah exploration, the Kaiparowits Plateau is seldom more than a looming presence, always visible at a distance, but seldom actually visited. Clarence Dutton, author of the definitive geological study of the high plateaus of southern Utah, pondered the Kaiparowits from a safe distance of 60 miles away on the crest of Arizona's Kaibab Plateau: "Due northward," he wrote, "rises the great wall of the Kaiparowits Plateau. This giant cliff is 60 miles in length and nearly 2,000 feet high. Throughout its course it wavers but little from a straight line . . . . "

IN BRIEF

Index Map: Area No. 39

Highlights: North of Lake Powell, the land rises dramatically to a series of high plateaus broken by long cliffs and rugged drainages. Ancient juniper forests, large raptor populations, excellent hunting, and spectacular geologic displays highlight this remote and seldom-visited region.

Guidebooks: Hall (1982)

Maps: USGS 1:100,000 Escalante, Smoky Mountain

Area of wilderness proposals in acres:

Unit	UWC	BLM
Burning Hills	68,400	0
Cave Point	4,800	0
Carcass Canyon	72,600	0
Fiftymile Bench	11,100	0
Fiftymile Mountain	173,900	91,361
Horse Spring Canyon	27,900	0
Nipple Bench	31,600	0
Squaw Canyon	11,200	0
Wahweap-Paradise Canyon	228,000	0
Warm Creek	21,000	0
TOTAL	650,500	91,361

Adjacent wild lands: Glen Canyon National Recreation Area

Escalante

To Boulder, Utah

12

Horse
Spring
Canyon

Canaan
Peak

Dixie National
Forest

B.L.M.

Mud Spring Canyon

Carcass Canyon

Collet Canyon

To Bryce Canyon NP

Hole-in-the-Rock

Kodachrome

Straight Cliffs

Basin

Paradise
Canyon

Rogers
Canyon

The Cockscomb

Fourmile

Navajo
Canyon

Bench

Cottonwood Creek

Warm
Cr.

Burning
Hills

Wahweap
Canyon

Squaw
Canyon

89

Nipple
Bench

Coyote Canyon

Big Water

Lake

Powell

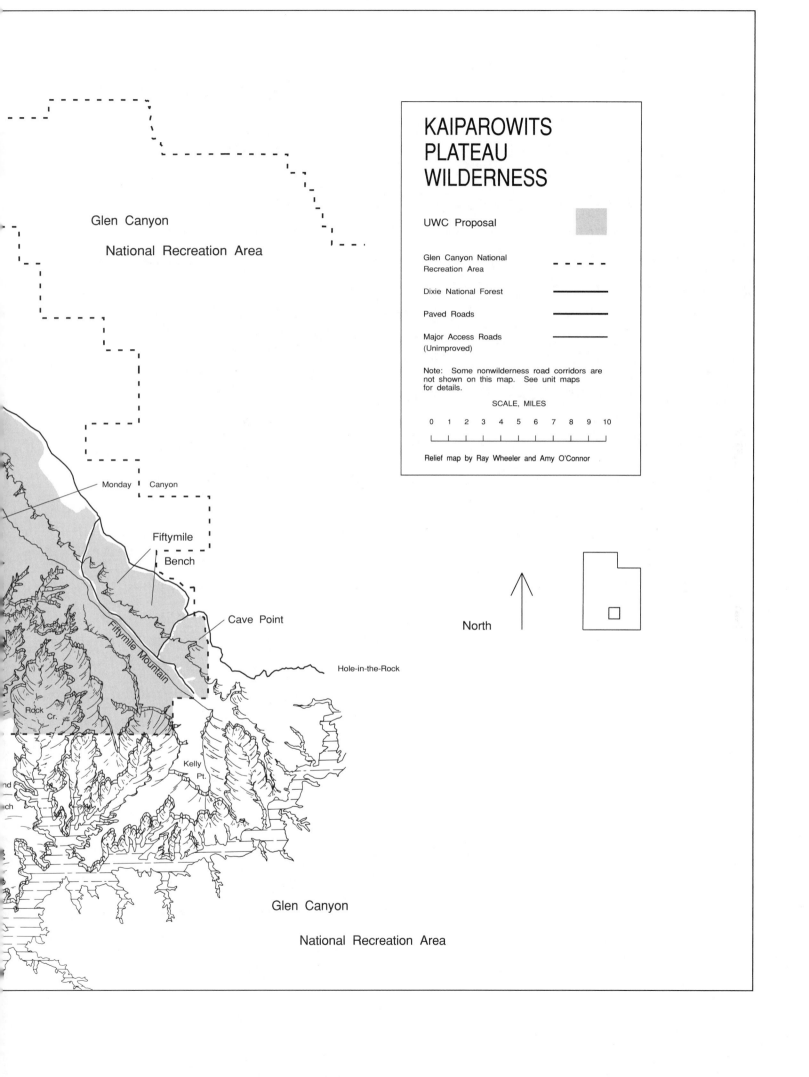

KAIPAROWITS PLATEAU WILDERNESS

UWC Proposal

Glen Canyon National Recreation Area

Dixie National Forest

Paved Roads

Major Access Roads (Unimproved)

Note: Some nonwilderness road corridors are not shown on this map. See unit maps for details.

SCALE, MILES

0 1 2 3 4 5 6 7 8 9 10

Relief map by Ray Wheeler and Amy O'Connor

Glen Canyon

National Recreation Area

Monday   Canyon

Fiftymile

Bench

Cave Point

Fiftymile Mountain

Hole-in-the-Rock

Rock Cr.

Kelly Pt.

Glen Canyon

National Recreation Area

North

The Utah Wilderness Coalition proposal would protect the sweeping vistas from Fiftymile Mountain and Fiftymile Bench, which form the eastern rampart of the Kaiparowits Plateau. The BLM failed to study the lower part of the Straight Cliffs in the Fiftymile Bench and Cave Point units (right edge of photo).

Tom Miller

Surrounded by the colorful canyons of the Paria, Escalante, and Colorado Rivers, the vast blue-green wedge of the Kaiparowits, with its wide, level benches, its broad canyons and harsh cliff-lines seems forbidding by contrast. Just reading place names on the map makes one's throat feel dry: Death Ridge . . . Carcass Canyon . . . Dry Bench . . . The Scorpion . . . The Burning Hills . . . Last Chance Gulch . . . Harvey's Fear. The geologist Herbert Gregory wrote in 1931 that " . . . vegetation in the Kaiparowits region has an unfriendly environment . . . . Many plants have no near neighbors; they stand as individuals in tracts of several acres or are present by twos or threes in areas of several square miles . . . . "

Yet the remoteness, the size, the harsh terrain, the heat, the aridity, the streams poisoned with alkali and arsenic, the wind, the silence when there is not wind, the overpowering solitude of the Kaiparowits—these are precisely the commodities which make it valuable. It is a fierce and dangerous place, and it is wilderness right down to its burning core.

Life in a Hard Place

The diverse landforms of the Kaiparowits, despite their harshness, host a remarkable variety of plants and animals. From south to north, the land rises 2,000 feet in a series of giant steps. Antelope graze in sage-dotted valleys on the southern perimeter. Grey shale badlands swarm against gold-colored cliff walls. As the valleys twist north into the rising land, they grow deeper and narrower, forming huge, branching canyon systems. Between the canyons lie the great benches of the Kaiparowits, carpeted with an ancient forest of juniper and pinyon pine. Still further north, the land rises to 7,000 feet at the northern rim of the Plateau. Deer, bear, cougar, coyote, bobcat, fox, and badger live in this high country, and its rugged cliffs and canyons are spotted with groves of fir, ponderosa pine, and spruce.

The first major environmental impact study of the region—the BLM's 1975 Kaiparowits Power Project EIS—noted the variety of species. "The Plateau is unique ecologically because there is a blending of both cold desert and warm desert species," concluded the study. "The harsh, arid terrain supports a surprisingly diverse population of small mammals," it continued, and " . . . the total number of [bird] species occurring in a year throughout the Kaiparowits area is surprisingly large."

Wildlife studies suggest that as many as 59 species of mammals, 200 species of birds, and 46 species of reptiles and amphibians may inhabit the Kaiparowits (BLM, 1976; 1986). Raptors are especially abundant—at least 22 varieties of hawks, eagles, and owls can be found on the Plateau. The very remoteness of this country is one of its greatest assets. Raptor populations, for example, "have not suffered the degree of loss common to many other areas," explains the Kaiparowits Project EIS, because "some of the major causes of mortality elsewhere are largely absent in the Kaiparowits area." Likewise, deer are abundant on Fiftymile Mountain, because "the inaccessibility of this high bench provides considerable protection from hunters." For plants, too, the Kaiparowits is a place of last refuge. Of the 841 plant species found on the Plateau, 42 are threatened or endangered, or are candidates for such listing—nearly half of those listed in Utah.

Culturally, as well as ecologically, the Kaiparowits is richly diverse. Situated at the intersection of three major prehistoric cultures, the Plateau has long been a magnet for archeological study. "From the first year of the Upper Colorado River Basin Archeological Salvage Project," wrote archeologist Elizabeth Lister in 1964, "it has been recognized that the Kaiparowits Plateau might contain important clues that would aid in answering questions in the archeology of the Southwest . . . . " At least 300 archeological sites have been recorded on the plateau, and in recognition of their scientific importance, the BLM has established a protection area called the Fiftymile Mountain Archeological District.

Coal Dreams

In the mid-1970s four of the West's largest utility companies launched a campaign to transform this wilderness into one of the largest industrial complexes in Utah. Their proposal—the Kaiparowits Power Project—called for the construction of a 3,000-megawatt power plant on Fourmile Bench, in the heart of the Kaiparowits. Coal for the plant would come from four underground mines in nearby Wesses Cove and on Smoky Mountain.

Today, to a visitor strolling among ancient pinyon pines on the proposed power plant site, the environmental impacts of the proposal are difficult to comprehend. Nine thousand acres of vegetation would have been destroyed during construction. A network of roads, power lines, pipelines, pumping stations, and coal slurry lines would have blanketed the western half of the Kaiparowits Plateau. A new road 67 miles long would have cut the Plateau in half, bringing the thunder of heavy truck traffic rolling across the heart of the area. Upper Wahweap Canyon would have become a 300-acre gravel quarry. A new road would have sliced the length of Wesses Canyon, destroying its natural springs and pools. One hundred and twenty million tons of solid waste would have been dumped in a 1,550-acre disposal area on Fourmile and John Henry benches. A new town of 20,000 would have wiped out 4,000 acres of critical antelope habitat on East Clark Bench.

The deer trotted away into the spruce, scarcely showing fear. Small game was abundant. Birds in flocks fluttered by at the approach of the horses . . . . Winding grey aisles of sage led back mysteriously; huge blocks of cliff choked some passages; caverns yawned. Along the outside of the main wall the scattered groups of oak, the lines of spruce, the dots of cedar looked as if they had been planted on the grey grassy level to insure the effect of stateliness, of park-like beauty.

Zane Grey
WILD HORSE MESA (1924)
[referring to Kaiparowits Plateau]

And there would have been the power plant—a blaze of lights invading the night sky, its 600-foot-high towers belching some 316 tons of pollutants *every* day into the clear air of southeastern Utah, sending a yellow haze drifting toward Bryce Canyon, Grand Canyon, Glen Canyon, and the Escalante River.

Yes, the Kaiparowits Plateau has coal—an estimated 15 billion short tons (Doelling and Graham, 1972). Only one half to one third of that coal is recoverable—perhaps 5 to 7 billion tons, or less than 4 percent of the nation's proven recoverable reserves. But only maximum development could justify the huge costs of construction in this remote region and the cost of transporting the coal to distant markets. The price of Kaiparowits coal would be the destruction of the wilderness character of the Kaiparowits Plateau.

Market Forces Halt Project

In April 1976, with demand for electrical power in southern California falling far short of projections, Southern California Edison abruptly backed out, and the Kaiparowits Power Project fell apart. Environmentalists were blamed for the project's demise. But in the end, economics determined the outcome.

The fundamental problem of Kaiparowits Plateau coal is the cost of getting it to market. With abundant and more accessible coal available elsewhere in the state and the nation, Kaiparowits coal may never be economic to mine. " . . . development of the Kaiparowits Plateau coal will face significant economic and environmental problems," explains the BLM in its 1986 Utah wilderness DEIS. "These problems include poor accessibility, lack of abundant water, high costs of underground mining, and competition from nearby areas where coal is more readily available and of better quality . . . . "

But risky economics and appalling environmental hazards alone may not prevent the development of Kaiparowits coal. If the developers cannot bring the power plants to the coal, then they may try to bring the coal to the power plants. In 1979, Union Pacific Railroad unveiled a proposal to build a new railroad across southern Utah and into the heart of the Kaiparowits coal fields. One year later, the U.S. Department of the Interior and the State of Utah conducted a major study of potential railroad and truck haul routes on the Plateau. "Despite delays, an agenda for development at Kaiparowits still exists," explains a study by the U.S. Geological Survey (Sargent, 1984). "Plans . . . . envisage shipment of coal to distant users by truck, conveyors, rail, and (or) slurry line."

The BLM Recommendation—Driven by Coal

The BLM wilderness review forcefully demonstrates that an agenda for developing Kaiparowits coal indeed still exists. When the agency announced its final wilderness inventory decisions in November 1980, it had cut nearly 400,000 acres of wild lands on the Kaiparowits Plateau.

According to the BLM, these lands lacked outstanding opportunities for solitude or primitive recreation. The Wahweap-Coyote roadless area, for example, was cut from the inventory because "although an opportunity for solitude is present, it is judged to be the equivalent of opportunities in other topographies of its kind . . . . " Solitude could not be found on the unit's extensive forested benchlands, the BLM concluded, because "the pinyon-juniper forest . . . does not offer superior visual screening on this terrain . . . . "

In the fall of 1980, Sierra Club representative Debbie Sease toured the Wahweap roadless area with Utah BLM state director Gary Wicks. Their helicopter touched down on the southern tip of Fourmile Bench. "We stood on the edge of far-as-the-eye-can-see, incredibly beautiful, utterly wild land," Sease recalls, "and I would say, 'Gary, why *are* you eliminating this?' And he'd say, 'Because there are no outstanding opportunities for primitive recreation.' And I'd say, 'And there's no outstanding opportunities for solitude, either?' And Gary would say, 'You're right. You can have solitude here, but it's not outstanding solitude.' And the man kept a straight face while he said that. Had the helicopter left us there . . . we would have known what outstanding solitude was all about."

Usurping the Role of Congress

The real reasons for the BLM's inventory omissions on the Kaiparowits had little to do with solitude. Wilderness study area designation would have been one more roadblock to the development of Kaiparowits coal. Though five BLM inventory team members had recommended WSA (wilderness study area) status for the majority of Kaiparowits wild lands, their recommendations were ignored by managers in the Cedar City district office. In effect, the local BLM managers assumed Congress's role, deciding what *ought* to be preserved, not just what *qualified* for preservation. "We tried to make the decision for somebody else, that we had no right to make," recalls one member of the inventory team. "We cut the pie the first time. If Congress never sees the whole pie, then they don't make decisions on it, do they? And that's exactly what happened."

The mismanagement of the BLM wilderness inventory on the Kaiparowits led environmentalists to appeal the agency's wilderness inventory decisions before the Interior Board of Land Appeals (IBLA) in 1981. To support their claim that six major roadless units had been overlooked, Utah conservation groups sent a small army of volunteers into the field. After reviewing their work—more than 200 pages of affidavits and 242 photographs—the IBLA returned a stunning verdict on the BLM inventory. In the largest reversal of an agency decision in the history of the IBLA, all 300,000 acres of appealed lands on the Kaiparowits were remanded to the BLM for reevaluation. Faced with the prospect of a lawsuit that could lock up the entire Kaiparowits region in litigation for years, the BLM reinstated nearly 80 percent of the appealed roadless areas to WSA status.

In 1986, when the BLM announced its draft wilderness recommendation for those Kaiparowits WSAs, few observers were surprised at the outcome. Of 12 key roadless units on the Kaiparowits Plateau, the BLM could find only two worth designating as wilderness. Virtually all proposed sites for power plants, railroads, coal mines, and coal transportation corridors had been omitted from the agency's wilderness recommendations on the Kaiparowits. Between the BLM's proposed Fiftymile Mountain wilderness unit on the northeast corner of the Plateau, and its proposed Wahweap wilderness unit on the southwest corner, some 450,000 acres of wild land had been zoned for industrial development. And in early 1990, the BLM announced that it would drop the Wahweap unit from its final wilderness recommendation, leaving only Fiftymile Mountain in its proposal.

Abundant Coal—Scarce Wilderness

The Utah Wilderness Coalition proposal for the Kaiparowits region is based on one simple premise: the land is superb wilderness and deserves to be protected as such. Wild areas as large as the Kaiparowits are extremely rare anywhere in the world. But coal and oil reserves such as those which may exist in the Kaiparowits region are small in comparison with those of other regions of the nation and the world.

Our 650,500-acre proposal would protect the sweeping vistas and the important archeological resources of Cave Flat and Fiftymile Bench. It would protect deer, bear, and cougar habitat among the rugged, forested cliffs and canyons along the rim of the Straight Cliffs. It would preserve thousand-year-old pinyon and juniper trees, and thousands of acres of critical winter forage for deer on the high benches at the interior of the Plateau. The Utah Wilderness Coalition proposal would ensure isolation for bighorn sheep in the rugged cliffs west of Glen Canyon, and would preserve critical antelope calving grounds in the valleys and badlands to the south. But most important, the Utah Wilderness Coalition proposal would preserve an opportunity to experience solitude, danger, excitement, and challenge found in few other places on earth.

Ray Wheeler

WAHWEAP-PARADISE CANYON UNIT

Highlights—The largest unit of the Kaiparowits wilderness, this expanse of wild country begins just 10 miles south of the town of Escalante and continues across Paradise Bench to the Wahweap Creek drainage northwest of Lake Powell. Long, winding canyons—in places narrow and intimate—dissect the plateau tops, offering both far-ranging vistas and remote hiking. The unit includes an area of ancient juniper trees on Fourmile Bench. The BLM dropped part of the unit (the Death Ridge WSA) in its wilderness study and recommended only 70,000 acres of the remainder (the Wahweap WSA) in 1986. The final recommendation omits the unit entirely. The unit is joined to the Grand Staircase wilderness at The Cockscomb, forming a huge wilderness expanse broken only by the Cottonwood Creek road.

Geology and landforms—The steeply dissected topography in the northern part of the unit is dominated by Death Ridge, at 7,956 feet one of the highest points in the Kaiparowits Plateau. Paradise Canyon and Escalante Canyon (a second one) cut through the high benches south of Death Ridge and converge to form Last Chance Creek in the Burning Hills unit. The land forms a staircase down toward the southwest, displaying the Carmel, Entrada, Dakota, Tropic, Straight Cliffs, Wahweap, and Kaiparowits formations. The BLM notes that the Wahweap Formation in the unit con-

In contrast to the forested top of the Kaiparowits Plateau, Coyote Creek flows past badlands such as these in the Wahweap unit. This unit was dropped from the BLM's wilderness recommendation and has since been proposed for such uses as filming motorcycle movies.

Jim Catlin

150

WILDERNESS AT THE EDGE

tains fossils. The Cockscomb, a prominent serrated ridge, lies at the western boundary.

Vegetation—The benchlands are heavily forested with pinyon pine, juniper, and in higher elevations, ponderosa pine. In the wash bottoms are serviceberry, snowberry, holly-grape, and buffaloberry, growing thick in places. Riparian vegetation grows along Wahweap and Tommy Smith Creeks as well as in Fourmile and Long canyons. The BLM lists Atwood's beardtongue (*Penstemon atwoodii*) on Death Ridge and in Right Hand Collet Canyon, and Cronquist aster (*Xylorhiza cronquistii*) in the southeastern part of its Death Ridge WSA; three sensitive plant species including *Cymopterus higginsii* (Higgin's biscuitroot), *Astragalus malacoides* (Kaiparowits milkvetch), and *Viguiera soliceps* (Paria sunflower) inhabit the Wahweap unit, according to the BLM. The Fourmile Bench Old Tree Area harbors a number of 1,400-year-old pinyon and juniper trees which have significantscientificvalue.

Wildlife—The transition from the hot, arid desert floor to the higher plateau country has created diverse habitats within the unit. Mule deer live here throughout the year; the tracks of black bear and mountain lion have been sighted in the northern part; there are even a few antelope on the lower, open benches. The BLM notes that bald eagles and peregrine falcons have been sighted in the unit.

Archeology and history—Inventories conducted for proposed coal-mining projects have identified numerous sites used by virtually every prehistoric Indian culture of the region. The sites are mostly suggestive of temporary hunting and gathering use rather than permanent dwellings, according to the BLM.

Recreation—Although few people visit the area due to its remoteness and lack of water, interesting hikes are available. Trap Canyon has a short "narrows," unusual in the Kaiparowits. The deeply incised Escalante and Paradise canyons offer a long loop trip; Paradise Canyon has narrow, convoluted sections and the western wall of Escalante Canyon has been likened to the Straight Cliffs. Views from Death Ridge take in the Henry Mountains, the Aquarius Plateau, and the whole of the Kaiparowits region. Wahweap, Tommy Smith, Fourmile Canyon, and Long Canyon have intermittent water. The stunning view of The Cockscomb entertains drivers on the Cottonwood Creek road, and the cliffs and benches rising beyond Lake Powell form a scenic backdrop to the reservoir.

BLM recommendation—In 1986, the BLM recommended only 70,380 acres of wilderness for its Wahweap WSA, and dropped the entire WSA from its final recommendation. The BLM dropped Death Ridge from wilderness study in 1980, claiming that the unit lacked outstanding opportunities for solitude. Conservationists appealed to the IBLA, pointing out that the size of the unit, its rough topography and winding canyons, and thick vegetation combined to give excellent solitude. The IBLA told the BLM to look at the unit again, and the agency reinstated it as a WSA. But in 1986, the agency omitted the unit from its recommendations, citing no specific reason. The agency left out 64,020 acres of the Wahweap WSA from its recommendation, excluding the upper canyons of Wahweap Creek and the northern part of the WSA. The BLM has also set aside an extensive area for pinyon-juniper chaining and sagebrush removal. Conservationists suspect that potential mineral resources underlie the BLM's decision. Exploration or development of these resources would entail high economic and environmental costs due to the remote, arid location; the area may never be suitable for mining regardless of wilderness designation.

Coalition proposal—We have identified a total of 228,000 acres that deserve wilderness designation. Our boundary follows narrow, little-used

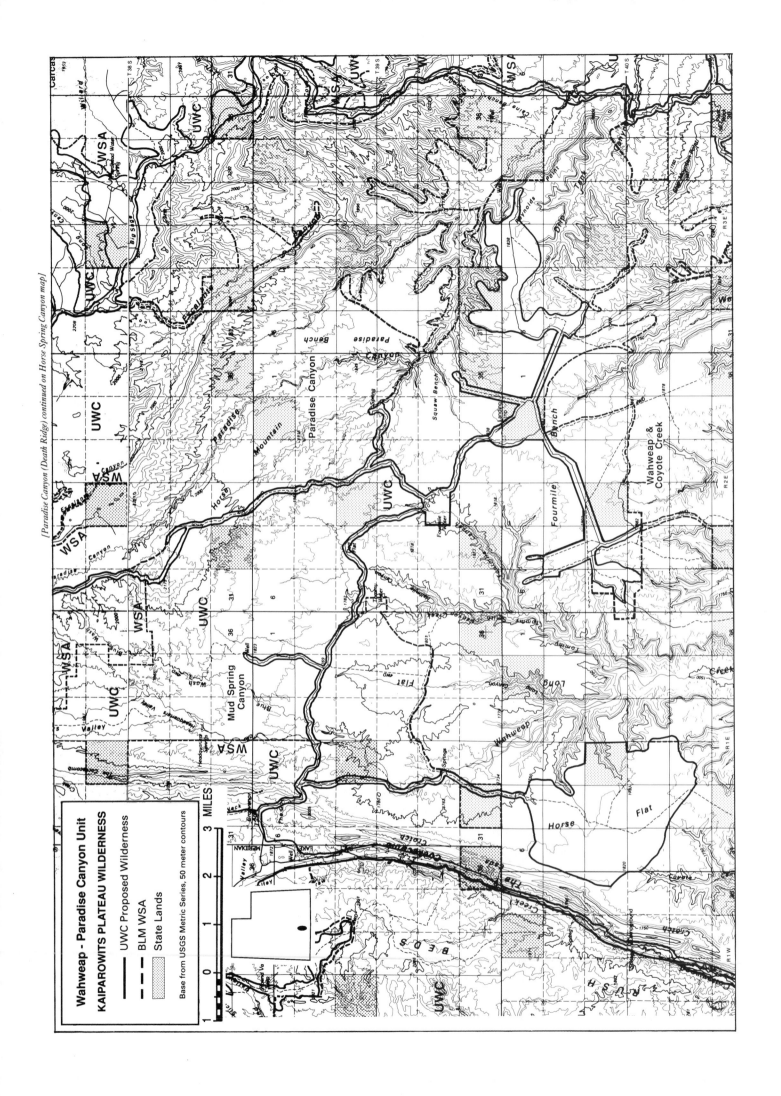

Wahweap - Paradise Canyon Unit
KAIPAROWITS PLATEAU WILDERNESS

— — UWC Proposed Wilderness
- - - BLM WSA
▨ State Lands

Base from USGS Metric Series, 50 meter contours

0 1 2 3 MILES

[Paradise Canyon (Death Ridge) continued on Horse Spring Canyon map]

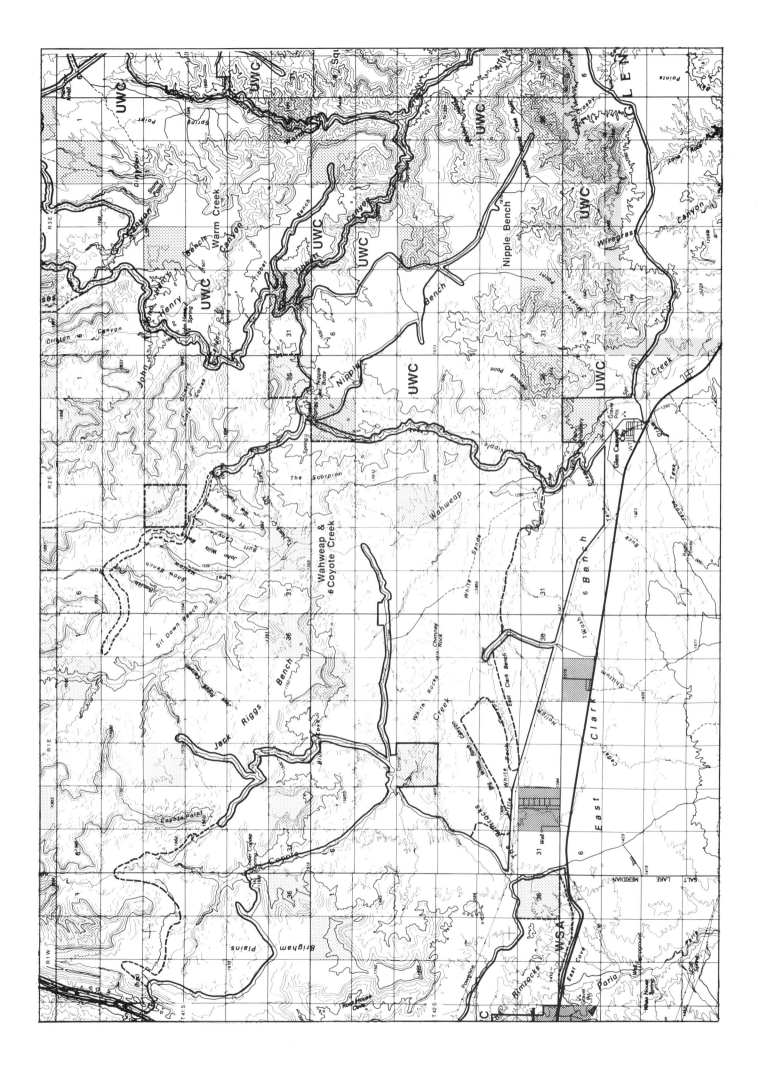

Hidden in the uplands of the Nipple Bench unit are significant paleontological finds, archeological resources, and the chance to experience complete solitude. The BLM, however, responding to plans for the now-defunct Kaiparowits Power Project, dropped the unit from its wilderness inventory.

Tom Miller

dirt roads, and excludes impacts along the periphery of the unit such as old chainings, seedings, and coal exploration tracks. We include undeveloped lands on Paradise Bench and Ship Mountain Point that connect the BLM's Death Ridge unit with its Wahweap WSA. We also include the Fourmile Bench Old Tree Area, which is absent from the BLM's recommendation. Primitive vehicle ways extend up Death Ridge and into Right Hand Collet Canyon and Escalante Canyon, but for most of their lengths, these ways are primitive, overgrown, and difficult to distinguish from the surrounding countryside. The known solitude and remoteness of this vast wild tract outweigh its speculative mineral values.

NIPPLE BENCH UNIT

Highlights—Nipple Bench abuts Glen Canyon National Recreation Area just north and east of Glen Canyon City. The bench offers a scenic view overlooking Lake Powell and the southern Kaiparowits Plateau, and is important habitat for big game. The mesa rim offers good hiking. The BLM dropped the unit in its initial wilderness inventory; we propose 31,600 acres of wilderness.

Geology and landforms—The prominent cliffs rising to the north above the Glen Canyon City-Smoky Mountain road (Route 277) are perhaps the most memorable part of this drive. Below the cliffs, isolated rocks sit on

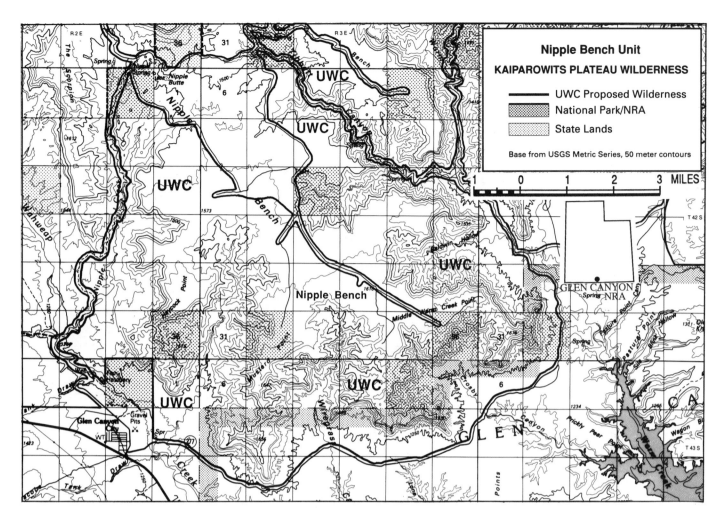

top of pedestals of mud and silt amid the badlands north of Lake Powell. Nipple Bench is an intermediate plateau, lying above these badlands and below the higher main plateau of the Kaiparowits. Nipple Canyon, shown on some maps as Lone Rock Canyon, forms the western boundary.

Plant communities—The lower badlands are almost devoid of vegetation; desert shrub species such as sagebrush, rabbitbrush, and shadscale grow in the higher areas.

Wildlife—The western part of the unit is antelope range (ERT, 1980, p. 3-21). Several springs located on the periphery of the unit are important for wildlife.

Archeology and history—Prehistoric site densities are expected to be high (more than 11 sites per square mile) on top of Nipple Bench, according to ERT (1980, p. 3-27). Sites would likely date from the Anasazi period. Studies for the Kaiparowits power project by the Museum of Northern Arizona located significant fossil vertebrates and plants in the north-central part of the unit. The investigators deemed these fossils to be of "major importance" (BLM, 1976, p. A-614). The fossils are in the Cretaceous Wahweap Formation, and include abundant fragments of turtle shells and dinosaurs, as well as several crocodile teeth. There is "an excellent chance that fossil mammals will eventually be discovered" here, the researchers noted.

Recreation—Hikes into rugged drainages below cliff walls begin along the road east of Glen Canyon City. The bench area can also be explored from a road leading from the north. This road goes to a scenic viewpoint at the southern cliff edge of Nipple Bench; it is cherrystemmed from our wilderness proposal.

BLM recommendation—The BLM claimed that the unit was impacted by mineral exploration, but these activities took place more than 20 years ago and are difficult to see on the ground. Nipple Bench was projected to have a water-supply pipeline and maintenance road as part of the Kaiparowits power plant (BLM, 1976); this may have influenced the agency to drop the unit.

Coalition proposal—We support designation of the natural portion of this unit as wilderness. The huge spaciousness of the bench offers heightened experience of solitude. Fewer than 300 acres of the unit are impacted. Our boundary cherrystems an often-used road across Nipple Bench to an overlook to the south. We also exclude about a thousand acres in the north-central part of the unit, where the BLM has been developing a water catchment system for livestock.

WARM CREEK UNIT

Highlights—Warm Creek is located in the heart of the Kaiparowits Plateau and is surrounded by the Wahweap-Paradise Canyon, Squaw Canyon, and Nipple Bench wilderness units. Its benches and canyon rims offer views across the southern edge of the plateau into the Glen Canyon National Recreation Area. A coal mine and processing facilities, formerly proposed here as part of the Kaiparowits Power Project, are once again proposed within the unit. Our wilderness proposal would preserve wildlife habitat, archeological resources, and backcountry recreation opportunities from further coal exploration that has thus far proven to be speculative.

Geology and landforms—John Henry and Wesses Canyons, which combine to form Warm Creek Canyon, separate the three major benches (Tibbets, John Henry, and Spring Point) that project into the unit from the central Kaiparowits Plateau. The benches, which, at an elevation of 5,000 feet lie below the higher parts of the Kaiparowits Plateau, are formed of the sandstones and mudstones of the Wahweap Formation of Cretaceous age; fossil vertebrates and plants are found in this formation. The canyons are cut into the Cretaceous Straight Cliffs Formation. Although the soils in the unit are fragile and susceptible to erosion, the Warm Creek drainage contributes relatively little sediment to Lake Powell (BLM, 1976, p. II-198). This may be due to the lack of human development in the unit.

Plant communities—Pinyon pine and juniper grow on benches, primarily in the northern part of the unit. Springs contribute to perennially moist areas in the upper parts of the main canyons, supporting tamarisk and a few cottonwood trees. The lower slopes are sparsely populated by grasses and shrubs such as shadscale, Mormon tea, fourwing saltbush, and sagebrush.

Wildlife—A small population of mule deer use the area, probably wintering in the canyons and moving to the higher benches in summer. The western part of the unit is habitat for antelope, which are commonly found farther to the west.

Archeology and history—Studies for coal development projects (BLM, 1976; ERT, 1980) indicate that prehistoric site densities are relatively high in parts of the unit, especially near springs which may have supported ancient agricultural uses. The sites consisted of lithic scatters (stone tool-flaking areas), campsites, and some rockshelters. One study (BLM, 1976, p. II-274) identified 26 sites within a single area proposed for coal mining, and an additional 17 sites adjacent to the mine. These studies, which covered less than 10 percent of the total area that would have been affected by coal mining, revealed over 600 prehistoric and historic sites.

Recreation—Warm Creek's location in the middle of the proposed Kaiparowits wilderness area gives it good opportunities for solitude. Views

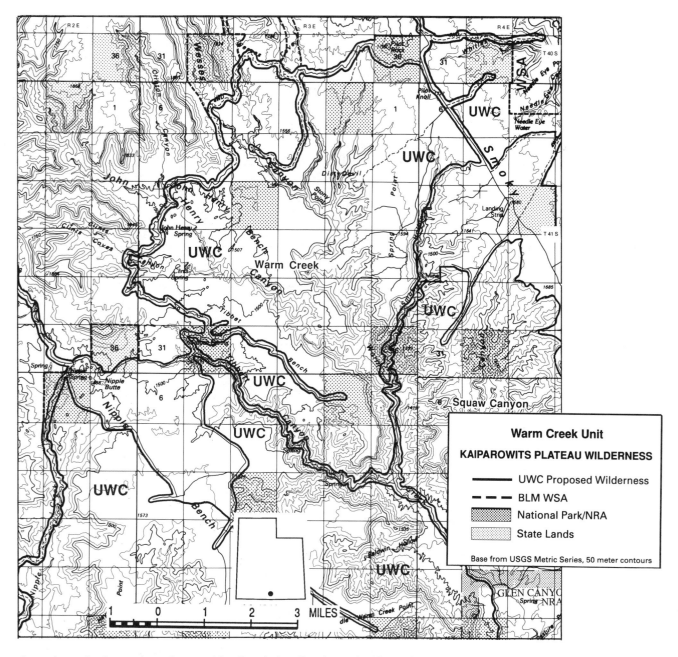

Warm Creek Unit

KAIPAROWITS PLATEAU WILDERNESS

——————— UWC Proposed Wilderness

– – – – – BLM WSA

National Park/NRA

State Lands

Base from USGS Metric Series, 50 meter contours

down into the lower benches and badlands leading into the Glen Canyon NRA are especially striking. The grand backdrop of the upper Kaiparowits Plateau is ever present to the north. Access is fairly easy from the dirt road up Smoky Hollow.

BLM recommendation—The BLM dropped Warm Creek from its wilderness inventory, claiming that coal exploration and engineering work for the Kaiparowits power project disqualified it for wilderness designation. But the old jeep tracks and drilling sites, located primarily in the northern and western parts of the unit, are slowly returning to a natural appearance after two decades of disuse.

Coalition proposal—We propose a 21,000-acre wilderness unit, taking in the undisturbed lands and excluding the primary vehicle ways that receive current use. Coal exploration tracks and scars across the sandy benches, the legacy of poor power-plant planning, should be allowed to fade. Our boundary excludes several primitive roads by cherrystems: one on Tibbet Bench that follows a pipeline from Tibbet Spring three miles to a stock watering reservoir and one on the north (North Branch Creek) four miles to a regularly used stock camp at a spring. The proposed Andalex coal mine would be located in Missing Canyon within the unit, but there

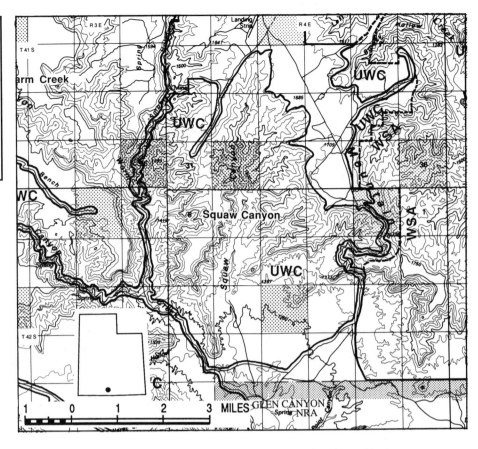

Squaw Canyon Unit

KAIPAROWITS PLATEAU WILDERNESS

——— UWC Proposed Wilderness

– – – BLM WSA

National Park/NRA

State Lands

Base from USGS Metric Series, 50 meter contours

1   0   1   2   3   MILES

is little market for coal from this region and the mine is unlikely to prove economic to operate. A new road is proposed down John Henry Canyon to provide access to the minesite.

SQUAW CANYON UNIT

Highlights—The south-central part of the Kaiparowits Plateau has dramatic vistas of isolated rock pillars, barren cliffs, and fluted canyon cliffs. The unit lies west of Burning Hills and east of Warm Creek. The BLM dropped the unit from review in its initial wilderness inventory; we recommend 11,200 acres for wilderness.

Geology and landforms—The unit is composed of steep, incised drainages with alternating short benches and cliffs which have carved out the west-facing side of Smoky Mountain. Smoky Hollow drains south along the western boundary of the unit to join Warm Creek. Squaw Canyon lies east of and parallel to Smoky Hollow in the center of the unit. The base of the cliffs in the unit is composed of Tropic Shale; the cliffs and bench tops are Straight Cliffs Formation. Smoky Hollow is the most scenic part of Smoky Mountain and possesses some of the most scenic vistas found in all of the Kaiparowits Plateau.

Plant communities and wildlife—Some pinyon and juniper grow on the Smoky Mountain bench in the northeastern part of the unit, with black-brush and sage predominating across most of the bench. The lower slopes are alkali scrub with barren shale badlands. Little information is available about the unit's wildlife resources; mule deer probably use the benches during the summer and the lower slopes during the winter.

Archeology and history—The unit is part of a larger area extensively used by the Kayenta Anasazi and later the Southern Paiute Indians; archeological site densities are expected to be moderate to high, based on studies for coal development in the area (ERT, 1980, fig. 3-6).

Recreation—Access is from a well-traveled secondary road leading 15 miles east and north from Glen Canyon City. As this road climbs up the

"Kelly Grade" to the top of Smoky Mountain, vistas open out across the cliffs and badlands of the unit. Hikes in Squaw Canyon begin from the Smoky Mountain bench on the north or from a primitive road leading up from Warm Creek on the south. This is rugged country and water is generally unavailable.

BLM recommendation—The BLM's initial inventory conclusion and rationale was terse for this area: "The naturalness of the unit has been impaired by extensive coal exploration activity and access roads." The BLM inventory map shows that these impacts are concentrated on the higher, flatter areas; there is a significant natural area in the lower and steeper parts of the unit. The agency probably dropped the unit because a coal haul route for the Kaiparowits power plant had been proposed across it.

Coalition proposal—Our field inventory shows that in the canyons themselves, there is almost no evidence of any human activity. The BLM simply failed to change its boundary to exclude only those significant human impacts as its inventory policy required. Coal exploration tracks northeast of the unit are still being used by vehicles and are excluded from our proposal.

BURNING HILLS UNIT

Highlights—Located in the core of the Kaiparowits Plateau between the Wahweap-Paradise Canyon and Fiftymile Mountain units, the Burning Hills unit rewards the visitor with treks down intimate, winding canyons and views across a rugged and colorful landscape. A 20-mile-long canyon system offers solitude, with water available in a few places. The unit is named for naturally occurring underground coal fires that have turned exposed hilltops red. The remaining coal seams have led the BLM to withhold a wilderness recommendation for the unit. But as in the rest of the Kaiparowits area, severe economic and environmental constraints render the coal of marginal value compared to the wilderness resource.

Geology and landforms—Two north-south ridges, Smoky Mountain on the west and Burning Hills on the east, are divided by a major canyon, Last Chance Creek, and its three large tributaries, Reese's Canyon on the east and Dry Wash and Drip Tank Canyon on the west. Last Chance Creek runs intermittently in its 20-mile course south to Lake Powell. The Burning Hills themselves are a series of pink, round-topped, rugged and steep hills, composed of Cretaceous strata, with many finger-like canyons below. Smoky Mountain has a precipitous, 800-foot-high cliff edge which forms a sheer wall much of the way to the floor of Last Chance Creek.

Vegetation—The typical pinyon-juniper forest of the Kaiparowits Plateau blankets the ridgetops in the north and west parts of the unit. In places mountain mahogany grows as tall as 15-20 feet. In the canyons and washes sloping off this plateau are found ancient juniper trees, scrub oak, and single-leaf ash, which turns golden-red in the fall. Rabbitbrush, serviceberry, blackbrush, and buffaloberry form a dense underscoring to the pinyon-juniper woodland. Small riparian areas line the canyon bottoms near springs, such as in Cigar Creek Canyon. The BLM notes the presence of two sensitive plant species: *Cymopterus higginsii* (Higgins' biscuit-root) on Smoky Mountain and *Penstemon atwoodii* (Atwood's beardtongue) in the north end of Dry Wash.

Wildlife—Mule deer are common here, and find winter range in the lower, southern exposures which stay clear of snow longer than the high plateau. The BLM lists cougar and various game birds as well, and suggests that some desert bighorn sheep introduced near Lake Powell may have migrated into suitable habitat within the unit. The BLM also notes that the sensitive Lewis's woodpecker and western and mountain bluebird

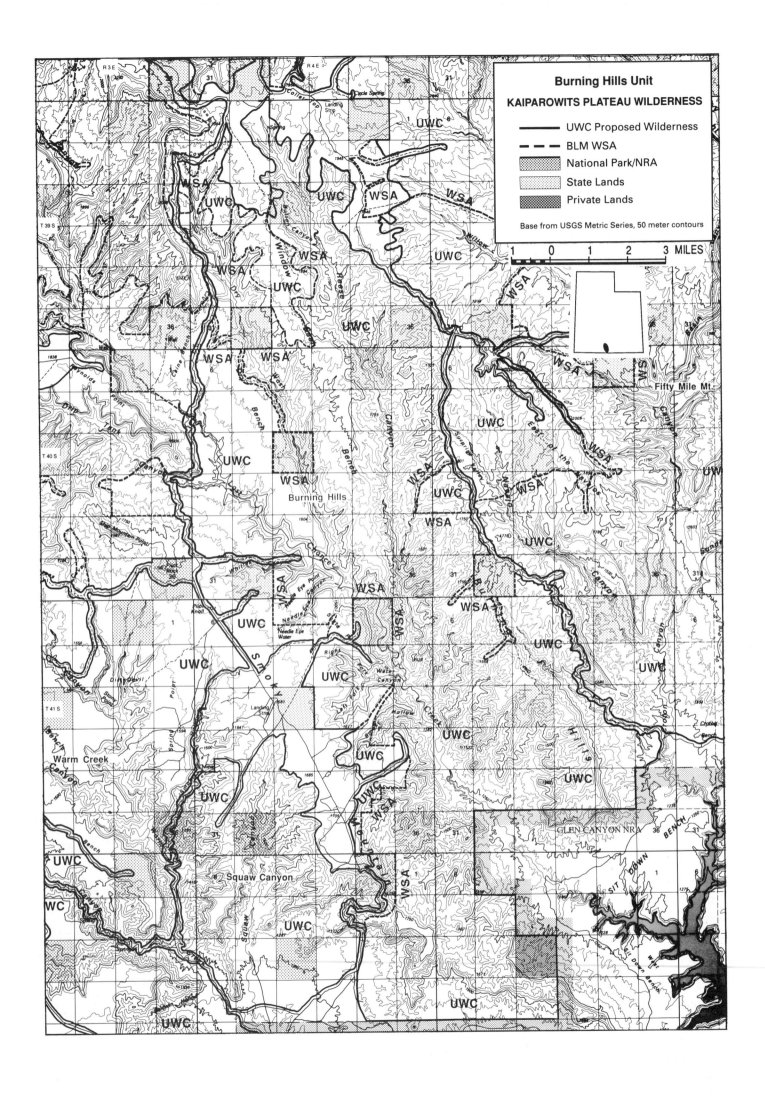

Burning Hills Unit

KAIPAROWITS PLATEAU WILDERNESS

—————— UWC Proposed Wilderness

– – – – – BLM WSA

National Park/NRA

State Lands

Private Lands

Base from USGS Metric Series, 50 meter contours

1   0   1   2   3   MILES

Fifty Mile Mt.

Burning Hills

Warm Creek

Squaw Canyon

GLEN CANYON NRA

are found in the unit, and that the endangered peregrine falcon and bald eagle found along Lake Powell may also use the unit.

Archeology and history—Our field researchers have found lithic scatters (stone chips, flakes, points, and scrapers) throughout the unit, including upper Reese and Last Chance canyons and the Burning Hills proper. Two rock shelters were also found.

Recreation—Remoteness, rugged topography, and dense vegetation on the bench tops and in the upper canyons make for outstanding opportunities for solitude. Water is limited, so day hikes and overnight trips starting from nearby roads are most suitable. The lower drainages are wide, deep, winding, and broken by numerous side drainages, with many opportunities for exploration. Hikes are possible down Last Chance Creek from the Smoky Mountain road, down Reese Canyon from near Collet Top, and in various smaller sidecanyons, notably Cigar Creek and Needle Eye. The bench tops are a good place to wander around, and the scorched, nearly barren Burning Hills themselves are a remarkable sight. Few people visit the unit at present.

BLM recommendation—After dropping Burning Hills from its wilderness inventory in 1980, the BLM designated a 61,550-acre WSA following formal appeals from Utah conservation groups. The agency recommended against wilderness for the WSA in 1986. No specific reasons were given, but its DEIS notes the presence of nearly 500 million tons of recoverable coal in the WSA. Seventeen pre-FLPMA coal leases cover 13,100 acres in the WSA, according to the BLM. The BLM's minerals consultant pointed out that any coal development here would encounter problems of "poor accessibility, lack of abundant water, high costs of underground mining, and competition from nearby areas where coal is more readily available and of better quality . . . . " (BLM, 1986).

Coalition proposal—We propose a 68,400-acre wilderness unit that forms a key part of our Kaiparowits Plateau wilderness. The unit is in a natural condition and offers fine solitude and recreation to the adventurous explorer. Intrusions include a few vehicle ways and oil drill pads around the periphery of the unit, and a few stock improvements, corrals, and an old cabin, all of which are listed by the BLM as "substantially unnoticeable" within its WSA. A mesa on the northern part of the unit, lying outside the WSA, has been partially chained but the remainder is natural and is included in our proposal. The potential for minerals other than coal are rated as unfavorable, and the unit has little promise of significant coal recovery. The outstanding wilderness values of Burning Hills clearly outweigh the limited development potential.

FIFTYMILE MOUNTAIN UNIT

Highlights—The scenic culmination of the Straight Cliffs, Fiftymile Mountain offers some of the most spectacular viewpoints on the Kaiparowits Plateau. The unit abuts wild lands in the Glen Canyon National Recreation Area that are recommended for wilderness designation by the National Park Service. Our proposal would preserve the diverse topography and landforms and varied wildlife habitat ranging from the high plateau to the desert environs of Lake Powell.

Geology and landforms—Deep canyons, upwarps, monoclines, and hogbacks contribute to the diverse topography of the unit. Included are 42 miles of the spectacular Straight Cliffs, the prominent wall that rises to the west of the Escalante country. Colorful exposures of the Navajo Sandstone are found in Rock Creek and Little Valley.

Plant communities—Most of the unit is covered with a pinyon-juniper forest, with the remainder in desert shrub and sagebrush vegetation types. The BLM (1986) notes that some canyons support aspen, maple, and oak, and upper Rogers Canyon supports Atwood's beardtongue, a sensitive species.

Wildlife—Fiftymile Mountain exhibits the diversity of wildlife found throughout the Kaiparowits Plateau. According to the BLM, the unit has habitat for as many as 45 species of mammals, 125 species of birds (including 13 species of raptors believed to nest in the unit), 17 species of reptiles, and 3 amphibians. Major game species are mule deer, cougar, and mourning doves. The unit includes some of the best habitat for mule deer on the Plateau. Peregrine falcon and bald eagle nest along Lake Powell to the south and have been sighted within the unit (BLM, 1986, p. 25).

Archeology and history—The Fiftymile Mountain Archeological District contains more than 300 sites, including Anasazi habitations and granaries (BLM, 1986).

Recreation—Diverse topography makes the Fiftymile Mountain unit conducive to solitude and wilderness activities. The unit is virtually unblemished, without a trace of roads or trails except at its boundaries. Extensive backpack trips through deep canyons and to spectacular vista points can be made here. Access is by jeep roads that form the northern and southern boundaries of the unit, branching off of the Hole-in-the Rock Road just south of Hurricane Wash and near the head of Sooner Gulch. Access from the west is more arduous, following two-wheel-drive and jeep roads leading west of U.S. Highway 89 at Glen Canyon City. Hall (1982) describes the hike to Navajo Point, which is the southeast tip of Fiftymile Mountain in the Glen Canyon NRA. The access trail up the Straight Cliffs is within this unit.

BLM recommendation—In 1986, the BLM recommended 92,441 acres for wilderness, but omitted major parts of the roadless area, including the face of the Straight Cliffs, the scenic walls of Collet Canyon, the area known as East of the Navajos, and the west side of Rogers Canyon—all despite the absence of identified conflicts with wilderness. The agency said these lands had "marginal wilderness quality"—in spite of the spectacular landforms and great solitude found in the area. The BLM's desire to encourage mineral development may be the real reason; the BLM allowed uranium exploration on the benches of the Straight Cliffs and in Rogers Canyon, consequently dropping much of the Straight Cliffs and Fiftymile Bench. (The mining road into Rogers Canyon has been abandoned and is largely reclaimed.) In several cases the BLM cherrystemmed impassable vehicle ways, such as a route from the Glen Canyon NRA into the southern part of the unit. The final BLM recommendation is expected to omit an additional 1,080 acres.

Coalition proposal—We support wilderness designation for 173,900 acres out of an original roadless area of 196,966 acres. Conflicts with wilderness designation are minimal. Oil and gas deposits, if present, are probably too small to recover; small, dispersed deposits of uranium, if they exist, will not be economic to mine in the foreseeable future. The BLM (1986, p. 35-36) considers coal production in the WSA unlikely in the near future because of high production costs and remote markets.

FIFTYMILE BENCH AND CAVE POINT UNITS

Highlights—At the foot of the southern Straight Cliffs above the lower Escalante canyons lie BLM wild lands separated from the surrounding vast wilderness only by primitive roads. The Escalante wilderness lies just to the northeast across the Hole-in-the-Rock Road; the drainages of Fortymile Gulch and Willow Creek begin in these units. The Fiftymile Mountain unit of the Kaiparowits wilderness rises to the south and west. Wilderness designation for these units will help to ensure that these essentially unbroken wild regions are not separated by inappropriate development. The BLM dropped both units from its wilderness inventory.

Geology and landforms—A thousand-foot-high cliffline of the Summerville, Morrison, and Dakota formations runs the length of these units, separating the Tropic Shale on Fiftymile Bench from the Entrada Sandstone canyons and sandy flats along the Hole-in-the-Rock Road. This cliffline is in turn dwarfed by the rampart of the Straight Cliffs rising above.

Plant communities and wildlife—Shadscale, blackbrush, ricegrass, and other species characteristic of these dry cliffs and foothills predominate. Mule deer and small mammals and other animals typical of desert benchlands are found here. The unit is probably an important transition zone for wildlife, containing forage that does not grow on the lower benches, and may serve as winter range for mule deer.

Recreation—Hikes along the cliffline reward visitors with grand vistas of the Escalante Canyons and much of southern Utah. The units are the foreground for views from Fiftymile Mountain and a scenic backdrop for the lower Escalante Canyons.

BLM recommendation—The BLM claimed that Fiftymile Bench was "heavily intruded from mineral exploration." It offered no description of the kind and location of impacts. Our field checks show that impacts are limited to less than 3 percent of the total Bench area. Those impacts are

The Kaiparowits wilderness can be intimate as well as intimidating; this sandstone outcrop is found in the Cave Point unit below Fiftymile Mountain.

Jim Catlin

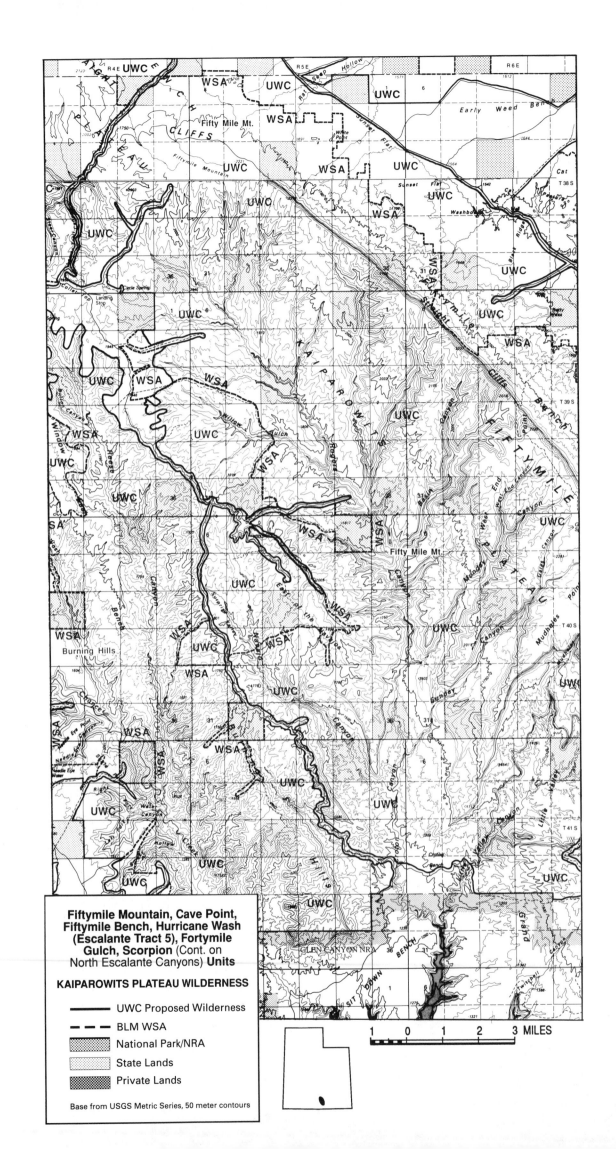

**Fiftymile Mountain, Cave Point,
Fiftymile Bench, Hurricane Wash
(Escalante Tract 5), Fortymile
Gulch, Scorpion** (Cont. on
North Escalante Canyons) **Units**

KAIPAROWITS PLATEAU WILDERNESS

——————— UWC Proposed Wilderness

– – – – – – BLM WSA

National Park/NRA

State Lands

Private Lands

Base from USGS Metric Series, 50 meter contours

1   0   1   2   3 MILES

not significant when compared with the surrounding wilderness area. In Cave Point, the BLM found no outstanding opportunities for solitude or primitive recreation, despite the unit's location at the center of Utah's largest expanse of wild lands, and its proximity to recommended wilderness in the Glen Canyon NRA. Although it acknowledged that "excellent panoramas of the Escalante River drainage and the Henry Mountains are possible from the top of the Fiftymile Bench" and noted the presence of spectacular 100-foot-high pedestal rocks, it classified them as "supplemental values" only.

Coalition proposal—Wilderness designation for 11,100 acres in Fiftymile Bench and 4,800 acres in Cave Point is needed to protect the scenic and recreational values of the Kaiparowits and Escalante wild regions.

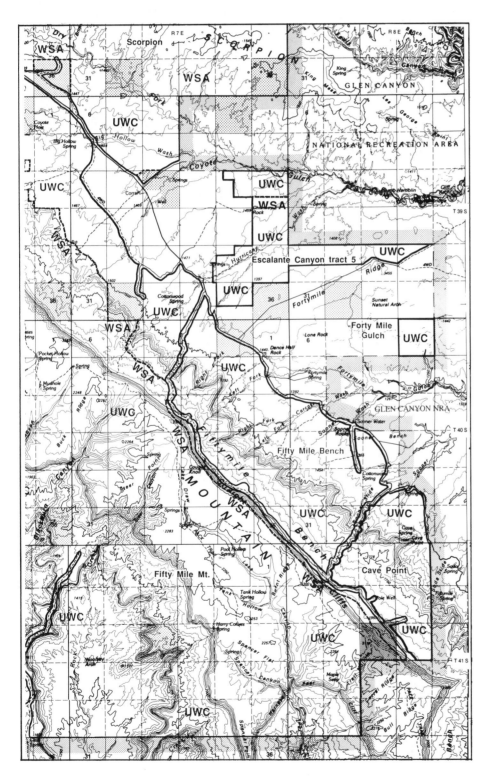

Water developments at Cottonwood Spring and Pole Well are excluded by cherrystems.

CARCASS CANYON UNIT

Highlights—The 2,000-foot-high Escalante Rim, the prominent escarpment west of the Hole-in-the-Rock Road, forms the backbone of this unit, located just south of the town of Escalante. Nearly 50 miles of deeply entrenched canyons, some more than 700 feet deep, cut through this northeastern rampart of the Kaiparowits Plateau. The BLM recommended against wilderness despite finding "outstanding" opportunities for solitude and primitive recreation in its 46,711-acre WSA. Our proposal includes the WSA, the adjacent Devils Garden study area, and additional wild lands.

Geology and landforms—The Escalante Rim, the northernmost part of the Straight Cliffs, rises to 7,500 feet in elevation and dominates the western view from the Escalante River canyons. The base of the rim grades out into gently rolling terrain cut by small canyons and washes, leading east to the oddly shaped arches and rock formations called Devils Garden, just off the Hole-in-the-Rock Road. Behind the rim, Carcass Canyon and Collet Canyon cut into the Kaiparowits Plateau, exiting the Straight Cliffs and forming Twentymile Wash. Avery Wash, which runs north to the town of Escalante, forms the western boundary of the unit.

Vegetation—Pinyon pine and juniper grow throughout most of the unit, except on nearly barren cliffs and the lower outwash benches below the rim. Some Douglas fir and ponderosa pine grow on the plateau. The BLM lists Atwood's beardtongue, a sensitive species, in the unit.

Wildlife—The cliffs of the unit are home to eight species of raptors, including the golden eagle, according to the BLM. Mule deer live throughout the unit and are prey for the occasional mountain lion.

Archeology and history—Scattered evidence of prehistoric use exists here, and the BLM notes that eight archeological sites have been recorded in its WSA.

Recreation—Canyon and ridge walking through broken terrain is available, with excellent views out across the Escalante canyons from the Escalante Rim. The BLM says that "The opportunity to explore in a primitive, unconfined recreational sense is considered outstanding." The constantly changing topography of mesas, slickrock ridges and domes, sand, and slickrock wash bottoms provide the challenge and visual interest to make excellent opportunities for foot travel and photography. Devils Garden, a compact area of unusual rock formations including Metate Arch, is popular with local and distant visitors alike. A small picnic area just off the Hole-in-the-Rock Road gives access to Devils Garden and the surrounding wilderness.

BLM recommendation—One of the least understandable nonwilderness recommendations in the State, the 46,711-acre Carcass Canyon WSA was highly rated in the BLM's 1986 DEIS. The agency, prodded to study the area by conservationists' appeals, found a "high quality of naturalness" throughout the area and "outstanding opportunities for solitude" in most of the area. Benchlands and ridges were downrated for solitude, yet the size of the area and the relative scarcity of visitors ensures solitude throughout. The BLM rated recreation highly: "The exploration-hiking opportunity is outstanding in complex canyon systems, along the top of the Straight Cliffs, and on the narrow ridges in the WSA"—in short, virtually the whole area. The reader of the 1986 DEIS is left to conclude what the agency will not state—that the potential to mine up to 200 million tons of coal, though currently infeasible, prompted its nonwilderness recommendation.

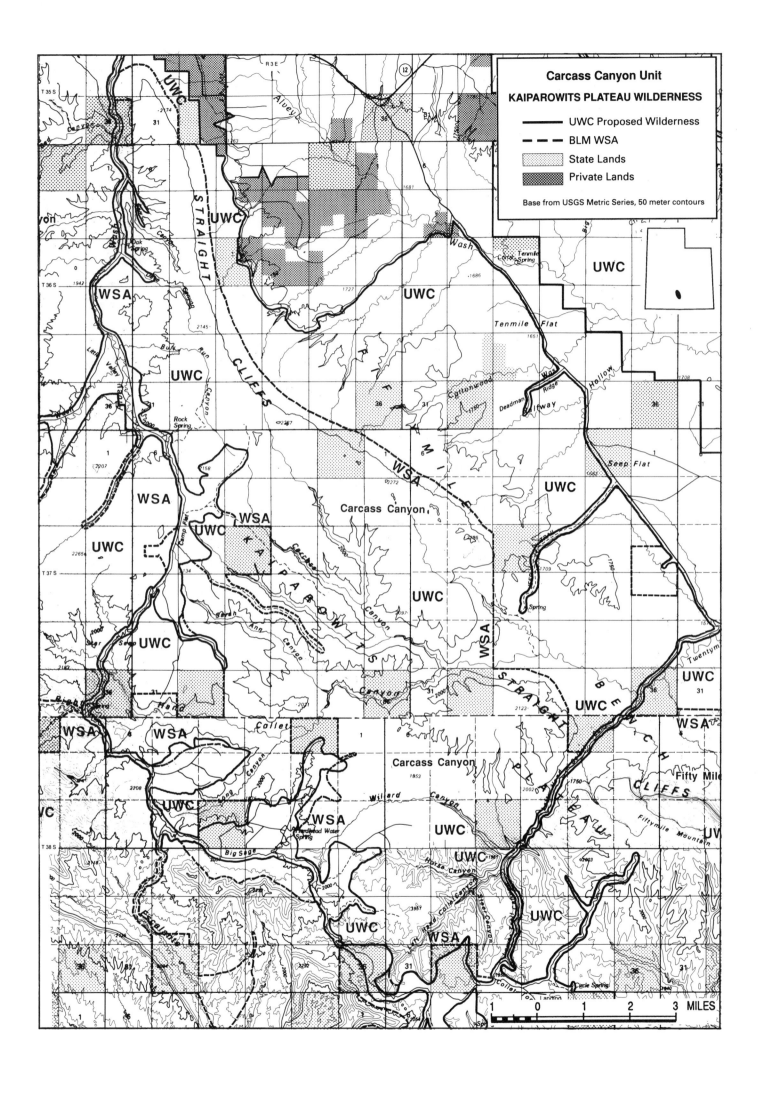

Carcass Canyon Unit

KAIPAROWITS PLATEAU WILDERNESS

———— UWC Proposed Wilderness

------ BLM WSA

State Lands

Private Lands

Base from USGS Metric Series, 50 meter contours

MILES

Coalition proposal—We propose a 72,600-acre wilderness, including the BLM's WSA, the Devils Garden Instant Study Area (excluding the small picnic area), and the washes and benches lying at the foot of the Straight Cliffs. A small, unnamed canyon between Carcass Canyon and Sarah Ann Canyon is also included; the BLM identified a road here but fieldwork indicates it's a sandy, but interesting, wash. Our boundary includes natural lands interrupted only by cherrystems above Seep Flat (at the eastern edge of the unit) and north of Hardhead Water Spring (at the southern edge). Mineral resources other than coal are unproven, according to the BLM's analysis. Some underground coal mining could be done from surface facilities outside the unit, but the high scenic and recreational value of the area, along with the dubious economics of mining, points to wilderness designation.

HORSE SPRING CANYON UNIT

Highlights—Like the rest of the Kaiparowits Plateau, Horse Spring Canyon is wilderness in the classic sense—unknown, little visited; a refuge for wildlife and an adventurer's destination. In its many alcoves and canyons one can find a natural arch, petrified wood, and Indian rock art. The BLM deprived Horse Spring Canyon of interim protection by claiming its solitude and recreation opportunities were not outstanding when compared to nearby slickrock areas.

Geology and landforms—Mitchell, Willow Spring, and Horse Spring canyons and their many tributaries wind through the alternating sandstones

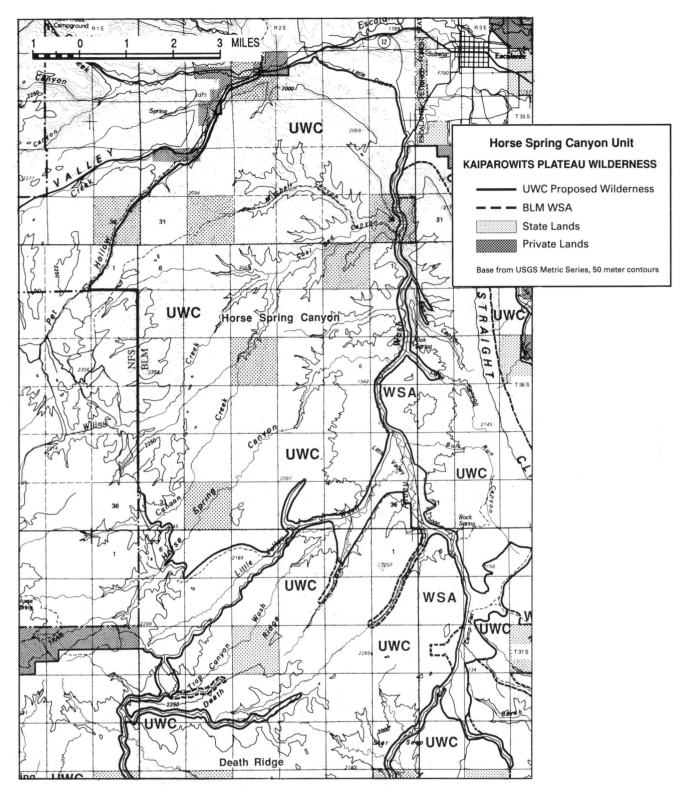

Horse Spring Canyon Unit

KAIPAROWITS PLATEAU WILDERNESS

UWC Proposed Wilderness
BLM WSA
State Lands
Private Lands

Base from USGS Metric Series, 50 meter contours

and softer strata of the Straight Cliffs Formation. The canyons are separated by forested bench tops.

Plant communities and wildlife—A dense pinyon-juniper forest mixed with sagebrush and ponderosa pine covers the unit. Atwood's beardtongue and the sweetvetch *Hedysarum boreale*, candidate species for threatened or endangered listing, are found in the unit. Mule deer and, occasionally, cougar are found in the unit.

Archeology and history—The BLM reports petroglyphs, pictographs, granaries, cave habitation sites, and open campsites.

Recreation—The twisting sidecanyons in this unit often narrow to five feet in width. Hiking can be rugged here, with boulders and fallen trees blocking the path. But these features also make for challenging and outstanding hiking, while providing both natural beauty and solitude. Hikers, backpackers, and horseback riders in this unit will find not only some beautiful wild country but if they look closely, they may spot Indian rock art, granaries, and petrified wood and fossils. Horizon Arch and other natural rock openings are also waiting to be found. The Alvey Wash Road leading southwest from Escalante gives access to the east side of the unit. The mouth of Willow Creek Canyon is about four miles from town; the mouth of Horse Spring Canyon, about seven miles.

BLM recommendation—In its 1980 intensive inventory decision, the BLM bisected this unit along an impassable and substantially unnoticeable vehicle way in Mitchell Canyon and decided that it lacked outstanding opportunities for solitude or primitive recreation. Conservationists appealed this decision to the IBLA which remanded the case to the BLM for further evaluation. The agency again found no outstanding opportunities claiming that "superior examples" of solitude in similar terrain were found "along the Table Cliffs Plateau, Escalante Mountain, Canaan Peak, and the Aquarius Plateau"—all Forest Service areas which that agency had not been recommended for wilderness. Conservationists appealed again. The IBLA affirmed the BLM's decision this time, saying that the "BLM necessarily makes subjective judgments which are entitled to considerable deference when challenged on appeal." Conservationists continue to be amazed at the way in which the BLM used its "subjective" judgment to exclude lands with perceived coal and uranium conflicts.

Coalition proposal—The Coalition proposes a 27,900-acre wilderness unit to protect this northern corner of the Kaiparowits Plateau. It contributes to the diversity of the larger wilderness area with its relatively wet, northeast-flowing canyons. It is tied to the rest of the Kaiparowits wilderness by its proximity to the Wahweap-Paradise Canyon unit on the south and the Carcass Canyon unit on the east.

THE ESCALANTE CANYONS WILDERNESS

Summary

Just four generations ago the Escalante River was unknown to the outside world. Hidden in a remote basin in south-central Utah, ringed by formidable cliffs and impassable canyons, the river was unmapped and unnamed until 1872. A century later the Escalante River basin remains one of America's most remote and mysterious landscapes, if somewhat better known. Rising in the lake-dotted meadows of the Aquarius Plateau, the Escalante River descends a vertical mile on its 125-mile journey to Glen Canyon, tumbling through forests of aspen and ponderosa before entering the vast expanse of bare rock that forms the floor of the river basin. Into that stone floor the river and its tributary streams have carved a thousand-mile labyrinth of interconnected canyons.

Some 400,000 acres of the Escalante wild lands are protected within Capitol Reef National Park and the Glen Canyon National Recreation Area. While the Park Service will prohibit any new development on at least 90 percent of its share, the BLM and Forest Service together plan to open two-thirds of their roadless lands in the region for mineral exploration, timber cutting, and the construction of hundreds of miles of associated roads.

Under the Rim of the Aquarius

Boulder Mountain is the brooding giant of southern Utah landforms. To travel anywhere near it is to experience its gravitational pull. On its long axis, the mountain is 25 miles in diameter. A walk around its base would be a journey of more than 100 miles. Its summit, roughly 12 miles in diameter and 50,000 acres in size, is the eastern extension of the Aquarius Plateau. Aquarius is Latin for "water-bearer," and the name is most fitting. Sailing among the clouds at an elevation of 11,000 feet, the plateau's broad, level, glacier-scoured surface collects moisture in hundreds of shallow lakes, and divides it among four major watersheds.

"The Aquarius should be described in blank verse and illustrated upon canvas," wrote the 19-century geologist Clarence Dutton. "The explorer who sits upon the brink of its parapet looking off into the southern and eastern haze, who skirts its lava cap or clambers up and down its vast ravines, who builds his camp-fire by the borders of its snow-fed lakes or stretches himself beneath its giant pines and spruces, forgets that he is a geologist and feels himself a poet."

A Thousand-Mile Maze

From the southeastern rim of the Aquarius, Dutton could see out over the Escalante River basin, whose floor lay more than 5,000 feet below him. The basin is ringed by gargantuan landforms. To the west lie the Escalante Mountains and the Table Cliff Plateau. To the south, the 2,000-foot-high wall of the Straight Cliffs runs for 50 miles to the brink of Glen Canyon. To the east, the blue-green domes of the Henry Mountains loom above the 1,000-foot-high, 100-mile-long hogback called Capitol Reef. At the center of the basin lies the maze of canyons carved by the Escalante River and its tributaries.

A century after Dutton's visit, this remarkable landscape still retains its primeval character. Roads, mining, agriculture, and logging have nibbled around its edges, but the vast majority of the region—nearly one million acres of Forest Service, Park Service, and BLM-managed public land—remains wild. The well-watered canyons of the Escalante have inspired a guidebook featuring 350 miles of backcountry hiking routes (Lambrechtse, 1985). In springtime, adventurous river-runners boat the Escalante in kayaks, canoes, and small rafts. Wildlife is abundant and diverse. The region provides habitat for as many as 270 species of mammals, birds, reptiles, amphibians, and fish, according to the BLM. Rainbow, cutthroat, and brown trout dart in its streams and lakes. Deer, bear, cougar, and elk roam its forested highlands. Coyote, antelope, and bands of wild horses can be found in its valleys, and desert bighorn sheep scramble among its cliffs and canyons.

Above all, the Escalante wilderness has beauty. There are slot canyons 100 feet deep narrowing down to 10 inches in width. There are cliff walls honeycombed with grottoes, alcoves, and caves. There are smooth-walled amphitheaters muraled with desert varnish and patterned with conchoidal fractures, swirls of crossbedding, and prehistoric rock art. There are rincons, natural bridges, arches, fins, domes, pinnacles, sinkholes, solitary monoliths of sculptured stone. There are cool canyon bottoms, clear springs, groves of whispering cottonwood. Above the canyon rims there are sweeping terraces of cream and rose-colored stone. Still higher there are forests of ponderosa and aspen, and finally, above all else—the roof of one world and the floor of another—the mosaic of forest, lake, and meadow, at the summit of the Aquarius Plateau.

Escalante National Monument—the 4.5-million-acre-Solution

Such landforms have made the Escalante wilderness one of the natural wonders of the West. It is a popular destination for Utahns and for visitors from all over the nation and world. Utahns have long admired this

IN BRIEF

Index Map: Area No. 40

Highlights: Famed for their enchanting glens and hanging gardens carved into a sandstone desert, the Escalante River Canyons attract hikers from all over the world. Crucial pieces of this wilderness are open to development that would sever the unbroken sweep of wilderness from Boulder Mountain to Lake Powell.

Guidebooks: Lambrechtse (1985), Hall (1982), Kelsey (1986a)

Maps: USGS 1:100,000 Escalante, Smoky Mountain, Hite Crossing, Loa

Area of wilderness proposals in acres

Unit	UWC	BLM
Colt Mesa	23,500	0
Dogwater Creek	3,500	0
Fortymile Gulch	640	0
Fremont Gorge	19,400	0
Hurricane Wash (Escalante Tract 5)	4,300	760
Long Canyon	16,400	0
N. Escalante Canyons	144,000	91,558
Notom Bench	8,400	0
Phipps-Death Hollow	43,500	39,256
Scorpion	38,100	14,978
Steep Creek	34,400	20,806
Studhorse Peaks	19,500	0
TOTAL	355,640	167,358

Adjacent wild lands: Dixie National Forest; Glen Canyon National Recreation Area; Capitol Reef National Park

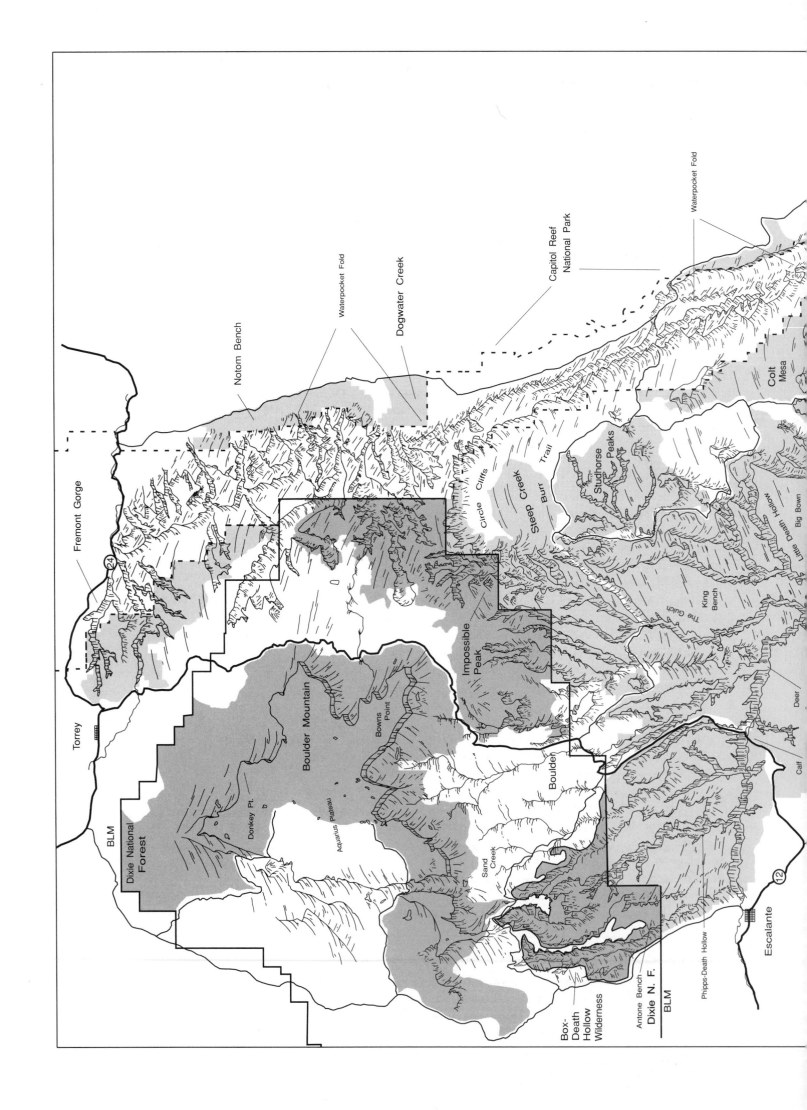

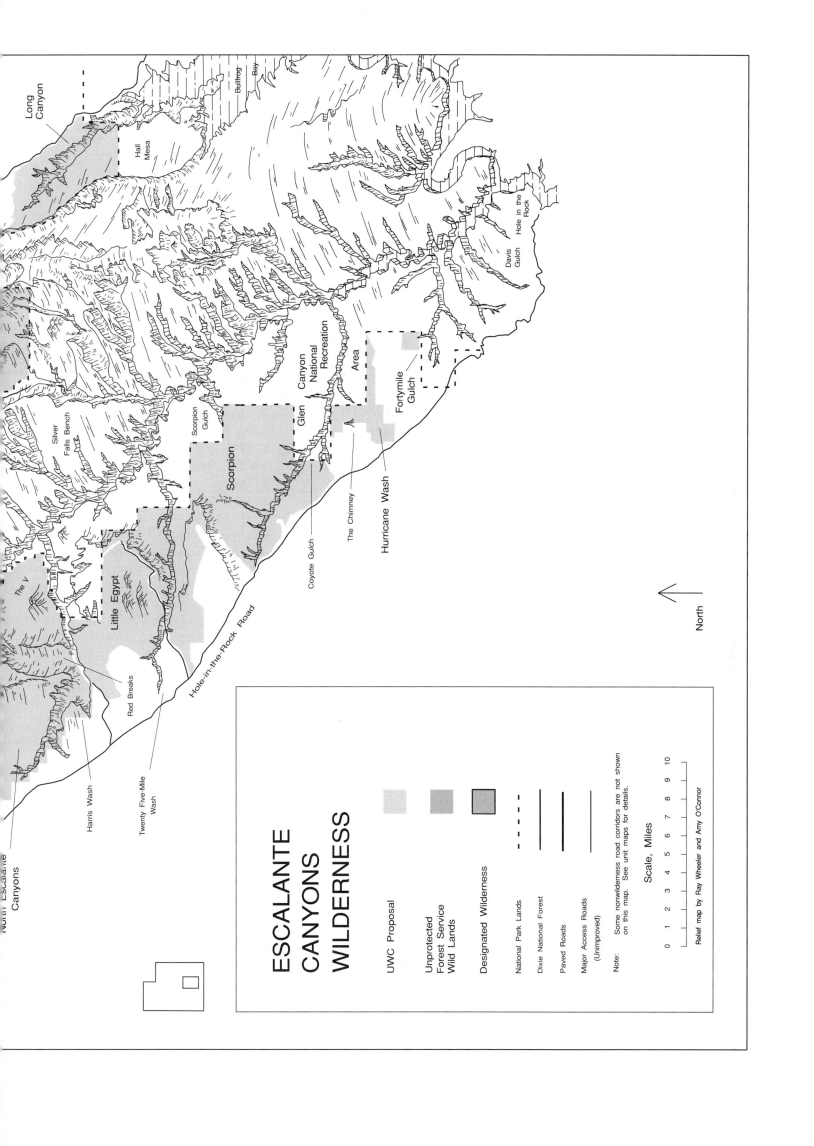

ESCALANTE CANYONS WILDERNESS

UWC Proposal

Unprotected
Forest Service
Wild Lands

Designated Wilderness

National Park Lands

Dixie National Forest

Paved Roads

Major Access Roads
(Unimproved)

Note: Some nonwilderness road corridors are not shown
         on this map.   See unit maps for details.

Scale, Miles

0 1 2 3 4 5 6 7 8 9 10

Relief map by Ray Wheeler and Amy O'Connor

North

Long
Canyon

Hall
Mesa

Bullfrog
Bay

Hole in the
Rock

Davis
Gulch

Fortymile
Gulch

Glen
Canyon
National
Recreation
Area

Scorpion
Gulch

Scorpion

Silver
Falls Bench

The V

Little Egypt

Red Breaks

Harris Wash

Twenty Five-Mile
Wash

Hole-in-the-Rock Road

Coyote Gulch

The Chimney

Hurricane Wash

North Escalante
Canyons

There is a fairy tale quality to that canyon. Escalante is sliced from beautiful rock that has been sculpted on a grand scale. Every side canyon conceals an arch or cave or vault in sandstone colors of cream, beige, salmon, pink, and brown. The bottom is gentle and generous, with green plants, willows, and cottonwood trees beside the river.

Kent Frost

MY CANYONLANDS (1971)

landscape, and they have repeatedly sought to protect the Escalante region within national parks or monuments. The first such proposal came in 1936, when the National Park Service identified a potential Escalante National Monument of 4.5 million acres, encompassing virtually the entire Colorado River canyon system between the towns of Escalante and Moab. Despite a favorable report by the Utah State Planning Board, which concluded that "the proceeds due directly or indirectly to tourist business will mean more to Southern Utah than those from any other use to which this barren and almost unproductive area may be put" (Richardson, 1965), powerful development interests eventually killed the proposal. But public support for protection remained strong. By the end of 1972, Federal legislation had added some 400,000 acres of Escalante wild lands to the National Park System within Capitol Reef National Park and the Glen Canyon National Recreation Area. And in 1984, Congress designated the 26,000-acre Box-Death Hollow Wilderness on National Forest land at the headwaters of the Escalante.

Despite such efforts, the majority of the Escalante wild lands—nearly 200,000 acres of Forest Service land and over 350,000 acres of BLM land—remains unprotected. And in recent years commercial development has accelerated. In 1980, the Forest Service suddenly raised timber sale volumes on the Dixie National Forest from 5 million to 20 million board feet per year. On Boulder Mountain the effect of the new harvest quotas was devastating. Between 1980 and 1987, loggers swept across its southern and western flanks, blading at least 100 miles of road and transforming 25,000 acres of ponderosa pine forest into a maze of logging roads, tree stumps, and slash.

During the next five decades, the Forest Service plans to allow 80 percent of the harvestable timber on the Dixie National Forest to be logged, according to a forest plan issued in 1986. More than 700 miles of roads would be constructed or upgraded. The plan's stated goal is to eliminate two-thirds of the remaining virgin timber, leaving old growth on less than 10 percent of the Forest.

At the headwaters of the Escalante, the planning documents call for a kind of logging blitzkrieg. When virtually every acre of harvestable ponderosa forest has been cut around the southern, eastern, and northern flanks of the Aquarius Plateau, the loggers will move up into the spruce and fir on its summit, where they will cut from rim to rim, slicing an estimated 60 miles of roads across 30,000 acres of lake-dotted forest.

BLM Wild Lands: The Missing Link

BLM wild lands are vital to the integrity of the Escalante region, for they lie at its center, linking the National Forest lands at the river's headwaters with the deep, scenic canyons within Glen Canyon National Recreation Area. They provide critical winter range for deer and elk which summer on the forested slopes of the Aquarius. Spanning the core of the Escalante River basin, they fill the view from any vantage point around its perimeter. The majority of hiking opportunities in the region lie on BLM lands, and a float trip down the Escalante—a candidate for Wild and Scenic River designation—is for most of its distance a journey through BLM-managed lands.

Unfortunately, while the BLM does recommend wilderness protection for the core of the Escalante Canyons, its would leave almost 200,000 acres of wild lands open to development—lands of critical importance to the scenic, recreational, and biological integrity of the entire region.

The BLM's development-oriented management philosophy may have severe consequences for the Escalante wilderness. In the southern portion

of the Circle Cliffs amphitheater, for example, the BLM would leave more than 60,000 acres of wild lands unprotected to allow the development of tar sand and uranium. The proposed tar sand development zone may reach southward from the rim of the Circle Cliffs to the Escalante River, overlapping 19,000 acres within the North Escalante Canyons WSA. This portion of the WSA contains four of the Escalante's most dramatic and beautiful tributary canyons: Horse Canyon, Wolverine Canyon, the North Fork of Silver Falls Canyon, and Little Death Hollow.

In its 1986 draft wilderness EIS, the BLM omitted the entire 19,000-acre segment from its proposed North Escalante Canyons wilderness—and left no doubt as to the reason for the omission. "The objective . . . is to analyze as wilderness that portion [of the WSA]...that would have the fewest conflicts with potential future mineral development," the draft EIS narrative explains. "The major area that would not be designated . . . is within the Circle Cliffs Special Tar Sand Area."

Such explanations suggest that the BLM's management philosophy is to allow development *wherever* it may appear feasible, no matter how profitless or destructive such development may be. Within the North Escalante Canyons WSA, the BLM is prepared to allow permanent scarring of 19,000 acres to recover an estimated 14 million barrels of oil—enough to meet the nation's current demand for less than one day.

Peekaboo Canyon is part of the thousand-mile-long labyrinth of canyons cut into the stone floor of the Escalante River basin. This haunting slot canyon was left out of the BLM's 1986 draft wilderness recommendation for the Scorpion unit, but public concern may have persuaded the agency to relent.

Bruce Barnbaum

Numberless tributary canyons open into [the Escalante River] along its course from both sides, so that the entire platform through which it runs is scored with a net-work of narrow chasms. The rocks are swept bare of soil and show the naked edges of the strata. Nature has here made a geological map of the country and colored it so that we may read and copy it miles away.

Clarence Dutton
GEOLOGY OF THE HIGH PLATEAUS OF UTAH (1880)

Should such development ever take place, its visual and environmental impacts could be devastating. In the forested valleys and high, narrow ridgetops at the headwaters of the Escalante, full-field development of carbon dioxide gas and associated oil deposits will require—at a minimum—97 production wells, 11 4-story compressor-dehydrator plants, 197 miles of power lines and pipelines and nearly 100 miles of new roads. The impacts from tar sand development would be even worse. According to a 1984 BLM environmental impact study, tar sand development in the Circle Cliffs could require the drilling of 27,000 injection and recovery wells across 49,000 acres of land. Developers would construct a 640-acre industrial park at the head of Wolverine Canyon, installing a power plant, a sewage plant, an air strip, and a work camp for 500 on-site construction workers. At any one time, some 200 wells would be active. Dozens of droning air compressors would raise ambient noise levels by 230 percent. The project would require hundreds of miles of new roads, some cutting up through the Circle Cliffs onto the benchlands that rim the Escalante River Canyon. The existing access road—the Burr Trail—would be widened, realigned, and paved to accommodate 140 truck-trips per day. Day and night, 18-wheel tanker trucks would roar up the steep grades, sending a low thunder echoing through the canyons of the Escalante.

Such proposals look far into an uncertain future. Under foreseeable market conditions, neither tar sand nor carbon dioxide is profitable to develop. Carbon dioxide gas, used to force heavy oil residues from depleted oil fields, must be transported at great cost to distant markets in Texas or California. Tar sand development is both costly and inefficient, recovering less than 30 percent of the in-place oil. And in the slow-growing forests of southern Utah, logging is notoriously unprofitable. On the Dixie National Forest, timber revenues have never matched the Forest Service's costs for the construction of new logging roads and the management of timber sales. The Forest Service is now losing a million dollars a year on the Dixie National Forest.

With wilderness values so exceptional—and development potential so marginal—one might expect that the Forest Service and the BLM would vigorously promote wilderness protection for the entire Escalante River basin. Unfortunately, intense lobbying by the mining and timber industries has persuaded both agencies to do just the opposite.

The BLM does recognize that the Escalante country is a scenic and recreational resource of national importance. In 1989 the agency floated a proposal to designate 470,000 acres surrounding the Escalante River as a National Scenic Area or National Conservation Area. But such designations do not preclude mining and new road construction—while wilderness designation most definitely does. And even if mining does not occur, leaving the wilderness open in anticipation of mining will also allow indiscriminate off-road vehicle use to damage vegetation, watersheds, and solitude.

The BLM's refusal to promote wilderness protection for the entire Escalante region is clearly rooted in a commitment to tar sand, uranium, oil and gas, and many other forms of development.

Unified Wilderness

The Utah Wilderness Coalition's 355,640-acre wilderness proposal for the Escalante region is rooted in a very different philosophy—a conviction that the scenic, biological, and recreational resources of the Escalante River basin are worthy of protection. Where the BLM envisions a patchwork of wilderness and development, the Coalition seeks to protect all lands which remain wild.

On the northeastern border of the Escalante country, the Coalition proposal would protect the wild Fremont River gorge, while the BLM envisions a penstock and hydroelectric power plant inside the 19,500-acre roadless area. Our proposal would protect 70,000 acres of roadless land adjacent to Capitol Reef National Park—while the BLM would allow uranium and petroleum exploration, tar sand development, and access for off-road vehicles along the park's borders. Along the southern perimeter of the Circle Cliffs Amphitheater, our proposal would protect over 60,000 acres in an area where the BLM would encourage uranium exploration and tar sand leasing. And along the southwestern border of the Escalante wilderness, our proposal would protect the 13,500-acre "Little Egypt" roadless area and the eastern portion of the Scorpion WSA—both earmarked for mineral exploration by the BLM.

From the lake country of the Aquarius Plateau to the heart of the Glen Canyon National Recreation Area, the Escalante River watershed is one wilderness. If it is to remain so, the current management philosophy of the BLM and the Forest Service must change. Both agencies pay lip service to the value of scenery, recreation, and wildlife. But under pressure from the mining and timber industries, both agencies have endorsed massive development projects in the heart of the Escalante wilderness. Only wilderness legislation can provide a mandate strong, comprehensive, and clear enough to insure permanent protection for one of the most beautiful natural areas in the nation.

Ray Wheeler

NORTH ESCALANTE CANYONS UNIT

Highlights—The North Escalante Canyons are the core of the Escalante wilderness. These canyons and the surrounding benchlands support diverse plant and animal life and hold significant geological formations, numerous archeological sites, and exceptional backpacking opportunities. The BLM's wilderness recommendation would leave important wild lands on the east side of the unit open to tar sand leasing and uranium exploration. We propose wilderness designation for 144,000 acres, including the Little Egypt unit which is connected via roadless lands in the Glen Canyon National Recreation Area.

Geology and landforms—Twenty miles of the Escalante River and scores of miles of narrow, winding sidecanyons highlight this unit. Within these canyons are arches, natural bridges, and alcoves; above the steep walls of Navajo Sandstone are scenic panoramas across an impossibly chopped and jointed landscape.

Plant communities—Most of the unit is slickrock that supports scattered pinyon and juniper trees and desert shrubs. (The pinyon-juniper forest is fairly thick on top of the Little Egypt mesa.) Riparian species grow along the Escalante River and its major sidecanyons. The unit may also support two sensitive plant species, according to the BLM: the Red Canyon catchfly (*Silene petersonii* var. *minor*) and the milkvetch *Astragalus barneby*.

Wildlife—Mule deer, cottontail, mountain lion and elk inhabit this unit. Mourning dove, waterfowl, and brown and rainbow trout can also be found here. Two endangered bird species, the bald eagle and peregrine falcon, are known to exist in this area, along with several sensitive species—the golden eagle, Lewis's woodpecker, and western and mountain bluebirds.

Archeology and history—The BLM identified 22 archeological sites in its WSA, including rock art, granaries, and shelters. Many more would be discovered if thorough surveys were undertaken. On lands south of Harris

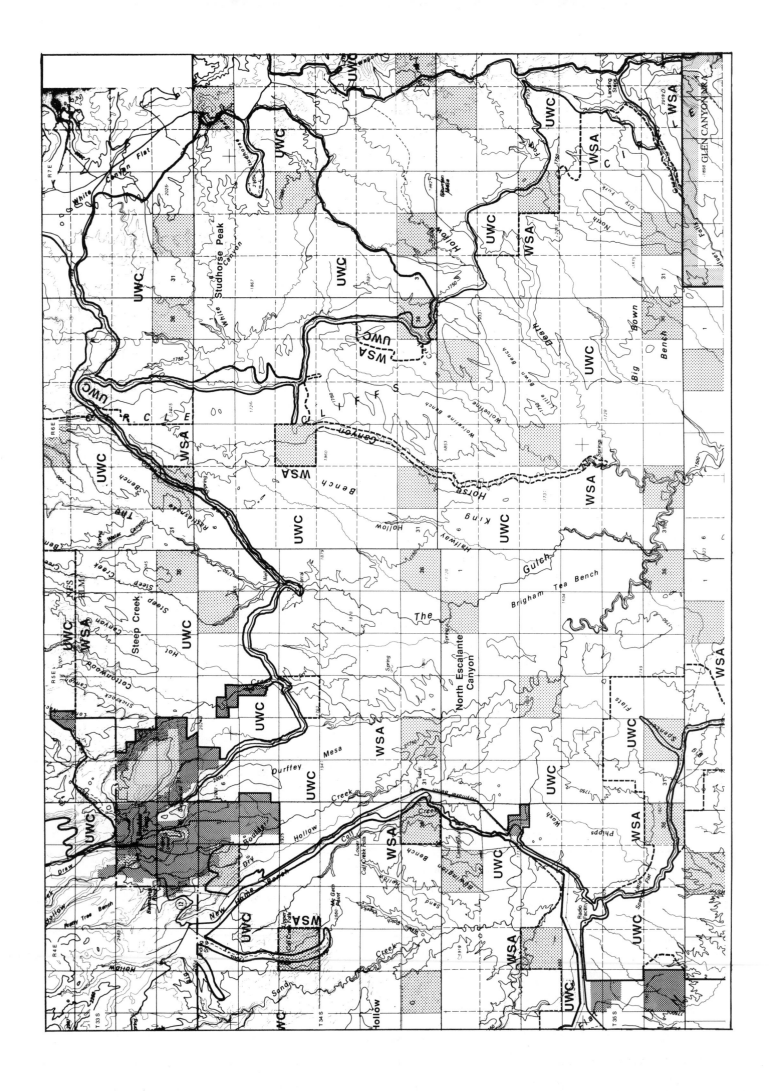

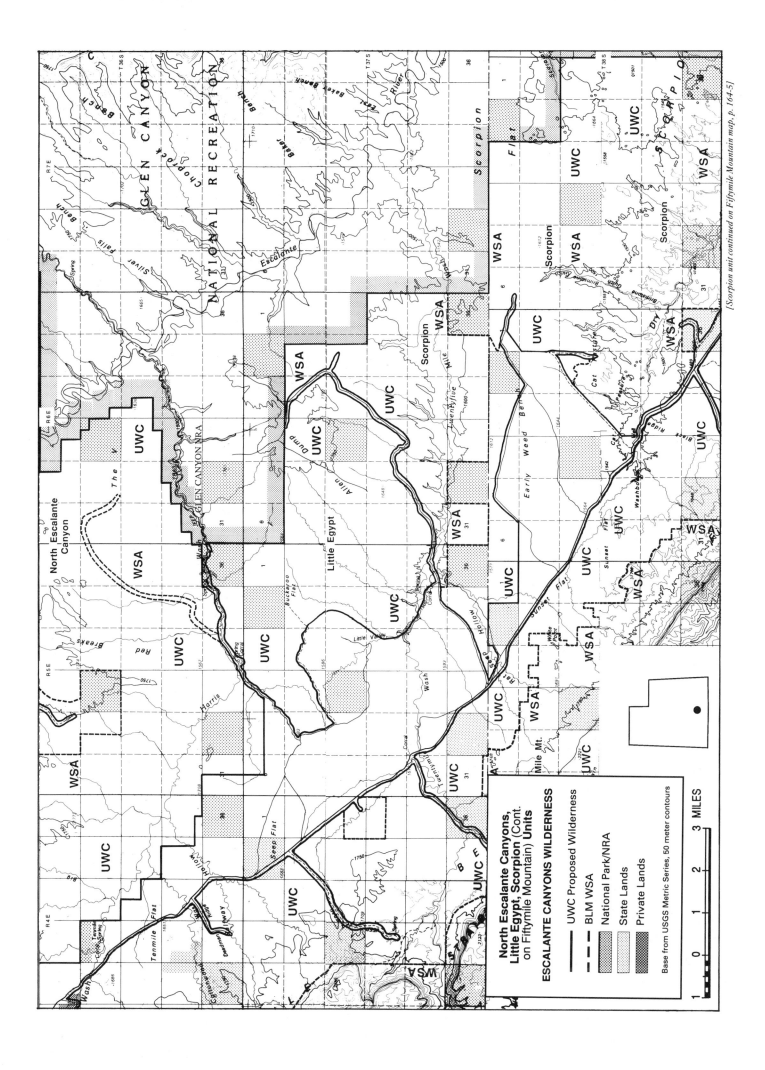

North Escalante Canyons, Little Egypt, Scorpion (Cont. on Fiftymile Mountain) Units

ESCALANTE CANYONS WILDERNESS

UWC Proposed Wilderness
BLM WSA
National Park/NRA
State Lands
Private Lands

Base from USGS Metric Series, 50 meter contours

0   1   2   3 MILES

[Scorpion unit continued on Fiftymile Mountain map, p. 164-5]

Wash that were dropped from the wilderness inventory, Coalition volunteers found 14 sites, chiefly lithic scatters, in a 1-day reconnaissance. Four of these are eligible for listing on the National Register. Unfortunately, these and other BLM lands south of Harris Wash, totalling 4,000 acres, were given to the State of Utah despite their known archeological sites. The Southern Utah Wilderness Alliance, a Coalition member group, has filed suit in federal court to rescind the illegal land transfer.

Recreation—This unit's breathtaking scenery, ample water, and notable geological and archeological features are accessible via dozens of hiking and backpacking trails. Little Death Hollow, which crosses the center of the BLM excluded area, offers an exciting "narrows" hike. A section of Harris Wash, the second most popular (after Coyote Gulch) access route to the Escalante River, passes through a section of this unit that was omitted from the BLM's wilderness inventory.

BLM recommendation—The BLM initially recommended wilderness for only 100,300 acres; its final recommendation pares this down another 8,700 acres. The agency excluded lands in the vicinity of Little Death Hollow and Big Bown Bench for the stated reason of allowing development of the Circle Cliffs Special Tar Sand Area (BLM, 1986, p. 9). Tar sand extraction would represent a profoundly destructive attack on the surrounding ecosystem (see area overview). The deposit, moreover, is of low quality and is not feasible to develop under foreseeable conditions (see Minerals section). Uranium was also cited as a conflict with wilderness but commercial deposits are unlikely. The BLM also recommends the creation of a half-mile-wide non-wilderness zone along the Burr Trail "to avoid conflict with potential realignment and paving" of the road. Finally, the BLM omitted 13,000 acres around Little Egypt and Harris Wash, claiming that it lacks naturalness and outstanding opportunities for solitude.

Coalition proposal—We propose wilderness designation for 144,000 acres, making minor boundary adjustments to exclude human impacts around the perimeter. We include 19,000 acres around Little Death Hollow which is of great value for primitive outdoor recreation and wildlife. Our boundary cherrystems access roads to and on Big Spencer Flats, rather than excluding a large area surrounding the road which would open up a major island of nonwilderness. A vehicle way on the "V" is rapidly being reclaimed by erosion and drifting sand. The vehicle route down Horse Canyon is mostly in the wash bed and would return to a natural condition if left undisturbed; this access route to the Escalante River is most appropriate for foot and horse travel. The Harris Wash-Little Egypt tract, which adjoins the Glen Canyon NRA, is overall in a natural condition; a seismograph line included in this tract is almost impossible to spot on the ground and represents a minor intrusion on the landscape. Harris Wash itself is included downstream from the existing trailhead access. The drainages and open benchlands throughout this unit provide excellent solitude. Finally, the 4,000 acres of public land south of Harris Wash that were given to the State of Utah are included, pending the outcome of the lawsuit seeking to block the transfer.

SCORPION UNIT

Highlights—The 38,100-acre Scorpion unit is located 25 miles southeast of Escalante and borders proposed wilderness to the east in the Glen Canyon NRA. Access is from the Hole-in-the-Rock Road or from the Escalante River. Twisting, narrow canyons, a perennial stream, endangered and sensitive bird species, and outstanding backcountry recreation opportunities make this a key unit of the greater Escalante wilderness.

Boating the Escalante River in small rafts or kayaks lets one enjoy the canyon without wading through the ever-present tamarisk. The week-long trip is best at high water and can require a strenuous haul out via Fortymile Ridge.

Fred Swanson

Geology and landforms—Nearly 60 miles of sinuous canyons are carved into the Mesozoic rocks of the Glen Canyon Group in this unit. Twenty-Five Mile Wash and Dry Fork Coyote Gulch gain most of their depth here, while Scorpion Gulch itself begins in a dramatic pouroff: all three flow east into the Escalante River in the Glen Canyon NRA. The tributaries of these drainages "exhibit concentrations of deep slots that are not equaled elsewhere in the Escalante River drainage" (BLM, 1986, p.16). The rocky benchlands developed on the Navajo Sandstone offer spectacular views into the canyons and across to the Waterpocket Fold and Fiftymile Mountain. Lower down in the main canyons, the deep reds of the Wingate Sandstone set a glowing backdrop for streamside vegetation.

Plant communities—Desert shrub vegetation predominates with its characteristic juniper, sage, Brigham tea, Indian ricegrass, and sand dropseed. Wildflowers including asters, gilia, and the dark-leaved *Datura* or jimsonweed stand out in sandy blows and hollows. Riparian vegetation follows the banks of Twenty-Five Mile Wash.

Wildlife—The diverse habitat ranging from sandy slickrock benches to grassy, trickling streams is home to as many as 50 species of mammals, 170 species of birds, 17 species of reptiles, and 5 species of amphibians, according to the BLM. The unit includes yearlong range for mule deer, winter range for a few mountain lion, and nesting areas for at least nine raptors. Bird species include the endangered bald eagle and peregrine falcon and four sensitive species: the golden eagle, Lewis's woodpecker, and the western and mountain bluebird. The perennial stream in Twenty-Five Mile Wash provides valuable habitat for a number of animals; small, evanescent waterpockets on the slickrock benchlands are also important water sources.

Archeology and history—The BLM (1986, p. 15) identified about 20 archeological sites, including occupation sites, campsites, and pictographs in the WSA; more would surface with a full inventory.

Recreation—Backpacking, horseback riding, hiking, sightseeing, and photographic opportunities are outstanding even for the Escalante country—the unit has been called "the best of the best." Brimstone Gulch and Spooky Gulch, tributaries to Dry Fork Coyote Gulch, offer challenging slot-canyon exploring; Scorpion Gulch and Twenty-Five Mile Wash are easier going but demand good routefinding skills to locate access points from the benchlands (see Lambrechtse, 1985). Nor should one forget the experience of hiking across the expansive slickrock benchlands, with their vistas of distant ridges, their intimate, sand-blown hollows, and delightful, unexpected waterpockets.

BLM recommendation—The BLM initially recommended only 9,620 acres of the 35,884-acre Scorpion WSA for wilderness designation, and excluded more than 4,000 acres of qualifying wild lands from the WSA. Superb hiking areas such as Dry Fork of Coyote Gulch, Scorpion Gulch, King Mesa, and Spooky and Brimstone Gulches were left out. (The final recommendation is expected to restore some 5,300 acres of these lands.) Potential uranium deposits may have led the BLM to recommend less than all of its WSA; no other minerals or other resources in the unit offer even remote development possibilities. The BLM notes that the eastern portion of the WSA is within the Greater Circle Cliffs probable uranium resource area, but any deposits at its fringe would be at depth and would involve high development and transportation costs.

Coalition proposal—We propose wilderness designation for the entire WSA along with 2,200 acres of additional qualifying land dropped in the inventory. Outstanding opportunities for recreation and solitude exist throughout the unit and it deserves protection from imprudent mineral exploration and other surface disturbance. Our proposal excludes the dirt road to the start of the cross-country hike to Scorpion Gulch.

HURRICANE WASH AND FORTYMILE GULCH UNITS

Highlights—The 4,300-acre Hurricane Wash unit (see Escalante Tract 5 on Fiftymile Mountain map, Kaiparowits area) features the upper reach of Hurricane Wash and a section of Coyote Gulch, which are the principal access routes into the famous lower canyons of the Escalante. The 640-acre Fortymile Gulch unit (also on the Fiftymile Mountain map) contains wild lands on the south slope of Fortymile Ridge. Containing superb wild country in its own right, these units complement the vast expanse of wilderness to the east in the Glen Canyon NRA.

Geology and landforms—Most of these units are covered with wind-blown sand and rock outcrops, but Hurricane Wash in the west cuts into the Entrada and Navajo sandstones, as does a corner of Coyote Gulch at the north end of the unit.

Plant communities—Desert shrub communities predominate at the higher elevations. Shrubs and grasses occur on benches above the streambeds, while cottonwood and willow grow along stream edges.

Wildlife—Hurricane Gulch offers yearlong mule deer habitat, and supports the sensitive western and mountain bluebirds (listed by the UDWR). Rare migrants through the unit, according to the BLM, include the endangered peregrine falcon and bald eagle.

Archeology and history—While the Hole-in-the-Rock Trail was under construction in 1879, the nearly 250 Mormon pioneers travelling to Bluff, Utah, camped at Fortymile Spring south and west of these units. They held meetings and dances in the shelter of Dance Hall Rock, designated as a historical site by the Secretary of the Interior in 1970.

Recreation—The popular 13-mile hike down Hurricane Wash to Coyote Gulch and the Escalante River begins in the Hurricane Wash unit. Coyote Gulch above Hurricane Wash tends to be less crowded than lower down and is well worth exploring, too. Water is present year round in Coyote Gulch and in Hurricane Wash starting just above the NRA boundary. These upper canyons offer high quality hiking, backpacking, horseback riding, sightseeing, and photography as well as great vistas from vantage points above the canyon walls. Lambrechtse (1985) describes the Hurricane Wash access to Coyote Gulch.

BLM recommendation—The BLM recommends only its 760-acre "Escalante Tract 5 Instant Study Area" (around Coyote Gulch) for wilderness designation. The agency did not study the rest of the Hurricane Wash unit, nor any of Fortymile Gulch. It violated its inventory policy by improperly drawing the study area boundary far from the edges of roads or other disturbances.

Coalition proposal—We propose wilderness designation for 4,300 acres in Hurricane Wash and 640 acres in Fortymile Gulch, complementing a much larger area of Park Service recommended wilderness in the Glen Canyon National Recreation Area and protecting a popular access route to the Escalante wilderness.

PHIPPS-DEATH HOLLOW UNIT

Highlights—The name "Death Hollow" is misleading, as this is a well-watered and inviting place. (The name may derive from the murder of one Washington Phipps along the Escalante River below Sand Creek.) The narrows of Death Hollow is a strenuous, though rewarding backpack trip; Calf Creek, in contrast, is one of the easiest and most popular short hiking trails in southern Utah. The BLM recommends 39,256 acres of its 42,731-

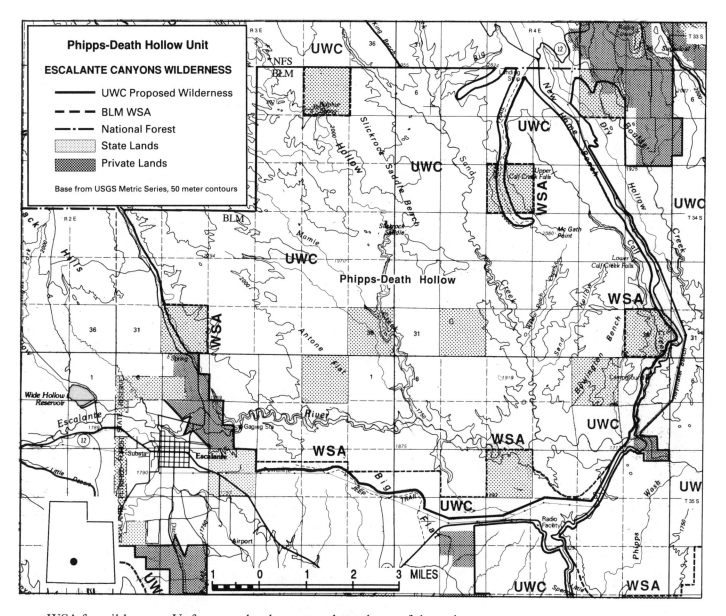

acre WSA for wilderness. Unfortunately, the agency leased part of the unit
for oil and gas exploration before it designated the Phipps-Death Hollow
Outstanding Natural Area in 1970. The Utah Wilderness Coalition
proposes 43,500 acres of wilderness, and a buyout or exchange of any oil
and gas leases which do not explicitly prohibit surface occupancy. The
designated Box-Death Hollow Wilderness on the Dixie National Forest,
an area similarly besieged by mineral development, is adjacent to the
BLM lands on the north.

Geology and landforms—Pure-white to golden Navajo Sandstone has
been eroded into expanses of slickrock and deep canyons by the Escalante
River, Mamie Creek, Sand Creek, and Calf Creek. The red layers of the
Carmel Formation cap the high mesas south of the Escalante River and between the tributary canyons. The ledges of the Kayenta Formation are exposed at the east edge of the unit along the Escalante River and in lower
Calf Creek Canyon.

Plant communities—Cottonwood trees, willows, and grasses line the 40
miles of perennial streams; hanging gardens dot the canyon walls. Pinyon-
juniper forests cover the flat-topped mesas. Most of the unit is exposed,
weathered slickrock. Death Hollow holds a relict plant community (BLM,
1986, p. 13).

Wildlife—The BLM (1986, p. 15) identified 21,200 acres of the unit as
important winter range for mule deer and 3,000 acres as important winter

The popular hike to Calf Creek Falls in the Phipps-Death Hollow unit is one of the most accessible scenic wonders of the proposed Escalante Canyons wilderness.

Bruce Barnbaum

range for elk. Over 15,000 acres on Antone Flat are unallocated for livestock use and are "designated especially for mule deer use." Mountain lions, golden eagles, American kestrels, Lewis's woodpeckers, and western and mountain bluebirds are also found here. Peregrine falcons and bald eagles are considered "rare migrants and possibly winter visitors" by the BLM (1986, p. 15). Rainbow and brown trout have become established in the creeks; the UDWR has stocked cutthroat trout in a segment of Calf Creek.

Archeology and history—Prehistoric sites include 6 campsites and 14 petroglyph and pictograph sites, according to the BLM (1986). The Friendship Cove Pictograph is nominated to the National Register. Historic sites include the Boulder Mail Trail (a good hiking route), and the Washington Phipps Grave.

Recreation—The strenuous 4- to 5-day backpack trip through Death Hollow, which begins on national forest wilderness to the north, has steep canyon walls to descend and deep, cold pools to ford or swim. It is considered a classic "narrows" hike. In contrast, the easy 3-mile walk to Calf Creek Falls from the campground on Highway 12 shows how accessible this wilderness can be. One can also backpack down the Escalante River from the town of Escalante to the Highway 12 bridge, or cross the Boulder Mail Trail intersecting Sand Creek and Death Hollow. The short, steep day hike to Upper Calf Creek Falls starts at an unmarked trailhead on Highway 12. Lambrechtse (1985) describes each of these hikes in detail.

BLM recommendation—The BLM's 39,256-acre recommended wilderness excludes the relatively flat pinyon-juniper uplands north of McGath Point, which are important winter range for elk and deer as well as a scenic overlook across the neighboring canyons. It also excludes a great slickrock area in the southeast corner of the unit. The agency argues that these are not lands "with the most outstanding wilderness characteristics" (BLM, 1986, p. 7)—a highly subjective judgment that ignores the ecological, scenic, and recreational diversity that these mesa tops add to the unit.

Coalition proposal—We propose wilderness designation for 43,500 acres—the entire BLM WSA as well as adjacent natural lands on the south. Included in our proposal, and absent from the BLM's, are the outstanding mesas and cliffs north of the Boulder-Escalante powerline. Congress effectively prohibited any new leasing for oil and gas on much of the unit when it designated the adjacent national forest lands as the Box-Death Hollow Wilderness in 1984. The BLM recognized this when it decided in 1988 not to offer new leases in the unit. But leases granted in 1969 still threaten, although they are being held in suspension until Congress decides whether to designate the BLM unit as wilderness. In this case, about 3,000 acres of those leases will be subject to drilling, which could cause permanent damage to the wilderness character of the area. These leases should be exchanged or bought out as part of wilderness legislation.

STEEP CREEK UNIT

Highlights—This 34,400-acre BLM unit anchors the Escalante wilderness, connecting it to the wild country on that great source of waters, the Aquarius Plateau. Beginning about two miles east of the town of Boulder, the unit stretches north from the Burr Trail to the forested slopes of Boulder Mountain and east to the cliffs of Capitol Reef National Park. A corridor between alpine country and deep slickrock canyons, this unit is a rich and diverse wilderness staircase. Steep Creek, along with the 2,900-acre Lampstand unit and contiguous wild lands in Capitol Reef National Park and the Dixie National Forest, forms a 170,000-acre roadless area.

Geology and landforms—Perennial streams flowing down from Boulder Mountain enter canyons entrenched in white Navajo and deep-red Wingate Sandstone. Deer Creek, Steep Creek, and The Gulch have year-round flows of clear, cold water—an important and vulnerable resource. Five springs rise within the unit. The Gulch leads up into the spectacular Circle Cliffs, where remarkable specimens of petrified wood can be seen in the Morrison and Chinle formations, some of the thick logs surviving intact to lengths of 60 feet or more.

Plant communities—Pinyon-juniper forest is prevalent in those areas which offer a foothold; much of the unit is slickrock. The BLM has identified riparian habitat along Deer Creek, Steep Creek, and The Gulch.

Wildlife—The UDWR has identified critical deer winter range and critical elk winter and calving habitat in this unit. Their presence brings in the

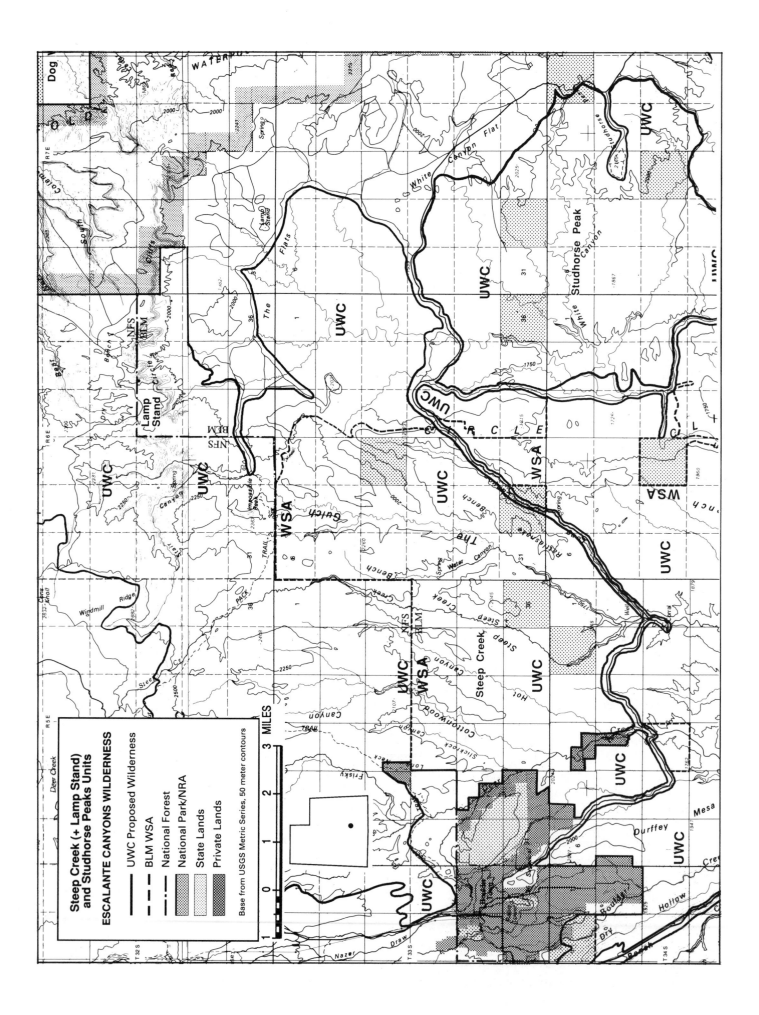

Steep Creek (+ Lamp Stand) and Studhorse Peaks Units

ESCALANTE CANYONS WILDERNESS

—— UWC Proposed Wilderness

--- BLM WSA

—·— National Forest

National Park/NRA

State Lands

Private Lands

Base from USGS Metric Series, 50 meter contours

0 1 2 3
MILES

mountain lions which roam throughout the unit. Deer Creek harbors rainbow and brown trout, and this and the other streams attract a variety of waterfowl. The BLM (1986, p. 16) notes that endangered peregrine falcon and bald eagle "are rare migrants and possibly winter visitors of the WSA." At least seven other raptors are known to nest in the unit, including the golden eagle and American kestrel. Lewis's woodpecker and western and mountain bluebirds, UDWR-listed sensitive species, inhabit the unit as well.

Archeology and history—The BLM estimates that half of the unit has medium site densities (11 to 49 sites per 23,000 acres). Densities for the rest of the unit are unknown. Several National Register sites have been found along the Burr Trail on the south boundary of the unit.

Recreation—The Burr Trail, in its present unpaved condition, affords easy access to a variety of hiking routes in the Steep Creek unit. Ideal day hikes begin from the Burr Trail, with well-watered canyons offering many opportunities for casual or more intensive exploration (see Lambrechtse, 1985, and Kelsey, 1986a). Horseback riding, photography, fishing, backpacking—diverse primitive recreation possibilities are available here. For those who seek remote, isolated campsites, the benches between the canyons offer solitude and good vistas. Red, orange, purple, and white rock formations, as well as Lamanite Natural Bridge, offer spectacular sightseeing.

BLM recommendation—The BLM recommended 18,350 acres of its 21,896-acre WSA for wilderness designation in 1986, and has indicated it will add about 2,500 acres to that recommendation in 1990. Areas in the northeast and southwest corners were recommended "nonsuitable," as was a strip along the Burr Trail to provide for road expansion and a utility corridor. The BLM chose this partial wilderness alternative to exclude 1,280 acres of mining claims (which are not producing and are likely to produce little in the future) and to delete lands it claimed did not have "the most outstanding wilderness characteristics" (BLM, 1986, p. 6). The excluded lands are eminently wild, rugged, and scenic. The agency deleted them simply to avoid the slightest conflict with existing mining claims of unknown validity. The BLM (1986, p. 10) assessed the uranium development opportunities of the unit as "not significant." The Lampstand unit was dropped from the BLM's inventory.

Coalition proposal—We support a 34,400-acre wilderness, comprising 31,500 acres in Steep Creek and 2,900 acres around The Lampstand. Our boundary extends to the edge of the Burr Trail in order to preserve the road as a scenic, low-speed backcountry access route and to protect the adjacent wild lands from commercial development and ORV abuse. Narrow canyons with sheer walls and steep grades make the road inappropriate as a paved highway. Adjacent wild lands on the Dixie National Forest should also be designated to protect water quality and the ecological diversity of the Escalante canyons.

STUDHORSE PEAKS UNIT

Highlights—The Studhorse Peaks unit (see map, North Escalante Canyons unit) is an upland area of pinyon-juniper forest located in the center of the scenic Circle Cliffs, just south of the Burr Trail. These prominent buttes rise directly above the road as you head west from Capitol Reef National Park. Part of the larger Escalante wild region, the unit is separated from the North Escalante Canyons unit only by the primitive road in Horse Canyon Wash. While the BLM failed even to study the area, the Coalition proposes a 19,500-acre wilderness.

The top of the Studhorse Peaks, a short hike off of the Burr Trail, affords a commanding view of the entire Circle Cliffs amphitheater.

Fred Swanson

Geology and landforms—Three main canyons drain east to west across the unit to Horse Canyon (along the west boundary). White Canyon, at the center of the unit, is the largest. The Studhorse Peaks are a series of flat-topped buttes that form a ridge at the eastern boundary of the unit. Most of the unit is the red Moenkopi Formation, which forms low rims and ledges, but the peaks are capped by the light-colored Shinarump Conglomerate. White Canyon cuts through the Kaibab Limestone to the Coconino Sandstone—the oldest stratum in the Escalante wilderness.

Plant communities—An extensive pinyon-juniper forest covers the uplands on the east, grading to shrub lands closer to Horse Canyon. On top of the peaks are pockets of Gambel oak in protected sand hollows.

Wildlife—The UDWR has identified critical elk calving habitat on the northwest edge of the unit.

Archeology and history—The area shows evidence of hunting use by prehistoric people, but no recorded surveys are available.

Recreation—Most visitors bypass this unit on their way to Capitol Reef National Park or the Escalante Canyons, so a hike down White Canyon or up one of the Studhorse Peaks will guarantee you solitude. The 360-degree view from the peaks encompasses the southern part of Capitol Reef National Park, the Henry Mountains, Navajo Mountain, Powell Point on the Table Cliff Plateau, the Circle Cliffs, and Boulder Mountain.

BLM recommendation—The BLM released this unit from further consideration in the initial inventory, claiming it lacked naturalness and opportunities for solitude or primitive recreation. Although about 2,200 acres of the BLM's 22,700-acre inventory unit are impacted, the remainder are clearly natural. The dense pinyon-juniper forest and the incised, branching canyons ensure solitude. The unit's location in a tar sand district may also have affected its disposition in the wilderness review (see area overview).

Coalition proposal—We recommend that the Studhorse Peaks unit be designated wilderness to preserve one of the Escalante's relatively unknown roadless areas. Our boundary excludes the main uranium exploration roads around the eastern peaks; minor bulldozer scars are located within the unit and are slowly healing.

COLT MESA UNIT

Highlights—Deer Point, in the southeastern part of this unit, is one of the highest points on the Waterpocket Fold, the geologic feature that Capitol Reef National Park was established to protect. In addition to outstanding vistas from the top of the Fold, there are excellent hiking and exploring opportunities in canyons cut into the oldest rock formations in the Escalante wilderness. The BLM failed even to designate a WSA, although the Park Service, in a memo to the BLM, stated that the unit "would enhance the wilderness characteristics of the adjoining Capitol Reef National Park." We recommend a 23,500-acre wilderness unit.

Geology and landforms—The spectacular monocline of the Waterpocket Fold tops out at Deer Point (7,243 feet) in the southeast corner of the unit. From this boomerang-shaped mesa the Colorado Plateau spreads out in every direction: eastward are views across Capitol Reef National Park, past the great curved line of Strike Valley, to the deeply etched mesas and rounded peaks of the Henry Mountains. To the west lie the escarpment of the Circle Cliffs, the dissected canyons of the Escalante River drainage, and rising beyond, the Straight Cliffs of the Kaiparowits Plateau. The slickrock summit of Deer Point is surrounded by colorful clay badlands of the Chinle Formation. The northwest four-fifths of the unit is mostly red-brown ledges and slopes of the Moenkopi Formation with the inner gorges of the upper Moody Canyons cutting into the relatively harder Kaibab Limestone and Coconino Sandstone, the oldest layers exposed in this region.

Plant communities—Pinyon-juniper is the major vegetation type. According to the U.S. Fish and Wildlife Service, the threatened Jones cycladenia (*Cycladenia humilis* var. *jonesii*) may be found in the southern half of the unit.

Wildlife—Raptors, including golden eagles, nest here and winter migrants include the endangered peregrine falcon and bald eagle. The UDWR classifies the southern third of the unit as a peregrine use area. Bighorn sheep have been reintroduced in the area and probably use this unit.

Recreation—The hike to Deer Point, though not well known, rewards the adventurous scrambler with a panoramic view of southern Utah. The unit offers excellent opportunities for exploring, sightseeing, and backpacking in its Chinle badlands, pinyon-juniper forested rims and washes, and sandstone gorges. Lambrechtse (1985) describes the access to Deer Point via Middle Moody Canyon. General access to the unit is from the Moody Creek road south of the Burr Trail.

BLM recommendation—The BLM dropped the unit during its intensive inventory, claiming it lacked outstanding opportunities for solitude and primitive recreation. It ignored one of the most outstanding vistas in southern Utah, the unit's contiguity with a park system area recommended for wilderness, and over 2,000 feet of elevation change. The Interior Board of Land Appeals strongly criticized the BLM for confusing outstanding "topographic or vegetative screening" with solitude in other

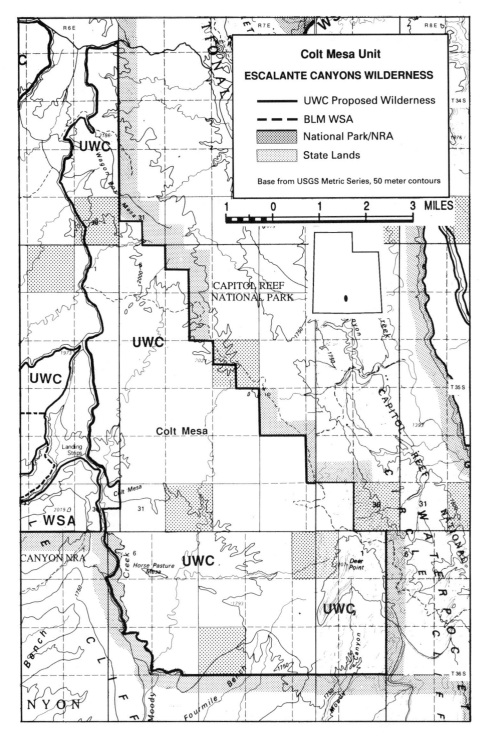

The legend of the map reads:

Colt Mesa Unit

ESCALANTE CANYONS WILDERNESS

— UWC Proposed Wilderness

--- BLM WSA

National Park/NRA

State Lands

Base from USGS Metric Series, 50 meter contours

inventory units. As a result, many areas dropped for the same reasons are now back in the wilderness review. The BLM decided that 18,230 acres were in a natural state; 1,690 acres were "unnatural" and 4,080 acres were excluded by drawing the northern boundary on a largely reclaimed jeep trail that periodically floods and is indistinguishable from the surroundings. The BLM found that "Ways north of Deer Point are impassable to vehicles, are rehabilitating naturally, and are not considered to significantly impact naturalness." Perceived conflicts with tar sand development may have motivated the agency to drop the area from study (see area overview).

Coalition proposal—We propose 23,500 acres for wilderness. High mesas, sandstone cliffs, and incised streambeds provide good topographic screening; the more open areas of the unit offer solitude simply because of their remoteness. The unit is generally undisturbed; the 1,690 acres the BLM felt were unnatural contain old mining scars from the 1950s that are slowly being reclaimed. These scars are excluded from our proposal where they are evident. The Congress, not the BLM, must determine whether the slim economic potential of tar sand outweighs the unit's value as a link between Glen Canyon NRA and Capitol Reef National Park. The wildlife, scenery, and solitude found here know no boundary lines.

LONG CANYON UNIT

Highlights—Capitol Reef National Park is the western boundary of this 16,400-acre unit; Glen Canyon NRA adjoins the southern boundary. Long Canyon is part of the 600,000-acre Escalante roadless area located between the Burr Trail and the Hole-in-the-Rock Road. Its multi-hued badlands add to the diversity of this wilderness with the youngest sedimentary rocks in the region. Although the BLM found the unit to be natural, it alleged that it lacked outstanding opportunities for solitude and primitive recreation. We propose wilderness designation to protect these scenic badlands and areas of sensitive soils adjacent to the park and the NRA.

Geology and landforms—Long Canyon (not to be confused with the Long Canyon farther west on the Burr Trail) is five miles long and over 600 feet deep. It cuts through the Upper Jurassic Entrada and Summerville formations. Hall Mesa and Middle Point on either side of Long Canyon have Morrison Formation badlands. A half-mile-wide finger of the unit extends north along the eastern boundary of the park and on Big Thompson Mesa; it includes Mancos Shale badlands.

Plant communities and wildlife—Sparse desert shrubs and grasses, principally blackbrush, shadscale, saltbush, and Mormon tea, are found throughout the unit. Juniper trees dot the northern portion. Mule deer live in the unit, but little else is known about its wildlife.

Recreation—Long Canyon is accessible from the Burr Trail along most of the eastern boundary and from the spur to the overlook of the Waterpocket Fold on Big Thompson Mesa. The unit receives little recreational use.

BLM recommendation—The BLM did not designate a WSA in Long Canyon. While most of the unit is in a natural condition (the only imprints are along the Burr Trail) the BLM claimed the unit did not have outstanding opportunities for solitude due to a lack of vegetative screening and topographic relief. This conclusion is unsupportable: the northern edge of the unit is a juniper-covered mesa top that provides vegetative screening and the southern end has over 1,000 feet of topographic relief from the bottom of Long Canyon to the top of Hall Mesa and Middle Point. Also relevant is the unit's location adjacent to a much larger wild area.

Coalition proposal—A 16,400-acre wilderness unit is needed to ensure protection of this unit's scenery and sensitive soils from speculative mineral exploration and ORV abuse. The unit is a logical extension of wild land in the adjacent Glen Canyon NRA and Capitol Reef National Park.

NOTOM BENCH AND DOGWATER CREEK UNITS

Highlights—Between Capitol Reef National Park and the Notom Road, on the rolling eastern foothills of the Waterpocket Fold, lie BLM wild lands that should be protected as part of the roadless area extending into the park. Outstanding hikes into the park begin in the washes and canyons of these units. An 8,400-acre Notom Bench and a 3,500-acre Dogwater Creek wilderness unit are essential for continued undeveloped recreation access to the adjoining park wild lands. The BLM dropped both units from its wilderness inventory.

Geology and landforms—The eastern flank of the Waterpocket Fold runs through both units. Notom Bench slopes steadily up into Capitol Reef and

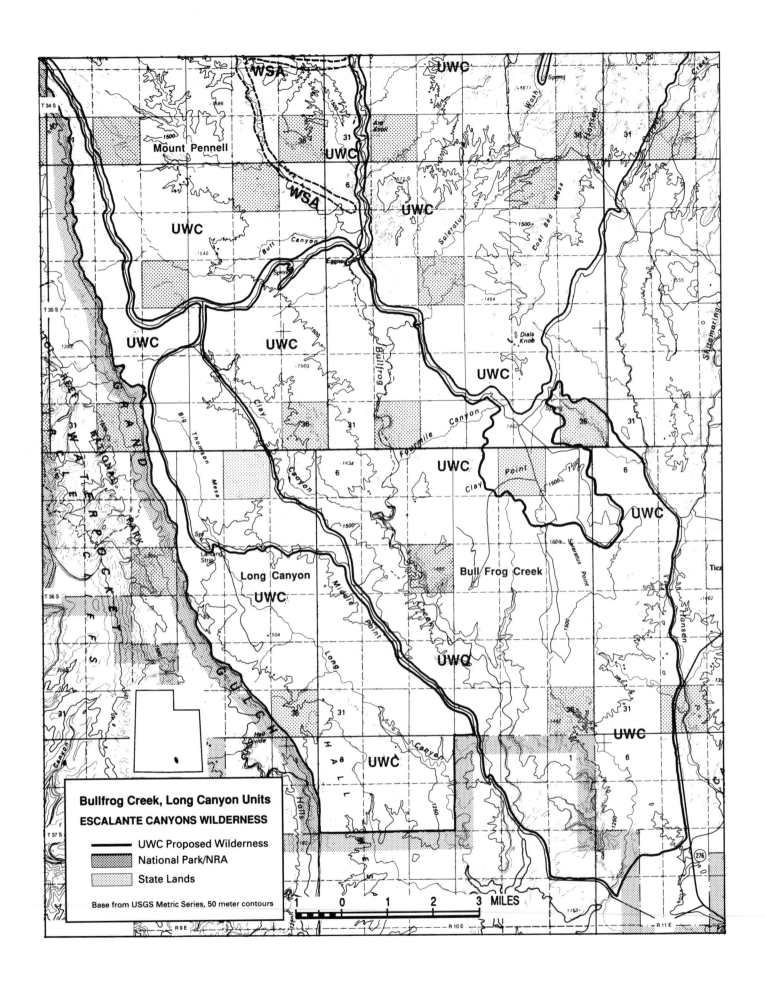

Bullfrog Creek, Long Canyon Units

ESCALANTE CANYONS WILDERNESS

—— UWC Proposed Wilderness

▨ National Park/NRA

░ State Lands

Base from USGS Metric Series, 50 meter contours

1   0   1   2   3   MILES

is cut by several major washes. Dogwater Creek is more open and flat, presenting a spacious appearance, and is especially scenic when viewed in the evening from near the Sandy Ranch on the Notom Road.

Plant communities and wildlife—Sparse vegetation is found here, primarily scattered pinyon pine and juniper with associated desert shrubs such as blackbrush and rabbitbrush. Occasional mountain mahogany and boxelder are found in the normally dry washes. Thorough wildlife inventories are lacking, but the units probably provide winter range for mule deer using the adjacent uplands.

Recreation—The narrow canyons of Burro, Cottonwood, and Fivemile washes and Sheets Gulch, which are increasingly popular with visitors to Capitol Reef National Park, are accessible through the Notom Bench unit. These canyons begin to "slot up" within the BLM lands. Each offers rather intense hiking, with Burro the easiest and Cottonwood and Fivemile the hardest; chockstones, pouroffs, and cold pools challenge the hiker. Outside these washes, east-facing slopes offer grand vistas of the Henry Mountains and their flanking reefs, mesas, and cliffs.

BLM recommendation—The only impacts are several substantially unnoticeable ways and an abandoned reservoir. The BLM dropped both units for lack of outstanding opportunities for solitude and primitive recreation, thus ignoring the incised canyons, undulating topography, and general lack of visitors that make backcountry travel here rewarding. The adjacent Park Service wilderness proposal mandates similar consideration of BLM lands. A letter from the Regional Director to the Utah State BLM Director specifically singled out Notom Bench as a victim of BLM's "narrow view of wilderness criteria for outstanding opportunities for solitude . . . we believe [this unit] would enhance the wilderness characteristics of the adjoining Capitol Reef National Park."

Coalition proposal—We recommend that the 8,400-acre Notom Bench unit and 3,500-acre Dogwater Creek unit be designated wilderness as logical extensions of wild lands in Capitol Reef National Park. State lands sold recently to Oak Creek Ranch are omitted from our proposal.

FREMONT GORGE UNIT

Highlights—The 19,400-acre Fremont Gorge unit offers outstanding hiking and fishing along a major river, and is easily accessible from Highway 12 southeast of Torrey. The unit adjoins proposed wilderness in Capitol Reef National Park; its preservation would safeguard an important stretch of wild river with its surrounding rugged benchlands. A proposed hydroelectric project would essentially dewater the river in this unit and drastically affect riparian vegetation in Capitol Reef.

Geology and landforms—The Fremont River and Sulphur Creek pass through deep gorges in Kaibab Limestone and Coconino Sandstone on the west side of the Waterpocket Fold. The combination of a high-gradient river in a deep, narrow gorge, beginning at the relatively high elevation of 6,600 feet, makes Fremont Gorge unlike any other canyon in Southern Utah. The benchlands above the canyons have ledges and shallow drainages in the red-brown Moenkopi Formation.

Plant communities—Pinyon, juniper, and grasses dominate the high, rocky areas while diverse deciduous shrubs and trees maintain a hold in the shaded canyons and along the waterways. Six miles of the Fremont River as well as Sulphur Creek and its tributaries support undisturbed riparian vegetation.

Wildlife—The BLM called its WSA "critical deer winter range" as well as home to coyotes, foxes, squirrels, rabbits, badgers, and many bird species, including, most likely, bald eagles and peregrine falcons.

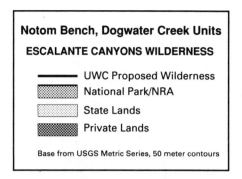

Notom Bench, Dogwater Creek Units
ESCALANTE CANYONS WILDERNESS

— UWC Proposed Wilderness
National Park/NRA
State Lands
Private Lands

Base from USGS Metric Series, 50 meter contours

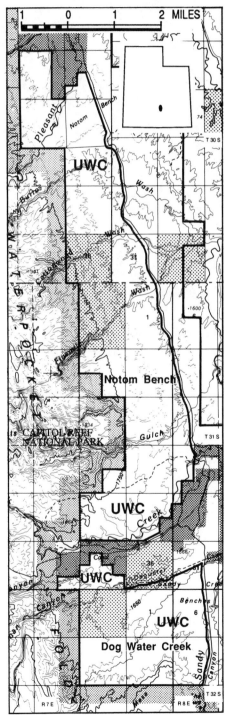

The eastern flank of the Water-pocket Fold (left foreground) is BLM land in the Notom Bench unit. Wilderness designation of this unit is needed to protect the approaches to the Fold, including several spectacular slot canyons.

Tom Miller

Archeology and history—The Fremont River gorge contains an interesting pictograph panel, probably of Fremont origin. Part of the unit has been surveyed in connection with the proposed Fremont River dam but data from those surveys are not published.

Recreation—A fast-moving desert river in a deep gorge, numerous sidecanyons, excellent fishing, hiking, seasonal waterfalls and solitude make this unit different from lower-elevation sandstone canyons. Hikers and anglers can follow the Fremont River from Highway 12 all the way through the gorge into Capitol Reef National Park. This long day hike is best done when water levels are low; high runoff makes stream crossings cold and tricky. Sulphur Creek is easier hiking; excursions into its wild forks start at the park visitor center. See Kelsey (1986a) for more information.

BLM recommendation—The BLM recommends no wilderness for its 2,540-acre Fremont Gorge WSA, which actually contains none of the Fremont Gorge. The BLM originally identified an 18,500-acre inventory unit, but split it in two and rejected one unit, overstating the significance of human imprints and disregarding the natural integrity of the river gorge. The resulting small WSA excludes large natural areas, its boundary following section lines instead of physical features. The BLM may have shrunk its WSA to allow for a hydropower plant proposed by the Wayne County Water Conservancy District. In March 1987, the Federal Energy Regulatory Commission issued a preliminary three-year permit for studies

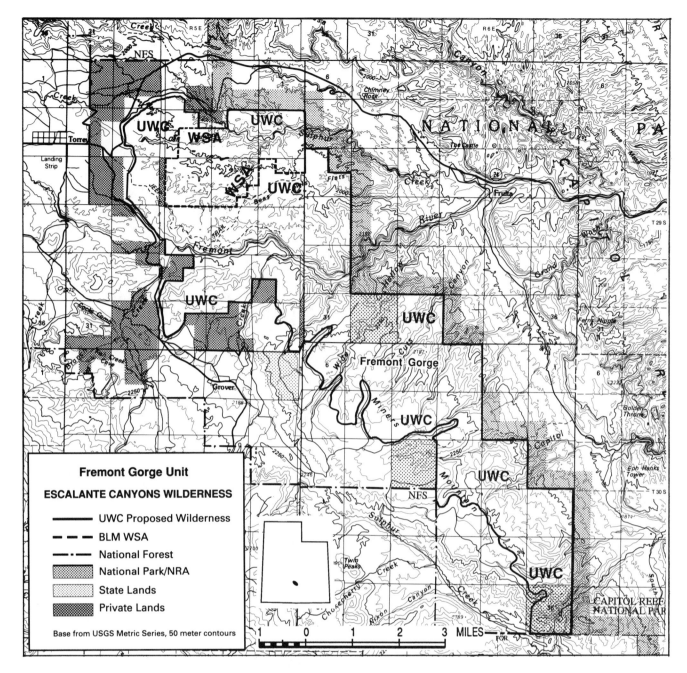

Fremont Gorge Unit

ESCALANTE CANYONS WILDERNESS

——————— UWC Proposed Wilderness

– – – – BLM WSA

–·–·– National Forest

National Park/NRA

State Lands

Private Lands

Base from USGS Metric Series, 50 meter contours

on the environmental impacts and economic feasibility of the project, which would include a 110-foot-high dam and reservoir west of Torrey, a reregulating dam where Highway 12 crosses the river southeast of Torrey, and a power plant in the heart of the Fremont Gorge, just west of the park boundary. A pipeline and road would lead from the dams to the power plant, taking nearly all the river's flow. Most of the trout fishery and much of the riparian vegetation along five miles of river below Highway 12 would be wiped out.

Coalition proposal—These 19,400 undisturbed acres are a significant component of an integrated wilderness area along Capitol Reef. The geologic features of the Waterpocket Fold and the Fremont River cutting through the Fold offer first-rate opportunities for solitude. Additional wild lands on Miners Mountain complete protection for the crest of the Fold. The unit has little potential for leasable or salable minerals. An old telephone line, which was at least part of the BLM's rationale for partitioning this unit, has been abandoned, the wires removed, and the poles taken down in all but the most inaccessible areas.

THE HENRY MOUNTAINS WILDERNESS

Summary

In the rectilinear landscape of southern Utah's canyon country, the Henry Mountains are a novelty—huge purple domes looming strange and silent above the mesas and badlands that surround them. Between the high peaks of the Henrys and Capitol Reef National Park to the west, there are almost 350,000 acres of BLM-managed wild lands. It is one wilderness, spanning an exceptional variety of landforms and ecosystems. From the summit of 11,000-foot-high Mt. Pennell, the landscape plunges away to the west, dropping 6,400 feet, leveling out, then climbing 2,000 feet to the crest of the Waterpocket Fold. The panorama across this huge natural basin is one of the most dramatic and beautiful on the Colorado Plateau. It is also one of the most threatened.

The BLM would designate less than one-third of the region as wilderness, zoning the remainder for up to 40,000 acres of coal mining or deforestation. The Utah Wilderness Coalition proposal would protect all that remains of the Henry Mountains wilderness, from the crest of the mountain range to the summit of the Waterpocket Fold.

Frustrated Volcanoes

There is something mysterious about the Henry Mountains; something incongruous, something odd, something alien. Anyone who encounters them, hovering like spaceships over the lunar landscape of desert badlands surrounding them, gleaming with fresh snow or brooding in lavender tones under an umbrella of storm clouds, receives an immediate and lasting impression that they do not quite belong where they are. "They are by far the most striking features of the panorama," observed the geologist Clarence Dutton, "on account of the strong contrast they present to the scenery about them. Among innumerable flat crest-lines terminating in walls, they rise up grandly into peaks of Alpine form and grace like a modern cathedral among catacombs—the gothic order of architecture contrasting with the elephantine."

It was the geologist Grove Carl Gilbert who revealed that the Henry Mountains are indeed visitors from another world—or inside our own. They are frustrated volcanos—huge blisters in the earth's crust, formed when molten lava, boiling upward from the underworld, encountered a roof of sedimentary rock so thick and so tough that it could bend upward, forming a dome, without rupturing and allowing the lava to escape to the surface. Gilbert coined the term "laccolite" (changed later to "laccolith") to describe the phenomenon. After the mountains were in place, erosion gradually removed the surface rocks, revealing the volcanic core of the range.

The Henrys are an ecological as well as a geological anomaly. "Projecting so far above the surface of the desert, they act as local condensers of moisture, and receive a generous supply of rain," noted Gilbert. "Springs abound upon their flanks, and their upper slopes are clothed with a luxuriant herbage and with groves of timber." While the Mancos Shale badlands at their feet are among the most biologically barren places on earth, the high peaks of the Henrys harbor forests of juniper, pinyon, ponderosa, fir, spruce, aspen, and bristlecone pine. Such ecological diversity supports a wide variety of plant and animal species. Some 700 plant species exist in the BLM's Henry Mountains planning unit, including 14 species listed as threatened or endangered. The Utah State Department of Natural Resources has identified 62 "high interest species" of wildlife in

IN BRIEF

Index Map: Area No. 41

Highlights: The prominent peaks of Mts. Ellen, Pennell, and Hillers are flanked by austere badlands and pinyon-juniper forests that provide important winter range for large mammals. The BLM excluded from wilderness study large areas corresponding with mineral deposits.

Guidebooks: Kelsey (1987a)

Maps: USGS 1:100,000 Hanksville, Hite Crossing, Loa, Escalante

Area of wilderness proposals in acres:

Unit	UWC	BLM
Bull Mountain	12,400	11,800
Bullfrog Creek	36,900	0
Mt Ellen-Blue Hills	116,900	65,804
Mount Hillers	18,600	16,360
Mount Pennell	141,200	25,800
Ragged Mountain	23,300	0
TOTAL	349,300	119,764

Adjacent wild lands: Capitol Reef National Park, Glen Canyon National Recreation Area

Storm over the Henry Mountains.

Stu Levy

the Henry Mountains region, including beaver, deer, cougar, bighorn sheep, and a herd of more than 300 buffalo—the largest free-roaming, hunted buffalo herd in the nation. The mountain range, together with the benchlands and valleys on its flanks, provides 100,000 acres of critical summer and winter range for deer and buffalo.

A Cluster of Small Circles?

Remote, silent, beautiful, the Henry Mountains region has long been recognized as an important natural and recreational area. Over 50 years ago, the Department of the Interior included virtually the entire Henry Mountains region, from Glen Canyon to the Waterpocket Fold, in its proposal for a 4.5-million-acre Escalante National Monument. The proposal was defeated by powerful development interests, and portions of the region have since been scarred by mining and livestock developments. Yet even today, most of the Henry Mountains region—350,000 acres in all—remains wild.

In 1979, when the Bureau of Land Management began its inventory of Utah wild lands, the Henry Mountains region was a prime candidate for wilderness study. But by the fall of 1980, when the BLM completed its inventory, something had gone wrong. The BLM had arbitrarily omitted over 240,000 acres of wild lands from its wilderness inventory—more than two-thirds of the Henry Mountains wilderness. Ignoring hundreds of thousands of acres of rugged mesa, canyon, and badlands terrain, the BLM

Hanksville

95

24

Sweetwater Creek

Bull Mountain

Mt. Ellen

Ragged Mountain

Mt. Pennell

South
Caineville Mesa

Capitol Reef
National Park

Blue Hills
Badlands

Thompson
Mesa

Wildcat Mesa

Notom Road

Tarantula
Mesa

Capitol Reef
National Park

Burr Trail

W A T E

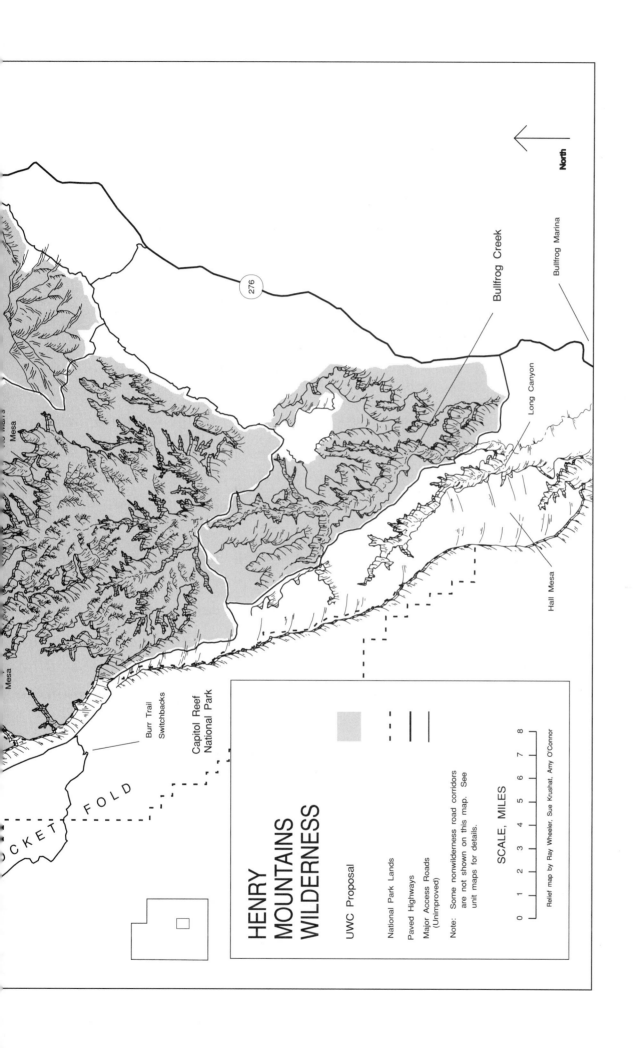

North

276

Bullfrog Creek

Bullfrog Marina

Long Canyon

Hall Mesa

Mesa

Mesa

POCKET FOLD

Burr Trail
Switchbacks

Capitol Reef
National Park

HENRY
MOUNTAINS
WILDERNESS

UWC Proposal

National Park Lands

Paved Highways

Major Access Roads
(Unimproved)

Note: Some nonwilderness road corridors
are not shown on this map.   See
unit maps for details.

SCALE, MILES

0   1   2   3   4   5   6   7   8

Relief map by Ray Wheeler, Sue Krushat, Amy O'Connor

had reduced a vast natural area to a cluster of small circles drawn around the summits of four high peaks in the range. All else had been dropped from the inventory.

In the two largest wilderness inventory units in the region—Mt. Ellen and Mt. Pennell—the BLM dropped more than 100,000 acres of land which the agency itself had acknowledged to be free of human impacts. Utah conservationists were astonished at the omissions. The BLM had dropped from the inventory some of the most beautiful, interesting, and important wild lands in the region, including some 50,000 acres surrounding Thompson, Wildcat, and South Caineville mesas and the eerie Blue Hills badlands, 15,000 acres of critical buffalo winter range on Swap Mesa, 37,000 acres of deep canyons along lower Bullfrog Creek, and 65,000 acres of Mancos Shale badlands south of Swap Mesa and Mt. Pennell.

Successful Appeals

In making the cuts, the BLM had repeatedly violated both the law and its own inventory policies, which clearly state that the agency must identify *all* lands with wilderness character as part of its inventory. In 1981, Utah conservationists appealed the BLM's inventory decisions, and in 1983, the Interior Department's Board of Land Appeals found the BLM in error on nearly 90 percent of the lands under appeal in the region. The IBLA directed the BLM to reconsider its decisions. The BLM reconsidered—and once again dropped the same lands from the inventory. *Once again* Utah conservationists appealed, and *once again* the IBLA found the BLM decision in error. This time the IBLA simply ordered the BLM to add 65,000 acres to the Mt. Ellen and Mt. Pennell WSAs.

But appeals could not force the BLM to acknowledge the outstanding character of the Henry Mountains wilderness. When the agency announced its draft wilderness recommendation in February, 1986, its meager 87,280-acre wilderness proposal omitted nearly 300,000 acres of wild lands surrounding the Henry Mountains—roughly three-quarters of the Henry Mountain wilderness. The Ragged Mountain, Long Canyon, and Bullfrog Creek roadless areas should be open to development, the BLM decided. For the Mt. Pennell wilderness inventory unit, a 141,000-acre roadless area of stunning beauty and diversity, the BLM recommended no wilderness at all. The agency finally added a small part of Mt. Pennell, and increased the size of its Mt. Ellen recommendation, only following strong public protest.

Why has the BLM so tenaciously opposed wilderness designation in the Henrys? The answer lies buried in the agency's planning documents. At the time of the wilderness inventory, the nation was in the midst of an energy crisis, and the Carter Administration had identified coal as the fuel of the future. The mesas and badlands bordering the Henry Mountains on the west—the lands repeatedly dropped from the BLM's wilderness inventory, and from its draft wilderness recommendations—contain coal.

By 1981, the BLM had completed a study which determined that over 100,000 acres within the Henry Mountains coal field should be opened to coal leasing, including 22,000 acres found suitable for strip mining. Had these lands been included within the Mt. Ellen and Mt. Pennell WSAs, they would have been closed to strip mining until the Congress could determine whether they should be protected as wilderness. Instead, all lands found suitable for coal development were summarily dropped from the two WSAs.

Ironically, the BLM was zoning for strip mining on a coal field that is of negligible value in comparison to the nation's vast coal reserves—and to the scenic and recreational value of the wild lands which would be permanently scarred by strip mining. In total, the Henry Mountains coal field contains an estimated 230 million tons of recoverable coal—but that coal may not be feasible to mine at all, given the aridity of the area and the distance to markets.

"Treating" the Range

Meanwhile, the BLM's desire to promote huge increases in the number of livestock on the range had begun to influence its wilderness recommendations for the Henry Mountains WSAs.

By 1983, when the agency completed its Henry Mountains Grazing Environmental Impact Study (BLM, 1983b), it was clear that the range was seriously overgrazed. "Evidence of overgrazing still exists," stated the EIS. "Non-native, weedy annual plant species have become established; cheatgrass, Russian thistle, sunflowers, and various unpalatable mustards are common. There has been a gradual replacement of herbaceous species by woody species of lower forage value."

Throughout large portions of the Henry Mountains planning unit, overgrazing was so severe that it had caused serious soil erosion. The EIS identified more than 50,000 acres of rangelands in the planning unit as being in "severe" or "critical" erosion condition. A study of 46 streams in the planning unit revealed that over 50 percent of their riparian habitat was in poor condition due to overgrazing.

The problem is simple and clear: there are too many animals for the range. Since the passage of the Taylor Grazing Act in 1934, the BLM had made reductions in the number of livestock, yet the range remained overgrazed. Recent BLM trend studies had shown that range conditions are improving on less than one-third of the study plots—and are *declining* on 20 percent. "The current numbers of big game (particularly bison) and allotted numbers of livestock presently overuse available forage in key . . . areas," concluded a 1988 BLM planning document. "Continuation of heavy use in these areas . . . will necessitate a reduction in the numbers of livestock and/or bison if ranges are to be protected."

While buffalo and deer have high visibility in BLM grazing studies, their numbers are negligible in comparison to livestock. In 1983, the BLM estimated that throughout the Henry Mountains planning unit, forage use by livestock was *six times* the use by wildlife. While the Henry Mountains buffalo herd numbers between 300 and 400 animals, and the Henry Mountains deer herd may have a population of several thousand, the 58 livestock permittees in the planning unit are running approximately *15,000* cattle and sheep on the range.

If there are too many animals for the available forage, the solution would seem as elementary as the problem: reduce the number of animals. But the BLM's management prescription for the Henry Mountains planning unit is precisely the opposite. In 1984, the agency announced that its long-term forage allocation for livestock throughout the planning unit would be *an increase of 89 percent over 1983 levels of use*. If implemented, the plan could nearly double the number of livestock on the range.

To support the increase in livestock, the BLM proposes to increase the amount of available forage by means of "vegetation treatment projects," in which blocks of pinyon-juniper forest would be destroyed by chaining or burning to create new artificial pastures for livestock. The Henry Mountains Grazing EIS (BLM, 1983b) proposed over 24,000 acres of such treatments, scattered across the forested flanks of the range. While the treatment projects were billed as habitat for wildlife, the BLM's own documents reveal that 82 percent of the additional forage would be consumed by livestock.

At the time of [the Henry Mountain's] discovery by Professor Powell the mountains were in the center of the largest unexplored district in the territory of the United States—a district which by its peculiar ruggedness had turned aside all previous travelers.

Grove Karl Gilbert

GEOLOGY OF THE HENRY MOUNTAINS
(1877)

Where proposed range treatment projects lay within wilderness study areas, the BLM's solution was simple: lands identified for range treatment would not be recommended for wilderness. Thus in 1986 the agency recommended "no wilderness" for the entire 74,000-acre Mt. Pennell WSA in part because of a single proposed range treatment project—variously depicted as 1,000 to 5,000 acres in size—on the wild southwestern flank of the mountain. The BLM announced in 1990 that it would recommend 25,800 acres of its WSA. But in all, over 4,000 acres of proposed treatments lie within the Henry Mountains WSAs.

Wilderness designation will not eliminate livestock grazing in the Henry Mountains. The Wilderness Act allows grazing to continue at existing levels of use in designated wilderness areas. Instead, wilderness designation will help to ensure the long-term productivity of the range by preventing destructive developments such as strip mining and by placing upper limits on the number of animals on the range.

Strip Mining or Wilderness?

For the Henry Mountains wilderness, the choices for the future are clear. The BLM would allow at least 40,000 acres of strip mining and deforestation to scar the landscape between Capitol Reef National Park and the high peaks of the Henrys. By contrast, the Utah Wilderness Coalition proposal would protect long-term values, including wildlife habitat, scenic vistas, and the region's great potential for attracting tourism.

The Coalition's 349,300-acre proposal would protect over 230,000 acres of superb natural landmarks which the BLM would zone for development. It would protect a complete ecological spectrum, ranging from the

Although the BLM omitted South Caineville Mesa from its 1986 draft wilderness recommendations, letters written to the agency by concerned citizens may persuade it to protect this landmark. The BLM, however, did not even study the wild lands at the base of the mesa.

Bob Bauer

windswept alpine zone at the summit of Mt. Ellen, down through the forests of spruce, aspen, ponderosa, and pinyon pine, to the badlands surrounding the range. It would protect South Caineville Mesa, one of the largest relict plant areas in the state. It would protect the strange and beautiful Blue Hills badlands, and the lonely promontories of Wildcat, Thompson, Tarantula, and Swap mesas. It would protect tens of thousands of acres of critical winter habitat for buffalo and deer. Above all, it would protect the silence, mystery, and strange, compelling beauty of these visitors from another world.

Ray Wheeler

MT. ELLEN-BLUE HILLS UNIT

Highlights—Two distinct landforms and vegetative areas characterize the unit: the virtually barren Blue Hills badlands and the 11,000-foot peaks of Mt. Ellen, which support dense pinyon-juniper, aspen, and spruce-fir forests. In juxtaposition, Mt. Ellen and the Blue Hills form a single roadless area—one of the largest in Utah—of spectacular ecologic, scenic, and recreational diversity. Mt. Ellen is a stunning backdrop for Capitol Reef National Park's slickrock domes and cliffs and for the nearby Escalante, San Rafael Swell, and Dirty Devil wilderness areas. The BLM's recommended wilderness unit excludes the spectacular mesas and badlands in the western part of the unit for the sake of insignificant coal deposits and uranium exploration. The Utah Wilderness Coalition's 116,900-acre proposal would protect sensitive watersheds, wildlife habitat, and relict plant communities.

Geology and landforms—Mt. Ellen, at 11,615 feet, is the highest peak in the Henry Mountains. From the summit of its long, rolling ridge unfolds a panorama of dissected canyon country and mountain ranges. To the west of the peak are the mesas and badlands of the Blue Hills, carved into the Mancos Shale. These stark erosional features have been described as "ever so much badder than Badlands National Monument" (Hunt, 1980). Fossilized shark teeth are found here. The entire area has fascinated geologists ever since G.K. Gilbert's landmark 1875 monograph on the Henrys. Gilbert proposed a new theory of mountain uplift, the laccolith, now understood to have formed the La Sal and Abajo Mountains as well.

Plant communities—Life zones ranging from the Upper Sonoran to Hudsonian are represented here. Aspen, subalpine fir, Douglas fir, and ponderosa pine dominate the slopes of Mt. Ellen; these are interspersed with windswept grasslands. Bristlecone pine grow on the highest slopes. A pinyon-juniper forest mantles the base of the mountain, grading into desert shrubs and eventually the utterly barren land of the Blue Hills. The BLM has designated South Caineville Mesa as an Area of Critical Environmental Concern (ACEC) because of its near-relict plant community. The mesa, which has not been grazed since 1950, supports abundant bunchgrasses (found in minimal densities on grazed lands) along with sagebrush, saltbush, and dwarf mountain mahogany. A 3,680-acre area, the Gilbert Badlands of Mancos Shale, harbors a unique relict plant community of mat saltbush.

Wildlife—The slopes of Mt. Ellen provide critical habitat for the nation's only free-roaming, hunted buffalo herd. Mule deer, pronghorn antelope, and cougar also live here along with various small mammals and birds. The mesas offer fine promontories from which to watch raptors soar along a main hawk migration route. Virtually all species of raptors can be seen during the migration season including golden eagles and prairie falcons.

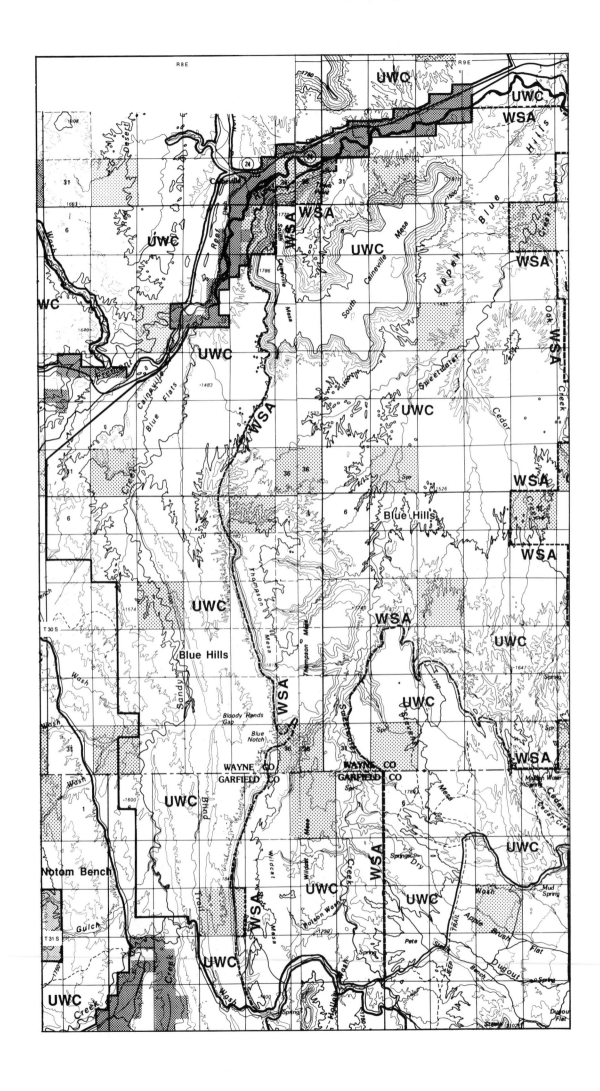

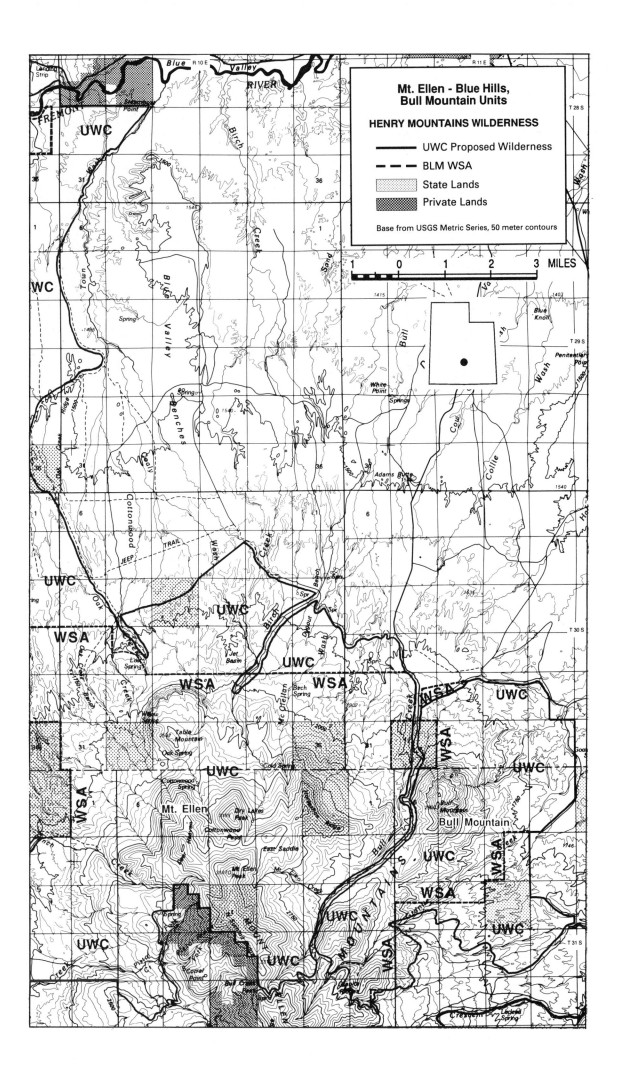

Mt. Ellen - Blue Hills,
Bull Mountain Units

HENRY MOUNTAINS WILDERNESS

—————— UWC Proposed Wilderness

- - - - - - BLM WSA

State Lands

Private Lands

Base from USGS Metric Series, 50 meter contours

1   0   1   2   3   MILES

The top of South Caineville Mesa—surrounded by some of the "baddest" badlands anywhere—is one of the largest relict plant areas in Utah. In the distance are North Caineville Mesa and Factory Butte in the proposed San Rafael wilderness.

Tom Miller

Archeology and history—Although detailed surveys have not been done, the BLM (1986) notes 7 campsites and chipping sites around Mt. Ellen and 29 similar sites in the Blue Hills. An old stone herder's cabin on South Caineville Mesa, a lonely outpost, has been nominated to the National Register.

Recreation—The summit of Mt. Ellen is a relatively easy jaunt along the ridge north from Bull Creek Pass; when snow blocks the road, ascents may be made from Lonesome Beaver Campground. Extended backpacking trips are possible via the Sweetwater Creek drainage or around the lower elevations of Mt. Ellen. The BLM notes that there are 60 miles of hiking routes in its WSA alone. Detailed hiking information is found in Kelsey (1986a; 1987a).

BLM recommendation—The BLM recommended wilderness designation for Mt. Ellen itself, part of the Blue Hills, and connecting benchlands. Areas of equal wilderness values were split off and deleted. Some 7,300 acres were to be added to the recommendation in 1990—still a fraction of the omitted lands. The boundary proposed in 1986 skirts South Caineville Mesa with no difference in naturalness between the part deleted and that remaining in the WSA. The Blue Hills were also split through completely natural areas. These deletions closely follow the lines of mineral leases and claims. Most of the BLM's boundary follows section lines deleting magnificent portions of the Blue Hills from wilderness designation. The BLM proposal also deleted the important buffalo habitat found on the scenic Thompson and Wildcat Mesas. In violation of its wilderness study policy, the BLM has allowed bulldozing of a forest, construction of a reservoir, and construction of a new road. Instead of insisting on reclamation of these intrusions, the agency plans to drop the affected lands from its wilderness proposal. On the southeast corner of the WSA, the BLM illegally chained about 300 acres during the wilderness study. The agency recommended this portion for wilderness in 1986, claiming that it had been rehabilitated, but its final proposal is expected to omit the area.

Coalition proposal—We propose wilderness designation for 116,900 acres, including areas excluded by the BLM (South Caineville Mesa, Thompson Mesa, Wildcat Mesa, Upper Sweetwater Creek, Oak Creek Ridge, and Cedar Creek). Dry drill holes and detailed geologic information substantiates the conclusion that there are no significant oil or gas conflicts within the area. Most of this unit is in a completely natural condition. The BLM lists 12.8 miles of ways, 2.5 miles of fence, and six livestock reservoirs within its WSA. Exxon cleared several acres and reconstructed nearly a mile of road to drill for oil and gas; there was no production, and the area was revegetated. The only impact on the 4,000-acre South Caineville Mesa is an historic stone shack near the mesa's southeastern ridge. The steep canyon, which serves as the only major access route to South Caineville Mesa, contains an eroded stock trail which has a minimal effect on naturalness. East of the mesa, our boundary follows a pipeline and access roads north to near the Fremont River. Wildcat Mesa is also substantially natural. In its intensive inventory documents, the BLM mentions no impacts on naturalness in the Upper Sweetwater Creek drainage or the deleted areas near Cedar Creek and Oak Creek Ridge.

BULL MOUNTAIN UNIT

Highlights—The granite-cliffed dome of Bull Mountain (see Mt. Ellen map) is the northeast buttress of the Henry Mountains and a landmark for visitors to the surrounding canyons and deserts. Bull Mountain's striking landscape offers great vistas across the northern Colorado Plateau, excellent day hikes beginning from an established BLM campground on the west boundary, and crucial summer range for deer and bison. Bull Mountain is separated from the Mt. Ellen-Blue Hills unit on the west and the Ragged Mountain unit at two points on the south by only narrow unpaved roads. The Utah Wilderness Coalition proposes designation of 12,400 acres. The BLM recommends 11,800 acres, omitting scenic lands on the east side of the mountain.

Geology and landforms—Like the other peaks in the Henry Mountains, Bull Mountain is the core of an igneous intrusion exposed by erosion of overlying sedimentary rocks. It is a bysmalith, in which the overlying rocks were lifted not by folding but by faulting, giving it steeper slopes than other peaks in the Henrys. Bull Mountain's golden cliffs and high ridges dominate the western half of the unit, while low-lying badlands and rims characterize the eastern half. Elevations vary from 5,000 feet in the northeast to 9,800 feet in the southwestern corner on Wickiup Ridge. Bull Creek drains along the western boundary and Granite Creek along the eastern side of the mountain. Granite Creek is the headwaters for Beaver Wash, a riparian area designated as an ACEC in the Dirty Devil proposed wilderness.

Plant communities—Stands of aspen, ponderosa pine, and fir grow at higher elevations, but pinyon-juniper and shrub-grass communities dominate the unit. Barren cliffs and badlands cover large areas, as well. The Cronquist wild-buckwheat (*Eriogonum cronquistii*), a sensitive species, occurs here.

Wildlife— The BLM identified 4,550 acres of crucial deer summer range and 7,000 acres of crucial bison summer range in the WSA. The bison summer range is in the western side of the unit, and the deer summer range is in the southwestern part (BLM, 1983b, p. 53, p. 51). All non-WSA lands and the northeastern quarter of the WSA are yearlong antelope habitat (BLM, 1983b, p. 55).

Recreation—Visitors to Bull Mountain enjoy excellent hiking, climbing, camping, geologic sightseeing, and wildlife viewing. The summit offers superlative views south and west to other peaks in the Henry Mountains, east to the Dirty Devil Canyons, and north to the Muddy Creek badlands and San Rafael Reef. The hike to the summit of Bull Mountain begins from the Lonesome Beaver campground (Kelsey, 1987a). The hike down Wickiup Ridge (a ridge with several peaks connecting Bull Mountain's summit with Mt. Ellen to the southwest) and Granite Ridge goes through a delightful aspen forest with distant views.

BLM recommendation—The BLM recommends its 11,800-acre WSA for designation but fails to recommend several hundred acres that were improperly released from study during the wilderness inventory. In its 1980 intensive inventory decision, the BLM exaggerated the extent of impacts in the eastern portion of the unit. It excluded the claimed impacts and three state sections by drawing a straight-line boundary, thus violating inventory policy by not placing its WSA boundary at the edge of physical disturbance. The land excluded from the BLM's recommendation are almost entirely scenic, highly erosive Morrison badlands that are the foreground for views from Bull Mountain.

Coalition proposal—We propose wilderness designation for the entire 12,400 acres of wild lands around Bull Mountain to protect outstanding scenic values, sensitive watersheds, and important wildlife values. These lands have insignificant mineral potential; the entire unit should be protected from ORV abuse, unwarranted mineral exploration, and destructive chainings in order to protect overriding natural values.

RAGGED MOUNTAIN UNIT

Highlights—This unit contains the most visually striking example of the geologic forces that created the Henry Mountains. Rock layers pushed upward by molten rock form concentric circles of cliffs and canyons at the center of the unit. Ragged Mountain offers scenic vistas of this uplift as well as other peaks in the Henrys and across the surrounding deserts. While the BLM did not designate Ragged Mountain as a WSA, we propose a 23,300-acre unit to protect this central link in the Henry Mountain wilderness.

Geology and landforms—Like Bull Mountain, Ragged Mountain itself is a bysmalith (an igneous intrusion with faulted sides). Just to the east, though, at the center of the unit is what may be the best expression in the Henry Mountains of a laccolith's doming effect on overlying sediments (see area overview). Here, The Block, a 7,646-foot peak, is surrounded by rings of Dakota, Morrison, Summerville, Entrada, Carmel, and Navajo formations. The harder layers form cliffs facing toward the Block. Canyons in the softer formations meet in Pyserts Hole east of the Block. Elevations vary almost 4,000 feet from 5,200 feet in North Wash on the eastern boundary to 9,113 feet at Ragged Mountain. Pennellen Pass, the low point on the ridge between Mt. Pennell and Mt. Ellen, lies on the western boundary of this unit.

Plant communities—Pinyon and juniper forest predominates at higher elevations on the west; desert shrubs and grasses at lower slopes on the east.

Wildlife—The BLM identified the western half of the unit as crucial summer range for bison and the south-central portion as crucial winter range for deer (BLM, 1983b, p. 51, 53).

Recreation—Hikes through Pyserts Hole to Raggy Canyon and other drainages around The Block begin from the Crescent Creek road on the eastern side of the unit (this road joins Highway 95, 26 miles south of Hanksville just north of the junction of Highways 95 and 276). Ragged Mountain is most easily climbed from Garden Basin on the northwestern side of the mountain.

BLM recommendation—The entire unit was released from wilderness review during the intensive inventory. The BLM claimed that only 15,000

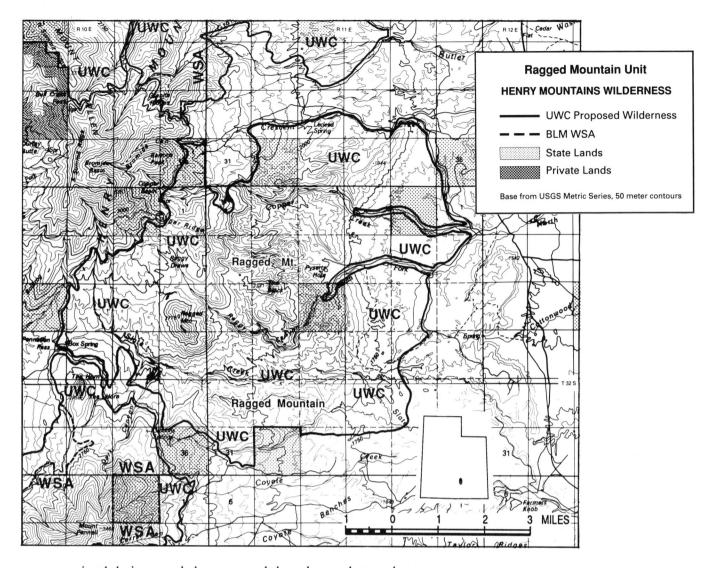

Ragged Mountain Unit

HENRY MOUNTAINS WILDERNESS

———— UWC Proposed Wilderness

– – – BLM WSA

State Lands

Private Lands

Base from USGS Metric Series, 50 meter contours

acres retained their natural character and then dropped even that acreage by misapplying the outstanding opportunities criterion. In its November 1980 intensive inventory decision the agency found that opportunities for solitude "are less than outstanding on the majority of the unit due to poor vegetative screening." On the basis of this statement, the BLM violated inventory policy in two ways: (1) outstanding opportunities need only be present in part of the unit in order to qualify the entire unit for wilderness study and (2) vegetative screening is not the only factor in outstanding solitude; the unit's large size, blocked configuration, and rugged topography should also have been considered. Moreover, the vegetative screening provided by the unit's dense pinyon-juniper forest contributes to outstanding opportunities for solitude. The decision ignored the outstanding recreation values of the unit's spectacular geologic formations and scenic vistas.

Coalition proposal—A 23,300-acre Ragged Mountain wilderness unit connecting the northern and southern peaks of the Henry Mountains should be designated to protect scenery, recreation, wildlife, and watershed values. The BLM has dropped its proposals for chainings within this unit, removing the only conflict with wilderness.

MT. PENNELL UNIT

Highlights—The second highest peak in the Henry Mountains, Mt. Pennell crowns an area of great topographic and ecologic diversity. Averaging 12 miles east-west and 14 miles north-south with nearly 7,000 feet of relief, this is an awe-inspiring landscape of badlands, mesas, and mountains. From atop Mt. Pennell's summit at 11,371 feet, stunning vistas reveal how the badlands and mesas link the Henry Mountains to Capitol Reef National Park. None of this landscape was included in the BLM's 1986 recommendation, and a mere 25,800 acres was to be included in the agency's final recommendation. The Utah Wilderness Coalition proposal for designation of 141,200 acres as wilderness would safeguard it in its entirety.

Geology and landforms—The expansive badlands in the southern half of the unit vary from relatively flat or rolling to extremely rugged. These badlands, with their abstract forms and stark shadows, offer outstanding sightseeing and photography. In the northwest quarter, Swap Mesa and Cave Flat are an intermediate step between the gray Mancos Shale badlands below and the light-colored high cliffs of the Mesa Verde Group surrounding Tarantula Mesa above. Mt. Pennell rises over all in the northeastern quarter, its igneous core exposed by the erosion of the overlying sediments. All but the northeastern and northwestern edges drain into Bullfrog Creek, which runs from north to south through the center of the unit. The BLM (1986, p. 14) rates 11 percent of the unit as in a critical erosion condition and 55 percent as moderate.

Plant communities—The gentler badlands have shadscale, blackbrush, and grasses while the more rugged areas are barren. The mesas and the lower slopes of Mt. Pennell support pinyon-juniper forests; the higher slopes, oakbrush, aspen, and fir. The endangered Wright's fishhook cactus (*Sclerocactus wrightiae*) is found in the unit; Cronquist daisy (*Eriogonum cronquistii*) and Winkler cactus (*Pediocactus winkleri*), candidates for threatened or endangered listing, may be present. Five perennial streams and 11 springs support 38 acres of riparian vegetation (BLM, 1986, p. 14-15).

Wildlife—The BLM (1986, p. 17) has identified at least 48,000 acres of the unit as "crucial-critical deer and/or bison range" and notes that mountain lions and coyotes are also present.

Recreation—Mt. Pennell offers excellent opportunities for primitive and unconfined recreation, including rock climbing, backpacking, day hiking, nature study, photography, wildlife viewing, and even mountain skiing in winter. The five-mile-long route up Mt. Pennell, outlined in Kelsey's guide (1987a), climbs more than 3,500 feet. The diorite outcrop called The Horn is an excellent place to rock climb, offering smooth vertical faces as well as tamer hiking routes from the north and west (Kelsey, 1987a). The badlands offer excellent day hiking and photography opportunities.

BLM recommendation—The BLM initially recommended none of its 74,300-acre WSA for wilderness designation and excluded an equal amount of wild land from the WSA. The final proposal is expected to be 25,800 acres. The non-WSA lands consist of about 33,000 acres in the Pennell Creek and Saleratus Wash badlands south of Mt. Pennell and about 40,000 acres on and north of Tarantula Mesa. The agency claimed (in its 1980 intensive inventory and 1983 reinventory decisions) that the Pennell Creek and Saleratus Wash badlands lacked outstanding solitude or primitive recreation. The "exploration disturbances" in the Saleratus Wash area are decades-old bulldozer tracks on highly erodible shales which are now largely unnoticeable. These extensive badlands are some of the most rugged terrain in all of Utah and provide solitude and beauty rivalling any wild place in America. The lands on and north of Tarantula Mesa were excluded for no stated reason in the BLM's 1980 intensive inventory decision. By excluding the chained portions of the mesa, our proposal retains the nearly pristine forest on the western and northern spurs of the mesa and the huge canyons cutting into its northern face—Divide, Spring, Five, and Seven canyons.

The BLM also gave no explicit rationale for recommending none of the WSA lands for wilderness designation. The 1,270 acres of strippable coal on Cave Flat are designated unsuitable for leasing by the BLM because of critical bison range and low oil and gas potential, and because hardrock mineral deposits "have been studied extensively since the 1890s and have remained subeconomical to develop due to their limited extent and quality" (BLM, 1986, p. 16-17). Twelve hundred acres are identified for potential chaining on the west side of Mt. Pennell, but this is hardly an excuse for not designating the other 73,000 acres of the WSA. The key to the BLM's reasoning lies not in its evaluation of resource conflicts, but in its evaluation of the wilderness resource itself. First, it claimed that 3,300 acres do not meet the naturalness criterion because of 12 miles of ways and 29.1 miles of roads (BLM, 1986, p. 19). These are, in fact, bulldozer tracks and vehicle ways which are largely unnoticeable in the context of the surrounding wild lands. Then the BLM claimed that only 17,800 acres have outstanding solitude and primitive recreation. Predictably, the outstanding area is found only on Mt. Pennell and not on Swap Mesa or the badlands south of Swap Mesa. Those areas were added to the WSA only after two conservationist appeals and a reversal by the IBLA. The BLM's unwillingness to recommend designation for this WSA is nothing less than an unwillingness to admit it was wrong. It also reflects the antipathy of the agency's politicized line officers to wilderness even in the absence of substantive conflicts.

Coalition proposal—At 141,200 acres, Mt. Pennell is the largest unit in our proposed Henry Mountains wilderness. This breathtaking landscape clearly deserves protection for its own sake and to complement the adjacent wild lands in Capitol Reef National Park. Our proposal includes important wildlife habitat, the unchained portions of Tarantula Mesa, and the magnificent escarpments surrounding Spring Canyon.

BULLFROG CREEK UNIT

Highlights—Bullfrog Creek (see map of Long Canyon, Escalante area) is an intermittent stream that begins high on the western slopes of the Henry Mountains and flows south for 30 miles to the reservoir in Glen Canyon. Most of the first 18 miles lie in the badlands of the Mt. Pennell wilderness unit, the next 10 miles in an eye-popping thousand-foot-deep canyon in this unit, and the last 2 miles in the adjacent Glen Canyon National Recreation Area. The BLM released this unit from further wilderness consideration in its 1979 initial inventory. The Utah Wilderness Coalition proposal would preserve nearly the entire wild course of the creek, interrupted only by chainings on the headwaters, the unpaved Starr Springs-Eggnog road, and the Burr Trail.

Geology and landforms—The canyons of Bullfrog Creek and its western tributary, Clay Canyon, are in the reddish-brown Entrada Sandstone and the chocolate muds of the Summerville Formation. The benches above the canyons, Middle Point and Clay Point, are in the colorful conglomerates, clays, and sandstones of the Morrison Formation, the light-colored Dakota Sandstone, and the lower layers of the gray Mancos Shale badlands (Hintze, n.d.). About 7,000 acres of this unit on Clay Point were identified as part of a 10,000-acre fossil plant locality by three Brigham Young University scientists (Welsh and others, 1980). They noted:

> The Salt Wash and Brushy Basin Members of the Morrison Formation are here exposed very well and contain an unusual concentra-

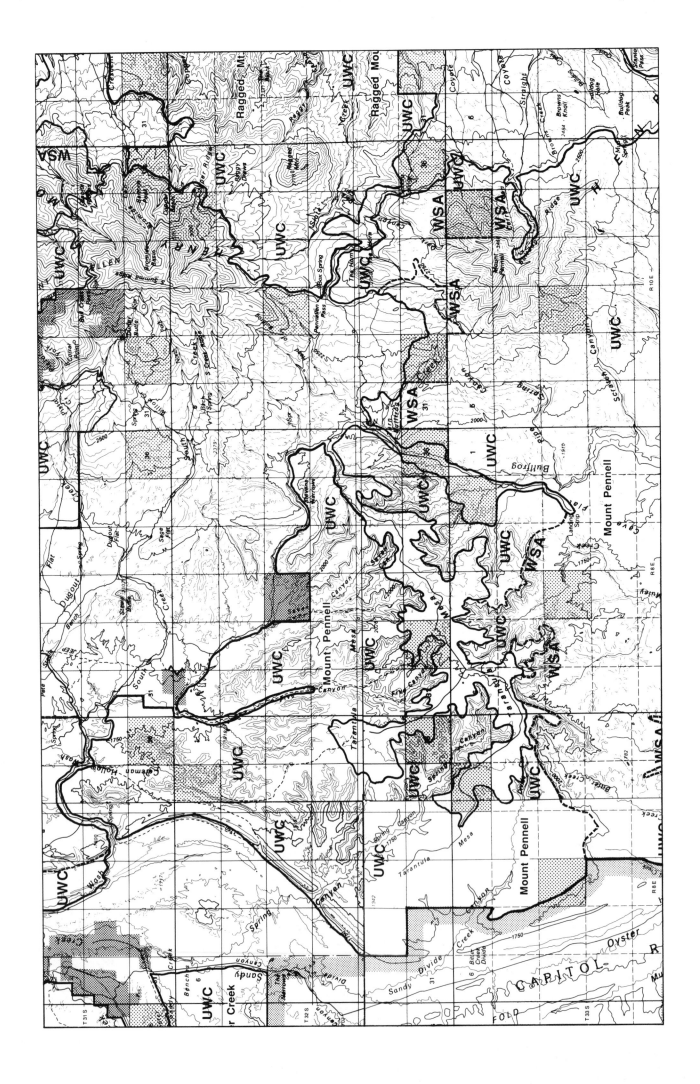

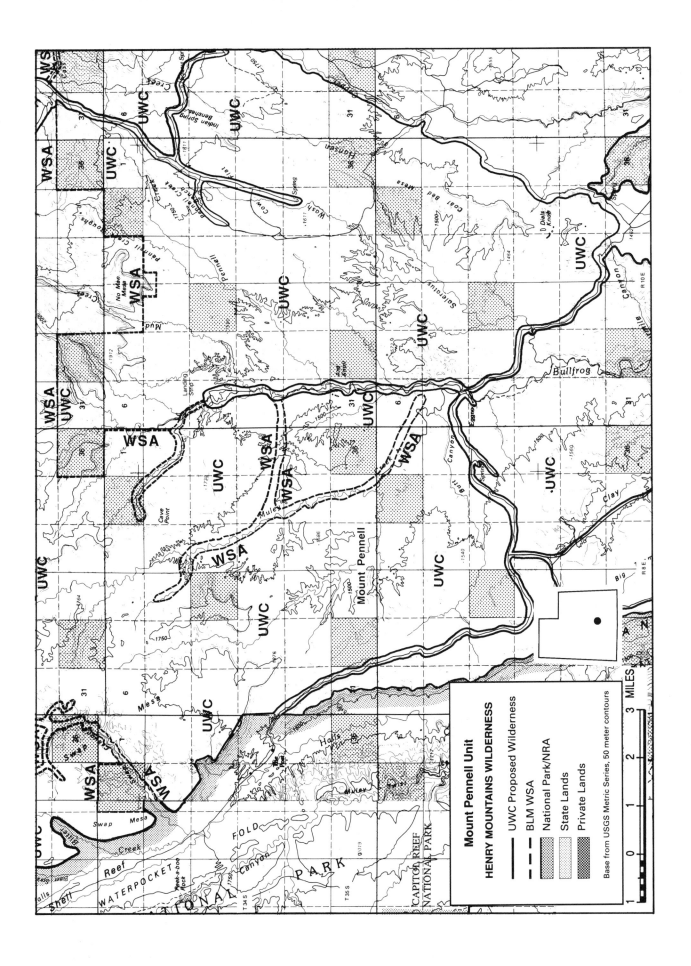

Mount Pennell Unit

HENRY MOUNTAINS WILDERNESS

	UWC Proposed Wilderness
	BLM WSA
	National Park/NRA
	State Lands
	Private Lands

Base from USGS Metric Series, 50 meter contours

0   1   2   3 MILES

Rock climbers as well as hikers are attracted to the east face of The Horn, a diorite outcrop northeast of Mt. Pennell (background).

Michael R. Kelsey

tion of fossil wood . . . . It is principally to preserve some remnant of the large logs of this extensive Jurassic fossil conifer community that this area is proposed. Triassic fossil woods are well represented in the park system by Petrified Forest National Park but the equally, if not more, significant Jurassic woods, such as represented here, have not been placed under some protective umbrella . . . . Primary concern here is for the rapid disappearance of the fossil wood from this Jurassic unit. Nowhere in the park system are extensive Jurassic fossil petrified forests preserved, yet this area, in which Morrison wood is abundant, is now being rapidly gleaned by rock hounds with extensive utilization of off-road vehicles.

Plant communities and wildlife—Sparse desert shrubs, mostly shadscale and blackbrush, cover most of the unit. Large areas are barren. Pinyon and juniper trees are found on the upper benches. The bench areas offer winter range for mule deer; the flats in the southeastern part of the unit are yearlong range for antelope (BLM, 1983b).

Recreation—In addition to the outstanding opportunities for geologic sightseeing on Clay Point described above, the unit also offers outstanding hiking, backpacking, and photography in Bullfrog Creek canyon and Clay Canyon and on the rims of the canyons. The Burr Trail (which begins on Highway 276 six miles north of Bullfrog Marina) gives access to the western rim of the canyons. This road crosses Bullfrog Creek below the unit in Glen Canyon National Recreation Area. The Eggnog crossing of Bullfrog Creek on the north boundary is on the road that leads west and south from the BLM's Starr Spring Campground (which is reached from Highway 276 between mile posts 17 and 18) to the Burr Trail.

BLM recommendation—The BLM did not designate Bullfrog Creek as a WSA, alleging that it had lost its natural character due to mineral exploration and off-road vehicle use.

Coalition proposal—Our field work shows that only 3,000 acres of the BLM's 24,000-acre inventory unit (on the northern part of Clay Point and Hansen Canyon) are unnatural. Additional wild lands the BLM did not inventory bring the size of this unit to 36,900 acres. In the mid-1950s, a jeep track was put down Bullfrog Creek from Eggnog on the north. This has not been passable for more than 10 years, and there is little evidence of

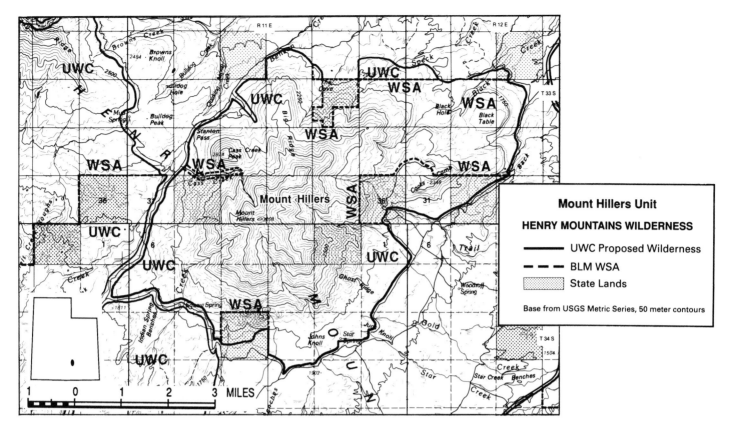

the vehicle way today. There are two 1/4-mile-long vehicle tracks across the benches to Clay Seep and Thompson Seep. These unmaintained and rarely used short tracks are also insignificant intrusions.

MT. HILLERS UNIT

Highlights—The third highest peak in the Henry Mountains, Mt. Hillers is located between Mt. Pennell and the Little Rockies; as such it links the Henrys with the Glen Canyon proposed wilderness. The 18,600-acre unit offers fine scenery, hiking, and camping as well as important big game habitat. Mt. Hillers rises prominently to the west of Utah Highway 276 between Highway 95 and Bullfrog. A well-maintained gravel road leads from the highway to the BLM's Starr Spring Campground, a good place to begin a climb of the mountain. A dirt road circles west from Starr Spring to the north side of the mountain to two other starting places for climbing Mt. Hillers: Woodruff Stone Cabin and Cass Creek.

Geology and landforms—The exposed igneous ridges of Mt. Hillers illustrate the geologic forces that formed this laccolithic mountain range. As in all of the Henrys, views from the top are outstanding. The Pink Cliffs, large slabs of Navajo Sandstone tilted up by the igneous intrusion on the south slope of the mountain, are highly scenic and geologically interesting.

Plant communities—Douglas fir, ponderosa pine, and bristlecone pine grow on the steep slopes of the mountain.

Some of the densest pinyon-juniper forest in the Henry Mountains is found on the bench areas of this unit.

Wildlife—Mt. Hillers' lower pinyon-juniper benchlands are critical deer habitat. The entire mountain is potential habitat for desert bighorn sheep. A few buffalo graze the unit as well.

Archeology and history—The BLM notes that there are 20 archeological sites within its WSA, all temporary occupation sites. Additional sites may well be discovered on the lower slopes of the mountain.

Recreation—There are several routes to the summit of Mt. Hillers which vary in difficulty and length. Hillers is a steep climb; Kelsey (1987a) outlines three routes to the top, ranging up to five miles in length. The terrain offers considerable variety—cliffs, canyons, and fins abound on the south side of Mt. Hillers. The lower benchlands are heavily forested with pinyon-juniper, and there are many suitable sites for camping in addition to Starr Spring. There are also a few other springs noted by Kelsey.

BLM recommendation—The BLM proposes 16,360 acres of wilderness, dropping much of the benchland surrounding the peak. The agency claims that these benchlands have limited topographic and vegetative screening. Its rationale may have more to do with proposed forest chainings and vegetative manipulation projects. Mineral potential is negligible; the BLM's evaluation notes that deposits of uranium, the mineral most likely to occur in the unit, would be scattered and small. Some post-FLPMA oil and gas leases exist in the unit but the BLM's consultant deemed the probability of finding deposits low.

Coalition proposal—Our 18,600-acre proposed wilderness includes the lower benchlands dropped by the BLM, which provide important wildlife habitat and contribute to the ecological integrity of the proposal. The stands of pinyon and juniper on these benchlands, broken by numerous small canyons, offer privacy to hikers, contrary to the BLM's claim. Several projects (a bulldozer track and a pipeline to a spring) are included within our proposal; these were constructed by the BLM during the wilderness review, despite requirements to protect the WSA, and thus do not warrant a boundary change. The inclusion of these benchlands would create a more logical wilderness unit instead of an isolated mountaintop.

THE DIRTY DEVIL WILDERNESS

Summary

Southeast of Hanksville, Utah, the Dirty Devil River winds for 90 miles through one of the most rugged and remote landscapes of the American West. Over millions of years this small desert stream has carved for itself a many-roomed mansion, a canyon system that sprawls across 500 square miles between Utah Highway 24 and Lake Powell.

The primitive beauty of the Dirty Devil country has inspired proposals for national monument, national park, and wild and scenic river designations. In 1965 some 50,000 acres surrounding the lower Dirty Devil River canyon were included in the Glen Canyon National Recreation Area. The remainder of the canyon system lies on BLM land. Yet, despite strong public support for protecting the entire region, the BLM has failed to recognize its importance. The agency's wilderness recommendations omit two-thirds of the BLM-managed wild lands in the Dirty Devil region. Instead of protecting these lands, the BLM proposes to open them for uranium and tar sand development, creating a 100-square-mile mining and industrial zone at the heart of the canyon system.

Such development would destroy forever the primitive character of the Dirty Devil region. It is one wilderness, with a scenic, recreational, and bioregional integrity that reaches from canyon rim to canyon rim. The Utah Wilderness Coalition's 263,500-acre proposal would protect that integrity for future generations.

At the Edge of The Block

Deep within the Dirty Devil River canyons lies a mesa called "The Block." It is a formidable object, a thousand-foot-high fortress with cliff walls curving inward to form deep bays and coves and reaching outward as jetty-like arms. A dense forest of juniper and pinyon pine carpets the

IN BRIEF

Index Map: Area No. 42

Highlights: From Hanksville to Lake Powell, the Dirty Devil River flows through some of the most remote Utah canyons. Old uranium-mining scars and tar sand deposits led the BLM to drop large acreages, but the area's size, ruggedness, and recreational attractions deserve protection.

Guidebooks: Kelsey (1987a)

Maps: USGS 1:100,000 Hanksville, Hite Crossing

Area of wilderness proposals in acres:

Unit	UWC	BLM
Dirty Devil- French Spring	175,300	72,110
Fiddler Butte	88,200	32,700
TOTAL	263,500	104,810

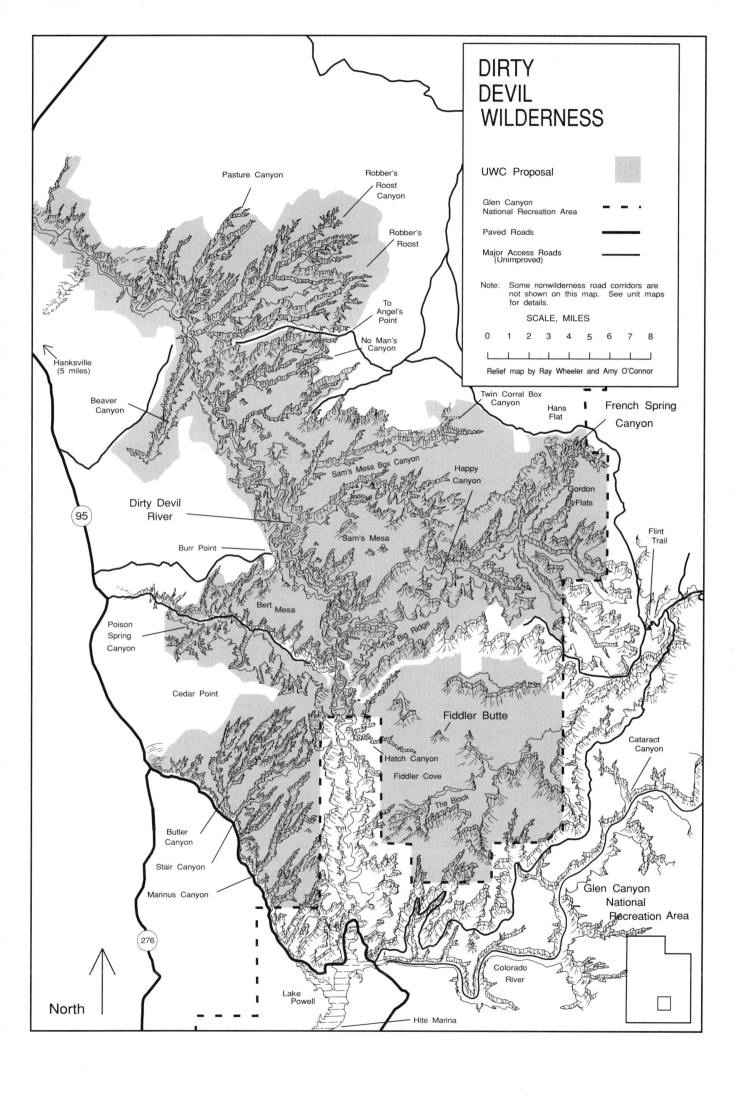

**DIRTY
DEVIL
WILDERNESS**

UWC Proposal

Glen Canyon
National Recreation Area

Paved Roads

Major Access Roads
(Unimproved)

Note: Some nonwilderness road corridors are
not shown on this map. See unit maps
for details.

SCALE, MILES

0 1 2 3 4 5 6 7 8

Relief map by Ray Wheeler and Amy O'Connor

Pasture Canyon

Robber's
Roost
Canyon

Robber's
Roost

To
Angel's
Point

No Man's
Canyon

Hanksville
(5 miles)

Beaver
Canyon

Twin Corral Box
Canyon

Hans
Flat

French Spring
Canyon

Bull Pasture

Sam's Mesa Box Canyon

Happy
Canyon

Gordon
Flats

Flint
Trail

Dirty Devil
River

Sam's Mesa

Burr Point

Bert Mesa

Poison
Spring
Canyon

The Big Ridge

Cedar Point

Fiddler Butte

Cataract
Canyon

Hatch Canyon

Fiddler Cove

The Block

Butler
Canyon

Stair Canyon

Marinus Canyon

Glen Canyon
National
Recreation Area

95

276

Colorado
River

Lake
Powell

Hite Marina

North

5,000-acre mesa top. Deer, bighorn, and an occasional human visitor climb the single foot trail that leads up through the cliffs to the summit.

To stand at the northern edge of The Block on a hot, stormy summer night is an experience akin to extraterrestrial travel. A warm wind roars through the forest, pushing a low ceiling of fast-moving clouds. At one's feet lies an abyss of empty black air. Distant thunder rolls in from all points of the compass, and flashes of lightning ring the horizon.

One by one, the landmarks burn with light. To the north lies The Big Ridge, a thousand-foot-high, fifteen-mile-long land bridge that forms the northern wall of Fiddler Cove. Massive buttes and pyramids rise from the floor of the Cove and, at its center, spiked by a lightning-strobe, stands Fiddler Butte, a sphinx-like monolith 900 feet high. Thunder rolls across the Cove, roaring like surf against its walls. To the west, the Henry Mountains seem to rise and fall against a backdrop of intermittent green light. On the northern horizon, a pink flash silhouettes the San Rafael Reef, Factory Butte, and the black hulk of Thousand Lake Mountain.

Somewhere below, lost in shadow, the Dirty Devil River trickles quietly between 500-foot-high canyon walls on its 90-mile journey from Hanksville to the Colorado River.

Abundant Wilderness

For centuries the Dirty Devil canyon system has been a barrier to civilization, a 300,000-acre wilderness suspended between sheer walls. It remains so today. Here one can find, in abundant supply, all that one could hope for in wilderness. The landscape is an infinite series of novel and beautiful shapes. There are colorful cliffs, winding slot canyons, rincons, alcoves, pools, waterfalls, buttes, towers, domes, spires, and arches. During the spring snowmelt boaters ride the length of the river in kayaks and canoes. Hikers and climbers find still more adventure; a recent guidebook (Kelsey, 1987a) features 200 miles of backcountry hiking routes within the Dirty Devil canyon system.

The entire Dirty Devil area provides important habitat for wildlife. Herds of antelope roam the plateau country along both canyon rims. Remote sidecanyons harbor rare populations of beaver, desert bighorn sheep, and at least nine species of plants and animals which the BLM has identified as "sensitive." Prehistoric artifacts are abundant here, as they are throughout the Colorado Plateau. Recent studies by the National Park Service and the BLM (1984) suggest an average density of 24 archeological sites per square mile, or up to 11,000 rock shelters, campsites, lithic scatters, stone tool quarries, and petroglyph sites throughout the Dirty Devil region.

Since the 1930s, there has been a series of proposals for preserving the primitive character of the Dirty Devil canyons. In 1936, Wilderness Society founder Bob Marshall identified the Dirty Devil canyons as an integral part of the 8.9-million-acre Colorado River canyons roadless area—the largest remaining block of wilderness in the lower forty-eight states. In the same year, the U.S. Department of the Interior launched a proposal to create a 4.5-million-acre Escalante National Monument in Utah. The monument's western boundary would have included nearly 200,000 acres surrounding the lower Dirty Devil River canyon. A 1961 proposal by Interior Secretary Stewart Udall would have included some 37,000 acres of the Dirty Devil region within Canyonlands National Park. In 1970, the BLM identified a candidate Dirty Devil primitive area of over 300,000 acres, and by 1979 the National Park Service had identified the entire length of the Dirty Devil River as a potential addition to the National Wild and Scenic River System.

The Dirty Devil River has been nominated for Wild and Scenic River designation. More than 200 miles of backcountry hiking routes are found within its canyon system.

Ray Wheeler

The Mining Invasion

Each new protection plan met with opposition from developers and a tangle of bureaucratic red tape. Meanwhile, even as the BLM began its inventory of potential new wilderness areas in Utah, powerful new forces had begun to influence the agency's planning process. A worldwide energy crisis had caused uranium and oil prices to skyrocket, and mineral exploration companies descended upon the Dirty Devil region. Between 1976 and 1980, the Cotter Corporation alone bladed more than 50 miles of roads and trails and punched hundreds of exploratory wells within the BLM's Dirty Devil wilderness inventory unit. The company "upgraded" 20 miles of abandoned uranium exploration trails and sliced more than 30 miles of new roads into pristine canyons and mesa tops.

Virtually all of the new roadwork was illegal, for Cotter Corporation had failed to apply for road right-of-way and drilling permits, as required by law. Where such developments might permanently impair the wilderness character of lands under review, they were strictly forbidden by the BLM's wilderness inventory regulations. Yet only after conservationists discovered the new roads did the BLM finally intervene. A 1979 BLM lawsuit forced the company to fully reclaim any new roadwork within the Dirty Devil WSA. Faced with the costs of repairing its damage—and a sharply declining market for uranium—Cotter abruptly canceled its exploration program.

Meanwhile the BLM was conducting its wilderness inventory. In response to the pressure from Cotter, the agency rushed to eliminate huge blocks of land from the inventory. During a special "accelerated inventory," the BLM reduced the original roadless area of more than 400,000 acres to three separate fragments: a 61,000-acre Dirty Devil WSA, a 25,000-acre French Springs-Happy Canyon WSA, and a 27,000-acre Fiddler Butte WSA. Between the three WSAs, and precisely at the center of the Dirty Devil canyon system, the BLM dropped from wilderness study nearly 100,000 acres, *including a 16-mile-long segment of the Dirty Devil River itself*. The lands omitted contained many of the region's most striking landmarks, including Sam's Mesa, lower Happy Canyon, The Pinnacle, The Big Ridge, The Block, Fiddler Cove, and Fiddler Butte.

Thus began an eight-year-long war of wills between Utah conservationists and the BLM. Instead of blocking new development on lands under study for wilderness designation, the BLM had become an agent for development. Even *inside* its three wilderness inventory units, the BLM continued to authorize the construction of new roads, new drillpads, mine assessment work, and reservoir construction. Yet the BLM's mandate to preserve wilderness was clear and direct. Congress had specifically instructed the agency to protect *all* of its wild lands from new development while they remained under wilderness review. Utah conservationists fought back with protests and formal appeals. In 1983 and 1985, they won important victories before the Interior Board of Land Appeals (IBLA). *The BLM had demonstrated no good reason*, the IBLA ruled, *for omitting Fiddler Butte from the Fiddler Butte WSA.* The two successful appeals ultimately forced the BLM to add 47,000 acres to the WSA.

Red Carpet for Tar Sand?

Uranium exploration, wildcat oil wells, new road and reservoir construction—all were serious threats to the primitive character of the Dirty Devil canyons. But by 1982, there was a new and far more dangerous threat. A coalition of 15 petroleum companies filed a proposal to develop a 66,000-acre tar sand mining complex spanning French Springs Canyon, Happy Canyon, The Big Ridge, and Fiddler Cove. The proposed development would have transformed the Dirty Devil region into a huge mining and industrial complex, causing environmental damage so thoroughly catastrophic that the BLM's 400-page environmental impact statement required more than 50 pages merely to describe it.

Over the 160-year life of the project, a total of 35,000 injection and production wells would be bored throughout 54,000 acres of land. Subterranean explosions and fires would cause extensive subsurface fracturing over 39,000 acres, destroying natural aquifers and causing subsidence rockfalls and steam blowouts on cliff faces. More than 30,000 acres of soil would be disturbed, and 14,000 acres of land would be stripped completely of vegetation. Some 2,000 archeological sites would be disturbed. There would be a dam and reservoir on the Dirty Devil River and a water pipeline running the length of Happy Canyon. Hundreds of miles of roads would be built throughout Happy and French Springs canyons, The Big Ridge, and Fiddler Cove. There would be a bridge over the Dirty Devil River, and the Flint Trail—a narrow, winding, adventurous jeep trail that climbs to the top of the Orange Cliffs—would be crowned, ditched, and paved to accommodate some 600 vehicles per day.

On-site facilities would include five steam generation plants, an electrical power plant, coking, sulphur recovery, and sewage plants, oil storage tanks, a reservoir, and a solid waste dump. Noise levels would be high enough to cause hearing impairment within 600 feet of the extraction zone. The refinery's stack would dominate the western horizon of Canyonlands National Park, sending up a smoke plume by day and a halo of artificial lighting by night. Its emissions would regularly violate federal air quality standards within Arches and Canyonlands National Parks. Traffic, habitat disturbance, and noise would drive bighorn sheep, peregrine falcon, and other sensitive species of wildlife out of the region.

Even before the BLM had completed its environmental impact statement, a sharp downturn in worldwide oil prices put a sudden end to tar sand development in Utah.

In comparison to world oil reserves and national consumption, the entire oil reserves of the Dirty Devil region, even under the most optimistic estimates, are but a drop in the bucket. And oil from tar sand is much too costly to be economically viable in the foreseeable future. But if the world's resources of cheaper oil were depleted before alternative energy sources became viable, there could once again be a push to exploit the Dirty Devil tar sand deposits.

Conservation or Exploitation?

The energy companies—and the BLM—are betting on another energy crisis. They are betting against energy conservation, and they are betting against cleaner and more economical sources of energy. The BLM seems committed to tar sand development in the Dirty Devil region no matter what its environmental effect. That commitment is abundantly clear in the agency's wilderness recommendations. The BLM would omit 40,000 acres from the Fiddler Butte WSA so as "to reduce tar sand conflicts," as the recommendation flatly states. Most of the 25,000-acre French Springs WSA would be opened to development. "About 20,460 acres of the WSA are involved in lease conversion application for tar sand development," the BLM explained. "Development work, extraction, and patenting would be allowed . . . . "

Such development would destroy the wilderness character of the entire region. The Dirty Devil canyon system is one wilderness, with an esthetic and physical integrity that would be lost forever to a 60,000-acre tar sand mining complex. Gradually, after decades of erosion, the scattered mining impacts of the 1950s and the 1970s are being reclaimed and revegetated. Mudslides and gullies are slowly obliterating the Cotter Corporation's illegal road work on Sam's Mesa, in Happy Canyon, and along the Dirty Devil River gorge between Happy Canyon and Twin Corral Canyon. The Dirty Devil canyons remain triumphantly wild.

While the BLM has failed to recognize the importance of protecting the entire canyon system, the Utah Wilderness Coalition has made region-wide integrity its primary goal. Our 263,500-acre wilderness proposal would protect the entire Dirty Devil wilderness, healthy and intact, for future generations to explore.

Ray Wheeler

DIRTY DEVIL-FRENCH SPRING UNIT

Highlights—In the 1890s, the Dirty Devil canyons were a hideout for Butch Cassidy and the Wild Bunch. Today these canyons still remain off the beaten path—a place to elude civilization. There are 40 miles of river canyon and eight major sidecanyons up to 15 miles long with high, curved sandstone walls rivalling the Escalante in beauty. The BLM's 72,110-acre proposal leaves out spectacular Happy Canyon, the expansive tops of Sam's Mesa and the Big Ridge, and 16 incomparably beautiful miles of the river itself. The agency excluded these lands because of old roads which are now impassable, and because of highly unlikely tar sand development. By including them, the Utah Wilderness Coalition's 175,300-acre proposed Dirty Devil-French Spring unit, along with the Fiddler Butte unit, would protect the river's entire length from Hanksville to Lake Powell and all of its sidecanyons.

Geology and landforms—Motorists on Utah Highway 95 south of Hanksville scarcely suspect that the low, reddish hills rising to the east conceal a vast canyon system lying beyond. The Dirty Devil River and its tributaries have carved as deep as 2,000 feet into the gently uplifted land, leaving a retreating series of cliffs and benches, a classic example of canyon lands topography. The slickrock sandstones of the Glen Canyon Group (Wingate, Kayenta, and Navajo formations) dominate the unit, but the lower river canyon and Happy Canyon have wide valleys in the Chinle clays and

Instead of blocking new development on lands under study for wilderness designation, the BLM had become an agent for development. Even inside its three wilderness inventory units, the BLM continued to authorize the construction of new roads, new drillpads, mine assessment work, and reservoir construction.

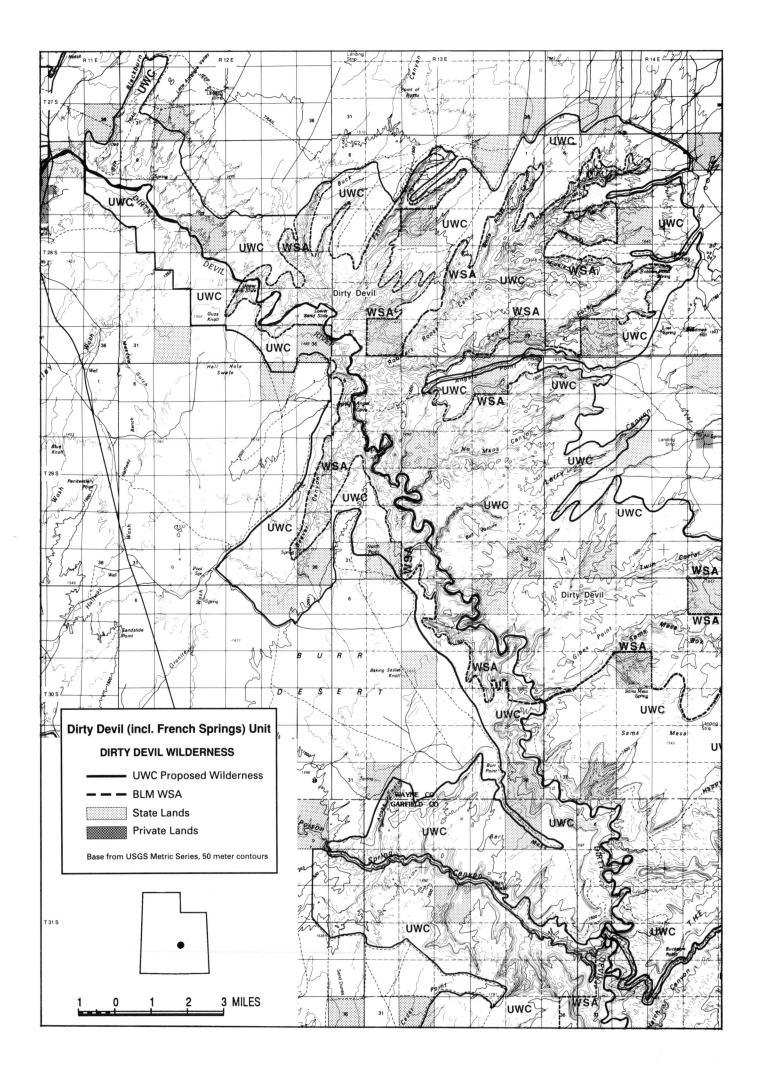

Dirty Devil (incl. French Springs) Unit

DIRTY DEVIL WILDERNESS

——— UWC Proposed Wilderness

– – – BLM WSA

State Lands

Private Lands

Base from USGS Metric Series, 50 meter contours

1 0 1 2 3 MILES

spectacular narrows in the White Rim sandstone. Dinosaur footprints are exposed on sandstone slabs in the unit.

Plant communities—This is arid country broken by a handful of seeps and springs that support lovely hanging gardens and by the willow- and tamarisk-lined Dirty Devil River. Much of the unit is bare rock and sand. Large Fremont cottonwoods are found in sidecanyons, such as Robbers Roost, where flash floods and their remnant pools are the main water source. Elsewhere the overpowering dryness leaves the land to well-adapted species such as blackbrush, saltbush, shadscale, and ephedra, with juniper and pinyon growing at higher elevations and on mesa tops to the east. Sam's Mesa and The Big Ridge contain relict plant communities. Beaver Wash Canyon has 4,800 acres of near-relict riparian vegetation; although grazed by cattle, this clear-watered canyon supports willow, cattail, and sedge and provides excellent habitat for beaver and migratory waterfowl.

Wildlife—Animals are similarly limited by scarce water here: there are some deer and antelope, and possibly desert bighorn sheep. A rare population of beavers has created dams along verdant Beaver Wash. Golden eagle use the area, and its cliffs provide excellent nesting sites for the endanger-

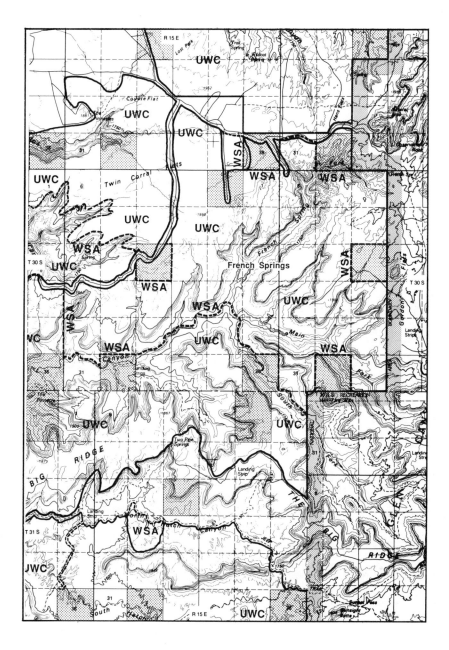

ed peregrine falcon, although no use is documented. The BLM notes that Bell's vireo, a sensitive species, may also be found here.

Archeology and history—A relic of the Old West, the Dirty Devil wilderness provided a haven for bygone outlaws. Less well documented are rock art sites, granaries, and lithic scatters, some dating back to Archaic times. The limited surveys that have been done indicate that the entire unit probably contains thousands of sites, mostly those used by a nomadic rather than settled people.

Recreation—The Dirty Devil River, a candidate for wild and scenic listing, may be floated during high runoff in kayaks, canoes, or small rafts; it makes an excellent backpack, too, either as a week-long trip down its entire length or as shorter trips via its sidecanyons. Kelsey (1987a) describes 11 hikes within the unit, some requiring skilled routefinding. The casual visitor can appreciate the magnificent view out over the canyons from Burr Point, at the end of a fairly good dirt road leading west from Highway 95 about 15 miles south of Hanksville. A pathway marked by stone cairns leads to the river from Angels Point.

BLM recommendation—The BLM recommends designating the 61,000-acre Dirty Devil WSA and 11,110 acres of the 25,000-acre French Spring-Happy Canyon WSA. More than 83,000 acres, however, were not even studied. In the late 1970s, the Cotter Corporation illegally built over 20 miles of roads for uranium exploration in the southwestern portion of the unit. In the same area, old exploration roads and landing strips built in the 1950s had largely returned to nature and were impassable when FLPMA was passed in 1976. (The BLM's inventory policy required WSA boundaries to be based on the extent of impacts when FLPMA was passed.) But the BLM, in its answers to protests and an appeal by the Sierra Club, simply cited their mere existence as a reason for dropping the very center of the Dirty Devil canyons from further wilderness consideration and coincidentally dropping most of the new roads, too. It did this despite the requirements of the inventory policy to document the extent and nature of impacts at the time of FLPMA's passage. The new roads built by Cotter began to return to nature, too, so that vehicles once again could not reach Sam's Mesa or travel the roads in Happy Canyon or along the river—at least until Wayne County road crews, acting without legal authorization, at-

Larry Canyon is one of the more remote reaches of the Dirty Devil canyon system.

Michael R. Kelsey

tempted to reconstruct parts of these roads onto Sam's Mesa. Because these roads traverse lands vital to the integrity of the region, they should be allowed to revegetate naturally.

Coalition proposal—We propose a 175,300-acre wilderness unit. Commercial resources of hard-rock and leasable minerals are unlikely, according to the BLM, and the removal of energy minerals (including tar sand and uranium) would be prohibitively expensive and damaging to the environment (see area overview). Some old uranium exploration roads and landing strips from the 1950s are included, as is Cotter Corporation's illegal "upgrading" of those scars in the 1970s. Those roads are returning to nature and are generally impassable by vehicles. Rather than fracture the wilderness at Sam's Mesa (which was included in the BLM's draft WSA boundary in 1979), we propose a unified wild area surrounding the Dirty Devil and all of its major sidecanyons from just below Hanksville to the Fiddler Butte unit and the Glen Canyon National Recreation Area. Unlike the BLM's recommendation, our proposal includes undisturbed mesas, benches, cliffs, and canyon bottoms.

FIDDLER BUTTE UNIT

Highlights—The Fiddler Butte unit is as remote and seldom visited as the Dirty Devil unit just to the north. Only the extremely rough Poison Spring/North Hatch Canyon dirt road separates the two. Fiddler Butte is an integral part not only of the Dirty Devil wilderness, but also of the greater Canyonlands wild region: the Maze roadless area lies just to the east (across another dirt road) in the Glen Canyon National Recreation Area and Canyonlands National Park. The eastern half of the unit was part of Canyonlands National Park as originally proposed by the Department of the Interior in 1962, before that proposal was pared down in response to opposition from resource interests. The entire unit is still of national park quality, but the BLM recommends leaving most of the lands open to tar sand leasing. The agency recommends only 5,700 acres of isolated mesa tops in the eastern half of the unit and 27,000 acres in the western end for protection. The awesome emptiness of the benches surrounding the Block—the essence of the area's wildness—would be unprotected. In contrast, the 88,200-acre Utah Wilderness Coalition proposal would protect the complete wild area.

Geology and landforms—Two very different topographic aspects are found in the unit. The Dirty Devil River's stupendous 2,000-foot-deep canyon divides the unit. East of the river, The Block, an impressive, almost inaccessible mesa of Navajo Sandstone, rises out of the broad Moenkopi clay benches. West of the river long, straight canyons cut down through Wingate and Navajo sandstone cliffs to North Wash.

Plant communities—Vegetation is similar to the Dirty Devil unit, with desert shrubs on lower elevations and a near-relict pinyon-juniper and sagebrush-grassland community atop The Block. Tamarisk, willow, and other riparian species grow along the river bottom. The BLM notes that two sensitive plant species, the milkvetches *Astragalus monumentalis* and *Astragalus rafaelensis*, may grow here. A few springs and seeps in the heads of the canyons have created small patches of greenery. The two mesas known as The Block, which cover 4,200 acres and are connected by a narrow strip of land, were grazed lightly by sheep in the early 1900s. Domestic livestock have not been on the mesas for a number of years, and the land has restored itself to near relict quality (Tuhy and MacMahon, 1988).

Wildlife—Nearly all of the unit is range for desert bighorn sheep, which have been reintroduced nearby. Golden eagles (listed as sensitive) use the entire unit. Endangered peregrine falcon may also use the unit,

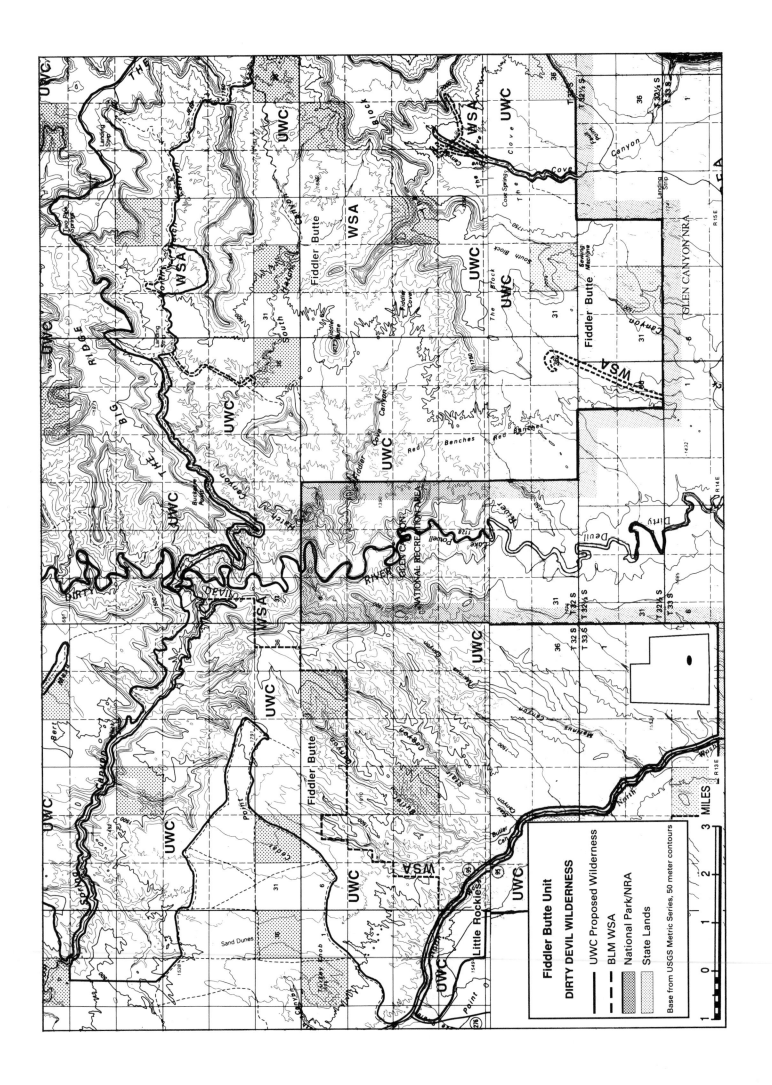

Fiddler Butte Unit

DIRTY DEVIL WILDERNESS

UWC Proposed Wilderness

BLM WSA

National Park/NRA

State Lands

Base from USGS Metric Series, 50 meter contours

MILES

which is "excellent habitat" for them, according to the BLM. The endangered bald eagle and sensitive Bell's vireo also may be present.

Archeology and history—Petroglyphs and temporary occupation sites (camping grounds and stone chipping areas) are known to occur in the unit; probably only a few of many have been located. These are probably of pre-Anasazi (Archaic) time, according to the BLM.

Recreation—The Block is probably one of the least-visited mesas of its size; views to the north across Fiddler Cove and across the Cove to the south are breathtaking (see area overview), as are the views from Cedar Point across the river canyon to The Block. The canyons that flow into North Wash make fine day hikes from Highway 95. Float trips on the Dirty Devil River pass through the unit before entering Glen Canyon NRA. Kelsey (1987a) describes hikes to the Block and in Butler, Stair, and Marinus canyons.

BLM recommendation—The BLM recommends wilderness for only 32,700 acres of this unit, claiming that the rest has less than outstanding wilderness characteristics and has potential for tar sand development. We believe that tar sand has blinded the BLM to the unit's wilderness values. The lands not recommended for designation include Fiddler Butte, the unit's namesake, and the expansive benches surrounding The Block, which connect it with the Colorado River canyon to the south and the Dirty Devil Canyon to the west. Additional lands were dropped south of The Block and on Cedar Point in the northwestern part of the unit owing to old scars from mining operations. Significant mineral production from those lands is unlikely; the old roads should be allowed to continue their return to nature.

Coalition proposal—Our 88,200-acre proposed wilderness unit includes the entire WSA and additional wild lands northwest of the WSA on Cedar Point. The entire unit is a critical scenic, recreational, and ecologic link between the Dirty Devil canyons to the north and the Glen Canyon NRA.

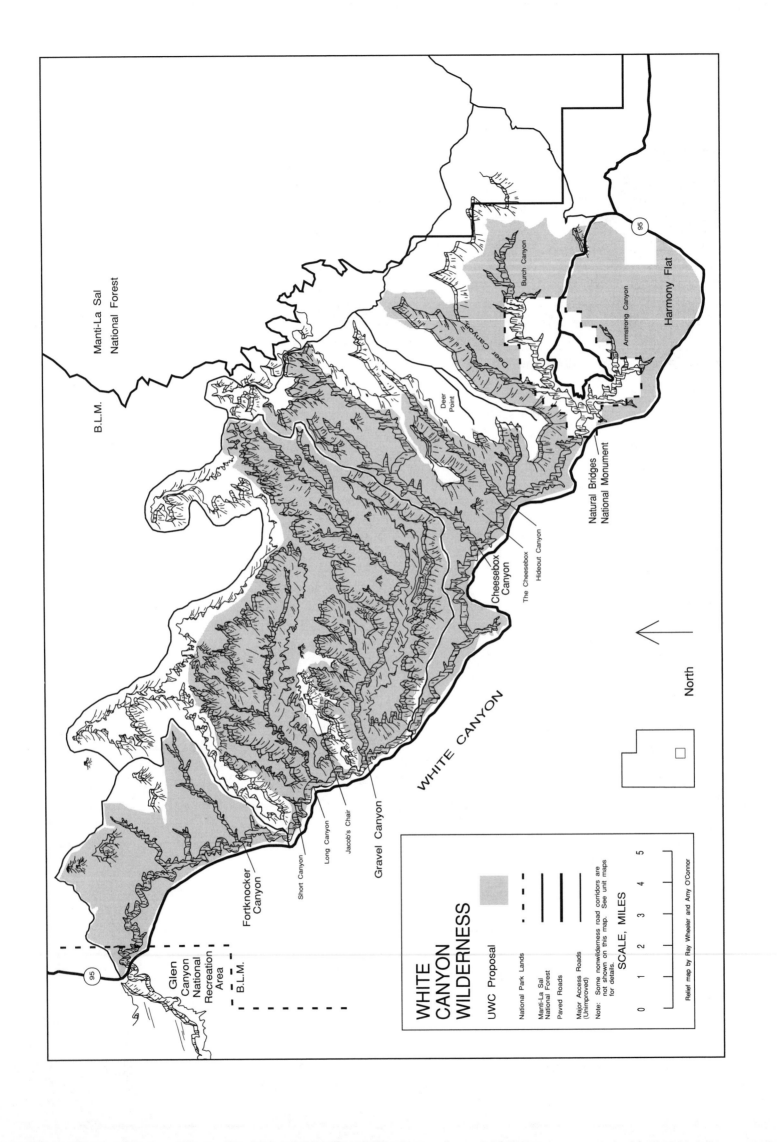

Manti-La Sal
National Forest

B.L.M.

Glen
Canyon
National
Recreation
Area

B.L.M.

Fortknocker
Canyon

Short Canyon

Long Canyon

Jacob's Chair

Gravel Canyon

WHITE CANYON

North

WHITE
CANYON
WILDERNESS

UWC Proposal

National Park Lands

Manti-La Sal
National Forest

Paved Roads

Major Access Roads
(Unimproved)

Note: Some nonwilderness road corridors are
        not shown on this map. See unit maps
        for details.

SCALE, MILES

0   1   2   3   4   5

Relief map by Ray Wheeler and Amy O'Connor

Cheesebox Canyon

The Cheesebox

Hideout Canyon

Natural Bridges
National Monument

Deer Canyon

Deer
Point

Burch Canyon

Armstrong Canyon

Harmony Flat

95

95

THE WHITE CANYON WILDERNESS

Summary

Each year nearly 100,000 visitors explore Natural Bridges National Monument, searching for the solitude, beauty, and silence that are unique to the Colorado Plateau. Few of these visitors realize that the 7,800-acre monument is surrounded by 85,000 acres of BLM wild lands in the upper drainages of White Canyon. On most of its wild lands the BLM has made some gesture of recognition, however faint, for outstanding wilderness values. But when the BLM announced its draft wilderness proposal for Utah in February of 1986, *not one acre* of the White Canyon complex was recommended for wilderness designation. And that recommendation will likely be repeated when the agency releases its final wilderness proposal in the fall of 1990.

Wilderness designation for the White Canyon area would protect outstanding backcountry canyoneering opportunities, thousands of acres of important habitat for desert bighorn sheep, and many ancient cultural resource sites, as well as complementing wild lands within Natural Bridges National Monument.

Classic High Desert

Between U.S. Highway 95 to the south, the rim of Dark Canyon to the north, the Elk Ridge road to the east, and Lake Powell to the west lie 85,000 acres of pristine wild lands administered by the BLM. Most of this broad plateau is covered with pinyon and juniper and studded with thousand-foot-high mesas and buttes. Deer, coyote, and desert bighorn sheep roam the rugged landscape. Raptors comb the air along the canyon rims.

White Canyon has carved a maze of canyons into the Cedar Mesa Sandstone that underlies the plateau. These canyons are among the world's foremost displays of erosional sculpting, and the upper part of White Canyon was included within Natural Bridges National Monument in recognition of this character. The canyons on the BLM lands are more intimate and challenging, though no less deserving of recognition. They alternately narrow down into cool, dark, armspan-width slots—and then widen again into coves littered with 40-ton houserocks and pocket forests of cottonwood, ponderosa, and fir.

The canyon walls are honeycombed with alcoves, arches, windows, hanging gardens, and grottoes; the canyon floors are riddled with potholes. In places springwater forms deep pools, and occasional rainstorms bring torrents of floodwater raging through boulder gardens and thundering over pouroffs in spectacular waterfalls. Well over 100 miles of narrow, winding canyons in the White Canyon system form a network so labyrinthine that backpacking trips of two and three weeks can scarcely begin to touch its recreation potential.

As in much of the Cedar Mesa region, archeological values are high. Remnants of the ancient Anasazi culture, ranging from scattered stone-working sites to impressive cliff dwellings, are located throughout the proposed wilderness. The BLM notes in its wilderness DEIS that "no significant archeological work has been conducted" in Cheesebox Canyon, the area's sole WSA. However, the BLM goes on to say that if such inventories were made, they probably would disclose 600 sites in the WSA alone, up to 400 of which could be eligible for listing on the National Register of Historic Places.

Isolation and rugged topography have protected the area from the vandalism that has scarred so many of southeastern Utah's irreplaceable ar-

IN BRIEF

Index Map: Area No. 43

Highlights: The serpentine canyons that flow into White Canyon near Natural Bridges National Monument are a natural continuation of the monument, but have been completely neglected in the BLM's wilderness review.

Guidebooks: Hall (1982), Kelsey (1983, 1986a)

Maps: USGS 1:100,000 Hite Crossing, Blanding

Area of wilderness proposals in acres:

Unit	UWC	BLM
Cheesebox Canyon	28,500	0
Harmony Flat	9,100	0
Fortknocker Canyon	12,400	0
Gravel & Long Canyon	35,000	0
TOTAL	85,000	0

Adjacent wild lands: Natural Bridges National Monument

Gravel Canyon—a major tributary of White Canyon.

Ray Wheeler

cheological sites. That isolation may change, however, if the wildness of the area is not formally protected.

Wilderness Recognized—Except by the BLM

The exceptional wilderness character of the White Canyon area has long been recognized. In the 1930s, the Interior Department identified the White Canyon region as part of a proposed 4.5-million-acre Escalante National Monument. More recently, the National Park Service identified the entire length of White Canyon, from Natural Bridges National Monument to Glen Canyon National Recreation Area, as a candidate for wild and scenic river designation. In 1979, Park Service officials proposed the acquisition of adjacent lands to protect the viewshed of Natural Bridges National Monument, and the National Parks and Conservation Association has since recommended the addition of 30,000 acres to the national monument.

The BLM has recognized that most of the White Canyon wilderness provides critical lambing and rutting habitat for desert bighorn sheep. But the BLM does not share the concern of other agencies and citizens for the wilderness resource of White Canyon. In 1979, the BLM dropped four of five White Canyon roadless units from its wilderness inventory, claiming that they "clearly and obviously lack wilderness character." In 1986, the BLM insisted that Cheesebox Canyon was also unworthy of wilderness designation. Strange indeed, for the Cheesebox WSA is geologically, biologically, and topographically a natural extension of the wild lands within Natural Bridges National Monument.

The BLM claimed that the White Canyon area lacked wilderness character because of old mining scars around the perimeter of the canyon system. But extensive ground and aerial reconnaissance by Utah Wilderness Coalition volunteers in the spring of 1985 proved that most of these mining impacts are minimal or have been obliterated by erosion. The rest were easily excluded from the Coalition's wilderness proposals through minor boundary adjustments.

Hundreds of Wells Authorized

Why has the BLM overlooked the wilderness potential of White Canyon throughout a decade of wilderness inventory and study? In 1979, when the BLM removed the White Canyon roadless units from its wilderness inventory, the nation was in the throes of an energy crisis, and the agency was under intense pressure to permit mineral exploration inside the roadless area. Between 1979 and 1983, in the Cheesebox Canyon inventory unit alone, the BLM authorized the drilling of more than 200 new uranium exploration holes and the construction of 10 miles of new seismic lines. Fortunately, as a result of protests, appeals, and a decline in energy prices, few of the authorized actions were ever undertaken.

Though the energy crisis has abated for the moment, new mining exploration proposals for the White Canyon wilderness may develop at any time. Meanwhile, so-called "range improvements" are the order of the day in the BLM's planning documents for the region. In 1985, the BLM proposed to build an 18-foot-wide, 8-mile-long stock driveway into the heart of the Gravel and Long Canyon roadless area. If constructed, the new road would invite vehicular traffic into the center of this wild area. Elsewhere inside the proposed White Canyon wilderness, the BLM proposes to chain down as much as 7,000 acres of pinyon-juniper forest (BLM, 1987b). Such developments will damage the region's extensive archeological resources, destroy critical habitat for desert bighorn sheep, and draw off-road vehicle traffic ever deeper into the roadless areas.

Although the White Canyon wilderness inventory was largely abandoned in order to promote energy exploration, the oil, gas, and uranium resources of this region are marginal at best. The BLM's San Juan Resource Management Plan rates the White Canyon region as low for oil, gas, uranium, and other hardrock minerals. According to the BLM, there are no coal, potash, geothermal, or other leasable minerals. "... all wells that have been drilled in this general area are now abandoned," the BLM said in its analysis of the Cheesebox Canyon WSA. "If oil and/or gas existed ... in the WSA, there is a good chance that it has drained away ... "

Wilderness Proposal Complements Park Lands

The Utah Wilderness Coalition proposes 85,000 acres of wilderness designations in White Canyon comprising four units. Since the White Canyon system is traversed by two low-grade dirt roads, the Coalition has used the road corridors as boundaries for three contiguous proposed wilderness units west of Natural Bridges National Monument. A fourth proposed wilderness unit abuts Natural Bridges on the southeast. Together these units would protect the recreational, cultural, and wildlife resources of the White Canyon area and would complement the purposes for which Natural Bridges National Monument was designated.

Ray Wheeler

CHEESEBOX CANYON AND HARMONY FLAT UNITS

Highlights—These roadless lands surround additional wild country within Natural Bridges National Monument. A primitive road separates Cheesebox Canyon from the Gravel and Long Canyon unit to the west. Wilderness designation is needed to protect these lands for their primitive recreation opportunities, archeological sites, and wildlife habitat. Further vehicle access and mineral exploration would jeopardize these resources. We propose 28,500 acres of wilderness for Cheesebox Canyon and 9,100 acres for Harmony Flat.

Geology and landforms—Tributaries of White Canyon have cut into the massive Cedar Mesa Sandstone throughout the forested benchlands surrounding Natural Bridges National Monument, forming Cheesebox, Hideout, and Deer canyons in the Cheesebox unit and Armstrong and Tuwa canyons in the Harmony Flat unit. The Cheesebox, a prominent butte visible from Highway 95, is a monument to the forces that stripped away hundreds of feet of overlying rocks, exposing the present plateau.

Plant communities—An extensive pinyon-juniper forest covers the benchlands, while cottonwoods and other riparian plants grow along White Canyon, an ephemeral stream.

Wildlife—Mule deer, mountain lion, bobcat, and a variety of smaller animals find habitat here. The western half of the Cheesebox unit is year-long habitat for the desert bighorn sheep and also provides crucial rutting and lambing areas. Harmony Flat contains crucial deer winter range, according to the UDWR. The BLM notes that bald eagles use the area in the winter.

Archeology and history—Thorough inventories have not been done, but 12 archeological sites, chiefly cliff dwellings and granaries, have been documented within the Cheesebox Canyon WSA (BLM, 1986). Many more sites of all types—as many as 600 in the WSA alone, according to the BLM—would probably be found if full surveys were undertaken. Harmony Flat has numerous sites of both Basketmaker and Pueblo age.

Recreation—More than 35 miles of canyon-bottom travel is possible, ranging from easy walks and horse trips along the bottom of White Canyon

White Canyon and its tributaries are among the world's foremost examples of erosional sculpting. Although the upper part of White Canyon is included within Natural Bridges National Monument, the BLM would not protect any of the lower canyon, shown here within the Cheesebox Canyon unit.

Fred Swanson

to narrow, pouroff-ridden slots requiring rope work. Convenient access is available from Utah Highway 95, where short spur roads lead down into White Canyon. Deer, Armstrong, and Tuwa canyons are accessible from within the National Monument, the latter two forming a good loop hike by cutting across the mesa top between them.

BLM recommendation—The BLM did not study nearly half the roadless lands in the Cheesebox unit, claiming that human impacts disqualified 12,000 acres in White, K and L, Hideout, and Deer canyons. The WSA boundary shrinks back from Natural Bridges National Monument, evidently in order to exclude three sections of state lands (see map). Instead of fragmenting the roadless area, the BLM should pursue an exchange of the state sections to consolidate BLM lands connecting Cheesebox and White canyons with the national monument. In 1986, the agency suggested that outside sights and sounds, chiefly traffic on nearby Highway 95 and visual intrusions from 20-year-old mining operations, compromise the solitude and naturalness found in the WSA. But Congress has repeatedly held this "sights and sounds" argument to be invalid, pointing out that wilderness areas that happen to be close to highways or towns hold value to the public because of their accessibility. The agency found nearly all of the Harmony Flat unit to be natural but could find no outstanding solitude or primitive recreation possibilities, despite the extensive pinyon-juniper forest and incised canyons. It stated in a 1981 letter that the unit's proximity to the national monument is "totally irrelevant," despite a Park Service statement in 1979 that "We concur in the BLM's designation of [the initial inventory unit] for further wilderness study and would consider lands within the Monument contiguous to this area as possible wilderness."

Coalition proposal—We have included several thousand acres in the Cheesebox unit that the BLM excluded from study; the intrusions are minimal, consisting mainly of old, eroding mineral-prospecting roads and cattle driveways. Imprints in Harmony Flat consist of six miles of cleared fenceline running along Highway 95, an old, closed-off access road from the highway to Owachomo Natural Bridge (now shown as a "foot trail" on the USGS map), and a road leading to forest chainings in a state section on the east. The Department of Energy's analysis of uranium potential indicates small, low-grade deposits only; most of the uranium-bearing rocks have already been prospected. Potential for other minerals and oil and gas

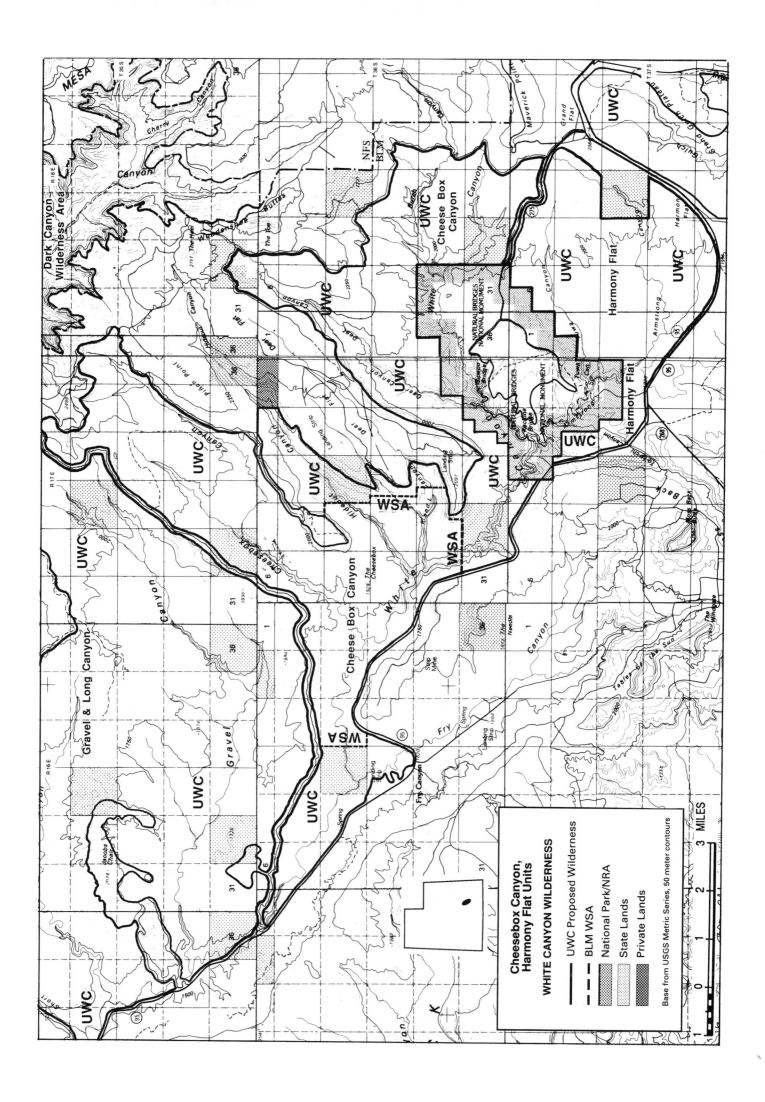

Cheesebox Canyon,
Harmony Flat Units

WHITE CANYON WILDERNESS

	UWC Proposed Wilderness
---	BLM WSA
	National Park/NRA
	State Lands
	Private Lands

Base from USGS Metric Series, 50 meter contours

0   1   2   3   MILES

in the unit is low, according to the BLM. Both units should be designated as wilderness together with roadless lands within the national monument to allow coordinated management of these outstanding wild lands regardless of jurisdictional lines.

GRAVEL CANYON AND FORTKNOCKER CANYON UNITS

Highlights—The northern half of the White Canyon complex has crucial bighorn sheep habitat, important archeologic resources, and some of the most challenging canyoneering in the state—all located just off Highway 95. Neither unit was designated a WSA by the BLM. We propose 35,000 acres of wilderness in Gravel and Long Canyon and 12,400 acres in Fortknocker Canyon.

Geology and landforms—Gravel Canyon and its neighbor to the north, Long Canyon, wind through wide benchlands surrounded by thousand-foot-high red mesas and buttes. Both canyons feed into White Canyon, as does Fortknocker Canyon farther downstream. In all, over 60 miles of narrow canyons wind through these units, a superb example of erosional sculpting of the Cedar Mesa Sandstone. The benchlands and mesas between the canyons form the spectacular vistas from the Highway 95 scenic corridor. The BLM designated an Area of Critical Environmental Concern for scenic values here.

Plant communities—The rocky benches in these units are covered with pinyon and juniper trees, with blackbrush, yucca, beavertail cactus, and associated desert shrubs also present. Soils are relatively undisturbed and thick cryptogam is common. Portions of these units have unusually healthy plant communities. Hanging gardens are found at seeps in some of the sidecanyons.

Wildlife—Desert bighorn sheep use most of these units yearlong; they also find critical rutting and lambing habitat here. Riparian habitat exists in the intermittently flowing White Canyon.

Archeology and history—Like much of the Cedar Mesa region, these units have important remains of the Anasazi culture that depend on isolation and remoteness as protection from vandalism.

Recreation—These canyons are all accessible from White Canyon, which can be entered by a dirt road two miles downstream from the mouth of Long Canyon. Primitive roads that cross White Canyon about two miles upstream from the mouth of Gravel Canyon and about four miles below the mouth also give access to the benchlands. County road 208, beginning six miles south of Hite Crossing, gives two-wheel-drive access to the upper forks of the Fortknocker Canyon unit. This area offers outstanding hiking, climbing, and photographic opportunities, including multi-day trips through canyons that twist for many miles. Good views of the Henry Mountains and Little Rockies are found on the benchlands. Driving the roads that encircle the units gives little forewarning of the deep canyons that incise the plateau. Kelsey (1986a) says the challenging hike/swim through the "Black Hole" of White Canyon in the Fortknocker Canyon unit is one of the best in the Colorado Plateau region. The National Park Service identified White Canyon as a potential wild and scenic river in its 1982 National Rivers Inventory, stating that it is an "excellent example" of an intermittent stream.

BLM recommendation—The BLM released both units from wilderness review in the initial inventory in 1979. The agency recognized the wilderness character of the canyons but vastly overstated the mining intrusions on the tablelands above the canyon. Proposed "range improvements" and ORV damage are serious threats to the wilderness. In 1986, the BLM proposed to construct an eight-mile-long stock driveway into the heart of the

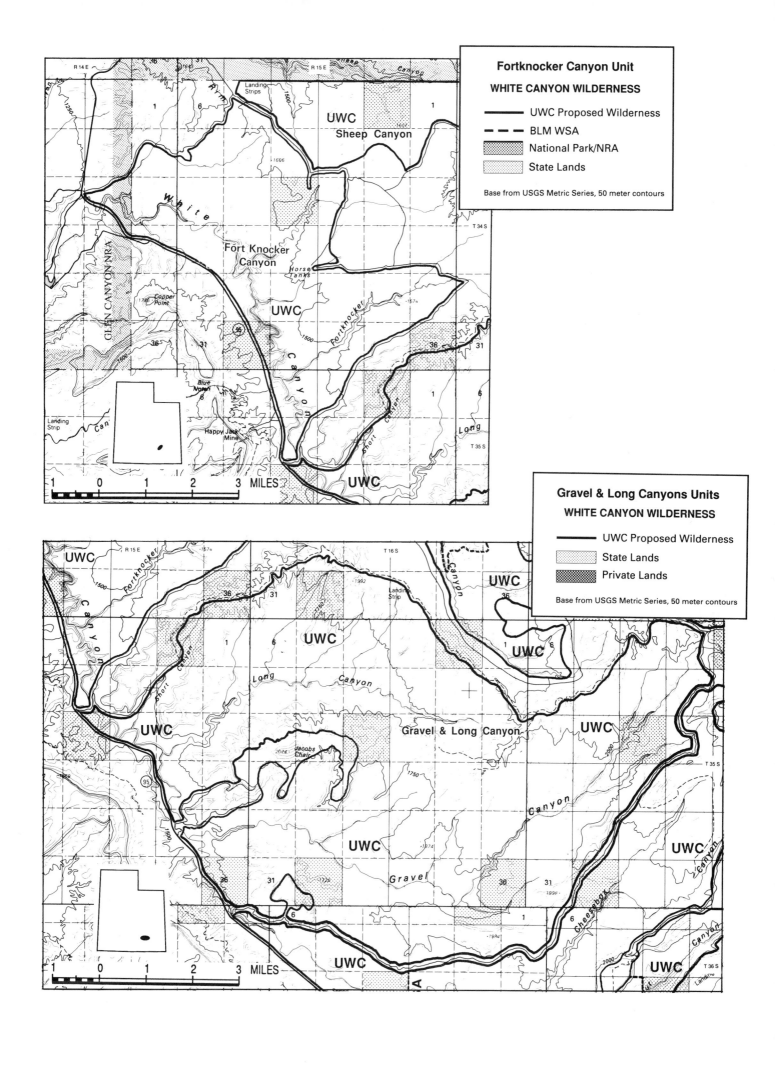

Fortknocker Canyon Unit

WHITE CANYON WILDERNESS

——— UWC Proposed Wilderness

– – – BLM WSA

National Park/NRA

State Lands

Base from USGS Metric Series, 50 meter contours

Gravel & Long Canyons Units

WHITE CANYON WILDERNESS

——— UWC Proposed Wilderness

State Lands

Private Lands

Base from USGS Metric Series, 50 meter contours

unit, and has identified parts of the unit as suitable for pinyon-juniper chaining. The driveway was dropped after conservationists protested the proposal, but such range developments remain on the BLM's agenda. The BLM's long-standing desire to promote mineral development in the area may also have motivated its release from wilderness study.

Coalition proposal—We recommend 35,000 acres of wilderness in Gravel and Long Canyon and 12,400 acres in the Fortknocker Canyon unit. Although mining exploration has left scars around the edge of these units, we have excluded the significant damage by means of boundary adjustments and cherrystems. Our field work in this area, including hiking the canyons and mesas and three flying trips specifically checking for human intrusion, indicates that the impacts are limited to an area around Jacob's Chair and one other location along the southern boundary. Mineral potential is low; the units have been prospected extensively to no effect.

THE GLEN CANYON WILDERNESS

"Awe was never Glen Canyon's province. That is for Grand Canyon. Glen Canyon was for delight."

So Wallace Stegner ("Glen Canyon Submersus," 1980) described the river journey only a few hundred boaters had known.

"Floating down the river one passed, every mile or two on right or left, the mouth of some side canyon, narrow, shadowed, releasing a secret stream into the taffy-colored, whirlpooled Colorado . . . . Every such gulch used to be a little wonder, each with its multiplying branches, each as deep at the mouth as the parent canyon . . . . Silt pockets out of reach of flood were gardens of fern and redbud; every talus and rockslide gave footing to cottonwood and willow and single-leafed ash; ponded places were solid with watercress; maidenhair hung from seepage cracks in the cliffs."

In March, 1963, the gates closed on the newly constructed Glen Canyon Dam, briefly interrupting a geologic process that had begun in the Jurassic Period. The windblown, crossbedded sands of the Navajo Sandstone, laid down in a desert climate more than 150 million years ago, had since been carved by the Colorado River into a hauntingly beautiful canyon. Now that canyon lies under the waters of Lake Powell, filling with sediment. The lake and its shoreline marinas have become one of most visited units of the National Park System, but a handful of pioneer river runners remember Glen Canyon of the Colorado as the very heart of earthly paradise.

The Canyon Returns

The reservoir and its accumulating sediments are a brief chapter of geologic evolution. Geologists predict that in a few centuries, Lake Powell will be a flat expanse of mud, sand, and boulders, with buried layers of human detritus. A few centuries more, and the dam will breach, beginning the cycle of erosion once again—this time rapidly returning Glen Canyon to its former contour. Willow, cottonwood, and tamarisk will once again colonize the riverbanks; hanging gardens will grow on slickrock walls. Beaver, lizards, and bighorn sheep will return to their former haunts. If human beings are still seeking silence, solitude, and beauty, they too will return.

The Utah Wilderness Coalition's BLM wilderness proposal stands for the long view: the notion that we humans, being brief tenants on the planet, ought to leave a bit of the Earth as we found it. Our Glen Canyon wilderness proposal, in turn, stands for a corollary: that having altered most of the face of this lovely planet, we ought to *return* some small part of it to its former grace.

IN BRIEF

Index Map: Area No. 44

Highlights: Once a single wilderness joined at the Colorado River, this area now flanks Lake Powell with Navajo Sandstone canyons, open plateaus, and volcanic peaks. The BLM gives only partial protection to the wilderness qualities of this area.

Guidebooks: Hall (1982), Kelsey, (1987a)

Maps: USGS 1:100,000 Hite Crossing, Navajo Mountain

Area of wilderness proposals in acres:

Unit	UWC	BLM
Little Rockies	60,000	38,700
Mancos Mesa	108,700	51,440
TOTAL	168,700	90,140

Adjacent wild lands: Glen Canyon National Recreation Area

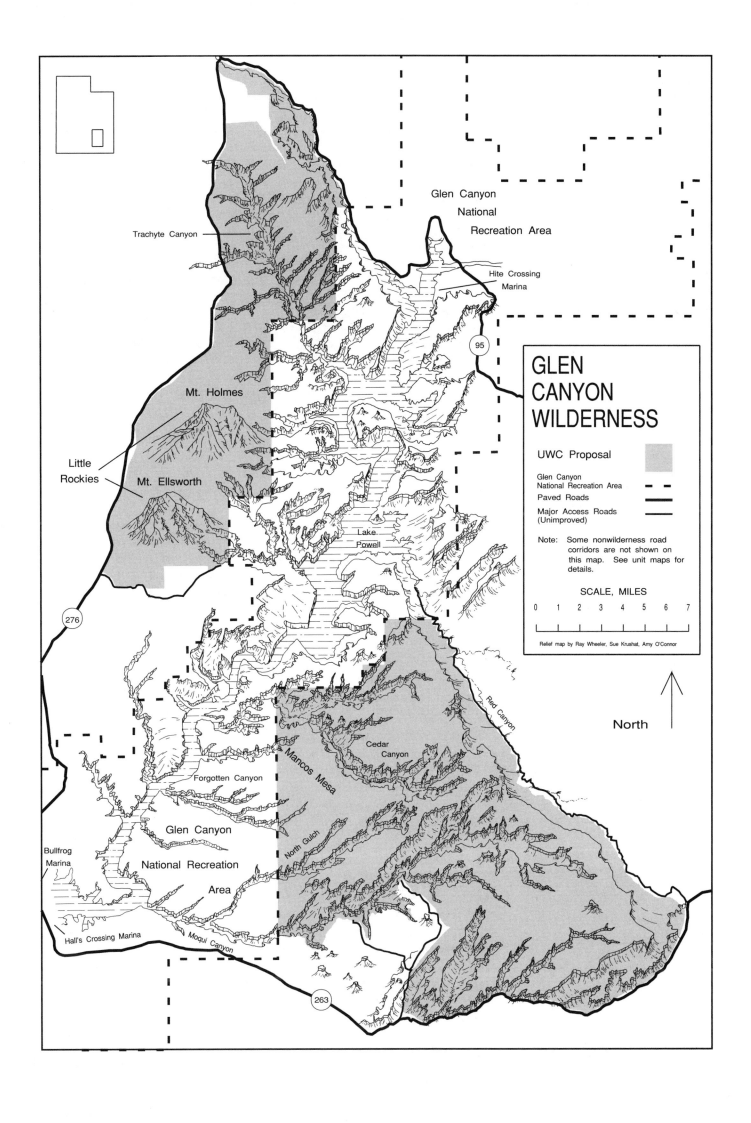

Trachyte Canyon

Glen Canyon

National

Recreation Area

Hite Crossing
Marina

95

Mt. Holmes

Little
Rockies

Mt. Ellsworth

Lake
Powell

276

GLEN
CANYON
WILDERNESS

UWC Proposal

Glen Canyon
National Recreation Area

Paved Roads

Major Access Roads
(Unimproved)

Note: Some nonwilderness road
corridors are not shown on
this map. See unit maps for
details.

SCALE, MILES

0   1   2   3   4   5   6   7

Relief map by Ray Wheeler, Sue Krushat, Amy O'Connor

North

Red Canyon

Cedar
Canyon

Mancos Mesa

Forgotten Canyon

North Gulch

Glen Canyon

Bullfrog
Marina

National Recreation

Area

Hall's Crossing Marina

Moqui Canyon

263

Country to lose yourself in: slick-rock and sand dunes dominate the seldom-visited expanse of Mancos Mesa. The sandstone ridges of the Nokai Dome unit are in the background.

Jeff Garton

The Utah Wilderness Coalition Proposal

It is an audacious idea. Lake Powell, not Zion, Bryce, or Arches, is Utah's premier tourist attraction. Proposals to milk still more money from its sterile shores have been made; the State of Utah has proposed Federal land swaps to permit the construction of as many as six new marinas. The cool, echoing recesses of Glen Canyon are a nostalgic memory for only a few.

Someday, however, the Colorado River will resume its ancient work. Until that day, we propose to dedicate wilderness on each side of the river as a memorial to the lost canyon, and to its eventual, inevitable return.

We include the Little Rockies in our proposed Glen Canyon wilderness because its canyons flow directly into the former course of the Colorado River. From high points in the unit one looks across Lake Powell to the remote, mysterious expanse of Mancos Mesa, the companion unit in the Glen Canyon area. Together these units make up 168,700 acres of BLM wild lands.

One day our descendants will be able to walk down Ticaboo Canyon, cross the muddy Colorado, and walk up Red Canyon below the imposing cliffs of Mancos Mesa. Along the way they will notice old banks of silt perched above the streambed. Perhaps they will see a plastic sixpack ring or an old bleach bottle poking out of the cutbank, and remember the brief moment in geologic time when humankind tried to remake a river.

Fred Swanson

MANCOS MESA UNIT

Highlights—The largest isolated slickrock mesa in southern Utah, Mancos Mesa's 180-square-mile table-top is bounded on every side by 1,000- to 1,500-foot-high cliffs. In a 1971 plan, the BLM recommended closing the entire mesa and Moki Canyon to mining and roadbuilding to protect a plant and animal community unusual for its large area without significant human disturbance. The BLM failed to withdraw the area from mineral entry, however, and from 1976 to 1979, extensive roadbuilding and uranium drilling (in violation of FLPMA's interim protection provisions) on the eastern third of the mesa left substantial scars. No economically significant mineral discoveries were made, and the roads were blocked to allow reclamation. The western half of the mesa is in the Glen

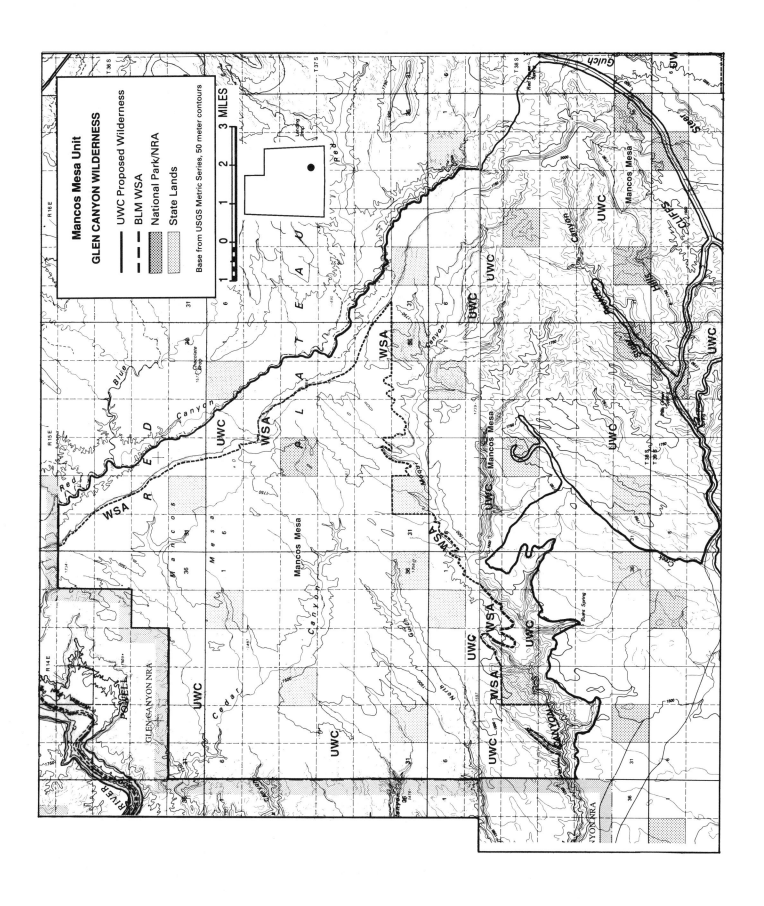

Mancos Mesa Unit
GLEN CANYON WILDERNESS

UWC Proposed Wilderness
BLM WSA
National Park/NRA
State Lands

Base from USGS Metric Series, 50 meter contours

0   1   2   3 MILES

Canyon NRA and is recommended by the Park Service for wilderness designation. The BLM initially recommended 46,120 acres for wilderness but left the entire southeastern portion and all of Moki Canyon unprotected. The final recommendation is expected to be 5,320 acres larger. The Coalition's 108,700-acre proposal would protect the entire mesa top, Moki Canyon, and about 40,000 wild acres south of Moki Canyon. The entire unit is yearlong bighorn sheep habitat (most of it is also crucial habitat).

Geology and landforms—The mesa top is roughly triangular in shape with Moki Canyon on the south as the base, Red Canyon as the northeast side, and the drowned Colorado River gorge as the northwest side. Cedar Canyon and North Gulch cut east to west across the width of the mesa. The entire unit is dominated by Navajo Sandstone with extensive areas of slickrock and dune sand. Cedar, Moki, and Steer Pasture canyons have deep inner canyons in the Wingate Sandstone. Windblown sand offers access into the canyons in places, notably at the "Sandslide" in Moki Canyon. There is water in several springs in the canyon bottoms.

Plant communities—The higher elevations on the east support pinyon and juniper, grading down through blackbrush, yucca, and Mormon tea to barest desert on the west. Riparian communities near the springs harbor cottonwood, oak, ash, willow, and watercress. Thanks to its inaccessibility, Mancos Mesa contains one of the few relict plant communities left in Utah. A 1970 BLM staff report described the mesa as a "near pristine example of the northern reaches of the upper Sonoran life zone." At that time, all but perhaps the northern tip of Mancos Mesa was in relict condition. (Grazing has since been expanded, however.) Valuable as a comparison area, the remaining relict community supports native perennial grasses, shrubs and some cacti. The report states that "Mancos has been isolated from the noticeable influences of man except limited grazing. Plant and animal communities are generally proceeding in a natural, unaltered environment, and few areas remain which offer pristine associations."

Wildlife—The BLM has designated the entire unit as yearlong bighorn habitat and the northern three-fourths as crucial desert bighorn sheep habitat (BLM, 1987b). This is an important native herd and supplies bighorns for transplant to other areas of Utah. Mule deer also live here, with bucks often of trophy size. Ringtail cat, mountain lion, bobcat, fox and coyote fill out the list of mammalian predators. The unit may also be peregrine falcon habitat. A number of reptiles inhabit the unit as well, including the chuckawalla lizard, unknown in most of Utah.

Archeology and history—Extensive archeological remains span 2,000 years of history and five different cultures. Lithic scatters, fireplaces, pithouses, kivas, and storage structures remain from the Basketmaker II and III, as well as the later Pueblo I, II, and III civilizations. A 1983 BLM memo states that Mancos Mesa "potentially contains numerous pristine cultural resources" and could contribute significant information on the livelihood of these peoples. In the lower reaches of Moki Canyon, the Park Service has documented dozens of Anasazi sites on NRA and BLM lands.

Recreation—Numerous remote, unnamed canyons await exploration, but gaining access to them is part of the challenge. Slickrock and sand dunes make for interesting hiking on the mesa top. Access is via a dirt road down Red Canyon or from Highway 263 between Clay Hills Divide and Halls Crossing.

BLM recommendation—The BLM recommended designation for 46,120 acres in 1986. Its final recommendation is expected to include 5,320 acres on the east end of the mesa that were left out of the draft recommendation. The agency improperly excluded 57,000 acres from study in its 1979 initial inventory decision as a result of mining exploration roads that had been constructed in violation of its wilderness inventory policy. A 1971 BLM management framework plan recommended that primitive qualities throughout the unit be protected "from mining and associated activities, roadbuilding, and mechanized travel of all forms."

Coalition proposal—We propose 108,700 acres of wilderness, with boundaries following natural features and including complete drainages wherever possible. Several vehicle tracks branch off the one passable road into the Burnt Spring area south of Moki Canyon, and the two that have noticeably impinged on the unit have been cherrystemmed out of the proposal. The vehicle track down the sand slide into Moki Canyon should be reclaimed (the BLM is considering proposals to do so at its WSA boundary on the north side of the canyon). The eastern boundary includes the land down to the road in Red Canyon, excluding areas of old mining impacts. These cliffs as well as the colorful escarpments of the Clay Hills and the Red House Cliffs in the southeast are beautiful, unusual, and completely natural and deserve protection. The mineral exploration of the late 1970s did not uncover any commercial deposits.

LITTLE ROCKIES UNIT

Highlights—While the peaks of the Little Rockies are geologically similar to the Henry Mountains, we include them in our proposed Glen Canyon wilderness because they are surrounded by slickrock canyons that—like those in Mancos Mesa—flow directly into the former course of the Colorado River in Glen Canyon. From high points in the unit one looks southeast across Lake Powell to the remote, mysterious expanse of Mancos Mesa, the companion unit in the Glen Canyon area. We propose 60,000 acres of wilderness to protect the rugged peaks of Mt. Holmes and Mt. Ellsworth, 50 miles of narrow, inviting canyons, and Navajo Sandstone slickrock. Access is easy from Utah Highway 276 which forms the unit's western boundary; the Glen Canyon National Recreation Area, through which the unit's canyons flow on their way to Lake Powell, forms the eastern boundary. The northern boundary is the high cliffs that line Highway 95 along North Wash before it reaches Lake Powell.

The south face of Mt. Holmes in the Little Rockies unit.

Fred Swanson

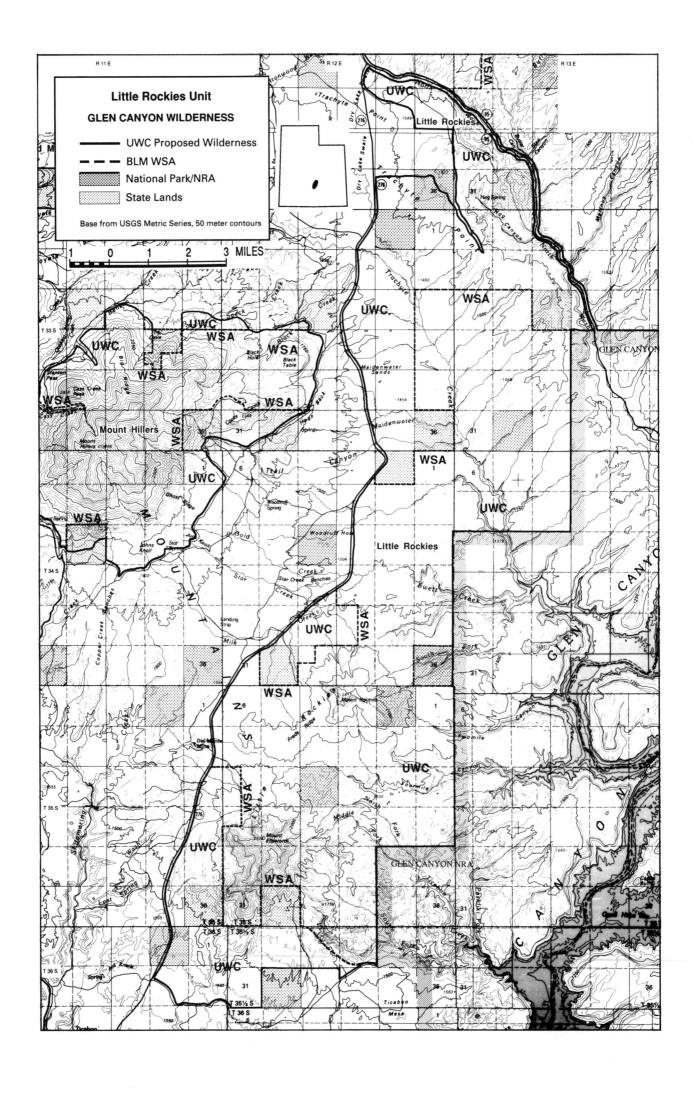

Little Rockies Unit

GLEN CANYON WILDERNESS

——— UWC Proposed Wilderness

- - - BLM WSA

National Park/NRA

State Lands

Base from USGS Metric Series, 50 meter contours

1   0   1   2   3   MILES

Geology and landforms—The Little Rockies were formed when an igneous intrusion pushed up flat-lying sedimentary rocks, forming a laccolithic dome similar to the nearby Henry Mountains. Erosion has since carved the laccolith into the prominent peaks of Mt. Ellsworth (8,295 feet) and Mt. Holmes (7,930 feet). Dikes and sills associated with the laccolith are exposed on the flanks of the peaks; light-colored diorite boulders eroded from the intrusive stock lie in the canyon bottoms. The Navajo Sandstone crops out around the peaks and is eroded into fins and pouroffs. The peaks were designated a National Natural Landmark in 1975 for their outstanding geologic features. One perennial stream, Trachyte Creek, drains the northeastern part of the unit, and a half-dozen small, ephemeral streams drain either into Trachyte Creek or directly into Lake Powell.

Plant communities—Since much of the unit is mountain slopes and slickrock, vegetation is sparse and consists primarily of desert shrubs such as blackbrush, Mormon tea, and shadscale, with juniper and pinyon pine scattered about. A few ponderosa pine cling to the north side of Mt. Ellsworth, where precipitation is higher and evaporation lower. Small areas of riparian vegetation are found along Trachyte Creek and in the canyon bottoms. The BLM (1986, p. 8) mentions one candidate threatened or endangered plant species, Hole-in-the-Rock prairie clover (*Dalea epica*), that grows in the southern part of the unit. The Maidenwater Sands hosts a natural plant community.

Wildlife—The endangered golden eagle has been sighted in the unit, according to the BLM, and a small band of desert bighorn was reintroduced to the area in 1985.

Archeology and history—Although the BLM has not finished an archeological resources inventory, it is likely that a variety of prehistoric occupation or hunting sites will be found, based on surveys in the adjacent Glen Canyon National Recreation Area.

Recreation—The unit's rough topography, broken by canyons and washes, is conducive to long day hikes and short backpack trips. Few people as yet explore this area. Trail and Swett canyons offer the easiest access to lower Trachyte Creek; Maidenwater and Woodruff canyons, narrower and more intimate, have interesting narrows and pouroffs to negotiate. Farther south, Fourmile and Ticaboo canyons offer long, remote canyons. A hike up Mt. Holmes or Mt. Ellsworth gives great views of most of the mountain ranges and canyon systems of south-central Utah. Hog Canyon, easily accessible from Highway 95 in North Wash, has a small spring at its head. All of these hikes are described in Kelsey (1987a); Hall (1982) describes a hike in Swett Canyon.

BLM recommendation—The BLM's 38,700-acre WSA, all of which it is recommending for wilderness, excludes wild lands on the north around Trachyte Point, the North Wash cliffs, and Maidenwater Canyon, and on the south near Ticaboo Mesa. The BLM held that mineral exploration roads and seismic lines put in before wilderness studies began marred natural qualities, but in a few places the WSA boundary was contracted far more than necessary. No significant mineral resources have been found, and the overall impact of exploration on the unit has been minor.

Coalition proposal—We propose a 60,000-acre wilderness, taking in 21,300 acres that were excluded from the WSA, including the scenic canyon of lower Maidenwater Creek, Hog Springs Canyon (excluding the trailhead facilities), and the south slopes of Mt. Ellsworth. The unit is virtually unblemished. A Park Service radio transmitter, which occupies a small site atop Mt. Ellsworth and is reached by helicopter, would be allowed to remain. A little-used four-wheel-drive road runs to an old mine on the northwest side of Mt. Ellsworth. A vehicle way on Trachyte Bench

Remember these things lost. The native wildlife; the chance to float quietly down a calm river, to let the current carry you past a thousand years of history, through a living canyon of incredible, haunting beauty.

David Brower

THE PLACE NO ONE KNEW—GLEN CANYON ON THE COLORADO RIVER (1963)

was built in 1979 during the wilderness review. Now unused and returning to a natural condition, most of the route is over sandy scrub terrain, and there are no permanent scars. Other signs of mineral exploration on Trachyte Bench and Ticaboo Mesa are excluded from our proposal, without deleting large areas of natural terrain as the BLM has done.

THE SAN JUAN-ANASAZI WILDERNESS

Summary

As the San Juan River winds past the small towns of Bluff and Mexican Hat, it meets sandy washes and tortuous canyons descending from pinyon-covered highlands. The intermittent streams that carved these canyons—Comb Wash, Johns and Slickhorn canyons, Grand Gulch, Steer Gulch and Whirlwind Draw, Mikes Canyon—also endowed them with dramatic geologic features. Buttes and arches, rincons, pinnacles, and palisades are carved into the cinnamon-tinted Cedar Mesa Sandstone and the dark-red sandstones and shales along the San Juan River.

It is difficult to imagine the Mormon pioneers crossing this rugged country in horse-drawn wagons, coming upon half-mile-wide gashes stretching across the landscape. Their route to the settlements at Bluff is now a historic trail. Archeological researchers are uncovering evidence of far older roads used by the enigmatic Anasazi Indian culture, which occupied most of this area.

Today the San Juan-Anasazi wilderness is one of the most popular destinations in Utah for backcountry visitors. Canyon adventurers often see Anasazi ruins as they hike through this enormous outdoor museum. The area is also biologically diverse, with streams and riparian vegetation complementing the lovely forests of Cedar Mesa and providing habitat for wildlife including deer, cougar, and many bird species.

As in much of southeastern Utah, unrestricted vehicle access has allowed pothunters to vandalize ancient ruins and off-road-vehicle users to tear up fragile soils. To protect the public's land from the abuses of the few, the Utah Wilderness Coalition proposes 395,800 acres of wilderness in seven units, ranging from the wide-open slickrock of Nokai Dome to the startling bare-rock spine of Comb Ridge.

Anasazi Country

Although the Anasazi left the area 700 years ago, their traces still exist in such deep canyons as Arch, Slickhorn, Grand Gulch, Fish, Owl, and Mule. Cliff dwellings made of mud and stone perch like swallow's nests on south-facing canyon exposures. In several canyons, stone towers once housed the Indians, and on the ground nearby, scatterings of broken pottery, along with corncobs and gourds desiccated by a thousand summers, hint at the daily lives of these desert dwellers. Circular kivas where the Anasazi gathered underground for religious ceremony, and curious pictographs on the sandstone walls are evidence of their spiritual legacy.

Recently discovered along Comb Wash near the mouth of Arch and Mule canyons is a continuous series of sites that the Anasazi used intensively. Some of these structures may have rivaled those found at Chaco Canyon, according to a BLM archeologist. The area has been likened to a prehistoric city whose presence was unsuspected a few years ago. An ancient road system that apparently connected habitation sites may change our fundamental understanding of the Anasazi culture. Much remains unknown about the Anasazi, and many potentially important archeological sites await discovery. Accordingly, it is important to protect this former homeland of the Anasazi from indiscriminate development.

IN BRIEF

Index Map: Area No. 45

Highlights: Once a center of the ancient Anasazi, this area now attracts hikers and boaters who enjoy viewing the remains of this mysterious culture. Wilderness designation would help protect archeological sites, desert bighorn habitat, and remote canyons and mesas.

Guidebooks: Hall (1982), Kelsey (1986a)

Maps: USGS 1:100,000 Blanding, Bluff, Navajo Mountain

Area of wilderness proposals in acres:

Unit	UWC	BLM
Arch and Mule Canyons	15,300	5,990
Comb Ridge	15,000	0
Fish & Owl Creek	59,000	40,160
Grand Gulch	139,800	105,520
Nokai Dome	93,400	0
Road Canyon	60,100	52,420
San Juan River	13,200	0
TOTAL	395,800	204,090

Adjacent wild lands: Glen Canyon National Recreation Area; Manti-La Sal National Forest

The concentration of archeological sites in this region, up to several hundred per square mile, may be as great as anywhere in the United States. Unfortunately, most of these sites are vulnerable to pothunters, and many of the important ruins have been vandalized already. Looters continue to steal valuable artifacts, yet the BLM is not adequately funded, staffed, or motivated to protect the cultural values on its lands. Although the BLM established the 33,000-acre Grand Gulch Primitive Area in 1974 to protect the archeological resources of the area, little money is allocated to protect the sites through education and law enforcement.

The BLM recently proposed to manage 400,000 acres of Cedar Mesa as a National Conservation Area (NCA). Accompanying this congressional designation would be increased funding to stabilize ruins, additional rangers to educate people and protect sites, a visitor center, and better trail management. However, the NCA would not necessarily preclude motorized access to sensitive archeological sites, limit mining exploration and development, or disallow "chaining" projects, which uproot trees and may destroy archeological sites to create artificial cattle pasture. If the legislation were accompanied by wilderness designation, these problems could be overcome.

Much of Cedar Mesa's cultural heritage is unprotected. If local officials had their way, it is likely that several of the ancient Anasazi roads would become county roads for automobiles, and much of Cedar Mesa would be open for unrestricted oil and gas development. The Utah Wilderness Coalition's proposal will help protect many of the ancient roads and structures by making them less easily accessible to vandals. The UWC proposal would also preclude new road construction in the wilderness.

Booming Recreation

Recreational use in the Cedar Mesa canyons has skyrocketed in recent years. Grand Gulch had only 2,000 recorded visitors in 1974. Ten years later nearly 20,000 visitors were registered. Fish and Owl canyons, which offer a convenient loop hike, had 2,500 recreation visitor days in 1980; in 1984, 6,160 visitor days were recorded. Commercial outfitting in these canyons has also increased in recent years, offering many who would not otherwise visit this remote and rugged country the opportunity to do so. Even in the lesser known canyons, use is increasing and the most delicate archeological sites are being visited regularly. A few of these sites have been inadvertently damaged.

In contrast to these busy canyons, the western part of the San Juan-Anasazi wilderness, the remote and austere Nokai Dome unit, is visited infrequently and offers complete solitude. Adjacent to the San Juan arm of the Glen Canyon National Recreation Area, this unit contains the long, deep forks of Mikes Canyon and the rolling slickrock-and-sand expanse of Grey Mesa, which the historic Mormon Trail traverses.

Arch Canyon—Focus of Conflict

The greatest controversy over the use of this area, however, is on its northeastern edge below the Abajo Mountains. Arch Canyon, a deep sandstone gorge that contains three natural stone arches, many archeological sites, several interesting sidecanyons, a perennial stream, and a variety of wildlife, was recommended for designation as a National Monument by the National Park Service in 1937. Its appeal as a recreational area is undeniable, and it is heavily used by hikers, hunters, and horse riders. Unfortunately, Arch Canyon has also come to symbolize the difficulties facing the public's wild lands. The canyon's solitude, archeological values, and riparian areas are threatened by growing off-road vehicle use.

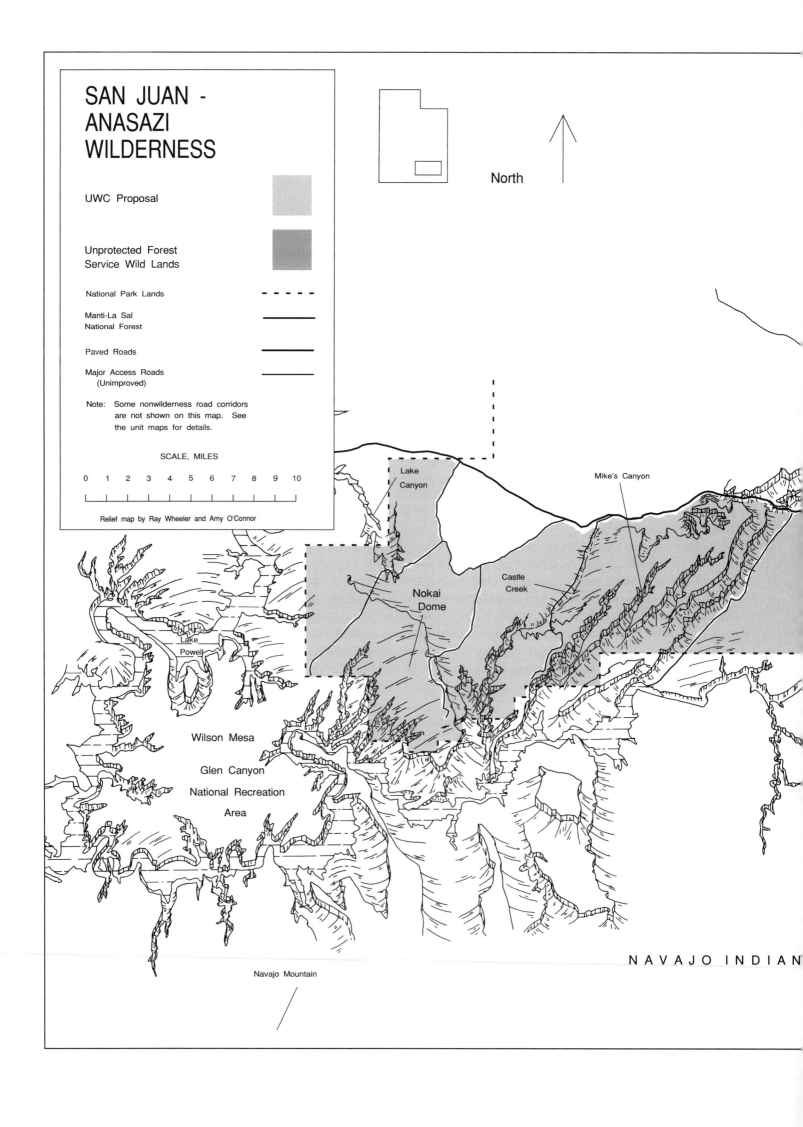

SAN JUAN - ANASAZI WILDERNESS

UWC Proposal

Unprotected Forest
Service Wild Lands

National Park Lands

Manti-La Sal
National Forest

Paved Roads

Major Access Roads
(Unimproved)

Note: Some nonwilderness road corridors
are not shown on this map. See
the unit maps for details.

SCALE, MILES

0 1 2 3 4 5 6 7 8 9 10

Relief map by Ray Wheeler and Amy O'Connor

North

Lake
Canyon

Mike's Canyon

Nokai
Dome

Castle
Creek

Lake
Powell

Wilson Mesa

Glen Canyon

National Recreation

Area

Navajo Mountain

NAVAJO INDIAN

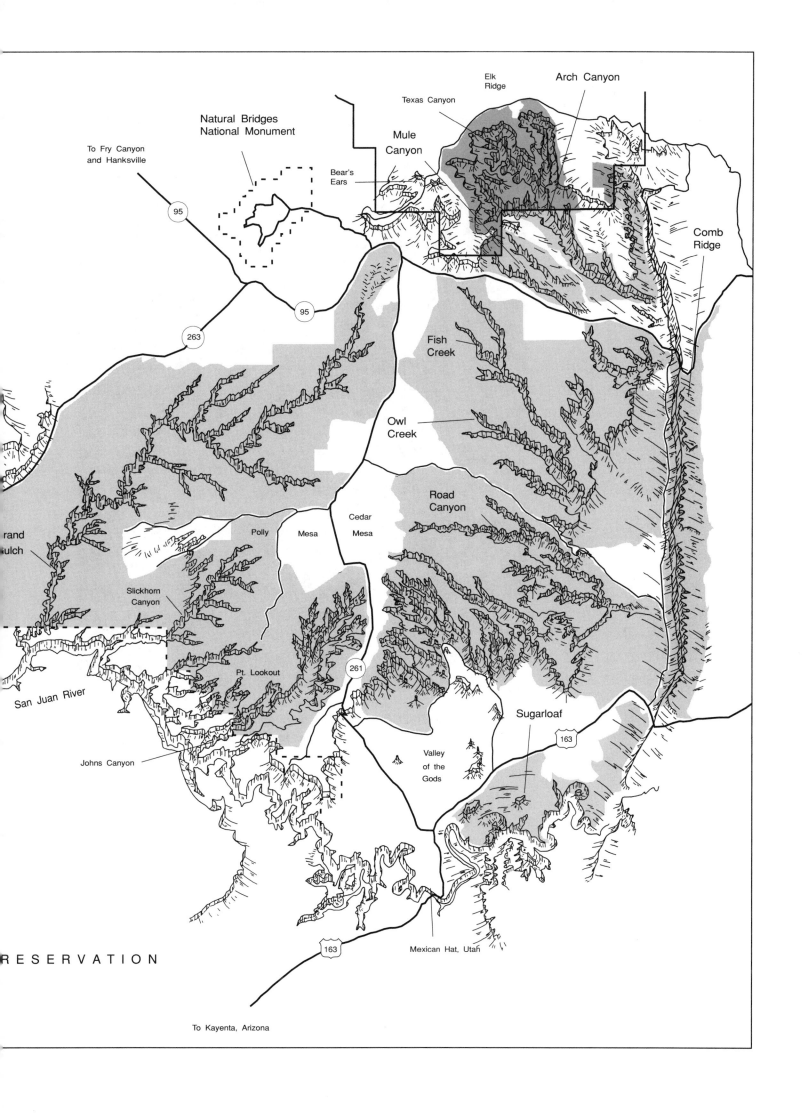

Natural Bridges
National Monument

To Fry Canyon
and Hanksville

Elk
Ridge

Arch Canyon

Texas Canyon

Mule
Canyon

Bear's
Ears

95

95

263

Comb
Ridge

Fish
Creek

Owl
Creek

Road
Canyon

rand
ulch

Polly
Mesa

Cedar
Mesa

Slickhorn
Canyon

261

San Juan River

Pt. Lookout

Sugarloaf

163

Johns Canyon

Valley
of the
Gods

RESERVATION

163

Mexican Hat, Utah

To Kayenta, Arizona

Huge stone monoliths line the course of Arch Canyon as it drops from the Abajo Mountains. This wild area was overlooked by both the Forest Service and the BLM in their wilderness reviews—partly because each agency managed only half of the canyon. The Utah Wilderness Coalition proposal recognizes the integrity of the whole canyon system.

Tom Miller

Narrow canyon bottoms with delicate riparian areas such as in Arch Canyon are simply no place for motorized vehicles or heavy cattle grazing. In 1989, the Chrysler Corporation began sponsoring an annual "Jeep Jamboree" in Arch Canyon. This gathering of ORVs threatens to tear up wild country and damage natural resources on a regular basis. Conservationists are fighting to keep repeated vehicle use from creating a road up Arch Canyon, and have asked the BLM to reduce or eliminate livestock grazing in Arch Canyon (whether or not it is designated wilderness). The Grand Gulch Primitive Area, which has been managed to exclude domestic livestock and ORVs, offers a good example of what such management can do in just a few years. In Grand Gulch, the grasses are denser and more diverse, streamside vegetation more luxuriant, erosion diminished, and wildlife more abundant than in nearby canyons.

The Utah Wilderness Coalition Proposal

The Utah Wilderness Coalition advocates leaving the San Juan-Anasazi area as close to its natural condition as possible by designating a wilderness area of 395,800 acres. The BLM would protect only 204,090 acres, missing all of the Nokai Dome unit, all of Arch Canyon, the wild slopes north of the San Juan River between Bluff and Mexican Hat, and much roadless land in three of the four remaining units. Full protection of the area is needed to safeguard its priceless archeological resources and ensure opportunities for low-impact backcountry recreation.

Mike Medberry

NOKAI DOME UNIT

Highlights—Sixty miles west of Blanding lies the 93,400-acre Nokai Dome unit, one of the most remote areas in Utah. Contiguous with the San Juan River arm of the Glen Canyon National Recreation Area, this rugged and lonely land contains numerous deep canyons, scenic expanses of slickrock, and breathtaking vistas of the surrounding country. Experienced hikers will find challenging terrain in Mikes, Castle, and Lake canyons, and desert bighorn find here their yearlong habitat.

Geology and landforms—A vast expanse of sandstone of the Mesozoic and Paleozoic eras, the Nokai Dome unit slopes gradually down to Lake Powell. Slickrock and sandblow dominate the uplands. Mikes Canyon and Castle Creek, which both harbor rare spring-fed streams, have cut cliffs into the sandstone. Lake Canyon provides a water source in the northwestern corner. Views from Nokai Dome include Navajo Mountain to the southwest, the Waterpocket Fold to the northwest, and the spires of Monument Valley to the south. Highway 263, which is the northern boundary of the unit, is managed as a scenic highway corridor.

Plant communities—Some pinyon-juniper is found at higher elevations, but blackbrush and associated desert shrubs dominate the unit. Small but delightful areas of riparian habitat are found in the bottom of Mikes, Castle, and Lake canyons and some of their tributaries. The Clay Hills support some grassy parks.

Wildlife—The Nokai Dome unit is part of the yearlong habitat of the desert bighorn sheep (BLM, 1986a, p. 3-43) and is also habitat for a number of desert species, including the endangered peregrine falcon. Beaver are found in riparian areas.

Archeology and history—Although this unit has not been thoroughly inventoried, it was used by Archaic, Basketmaker, and Anasazi cultures. The lower canyons have numerous storage structures and some habitation sites; stone chipping and camping sites are found on the benchlands. The historic Hole-in-the-Rock Trail, where a group of Mormons trekked to Bluff, Utah, cuts across the western portion of the unit.

Recreation—Visitation to Nokai Dome is limited owing to its remote and untamed nature. Water is limited to a few cliffside springs and the lower reaches of the canyons, but if one is well prepared, there are exceptional hiking and backpacking opportunities. Mikes Canyon can be reached via its upper tributaries or overland from the Clay Hills road; Castle Creek and Nokai Dome itself can be reached via four-wheel-drive routes. The solitude in this unit is almost more than one can bear. The views of the Henrys, the Little Rockies, Lake Powell, and the surrounding countryside are unparalleled in the Plateau country.

BLM recommendation—The BLM declined to study this vast expanse of wild land for its wilderness potential, claiming that the area was heavily impacted by mineral exploration. It divided the unit into four small parcels and dropped each from its wilderness inventory. The subdivision of the unit along various vehicle ways violated the BLM's wilderness inventory policy. The Hole-in-the-Rock Trail, a four-wheel-drive vehicle route, is not maintained as a road. The way along Castle Creek follows a sandy

Southeastern Utah seems destined to have many visitors who are attracted by the scenery of a region remote from main lines of travel . . . . the exceptionally interesting trail through the Clay Hills, Castle Wash, Wilson Mesa, and across the San Juan to Navajo Mountain, and the trail through the Henry Mountains and the Kaiparowits region to Escalante, are feasible for adventurers who place unusual experiences above daily comforts.

Herbert Gregory

THE SAN JUAN COUNTRY (1938)

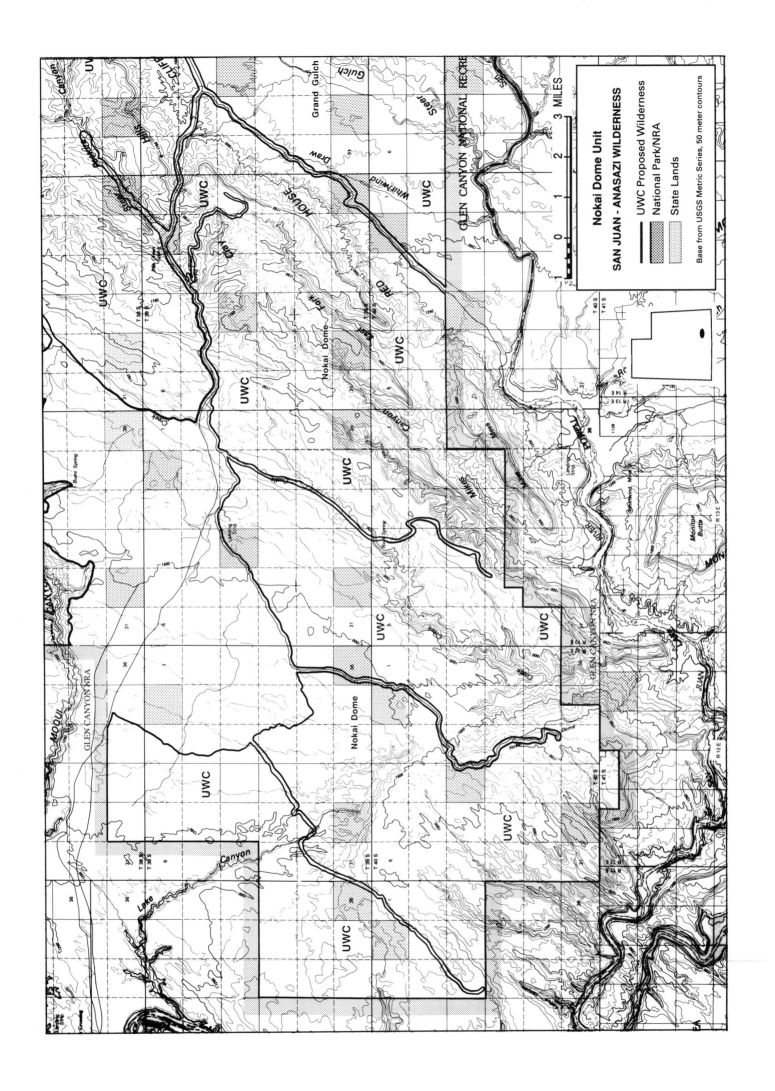

Nokai Dome Unit

SAN JUAN - ANASAZI WILDERNESS

UWC Proposed Wilderness

National Park/NRA

State Lands

Base from USGS Metric Series, 50 meter contours

0   1   2   3   MILES

wash impassable to passenger vehicles. A mineral exploration road up onto Nokai Dome itself was bladed in places but is now limited to four-wheel-drive vehicles.

Coalition proposal—We propose 93,400 acres of wilderness. Our boundary cherrystems the vehicle ways noted above, including the historic Mormon Trail, a popular off-highway route in the area. Mining exploration tracks and drill pads in the unit are largely overgrown, eroded, or blown over with sand and do not significantly affect the unit's wildness. If natural reclamation were given some assistance, these scars would continue to fade. Rather than cast out the entire unit because of past bulldozing and drilling in a few areas, we should allow the tremendous wild character of the region to reestablish itself.

GRAND GULCH UNIT

Highlights—Grand Gulch, one of the most popular hiking areas in the state, is the centerpiece of the 139,800-acre Grand Gulch roadless area. Other, less-visited canyons are also cut into the broad upland that slopes southwest from Highway 95 to the San Juan River. The unit has hundreds of miles of canyons and sidecanyons, thousands of archeological sites (many of them threatened by abuse and misuse), and important desert bighorn habitat.

Geology and landforms—Johns Canyon, Slickhorn Canyon, and Grand Gulch are cut into the 800-foot-thick Cedar Mesa Sandstone of Permian age. These canyons have also exposed older Pennsylvanian rocks in their lower stretches before reaching the San Juan River. Deep overhangs and alcoves line these canyons and their tributaries, many of which shelter Anasazi dwellings. Downstream from Grand Gulch, Steer Gulch and Whirlwind Draw enter the San Juan. The broad upland benches that separate the canyons range in elevation from 6,600 feet in the northeast at Grand Flat to 4,100 feet in the southwest at the Clay Hills road.

Plant communities—A pinyon-juniper forest dotted with sagebrush parks covers more than half of the unit. The more arid blackbrush-desert shrub community is found at lower elevations to the southwest. Grand Gulch, Slickhorn, and Johns Canyon flow during most of the year and contain riparian habitat such as cottonwood and willow. The BLM's WSA includes four sensitive species, the milkvetches *Astragalus cottamii* and *Astragalus monumentalis*, the Kachina daisy (*Erigeron kachinensis*), and the death camas (*Zigadenus vaginatus*) (BLM, 1986, p. 15.)

Wildlife—The unit encompasses nearly 3,000 acres of crucial deer winter range, according to the BLM, and mule deer inhabit some of the canyons year round. Although bighorn have not been abundant in recent years, 3,900 acres of crucial bighorn range are also found in the unit. Spotted skunk and ringtail cat live in the wetter canyons, and the unit is home to a number of small mammals and birds. The endangered bald eagle spends its winters here.

Archeology and history—This unit houses a "wealth of pristine Anasazi cultural resources" (BLM, 1986, p. 19). Nearly 600 archeological sites have been recorded from both the Basketmaker and Pueblo cultures of the Anasazi, and the BLM estimates that its WSA alone may contain more than 11,000 additional unrecorded sites, three-fourths of which could be eligible for the National Register. Unfortunately, vandalism is a serious problem, and the footfalls of thousands of well-meaning visitors have also disturbed many sites. Elsewhere in the unit, the Hole-in-the-Rock Trail marks the passage of early Mormon settlers on their way to Bluff, Utah, in 1879.

Overpowering solitude can be found out on the slickrock mesas of Nokai Dome. Navajo Mountain is among the many distant landmarks visible from this unit.

John P. George

Recreation—Hiking, backpacking, camping, horseback riding, and the study of archeology and nature drew an estimated 20,000 visitor days of use in 1985, up from 2,000 a scant 11 years earlier (BLM, 1986, p. 20). The BLM has attempted to redirect some traffic to neighboring wild lands that offer equally grand hiking and greater solitude; we suggest visiting Grand Gulch during the late fall or early spring, when crowds are smaller and the lighting on the rocks is sublime. Alternatively, try the outlying canyons such as Steer Gulch or Whirlwind Draw. In past years, a permanent BLM ranger, assisted by six or seven temporary staff, were on hand to manage traffic and educate visitors about protecting the Anasazi ruins. Recent budget cuts have left only one seasonal ranger and some volunteers—hardly the protection this superb area deserves. All this at a time when the agency is drawing plans for huge, budget-draining forest chainings elsewhere in the area.

BLM recommendation—The BLM recommends that all of its 105,520-acre WSA be designated wilderness. But the agency dropped from its initial inventory 40,000 acres of roadless lands, including the upper part of Grand Gulch and the western part of the area around Steer Gulch and Whirlwind Draw. There are no known mineral conflicts in this area, and it is as wild as the WSA—perhaps more so.

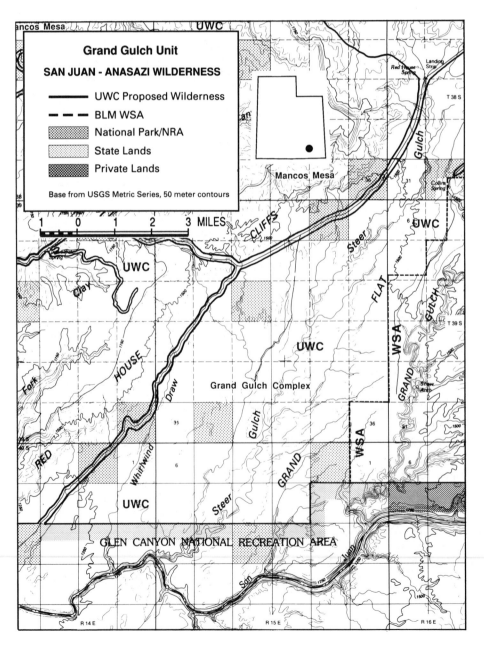

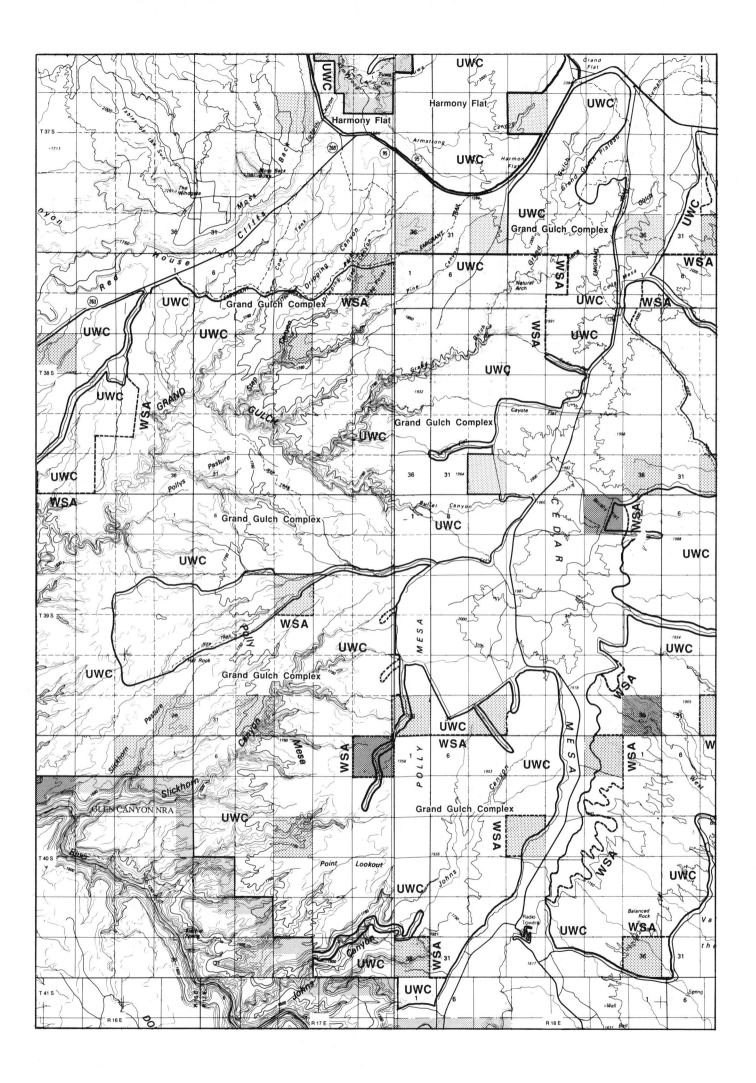

Wilderness designation, by excluding vehicles, would aid efforts to preserve Cedar Mesa's priceless archeological sites. Pothunters and vandals generally rely on mechanized access.

Fred Swanson

Coalition proposal—We propose a 139,800-acre wilderness unit, including the roadless land that the BLM dropped from its inventory. A half-dozen old vehicle ways, totalling about 16 miles in length, are included in both the BLM's proposal and ours. The BLM has closed these to vehicle use. The unit retains its overall sense of naturalness and remains the central part of our San Juan-Anasazi wilderness, linking the slickrock mesas of the Nokai Dome unit with the rest of Cedar Mesa to the east.

FISH AND OWL CREEK CANYONS UNIT

Highlights—The canyons of Fish Creek and Owl Creek, as well as the less well-known but also beautiful canyons of Dry Wash and lower Mule Creek, harbor important archeological resources worthy of protection. Our 59,000-acre wilderness unit would help protect these endangered resources as well as a popular backpacking area. The unit is located in the southeastern part of Cedar Mesa and forms a wilderness stretching from Comb Ridge to the Grand Gulch Plateau. The unit is encircled by the rest of the San Juan-Anasazi wilderness and is separated from the Comb Ridge and Road Canyon units by only a single dirt road.

Geology and landforms—Fish Creek and its western tributary, Owl Creek, are steep-sided, narrow canyons cut into the southeast-dipping Cedar Mesa Sandstone, the only formation with significant exposure in the unit. Dry Wash and lower Mule Canyon drain the eastern part of the unit and, like Fish Creek, flow to the southeast into Comb Wash. In places the slickrock walls are 600 to 800 feet high; prominent arches also occur. The continuous vertical cliffs formed in the Cedar Mesa Sandstone permit access into the canyons only at a few breakdowns. The twists and turns of the canyons give an intimate feeling, whereas on the mesa tops one can see across the canyons to the imposing west face of Comb Ridge.

Plant communities—Dense stands of pinyon and juniper cover most of the uplands in the unit, broken by sagebrush parks and some expanses of bare slickrock. This is the forest that lends all of Cedar Mesa its inviting appearance, less harsh than lower-elevation desert canyons. The BLM (1986) reports four candidate threatened and endangered species, the milkvetches *Astragalus cottamii* and *Astragalus monumentalis*, the Kachina daisy (*Erigeron kachinensis*), and the death camas (*Zigadenus vaginatus*). Riparian habitat is found along the creek bottoms; the BLM (1986a) lists a potential Area of Critical Environmental Concern for riparian habitat in Fish Creek, Owl Creek, and Butler Wash.

Wildlife—The unit provides seasonal habitat for mule deer and the endangered bald eagle. Petroglyphs indicate that the area was once desert bighorn habitat; their reintroduction should be considered.

Archeology and history—The entire unit was heavily used for agriculture by the Anasazi people; near-perfect kivas and cliff dwellings can be found in Fish and Owl Creek, as well as numerous burial and chipping sites. Undisturbed Basketmaker sites are also present. The mesa tops above Mule Canyon and the cliff walls themselves contain one of the greatest densities of archeological sites in the United States. The historic Hole-In-The-Rock pioneer trail forms the southwestern boundary of the unit.

Recreation—Fish and Owl Creek Canyon are among the most popular backpacking areas on Cedar Mesa. Multi-day backpacking trips take in a loop of these canyons, passing through twisting, narrow slickrock walls. For years the BLM encouraged use of this area as an "overflow" from Grand Gulch. Use has increased steadily from about 2,500 visitor-days in 1980 to 6,160 in 1984 (BLM, 1986, p. 18). Outfitting makes up a significant proportion of these totals. Lower Mule and Dry Wash canyons are shorter, less traveled, and provide outstanding opportunities for solitude on day

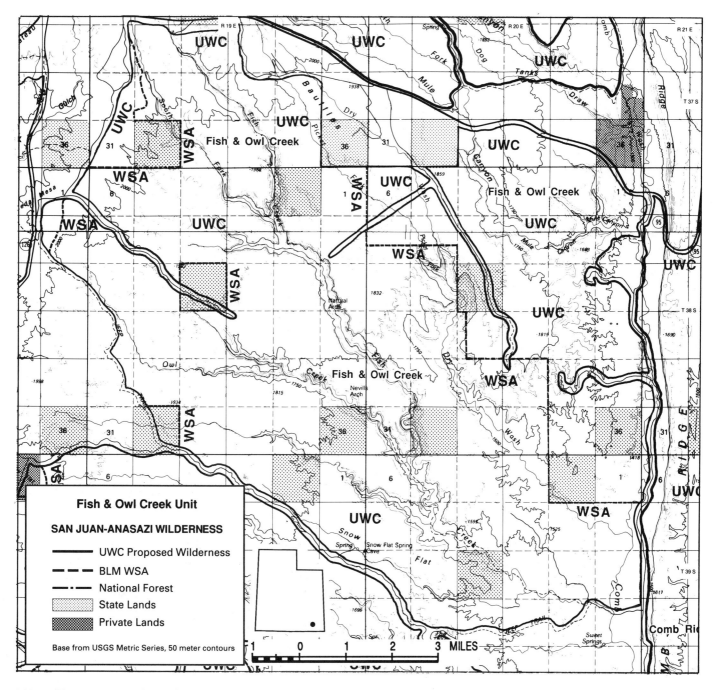

hikes. The mouths of all of these canyons can be reached by hiking west
from the dirt road that runs along Comb Wash between Utah Highway 95
and U.S. 163. This road is passable to two-wheel-drive vehicles in dry
weather, but rainstorms may necessitate four-wheel-drive. Cars can also be
parked at the Kane Gulch Ranger Station atop Cedar Mesa on Utah 261
for round-trip hikes through Fish and Owl Creek Canyon.

BLM recommendation—The BLM initially recommended that 35,220
acres out of its 46,440-acre WSA be designated as wilderness. Its final recommendation is expected to be 40,160 acres. Following agency custom,
the slightly less rugged eastern parts of the unit were excluded, part during the initial inventory and part during the WSA study. Much of this area
is proposed for costly, destructive forest chaining. The BLM's arbitrary
WSA boundary left out the archeologically rich lower part of Mule Canyon, as well as Baullie's Bench and Dry Wash. The claim was that these
areas lacked outstanding opportunities for solitude. Oil and gas leases
cover much of the unit, despite its high wilderness values; in fact, the
BLM has allowed drilling in an area they had recorded as habitat for the

endangered bald eagle. However, the potential for mineral resources is low due to unfavorable geologic conditions.

Coalition proposal—We propose a 59,000-acre wilderness unit, restoring to protection the lands BLM deleted in lower Mule Creek, Dry Wash, and Baullie's Bench. Despite the agency's claim, excellent solitude is to be found on those lands, not just in areas of dense vegetation or behind steep canyon walls. Like the mesa tops, the natural open areas surrounding the mouths of the canyons are integral to the unit. Our proposal excludes intrusions along the seven-mile-long Comb Wash overlook road, which extends between Dry Wash and Mule Canyon. A cherrystem excludes the two-mile-long road extending west from the eastern boundary and a two-mile-long road extending northwest between Fish Creek and Dry Wash.

ROAD CANYON UNIT

Highlights—This 60,100-acre unit, which forms the south-central block of the San Juan-Anasazi wilderness, includes the narrow slickrock canyons of Road Canyon and Lime Creek. The unit's name is a misnomer; there are no roads in Road Canyon. The unit is separated from the adjoining Comb Ridge and Fish and Owl Creek units by a single four-wheel-drive road. A two-wheel-drive road taking off from the Valley of the Gods loop road (off of U.S. Highway 163 and Utah 261 north of Mexican Hat) gives access to the main fork and west fork of Lime Creek Canyon. The upper ends of these canyons as well as Road Canyon itself can be reached from Utah 261 on top of Cedar Mesa, and the mouths of Road and Barton canyons can be reached from U.S. 163 via a dirt road that begins just north of the bridge over Comb Wash.

Geology and landforms—The edge of Cedar Mesa, which bisects this unit, abruptly drops 1,000 feet in places. The view from the mesa rim takes in the isolated monoliths and rock fingers of the Valley of the Gods, the huge Raplee Anticline rising over the San Juan River, and distant mountains in Colorado and New Mexico. (Summer visibility averages 100 to 130 miles.) Cutting across the mesa top are narrow, sinuous stair-stepped sandstone chasms, in their upper reaches 600 to 800 feet deep. To the south these canyons enter an area of brittle, deep red to purple Halgaito Shale before draining out into the expanse of the Valley of the Gods. A beautiful variety of colors and erosional forms is found here.

Plant communities—The pinyon-juniper forest of Cedar Mesa carpets the upper parts of the unit with its dark, velvety green. As this plateau breaks off into canyon and desert floor, the forest is replaced by desert shrubs. According to the BLM, two threatened or endangered candidate species, the milkvetch *Astragalus cronquistii* and the daisy *Erigonum clavellatum* may live in the unit (BLM, 1986, p. 16).

Wildlife—Like the Fish and Owl Creek unit to the north, Road Canyon is populated by a typical variety of wildlife, including the elusive cougar, some deer, and migrant bald eagles. Bighorn sheep have used the area in former years, according to the BLM (1986); however, there are no plans to reestablish their populations.

Archeology and history—There are well-preserved Anasazi and Basketmaker sites in the canyons and mesa tops. Limited surveys in the area suggest that the unit may contain more than 6,000 archeological sites, with more than 4,000 possibly eligible for the National Register (BLM, 1986, p. 21). The historic Hole-In-The-Rock Trail, a Mormon pioneer route, borders the unit on the northeast.

Recreation—Road Canyon and Lime Creek Canyon, the two major drainages in the unit, offer excellent overnight hikes. Far fewer people

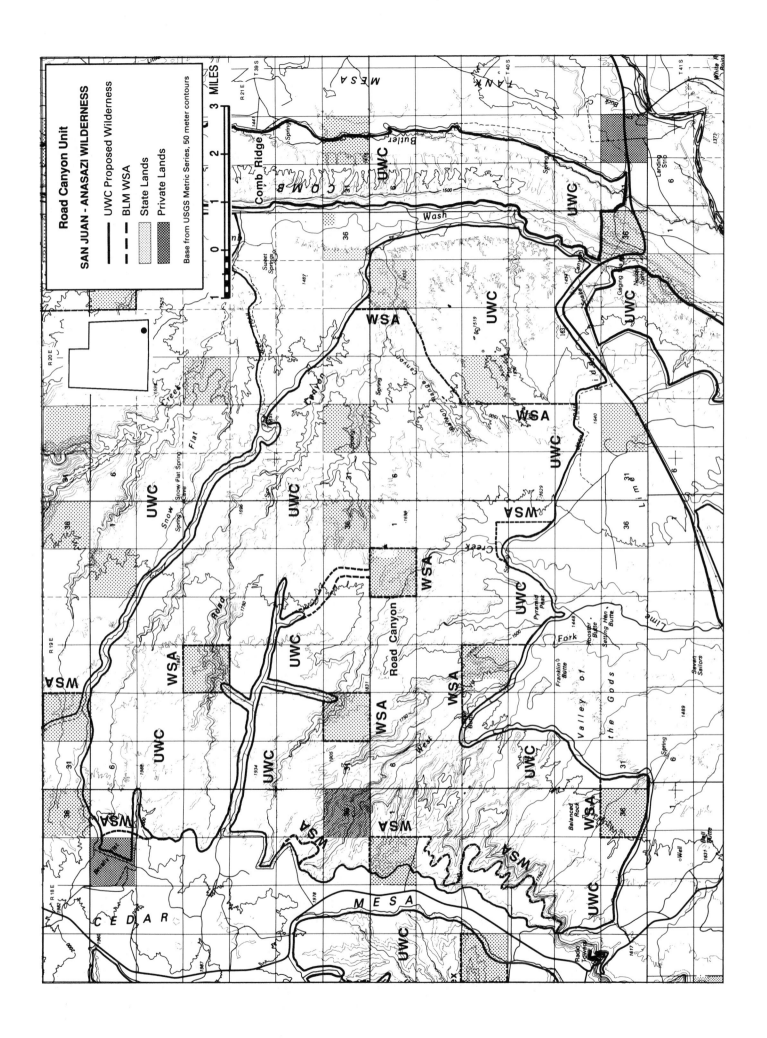

Road Canyon Unit

SAN JUAN - ANASAZI WILDERNESS

— UWC Proposed Wilderness
--- BLM WSA
State Lands
Private Lands

Base from USGS Metric Series, 50 meter contours

MILES
3 2 1 0 1

visit this unit than the neighboring Grand Gulch and Fish and Owl Creek units. The BLM estimates use at only a few hundred visitor days per year, most of which are part of the educational programs of the National Outdoor Leadership School. The full length of Road and Lime Creek canyons can be hiked, although a 50-foot pouroff in lower Lime Creek requires routefinding through a natural rock tunnel. The strange, multicolored badlands between Barton Canyon and Comb Wash make fascinating exploration.

BLM recommendation—To its credit, the BLM recommended 45,720 acres of its 52,420-acre WSA for wilderness, and has announced that it will recommend all of the WSA in its final EIS. Earlier, the BLM had inexplicably dropped from its inventory the benches and badlands between Barton Canyon and Comb Wash. There are numerous oil and gas leases in the unit, but their development potential appears to be low.

Coalition proposal—We propose a 60,100-acre wilderness unit encompassing the desert benchlands that the BLM deleted, including some of the pinnacles, escarpments, and peaks within the Valley of the Gods. The rolling landscape provides excellent screening from other users, enhancing the sense of seclusion. Wilderness designation is needed to prevent ORV use from disturbing fragile soils and solitude. Our proposal cherrystems the dirt road running between Road and Lime Creek canyons. There appear to be no other conflicts with wilderness designation.

SAN JUAN RIVER (SUGARLOAF) UNIT

Highlights—The float trip down the San Juan River from Bluff to Mexican Hat passes between the Navajo Reservation and BLM land to form the southernmost boundary of the San Juan-Anasazi wilderness. The BLM side was not studied for its wilderness potential, despite its high scenic and recreational values. The unit also includes the plateau between the river and Highway 163. A hiker can travel a portion of the waterway by entering the canyon where the river exits from the Raplee anticline, known locally as the Navajo Rug, and the upland region can be reached from the north by dirt roads leaving Highway 163 near the crest of Lime Ridge. An alternative take-out is near Mexican Hat Rock, where a rough sandy road reaches the river and forms the downstream unit terminus.

Geology and landforms—The San Juan River cuts deeply through Pennsylvanian sedimentary rocks some 300 million years old. The Lime Ridge and Raplee anticlines are bisected by the river and form walls up to 800 feet high. Bioherms—ancient mudbanks with heavy concentrations of algae and other fossils—can be found along the canyon bottom. An enormous abandoned river meander, with the imposing pinnacle of Sugarloaf Butte rising from its center, lies in the interior of the unit. The sandy bottomed river falls at a rate greater than that of the Colorado River in the Grand Canyon, and the combination of high gradient and heavy sediment loading results in sand waves, an uncommon phenomenon. For details on the geology of the area see Baars (1986).

Plant communities—The mesas above the river are dominated by desert shrubs spaced widely apart on the often rocky soils. Some riparian vegetation is found along the river, with shady cottonwood stands near the upstream boundary of the unit. Box elder grows along some lazy turns of the canyon, and tamarisk is ever-present.

Wildlife—Fox, coyotes, lizards, mountain lions, bighorn sheep, snakes, and eagles can be found in the unit. The river holds a population of channel catfish, among other aquatic species.

Archeology and history—A unique Clovis point hunting site thousands of years old has been found on the edge of the unit on Lime Ridge. The An-

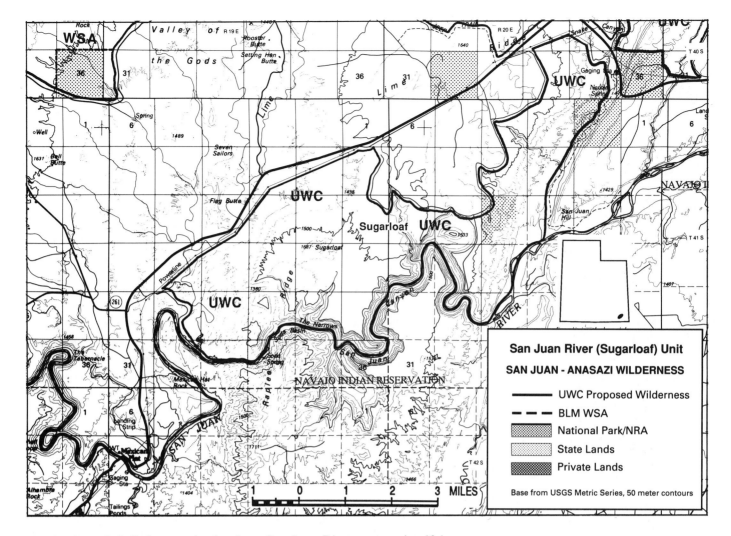

San Juan River (Sugarloaf) Unit
SAN JUAN - ANASAZI WILDERNESS

———— UWC Proposed Wilderness
– – – BLM WSA
National Park/NRA
State Lands
Private Lands

Base from USGS Metric Series, 50 meter contours

asazi culture left little trace in the deep San Juan River canyon itself, but there are extensive rock art panels upstream from this unit and numerous cliff dwellings across the river on the Navajo Reservation in Chinle Wash. (Permission should be obtained before visiting those sites.)

Recreation—The San Juan River is a popular float trip, with warm water and red rock scenery. The river is traveled by raft, kayak, and canoe; however, there are some rapids on this stretch, and any trip should include experienced river runners. Commercial outfitters offer guided trips. The float from Bluff to Mexican Hat can be done as a day or overnight trip. A hike across the plateau from Highway 163 towards Sugarloaf Butte provides stunning and seldom seen vistas down into the river canyon. Also worthy of a visit from the plateau is the abandoned rincon, which drops suddenly and spectacularly from the surrounding mesa.

BLM recommendation—The BLM inexplicably failed to give this unit WSA status. It exaggerated the extent of a few localized impacts and incorrectly mapped nonexistent roads. It appears that the agency may have gotten carried away with a marking pen and cut the unit in half by drawing a road which, if it actually existed, would run from Highway 163 off the top of Lime Ridge and over several hundred feet of airspace above the river. Perhaps a developer would dream of such an architectural feat, but you'll find only the wide-open skies over the unit.

Coalition proposal—We propose that 13,200 acres of the San Juan River Canyon be protected along the river from Comb Wash to Mexican Hat Rock and out to Highway 163 and the highway powerline corridor. Our unit would protect the multi-colored patterns formed by overlapping uplifted rocks on the west side of Comb Wash which have at various times

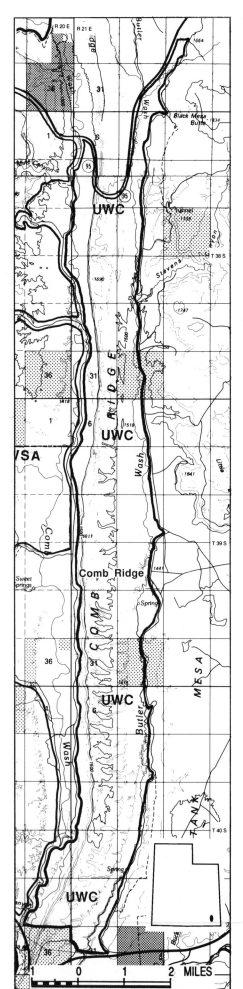

been threatened by strip mining proposals. The unit would also help preserve the San Juan River corridor to ensure that a wilderness trip remains possible. The canyon has been considered as a reservoir site, although there are no serious proposals at this time. Our proposal cherrystems the dirt roads atop Lime Ridge.

COMB RIDGE UNIT

Highlights—The scenic culmination of a drive on Utah's Highway 95 is the climb over Comb Ridge, one of the Southwest's most spectacular geologic features. But those who get out of their vehicles and wander south along the ridge discover still more magnificent vistas, as well as hidden side-canyons offering quiet seclusion. We propose a 15,000-acre wilderness unit, about 15 miles long by 1-1/2 miles wide, forming the eastern border of the San Juan-Anasazi wilderness. Access is easy from Highway 95 at the unit's north end or Highway 163 at its south end, and from the dirt road along Butler Wash. The approach to the ridge's sheer western wall is best left to the hawks and eagles that frequent the unit.

Geology and landforms—Comb Ridge is a 600-foot-high sandstone monocline that runs in a north-south direction for nearly 90 miles, curving west past Kayenta, Arizona. The ridge's greatest expression is within the proposed wilderness unit, where its near-vertical western wall and gentler eastern slope are visible from many vantage points in the region. From its top are 360-degree views taking in the Abajos, Cedar Mesa, the patterned badlands below Bartlett Canyon, the spires of Monument Valley, and the Mule's Ear above the San Juan River. Comb Ridge itself is visible stretching toward the Abajos to the north and the San Juan River to the south. The east flank of the ridge is cut by many short canyons, most of them straight, narrow, and secluded.

Plant communities—Only the occasional hardy shrub or juniper grows on the exposed sandstone of Comb Ridge. The more gradual eastern slope, however, hosts a scattering of pinyon and juniper trees and their associated desert shrubs.

Wildlife—Comb Ridge is prime raptor habitat and the birds can be seen wheeling and diving along the precipitous face of the ridge. Deer also inhabit the unit.

Archeology and history—Archeological sites are found in rifts along the side of the ridge. In places Anasazi footholds are cut into the stone.

Recreation—A hike up the sloping slickrock to the edge of Comb Ridge pays off in fabulous views. Hikers can track the high edge of the ridge for most of the unit's 15-mile length but should use discretion and choose their route carefully. The west face of the ridge offers challenging rock climbs for expert climbers. While the top of the ridge draws attention with its high profile, the short, narrow sidecanyons on its eastern flank are subtle and secret. A shady green pool lies below Monarch Cave, awaiting swimmers on a scorching afternoon.

BLM recommendation—The BLM dropped Comb Ridge from its wilderness inventory, alleging that the unit is too small to offer solitude and primitive recreation. But exploration of the unit reveals just those qualities: it is extremely rugged and the topography provides secluded spots as well as grand vistas, with plenty of challenge for hikers and climbers.

Coalition proposal—We propose a 15,000-acre wilderness unit and know of no conflicts with wilderness designation.

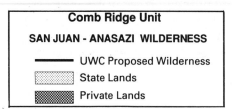

Comb Ridge Unit

SAN JUAN - ANASAZI WILDERNESS

——— UWC Proposed Wilderness

State Lands

Private Lands

ARCH AND MULE CANYONS UNIT

Highlights—This 15,300-acre unit begins as a slice through a great dome of slickrock rising above Comb Wash and then trails up into tall groves of ponderosa pine where impressive natural arches stand. The upper four miles of Arch Canyon are part of a roadless area under Forest Service management. Undisturbed cliff dwellings in both Arch and Mule canyons bespeak the Anasazi culture. Hiking opportunities are excellent, and the scenery is unmatched. The National Park Service recommended National Monument protection for Arch Canyon as early as 1937. Access is from Highway 95 and the road up Comb Wash.

Geology and landforms—Three sandstone arches as well as fins, spires, and alcoves are found in Arch Canyon. The first arch, as one heads up the canyon, is found near where Texas and Butts canyons split from the main canyon. Farther up the canyon, the 1,000-foot-deep gorge is filled with thin ridgelines and buttresses, the source of two more arches. The unit includes the mesas above the branches of Arch Canyon as well as the tight canyons draining off of the east side of Little Baullie Mesa into Trail Canyon. Along Trail Canyon are views of the Abajo Mountains to the north and the sheer face of Comb Ridge to the east. The two forks of Mule Canyon are lined with cliffs of striated red-and-white sandstone.

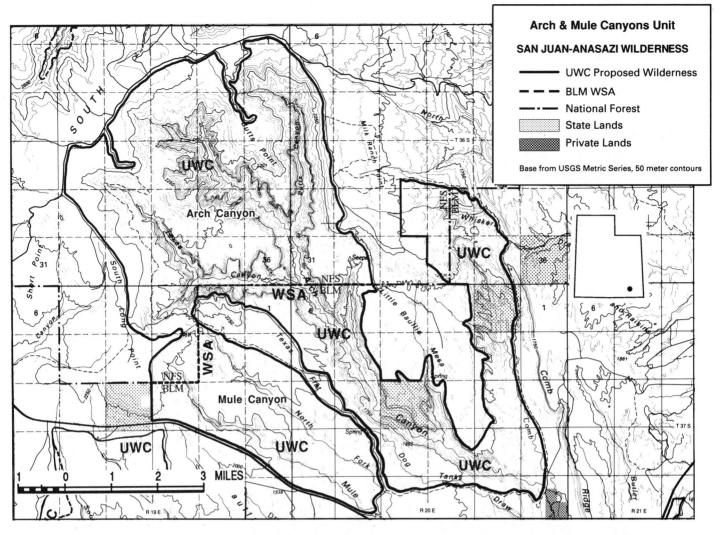

Plant communities—Near the mouths of the canyons are large cottonwoods, aspens, and other riparian species. Virgin ponderosa pine and Douglas fir line the canyon rims, while thick stands of Gambel oak carpet the slopes. Small pockets of maple provide a splash of red fall color in the canyons. On the mesas above the canyons, the vegetation is a mix of pinyon-juniper, Gambel oak, and sagebrush. The milkvetch *Astragalus cottamii*, a sensitive species, may occur in the unit as well, according to the BLM. Wildflowers carpet the red, sandy soil in May and June with pink, blue, and yellow.

Wildlife—These canyons provide yearlong range for mule deer and may support some bighorn sheep. Bobcat, mountain lions, coyote, and ring-tailed cat make their homes here. Numerous bird species populate the unit, the raptors nesting in the towering cliffs. Bald eagles may pass through the unit, according to the BLM.

Archeology and history—Numerous cliff dwellings and granaries are preserved high on the red-rock canyon walls. Multi-level dwellings and kivas are found throughout the unit in south-facing alcoves. Ground level sites can be found near the mouth of Arch Canyon. According to the BLM, 52 prehistoric sites have been recorded in the unit, but our field work indicates that more exist. A few sites occur on the tablelands above the canyon.

Recreation—Access is easy, water is readily available, and good campsites are abundant, making for pleasant, easy hiking and backpacking. Hall (1982) and Kelsey (1986a) both describe hikes here. A number of tributaries to Arch Canyon provide possibilities for side trips. Numerous small waterfalls and deep pools are enjoyable rest spots. Horseback riding, rock climbing, photography, birdwatching, and nature study are all possible here. In the early 1970s, the BLM proposed Outstanding Natural Area status for Arch Canyon, based on its extraordinary opportunities for solitude and primitive recreation.

BLM recommendation—The BLM recommends all of its 5,990-acre Mule Canyon WSA for wilderness designation. But the agency dropped Arch Canyon from wilderness study, alleging "irregular configuration" and "inadequate natural screening" in the eastern part. The BLM originally considered Arch Canyon along with Mule Canyon as a single roadless area. It later argued that a single section of state land divided Arch Canyon into two small parcels, and that a road along Texas Flat split Arch Canyon from Mule Canyon. The state section is undeveloped and does not impair the natural qualities of the unit. The Texas Flat road has washed out above (to the west of) Texas Flat and no longer divides the unit. Moreover, the BLM ignored contiguous National Forest roadless lands to the north. At the time of these decisions, the BLM wilderness coordinator's spouse had mining claims within the area and headed a group that sought to prevent protection of Arch Canyon so that it could use ORVs within the canyon.

Coalition proposal—We propose that 15,300 acres be designated wilderness. The 16,000 acres of contiguous national forest land to the north make a large, intact roadless area. A jeep trail in the lower end of Arch Canyon, where vehicles have driven up the streambed, is largely unnoticeable and would be washed away with seasonal flooding if vehicle use were discontinued. It would be a tragedy to permit the continued erosion of wilderness values in this area, once considered for National Monument status.

THE SQUAW-CROSS CANYONS WILDERNESS

Summary

Many of the most striking monuments of the Anasazi culture are located on the Colorado-Utah state line between Cortez and Monticello. Several large Anasazi towns are set aside in Hovenweep and Yucca House National Monuments. But these are tiny enclosures only tens or hundreds of acres in size that contain none of the habitat in which the Anasazi thrived. Unrecorded and unprotected cultural sites abound in the wild canyons surrounding these better known attractions. The proposed Squaw-Cross canyons wilderness, located a short distance north of the scattered units of Hovenweep National Monument, would protect these remnants of Anasazi culture. Our proposal encompasses three WSAs combined into two wilderness units, Squaw-Papoose Canyons and Cross Canyon, 7,580 acres of which lie in Utah and 26,890 acres in Colorado. Both units were evaluated for wilderness by the Montrose, Colorado, district of the BLM.

Hikes Among the Ruins

Cross, Squaw, and Papoose canyons provide uncommon opportunities for extended hikes in a setting with abundant, undisturbed cultural sites. Photography and birdwatching are frequent uses of the area, as is hunting for mule deer in the fall. The rugged terrain offers challenging hiking, climbing, and backpacking away from the signs of modern civilization; the prospect of finding the remains of an ancient civilization adds to the visitor's experience. Campsites are plentiful, both on the canyon rims and on the canyon floor. Natural overlooks provide excellent vantage points for observation and photography.

The canyons generally parallel each other, trending northeast to southwest as they cross the Colorado-Utah border. Squaw and Papoose canyons join near the southern boundary of that unit, running for 15 miles in all. The canyons begin as rocky arroyos but cut rapidly into the Dakota Sand-

IN BRIEF

Index Map: Area No. 46

Highlights: These roadless lands north of Hovenweep National Monument contain significant prehistoric Anasazi Indian sites, as well as excellent wildlife habitat and hiking opportunities. Wilderness designation would help preserve cultural, recreational, and ecological values as important as those found within the national monument.

Maps: USGS 1:100,000 Blanding, Bluff, Dove Creek, and Cortez

Area of wilderness proposals in acres (Utah):

Unit	UWC	BLM
Cross Canyon	1,000	0
Squaw & Papoose Canyons	6,580	0
TOTAL	7,580	0

Adjacent wild land: Colorado BLM

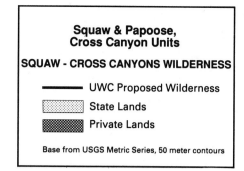

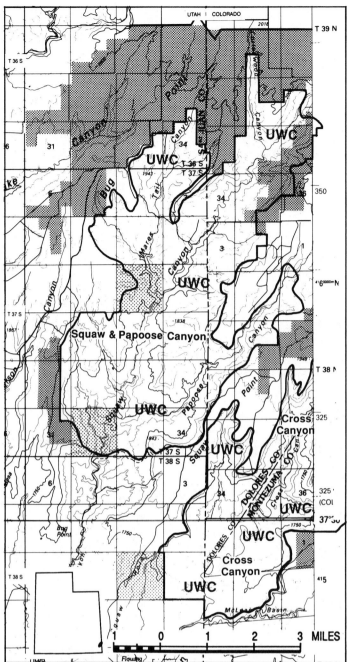

stone and Morrison Formation to form rugged, steep canyon walls of exposed rock outcrops, boulders, and talus slopes. Access is via several two-wheel-drive roads turning west off U.S. Highway 666 near Dove Creek, Colorado. Road spurs lead to a number of jumping-off points into the canyons.

Cross Canyon runs parallel to and 3 miles east of Squaw and Papoose canyons, separated by only a wide road right-of-way at their closest point. The lower end of the canyon crosses the Utah-Colorado state line about 25 miles northwest of Cortez, Colorado. Cross Canyon is only 3 miles north of the Cutthroat Castle group of ruins in Hovenweep National Monument and is almost adjacent to the BLM's Lowry Ruins National Historic Landmark. Access is via any of several roads turning west off U.S. Highway 666 near Cahone, Colorado. The road to Lowry Ruins is a good route to the rim of the Ruin or Cow Canyon tributaries.

Diverse Biota

A wide variety of vegetation occurs in the area, with pinyon-juniper forest and sagebrush dominating the canyon rims and mesas, and rabbitbrush, Mormon tea, mountain mahogany, Gambel oak, serviceberry, and cliffrose on the slopes. Vegetation is thicker along the canyon floors with numerous grasses, cactus, and yucca; wildflowers such as Indian paintbrush, penstemon, yarrow, phlox, and lupine; and riparian flora including rushes, sedges, cattails, willows, tamarisk, box elder, and cottonwoods. Old cottonwood trees line Cross Canyon, fed by streams that in some areas feature inviting pools and waterfalls.

The area supports numerous species of wildlife, many of which have been displaced from the surrounding uplands by agricultural and other development activities. Larger mammals include deer, mountain lion, and black bear. The diverse topography allows for an abundance of bird species including resident golden eagles and migratory bald eagles. Peregrine falcons may occasionally visit the area. Squaw and Papoose canyons have an abundant and diverse reptile and amphibian population, including many rare and localized species and subspecies. The long riparian area formed by Cross Canyon and Cahone Canyon is a haven for wildlife but also was source of sustenance for the ancient Anasazi.

Hidden Archeology

The canyons of Squaw, Papoose, Cross, Cahone, and their many smaller tributaries (including the aptly named Ruin Canyon) have thousands of recorded and unrecorded Anasazi cultural sites, the legacy of a culture that flourished here from about 450 A.D. to 1300 A.D. Surveys have shown high numbers of small cliff dwellings, well-hidden masonry structures, great kivas, towers, and water control devices. A wide variety of pictographs and petroglyphs are hidden among the rocks and cliffs. An intact square tower similar to those found at Hovenweep is found in the area. Cultural site densities range from 40 to 100 sites per square mile, some of the richest locations in the entire Southwest.

Yet much of this rugged, wild area is unexplored and uninventoried. The BLM, in its San Juan/San Miguel Resource Management Plan (1984), notes that the "interpretive and scientific potential of these canyons is as yet untapped." For example, although only 750 acres of Cross Canyon have been intensively inventoried, there are at least 151 recorded sites, which include 88 pueblo habitation sites and 19 rockshelters. The undiscovered potential is immense; the BLM considers these canyons to be of probable national importance based on their cultural resources and their position near the northern edge of Anasazi agriculture. In a region famed for archeology, the canyons of the proposed wilderness harbor significant archeological resources that complement the protected sites such as Hovenweep National Monument. This and other well-known sites are extremely small in area. Those sites give no feel of the country or the hardships overcome by the Anasazi in establishing their culture.

In the late 1970s, the idea of an Anasazi National Conservation Area was broached, later followed by the BLM's identification of the area as the Anasazi Culture Area of Critical Environmental Concern (ACEC). The ACEC title, while giving the impression of protection, simply approved the status quo of continuing mineral leasing and development while offering no new protection to the lands within it. Most recently, Congress has authorized the study of an Anasazi Culture National Park which might encompass lands in the vicinity. Unfortunately, few have offered the time-tested solution of simple wilderness designation.

Squaw-Cross Canyons are among the richest archeological locations in the Southwest, with masonry structures similar to those at nearby Hovenweep National Monument.

Red Wolfe

Resolving Mineral Conflicts

Despite the area's preeminent archeological resources, the BLM has leased much of it for oil and gas; about 60 percent of Cross Canyon and 20 percent of Squaw-Papoose Canyons are covered by pre-FLPMA oil and gas leases (mostly in the northern end). The area has been crisscrossed many times by repeated geophysical exploration. The Morrison Formation and Dakota Sandstone may contain oil, gas, uranium, and coal; deep formations in the area have been drilled for carbon dioxide. There has been exploration for uranium, and there are about 440 mining claims in the unit, although the deposits are low-grade and there has been no production.

As a result of the mineral industry's interest, the BLM has recommended the entire area—three WSAs in all—as unsuitable for wilderness. But the agency perceives a greater conflict than in fact exists. Due to the inaccessibility of the canyon floor and the unit's relatively narrow width, slant drilling into formations underlying the area is possible from the canyon rims outside the wilderness boundaries. This practice has been used by several oil and gas operators in the area in order to avoid destructive road construction below the canyon rim and to avoid destroying archeological sites.

The BLM has proposed placing all of the WSAs in either no-leasing or no-surface-occupancy leasing categories to limit damage from oil and gas exploration and development. The BLM wilderness study documents note that "if access is allowed into remote areas, damage to a large number of cultural sites from commercial pothunting will continue; impacts will be especially significant in the . . . Squaw/Papoose, Cahone, and Cross . . . canyons."

The existing leases could be allowed to expire without exploration; other options include negotiations with lease holders to secure no-surface-occupancy agreements, lease buy-outs, trades, and even voluntary preservation of sections of leases within the wilderness area.

The Utah Wilderness Coalition Proposal

We propose a wilderness area comprising two units, Squaw-Papoose Canyons and Cross Canyon, with a total of 7,580 acres within Utah. The Squaw-Papoose Canyons unit (6,580 acres within Utah) would protect the entire length of Squaw and Papoose canyons. Cross Canyon (1,000 acres within Utah) incorporates both the Cross Canyon and Cahone Canyon WSAs, joining the two by eliminating an abandoned jeep trail between them. Contiguous wild land in Colorado brings the size of both units to 34,470 acres. Together these units would greatly expand the protection afforded America's most magnificent and threatened cultural sites.

Mark Pearson

THE DARK CANYON WILDERNESS

Summary

Dark Canyon is arguably the wildest canyon in southern Utah. Its walls are consistently 1,500 to 2,000 feet high for its 30-mile length from the forests of Elk Ridge to Cataract Canyon. The upper half of Dark Canyon is already a 46,000-acre congressionally designated national forest wilderness area. The lowest several miles, in the Glen Canyon National Recreation Area, are proposed by the National Park Service for wilderness designation. The BLM recommends designation for all of its 68,030-acre WSA, including Dark Canyon and two canyons to the north, Bowdie and Gypsum. The Utah Wilderness Coalition proposes 130,200 acres including the lands the BLM recommends as well as rim lands above the canyons, spectacular prehistoric ruins in Ruin Canyon and Beef Basin Wash, deer winter range in Beef Basin, the Sheep Canyon unit adjacent to the Colorado River, and crucial bighorn habitat in Bull Valley and upper Cross Canyon adjacent to Canyonlands National Park.

Canyon Walls and Open Parks

Like the Colorado River in Cataract Canyon and the San Juan River below Mexican Hat, Dark Canyon cuts into the 300-million-year-old Honaker Trail Formation, one of the oldest rock layers exposed in southern Utah. This formation's mixed limestones, shales, and sandstones and the overlying Halgaito Shale and Cedar Mesa Sandstone form the cliffs and talus slopes of Dark, Gypsum, and Bowdie canyons. The non-WSA lands around Beef Basin on the north have Cedar Mesa Sandstone canyon walls and pinnacles with canyon bottoms and open parks in the Halgaito Shale and unconsolidated sand. The rock layers of the Dark Canyon area have been lifted and tilted up slightly to the east and south by the Monument Upwarp which extends from Monument Valley to Canyonlands National Park. Relatively rapid erosion across this uplift is responsible for exposing the Paleozoic formations that are generally deeply buried across the rest of southern Utah. In upper Cross Canyon and Bull Valley, rock layers above the unstable Paradox Formation salts have slumped toward the Colorado River leaving grabens—long parallel valleys—which extend northward into Canyonlands National Park.

Refuge for the Desert Bighorn

Riparian vegetation punctuated by cottonwoods grows in places along Dark, Gypsum, and Ruin canyons. A broad expanse of pinyon-juniper forest blankets the surrounding plateau. On the lower plateau in the western part of the area are enchanting "oriental gardens" of cacti and other wildflowers set among deep, undisturbed cryptogam. The milkvetch *Astragalus monumentalis* and the daisy *Erigeron kachinensis*, both sensitive species, may occur in the area, according to the BLM. This area, like much of the southern part of Canyonlands, is an important refuge for the desert bighorn sheep. The BLM has identified most of the area (except Middle Point, Fable Valley, Beef Basin, and the Sweet Alice Hills) as crucial desert bighorn sheep habitat. Middle Point and Fable Valley are yearlong bighorn habitat, and the Beef Basin area is crucial deer winter range (BLM, 1985). The UDWR has identified a peregrine use area on the northeast edge of the area. Other species listed by the BLM include mountain lion, bobcat, ringtail cat, great horned owl, American kestrel, canyon wren, mountain bluebird, collared lizard, and Hopi rattlesnake.

IN BRIEF

Index Map: Area No. 47

Highlights: One of the nation's first designated primitive areas, the deep gorge of Dark Canyon attracts hikers who savor its clear waterfalls and pools. Forested lands on the Dark Canyon Plateau should be added to the BLM recommendation.

Maps: USGS 1:100,000 Blanding, Hite Crossing

Area of wilderness proposals in acres:

Unit	UWC	BLM
Dark Canyon	126,500	68,030
Sheep Canyon	3,700	0
TOTAL	130,200	68,030

Adjacent wild lands: Manti-La Sal National National Forest (Dark Canyon Wilderness); Canyonlands National Park; Glen Canyon National Recreation Area

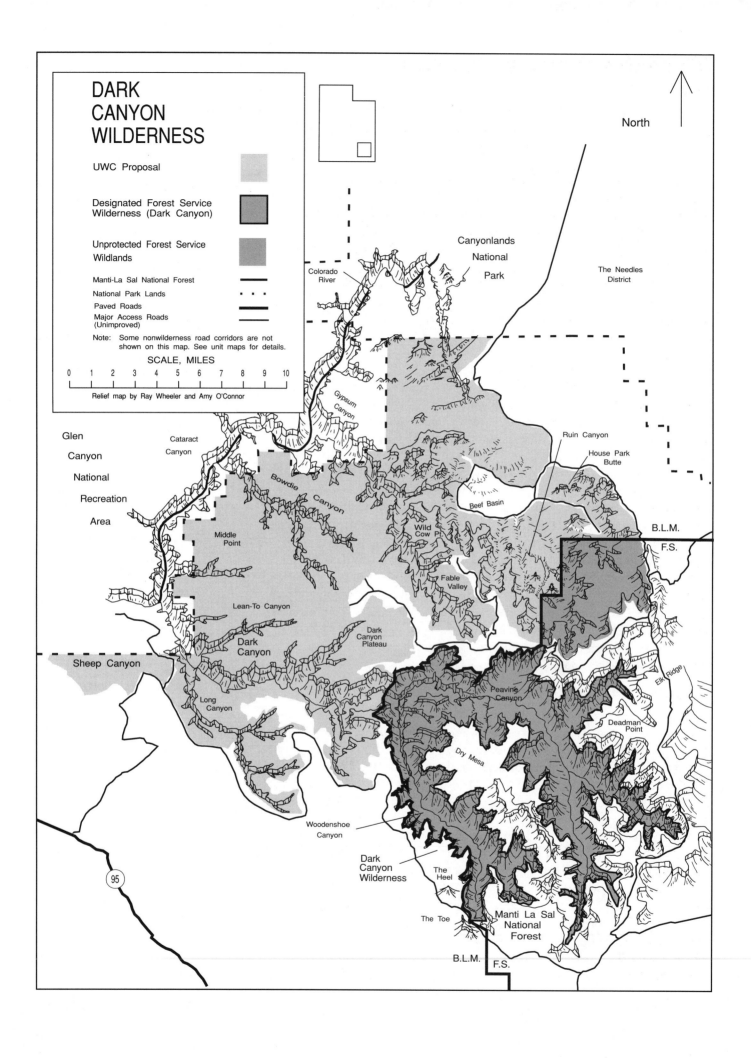

DARK
CANYON
WILDERNESS

UWC Proposal

Designated Forest Service
Wilderness (Dark Canyon)

Unprotected Forest Service
Wildlands

Manti-La Sal National Forest
National Park Lands
Paved Roads
Major Access Roads
(Unimproved)

Note: Some nonwilderness road corridors are not
shown on this map. See unit maps for details.

SCALE, MILES

0 1 2 3 4 5 6 7 8 9 10

North

Canyonlands
National
Park

The Needles
District

Colorado
River

Glen

Canyon

National

Recreation

Area

Cataract
Canyon

Gypsum
Canyon

Ruin Canyon

House Park
Butte

Beef Basin

B.L.M.

F.S.

Bowdie
Canyon

Middle
Point

Wild
Cow Pt.

Fable
Valley

Lean-To Canyon

Dark
Canyon
Plateau

Peavine
Canyon

Elk Ridge

Sheep Canyon

Dark
Canyon

Long
Canyon

Deadman
Point

Dry Mesa

Woodenshoe
Canyon

Dark
Canyon
Wilderness

The Heel

95

The Toe

Manti La Sal
National
Forest

B.L.M.

F.S.

Ancient Anasazi towers in Ruin Park could suffer from overuse and vandalism if vehicle access is allowed nearby. The Coalition's wilderness proposal, but not the BLM's, would protect these features.

Rodney Greeno

Spectacular Prehistory

Dark Canyon was heavily used by the Anasazi, and its size and remoteness have helped preserve its rich archeological heritage. The BLM has identified 32 sites in its WSA, primarily cliff dwellings and granaries, and has concluded that "because of the inaccessibility of Dark Canyon, this [area] potentially contains numerous pristine cultural resources" (BLM, 1986, p. 22). The BLM estimates that up to 2,658 sites could exist within the WSA, 1,773 of which could be eligible for the National Register. The non-WSA lands hold equally spectacular prehistoric sites. Beef Basin is a potential 35,000-acre National Register Eligible Archeological District: "The unique and accessible towers and other structures in Ruin Park are especially significant" (BLM, 1985). The BLM goes on to say of the Butler Wash area just to the north and east of Beef Basin that "particular management consideration is needed to ensure continued protection *if the area is not designated wilderness.*" (Emphasis added.) The Ruin Park towers and many other sites are in the Coalition-proposed Dark Canyon wilderness, but not in the BLM's recommended area. Continued isolation from vehicle access and large numbers of recreationists is the only hope for preserving these sites. Those who visit these ruins should refrain from touching them or walking in them.

The BLM captured the allure of Dark Canyon in a hiking guide it published: "Lower Dark Canyon is set apart by an abundant supply of clear, flowing water and deep crystalline plunge pools. The hiker walks to the music of water tumbling over pour offs and rolling gently downstream." This reach of the canyon has attracted hikers ever since it was designated a Primitive Area in 1970. This administrative designation, one of the first in the nation, was a first step toward permanent congressional protection as a Wilderness Area. In 1986, the BLM recommended that the entire primitive area, now a 68,030-acre WSA, be designated as wilderness.

The agency's recommendation, however, excludes 62,000 acres of adjacent natural lands with important wilderness values. It fragmenting a single roadless area into many small subunits and assessed the naturalness and opportunities for solitude and primitive recreation of each separately. Of course, these values appear lower when one looks only at pieces of the whole. The BLM appears likely to propose forest chainings on much of the omitted wild land.

As they drew up, the low wall of the aspen and pine-clad Sweet Alice Hills was behind them, cutting them off from the view to the east. Westward the land was afire . . . the pinks and reds of the fantastic rock formations to the west and north were weirdly lit by the dull red fire of the setting sun, while the dark fingers of the canyon that clawed toward the Colorado were simply black streaks through the canyon.

Louis L'Amour

Dark Canyon (1963)

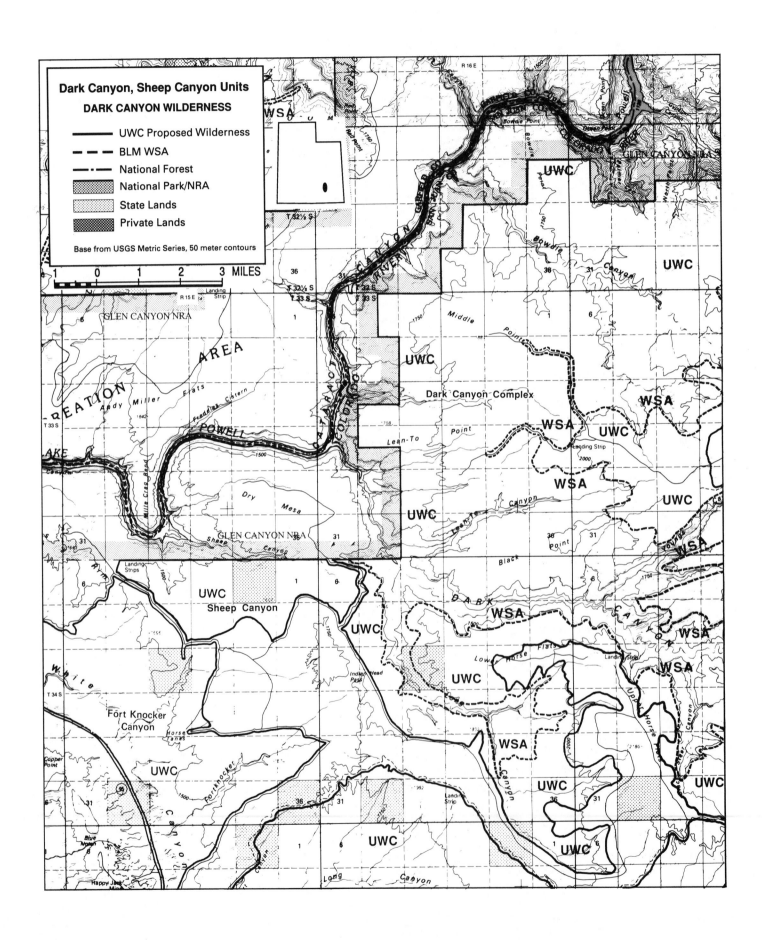

Dark Canyon, Sheep Canyon Units

DARK CANYON WILDERNESS

	UWC Proposed Wilderness
	BLM WSA
	National Forest
	National Park/NRA
	State Lands
	Private Lands

Base from USGS Metric Series, 50 meter contours

1 0 1 2 3 MILES

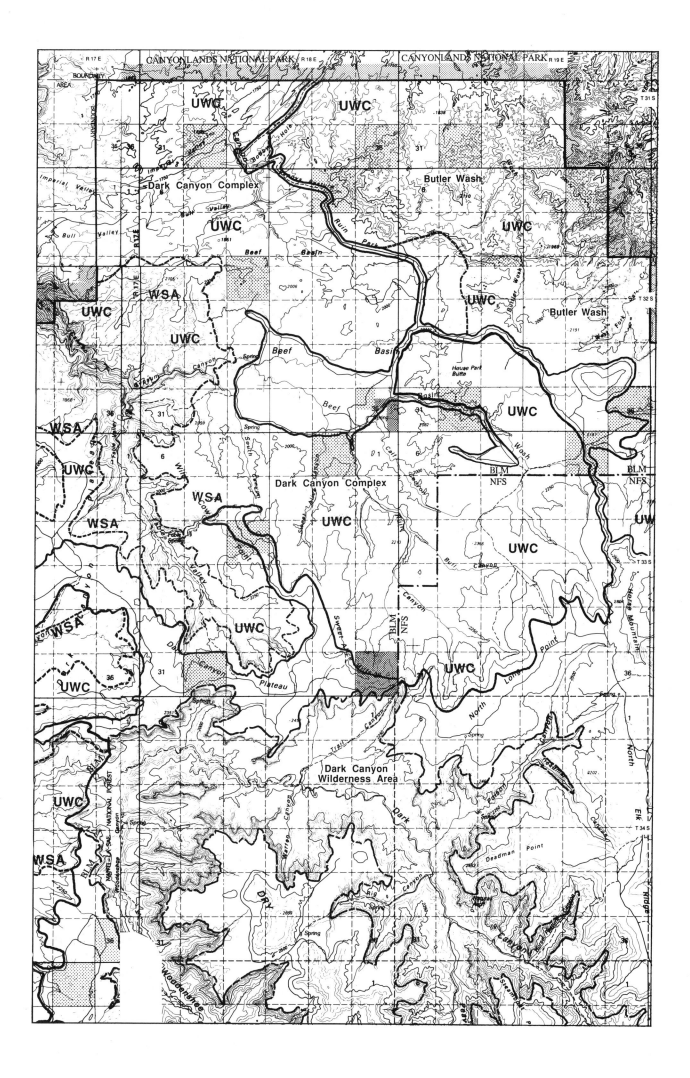

The Utah Wilderness Coalition Proposal

The Utah Wilderness Coalition supports wilderness designation for a 130,200-acre Dark Canyon wilderness to protect the entire area's extraordinary wildlife, cultural, and recreational values. Designating only the primitive area/WSA would risk losing the Anasazi sites and wildlife habitat of the plateau lands that surround the canyons. The proposed area includes the 3,700-acre Sheep Canyon unit on the west, which borders the popular Sundance Trail access to lower Dark Canyon.

The lands we propose to add to the BLM's recommendation have few signs of human activity. A loop road in Beef Basin and side roads into Ruin Canyon and Beef Basin Wash are excluded from our proposal. A three-mile-long way on Middle Point is cherrystemmed to a stock facility; beyond that point the way is little used and is largely reclaimed. Our boundary follows the edge of existing forest chainings whereas the BLM drew its boundary at the canyon rims. Mineral potential is low within the area; the BLM concluded that its WSA has a "low" potential for oil and gas, a "very low" potential for locatable minerals, and that there is no coal, potash, or other leasable minerals (BLM, 1986, p. 19). Based on information in the BLM's land use planning documents (BLM, 1985), these conclusions also apply to the part of our proposal located outside the WSA.

Rodney Greeno

THE CANYONLANDS BASIN WILDERNESS

Summary

The creation of Canyonlands National Park in 1964 protected the core of the Canyonlands Basin, a 1,200-square-mile amphitheater ringed by the Orange Cliffs. But the park does not span the entire basin from rim to rim. Indeed, the eastern quarter of the basin lies outside the park and is administered by the Bureau of Land Management (BLM) and the U.S. Forest Service. Here, nearly a quarter of a million acres of wild lands lie open to commercial exploitation. The Utah Wilderness Coalition's Canyonlands Basin wilderness proposal would protect 162,100 acres of BLM wild lands adjacent to the park's eastern edge plus an additional 70,000 acres of adjacent National Forest land. Our proposal would embody a 50-year-old dream of a Canyonlands wilderness reaching from rim to rim, encompassing its dramatic cliffs and its myriad stone towers—one of the largest and most intricate canyon systems in the world.

Discovery—1859

On a blazing afternoon in the summer of 1859, a U.S. Army reconnaissance unit led by Captain John S. Macomb discovered the landscape that is now Canyonlands National Park. According to F.A. Barnes, who researched the history of the expedition, the explorers approached from the east, skirting the Abajo Mountains and making a precarious descent into the canyon today called Harts Draw. At its mouth the canyon opened like a doorway cut through the wall of the Orange Cliffs. Here Macomb and his men halted to marvel at the view. Before them lay a vast amphitheater ringed by towering cliffs, cut by deep canyons, and studded with stone monuments.

Expedition geologist John S. Newberry was struck by what he saw. "No language is adequate to convey a just idea of the strange and impressive scenery," he wrote in his official report. "Toward the west the view reached some thirty miles, there bounded by . . . walls similar to those be-

IN BRIEF

Index Map: Area No. 48

Highlights: In the eastern quarter of the Canyonlands Basin, adjacent to Canyonlands National Park, lie unprotected BLM lands that are as wild and interesting as those found within the park. We propose wilderness designation for six parcels of BLM wild lands to protect their scenic, archeological, ecological, and recreational values.

Guidebooks: Barnes (1977), Kelsey (1986a)

Maps: USGS 1:100,000 La Sal, Blanding

Area of wilderness proposals in acres:

Unit	UWC	BLM
Bridger Jack Mesa	32,700	5,290
Butler Wash	28,300	24,190
Gooseneck	8,300	0
Harts Point	62,800	0
Indian Creek	27,000	6,870
Shafer Canyon	3,000	0
TOTAL	162,100	36,350

Adjacent wild lands: Canyonlands National Park, Manti-La Sal National Forest

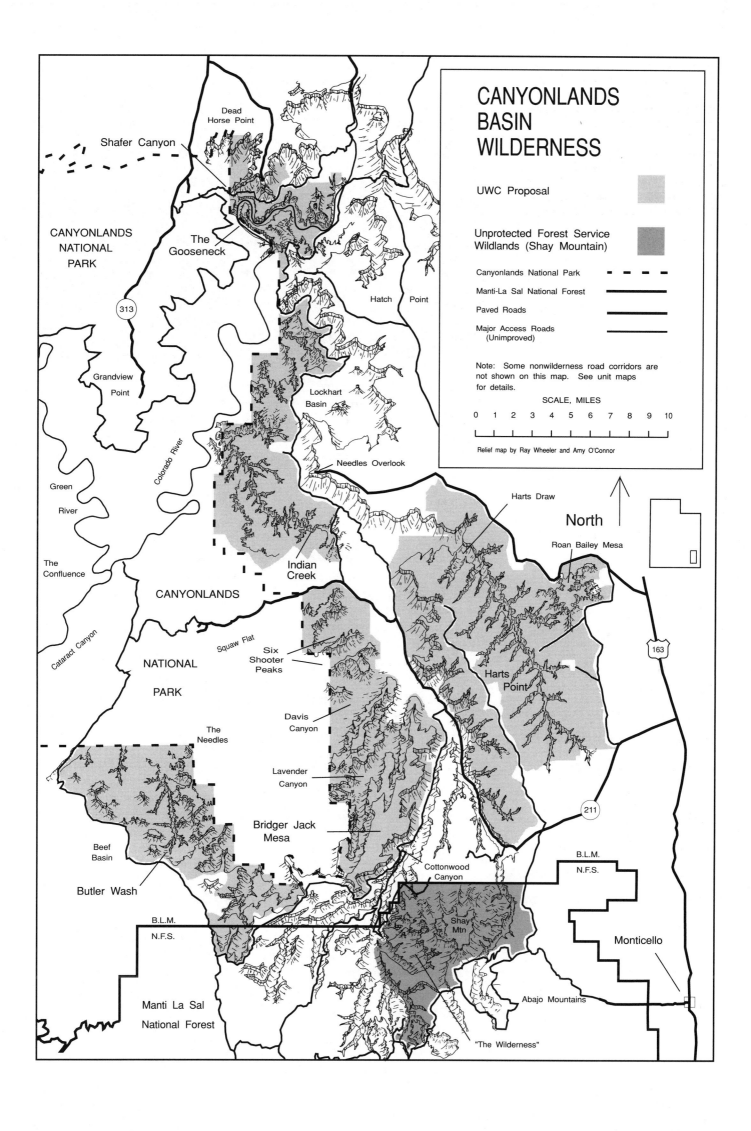

CANYONLANDS BASIN WILDERNESS

UWC Proposal

Unprotected Forest Service
Wildlands (Shay Mountain)

Canyonlands National Park

Manti-La Sal National Forest

Paved Roads

Major Access Roads
(Unimproved)

Note: Some nonwilderness road corridors are
not shown on this map. See unit maps
for details.

SCALE, MILES

0 1 2 3 4 5 6 7 8 9 10

Relief map by Ray Wheeler and Amy O'Connor

North

Shafer Canyon

Dead
Horse Point

CANYONLANDS
NATIONAL
PARK

The
Gooseneck

Hatch Point

313

Grandview
Point

Colorado River

Lockhart
Basin

Green
River

Needles Overlook

Harts Draw

The
Confluence

Roan Bailey Mesa

Indian
Creek

CANYONLANDS

163

Cataract Canyon

NATIONAL

Squaw Flat

Six
Shooter
Peaks

Harts
Point

PARK

The Needles

Davis
Canyon

Lavender
Canyon

211

Bridger Jack
Mesa

Beef
Basin

Cottonwood
Canyon

B.L.M.

N.F.S.

Butler Wash

Shay
Mtn

B.L.M.

Monticello

N.F.S.

Manti La Sal

National Forest

Abajo Mountains

"The Wilderness"

From this point the view swept westward over a wide extent of country, in its general aspects a plain, but everywhere cut deeply by a tangled maze of canyons, and thickly set with towers, castles, and spires . . . the most wonderful monuments of erosion which our eyes, already experienced in objects of this kind, had beheld.

John S. Newberry

REPORT OF THE EXPLORING EXPEDITION
FROM SANTA FE . . . (1876)

hind us . . . ." In every direction Newberry could see "columns, spires, castles, and battlement towers of colossal but often beautiful proportions."

Peering off to the southwest, Newberry could see "a long line of spires of white stone, standing on red bases, thousands in number, but so slender as to recall the most delicate carving in ivory . . . ." The "Needles" of Canyonlands National Park had made their debut.

Discovery—Today

Just a few miles north of the Macomb expedition route, on a promontory called Needles Overlook, the BLM has built a viewing balcony at the brink of the Orange Cliffs. Twenty thousand tourists visit the overlook every year. For them, as for Captain Macomb, the first view of the Canyonlands Basin is an act of discovery. They stand gripping the rail, hair streaming back in the wind, like sailors on the bridge of a ship. Far below them the basin's redrock floor rolls away to its opposite wall, miles distant on the western horizon.

A century has passed since the Macomb expedition put Canyonlands on the map, yet its landscape remains virtually unchanged. And for at least half a century, Americans have been reaffirming their desire to keep it that way.

Rim to Rim: the Dream that Refuses to Die

More than 50 years ago, Wilderness Society founder Bob Marshall made an inventory of the nation's remaining roadless areas. Marshall identified a roadless area of 8.9 million acres centered over the confluence of the Green and Colorado Rivers—the largest such area in the lower 48 states.

In 1936, the U.S. Department of the Interior tried to give substance to Bob Marshall's vision with a proposal to establish an Escalante National Monument of 4.5 million acres, reaching from Escalante to Moab, Utah, and spanning the Canyonlands Basin from rim to rim.

Powerful, development-minded opponents defeated the Escalante National Monument proposal. Yet nationwide support for protecting the canyonlands country continued to grow. In 1961 Interior Secretary Stewart Udall called for the creation of an 800,000-acre rim-to-rim Canyonlands National Park. Once again, would-be developers deflated the vision. When Congress finally established a Canyonlands National Park in 1964, it was a

dim shadow of former proposals. At 257,000 acres, it contained barely one-third of Udall's park proposal, less than 6 percent of the proposed Escalante National Monument, and less than 3 percent of Bob Marshall's 9-million-acre roadless area.

BLM Lands in the Canyonlands Basin

Today, along the eastern rim of the Canyonlands Basin, some 200,000 acres of wild lands remain outside the park, chiefly on BLM lands. These lands are the orphan children of the *real* Canyonlands National Park. Geographically, geologically, and esthetically, they are an integral part of the Canyonlands Basin and hold some of its finest attractions.

Northeast of the park lies the "Gooseneck," the famous hairpin turn in the Colorado River gorge that dominates the view from Dead Horse Point State Park. The Gooseneck is one of the most photographed features of the entire Canyonlands Basin. It is a river runner's doorway to Canyonlands National Park. Yet it remains outside the park boundary, and therefore is open to development.

Southeast of the Colorado River, along the eastern wall of the Canyonlands Basin, lies the Indian Creek roadless area. Indian Creek Canyon is the redrock fantasia that fills the view from Needles Overlook—a wonderland of hoodoos, spires, and knobs. It is rich in archeological sites, and it provides critical habitat for a small but growing population of desert bighorn sheep. A popular hiking area, it offers overflow camping when the Park Service campground at Squaw Flats is full. Indian Creek Canyon is as intriguing as any place within Canyonlands National Park, yet it, too, lies outside the park boundary.

Southeast of Indian Creek lies lovely Harts Draw, the route of the Macomb expedition. Graced with soaring natural bridges, a perennial stream, and abundant wildlife, Harts Draw complements Canyonlands National Park but, lacking formal protection, it is open for development.

THE COLORADO PLATEAU REGION

The Utah Wilderness Coalition proposal for the Canyonlands Basin is but the latest version of a dream shared by Utahns and canyonlands lovers all over the nation—the dream of a rim-to-rim wilderness as pristine as it was when Captain John Macomb first laid eyes on it. Unfortunately, the BLM recommends against wilderness designation for three-quarters of the wild lands along the eastern rim of the Canyonlands Basin.

Also excluded from the park are most of the familiar landmarks along its southeastern border, including Bridger Jack Mesa, Lavender and Davis canyons, and Sixshooter Peaks.

Farther south, at the headwaters of Indian Creek, the great forested island of Shay Mountain rises above the Needles district. Most of Shay Mountain lies on the Manti-La Sal National Forest and forms a 70,000-acre roadless area lacking formal protection. West of Shay Mountain, and due south of the park, are the colorful slickrock knolls and grassy parklands at the head of Salt Creek Canyon and Butler Wash.

Wilderness or Waste Dump?

What does it matter where the protective boundary happens to fall? For Utahns concerned about the threat of a nuclear waste dump next to Canyonlands, it matters a great deal.

In 1984, the U.S. Department of Energy identified the mouth of Davis Canyon, just outside Canyonlands National Park, as one of the prime candidate sites for the nation's first high-level nuclear waste dump. A *Salt Lake Tribune* poll found that Utah residents opposed the siting of a nuclear waste dump near Canyonlands by a ratio of *four to one*. Soon after, Utah Governor Scott Matheson held a press conference to declare his opposition to the dump. The Davis Canyon site "can never be acceptable," Matheson told reporters, because of its proximity to Canyonlands National Park.

A nuclear waste dump in Davis Canyon would have totally transformed the landscape along the eastern border of the park, bringing a floodlit 640-acre compound, a commercial-grade truck haul road, and a powerline and railroad marching over the land. Of two alternative proposed routes for the railroad, one would have run for 30 miles along the base of the Orange Cliffs, tunneling directly under the Canyonlands and Needles Overlooks. The second route would have followed in the footsteps of the Macomb expedition, blasting down into Harts Draw by means of a tunnel and issuing from its mouth.

In January 1987, Utah Congressman Wayne Owens introduced legislation to expand Canyonlands National Park by over 400,000 acres, more than doubling its size. Owens' bill would add virtually all the BLM-managed wild lands along the eastern rim of the Canyonlands Basin, including the Gooseneck, Indian Creek Canyon, Harts Draw, Butler Wash, and the head of Salt Creek Canyon—and the proposed nuclear waste dump sites in Davis and Lavender canyons. It was time, Owens explained, to preempt further discussion of a nuclear waste dump on lands that belonged within Canyonlands National Park.

The BLM Excises Wilderness

But expanding the park will be a long, uncertain process, and meanwhile the BLM lands surrounding the park remain in jeopardy. To safeguard these lands, the Utah Wilderness Coalition is proposing that 162,100 acres of BLM wild lands next to Canyonlands be designated as wilderness. Such designation would protect those lands whether they are ever added to the park.

The Utah Wilderness Coalition proposal for the Canyonlands Basin is but the latest version of a dream shared by Utahns and canyonlands lovers all over the nation—the dream of a rim-to-rim wilderness as pristine as it was when Captain John Macomb first laid eyes on it. Unfortunately, the wilderness recommendations of the BLM do not recognize that dream. The agency recommends *against* wilderness designation for three-quarters of the wild lands along the eastern rim of the Canyonlands Basin. Indeed, the BLM refused even to study the wilderness character of more than 70 percent of the BLM-managed wild lands bordering Canyonlands Park on the south and east.

During its wilderness inventory of 1979-80, the BLM rejected the entire roadless area surrounding Harts Draw as "clearly and obviously" lacking wilderness character. Yet the jeep trails and seismic lines the BLM identified as "significant human impacts" can easily be excluded by boundary adjustments around the perimeter of the unit, leaving 62,800 acres of wilderness at its core.

In similar fashion, the BLM omitted more than three-quarters of the Bridger Jack and Indian Creek roadless areas, and all of the Gooseneck roadless area, from wilderness study.

Mining Claims Motivate Exclusions

In March 1985, Clive Kincaid, former BLM wilderness coordinator in Arizona, explained to the House Public Lands Subcommittee why so much wild land had been omitted from the BLM's wilderness inventory of the Canyonlands Basin. Kincaid had spent more than a year investigating the BLM inventory process and had made a case study of the Indian Creek wilderness inventory unit. There the BLM had originally eliminated the entire roadless area from its wilderness inventory, then reinstated 7,300 acres after a BLM employee filed a formal protest. Kincaid testified that " . . .considerations other than the true presence or absence of wilderness character . . . motivated first the deletion of the entire unit and then the seemingly meaningless reinstatement of a small portion of the actual roadless area . . ." The agency's wilderness study area (WSA) boundary, he demonstrated, coincided precisely with the boundaries of mining claims— and eliminated 99 percent of the claims located within the roadless area.

Such exclusions of qualifying wilderness lands are illegal under the BLM's own wilderness inventory guidelines, which specify that the Congress, not the BLM, must weigh wilderness-for-development tradeoffs. The BLM's exclusion of mining claims from Indian Creek pre-empted Congressional review of those lands (see "The BLM Wilderness Review" chapter).

A similar explanation accounts for the elimination of more than 30,000 acres of wild lands surrounding Sixshooter Peaks, Lavender Mesa, and Lavender and Davis canyons. There, WSA designation would have blocked the siting of the proposed nuclear waste dump at the mouth of Davis Canyon. At the time of the BLM's wilderness inventory, during 1979 and 1980, the roadless areas bordering Canyonlands National Park were under study as a nuclear waste dump site, and the agency was under intense pressure to keep the entire region open for development.

The nation's first nuclear waste dump will not be located at the mouth of Davis Canyon, for after vigorous opposition from Utahns, the Department of Energy has selected a different site. But Davis Canyon may yet become a candidate site for a second, third, or fourth nuclear waste dump.

Only formal protective status can ensure that the entire Canyonlands Basin will be preserved, intact, for future generations to discover and enjoy. That is the dream embodied in the Utah Wilderness Coalition's wilderness proposal for the Canyonlands Basin.

Ray Wheeler

SHAFER CANYON AND GOOSENECK UNITS

Highlights—Ten miles of the Colorado River flow between these units, which are adjacent to the northeast boundary of the Canyonlands National Park. The river, a popular float trip, is the wild entrance to the 700,000-acre

The Gooseneck of the Colorado River, as seen from Dead Horse Point, is one of the world's premier views. But neither Shafer Canyon (shown entering from the right) nor the lands across the river were studied for their wilderness potential by the BLM.

Fred Swanson

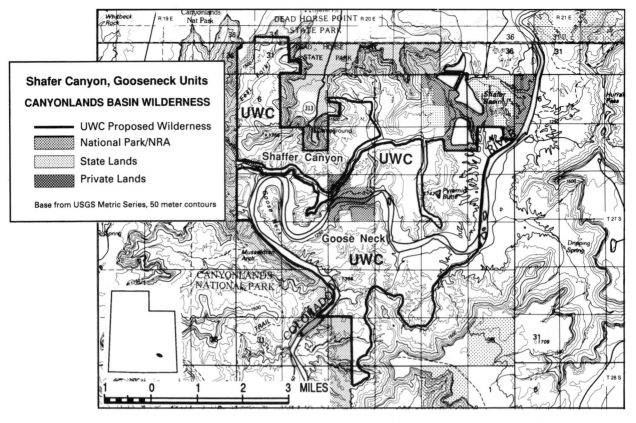

Shafer Canyon, Gooseneck Units

CANYONLANDS BASIN WILDERNESS

UWC Proposed Wilderness
National Park/NRA
State Lands
Private Lands

Base from USGS Metric Series, 50 meter contours

roadless area which includes much of the park and its surrounding BLM wild lands. The Gooseneck is an outstanding scenic feature viewed from Dead Horse Point State Park; Shafer Canyon is the foreground for this view. The BLM alleged that these spectacular units lacked wilderness character. We propose 8,300 acres of wilderness for the Gooseneck unit and 3,000 acres below the White Rim jeep trail for the Shafer Canyon unit.

Geology and landforms—These units lie on both sides of the Gooseneck of the Colorado River, a three-mile-long loop that can be seen 1,800 feet below Dead Horse Point State Park. Shafer Canyon also takes in seven additional miles of deeply entrenched canyon walls towering 1,500 feet above the Colorado River and the rugged cliffs and benchlands north of the river. The units are part of the view from Dead Horse Point, one of the premier vistas in the world. Petrified wood and fossils in the Honaker Trail Formation provide a valuable source for geologic study and sightseeing.

Plant communities—Desert shrub vegetation covers the area, including blackbrush, shadscale, and Indian ricegrass. Tamarisk, willow, and other riparian species line the Colorado River.

Wildlife—The Colorado River supports the endangered bonytail chub and Colorado squawfish. The UDWR identifies the units as a peregrine falcon use area and part of the Gooseneck unit as yearlong bighorn habitat.

Archeology and history—The primitive track leading to the narrowest part of the Gooseneck dates back to cattle-rustler days, according to the BLM; stolen cattle and horses were hidden there until they could be resold.

Recreation—The Colorado River is a favorite for float trips continuing into Canyonlands National Park. This portion of the river is listed on the Department of the Interior's Nationwide Rivers Inventory. The majestic slickrock canyon walls offer outstanding opportunities for photography, sightseeing, and the study of petrified wood and fossils. The benchlands surrounded by towering cliffs offer outstanding opportunities for solitude.

The exceptional scenic qualities of the area attract photographers and hikers alike.

BLM recommendation—The BLM dropped both units from wilderness study. The agency claimed that the Gooseneck unit lacked natural character; its inventory documents show two drill holes, two gully plugs, three seismic lines and 4.4 miles of vehicle track. Our field checks indicate that these occupy a total of 22 acres, not the 1,800 acres the BLM claims. Moreover, most of these impacts are not noticeable to the wilderness visitor. The drill sites are more than a decade old and are no longer evident, and the gully plugs are small and appear natural. In many places one must look long and hard to find the vehicle track, since it has been maintained only by the passage of vehicles. The BLM claimed that Shafer Canyon lacked outstanding opportunities for solitude due to the irregular configuration of the adjacent state park, which comes within half a mile of bisecting the unit. The BLM ignored the protected status of the adjacent state lands and the proposed wilderness in Canyonlands National Park. The BLM also failed to assess the geologic, scenic, and recreational value of the unit.

Coalition proposal—The importance of both of these units for outstanding vistas, river recreation, and the opportunity for scientific study qualifies them for wilderness designation. When considered with the adjacent park lands, the units have added value for these activities. Mineral development potential is low in both; the potash mine in Shafer Basin lies well to the northeast.

INDIAN CREEK UNIT

Highlights—West of the Needles Overlook, a breathtaking assemblage of eroded pinnacles and twisting canyons composes the 27,000-acre Indian Creek unit. This maze of redrock was proposed for inclusion in Canyonlands National Park in 1962 but was dropped for political reasons. In addition to its magnificent geology, Indian Creek encompasses numerous archeological sites, thriving wildlife habitats, and many opportunities for primitive recreation. Its two perennial streams contrast wonderfully with the dry surroundings of Canyonlands National Park.

Geology and landforms—Four steep-walled canyons—Lockhart, Horsethief, Rustler, and Indian Creek—cut through the Cutler Formation and into the Honaker Trail Formation. In 1976, the BLM recommended a primitive area here, noting that it "exhibits severely eroded patterns of canyons and knobs and pinnacles . . . The surface erosion creates a maze of minor canyons with hues varying from purple to buff and a pattern of light and shadows that changes with the hour of the day."

Plant communities—Much of the unit is bare slickrock, but its scattered benches support typical desert shrubs, and Indian Creek and Rustler canyons are lined with riparian species. The milkvetch *Astragalus monumentalis*, a sensitive species, may occur here, according to the BLM.

Wildlife—The unit affords crucial habitat for desert bighorn sheep, according to the BLM, as well as habitat for coyotes, cottontail, whitetailed antelope squirrels, and Ord kangaroo rats. Its skies are home to ravens, rockwren, ash-throated flycatchers, larks, black-throated sparrows, mourning doves, and chukar. The UDWR has classified the southern fifth of the unit a use area for the endangered peregrine falcon. Numerous species of lizards, such as the side-blotched, the northern whiptail, and the sagebrush, are common as well.

Archeology and history—Plentiful examples of Indian rock art, dwellings, and granaries are found here. The BLM has estimated that there could be over 100 archeological sites within its small WSA alone; the area outside the WSA may contain an even greater number. The unit encompasses several historical sites, including the route of the first white explorers in the Canyonlands Basin.

Recreation—Indian Creek offers an interesting hike down a scenic canyon away from the crowds in the nearby National Park. It begins where the rocky dirt road leading north from Highway 211 crosses Indian Creek, or alternatively 10 miles beyond this crossing at Rustler Canyon, which gives access to lower Indian Creek. The perennial streams with their occasional pouroffs, sandy benches, and Anasazi ruins make for easy, enjoyable hiking.

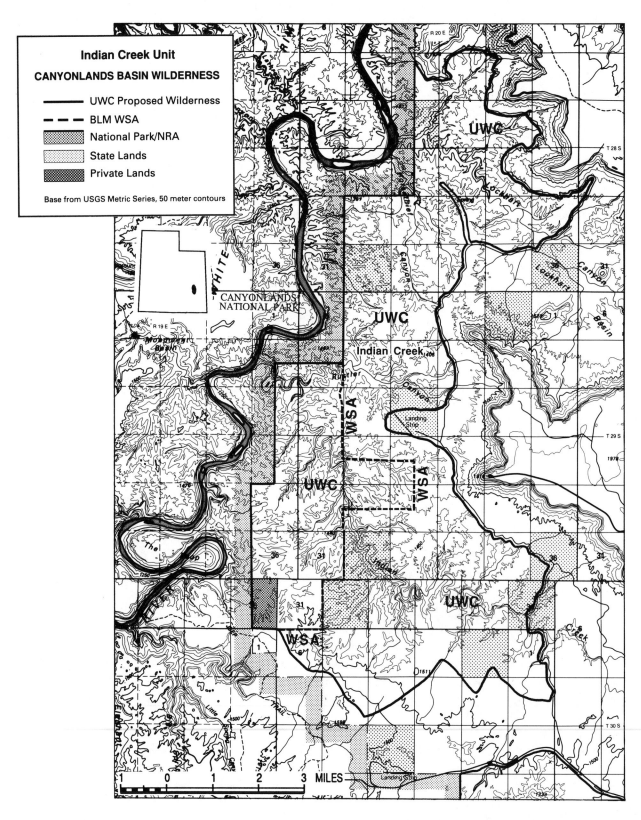

Indian Creek Unit

CANYONLANDS BASIN WILDERNESS

——— UWC Proposed Wilderness

– – – BLM WSA

National Park/NRA

State Lands

Private Lands

Base from USGS Metric Series, 50 meter contours

1   0   1   2   3 MILES

BLM recommendation—The BLM recommends wilderness for its 6,870-acre Indian Creek WSA, leaving the remaining 20,000 acres open to potential mining and ORV use. The agency cites old roads and an airstrip as disqualifying intrusions. Our fieldwork shows that the "roads" are merely vehicle ways and occupy only a small area, and the airstrip could have easily been excluded with a small boundary modification. A more likely reason for the exclusion is the presence of mining claims and mineral leases for copper, vanadium, potash, and uranium. The BLM cut all but one percent of these claims out of its WSA, zoning the remainder for development.

Coalition proposal—Our 27,000-acre proposal would protect Indian Creek's most important wilderness values—including the archeological sites, wildlife habitat and recreational lands that lie outside of the WSA. Mineral resources in this unit could be developed only at great economic and environmental cost in this dry, remote area; better sources lie in other, developed areas. Although ORVs are currently allowed entry, the topography makes most of the area impassable to motorized vehicles. Indian Creek is a delightful complement to the dry expanses of the surrounding Needles District and should be protected in its entirety.

HARTS POINT UNIT

Highlights—Harts Point, a 5-mile-wide plateau, reaches north from the base of the Abajo Mountains 12 miles into the Canyonlands Basin. Thousand-foot-high cliffs surround the point on three sides: on the west they are the east wall of Indian Creek Canyon and a scenic backdrop for travellers on Highway 211 (the main road to the Needles District of Canyonlands National Park); on the north and east the cliffs form the southwest wall of Harts Draw, one of the least-known slickrock canyon systems in southern Utah. Indian Creek State Park is adjacent to the Harts Point unit on the west and the BLM's Windwhistle Campground (part of the Canyon Rims Recreation Area) is adjacent on the east. The BLM failed even to designate Harts Point as a WSA, while the Utah Wilderness Coalition proposes a 62,800-acre wilderness unit to protect critical deer winter range, riparian habitat, archeological values, scenic vistas, and primitive recreation.

Geology and landforms—The walls of Harts Point and Harts Draw are of the classic southern Utah sequence: Navajo Sandstone cliffs on top separated from Wingate Sandstone cliffs below by a Kayenta Formation bench. Upper Harts Draw and its tributaries cut through these rock layers in narrow, well-watered canyons. Lower Harts Draw opens into a wider canyon bounded by monumental Wingate cliffs as it cuts into the softer Chinle Formation shales.

Plant communities—A dense pinyon-juniper forest and sagebrush cover Harts Point and the eastern rim of Harts Draw. The canyon bottoms have desert shrubs and grasses, with cottonwoods and other riparian vegetation lining the course of Harts Draw and many of its sidecanyons.

Wildlife—The BLM (1985) has identified a critical deer winter range over Harts Point and upper Harts Draw as well as aquatic and riparian habitat in upper Harts Draw. The eastern part of Harts Draw attracts some elk during the winter, and cougar have been sighted in the unit.

Archeology and history—Twelve thousand acres in the southwest part of the unit, adjacent to Newspaper Rock State Park, have been identified by the BLM (1985) as part of a potential area of critical environmental concern for cultural resources. Harts Draw is believed to be the route of the Macomb Expedition, the first known exploration of the Canyonlands Basin by white people.

Recreation—The large size of the Harts Point unit and its 1,500 feet of vertical relief provide outstanding opportunities for solitude and primitive

I looked more closely at the distant inner gorge rim with our binoculars. The canyon's trickling stream didn't reach the rim, but instead disappeared into a big hole many yards back from the rim. It reappeared in a huge alcove below the rim, then plunged down an undercut cliff into an immense pool of water surrounded by trees, shrubs and grasses. Most certainly the isolated rim of rock was a natural bridge, one never before reported.

F.A. Barnes

CANYON COUNTRY ARCHES AND BRIDGES (1987)

Pothole arch (properly speaking, a natural bridge) in Bobbys Hole Canyon, a tributary of Harts Draw.

Ray Wheeler

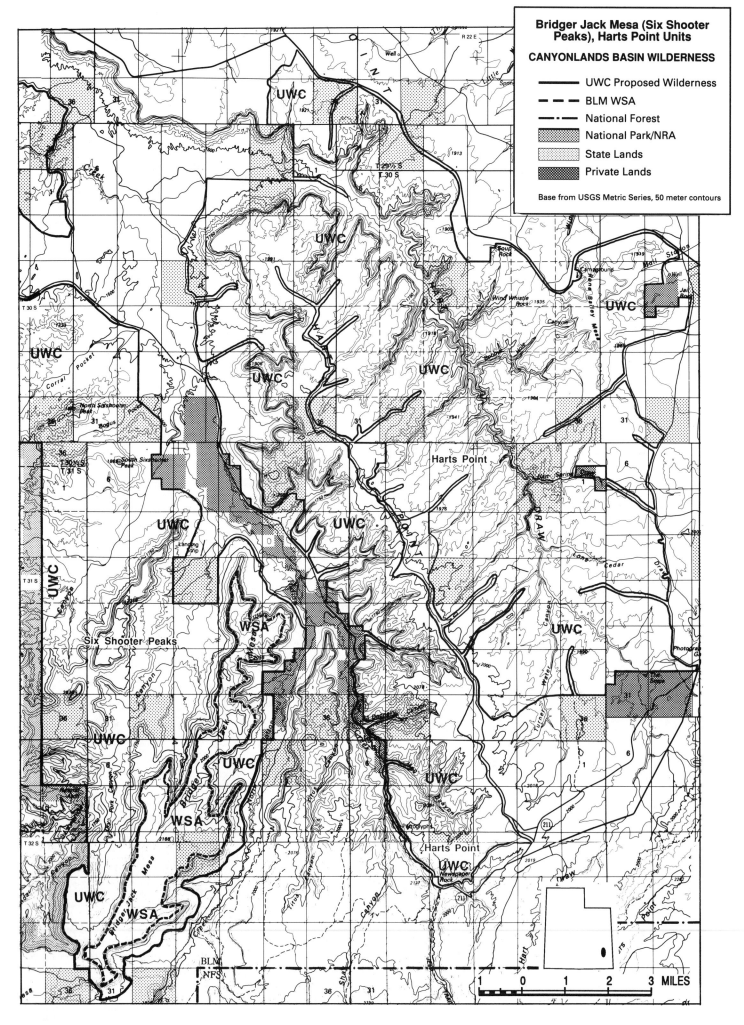

Bridger Jack Mesa (Six Shooter Peaks), Harts Point Units

CANYONLANDS BASIN WILDERNESS

————	UWC Proposed Wilderness
– – – –	BLM WSA
–·–·–	National Forest
▨	National Park/NRA
▨	State Lands
▨	Private Lands

Base from USGS Metric Series, 50 meter contours

recreation, including hiking, backpacking, rock climbing, and exploration of historic trails. Windwhistle Campground on the Needles Overlook highway is the start of day hikes into Bobbys Hole Canyon and along the east rim of Harts Draw. A dry waterfall through a pothole arch blocks access to Harts Draw from upper Bobbys Hole Canyon, but there is a route into lower Bobbys Hole and Harts Draw from the ridge west of Windwhistle Campground (see Kelsey, 1986). In Harts Draw and its sidecanyons rock and log trails over the slickrock were constructed long ago for horse and cattle use. Aqueduct Arch, in a western sidecanyon of Harts Draw, is accessible from the road on Harts Point (Barnes, 1977).

BLM recommendation—The BLM released Harts Draw from wilderness consideration in a 1979 initial inventory decision. The agency exaggerated the extent of impacts in its 54,000-acre inventory unit to find it "clearly and obviously lacking in wilderness character."

Coalition proposal—Our 62,800-acre proposal excludes all substantially noticeable developments by cherrystemming the deadend road and associated range improvements on Harts Point as well as other peripheral mining and range impacts. This leaves a large, manageable wilderness unit which would protect archeologic, scenic, and recreational values as well as riparian habitat and crucial deer winter range along the eastern wall of the Canyonlands Basin.

BRIDGER JACK MESA UNIT

Highlights—Bridger Jack Mesa is the eastern third of a 110,000-acre roadless area that extends across the southeastern corner of Canyonlands National Park to include the Butler Wash BLM wilderness unit. This unit's stunning scenery (including Lavender and Davis canyons and the famous Sixshooter Peaks), relict plant communities, crucial mule deer winter range, and important archeological values should have placed it within the original park boundary; recently proposed legislation would have done just that. Meanwhile, the Utah Wilderness Coalition proposes a 32,700-acre BLM wilderness unit to complement the existing park lands.

Geology and landforms—Bridger Jack Mesa and its companion mesa to the north, Little Bridger Jack (unnamed on topographic maps) dominate the unit; North and South Sixshooter Peaks are prominent landmarks to the north of these mesas. Davis and Lavender canyons separate the mesas and extend into Canyonlands National Park. Layers of Triassic rock, including the Moenkopi and Chinle formations and the Glen Canyon Group have been carved into spectacular cliffs and valleys.

Plant communities—The mesa tops are covered by a pinyon-juniper forest; the broad canyon bottoms by sparse sagebrush and grasses. Riparian habitat is found in Davis, Lavender, and North Cottonwood canyons. The top of Bridger Jack Mesa has small, open, grassy parks among dense stands of pinyon pine. Little grazing of domestic stock has taken place here in recent decades, permitting the recovery of diverse grasses and shrubs. One researcher compiled a preliminary list of about 50 species. The mesa has been listed as a federal Research Natural Area because of its relatively undisturbed plant communities, including a small, relict stand of Douglas fir. Bridger Jack Mesa was proposed, but was never officially listed, as an Outstanding Natural Area by the BLM in the early 1970s. Northwest of Bridger Jack Mesa lies Lavender Mesa, a 640-acre gem that has escaped any human impact. The unit's mesa tops are of great value for the scientific study of essentially undisturbed grasslands and woodlands and can teach us what the land was like before the arrival of domestic livestock in the mid-1800s.

Wildlife—The unit's climax pinyon-juniper forest, grassy areas, and revegetated burned areas provide good habitat for a wide variety of animal life. The BLM lists 2,700 acres of its Bridger Jack Mesa WSA as crucial winter range for mule deer, and bobcats and coyotes inhabit the mesa as well. The UDWR has mapped the western half of the unit as a peregrine falcon use area. Golden eagles may nest on Bridger Jack Mesa; other raptors include red-tailed hawk, American kestrel, and Cooper's hawk.

Archeology and history—Because of its remote location, the unit includes numerous untouched cultural resources. Some of the finest rock art in the country is found in Lavender Canyon; notable ruins are found here also. The unit is in a transition zone between the Fremont and Anasazi cultures; Ute/Navajo peoples may have used the unit as well. The BLM (1986) states that, based on studies of similar areas, the 5,290-acre WSA alone might possess 125 archeologic sites, 80 of which could be eligible for the National Register. The agency (1986, p. 12-13) states that "the cultural significance of the WSA lies in the potential for answering settlement and subsistence questions in this little understood area." The unit also contains historic evidence of early-day cattle grazing; the BLM notes that primitive tools used to construct small trails and reservoirs remain to this day on the mesa.

Recreation—Vistas from the unit are outstanding, often extending over 100 miles during the summer and even farther in the winter. Opportunities for hunting, photography, backpacking, sightseeing, and other forms of primitive recreation are plentiful.

BLM recommendation—In violation of its wilderness inventory policy, the BLM divided the unit into three separate areas: Sixshooter Peaks, Little Bridger Jack, and Bridger Jack Mesa. It then dropped the first two from study with the dubious claim that solitude and recreational possibilities were not outstanding. The BLM then pared away 2,600 acres of scenic cliffs from Bridger Jack Mesa, claiming impacts from mining. Our field investigations show that only a small fraction of the acreage dropped has any intrusions within it, and all of it has outstanding opportunities for solitude and primitive recreation.

Coalition proposal—We propose 32,700 acres for wilderness designation, including Bridger Jack Mesa (with the surrounding scenic cliffs), Little Bridger Jack Mesa, and North and South Sixshooter Peaks. The BLM rates its WSA unfavorable for mineral development.

BUTLER WASH UNIT

Highlights—Lying adjacent to Canyonlands National Park, the Butler Wash unit contains the same spectacular scenery for which the park was designated. Fortunately, the BLM recommends most of the unit for wilderness designation: 24,190 acres compared to the Utah Wilderness Coalition's 28,300-acre proposal. The unit's scenery, recreational opportunities, and archeological resources clearly deserve protection as wilderness.

Geology and landforms—The upper forks of Salt Creek in the eastern half of the unit and Butler Wash in the western half lie in 600-foot-deep canyons of Cedar Mesa Sandstone. The canyons are wider in the Butler Wash area and relatively shallow in the far western end of the unit.

Plant communities—Most of the unit is covered by a pinyon-juniper forest, but large areas are slickrock. There are small areas of sagebrush and grasses. Riparian vegetation is found along Butler Wash and the West Fork of Salt Creek. *Astragalus monumentalis,* a species of milkvetch being considered for threatened or endangered listing, may be present within the unit, according to the BLM.

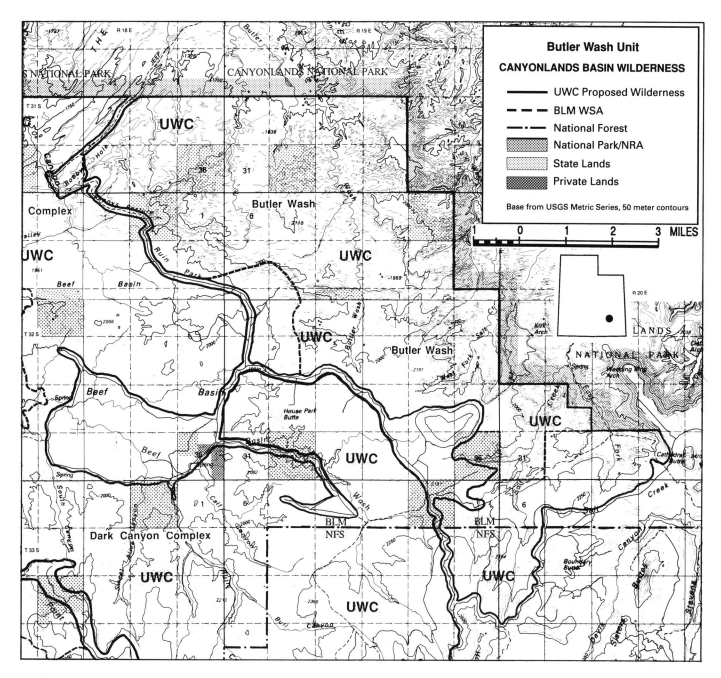

Wildlife—The relatively open country on the west and southwest sides of the unit provides winter habitat for mule deer. Other species in the unit, according to the BLM, include bobcat, mountain lion, coyote, and several species of raptors including red-tailed hawk, American kestrel, and Cooper's hawk.

Archeology and history—The BLM (1986, p. 13) reports that: "Because of the relative difficulty in access into the Butler Wash, it potentially contains numerous pristine cultural resources . . . . The WSA is located in a transition area between Fremont and Anasazi cultural groups. Scientifically, the cultural significance of this WSA lies in the potential for better understanding the interrelationship between these people. The unique rock art in this area quite possibly holds the key toward establishing the nature of this contact." There are at least seven recorded prehistoric sites. A stock trail and brush fence are remnants of historic cowboy use.

Recreation—Extended hiking and backpacking trips down the forks of Salt Creek and Butler Wash start from the Cottonwood Canyon-Beef Basin road which forms the south boundary of the unit. (The road begins at Dugout Ranch on Highway 211.) Barnes (1977, p. 131-133) describes access to upper Salt Creek.

BLM recommendation—The BLM recommends wilderness designation for 24,190 acres—all of its 22,030-acre WSA plus 2,160 acres in the upper East Fork of Salt Creek, the latter added following recommendations from outside the agency to protect adjacent park values.

Coalition proposal—We recommend that 28,300 acres be designated as wilderness, including scenic Pappys Pasture and the northern parts of House Park and Ruin Park. (The rest of House Park and Ruin Park are in our Dark Canyon proposal, separated from Butler Wash by a road.) These three areas were dropped from the WSA in the BLM's 1980 intensive inventory. The boundary should be expanded to include these natural areas and the important wildlife and archeological resources within them.

THE BEHIND THE ROCKS WILDERNESS

Summary

The high cliffs that bound the Moab Valley on the southwest have been fractured, folded, and eroded into a beautiful labyrinth of domes, fins, arches, and deep canyons with perennial springs, hanging gardens, plunge pools, and rich riparian habitat. Numerous routes into this complex, visually stunning area are easily accessible from Moab and are increasingly used by both locals and visitors.

The proposed 51,100-acre Behind the Rocks wilderness area is divided into four units: Goldbar Canyon, north of the Colorado River; Behind the Rocks and Hunters Canyon south of the river, separated by the Pritchett Canyon jeep way; and Hatch Wash still farther south and to the west of the Kane Springs Canyon road. The BLM dropped three of these units from wilderness study altogether and dropped contiguous natural areas from the fourth. The agency failed to exclude impacted areas from its WSA boundaries, exaggerated minor impacts, and subdivided contiguous natural areas along topographic lines.

The Utah Wilderness Coalition proposal would restore the natural boundaries of the Behind the Rocks area to meet the legal requirements for wilderness. The area concentrates geological and cultural features found in Arches National Park to the north and the Needles District of Canyonlands National Park to the south, providing outstanding backcountry recreation and solitude in first-class scenery immediately outside the town of Moab.

Arches Meets Canyonlands

The Moab Rim is topped with domes and fins of Navajo and Entrada sandstones, with drainages cutting into the multi-hued Kayenta Formation and then the red cliff-forming Wingate Sandstone beneath. The concentration of arches in the proposed Behind the Rocks wilderness is similar to that in Arches National Park, with over 20 major, named arches and at least that number of unnamed arches known within the area, with more being discovered each year. As in Arches National Park, most arches are in the Navajo and Entrada. Unlike Arches, at least one large arch also occurs in the Kayenta Formation in the Goldbar unit, similar to the Cassidy and Hickman Arches in Capitol Reef National Park.

The top of Goldbar Canyon, Hunters Canyon, and Hatch Wash bears a remarkable resemblance to the area of Capitol Reef National Park traversed by the Frying Pan Canyon Trail between Grand Wash and the Fremont River. Potholes abound in the tops of Navajo Sandstone domes and smaller canyons. There are exposures of Navajo fins in the Klondike

IN BRIEF

Index Map: Area No. 49

Highlights: Just west of Moab, behind the 1,800-foot-high Moab Rim, lies an area of petrified sand dunes that have been carved along jointing fractures into a maze of hidden mini-canyons. Called "Behind the Rocks," this area offers secluded hiking just a few miles from town. Other units of the proposed wilderness to the west and south take in canyons with perennial streams and areas of slickrock with large sandstone arches.

Guidebooks: Barnes (1977), Hall (1982), Kelsey (1986a)

Maps: USGS 1:100,000 Moab, LaSal

Area of wilderness proposals in acres:

Unit	UWC	BLM
Behind the Rocks	20,300	12,635
Goldbar Canyon	12,500	0
Hatch Wash	14,300	0
Hunters Canyon	4,000	0
TOTAL	51,100	12,635

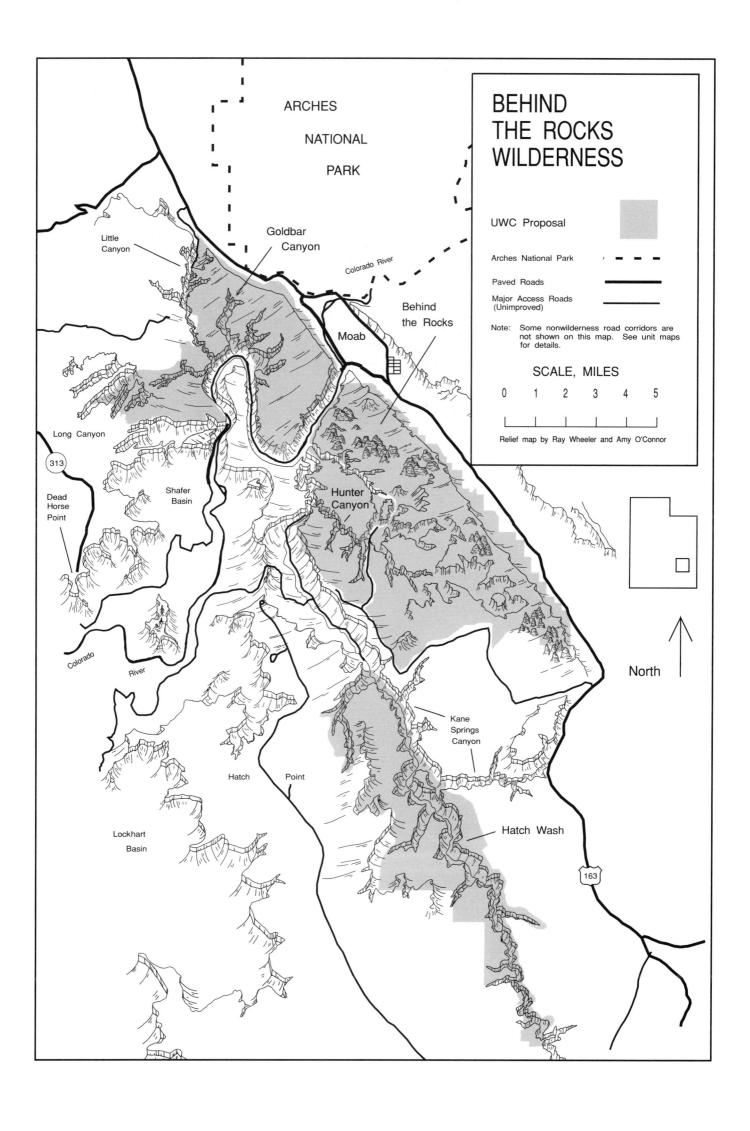

BEHIND
THE ROCKS
WILDERNESS

UWC Proposal

Arches National Park

Paved Roads

Major Access Roads
(Unimproved)

Note: Some nonwilderness road corridors are
not shown on this map. See unit maps
for details.

SCALE, MILES

0   1   2   3   4   5

Relief map by Ray Wheeler and Amy O'Connor

ARCHES

NATIONAL

PARK

Little
Canyon

Goldbar
Canyon

Colorado River

Behind
the Rocks

Moab

Long Canyon

313

Dead
Horse
Point

Shafer
Basin

Hunter
Canyon

Colorado

River

Kane
Springs
Canyon

Hatch   Point

Lockhart
Basin

Hatch Wash

163

North

On the ground one can easily lose the thread of Behind the Rocks' sandstone labyrinth. Easily accessible by passenger car or jeep from the town of Moab (upper right), the fins themselves are negotiable only on foot.

Tom Miller

Bluffs area of Arches National Park, but the area of fins dominating Behind the Rocks is much larger.

Where canyon drainages penetrate the Wingate Sandstone, pouroffs form into 400- to 1,000-foot-deep, sheer-walled canyons, often exposing perennial springs at the bottom of the Kayenta Formation. Lower Pritchett, Hunters, Kane Springs, and Hatch canyons penetrate the Wingate, with only Pritchett lacking perennial water.

Behind the Rocks was inhabited extensively by the Anasazi and Fremont Indians, the two cultures apparently overlapping here. Petroglyph panels, habitation caves, stone ruins, and chert-knapping middens abound throughout the area, as they do to the south in Indian Creek and Salt Creek in the Canyonlands area.

Because the deep canyons are sinuous and typically thick with riparian vegetation while the majority of the country is a whimsical labyrinth of domes, fins, arches, spires, and potholes, one rarely encounters other visitors. It is rare to find a natural area with as much geological and cultural interest so close to a town with extensive visitor facilities. One can spend weeks in Behind the Rocks exploring new routes amid real solitude.

Speculative Hopes

Why did the BLM overlook the wilderness values of the Behind the Rocks, dismissing most of the qualifying lands from the wilderness inventory?

Around 1979, when the BLM dropped 7,365 acres from the Behind the Rocks WSA and dropped the remaining units from wilderness consideration, the nation was in the throes of an energy crisis. The "Sagebrush Rebels," those opposed to federal control of public lands, had captured the local political structure. Oil and gas exploration roads were approaching the wilderness across Flat Iron Mesa and Hatch Point in the south and in the Little Canyon drainage to the east. Moabites staked mineral claims all over exposures of Navajo and Kayenta formations, despite the fact that the uranium-bearing Chinle Formation was a thousand feet down and the potash-rich Paradox Formation was over three thousand feet down. Moreover, the country was too rough for surface access to do exploratory drilling, much less profitable extraction if any commercial-grade deposits were found.

Wilderness designation, which would limit such speculation, was viewed with overt hostility. In the Moab area, the BLM coordinator for the wilderness inventory was married to the geologist for a mining company who also had thousands of claims filed in his own right and was the president of the local off-road vehicle club. Conservationists soon noted how the BLM's claims of a lack of wilderness values coincided with areas in which this individual had mineral or ORV route interests.

For the three units dropped from the wilderness inventory, the BLM cited impacts from mineral exploration roads on the relatively accessible areas to the south, west, and east of the units but did not adjust the boundaries to embrace natural areas too rough for roads to penetrate, excluding the areas with substantially noticeable impacts, as the Utah Wilderness Coalition has done in this proposal. ORV routes over slickrock—which are rarely noticeable even on the ground—were called "roads." These exaggerated impacts were used to disqualify part of the Goldbar Canyon and split off the northern portion of the Behind the Rocks unit. A largely invisible, abandoned drill road (located half on slickrock) and the presence of two state sections were used as rationale for dropping Hunters Canyon. The entire east face of the Moab Rim was dropped from the Behind the Rocks unit on the dubious rationale that, being a vertical cliff from which one could see the Moab Valley, it did not offer solitude and other wilderness values.

Claims of resource conflicts in the Behind the Rocks area rest on fantasy. The proposed wilderness units are ringed with dry oil and gas holes. Any extractable minerals underneath the units, however rich, face formidable costs for exploration and extraction and cannot compete with other, non-wilderness areas with equivalent mineral resource potential. Most of the topography is too rough for a horse or mule, much less a motorized vehicle.

The Utah Wilderness Coalition Proposal

The four units of our 51,100-acre Behind the Rocks proposed wilderness would protect outstanding recreational, geological, cultural, and riparian wildlife resources and form a bridge between Arches National Park to the north and the Needles District of Canyonlands National Park to the south. The wilderness would be a strong recreational asset for the Moab area and all of Utah.

Lance Christie

GOLDBAR CANYON UNIT

Highlights—Northwest of Moab, where the Colorado River flows through the cliffs of The Portal, the 12,500-acre Goldbar Canyon unit is set into a great bend of the river. Its north edge lies west of Arches National Park across Highway 191, and it shares the character of the park, containing several major arches. Goldbar Canyon completes the stretch of wild land from Arches to Behind the Rocks and Hunters Canyon south of the river.

Geology and landforms—Goldbar Canyon lies in a syncline, dipping in the middle and sloping gradually up on the east and west. The Navajo Sandstone crops out over most of the unit and is eroded into slickrock terraces, fins, and arches; the deeper canyons expose the Wingate Sandstone and the Kayenta Formation. Soils in the unit are classified in the critical erosion class, according to the Grand Resource Management Plan (BLM,

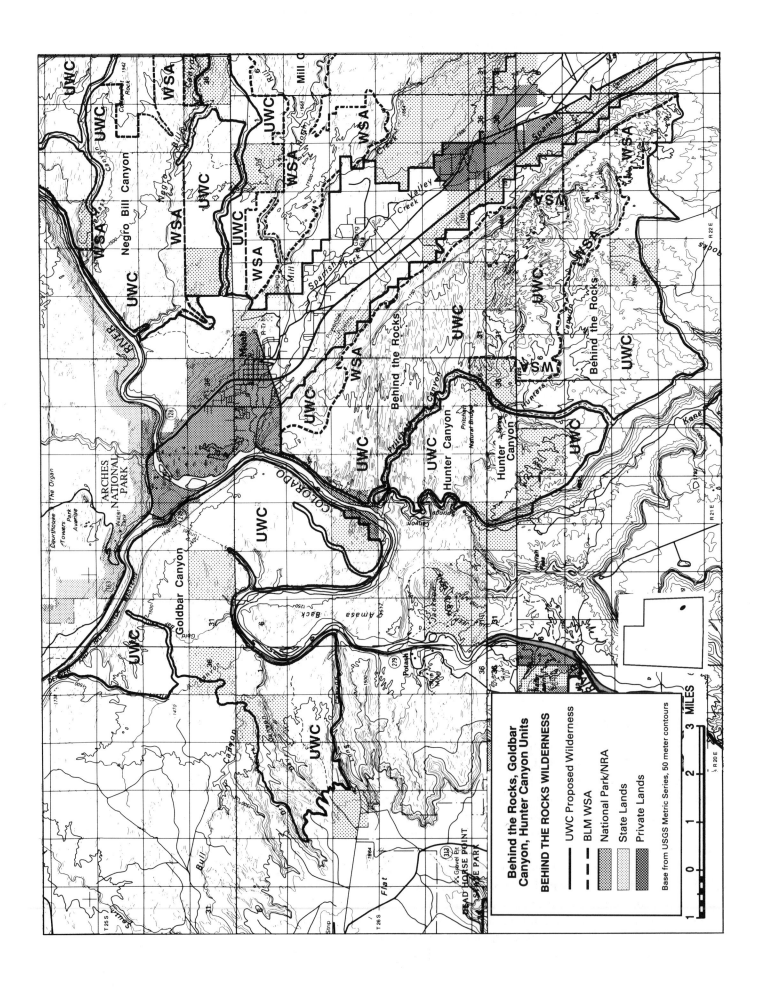

Behind the Rocks, Goldbar
Canyon, Hunter Canyon Units

BEHIND THE ROCKS WILDERNESS

UWC Proposed Wilderness

BLM WSA

National Park/NRA

State Lands

Private Lands

Base from USGS Metric Series, 50 meter contours

0   1   2   3   MILES

1983), creating hazards for potential development. Among the spectacular arches are Corona (sometimes called Little Rainbow Bridge, although it is not a true natural bridge), Bowtie, Little, and Jeep. A number of unnamed arches, natural bridges, and tunnels are found in the upper branches of Goldbar Canyon.

Plant communities—Mostly bare slickrock, the unit also supports pinyon pine and juniper as well as some blackbrush. Riparian growth winds along the bottoms of both Day and Goldbar canyons, and some hanging gardens color the canyon walls where seeps trickle down.

Wildlife—Bighorn sheep frequent the unit and are sometimes seen grazing on the cliffs and grassy areas above Highway 191. Mule deer also make their homes here, and coyotes, cottontails, foxes, and a variety of lizards inhabit the unit. The steep-walled canyons provide good nesting sites for raptors.

Archeology and history—In the southeast of the unit, near the Poison Spider jeep trail, is a rock slab of the Kayenta Formation imprinted with dinosaur tracks. (The Moab Chamber of Commerce has established a viewing point along Highway 163.) Also present in the southeast are petroglyph panels and several caves used by the Anasazi from which artifacts have been excavated. No archeological inventory of the unit has been completed.

Recreation—Easily accessible from Highways 163 and 279, Goldbar Canyon provides numerous hiking opportunities in rugged terrain. F.A. Barnes (1977), in *Canyon Country Hiking and Natural History*, describes hikes to Corona and Bowtie arches as well as on Poison Spider Mesa, and also mentions several arches in his 1987 book *Arches and Bridges*. This is a good place to explore for unusual geological formations. High points in the unit offer panoramic vistas of the Colorado River gorge and Arches National Park. The maze of slickrock fins across the river in the Behind the Rocks unit is a breathtaking sight, and the feeling of solitude so close to Moab is quite remarkable.

BLM recommendation—The BLM did not study Goldbar Canyon for possible wilderness designation, beyond a cursory examination that focused on a few areas of impacts that are deleted from our proposal.

Coalition proposal—Our boundary excludes zones of human disturbance, including regularly used roads, two reservoirs, a landing strip and associated structure, two pipelines, three transmission lines, and popular mountain bike routes. There is a railroad tunnel beneath Poison Spider Mesa, but the undisturbed surface above the tunnel is included in our proposal. The most heavily used part of the jeep/mountain bike road onto Poison Spider Mesa is cherrystemmed from our proposal. The remaining 12,500 acres retain their pristine character. Designation of these wild lands would provide a "natural bridge" between Arches National Park and the Behind the Rocks and Hunters Canyon units, enhancing the wildness of the entire area.

BEHIND THE ROCKS AND HUNTERS CANYON UNITS

Highlights—Just beyond the 1,800-foot-high rim to the southwest of Moab lie almost 25,000 acres of Navajo Sandstone fins. These rock walls shelter narrow, secret desert gardens that invite discovery on foot. Easy access from Moab (via Highway 163 along the Colorado River and the Pritchett Canyon jeep way, which splits the two units) gives Behind the Rocks and Hunters Canyon special value to this recreation-oriented community.

Geology and landforms—Primarily exposed and eroded Navajo Sandstone, Behind the Rocks is a "50 square mile labyrinth of slickrock fins and

The Hunters Canyon unit, like the rest of Behind the Rocks, has a concentration of arches similar to that of Arches National Park.

Ray Wheeler

domes, arches, giant caverns, sand dunes, deeply cut canyons and lofty rimlands . . . ." (Barnes, 1977). The fins that dominate Behind the Rocks run from east to west and provide natural screening that creates a feeling of overpowering solitude. The fins extend west across Pritchett Canyon into the Hunters Canyon unit, giving way to the contorted domes, ledges, and numerous small canyons of the Kayenta Formation before reaching the sheer Wingate cliffs in Hunters and Kane Springs canyons. With rugged terrain and panoramic views of the Colorado River and southeastern Utah, these units offer a close look at unique erosional forms.

Plant communities—Pinyon pine and blackbrush grow between the bare rock fins, as well as some juniper and scattered riparian species, notably in Hunters Canyon. Hanging gardens are found at seeps, particularly in Hunters Canyon. The BLM lists three sensitive species: the milkvetch *Astragalus isleyi*, the milkweed *Asclepias cutleri*, and the death camas *Zigadenus vaginatus*.

Wildlife—The unit provides habitat for an impressive variety of wildlife. The BLM lists mule deer, coyote, bobcat, cottontail, chukar, and occasional cougar and desert bighorn sheep; the cliff faces provide nesting habitat for a number of raptors including red-tailed hawk, great horned owl, prairie falcon, and kestrel. Peregrine falcon are found in Hunters Canyon, according to the UDWR; golden eagle may also visit the units.

Archeology and history—The units are rich in history and prehistory. Five archeological sites have been reported in Behind the Rocks; the BLM estimates that six times that many sites may exist. A likely candidate for inclusion in the Register is the "Indian Fortress," which covers some five acres and includes much fine rock art and several historic inscriptions. A rock slab of Kayenta Formation is imprinted with dinosaur tracks in this area. Another interesting set of historic graffiti is found near Otho Arch, one of at least four spectacular natural arches found in the unit. The Old Spanish Trail is visible to the east from the Moab rim.

Recreation—The character of Behind the Rocks ranges from quiet, private canyons among the Navajo Sandstone fins, to vantage points on the Moab Rim that command panoramic views of southeastern Utah. Day hikes are especially popular here; short backpacks are possible, but water sources are few. Suggested hikes in Behind the Rocks and Hunters Canyon can be found in Barnes (1977), Hall (1982), and Kelsey (1986a). Rock climbs and scrambling are possible here. Not published are innumerable routes through a labyrinth of beautiful erosional forms between Hunters Canyon and Pritchett Canyon. These canyons are accessible from the jeep way along Pritchett Canyon or by a route from Tunnel Arch or Moonflower Canyon out of Kane Springs Canyon.

BLM recommendation—The BLM recommends wilderness for its 12,635-acre Behind the Rocks WSA. However, the agency dropped 7,365 acres from that unit in its initial inventory and dropped all of Hunters Canyon. The agency failed to draw a boundary that excluded the obvious impacts, and it downrated areas used by ORVs. The scenic eastern cliff viewed from Moab, as well as the northern cliff where the Colorado River enters The Portal, were deleted after the BLM split the inventory unit along a cliff face, claiming that the area just below the cliff rim lacked outstanding opportunities for solitude and primitive recreation. The northern part of the deletion was made to accommodate an ORV route over solid sandstone. The route cannot be followed without cairns; it is an insignificant intrusion on the landscape.

Coalition proposal—We propose 20,300 acres of wilderness in the Behind the Rocks unit and 4,000 acres in the Hunters Canyon unit. Both units qualify for wilderness designation, and their unique scenic, geologic, and archeologic features deserve protection. Our boundary includes the northern portion and eastern cliff of Behind the Rocks that the BLM deleted from study. The ORV route to the rim is part of a designated BLM hiking trail to Indian Fortress and Hidden Valley and should be limited to non-motorized use. Back of the Moab Rim, vegetated areas of blow sand between rock formations are being indiscriminately sterilized by ORV wheels.

Lower Hatch Wash as it enters Kane Springs Canyon. The wash is seldom visited despite its perennial stream lined with riparian vegetation. Perhaps the lack of public use is why the BLM did not study its wilderness potential.

Jim Catlin

HATCH WASH UNIT

Highlights—Hatch Wash lies about 20 miles south of Moab. Thirty miles of deep, twisting canyons wind though the unit, and lovely riparian vegetation borders the clear perennial stream that flows the length of the main canyon. Hatch Wash forms an isolated area of high recreational potential just east of Canyonlands National Park.

Geology and landforms—Hatch Wash, a major tributary to Kane Springs Canyon, dissects the broad plateau lying between Highway 191 and the Anticline Overlook road. The entire Glen Canyon Group is exposed in its cliff walls, down to the Chinle Formation. The Entrada Sandstone is also present. Several abandoned meanders, or "rincons," are found along the wash south of its junction with West Coyote Creek.

Plant communities—The perennial stream in Hatch Wash supports a dense cover of riparian vegetation described as "a narrow green paradise in between red canyon walls" (Kelsey, 1986a). The mesa top supports pinyon-juniper and various desert shrubs.

Wildlife—Maps compiled by the UDWR show peregrine falcon use along the north edge of the unit. The combination of cliffs overlooking a riparian area offers good nesting habitat and prey sources for the falcon.

Archeology and history—Petroglyph panels are scattered throughout the deep canyons.

Recreation—Hatch Wash may be entered from Kane Creek Canyon, which it joins, or by descending its upper sidecanyons. Access via Kane Creek is described by Barnes (1977); access via Threemile Creek is described by Kelsey (1986a). One of the BLM's few developed hiking trails follows Trough Springs Canyon at the northern edge of the unit. Despite the presence of water (the stream is particularly lovely in the late spring)

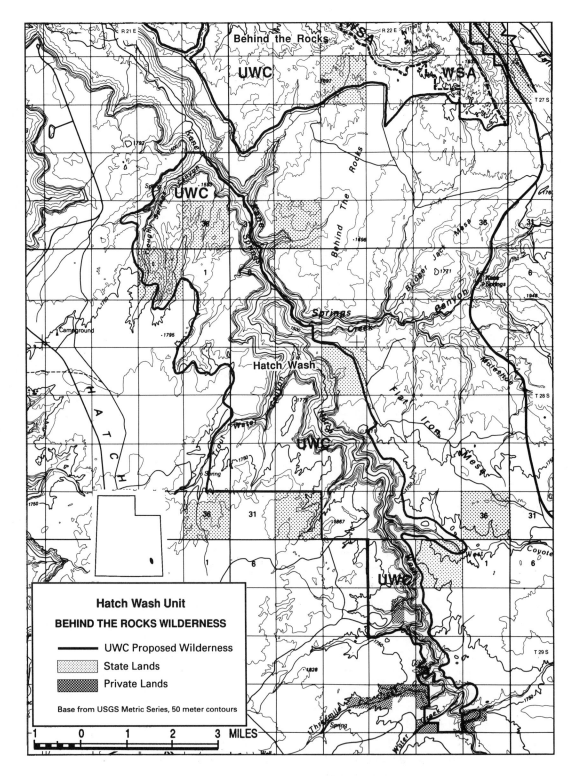

Hatch Wash Unit

BEHIND THE ROCKS WILDERNESS

—— UWC Proposed Wilderness

State Lands

Private Lands

Base from USGS Metric Series, 50 meter contours

1 0 1 2 3 MILES

and its proximity to Moab, Hatch Wash is not often visited and offers outstanding hiking and camping.

BLM recommendation—The BLM dropped the Hatch Wash unit from its initial wilderness inventory, saying it was "heavily intruded by access roads, ways, seismic lines, drilling activities and stock improvements." The BLM's inventory boundary took in many impacts on Flat Iron Mesa that could easily have been excluded, as in the Coalition proposal. The BLM's inventory document dryly notes that "opportunities for solitude are probably present, as are opportunities for primitive recreation." One wonders if the field investigation included a walk up Hatch Wash itself—the same canyon described by knowledgeable writers in such glowing terms.

Coalition proposal—After removing the road-marred higher benches and mesas from the proposal, a 14,300-acre wilderness unit remains. Public comments on the inventory uniformly noted the wild character of the unit and recommended its preservation. Small areas of private lands exist along the wash in the upper part of our proposal. They were once accessible by an old mining road up the lower part of the wash which is now thoroughly obliterated and visible only in sections. The inholdings are not currently being accessed by vehicle. A major highway was proposed up Trough Springs Canyon on the northern edge of the unit, connecting Kane Springs Canyon with the Anticline Overlook road. Local conservationists oppose this road as an unnecessary extension of motorized access into a wild area. The BLM has since dropped the idea.

THE LA SAL CANYONS WILDERNESS

Mid-July, 1957. Noon. A ranger at Arches National Park takes refuge from the 110-degree heat under the shade of his housetrailer's brush awning, and observes the 12,000-foot-high Sierra La Sal rising off to the southeast. The ranger is Edward Abbey, an unknown writer whose book *Desert Solitaire* will one day make him famous. In a passage from that book, written nine years later, he recaptures the view from his "shaded ramada:"

> The mountains are almost bare of snow except for patches within the couloirs on the northern slopes. Consoling nevertheless, those shrunken snowfields, despite the fact that they're twenty miles away by line of sight and six to seven thousand feet higher than where I sit. They comfort me with the promise that if the heat down here becomes less endurable I can escape for at least two days each week to the refuge of the mountains—those islands in the sky surrounded by a sea of desert. The knowledge that refuge is available, when and if needed, makes the silent inferno of the desert more easily bearable. Mountains complement desert as desert complements city, as wilderness complements and completes civilization.

Edward Abbey is gone, buried in an unmarked grave somewhere in the Arizona desert. But the mountains he once looked to for refuge remain on the horizon, just as they have for the past 20 million years.

Laccoliths and Salt Valleys

The La Sals are a "laccolithic" mountain range formed when molten volcanic rock, rising under great pressure from deep within the earth, uplifted the surface of the land into a group of huge domes. Later region-wide uplift, accelerating erosion, and nine periods of glaciation have sculpted those domes into elegant cone-shaped peaks cloaked with frost-rubble and ringed by glacial cirques and moraines.

The La Sal mountains not only complement the redrock desert below—they have shaped it as a potter shapes clay. Rising 6,000 feet above the surrounding landscape, the mountains mine water from the clouds and store it in snowfields and lakes. Spring-fed perennial streams radiate in every direction from the La Sals, each entrenched in a winding canyon carved through colorful rock. The La Sals are surrounded by a labyrinth of their own design.

Further complicating the topography, eight salt-dome-collapse valleys ring the mountain range. Each marks the location of a large underground salt deposit, emplaced under great pressure, which arched the overlying rock layers much as laccoliths do. The uplifts caused extensive fracturing

IN BRIEF

Index Map: Area No. 50

Highlights: The La Sal Mountains send their clear streams and spring water down to redrock canyons fringing the mountains, creating lovely hiking and verdant wildlife habitat. Located close to Moab, these wild areas enhance the community's appeal as a backcountry recreation center.

Guidebooks: Barnes (1977), Hall (1982), Kelsey (1986a), Nichols (1986)

Maps: USGS 1:100,000 Moab, LaSal

Area of wilderness proposals in acres (Utah):

Unit	UWC	BLM
Beaver Creek	28,200	0
Fisher Towers	15,100	0
Granite Creek	5,100	0
Mill Creek	15,700	9,780
Negro Bill Canyon	20,600	7,620
Mary Jane Canyon	24,200	0
Sewemup Mesa	600	0
TOTAL	109,500	17,400

Adjacent wild lands: Colorado BLM, Manti-La Sal National Forest

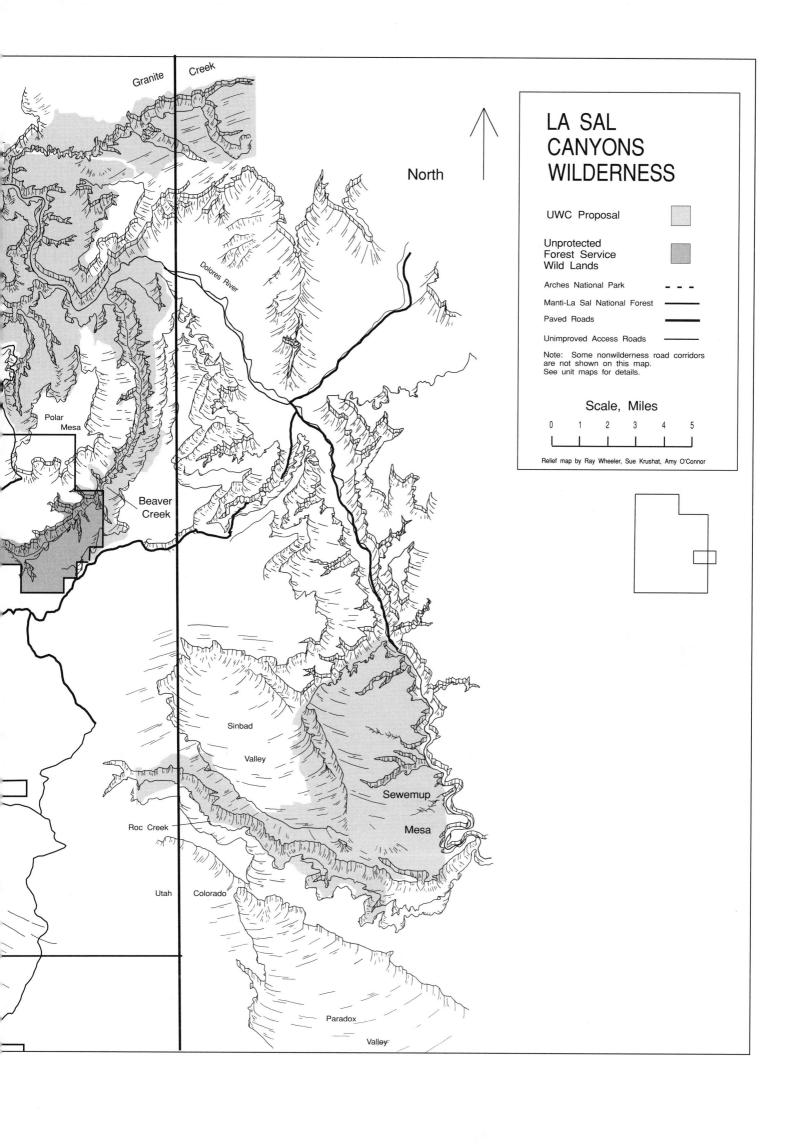

North

LA SAL CANYONS WILDERNESS

UWC Proposal

Unprotected
Forest Service
Wild Lands

Arches National Park - - -

Manti-La Sal National Forest ——

Paved Roads ▬▬▬

Unimproved Access Roads ——

Note: Some nonwilderness road corridors
are not shown on this map.
See unit maps for details.

Scale, Miles

0   1   2   3   4   5

Relief map by Ray Wheeler, Sue Krushat, Amy O'Connor

Granite Creek

Dolores River

Polar Mesa

Beaver Creek

Sinbad

Valley

Roc Creek

Sewemup

Mesa

Utah   Colorado

Paradox

Valley

of surrounding rock. Erosion has widened these fractures into narrow corridors separating huge fins of stone. Exposed to erosion on two sides, many of the fins have developed natural openings—windows, arches, and bridges. Within a 30-mile radius of the La Sal Mountains, there are hundreds of natural spans.

The rugged landscape which surrounds the La Sal mountain range is cut off from the outside world by the Colorado River on the north, the Dolores River on the east, and by the cliffs of Spanish Valley on the west. Remote, rugged, intact, the entire region retains, to this day, the feel of primeval wilderness. This is true despite the existence of scattered human impacts. A paved road cuts across the western shoulder of the La Sals. Several dirt roads encircle the mountain range at the 8,000 to 9,000-foot level. Parts of Castle and Professor valleys, which lie north of the mountain range along the Colorado River, are privately owned, as are several ranches on both the eastern and western slopes of the La Sals. Oil exploration and mining have left their mark in the glacial basins of the range, and small portions of the Manti-La Sal National Forest have been logged.

Why, despite such intrusions, does the entire La Sal region retain its primitive feel? Merely to set foot in this landscape is to know the answer immediately. Human impacts are small in comparison to the scale of the land. The complexity of the terrain makes travel adventuresome and slow. There are few roads, and between them lie almost 110,000 acres of undeveloped BLM land.

The Magic of Water

In pointed contrast to the works of man, the great peaks of the La Sals dominate the landscape. They loom above cliff wall and canyon rim, dominate every vista, and peek into every photograph. Even in the canyons below, where the mountains themselves are not visible, one can feel, hear, and see their presence in the perpetual magic of flowing water.

That water—together with the wildlife it supports and the scenery through which it flows—has made the La Sals region a mecca for outdoor enthusiasts. In the springtime, boaters flock to the Dolores River canyon, a candidate for wild and scenic river designation. Perennial streams and fine swimming holes attract hikers to Negro Bill, Mill Creek, and Beaver Creek canyons. More adventurous hikers scramble among the cracks and fins bordering the canyons, searching for rock art and natural spans. The region's dramatic stone monoliths, which include the Fisher Towers and Castle Rock, attract climbers from all over the country. There are excellent opportunities for fishing and hunting. Mill Creek, Beaver Creek, and Granite Creek are all stocked with trout. The La Sal Mountains provide summer range for large deer and elk herds which winter on the mesas and in the canyons below. The region is popular among deer hunters, and Utah Department of Wildlife Resources statistics suggest that it is one of the most productive cougar and bear management units in Utah.

Much of the La Sals region features terrain similar to that of Arches National Park, but with the added attractions of high mountain peaks, abundant water, and more diverse wildlife. Yet not one acre of the La Sals region has been protected as a national park, national monument, or wilderness area. For at least four decades, one of the most beautiful wild regions in the American West has gone unrecognized and unprotected even as it has been subjected to wave after wave of development threats.

Uranium prospectors swept through the La Sals region during the mining boom of the early 1950s, and mineral exploration has continued intermittently ever since, though rugged terrain has been an effective barrier to

development. But with time, as miners and loggers steadily expand the road network, the region will lose its wilderness character. Only national park or wilderness designation can save it.

Wilderness Shutout

Most of the La Sals region is federally owned public land. The high peaks and forested slopes of the La Sals lie within the Manti-La Sal National Forest and are surrounded by BLM lands. During the 1970s, both the Forest Service and the BLM conducted inventories of roadless lands in the region. By 1983 both agencies had completed preliminary wilderness suitability recommendations. The results were astonishing. Of more than 150,000 acres of roadless lands originally under study in the La Sals region, neither agency could find a single acre worthy of wilderness designation. Instead they recommended that the entire region be left open to mining and logging.

While the Forest Service recommended that small portions of the mountain range be designated as "scenic areas" and managed for minimum impact, it was obvious that almost all of the range would be open to mining and logging. The agency began selling timber on lands bordering the La Sals roadless areas even before its wilderness review was complete.

Meanwhile, the BLM was conducting its own wilderness review, with identical results. After inventorying six roadless areas totalling 130,000 acres, the BLM could find only 10,000 acres worthy of further wilderness study. Even this was too much for Moab miner George Schultz. Schultz owned mining claims in the vicinity of the new WSA, and on December 15, 1980, he filed a protest of the decision creating it. BLM wilderness coordinator Diana Webb reviewed the protest, and on January 13, 1981, she drafted a letter notifying Schultz that the agency would eliminate its sole

The leitmotif of east-central Utah: the La Sal Mountains, rising far above the Fisher Towers and the Colorado River. In these 8,000 vertical feet of relief are found desert badlands, vertical stone towers, stream-fed canyons, a mantle of spruce-fir forest, and alpine tundra.

Michael Newberry

Not one acre of the La Sals region has been protected as a national park, national monument, or wilderness area. For at least four decades, one of the most beautiful wild regions in the American West has gone unrecognized and unprotected even as it has been subjected to wave after wave of development threats.

remaining WSA in the La Sals region. The letter travelled by certified mail, but it might as well have been delivered by hand. Addressed to her husband, George Schultz, its destination was Diana Webb's own mailbox.

By such means the BLM eliminated from wilderness study more than 80,000 acres of wild lands surrounding the La Sal Mountains. The lands dropped from further review contained some of the most beautiful scenery in all southern Utah. Mill Creek Canyon, which borders the La Sals on the east, is a miniature Yosemite Valley walled by soaring cliffs and flat-sided domes of bare rock. Its neighbor, Negro Bill Canyon, features waterfalls, swimming holes, and Morning Glory Natural Bridge—the fifth widest natural span in America. North of the La Sal mountain range, in the Mary Jane Canyon and Fisher Towers roadless units, colorful cliffs and needle-sharp spires rise above the broad mirror of the Colorado River. Giant old-growth ponderosa pine and a rushing stream can be found in Beaver Creek Canyon, part of a 28,200-acre roadless area which straddles the 1,000-foot-deep Dolores River canyon north of the La Sals. North of the Dolores, lovely Granite Creek drops from pool to pool through a red-walled canyon filled with cottonwood and oak.

Bulldozers and Bomb Threats

If it is difficult to understand why the BLM omitted so much beautiful country from its wilderness inventory, the historical context helps. In 1979 and 1980, while the inventory was in progress, the West was in a mining boom. Since the construction of new roads—essential to mineral exploration and development in previously unroaded areas—is generally prohibited in wilderness study areas, the BLM's wilderness review was a constant frustration to miners. Inspired by Sagebrush Rebellion rhetoric, local mining boosters led a campaign against the wilderness review.

Matters came to a head when the BLM constructed a barrier to block off-road vehicle access to Negro Bill Canyon. At the direction of the Grand County commissioners, a county road crew promptly tore the barrier down. Twice the BLM replaced the barrier, and twice Grand County road crews destroyed it. A year later, the county commission sent a bulldozer into Mill Creek Canyon—a deliberate violation of federal law.

Emboldened by this example, local miners began a campaign of intimidation which included vandalism and death threats directed at BLM staff and local environmentalists. The campaign was a success. By February 1981, not one acre in the La Sals region remained under study for wilderness designation.

Ironically, even as the BLM capitulated, the mining economy of Moab was collapsing. Between 1979 and 1983 worldwide energy prices fell precipitously. By 1986, mineral exploration and production had virtually ceased in Grand County.

When Utah environmentalists learned that the BLM had abandoned its wilderness review in the La Sal region, they immediately filed appeals. An administrative law court directed the BLM to reconsider its decisions, and the agency established small WSAs in Negro Bill and Mill Creek canyons. Neither WSA was recommended for wilderness in the agency's 1986 draft wilderness EIS, but following voluminous comment from citizens the agency announced that it would recommend some wilderness for both canyons.

It is clear that both the BLM and the Forest Service intend to leave nearly all of the La Sals region open to development. In doing so they will sacrifice the needs of hunters and wildlife—of fishermen, climbers, swimmers, boaters, hikers, artists and poets—to promote an industry which has, at least temporarily, ceased to exist in the region.

The Utah Wilderness Coalition Proposal

In 1985, Utah environmentalists conducted their own inventory of the La Sals region. After extensive reconnaissance, they identified 109,500 acres in seven roadless areas which eminently qualify for wilderness protection.

The Utah Wilderness Coalition's proposal is based on a conviction that the beauty of the La Sals region is far more valuable than its marginal resources of uranium, oil, molybdenum, or timber. Even while the mining industry has gone bust, protected natural areas such as Arches and Canyonlands National Parks have been a powerful economic asset to the small town of Moab and all southern Utah. Wilderness, too, is valuable as an asset for the tourist economy, and it is still more valuable as an asset to the quality of life for Utah residents and the entire nation.

No one has better explained this highest value of the La Sals wilderness than Edward Abbey. If a piece of this region should ever become part of the National Wilderness Preservation System, it will be in some measure a tribute to his wisdom and passion and poetry, which so beautifully complements and completes the canyon country of southern Utah. For those who have read and loved Abbey's books, some part of these mountains, this desert, will always be the Edward Abbey Wilderness.

Ray Wheeler

MILL CREEK UNIT

Highlights—Abundant clear water rushing down from the La Sal Mountains toward the Colorado River creates habitat for a wealth of wildlife and fine opportunities for backcountry recreation. Vertical slickrock walls dotted with rock art, inviting swimming holes at spillovers, and some sublime camping sites in groves of cottonwood make Mill Creek a worthwhile destination for out-of-state hikers, as well as a delightful backyard wilderness for Moabites. This unit of the La Sal Canyons wilderness connects the Negro Bill Canyon unit on the north to the Horse Mountain-Manns Peak national forest roadless area on the east. The BLM studied Mill Creek, but in 1986 failed to recommend it for designation. The agency is expected to recommend a 9,780-acre wilderness in 1990. The Coalition proposes designation for 15,700 acres to protect Mill Creek's water, wildlife, archeology, recreation, and scenery.

Geology and landforms—Four miles of Mill Creek's 20-mile course from the 12,000-foot peaks of the La Sal Mountains to the Colorado River are in this unit. Here the creek has cut an inviting, 400-foot-deep canyon among massive Navajo Sandstone fins and domes. The unit also includes Mill Creek's north fork and a major sidecanyon, Rill Creek, making 20 miles of perennial stream in all. Elevations vary from 4,200 feet at the confluence of Mill Creek and the North Fork on the west to 7,000 feet on the rims of Wilson and South mesas on the east.

Plant communities—Nearly 3,000 feet of relief takes you from a pinyon-juniper forest on Wilson Mesa through blackbrush and sagebrush benchlands to the lush cottonwood- and willow-lined streams. Large areas of slickrock lack any vegetation.

Wildlife—The extensive riparian vegetation in this unit provides habitat diversity for wildlife. Mill Creek supports several species of fish and a healthy range and number of macroinvertebrates (BLM, 1986). Ephemeral potholes in the slickrock support cryptobiotic tadpole and fairy shrimp. The BLM identifies 5,580 acres as crucial winter range for deer. The UDWR designates the western two-thirds of the unit as a peregrine falcon use area. Golden eagles and other raptors are also found here, as well as elk, coyotes, bobcats, mountain lions, and possibly black bears.

Archeology and history—Cultural inventories have not been completed within the BLM's WSA, yet the 25 recorded sites suggest the archeological significance of this area. Ancient campsites, rockshelters, and rock art panels are scattered throughout the unit, most of Archaic and Fremont age. Fine pictograph panels are found along the North Fork, which, one hopes, visitors will leave unscathed. Pothunters, however, have left their telltale soil mounds in caves and overhangs.

Recreation—An abundant water supply makes for excellent camping and hiking. Swimming and wading on hot summer afternoons are favorite activities; however, backpacking is best in spring and fall. Two pouroffs along the lower North Fork must be passed, although most of Mill Creek and its tributaries offer flat, gentle hiking. Access is also possible from the Sand Flats road above Rill Creek, a tributary of Mill Creek.

BLM recommendation—Mill Creek has a history of controversy. In 1980, soon after the BLM had proposed Mill Creek as a 10,320-acre WSA, a Grand County Commissioner led a group of flag-waving locals into the WSA and bulldozed a 100-yard scar. The BLM took no action against the self-styled sagebrush rebels. Instead, after receiving a three-sentence protest from a local mine developer, the BLM dropped the WSA. Utah conservationists appealed and regained WSA status for the unit in 1983, although the new 9,780-acre WSA left out lands up to 2 miles from the nearest significant human impacts. The BLM also cherrystemmed the lower North Fork from the WSA, despite the inadvisability of vehicle use above the lower pouroff. In its 1986 DEIS, the BLM recommended against wilderness, citing (in an informal addendum to the DEIS) its oil and gas potential. But an abundance of dry holes in nearby areas, drilled into the most likely producing horizons, suggests that the BLM has overrated the likelihood of hydrocarbon production. Public support for wilderness has been high and the agency will likely recommend its 9,780-acre WSA for wilderness in its final EIS.

Coalition proposal—We propose 15,700 acres of wilderness, including important benchlands on the rims above the main fork of Mill Creek. Our boundary takes in some insignificant intrusions: three miles of seismic lines between the forks of Mill Creek, old placer mining near Wilson Mesa, an old vehicle track north of Rill Creek, and several other minor vehicle ways. The many recreational, cultural, and scenic qualities of the unit coupled with its diverse wildlife make Mill Creek a prime candidate for wilderness designation.

NEGRO BILL CANYON UNIT

Highlights—Negro Bill Canyon is one of the most popular day hiking areas near Moab, lying only two and a half miles east of town off Highway 128. Hikers are attracted by the canyon's spectacular sandstone walls, flowing water, cottonwood trees, and Morning Glory Natural Bridge, one of the largest natural rock spans in the world. Fed by groundwater from rain and snow falling on the La Sal Mountains, Negro Bill Canyon's six miles of perennial stream are an oasis for flora and fauna. Negro Bill Canyon is wedged between Mill Creek on the south and Arches National Park (across the Colorado River) on the northwest. The BLM initially opposed wilderness but public support has apparently changed the agency's mind. The Coalition proposes 20,600 acres of wilderness to protect this treasure of running water, greenery, and slickrock just minutes from Moab.

Geology and landforms—The proposed wilderness unit is a triangle of slickrock with the rim of Negro Bill Canyon as the base on the south, the

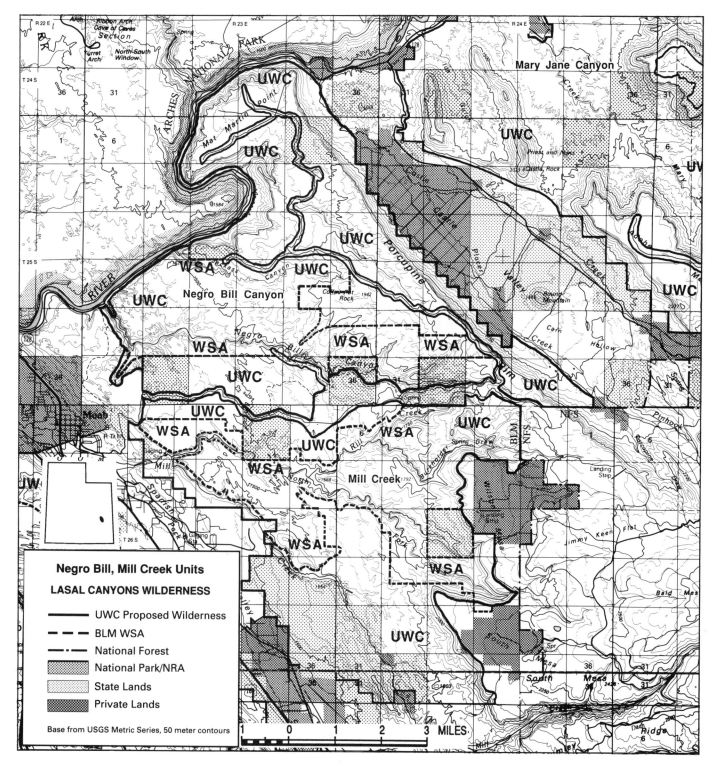

Negro Bill, Mill Creek Units

LASAL CANYONS WILDERNESS

—————— UWC Proposed Wilderness

– – – – – BLM WSA

–·–·– National Forest

National Park/NRA

State Lands

Private Lands

Base from USGS Metric Series, 50 meter contours

1 0 1 2 3 MILES

Colorado River gorge as the northwest side, and the 1200-foot cliff of Porcupine Rim dropping into Castle Valley as the northeast side. Negro Bill, Jackass, and Dripping Spring canyons cut east to west across the unit from the Porcupine Rim (at 5,400 to 7,000 feet) to the river gorge (at 4,000 feet). Navajo Sandstone fins and domes mark large areas of the unit. Most of the remainder is Kayenta Formation ledges and rims with Wingate Sandstone inner canyons in upper Negro Bill and Dripping Spring Canyon. Numerous springs and seeps provide a remarkable abundance of water.

Plant communities—Outside the large areas of slickrock, this unit is vegetated primarily with blackbrush and juniper. Six hundred acres of riparian growth line Negro Bill Canyon, and *Aquilegia micrantha*, a rare

Rill Creek, a tributary of the North Fork of Mill Creek, is one of many spring-fed streams that tumble from the flanks of the La Sals.

Fred Swanson

columbine, may be present in the colorful hanging gardens, according to the BLM.

Wildlife—Negro Bill Canyon's perennial stream and associated riparian vegetation provide important habitat for a great variety of wildlife, according to BLM data (1986). Beaver numbers have increased recently. Waterfowl, including mallard, blue-winged teal, and common merganser ducks, are seen even in summer. Bluehead sucker, roundtail chub, red shiner, fathead minnow and plains killifish are the most common native fish species. There are small numbers of game fish including large-mouth bass and green sunfish. The golden eagle is common in Negro Bill and the UDWR identifies the unit as a peregrine use area. The BLM identifies almost half of its WSA as critical deer winter range.

Archeology and history—A cowboy hideout and a petroglyph panel are known within the unit. The BLM estimates that the unit has 12 sites, 6 of which may be eligible for the National Register. Cultures known to have used the vicinity include Paleo-Indian, Desert Archaic, Fremont, Anasazi, and Ute. The canyon is named for William Granstaff, a farmer who was one of Moab's earliest settlers.

Recreation—Easily accessible from Moab, this canyon is a popular recreation site. The BLM (1986, p. 14) notes that a commercial horseback operation takes trips to Morning Glory Natural Bridge, and that "school groups frequently hike the canyon in conjunction with environmental studies."

BLM recommendation—The BLM recommended none of its 7,620-acre WSA in its 1986 DEIS, deferring to past local antagonisms that are no longer a factor. The final EIS will probably recommend all of the WSA. The BLM also alleged that a wilderness boundary would be difficult to identify; however, if the boundaries were expanded to include all the natural area surrounding the canyon (as required by the inventory policy), boundary definition would be much easier. The BLM (1986, p. 10) claimed that the WSA is moderately favorable for oil and gas, potash and uranium. However, in the Grand RMP (1983, p. 1-18 to 20), the BLM identified no areas of known ore grade uranium, no known potash deposits, and no oil and gas potential in the unit. Mineral prospecting in the area has not been successful and numerous dry holes indicate a low potential for hydrocarbons.

Coalition proposal—The Coalition proposes wilderness designation for the 20,600-acre Negro Bill Canyon unit, including the BLM's WSA, lower Jackass Canyon, and benchlands extending north and east to Porcupine Rim. Our boundary cherrystems two vehicle and mountain bike routes on Mat Martin Point and includes all lands that are in a natural condition north of the Sand Flats road.

MARY JANE CANYON UNIT

Highlights—The mesas that finger off of the La Sal Mountains between Castle Valley and the Fisher Towers guard a seldom visited slickrock canyon with a perennial stream. We propose a 24,200-acre wilderness unit that takes in this canyon (above the private lands at the Professor Valley Ranch), as well as part of the scenic Richardson Amphitheater and the famous rock towers of Castle Rock and the Priest and Nuns.

Geology and landforms—The broad, cliff-rimmed valley of Professor Creek, known in its upper reaches as Mary Jane Canyon, forms the center of the unit. The canyon is eroded into the White Rim Sandstone; the gentler valley slopes are Chinle and Moenkopi formations. Fisher Mesa with its sheer Wingate Sandstone cliffs reaches out to the north of the valley from the uplands of the La Sal Mountains, and Parriot and Adobe

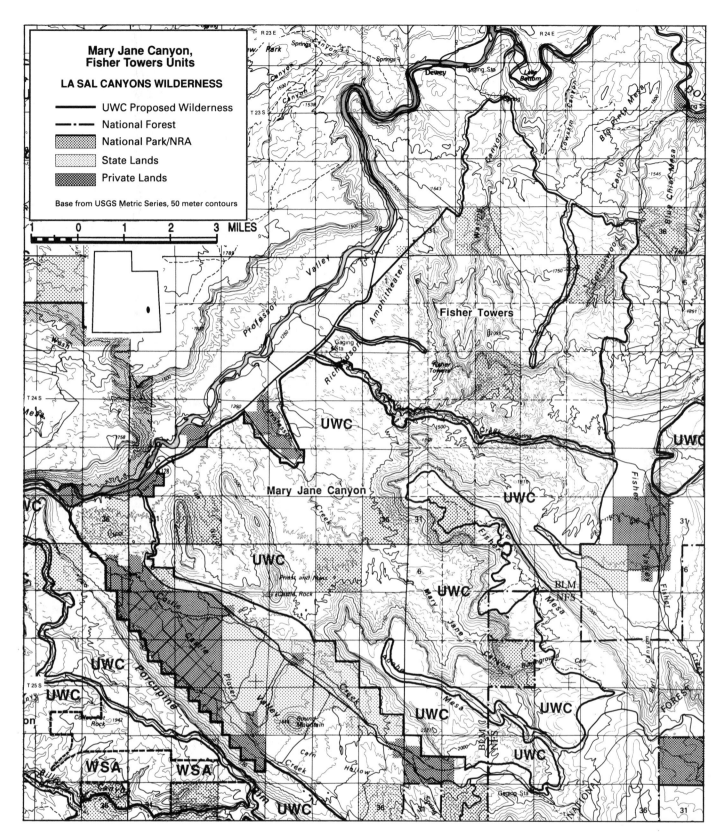

mesas separate the valley from Castle Valley to the south. Remnants of
the latter cliff have been eroded into the spectacular rock towers called
Castle Rock (Castleton Tower) and the Priest and Nuns. The Totem
Pole, another rock spire, rises immediately south of Onion Creek below
the Fisher Towers.

Plant communities—The lower slopes have a scattering of blackbrush
and other desert shrubs, with pinyon pine and juniper; on the mesas sagebrush flats alternate with pinyon-juniper forest. Much of the pinyon-
juniper forest on Fisher Mesa (outside the unit) has been chained.

Cottonwood, tamarisk, and other riparian species grow along Professor Creek, which is fed by springs higher in the mountains, and Douglas fir and aspen are found in the uppermost canyons.

Wildlife—A dozen or so elk and larger numbers of deer winter in Professor Valley. A few deer remain in the unit yearlong, whereas most deer and elk move up into the adjacent national forest during the summer.

Archeology and history—A historic wagon road connected Professor Valley and Castle Valley by way of the pass between Castle Rock and Adobe Mesa, but the route is little evident now. A petroglyph panel is located within the unit and has figures of bighorn and other creatures.

Recreation—Mary Jane Canyon merited mention in two guidebooks: Kelsey (1986a) calls it "a good example of a canyon narrows" and Barnes (1977) notes "the endless examples of unusual and lovely sandstone erosional forms." Castle Rock is well known among rock climbers as a spectacular, but not extreme, vertical climb. The narrows of Onion Creek, which divides this unit from the Fisher Towers unit, is also worth exploring.

BLM recommendation—The BLM dropped Mary Jane Canyon from its 1979 intensive wilderness inventory. The agency's field investigator found the unit to be primarily in a natural condition, but claimed that it lacked outstanding opportunities for solitude and primitive recreation. This determination was based on the alleged lack of topographic or vegetative screening. (When conservationists appealed similar BLM decisions in other inventory units, the IBLA ruled that the BLM's definition of solitude was excessively narrow.)

Coalition proposal—We propose a 24,200-acre wilderness unit, taking in the undeveloped canyon and valley and reaching up into the undisturbed portions of the mesa tops. Our proposal excludes proposed range facilities and maintained access routes on Adobe Mesa and chainings on Fisher Mesa. The canyon itself offers fine solitude as it twists through the eroded valley; the upper part of the canyon is somewhat difficult to traverse (see Kelsey, 1986a) and solitude is practically guaranteed here. The remainder of the unit is more open, but as in the Fisher Towers to the north the openness only adds to the sense of aloneness. The BLM's criteria for assessing solitude ignore the opportunities for exploring found here. Our proposal includes several old, unused vehicle ways that are largely reclaimed. Ways leading up from the Professor Valley Ranch, dating from the uranium exploration days of the 1950s, are largely revegetated or eroded away and are difficult to locate on the ground. A few small, abandoned uranium pits are found in the Chinle Formation north of the creek near the ranch. A vehicle way that is receiving some use loops through the Richardson Amphitheater off of Highway 128, reaching as far as the knolls below Fisher Mesa. This track was created by repeated ORV use, mostly motorcycles. It serves no comprehensible purpose and should be blocked off and turned back over to nature, which would quickly reclaim it.

FISHER TOWERS UNIT

Highlights—The fluted, dark-red spires of the Fisher Towers rise above the Colorado River 20 miles northeast of Moab. The combination of the sparkling river, spectacular redrock cliffs, and the snowcapped La Sal Mountains soaring above 12,000 feet creates a fairytale picture. One of the best known geologic formations in southern Utah, the Fisher Towers are also well known for advanced rock climbing. Unknown to many, however, is pristine 5-mile-long Waring Canyon, which begins just behind the cliffs north of the towers and drains into the Dolores River. The BLM exaggerated impacts and dropped this unit in the initial inventory. The Coali-

The Fisher Towers are recognized as a classic rock climb, but a foot trail around their base offers an easy view of these monoliths. Despite the area's popularity, the BLM did not examine its wilderness potential.

Bob Bauer

tion's 15,100-acre proposal excludes peripheral impacts and includes the imposing Towers and Waring Canyon with its stream.

Geology and landforms—Reminiscent of ancient Gothic cathedrals, the soaring redrock spires of the Fisher Towers are carved from siltstone of the Moenkopi and Cutler Formations. The Titan, tallest of the colorful formations, stands 900 feet above its base. Waring Canyon projects straight north from a Wingate Sandstone cliff that divides the unit, Richardson's Amphitheater slopes down to the Colorado River in the west, and perennial Onion Creek with its redrock grottoes winds in and out among badlands and cliffs along the southern border. Elevations vary from 4,400 to 7,000 feet.

Plant communities—Pinyon-juniper populates the eastern part of the unit while the western part is primarily barren cliffs and badlands. Richardson's Amphitheater, the lowest elevation in the unit, is covered with the blackbrush vegetation type, and riparian habitat follows the stream banks of Waring Canyon and Onion Creek. The scenic Onion Springs Badlands and rugged cliffs harbor an endangered plant community, and the western tip of the unit has the threatened *Cycladenia humilis* var. *jonesii*.

Wildlife—The northern half of this unit has been classified by the UDWR as a peregrine falcon use area. Sheer cliff walls provide prime nesting spots for this endangered species and other raptors. The UDWR has also identified the south edge as critical deer winter habitat.

Recreation—Foot travel ranges from the very easy to the extremely challenging. A gently graded, maintained foot trail begins at a parking lot at the Fisher Towers and winds around the pinnacles. The highest tower, the 900-foot-tall Titan, is listed in Roper and Steck's *Fifty Classic Climbs of North America* (Sierra Club Books, 1979); it was not climbed until 1962 when a National Geographic team spent three days ascending the mono-lith (see *National Geographic*, November, 1962). Eric Bjornstad, in *Desert Rock* (Chockstone Press, Denver, 1988), gives an extensive writeup of tech-nical climbing routes in Fisher Towers as well. To the north, Waring Canyon also offers outstanding hikes. The climb to the edge of Waring Mesa gives panoramic views of the Colorado River and the La Sal Mountains as well as the green meadows of Fisher Valley and the red sandstone cliffs of Richardson's Amphitheater. The easiest access is from the end of a graded dirt road off of Highway 128 to the picnic area and trailhead at the Fisher Towers. A road also follows Onion Creek at the south boundary of the unit, and Waring Canyon can be reached via a gravel road which leaves Highway 128 at the south end of Dewey Bridge. For details of the hike to Panorama Point see Barnes (1977).

BLM recommendation—In 1979, the BLM dropped the Fisher Towers unit from its wilderness inventory. The agency's brief field investigation, conducted by just one person, cursorily noted that, "The red rock cliffs here are striking." It went on to claim that the area was heavily impacted. The agency could simply have drawn a boundary to exclude the most significant human impact, instead of dropping the entire unit from study.

Coalition proposal—We propose that 15,100 acres be designated as wilderness. Our boundary excludes the significant human impacts. We include a cherrystem for the 2-1/2-mile-long graded dirt road from Highway 128 to the picnic area below the Fisher Towers. Our northern boundary is along an ORV road that follows a powerline, and the eastern boundary is the Top of the World ORV route; both routes are regularly used and pro-vide good access to the unit. Our boundary also excludes the drill sites and chained areas that the BLM cited in dropping its roadless area from study. Only a few old seismic lines and drill holes are within our boundary and do not constitute a significant intrusion. A BLM planning document (1983, p. 1-18, 20) indicates low potential for uranium, coal, potash, or oil and gas. This wild area is as spectacular as they come and would be one of the most easily accessible wilderness areas in the state.

SEWEMUP MESA UNIT

Highlights—Sewemup Mesa is perhaps the single most ecologically pris-tine area in the region, having been isolated from development by its al-most impassable belt of encircling sandstone cliffs. Most of the 21,335-acre unit lies in Colorado but a 600-acre portion of the Roc Creek drainage, a steep-walled canyon lined with Douglas fir and ponderosa pine, reaches into Utah. The unit is contiguous to 9,500 acres of national forest roadless land on the Manti-La Sal National Forest.

Geology and landforms—The most striking feature of Sewemup Mesa is its band of thousand-foot-high Wingate Sandstone cliffs, which encircle more than three-fourths of the unit. These cliffs rise out of the magnificent slickrock gorge of the Dolores River, towering above Sinbad Valley. The cliffs extend west up into the La Sal Mountains, forming Sinbad Ridge which forms the north wall of the 1,500-foot-deep gorge of Roc Creek. These features are named for Sinbad the Sailor and the giant bird of Arab legend.

Plant communities and wildlife—Huge ponderosa pines line the drainages on the mesa top and grow directly from the sandstone terraces along the mesa's western cliffs. The brilliant red walls of Roc Creek canyon are framed by green forests of Douglas fir and ponderosa pine. A pinyon-juniper forest covers the mesa. Peregrine falcons and golden eagles nest on the cliffs, and bald eagles winter along the Dolores River at the unit's eastern edge. Mountain lions prowl the mesa, and much of Sinbad

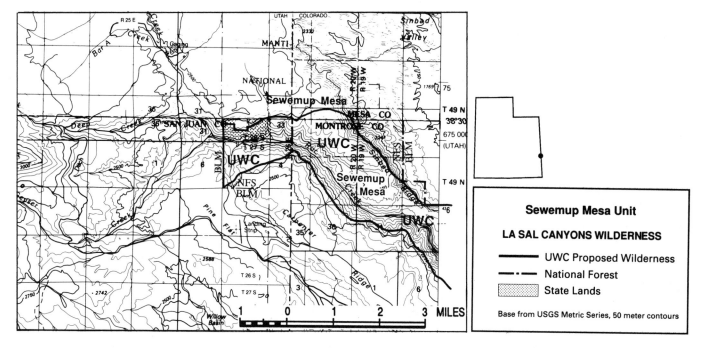

Sewemup Mesa Unit

LA SAL CANYONS WILDERNESS

— UWC Proposed Wilderness
-·- National Forest
▨ State Lands

Base from USGS Metric Series, 50 meter contours

Ridge and the mesa's lower slopes are important big game winter range for deer and elk.

Archeology and history—Sewemup Mesa derives its name from the cattle rustling days of the McCarty Gang. The rustlers are said to have burnt off and "sewed up" the cattle's rightful brands.

Recreation—Few places offer more exhilarating solitude than the edge of Sewemup Mesa's cliffs. In contrast to the mesa's towering heights, Roc Creek plummets 1,000 feet straight down, forming the largest canyon draining east from the La Sal Mountains. Access to the unit is primitive roads on the northwest (Beaver Creek area) and east (Gateway area).

BLM recommendation—The Colorado BLM recommended 18,835 acres of its 19,140-acre WSA for wilderness designation. But its WSA includes none of Sinbad Ridge or the Roc Creek drainage and does not extend into Utah.

Coalition proposal—We support the recommendations of Colorado conservationists for a 21,335-acre wilderness unit, including 600 acres within Utah. Our proposed unit includes all of Sinbad Ridge and the deepest part of the Roc Creek canyon, thus adding to the diversity of the unit and completing the connection with national forest roadless lands in the La Sals. Our boundary takes in a number of abandoned, impassable, and improperly mapped roads along Sinbad Ridge (mostly in Colorado) and in the saddle separating Sewemup Mesa and Sinbad Ridge. Our boundary follows the southern rim of Roc Creek canyon, adding 2,500 acres to the BLM's WSA and forming a topographically complete boundary along the rim instead of following the section lines of the national forest boundary.

BEAVER CREEK UNIT

Highlights—Beaver Creek flows out of the northern La Sal Mountains through a 12-mile-long slickrock gorge before emptying into the Dolores River. Located on the eastern border of Utah 25 miles northeast of Moab, the Beaver Creek wilderness unit also includes 6 miles of the Dolores River which have been recommended by the Park Service for Wild River designation. Cottonwood Canyon, with its tributaries Thompson and Burro canyons, and bench lands around Sevenmile and Steamboat mesas are also included. Peregrine falcon, elk, and deer find critical habitat in this remote area. Beaver Creek links the Granite Creek wilderness unit on the north and the Fisher Towers unit on the west to the Horse Mountain-Manns Peak national forest roadless area in the La Sal Mountains to the southwest. The BLM did not designate this stunningly diverse and beautiful area for wilderness study. The Coalition proposes designation for 28,200 acres of BLM land and 5,450 acres of adjacent national forest land.

Geology and landforms—Barnes (1977) describes Beaver Creek canyon as a "lovely, primitive, wooded gorge that winds between convoluted slickrock walls for 12 miles before joining the Dolores River gorge." The deep inner canyon exposes sheer walls of red Wingate Sandstone. The Kayenta Formation forms wide intermediate benches, and rising above are isolated mesas of pink, orange, and white Navajo and Entrada sandstones. The entire unit is tilted up to the La Sal Mountain laccolith to the south.

Plant communities—The unit contains many miles of riparian vegetation along the Dolores River and along Beaver and Cottonwood creeks. A transition zone from the Dolores River to the La Sal Mountains, the unit encompasses a wide variety of vegetation types. From low elevation blackbrush to mid-elevation pinyon-juniper, the unit reaches up into aspen, ponderosa pine and oak brush in the more mountainous south.

Wildlife—This unit possesses a "healthy and relatively undisturbed ecosystem with outstanding wildlife values," according to the National Park Service (1979). The endangered bald eagle lives in these canyons. The UDWR identifies the northern third of the unit as a peregrine use area and the southern half as critical deer winter range. Elk winter in upper Beaver Creek canyon and deer winter north of the Dolores River (BLM, 1983a, p. 1-16). The UDWR is introducing desert bighorn sheep into the area surrounding the Dolores due to its favorable habitat and relative isolation. Trout live in Beaver Creek.

Recreation—The Dolores River provides whitewater boating which is "challenging without being too severe" (National Park Service, 1979). Beaver Creek and eight other major sidecanyons afford outstanding hiking, backpacking, photography and nature study opportunities. Hiking and camping are excellent on the grassy benches with expansive vistas across the Dolores Triangle to the north, of the La Sal Mountains in the south, and to Colorado's Uncompahgre Plateau in the east. Access is by a graded road down the Dolores from Gateway, Colorado, to the mouth of Beaver Creek; the Castleton-Gateway gravel road into the upper end of Beaver Creek Canyon (avoiding posted private lands); and the Onion Creek Road to the head of Cottonwood Canyon and Thompson Canyon. Barnes (1977) describes the hike down Beaver Creek canyon; Nichols (1986) describes the float trip down the Dolores River.

BLM recommendation—In 1979, at the same time the Park Service was recommending the Dolores River for Wild River designation, the BLM was releasing the river canyon and surrounding lands as "clearly and obviously lacking wilderness character." The BLM exaggerated the extent of impacts within the unit and failed to consider a study area boundary which would have excluded major impacts.

Coalition proposal—We propose a 28,200-acre Beaver Creek wilderness unit along with 5,450 acres of adjacent national forest wild lands. Our proposal excludes ranch and farm development at the mouth of Beaver Creek as well as chainings on the rim of Beaver Creek and uranium impacts on Blue Chief Mesa and Polar Mesa. Old vehicle ways on Sevenmile Mesa are reclaiming naturally and are included in our proposal. On the east, the boundary follows the edge of old mining activities midway down the side of the mesa. Mineral prospects appear to be marginal, according to information in BLM documents (1983).

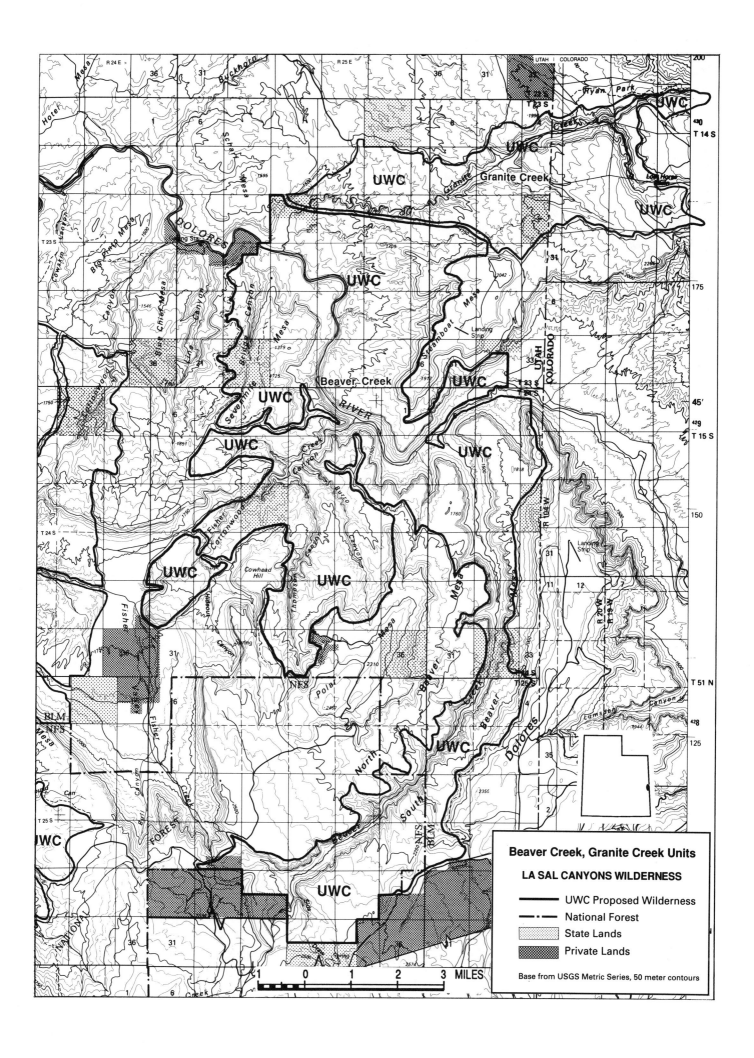

Beaver Creek, Granite Creek Units

LA SAL CANYONS WILDERNESS

—————— UWC Proposed Wilderness

—·—·— National Forest

State Lands

Private Lands

Base from USGS Metric Series, 50 meter contours

Wingate Sandstone cliffs frame the gorge of Beaver Creek as it spills from the north slopes of the La Sals. Few people traverse this wild canyon.

Tom Miller

GRANITE CREEK UNIT

Highlights—Granite Creek, a perennial stream that supports a trout fishery, flows into the Dolores River about 30 miles northeast of Moab. Hikes down Granite Creek can continue through Beaver Creek into the La Sal Mountains and across Mill Creek to Moab. The BLM refused to study this unit despite the recommendation of Colorado BLM staff. We recommend 5,100 acres of wilderness in Utah, with an additional 9,200 acres in Colorado.

Geology and landforms—Lower Granite Creek is a dramatic red Wingate Sandstone canyon, dotted with picturesque fins, columns, windows, and buttes. The canyon is named for exposures of ancient granitic rocks in the canyon bottom. The higher, eastern end of the canyon, which is cut into the Chinle and Cutler formations, is relatively open and straight, whereas the western end where it joins the Dolores River is so serpentine that the stream runs 7 miles to cover 3 straight-line miles.

Plant communities—The uplands above the canyon are covered with pinyon pine and juniper, with some ponderosa pine in the higher elevations. Lower down, in the western part of the unit, shrubs and grasses take over. The perennial stream in the canyon supports riparian species such as cottonwood and willow, with box elder and Gambel oak in drier sites.

Wildlife—Granite Creek has trout and several species of nongame fish, according to the BLM (1983a, p. 3-15). The unit provides critical winter range for mule deer and elk. Black bears, mountain lions, peregrine falcons, and bald and golden eagles also inhabit the unit.

Archeology and history—An old homestead is located along Granite Creek in the center of the unit. Its remnants of fences, corrals, and buildings add a historical flavor and do not detract from the canyon's overall appearance of naturalness.

Recreation—Granite Creek is a popular day hike for Dolores River boaters. A BLM staff report notes that the unit's "riparian vegetation, perennial stream, interesting and varied geology and wildlife provide for a very high capability to attract hikers and backpackers." The unit is part of the remote Dolores Triangle area known for its excellent backcountry hunting. Views from the upland slopes take in the high peaks of the La Sal Mountains to the south, and the desert slopes to the northwest.

BLM recommendation—The BLM did not establish a WSA for Granite Creek, despite its acknowledgment (in the 1980 intensive inventory decision) that "the unit appears to be generally natural." The agency claimed that the unit lacked outstanding opportunities for solitude. It offered, instead, to consider administrative designations such as an Area of Critical Environmental Concern (ACEC). But the BLM did not consider an ACEC for Granite Creek in its 1983 Grand Resource Area management plan and gave it no protection from mining, ORVs, or other development.

Coalition proposal—The riparian plant community and steep-walled canyon provide excellent opportunities for solitude in the upper and middle parts of the canyon. Farther downstream, the sharply meandering canyon with 200- to 300-foot-high walls also provides outstanding solitude. The BLM's inventory unit boundary traced an old road south from the north rim down into the canyon to the site of the old homestead, then followed the creek east to the south fork, eventually leaving the canyon. These roads are overgrown, blocked by landslides, and are washed out in three places. Our boundary incorporates these eroded roads and follows the north rim of the canyon, thus protecting the outstanding features of the canyon.

THE WESTWATER CANYON WILDERNESS

Summary

As the Colorado River enters Utah, it carves the first of the desert canyons for which it is famous, cutting deep into black Precambrian bedrock as well as exposing the bright reds and oranges of the overlying sandstones. These canyons draw over 20,000 boaters annually, most to tackle Westwater Canyon's challenging rapids, but others to delight in the scenery and wildlife of the gentle Ruby and Horsethief canyons upstream from Westwater.

The Colorado River wilderness encompasses two units, Black Ridge Canyons and Westwater Canyon, which include the stretch of river running from below Loma, Colorado to near Cisco, Utah. Our proposal will safeguard one of the most accessible wild canyons of the Colorado River. Boat launches are found at the Westwater Ranger Station and at the Loma highway interchange. The tributary canyons can be reached via Glade Park, Colorado, on county roads leading west to Coates Creek.

The River

Rather than skirt the broad uplift of the Uncompahgre Plateau, the Colorado River grinds straight through for 40 miles, carving Horsethief Canyon out of soft sediments, then moving through the underlying strata until in Ruby Canyon it reaches the black Precambrian granites that form the core of the plateau. The river then dives abruptly into the depths of Westwater Canyon, cutting a tight corridor through shimmering, smooth, fluted black schist. (After its exposure in Westwater, this bedrock does not reappear until the Inner Gorge of the Grand Canyon.) Far above are the bright red walls of the Wingate Sandstone and the cream-colored Entrada Sandstone. The short and riotous journey through Westwater ends in the gentle desert near Cisco.

Recreationists flock to the river from April through October. More than 15,000 user-days are recorded annually in Westwater Canyon, and 7,000 in Ruby and Horsethief canyons. Commercial outfitters offer trips ranging from one to four days in length. River runners test their skill against rapids with names such as Sock-It-To-Me, Skull, Big Hummer, and Funnel Falls.

Hikers wander through a maze of twisting tributary canyons, in which perennial streams display plunge pools and waterfalls. Black Ridge Canyons includes innumerable spires and pinnacles, a concentration of natural arches surpassed only by Arches National Park, and a huge 300-foot cavern cut by a stream meander in Mee Canyon. In fact, the Black Ridge Canyons unit is under study by the National Park Service as a potential addition to Colorado National Monument.

Biotic Refuge

Species of wildlife that have been largely extirpated from native habitat elsewhere have found a home in these river canyons. Four species of threatened or endangered fish (humpback chub, Colorado River squawfish, bonytail chub, and razorback sucker) have been found in the Colorado River within the proposed wilderness. Numerous bald eagles winter along the river; this stretch includes the only pair of nesting bald eagles in Utah. Golden eagles nest at various sites within the area. Several pairs of great blue herons also nest along the river. The area is along the whooping crane's migration route. Even a rare butterfly (*Papilio indraminori*) has made its home here.

IN BRIEF

Index Map: Area No. 51

Highlights: The exciting whitewater run through Westwater Canyon contrasts with the Colorado River's gentle flow in Ruby and Horsethief canyons. These superb float trips take you past a series of sidecanyons well worth exploring. The Utah and Colorado BLM, to their credit, have recommended most of this area for wilderness.

Guidebooks: Nichols (1986)

Maps: USGS 1:100,000 Westwater, Grand Junction, Moab

Area of wilderness proposals in acres (Utah):

Unit	UWC	BLM
Black Ridge Canyons	5,100	5,100
Westwater Canyon	32,500	26,000
TOTAL	37,600	31,100

Adjacent wild lands: Colorado BLM

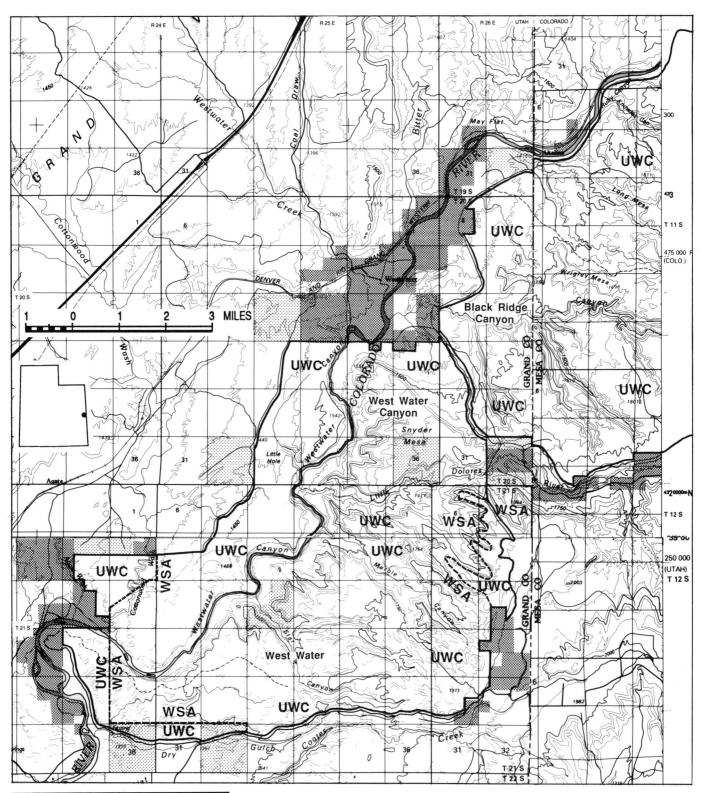

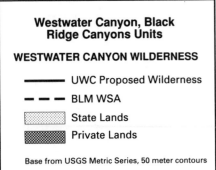

Westwater Canyon, Black Ridge Canyons Units

WESTWATER CANYON WILDERNESS

——— UWC Proposed Wilderness

– – – BLM WSA

State Lands

Private Lands

Base from USGS Metric Series, 50 meter contours

The Colorado Division of Wildlife has reintroduced desert bighorn sheep into the Black Ridge Canyons. The herd, now comprising 30-40 animals, was opened to limited hunting in 1988. Mountain lion roam the rugged recesses of the area. A large herd of elk winters on the south side of the river along the state line, which along with numerous deer draws many hunters.

The mesas and slopes of the area are covered with pinyon-juniper forest. Cottonwoods, willows, and tamarisk grow along the river and in the tributary canyons. Sagebrush, single-leaf ash, and mountain mahogany are found in drier areas, and occasional aspen grow near water sources.

Fossils and Hideouts

Several Fremont Indian rock art sites and campsites have been discovered within the area. Historic sites include the Miner's Cabin, built around 1912, a cave that was used as a hideout by two outlaws around 1913, and the grave of one of the outlaws, all in the Westwater unit. Black Ridge Canyons may hold paleontological interest, since it contains the same geologic formations that have yielded fossils in nearby Rabbit Valley.

Wild and Scenic

This is one of the few wild areas given something close to adequate recognition by the federal government. In 1975, Congress directed that this stretch of river be studied for possible inclusion in the federal Wild and Scenic Rivers System. The study, completed in 1979, recommended the entire stretch from Loma to Cisco (and beyond) for designation under the categories of Wild and Scenic. As of 1990, legislation was working its way through Congress that would designate a part of this stretch as a Wild River, but included no Scenic River designation for the remainder.

The BLM's Utah and Colorado offices have recommended most of the qualifying area for wilderness, leaving out only a few thousand acres on the periphery of Westwater Canyon. A 2,870-acre parcel in the southwest corner of the Westwater WSA was left out because of an infrequently used jeep trail; the local grazing permittee (Mountain Island Ranch) supports inclusion of the trail in the wilderness. Other areas were omitted merely because the BLM anticipated difficulty with locating boundaries—hardly an appropriate criterion. One of the deletions is well defined by a cliff face and mesa; another occurs in an area with little visitor use. Only minimal management techniques such as posting signs and constructing ORV barriers would be needed. Another parcel was not recommended because of "sights and sounds" of nearby ranching, impacts that Coalition observers believe have been exaggerated.

The Utah Wilderness Coalition Proposal

We propose 37,600 acres of wilderness in two units; an additional 68,800 acres lie in the Colorado portion of Black Ridge Canyons. The Coalition endorses the BLM's proposed wilderness boundaries and road closures for the Black Ridge and Black Ridge West WSAs in Colorado, joining the two WSAs into one unit (Utah acreage: 5,100). The adjacent 32,500-acre Westwater Canyon unit is separated from Black Ridge Canyons by a dirt road and is located entirely within Utah. Together, these units will protect the only undeveloped segment of the Colorado River under BLM jurisdiction.

Mark Pearson

The Colorado River cuts through dark Precambrian rocks in Westwater Canyon, attracting thousands of boaters each year.

Steve Howe

ARCHES-LOST SPRING CANYON WILDERNESS

Summary

Looking out to the east from the Devils Garden Campground in Arches National Park, the visitor sees a vast expanse that may appear to be a continuation of the park. Unfortunately it is not. This charming landscape with names to match—like Yellowcat Flat, Mollie Hogans, Fish Seep Draw, and Lost Spring Canyon—is BLM land. Despite a few old uranium mining tracks and a buried gas pipeline, this 16,900-acre area remains wild. Recommended by the Park Service as a complement to the adjoining park, Lost Spring Canyon was dissected during the BLM wilderness review. Split into two units during the initial inventory, it was then dropped altogether by Interior Secretary James Watt. A 3,880-acre fragment was

Lost Spring Canyon lies just east of Arches National Park and is the foreground for views from the Devils Garden area of the park (on skyline).

Clive Kincaid

reinstated to wilderness study after conservationists appealed. That tiny WSA is now recommended for wilderness by the BLM, but the remaining wild lands go unrecognized and unprotected.

The Canyon

Below the Mollie Hogans, the two high, flat-topped buttes that rise northeast of Arches National Park, Salt Wash begins to cut its way into the Entrada Sandstone. Some 14 miles downstream, passing in and out of the park, flowing past the trailhead to Delicate Arch, the wash finally enters the Colorado River amid a deep canyon. Two tributaries empty into upper Salt Wash from the east: Cottonwood Wash, a small, mostly unspoiled canyon, and the larger Lost Spring Canyon, deeply eroded into sculpted slickrock.

Surrounding the rims of these canyons are extensive plains of blackbrush—a sparse shrub that dots the desert with its evenly spaced growth, inviting the eye to the horizon. To the east, gentle grasslands rise beyond to the distant Highlands and the Dome Plateau. To the west the view rises with the rock as it climbs to the eroded spine of Devils Garden—a unique vantage on Arches National Park.

Lost Spring Canyon is eroded almost exclusively within the Slickrock Member of the Jurassic Entrada Formation, the rock unit in which the most famous of the park's arches are formed. Smoothly weathered walls, domes, and alcoves of this fine-grained rock give the area an intimate magic. Desert varnish stripes many of the cliffs with black and metallic blue tapestries. Emerald groves of cottonwood, with squawbush, desert holly, serviceberry, and other riparian species, contrast with the bare, salmon rock of the canyon.

In comparison with the adjacent national park, few people explore this area. Yet a hike up Salt Wash from the Delicate Arch trailhead and into Lost Spring Canyon, with its many coves and tributaries, can be fully as intriguing—and a lot less crowded—than hikes in the park. Covert Arch is an impressive feature within the BLM's WSA. In upper Fish Seep Draw, Behemoth Cave is worth exploring.

The Inventory

The colorful shale hills of the headwaters are dotted with old mines left over from the uranium boom of the 1950s, now crumbling slowly back into the desert. A few old dirt roads are fading away, one leading to a herder's cabin. These and other vehicle ways, seismic lines, and a buried gas pipeline were the BLM's excuse to drop most of the roadless area from wilderness study. During the initial inventory, the area was divided into two units, Lost Spring Canyon and Dome Plateau, the boundary following a thin wisp of a grassy way down Winter Camp Ridge, barely a mile from Delicate Arch.

The pinyon- and juniper-covered Dome Plateau reaches over 5,800 feet in elevation. Its edge forms sheer, 1,500-foot-high Wingate Sandstone cliffs that frame the Colorado River for more than 20 miles. Part of the plateau had originally been in Arches National Monument but was dropped when it became a National Park. The BLM also chose to drop this 20,000-acre area, citing intrusions that made up less than 12 percent of its area.

The agency then began to reduce and divide the smaller Lost Spring inventory unit, splitting it down the middle and then paring away its natural boundaries along section lines. Seismic lines, ranching operations, vehicle ways and drill holes were used to dissolve more of the unit. Many of the intrusions were so old or benign that they could not be located on

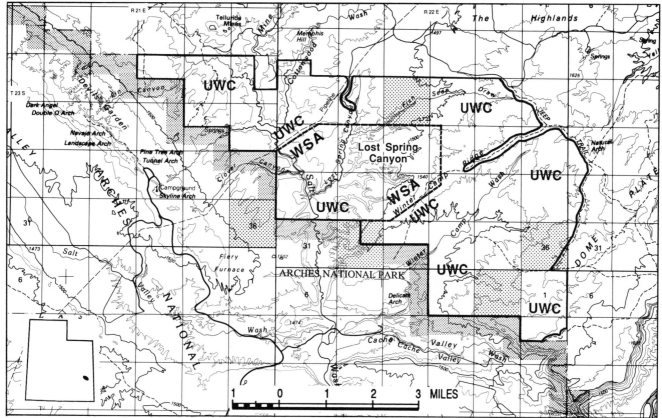

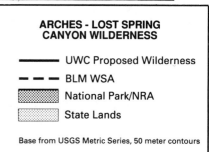

**ARCHES - LOST SPRING
CANYON WILDERNESS**

———— UWC Proposed Wilderness

– – – BLM WSA

▓▓▓ National Park/NRA

░░░ State Lands

Base from USGS Metric Series, 50 meter contours

the ground. Years of illegal motorcycle use down the gas pipeline road and into the park led the BLM to eliminate this part of the study area.

Aiding the inventory cuts was the BLM's definition of "solitude," which relied on topographic and vegetative screening. This little-visited, remote area looks out on miles and miles of open desert from the canyon rims—the definition of solitude. But the BLM concluded that "The configuration of the [northern] unit, even when considered in conjunction with the adjacent Arches N.P. wilderness proposal, is also not conducive to opportunities for solitude."

In a last insult, Interior Secretary James Watt dropped the 3,880 acres that remained in a move to excise all areas of less than 5,000 acres from wilderness study. Only a conservationist appeal reinstated the WSA.

Complement to the Park

During these years the Park Service expressed interest in the area as a complement to its 18,000-acre Devils Garden park wilderness proposal, located opposite Lost Spring Canyon and sharing the same Salt Wash watershed. The Park Service advised the BLM that " . . . portions of North Lost Spring Canyon offer outstanding opportunities for prime recreation and solitude when taken in conjunction with the park wilderness proposal. . . " As late as October, 1982, the Park Service stated, " . . . we are disappointed to see that [Lost Spring Canyon WSA] . . .is not recommended for wilderness . . . . The NPS continues to believe that a holistic approach can be made in many instances to integrate WSAs into other land use plans." The BLM never officially responded.

The Utah Wilderness Coalition Proposal

The 16,900 acres we propose for wilderness are undeveloped and under-recognized as a place worth exploring. Our proposal includes the upper part of a vehicle track across a sandy grassland on Winter Camp Ridge that is little used and is not maintained; the lower part is cherrystemmed. The gas pipeline that traverses the unit could be maintained from the existing right-of-way and closed to other vehicle use.

Lost Spring Canyon could be easily overlooked, as Secretary Watt would have preferred. Or it could be recognized and protected as a designated wilderness and as a potential addition to Arches National Park. Its remoteness, solitude, and integrity deserve no less.

Michael Salamacha

THE LABYRINTH CANYON WILDERNESS

Summary

Twenty miles south of the Interstate 70 bridge, the Green River sinks gently into the land, winding for 50 miles through a series of "bowknot" curves before entering Canyonlands National Park. This is Labyrinth Canyon, one of the last great wild rivers of the West, and an integral part of a 700,000-acre roadless region that includes Canyonlands.

Labyrinth Canyon's geological and archeological wonders are internationally recognized, and its recreational assets are extolled in a half-dozen guidebooks. The BLM's own planning documents emphasize the area's scenic and primitive character. Yet the BLM recommended wilderness designation *west of the river only*, cutting the canyon in two and leaving more than half of the Labyrinth Canyon wilderness open to roadbuilding, mineral exploration, hydropower development, and indiscriminate off-road vehicle use.

By contrast, the Utah Wilderness Coalition's 171,700-acre Labyrinth Canyon wilderness proposal would protect the entire canyon system, while excluding all significant human impacts.

Wild River Corridor

"There is an exquisite charm in our ride today down this beautiful canyon. It gradually grows deeper with every mile of travel; the walls are symmetrically curved and grandly arched, of a beautiful color, and reflected in the quiet waters . . . . We are all in fine spirits and feel very gay, and the badinage of the men is echoed from wall to wall."

Thus wrote John Wesley Powell, recalling his voyage of discovery through Labyrinth Canyon in 1869. For Powell, as for every river runner who has followed, the soaring sandstone walls, mirror-smooth water, and radiant gold light of Labyrinth Canyon have been irresistible.

Unique among Utah's wild rivers, the Green River through Labyrinth Canyon offers nearly 50 miles of smooth water unbroken by rapids or falls. It is a river runner's paradise. Guidebooks describe it in superlatives:

" . . . one of the finest river canyons I have floated in my twenty years of running rivers . . . calm and peaceful, a scenic wonder without parallel." (Verne Huser, *Canyon Country Paddles*)

" . . . the finest beginning canoe-camping trip in the state" (Gary Nichols, *River Runner's Guide to Utah*).

In 1974, an estimated 4,000 river runners boated the canyon, and according to the BLM, floatboating in Labyrinth has tripled since 1980.

Labyrinth Canyon is the last vestige of what Glen Canyon had once been—an elegant display of the power of a wild river cutting through the Navajo Sandstone, creating a textbook example of an entrenched meander. At Bowknot Bend, for instance, the Green River makes a nearly complete loop 7.5 miles long, doubling back to within just 1200 feet of itself. Throughout Labyrinth, the canyon walls are riddled with alcoves and caves. Stupendous natural bridges cling to the rim. A previously unreported double bridge was discovered in Labyrinth Canyon in 1986.

IN BRIEF

Index Map: Area No. 53

Highlights: The Green River offers a classic flatwater wilderness canoe trip from Trin-Alcove Bend to Mineral Bottom and on into Canyonlands National Park. Quiet water and hikes up numerous sidecanyons make Labyrinth a family favorite.

Guidebooks: Nichols (1986), Kelsey (1986, 1987a), Barnes (1977)

Maps: USGS 1:100,000 San Rafael Desert, Moab, Hanksville, La Sal

Area of wilderness proposals in acres:

Unit	UWC	BLM
Labyrinth Canyon	120,000	20,500
Upper Horseshoe Canyon	51,700	36,000
TOTAL	171,700	56,500

Adjacent wild lands: Canyonlands National Park; Glen Canyon National Recreation Area

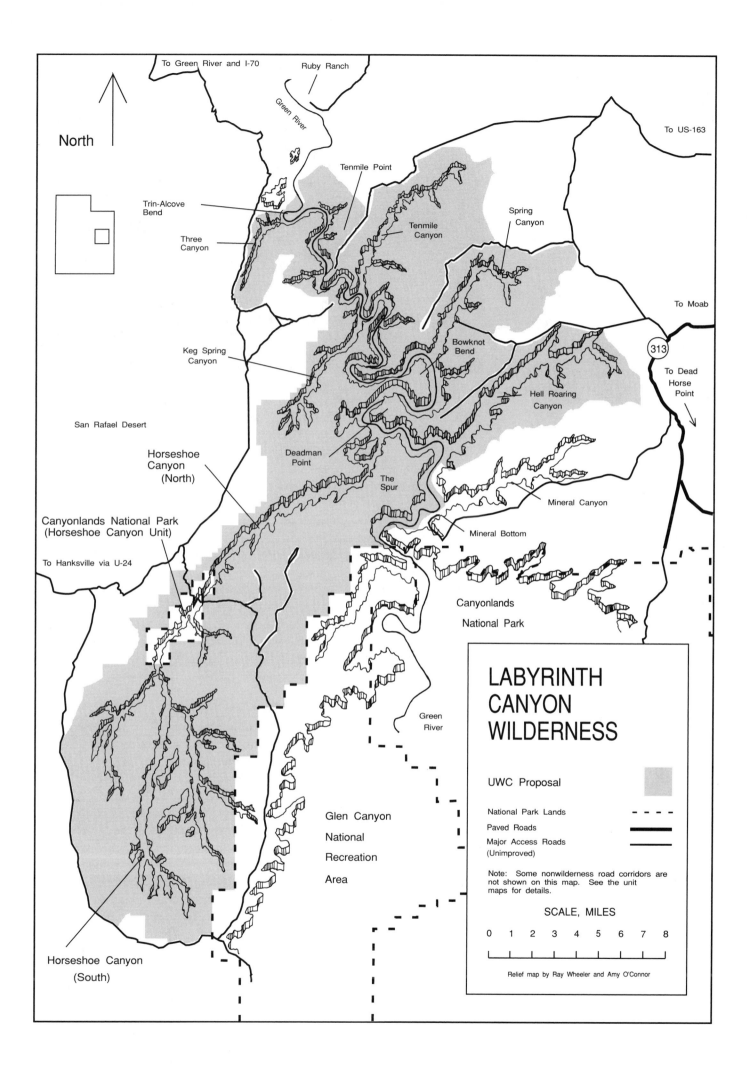

North

To Green River and I-70
Ruby Ranch
To US-163

Green River

Tenmile Point

Trin-Alcove
Bend

Three
Canyon

Spring
Canyon

Tenmile
Canyon

To Moab

313

Keg Spring
Canyon

Bowknot
Bend

To Dead
Horse
Point

San Rafael Desert

Hell Roaring
Canyon

Horseshoe
Canyon
(North)

Deadman
Point

The
Spur

Mineral Canyon

Canyonlands National Park
(Horseshoe Canyon Unit)

Mineral Bottom

To Hanksville via U-24

Canyonlands

National Park

Green
River

Glen Canyon

National

Recreation

Area

Horseshoe Canyon
(South)

LABYRINTH CANYON WILDERNESS

UWC Proposal

National Park Lands

Paved Roads

Major Access Roads
(Unimproved)

Note: Some nonwilderness road corridors are
not shown on this map. See the unit
maps for details.

SCALE, MILES

0   1   2   3   4   5   6   7   8

Relief map by Ray Wheeler and Amy O'Connor

About six miles below noon camp we go around a great bend to the right, five miles in length, and come back to a point within a quarter of a mile of where we started. Then we sweep around another great bend to the left, making a circuit of nine miles, and come back to a point within 600 feet of the beginning of the bend. In the two circuits we describe almost the figure 8. The men call it a 'bowknot' of a river; so we name it Bowknot Bend.

John Wesley Powell

CANYONS OF THE COLORADO (1895)

Like its geology, the biological and cultural resources of the Labyrinth wilderness are rich and diverse. Deer graze among tamarisk and willow along the river. Beaver glide across lagoons at the mouths of sidecanyons. A dozen species of fish, including the endangered Colorado squawfish, bonytail chub, and humpback chub, live in the river. Coyote, bobcat, fox, and desert bighorn sheep roam the sidecanyons and benchlands. Hawks, vultures, and golden eagles share the updrafts with recently reintroduced peregrine falcons. Pronghorn antelope graze among the dunes and slickrock domes along the canyon's rims.

Deep in Horseshoe Canyon, a 35-mile-long sidecanyon, lies the Great Gallery, one of the finest museums of prehistoric rock art in the American Southwest. A 2,500-acre unit of Canyonlands National Park protects the site, but the rest of the canyon, including less well known pictograph panels, remains unprotected. Elsewhere in the Labyrinth Canyon system archeologists have discovered human artifacts nearly 9,000 years old. Among and below the human artifacts they found the dung of mammoth, bison, camel, sloth, and an extinct species of horse.

The BLM's Fractured Wilderness Proposal

One might expect that the BLM would seek full wilderness protection for such an outstanding area as Labyrinth Canyon. But the BLM's wilderness proposal is actually a blueprint for development.

In 1979, during the early stages of its wilderness inventory, the BLM drew a roadless area boundary right up the bottom of Labyrinth Canyon. Since the Green River in Labyrinth is navigable to motorboats, the BLM concluded that it was owned up to the high-water mark by the State of Utah. Thus the Labyrinth wilderness was bisected, in the BLM's view, by a corridor of non-federal land. *West* of the river, the BLM identified two wilderness study areas (WSAs) spanning the length of Horseshoe Canyon, both of which it is now recommending for wilderness designation. *East* of the river, the agency further fragmented the area into three separate units, and immediately dropped all three units from its wilderness review.

Ironically, the BLM had earlier earmarked more than 14,000 acres in Tenmile and Hellroaring canyons—both east of the river—as potential primitive areas. " . . . Hellroaring and Tenmile are both still in a pristine status," one staff report concluded. "This, along with their natural ruggedness and beauty warrants consideration of the primitive area designation." The BLM created a "scenic river corridor" in 1977 to prevent oil and gas exploration within Labyrinth Canyon, and in 1979 it proposed the Green River in Labyrinth as a candidate for Wild and Scenic River designation.

The BLM's subsequent rationale for eliminating more than 30,000 acres of wild lands from its wilderness recommendation is far from convincing. "Opportunities for solitude and primitive recreation are probably present," explains the wilderness inventory evaluation sheet for the roadless area surrounding Tenmile Canyon, "however, the topography is typical of . . . the general area. Because the topography is typical, opportunities . . . are seen as average and not outstanding." Earlier BLM staff reports had reached precisely the opposite conclusion: "While there are other canyons of a similar nature in the general area, Tenmile is unique in that it still remains in an undisturbed condition."

Elsewhere along the east bank, the BLM claimed that the canyon had lost its naturalness as a result of uranium mining. During the past 40 years developers have riddled some of the benchlands near Labyrinth with vehicle ways and seismic lines, searching for oil, uranium, and potash deposits which they never seem to find. And during the 1950s, uranium prospectors pushed a jeep trail to the mouth of Spring Canyon and nine miles upstream along the east side of Labyrinth Canyon to a mining camp at the mouth of Hey Joe Canyon.

These mining relics have now been abandoned for a quarter of a century, and while some of them are still visible, they are insignificant in comparison to the vast canyon system surrounding them. In high water, portions of the trail to Hey Joe Canyon have been inundated by the Green River, and in places it has been covered by rock slides. It has never been maintained, and its eventual obliteration is inevitable.

Moreover, the BLM has included identical mining impacts within its Horseshoe Canyon WSA directly across the river, stating that they do not affect the outstanding wilderness character of the canyon. "Natural processes are slowly reclaiming the road cuts," concludes the DEIS. "The imprints are localized and do not detract from the WSA's natural character."

Held Open For Mining Exploration

If the east side of Labyrinth Canyon is just as rugged and primitive as the west side, and if the old mining remnants do not detract from its natural character, why has the BLM eliminated the entire east half of the canyon from its wilderness recommendations?

Behind the official rationale about "less than outstanding" wilderness values, there lies a more plausible explanation: during the wilderness inventory of 1979, BLM lands on the eastern perimeter of Labyrinth Canyon were intensively explored for potash and uranium. In 1977, the BLM had approved a proposal by Buttes Oil and Gas to develop a giant potash solution mining plant just east of the canyon. Wilderness studies would have restricted exploration for uranium and potash.

But even as Buttes began drilling its first exploratory wells in 1978, the market for domestic potash was collapsing. By 1986, Moab's nearby Texasgulf potash plant had laid off 375 of its 400 workers, and Buttes had mothballed the project near Labyrinth Canyon. Meanwhile, the price of uranium fell through the floor, forcing the closure of uranium mills throughout the southwest—including the Atlas uranium mill in Moab.

The BLM's analysis of the mineral potential of its Horseshoe Canyon WSAs demonstrates that the economic value of development in Labyrinth Canyon is negligible; years of exploration have yet to discover an economically developable resource. Even by the agency's own estimates, any

If the east side of Labyrinth Canyon is just as rugged and primitive as the west side, and if the old mining remnants do not detract from its natural character, why has the BLM eliminated the entire east half of the canyon from its wilderness recommendations?

deposits would be small. In the Horseshoe Canyon (South) WSA, "the likelihood for production of oil from tar sand is thought to be minimal;" the WSA "has low potential for . . . oil and gas;" there are "no known commercial deposits of locatable minerals," and "no known deposits of leasable minerals." As in the Horseshoe Canyon (North) WSA, oil and gas exploration has been uniformly unsuccessful, and "the extremely rugged surface in the majority of the WSA could make drilling uneconomical." As for potash: "the likelihood of this area being a target for exploration and possible development is very remote . . . . " The WSA is "considered geologically unfavorable for coal;" manganese deposits "are chiefly small and low grade," and copper deposits "would probably be small." In 25 years of uranium exploration and mining, three historic uranium mines in the WSA have produced "less than 100 tons of uranium ore," and "all surface deposits probably have been discovered."

Of all the development proposals for Labyrinth Canyon, perhaps the most questionable is one for a hydroelectric dam. Studies have identified two potential damsites which would flood Labyrinth Canyon, destroying yet another magnificent wild river to generate only 165 megawatts of power.

The Utah Wilderness Coalition Proposal

In Labyrinth Canyon, the choices for the future are clear. The BLM recommendation would leave the entire river corridor and the east half of the canyon open for development, as well as much of the west half. Future mineral exploration could scar Labyrinth and its magnificent sidecanyons—and still produce little or nothing of significance.

The Utah Wilderness Coalition seeks to preserve the wilderness character of the entire canyon system. We recommend wilderness designation for 171,700 acres in two units, Upper Horseshoe Canyon and Labyrinth Canyon. These units incorporate the following key areas omitted from the BLM's recommendation: Three Canyon, Tenmile Canyon, Hellroaring Canyon, Spring Canyon, and The Spur.

Ray Wheeler

LABYRINTH CANYON UNIT

Highlights—Labyrinth Canyon and its spectacular sidecanyons, arrayed along 46 miles of the Green River from Trin-Alcove Bend to Canyonlands National Park, dominate this 120,000-acre unit of the Labyrinth wilderness. Preserving this northernmost component of the wild Canyonlands region would ensure that the magnificent 120-mile wilderness float trip from below the town of Green River to the confluence with the Colorado River would remain peaceful and uncluttered by the artifacts of civilization. The unit joins the Upper Horseshoe Canyon unit at the detached part of Canyonlands National Park.

Geology and landforms—River runners enjoy the sight of Navajo Sandstone cliffs gradually rising out of the flat-lying desert as they float down the smooth waters of the Green. By Trin-Alcove Bend, the cliffs are an imposing barrier to overland travel. Additional access points are found at Tenmile, Spring, Hellroaring, and Horseshoe canyons. Above the canyons, rolling benchlands culminate in dramatic overlooks of the river. By the time the river reaches Mineral Bottom and Canyonlands National Park, the cliffs of the Wingate Sandstone are exposed high above.

Plant communities—The BLM identified 2,400 acres of relict plant communities on isolated, inaccessible mesas at Bowknot Bend and Horseshoe Bend. The unit also includes riparian, desert shrub, and grassland vegetation types. An endangered primrose (*Oenothera megalantha*) may occur in the unit. Prince's plume thrives in Spring Canyon, and cottonwood, sage, and Gambel oak grow in many of the lower sidecanyons.

Wildlife—Riparian areas along the Green River and major sidecanyons provide diverse habitat for many species of fish, waterfowl, reptiles, and mammals (see area overview). Desert bighorn sheep have been seen on the east side of the river and may have entered the west side of the unit from adjacent park land. Pronghorn and mule deer also live in the unit yearlong. The endangered Colorado squawfish is found in the Green River; the bonytail chub and humpback chub (also endangered species) may occur. Peregrine falcon and bald eagle may use the unit; the BLM identified potential peregrine falcon habitat in its Horseshoe Canyon (North) WSA and bald eagle habitat along the Green River. (The falcons were recently reintroduced to the unit.) The Fish and Wildlife Service indicates that the unit may be potential habitat for three candidate endangered species: ferruginous hawk, razorback sucker, and white-faced ibis.

Archeology and history—Early river explorers left inscriptions at Bowknot Bend and at several other locations along the Green River. The BLM notes several prehistoric sites, thought to be Anasazi, within its WSA and suggests that more sites may exist outside the WSA.

Recreation—An estimated 10,000 people enjoyed trips to the Labyrinth Canyon in 1982, and use (particularly by boaters) is increasing. In 1982, the National Park Service included this stretch of the Green River in its inventory of rivers eligible for Wild and Scenic designation. The river gives easy access to the lower parts of Labyrinth's sidecanyons, which offer good hikes. Most of these sidecanyons, notably Horseshoe and Tenmile, are also accessible from two-wheel-drive or jeep roads in their upper portions. Hiking the rim of Labyrinth Canyon provides dramatic views of cliffs, pinnacles, river bends (especially the famous Bowknot Bend), and a 60-foot natural bridge (Barnes, 1977).

BLM recommendation—More than three-fourths of the wild lands making up the Labyrinth Canyon unit were excluded from wilderness study by the BLM. What is left is a tiny 20,500-acre WSA (Horseshoe Canyon North) that takes in some of the wild lands to the west of the river. The BLM alleged that the lands it dropped were not natural—but the jeep trails and mining exploration scars are insignificant intrusions into an essentially wild landscape. Within the WSA, the BLM identified two seldom-traveled ways, three short livestock trails, three developed springs, one water pipeline, a mining trail, portals, tunnels, and several pieces of

At 2:05 p.m. we entered Labyrinth Canyon. This masterpiece of nature is well named. The river twists and turns sinuously. Red sandstone walls rising two hundred to four hundred feet surrounded us and hemmed in the river—what a quick change from open country into a canyon—but the water remained quiet and smooth.

Barry Goldwater
"DELIGHTFUL JOURNEY DOWN THE GREEN AND COLORADO RIVERS" (1940)

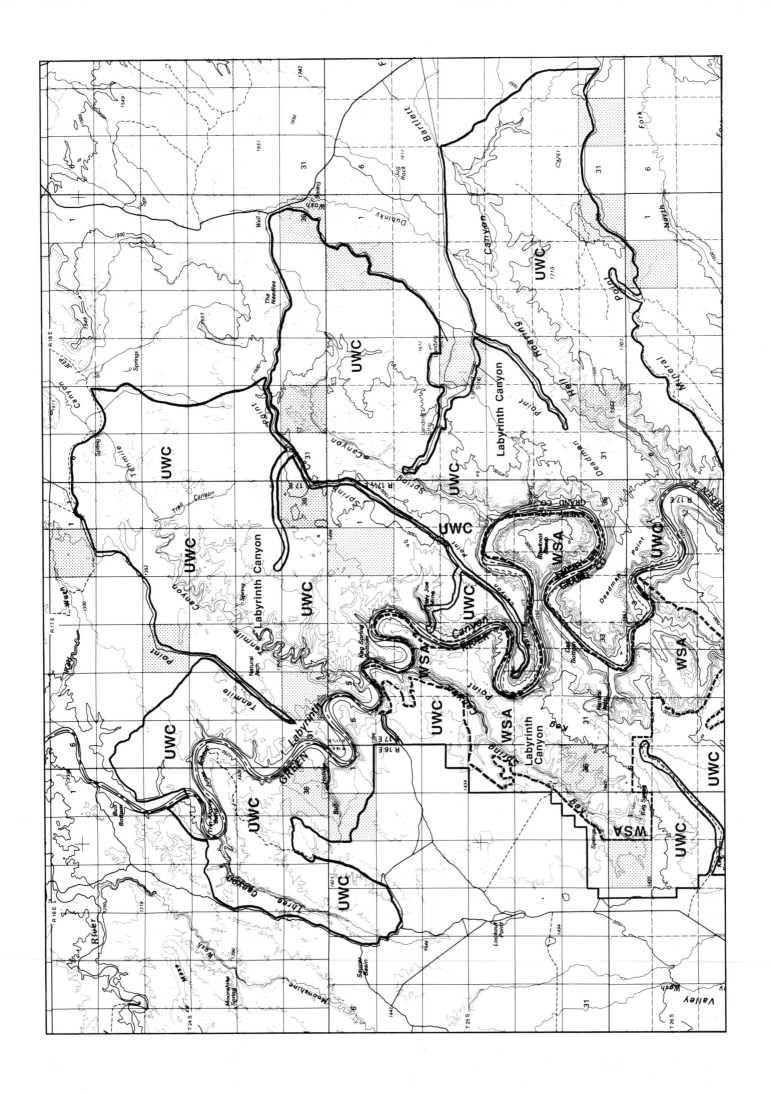

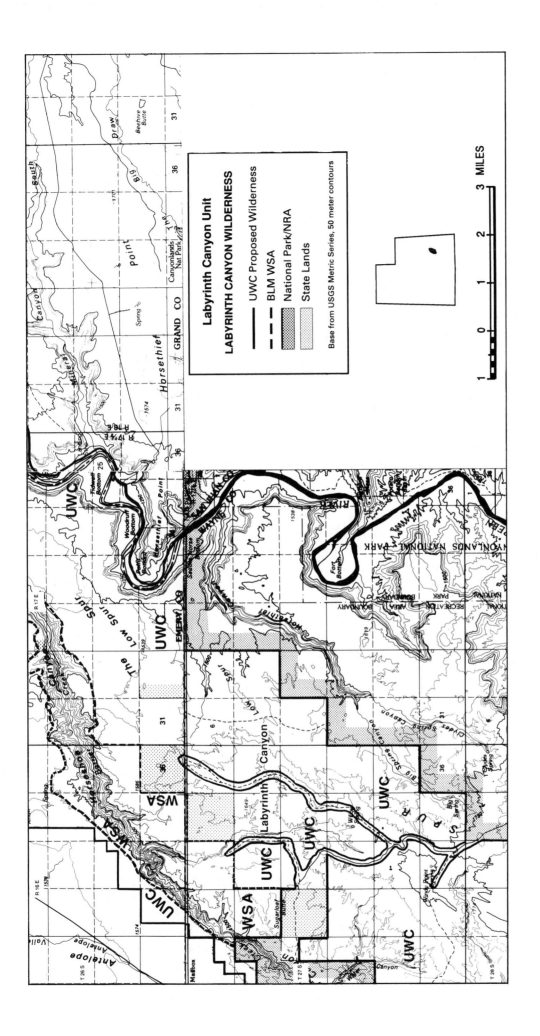

Labyrinth Canyon Unit

LABYRINTH CANYON WILDERNESS

UWC Proposed Wilderness
BLM WSA
National Park/NRA
State Lands

Base from USGS Metric Series, 50 meter contours

1   0   1   2   3
                              MILES

equipment. Intrusions outside the WSA are similar and should be included.

Coalition proposal—Our proposal takes in 120,000 acres of wild, undeveloped lands, skirting the significant impacts without dropping whole drainages (and the entire east bank of the river) as the BLM has done. Our boundary excludes cherrystemmed ORV routes at Tenmile Point, Spring Canyon Point, Deadman Point, Mineral Point, Mineral Canyon, and The Spur. The Spring Canyon trail to the mouth of Hey Joe Canyon is rapidly eroding and is impassable to all but the most determined four-wheelers. It should be closed at the south rim of Spring Canyon and allowed to be reclaimed by nature. The mining camp in Hey Joe Canyon is cherrystemmed from our proposal along the abandoned cable system that was used to supply it from the south rim of Hey Joe Canyon. The abandoned mining operations at Bowknot Bend, a minor intrusion, are included in both the BLM's and Coalition's proposals.

UPPER HORSESHOE CANYON UNIT

Highlights—The upper forks of Horseshoe Canyon gather in this 51,700-acre unit of our proposed Labyrinth Canyon wilderness. The unit borders Canyonlands National Park at the Horseshoe Canyon detached unit of the park. The Glen Canyon National Recreation Area forms the eastern boundary of the unit. Thus Horseshoe, like the Labyrinth Canyon unit to the north, is a significant part of a much larger wild region despite the political subdivisions.

Geology and landforms—Horseshoe is Labyrinth's largest sidecanyon, stretching 35 miles north from Hans Flat to the Green River. It cuts into the Navajo and Wingate sandstones, forming a deep gash in the surrounding benchlands. The grassy parks which separate the canyons feature views to the La Sal Mountains and the Book Cliffs. Tributary canyons to Horseshoe are less deep but offer remoteness and solitude.

Plant communities—Pinyon-juniper, desert grass, and blackbrush grow on the benchlands. This grassland vegetative community would add significantly to the diversity of the wilderness system.

Wildlife—Mule deer, antelope, fox, coyote, and badger live in the unit. The UDWR introduced desert bighorn sheep onto the nearby Orange Cliffs in 1982; the unit contains habitat for this species. Bell's vireo and golden eagle may occasionally be seen in the unit.

Archeology and history—The unique "Barrier Canyon" style of prehistoric rock art is largely confined to this unit and to the adjacent detached part of Canyonlands National Park. (One of the outstanding panels in the park unit was recently vandalized, demonstrating the importance of limiting vehicle access to this area.) Cowboy Cave contains some of the richest and oldest paleontological remains in the state. Scientific studies of this site have yielded important new data about large prehistoric mammals on the Colorado Plateau.

Recreation—A 35-mile hike down the length of the Horseshoe Canyon system begins at Hans Flat and ends at the Green River in our proposed Labyrinth unit. Many miles of sidecanyons can also be explored in Spur Fork, Moqui Fork, and Bluejohn Canyon. A two-wheel-drive road from Utah Highway 24 leading to Hans Flat at the Maze entrance to Canyonlands National Park gives access into the upper forks of Horseshoe Canyon. Routes begin at the Twin Corral Flats airstrip, Hans Flat, and the Head Spur. A trailhead located about six miles off of the Hans Flat road gives access to Horseshoe Canyon via the detached part of Canyonlands National Park. See also Kelsey (1986a, 1987a) and Barnes (1977).

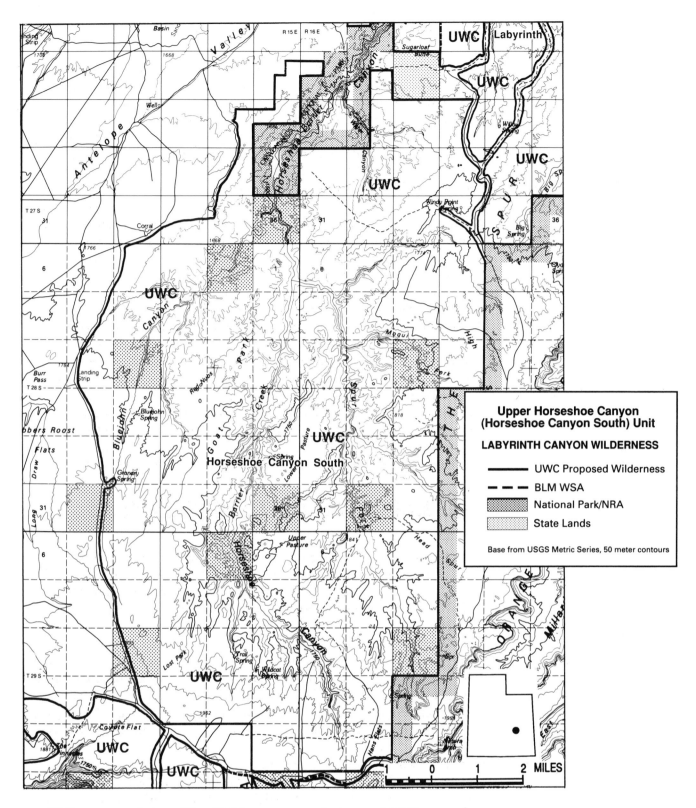

Upper Horseshoe Canyon
(Horseshoe Canyon South) Unit

LABYRINTH CANYON WILDERNESS

—————— UWC Proposed Wilderness

— — — — BLM WSA

▓▓▓▓ National Park/NRA

░░░░ State Lands

Base from USGS Metric Series, 50 meter contours

BLM recommendation—The BLM proposes to designate 36,000 acres of its 38,800-acre Horseshoe Canyon South WSA as wilderness. The agency claims that the 2,800 acres deleted from its recommendation, and 13,200 acres excluded from the WSA, have low wilderness values, lack topographic and vegetative screening, and are not natural. The BLM's exclusion of the northern fingers of the WSA on either side of a state section would allow for a new road or other development to separate this unit from the national park land to the north of the state section. The BLM identified a handful of "substantially unnoticeable" intrusions in its WSA: two miles of fence, three corrals, one reservoir, two drill sites, some improved springs, and 23 miles of ways in various stages of natural rehabilitation.

Coalition proposal—Our 51,700-acre proposed wilderness unit includes wild lands that the BLM needlessly excluded from its wilderness recommendation. These lands are important antelope and deer habitat; they were excluded by the BLM after it claimed (contrary to its wilderness study policy) that there was insufficient topographic and vegetative screening to permit solitude. The BLM also claimed that adjacent roads and corrals detract from solitude in this area. But the sense of solitude here is as great as in the area that the BLM recommends for wilderness. Our boundary cherrystems a road less than a mile long to Windy Point Spring on the northeast boundary and a road one-tenth of a mile long to Granary Spring on the west boundary. Outside the WSA, but within our proposal, is a two-mile-long jeep track across blown sand and grasslands on the Head Spur with no evidence of construction or maintenance, a three-mile-long vehicle way on the High Spur, and a 3.5-mile-long jeep track extending from the Windy Point Spring cherrystem to Water Canyon near the Canyonlands National Park boundary. These intrusions do not significantly detract from the naturalness of the area, and should be included in the wilderness. An old vehicle track beginning south of Granary Spring and leading northeast to the Red Nubs was illegally graded by a Wayne County road crew in the spring of 1990; this way was not maintained and had been receiving little use. The BLM acted quickly to halt the intrusion and required the county to revegetate the route. The route should be included in the wilderness in order to preserve the unit's wild interior and limit vehicle access to the pictograph panels in Horseshoe Canyon.

THE SAN RAFAEL SWELL WILDERNESS

Summary

Between the towns of Salina and Green River, Interstate 70 cuts through a great dome of uplifted sedimentary rock called the San Rafael Swell. Fifty miles long and thirty miles wide, the Swell rises 1,500 feet above the surrounding desert, forming one of the scenic and geological wonders of the world.

The San Rafael Swell is a world of jagged cliff faces, narrow slot canyons, and hidden valleys littered with domes and towers. Its landscape is an encyclopedia of earth history, displaying diverse exposed rock formations and erosional forms. It is a popular destination for hikers, climbers, and river runners. But the scenic beauty and historic solitude of the Swell is increasingly threatened by mineral exploration and indiscriminate off-road vehicle use.

Proposals for legislation to protect the San Rafael Swell have been made repeatedly during the past 50 years, culminating with recent proposals for a San Rafael National Park. Yet faced with a clear choice between protection and development, the BLM has zoned for development throughout the interior of the San Rafael Swell, refusing even to study the wilderness character of half a million acres of wild lands.

The Utah Wilderness Coalition's 752,900-acre wilderness proposal would safeguard the region now and complement any additional protections that may be afforded through National Park designation.

Geology Exposed

The San Rafael Swell is a microcosm of the entire Colorado Plateau: a huge basin ringed by highlands, studded with mesas and buttes, traversed by powerful, sediment-laden desert streams, and crisscrossed by canyon systems. Because uplift and erosion have been greater in the interior, the oldest rock formations are exposed in the core of the Swell, surrounded by concentric rings of younger rocks which radiate outward like waves in a pond.

Each rock formation has created its own unique world. In the heart of the Swell, two perennial streams have bored deeply into the rising land, revealing one of the oldest rock layers exposed in the region—the 250 million-year-old Coconino Sandstone. So narrow are these canyons, called "The Chute" and "The Black Box," that flood debris hangs from their walls 30 to 50 feet above the canyon floor.

Above the Coconino lies the Kaibab Limestone, a resistant layer which forms the broad floor of Mexican Bend, the hidden valley where the outlaw Butch Cassidy once left two posses eating his dust. Above the Kaibab lie the red beds of the Moenkopi and Chinle formations, forming the intricate, spired redrock mazes of Red Canyon, Penitentiary Canyon, and Keesle Country. Above the Chinle rise the petrified sand dunes of the Wingate, Kayenta, and Navajo formations. Smooth, hard, elegantly sculptured masses of bare rock, these formations form the great outer wall of the San Rafael Reef and the huge, monolithic buttes and towers in the interior of the Swell.

The rock formations collectively named the San Rafael Group lie for the most part outside the Swell. They include the colorful Entrada Sandstone, which forms the brilliant orange cliffs and towers of Cathedral Valley, Salt Wash, and the Red Desert, and the famous hoodoos of Goblin Valley, just south of the Swell. Higher still lie the psychedelic badlands of the Morrison Formation, an intricate "painted desert" littered with agate, chert, barite, celestite, geodes, gastroliths, dinosaur bones, and glittering shards of gypsum. South and west of the Swell, dark volcanic mountains loom over the badlands, radiating knife-sharp dikes, or fins, of jet-black basalt. And above all this, forming a sea of blue-grey hills to the south and east of the Swell, lies the Mancos Shale, at 65 to 100 million years the youngest rock in the region.

Habitat for Wildlife and Adventurers

This varied terrain supports an exceptional variety of wildlife. In recent years, the Utah Department of Wildlife Resources (UDWR) has established a population of more than 70 bighorn sheep in the Swell. The UDWR estimates the total carrying capacity of the Sids and Mexican Mountain WSAs alone at nearly 2,000 sheep. More than 300 antelope occupy the desert east of the Swell, occasionally venturing into its interior (BLM, 1986). In the jagged cliffs ringing Mexican Mountain, the UDWR has identified more than 11,000 acres of critical peregrine falcon habitat.

Not surprisingly, the San Rafael Swell also provides critical habitat for climbers, hikers, and boaters. Just three hours' drive south of Salt Lake City, the Swell is the nearest and most accessible part of southern Utah's canyon country for residents of the Wasatch Front. Its attractions are featured in at least six different guidebooks. Since 1986, Utah publishers have released three new books about the Swell, one of which describes more than 300 miles of hiking routes inside Utah Wilderness Coalition-proposed wilderness. By the turn of the century, according to BLM estimates, nonmotorized recreation in the Swell could increase to more than 10 times its current level.

Wilderness Recognized 50 Years Ago

Before 1970, the country surrounding the Swell was one of the most remote regions of the West, a 1.8-million-acre block of rugged and deso-

IN BRIEF

Index Map: Area No. 54

Highlights: Sawtoothed cliffs, slot canyons, and upland valleys make the "Swell" a scenic, geological, and recreational wonder. The BLM would designate wilderness only on its perimeter, leaving the interior open to indiscriminate off-road vehicle use and mineral exploration.

Guidebooks: Bauman (1987), Hall (1982), Kelsey (1986a,b), McClenahan (1986), Nichols (1986)

Maps: USGS 1:100,000 Huntington, Salina, San Rafael Desert, Loa, Hanksville

Area of wilderness proposals in acres:

Unit	UWC	BLM
Cedar Mountain	14,500	0
Devils Canyon	21,500	0
Hondu Country	18,900	0
Jones Bench	2,800	0
Limestone Cliffs	21,300	0
Mexican Mountain	102,600	46,750
Muddy Creek	246,300	56,735
Mussentuchit Badlands	23,000	0
Red Desert	36,800	0
San Rafael Reef	95,000	59,170
Sids Mountain	95,800	80,084
Upper Muddy Creek	17,000	0
Wild Horse Mesa	57,400	0
TOTAL	752,900	242,739

Adjacent wild land: Manti-La Sal National Forest; Capitol Reef National Park

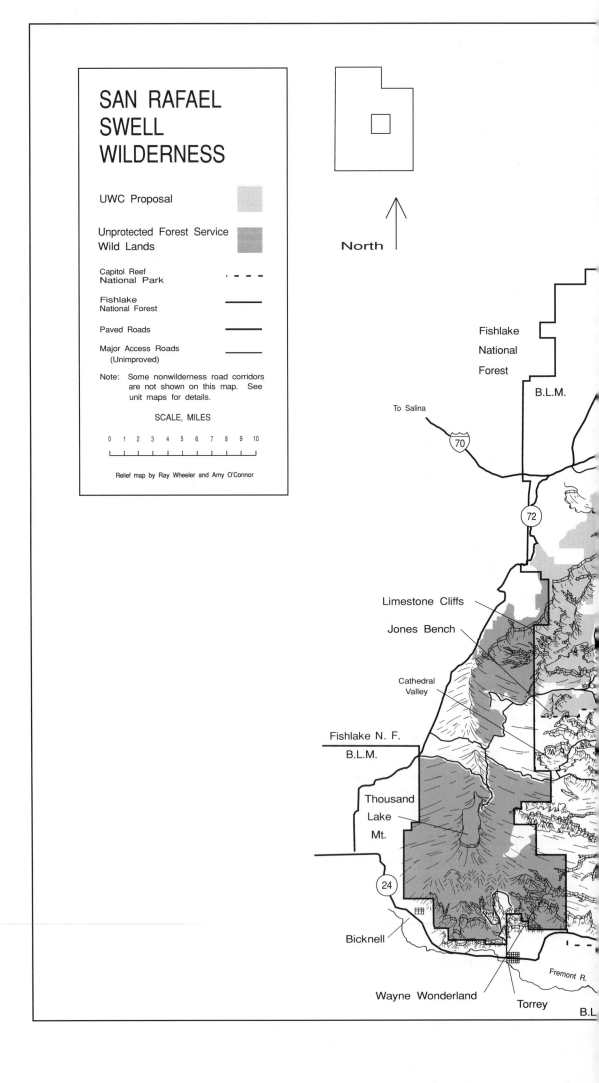

SAN RAFAEL
SWELL
WILDERNESS

UWC Proposal

Unprotected Forest Service
Wild Lands

Capitol Reef
National Park

Fishlake
National Forest

Paved Roads

Major Access Roads
(Unimproved)

Note: Some nonwilderness road corridors
are not shown on this map. See
unit maps for details.

SCALE, MILES

0 1 2 3 4 5 6 7 8 9 10

Relief map by Ray Wheeler and Amy O'Connor

North

Fishlake

National

Forest

B.L.M.

To Salina

70

72

Limestone Cliffs

Jones Bench

Cathedral
Valley

Fishlake N. F.

B.L.M.

Thousand

Lake

Mt.

24

Bicknell

Wayne Wonderland

Fremont R.

Torrey

B.L.

10

Sids Mountain

San Rafael
River

The Wedge

Buckhorn
Wash

Mexican
Mountain

Coal Wash

Eagle
Canyon

To Green
River

70

San Rafael
River

Upper
Muddy Creek

Devil's
Canyon

Eardly
Wash

The Dike

Hondu Country

San
Rafael
Reef

Cedar
Mt.

Muddy Creek
(The Chute)

Segers
Hole

Goblin
Valley
State
Park

24

sentuchit
lands

Slopes

Maroni

Wild Horse Mesa

Black
Mt.

Salt Wash

Muddy Creek

Factory
Butte

Dirty Devil River

Red
Desert

Skyline Rim

Fremont R.

Hanksville

95

North Caineville
Mesa

To Lake Powell

Capitol Reef
National Park

B.L.M.

late landscape reaching west to the forested ramparts of the Wasatch Plateau, and south into Capitol Reef National Park. But in 1970, with the completion of Interstate 70, access was improved and visitation dramatically increased, bringing a host of new development threats into the heart of the Swell. Mineral exploration accelerated during the late 1970s, and by 1982 off-road vehicle abuse had become a serious problem.

Recognizing the danger of such threats, Utahns and conservationists around the nation have repeatedly called for legislation to protect the San Rafael Swell. At least a dozen such proposals have been made in the past 50 years. The first proposal for a new national park in the vicinity came in 1935, when the Utah State Planning Board proposed a 360,000-acre "Wayne Wonderland" national park. In 1936, Wilderness Society founder Bob Marshall identified a roadless area of nearly 2 million acres in the San Rafael Swell—one of the 10 largest desert roadless areas in the nation. Between 1967 and 1973, a stream of BLM planning documents identified well over 250,000 acres of lands qualifying for primitive or natural area designation, and a 1972 study by Utah State University recommended primitive area designation for 307,000 acres (Dalton and Royer, 1972).

The unique geology of the San Rafael wilderness was again recognized in a 1980 Interior Department study that identified seven potential National Natural Landmark sites within and around the Swell. More recently, the Emery County Development Council has proposed national park designation for 210,000 acres in the northern San Rafael Swell. "While some people may boggle at the idea of another national park in Utah," commented Salt Lake City's *Deseret News*, "it can be argued that the Emery officials are too modest in their approach."

"The San Rafael country may be the best remaining unprotected desert land," explains *Deseret News* environmental reporter Joe Bauman, in his book *Stone House Lands*. "Yet it teeters on the verge of destruction . . . . A new national park, embracing the entire Swell, is the only solution."

IPP: The Phantom Power Plant

With such a long record of public outcry for protection, it is difficult to understand the BLM's limited wilderness recommendations for the San Rafael Swell. The BLM would protect only a narrow ring of wild lands around the perimeter of the Swell, while opening up virtually all of the interior—and nearly 300,000 acres bordering the Swell on the south and west—for massive industrial development. Indeed, of the more than 750,000 acres of wild lands within the San Rafael Region, the BLM omitted nearly two-thirds—almost 500,000 acres—from its wilderness inventory, refusing even to study its merits.

Why such an abbreviated proposal?

In 1979, while the BLM was conducting its wilderness inventory, the agency was embroiled in controversy over the siting of a proposed power plant just south of the Swell. The proposed 3,000-megawatt Intermountain Power Project (IPP), billed as the largest coal-fired power plant on earth, would have radically transformed the entire San Rafael region, bringing a network of railroads, smokestacks, power lines, pipelines, evaporation ponds, and a new town of 9,800 people into the heart of a BLM roadless area lying between the San Rafael Swell and northern Capitol Reef National Park.

The BLM was required by law to prohibit new development in roadless lands under study for wilderness. Since the proposed plant site lay in the heart of a 250,000-acre roadless area, wilderness study area (WSA) designation would have delayed or prohibited development of the site. To prevent delay, the Utah state office of the BLM requested and received

Opposite: the Mancos Shale badlands below North Caineville Mesa at the southern end of the San Rafael Swell are a supreme example of erosional sculpting. Other parts of these badlands are being scarred by off-road vehicles.

Tom Miller

One of the most spectacular small intrusion complexes in the Colorado Plateau is that in the Little Black Mountain, northeast of Capitol Reef National Park. Here a tremendous array of dikes, sills, and small laccoliths of black basaltic magma have been emplaced in the deep red and brown Triassic and Jurassic rocks along part of the Waterpocket Monocline. This complex is one of the most instructive and one of the most dramatic, easily seen complexes of igneous intrusions anywhere in the world.

Welsh, Hamblin, and Rigby

A SURVEY OF NATURAL LANDMARK AREAS OF THE NORTH PORTION OF THE COLORADO PLATEAU—BIOTIC AND GEOLOGIC THEMES (1980)

permission to conduct a special accelerated wilderness inventory in the vicinity of the proposed power plant site. Within 14 months, the agency had eliminated from wilderness study a large region surrounding the plant site and all potential railroad and power line corridors.

In all, the BLM cut 300,000 acres of wilderness lands from its inventory to clear a power plant site that would never be used. As early as 1977, Interior Secretary Cecil Andrus had gone on record opposing the Salt Wash IPP plant site, and a different site was eventually selected. "Andrus made it plain long ago that Salt Wash would never be approved because it's too close to Capitol Reef National Park," complained the *Deseret News* in January, 1979. "Yet the hasty decisions of the IPP review will stand as BLM recommendations to Congress on important wild lands."

Circular Dominoes

Utah BLM officials attempted to justify those recommendations by claiming that *in comparison* with each other, certain wilderness inventory units were not "outstanding." The agency cut the southwestern sector of the Muddy Creek roadless area from wilderness study, declaring that the spectacular dikes and sills surrounding Little Black Mountain "do not compare with those in the Cedar Mountain area." Just one year later, a National Park Service study identified the Little Black Mountain area as "one of the most instructive and one of the most dramatic, easily seen complexes of igneous intrusions anywhere in the world." Meanwhile, the Cedar Mountain roadless area was *also* cut from the inventory, after BLM inventory staff concluded that its landscape of colorful badlands, volcanic cliffs and dikes, was "not an outstanding scenic feature when compared with . . . such areas as . . . [the] San Rafael Knob." But just nine months later, the San Rafael Knob, too, was cut from the wilderness inventory, when BLM staffers discovered that Ranchers Exploration company had slashed 30 miles of new roads across the highest landmark in the San Rafael Swell.

The 'Dozers Move In

Cut from the inventory, these lands were now wide open for development of all kinds. Indeed, even while the entire region was under review, the BLM allowed large-scale mining exploration projects to be undertaken inside several key wilderness inventory units. By 1980, uranium exploration companies had constructed at least 40 miles of new roads—and bored hundreds of drill holes—in several key parts of the Muddy Creek wilderness inventory unit. Gulf Minerals Corporation, for example, bored dozens of test wells on the rim of Muddy Creek Canyon—then left the area, violating a signed agreement to reclaim all impacts. The purpose of such actions was obvious. "There appears to be a move to push roads into roadless areas . . . prior to study or designation," explained BLM area manager Sam Rowley in a memo to the file. Once roaded, an area could never again qualify for wilderness designation.

In the absence of wilderness designation, developments such as these may transform the San Rafael Swell from a natural wonder into an industrial mining complex. During the energy crisis of the 1970s, it appeared that tar sand exploration would trigger major new development projects in the heart of the Swell. Two proposals for tar sand development—both summarily approved by the BLM—suggest the scope of the damage which may result if tar sand are ever developed in the Swell. To recover an estimated 40 to 60 million barrels of bitumen from the tar sand in the heart of the Swell, Kirkwood Oil Company would drill more than a thousand injection and recovery wells. Underground explosions and fires would cause surface subsidence. A major industrial plant would be con-

struced, consisting of production and fuel storage tanks, a warehouse, a repair shop, a sewage plant, a network of pipelines connecting the wells, and housing for more than 200 workers. To transport the bitumen to Green River, a fleet of giant oil trucks would make 160 truck trips per day—one truck every 10 minutes, thundering across the interior of the San Rafael Swell—"raising safety problems," as the BLM's 1985 environmental assessment put it, "for tourists having to negotiate between large trucks at frequent intervals."

"This traffic," wrote author Joe Bauman in 1987, "plus the workers' off-duty play with ORVs, would wreck whatever solitude remained in the region." All this, to provide enough oil to meet the nation's demand for about four and a half days.

Since the mid-1970s, energy prices have fallen dramatically, and at present neither tar sand nor uranium production is economically feasible in Utah. But an increase in energy prices could bring the developers hurrying back.

Meanwhile, a new challenge to the San Rafael wilderness has arisen: off-road vehicles. Already Buckhorn Wash, the beautiful canyon separating the BLM's Sids Mountain and Mexican Mountain WSAs, has been devastated by off-road vehicle traffic. On a single spring weekend, BLM recreation planners have counted more than a thousand people camped along the Buckhorn Wash road. The entire canyon floor, from wall to wall, is crisscrossed with off-road vehicle tracks. Broken bushes, tree limbs, and beer cans litter the landscape.

The BLM's own planning documents repeatedly emphasize the importance of restricting motorized vehicles throughout the San Rafael Swell to existing roads and trails. In its comprehensive management plan for the San Rafael Swell, published in 1973, the BLM specifically recommended "that all vehicles should be confined to designated roads and trails . . . to

Muddy Creek exits the southern end of the San Rafael Swell in a stunning example of the power of a silt-laden desert stream. The Utah Wilderness Coalition proposal takes in Muddy Creek's hairpin meander in the foreground, the basin of Salt Wash, and Factory Butte and North Caineville Mesa in the background. In the distance is Mt. Ellen in the Henry Mountains. The BLM proposal would omit all but Mt. Ellen and the cliffs east (left) of Muddy Creek.

Ray Wheeler

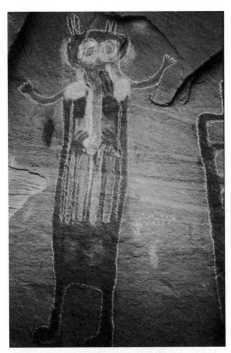

Ancient pictograph in Black Dragon Wash in the San Rafael Swell (Mexican Mountain unit). Easy access by road has resulted in vandalism of several pictographs in this panel, including the chalk outline shown here.

Harvey Halpern

prevent erosion and scarring due to overland vehicular traffic." Moreover, "abandoned roads and trails will be obliterated and revegetated. The fragile soils are highly erosive. Many of the most prominent examples of accelerated soil erosion started in ruts left by vehicles."

Yet the agency's wilderness recommendations systematically exclude huge tracts of land to allow off-road vehicle access. The BLM proposes to throw open some 15,000 acres of lands *inside* its Mexican Mountain and Sids Mountain WSAs to off-road vehicle use. Within the exclusion areas, the BLM explains, "Present ORV use could continue and expand . . . . No ORV trails . . . would be closed south of the San Rafael Bridge Campground, on Indian Bench, at Mexican Bend, or to Swasey's Leap." And in the Sids Mountain WSA, the BLM would create *22 miles* of motorized vehicle access corridors *straight into the center of the proposed wilderness, literally cutting it in half.* The principal objective of BLM's wilderness proposal for the area, explains the DEIS narrative, "is to . . . avoid conflicts with traditional ORV access routes."

The Utah Wilderness Coalition Proposal

"Something more important than the thrill of blasting across slickrock on a hot bike is at stake here," wrote Joe Bauman in 1986, in a plea for legislation to protect the San Rafael Swell. "Wild nature is priceless and irreplaceable."

We agree. The Utah Wilderness Coalition proposal will protect *all* of the San Rafael Swell's natural wonders. Each of the 14 units included within our proposed San Rafael Wilderness offers superb wilderness values—yet too few of them have been recognized by the BLM as candidates for wilderness designation. By extending wilderness protection to all deserving lands in the San Rafael Swell, we can yet preserve one of the nation's most important natural wonders.

Ray Wheeler

SIDS MOUNTAIN UNIT

Highlights—For most Utahns, this is the slickrock wilderness closest to home: the northern overlooks and trailheads of Sids Mountain are less than three-and-one-half hours' driving time from Salt Lake City. Part of the oft-proposed San Rafael National Park, sandstone-walled canyons wind northward from the Head of Sinbad at the center of the Swell to the Little Grand Canyon of the San Rafael River. Those who seek to float a wilderness river or to explore hidden mesas and canyons will not be disappointed—despite tragic overgrazing near streams and springs and an increasing off-road vehicle threat. The BLM recommends 80,000 acres for designation, but divided the unit with off-road vehicle corridors in canyon bottoms. The Utah Wilderness Coalition's 95,800-acre proposal would protect habitat for desert bighorn sheep and hikers by including these canyon bottoms. It would also add to the diversity of the unit by including colorful badlands at North Salt Wash on the northwest and bighorn sheep habitat at Cane Wash on the east.

Geology and landforms—Sids Mountain proper is actually a broad mesa, the highest among several that cover the unit. Knobs and buttes of Navajo Sandstone dot the uplands—some with unusual names given by pioneer stockherders. The mesas drop off into deep canyons with sheer Wingate Sandstone cliffs. A candidate for wild and scenic river designation, 16 miles of the San Rafael River flow through the northern part, forming the spectacular gorge deservedly called the Little Grand Canyon.

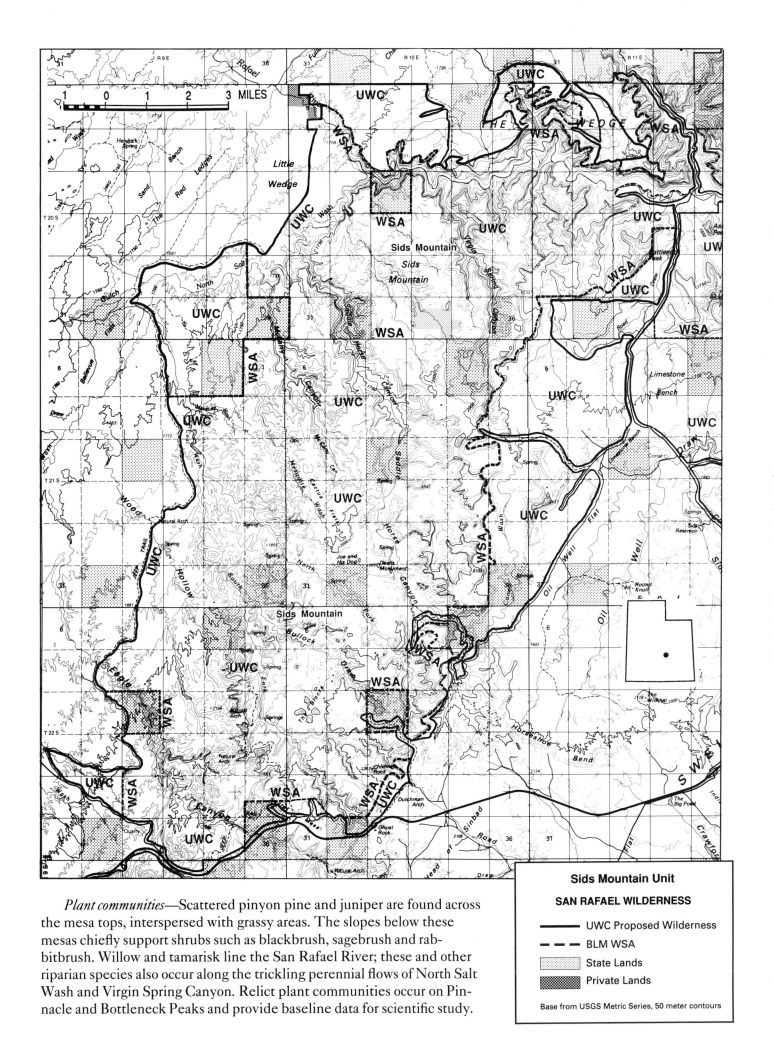

Plant communities—Scattered pinyon pine and juniper are found across the mesa tops, interspersed with grassy areas. The slopes below these mesas chiefly support shrubs such as blackbrush, sagebrush and rabbitbrush. Willow and tamarisk line the San Rafael River; these and other riparian species also occur along the trickling perennial flows of North Salt Wash and Virgin Spring Canyon. Relict plant communities occur on Pinnacle and Bottleneck Peaks and provide baseline data for scientific study.

Sids Mountain Unit

SAN RAFAEL WILDERNESS

——— UWC Proposed Wilderness

– – – BLM WSA

State Lands

Private Lands

Base from USGS Metric Series, 50 meter contours

The BLM notes that the unit includes habitat for a dozen rare plant species including cacti and milkvetches.

Wildlife—Sids Mountain provides crucial yearlong habitat for desert bighorn sheep, according to the BLM. The sheep were reintroduced in 1978 and 1979 and have more than doubled in population since that time to number about 60 at present (BLM, 1986, p. 18). Mule deer browse in the unit and attract occasional mountain lions. Raptors inhabit the unit yearround and golden eagles are especially prevalent. Bald eagles have been sighted west of the campground along the San Rafael River, the BLM notes. Waterfowl use the river as a refueling area during migration, and the UDWR has listed the entire unit as a peregrine use area.

Archeology and history—A superb Fremont Indian pictograph panel can be found just off the San Rafael River. The BLM also notes other remains of the Fremont culture, including a petroglyph and a granary. A historic cabin has recently been acquired in the north of the unit and an old mine of historical interest is located in its center.

Recreation—The 18-mile float trip down the San Rafael River from Fuller Bottom to the Buckhorn Wash bridge is particularly impressive, yet can be done in small rafts, kayaks, canoes, and even innertubes (see Nichols, 1986). Hikers also follow the river during low water, crossing its course many times. The San Rafael's twisting and colorful canyons and sheer sandstone walls have earned it a nomination for National Wild and Scenic Rivers designation. Away from the river, hiking and horseback riding afford spectacular panoramic vistas from the parklands above the canyon system (see Kelsey, 1986b). For those who prefer to stay near their car, the Wedge Overlook at the northern edge of the unit affords breath-taking views of the Little Grand Canyon and the Coal Wash Overlook on Interstate 70 looks out over the South Fork of Coal Wash and the Block Mesas. Because of its proximity to the Wasatch Front, Sids Mountain is expected to receive a dramatic increase in recreational use beyond its 1,000 visitor days per year as recorded by the BLM.

BLM recommendation—The BLM initially recommended wilderness for 78,408 acres of its 80,530-acre WSA, and is expected to recommend 80,084 acres in 1990. The agency excluded lands in upper Cane Wash and North Salt Wash from study by drawing straight line and topographic boundaries, contrary to its inventory policy. The North and South Forks of Coal Wash, Bullock Draw, and Saddle Horse Canyon were deleted from the 1986 draft recommendation to open up 25 miles of ORV corridors into the heart of the unit. ORV use would shatter the silence, damage vegetation, and disturb wildlife habitat in these wash bottoms. Mineral conflicts within the unit are insignificant, according to the BLM.

Coalition proposal—The Coalition proposes wilderness designation for 95,800 acres. Important for its spectacular maze of canyons, educational geology, numerous endangered and threatened plants, and bighorn sheep population, the entire Sids Mountain unit deserves protection. Off-road vehicle corridors contradict the definition of wilderness and have no place in the heart of the unit. Closure of these routes at the canyon rim, not at the wash bottom, is the only manageable wilderness boundary. We also include undisturbed lands north of the San Rafael River and west of the Wedge Overlook, but omit the roaded overlook itself.

MEXICAN MOUNTAIN UNIT

Highlights—Geologic wonders typify this unit: the northern reaches of the San Rafael Reef, the mysterious slot canyons of the Upper and Lower Black Boxes, a cliffline north of the river reminiscent of Capitol Reef National Park, Mexican Mountain itself, and countless canyons cutting across the northeast side of the Swell. The most unusual geologic feature in the unit is excluded, however, from the BLM's 46,750-acre recommendation: Windowblind Peak, one of the largest free-standing monoliths in the world. The 102,600-acre Coalition proposal includes Windowblind Peak and other lands at the west end of the unit. These lands are an important link to the Sids Mountain unit (across the Buckhorn Wash road) for the northern San Rafael desert bighorn sheep herd and are critical habitat for the endangered peregrine falcon. They are also an important part of the view from the Wedge Overlook and should be kept free from further off-road vehicle damage and development.

Geology and landforms—The unit displays a vertical mile of uplifted strata on the east flank of the San Rafael Swell, including deposits from the Pennsylvanian to the early Cretaceous. The Navajo Sandstone covers about one-fourth of the unit, chiefly in the northeast and east, where it is carved into colorful buttes surrounding Cottonwood and Spring canyons. Wingate Sandstone cliffs line the north side of the river for 20 miles below the bridge at Buckhorn Draw. Here the river enters the Upper Black Box, a forbidding slot canyon carved into dark Paleozoic rocks. The spectacular Mexican Bend, where the San Rafael River curves around the massive bulk of Mexican Mountain, can be viewed at the crest of the Horsethief Trail. The river exits the San Rafael Reef just north of Interstate 70 through the Lower Black Box. Windowblind Peak, a 1,200-foot-high tower located south of the San Rafael River at Buckhorn Wash, is visible from many vantage points throughout the Swell. Its name comes from its ability to block the sun in an otherwise open landscape.

Plant communities—The unit is composed primarily of pinyon-juniper forest on the uplands, shrubs and grasses at lower elevations, and riparian plants along streams and washes. Two endangered and six proposed or candidate plant species may grow in the unit.

Wildlife—According to the BLM, the unit encompasses more than one-fourth of the range for the North San Rafael desert bighorn herd and supports a few mule deer as well. Mountain lions hunt within the unit. The BLM has identified 11,290 acres of critical habitat for the endangered peregrine falcon in its WSA, along with a number of falcon and golden eagle nests. The endangered bald eagle has been sighted during its migration.

Archeology and history—Five archeological sites have been recorded but a thorough inventory has not been made, according to the BLM. The Old Spanish Trail, a mid 19th-century route from New Mexico to California, runs just north of the unit and a remnant may be within the WSA. Swasey's Leap, site of Sid Swasey's legendary horse jump across the Lower Black Box, is a favorite destination. Along Mexican Bend are remnants of an old corral and camp where the western outlaws, the Wild Bunch, frequently stayed. The abandoned Smith cabin and corrals on the eastern boundary record early use by livestock herders. An impressive pictograph panel is found along Black Dragon Canyon, but easy access by vehicles has led to some defacement of the panel.

Recreation—The Mexican Mountain unit offers countless recreational opportunities. Good access is available by a spur road which follows the San Rafael River for 15 miles below the bridge at Buckhorn Wash. This road provides access to the upper Black Box and Spring Canyon, both excellent hikes. Cottonwood Canyon, the historic Horsethief Trail, and the Lower Black Box are reached by good dirt roads branching off of Highway 6 or Interstate 70. The San Rafael River, under consideration for Wild and Scenic status, provides challenging kayaking and tubing during the spring runoff and into the summer. The unit's hiking is detailed in Hall (1982)

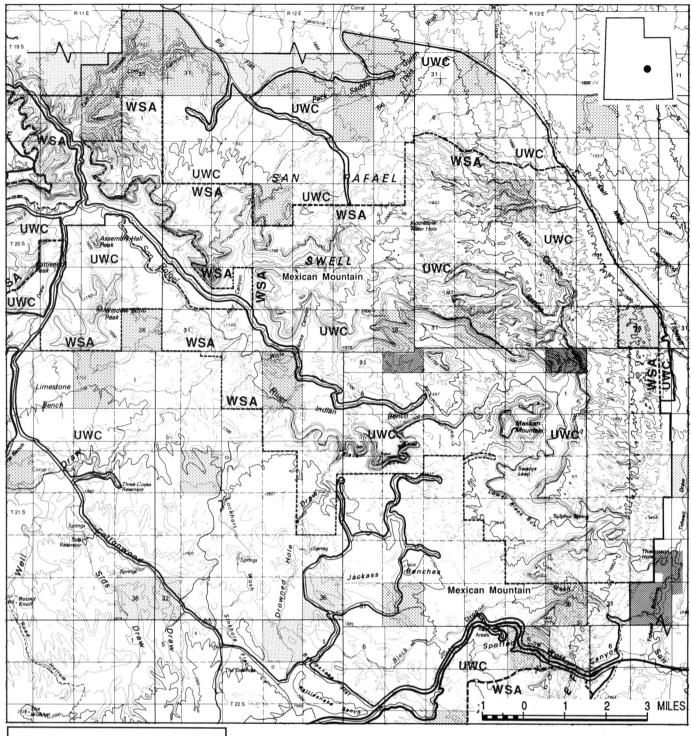

Mexican Mountain Unit

SAN RAFAEL WILDERNESS

——— UWC Proposed Wilderness

– – – BLM WSA

State Lands

Private Lands

Base from USGS Metric Series, 50 meter contours

and Kelsey (1986b); the float trip down the Black Box is described in Nichols (1986). Horse riding, rock climbing, fishing, hunting, rockhounding, and (occasionally) ski touring are available as well.

BLM recommendation—The BLM recommends wilderness for only 46,750 acres of its 59,600-acre WSA, omitting part of the western portion of the WSA and creating a broad vehicle corridor north of the San Rafael River all the way to Mexican Mountain—the very heart of the WSA. It also allows a cherrystem road to Swasey's Leap. The WSA itself excludes large areas on the north and south because of a claimed lack of naturalness. Uranium and tar sand deposits may have motivated the exclusions, even though mining is generally infeasible.

Coalition proposal—The Coalition proposes 102,600 acres of wilderness. The imposing geologic formations, important wildlife habitat, rich history and outstanding recreational opportunities of the unit need to be preserved for generations to come. Conflicts with wilderness designation are few. Some ORV use occurs around the San Rafael River campground and the spur road down the river, but nearby roads and trails along the Buckhorn Wash road would remain open to such use. Uranium and tar sand are found in the unit but their economic potential is low (see overview). Human intrusions are substantially unnoticeable in this huge landscape. Our boundary cherrystems the road along the San Rafael River (instead of deleting a broad swath five miles long as the BLM recommended), but includes old mining impacts (including bulldozer trails and an abandoned landing strip) at Mexican Bend as does the BLM. Our boundary includes Black Dragon Canyon to just below the well-known pictograph panel in order to protect the panel from further damage.

SAN RAFAEL REEF UNIT

Highlights—The San Rafael Reef, the steeply tilted slickrock cliffs forming the eastern edge of the San Rafael Swell, displays some of the most spectacular and educational geology in the country. Its hidden canyons and open benchlands offer excellent recreational opportunities, significant historical and archeological sites, and habitat for endangered plants as well as for golden eagles and desert bighorn sheep. A total of 95,000 acres should be protected, connecting the Mexican Mountain and Muddy Creek units to protect the entire length of the Reef.

Geology and landforms—The San Rafael Reef, a classic plunging anticline breached by numerous short canyons, rises abruptly from the desert west of the town of Green River and northwest of Hanksville. The unit displays fascinating rock formations including arches, caves, knobs, pinnacles, sheer cliffs, and water-filled potholes. Grape agate, a rare gem found in only a few areas of the country, is present in the unit, according to the BLM. Soils in half of the BLM's WSA would be highly erodible if disturbed (BLM, 1986, p. 9) and thus would limit development. Straight Wash cuts to the Pennsylvanian Hermosa Group, the oldest formation in the San Rafael Swell, and there are large exposures of Coconino Sandstone with narrow slot canyons.

Plant communities—Most of the unit is sparsely covered with a pinyon-juniper forest and associated desert shrubs. The remainder consists of grassland, shrub growth, and barren land. Eight rare plant species have been identified in the WSA (BLM, 1986, p. 10).

Wildlife—The BLM designated 27,311 acres of its WSA as high-priority desert bighorn habitat. Most of the South San Rafael desert bighorn sheep herd lives in the unit, which includes critical rutting and lambing grounds. Other mammals present, according to the BLM, include mule deer, coyotes, bobcats, cottontail rabbits, badgers, Ord kangaroo rats, gray foxes, kit foxes, and white-tailed antelope squirrels. The golden eagle, a sensitive species, inhabits the unit.

Archeology and history—Ancient Indian rock art can be found in several locations. Six sites have been recorded in the WSA, according to the BLM, which notes that additional undiscovered sites are likely to occur. Remnants of historic wagon trails can also be found.

Recreation—The proximity of the San Rafael Reef to Utah Highway 24 and Interstate 70 makes for easily accessible recreation. Backpacking, rockhounding, hiking, camping, rock scrambling, photography, and scenic viewing are all excellent in this area. The rugged topography permits the visitor to experience a high degree of solitude and challenge just a few miles from the paved highways. Hiking trips in the unit are described in Kelsey, (1986b) and in Joe Bauman's *Stone House Lands* (1987).

The Black Box of the San Rafael River in the Mexican Mountain unit. The river has cut into Paleozoic rocks, forming a gorge that challenges hikers and (during runoff) boaters in kayaks. To its credit, the BLM includes this canyon in its wilderness recommendation.

Rodney Greeno

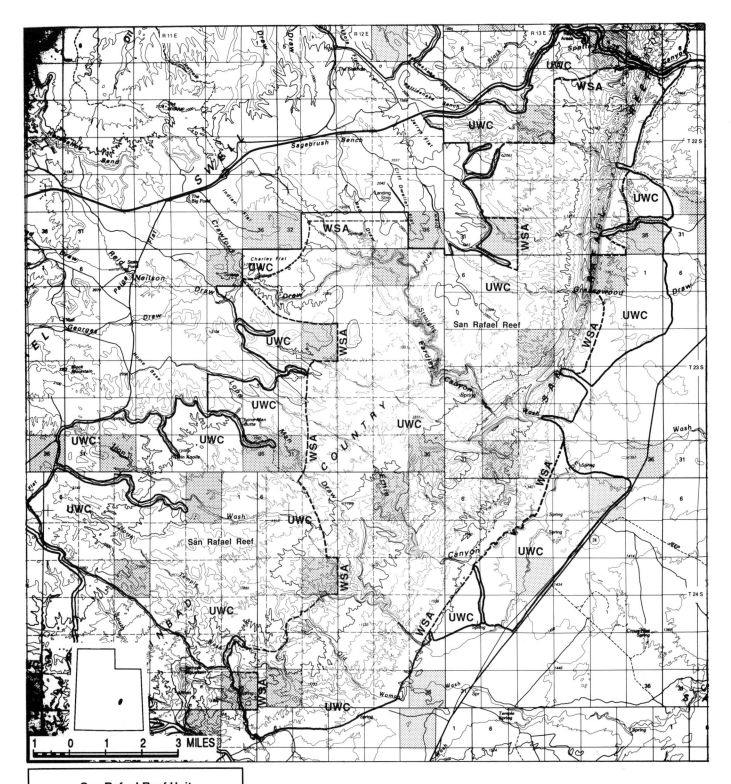

San Rafael Reef Unit

SAN RAFAEL WILDERNESS

———— UWC Proposed Wilderness

– – – BLM WSA

▨ State Lands

Base from USGS Metric Series, 50 meter contours

BLM recommendation—In its initial inventory, the BLM reduced the size of the unit from 101,270 acres to 63,264 acres, claiming it was retaining only the "areas of principal interest." As a result, its boundary crosses large natural areas averaging six miles from the original boundary road. The BLM then deleted 17,000 acres by exaggerating the extent of a few small intrusions, many of which show no evidence of construction and are almost completely reclaimed. In 1986, the BLM expanded its diminutive WSA from 55,540 acres to 59,170 acres and recommended wilderness for the entire area. The intrusions that the BLM used to justify its inventory deletions have but a minor effect on the unit's overall naturalness and solitude. For example, the BLM used two dirt jeep trails to drop over

3,000 acres of steep canyons just south of Interstate 70. The trails are less than 7 feet wide and total 5.5 miles in length; they occupy a total area of fewer than 6 acres. They are largely reclaimed since the construction of Interstate 70 which fenced them off and rendered them unusable to vehicles. The BLM deleted about 4,000 acres north of Temple Mountain, claiming that impacts separated this strip of land from the larger roadless area. But the impacts total fewer than 5 acres along a 4.5-mile-long reclaimed jeep trail. A section of state land was dropped for similar reasons.

Coalition proposal—The BLM states that its 55,540-acre WSA provides outstanding opportunities for solitude and important wildlife habitat. We agree, but the same applies to additional roadless lands west of the WSA and on benchlands beneath the Reef. The wilderness unit should be expanded to take in these lands. Habitat and recreational opportunities should be protected not just within the deep sandstone canyons, but also in the access gullies, the benches, and pinyon-juniper forest. All of these features work together to protect the character of the land and its inhabitants. Our 95,000-acre San Rafael Reef unit deserves wilderness status in order to preserve its crucial desert bighorn sheep habitat, its unique geology, and its outstanding solitude and primitive recreation values.

WILD HORSE MESA UNIT

Highlights—In the badlands between the San Rafael Reef and Capitol Reef National Park simple forms and solid colors combine in a landscape of barren purity. Highly susceptible to erosion when disturbed, these badlands should be off limits to vehicle use to protect scenery and downstream water quality. Wild Horse Mesa is adjacent to Goblin Valley State Park on the northeast and is separated from the Muddy Creek unit on the north and west by only a primitive road. Muddy Creek runs for about 30 miles through the unit. Unlike any area the BLM has recommended, this unit and the Muddy Creek unit include the full range of Jurassic and Cretaceous badland formations from the Carmel through the Morrison to the Mancos. Unfortunately, the BLM relied upon an obsolete power plant siting study to exclude Wild Horse Mesa from wilderness study. The Coalition proposes 57,400 acres for designation.

Geology and landforms—Smooth, wide-open badlands, crisscrossed by occasional deep canyons create a moon-like, otherworldly atmosphere. Jet-black stone pinnacles and "goblin" formations (like those in adjacent Goblin Valley State Park) add to the effect. The cliffs of the San Rafael Reef in the Muddy Creek unit rise to the north. The oldest formations (Carmel, about 180 million years old) are along the north and east sides of the unit, and the youngest (Mancos Shale—about 80 million years old) are on the south and west. (See Mussentuchit Badlands unit for discussion of sensitive soils which cover most of this unit.)

Plant communities—Much of the unit is barren, but greasewood is dominant along Muddy Creek and shadscale with galleta grass is found on the uplands. The endangered fishhook cactus *Sclerocactus wrightiae* may be present, according to the U.S. Fish and Wildlife Service. Riparian habitat is found along Muddy Creek.

Wildlife—The northern part of the unit is yearlong bighorn sheep habitat (BLM, 1988b, vol. 2, p. 71).

Recreation—During high water in the spring one can float the entire length of Muddy Creek to Hanksville, viewing the constantly changing colors and varied topography of the area. (See Upper Muddy Creek unit for further information.) Hiking, sightseeing, and photography opportunities are outstanding in the unit's cliffs and badlands.

BLM recommendation—The BLM rejected the entire inventory unit during a special accelerated study conducted in 1979 to make way for the proposed Intermountain Power Project. That power plant was subsequently located near Delta on the other side of the state, but the inventory decision was never revised (see area overview). According to the BLM, the unit was dropped because of the "extensive human activities" found in about one-third of the unit. These consisted of about 18 miles of vehicle ways, an area of contour furrows (1,000 acres), four stock reservoirs, and three miles of seismograph lines. These impacts are concentrated in the western part of the unit; most are near its edge. The entire eastern and southwestern portions of Wild Horse Mesa, on the other hand, were deemed "essentially natural" by the BLM. Still, despite the clearly limited extent of human impacts on the majority of the unit, the total area was determined to be lacking in basic wilderness attributes. The agency excluded the great wild badlands south and west of the Reef (including Wild Horse Mesa) from any conflict with the proposed Intermountain Power Project by concluding that only slickrock areas could be wilderness.

Coalition proposal—Our proposed 57,400-acre wilderness unit excludes the significant "human activities" that the BLM cited in dropping the unit from wilderness study. For example, the 1,000 acres of contour furrows, as well as an area of mining impacts, are both isolated at the extreme north boundary of the roadless area and are excluded by minor boundary adjustments. Further, the vehicle ways described by the BLM are 25 years old and have grown over or simply disappeared due to erosion, making them practically invisible to anyone on the ground. They do not represent an impact so severe that Wild Horse Mesa should be denied wilderness status.

MUDDY CREEK UNIT

Highlights—Reaching from the interior of the San Rafael Swell to the northeast corner of Capitol Reef National Park, Muddy Creek is the second largest block of undeveloped BLM land in Utah. Within this huge area every landform found in the San Rafael region is represented: 200 million years of geologic history from the Permian Coconino Sandstone to Tertiary igneous intrusions folded and carved into towering mesas, sweeping badlands, impassable reefs, slickrock domes and canyons, and random black walls. The BLM's 56,735-acre proposal includes only the San Rafael Reef (Crack Canyon WSA) and the upper Muddy Creek Gorge (Muddy Creek WSA) while excluding most of the unit's many outstanding geologic features: Factory Butte and Little Black Mountain, lower Muddy Creek Gorge, Segers Hole, the Moroni Slopes, Sinbad Country, North Caineville Mesa and Reef, Hebes Mountain, and Salt Wash. The 246,300-acre Coalition proposal would protect the full scientific, ecologic, watershed, scenic, and recreational values of this incomparable landscape.

Geology and landforms—The center of this unit at the junction of lower Muddy Creek Gorge and Segers Hole is the southwestern tip of the oval-shaped San Rafael Swell uplift. From this point, great Wingate and Navajo sandstone cliffs run north along Muddy Creek and east along the San Rafael Reef defining the southern and western limits of the Swell. Inside these cliffs to the east and north is the Sinbad Country. Here Muddy Creek's tributaries have cut myriad small, twisting canyons through the reddish-brown Moenkopi Formation. Muddy Creek cut deeper into the gray Kaibab Limestone with spectacular inner gorges in the slickrock Coconino Sandstone. Outside the Wingate and Navajo cliffs, upper Mesozoic badlands interrupted by small igneous intrusions extend south to the Fremont River and west to Cathedral Valley in Capitol Reef National Park (see Wild Horse Mesa and Cedar Mountain units).

Plant communities—Rock outcrops and barren land predominate, with sparse desert shrubs and grasses (principally shadscale and galleta) across much of the unit. A low-growing pinyon-juniper forest covers the Sinbad Country. Scattered pinyon and juniper trees are also found in the Reef and on higher rims west of Muddy Creek. Cottonwoods occur in small groves along many canyon and wash bottoms. Five candidate, one proposed, and two listed threatened or endangered plant species are known within or near the unit, according to the BLM. Hebes Mountain has a 650-acre relict plant community. Because no water occurs on the mountain, it is not likely that grazing has ever taken place here. Tall grasses such as ricegrass and galleta, as well as shadscale and juniper, grow here.

Wildlife—The UDWR and BLM have identified the higher parts of this unit in the Crack Canyon WSA as "high-priority desert bighorn sheep habitat" with "habitat for about 32 percent of the desert bighorn sheep in the south San Rafael herd" (BLM, 1986, p. 14-15). The UDWR identified the northeastern part of the unit (the Moroni Slopes) as critical yearlong habitat for desert bighorn sheep. Mule deer, wild horses, gray fox, kit fox, and smaller mammals inhabit the unit. Raptors include bald and golden eagles, ferruginous hawks, and rough-legged hawks.

Archeology and history—Several archeological sites including rock art and a structure are known, but the full extent of cultural resources is unknown.

Recreation—The rugged terrain offers unforgettable opportunities for solitude and primitive recreation. Activities include hiking, backpacking, sightseeing, photography, geologic study, and horseback riding. (See Upper Muddy Creek unit for description of float trips down Muddy Creek.)

BLM recommendation—The agency recommends only 56,735 acres in its two WSAs (Crack Canyon and Muddy Creek) for designation. Instead of recognizing the national and international significance of this wilderness resource, the BLM concluded in its 1979 inventory that about 152,000 acres, including the area surrounding the proposed Salt Wash site of the Intermountain Power Project (IPP), lacked wilderness character. Another 36,000 acres were excluded in the 1980 intensive inventory decision. The areas deleted are described in detail below. The first six were part of the Muddy Creek/Moroni Slopes special inventory unit that was released in

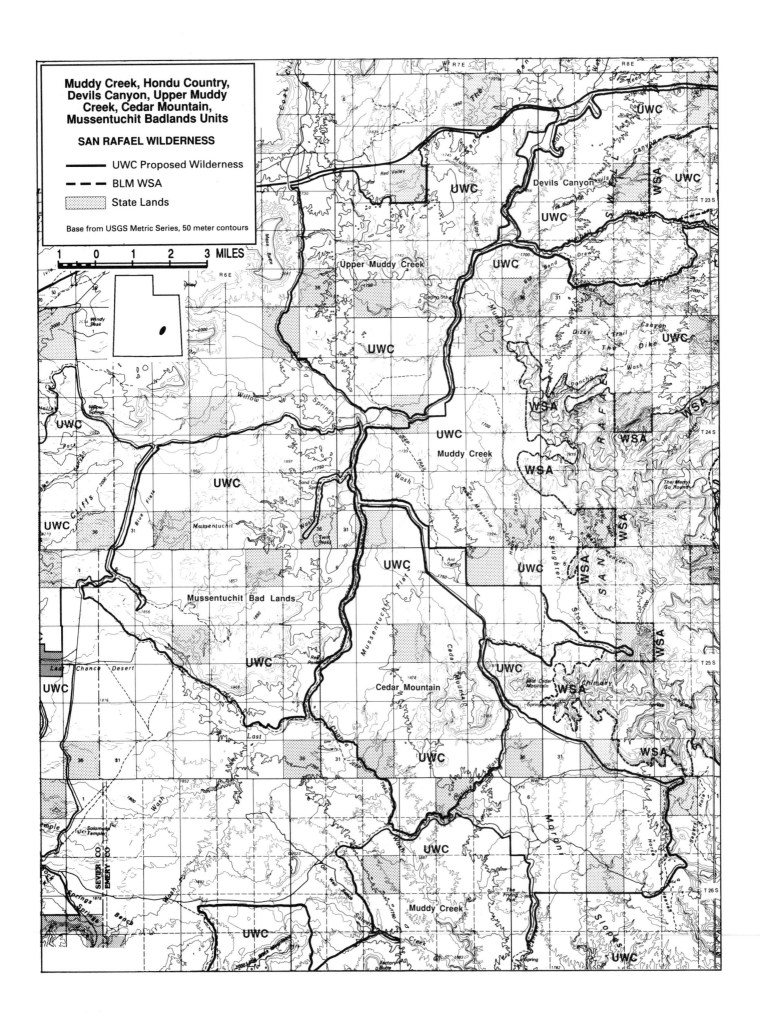

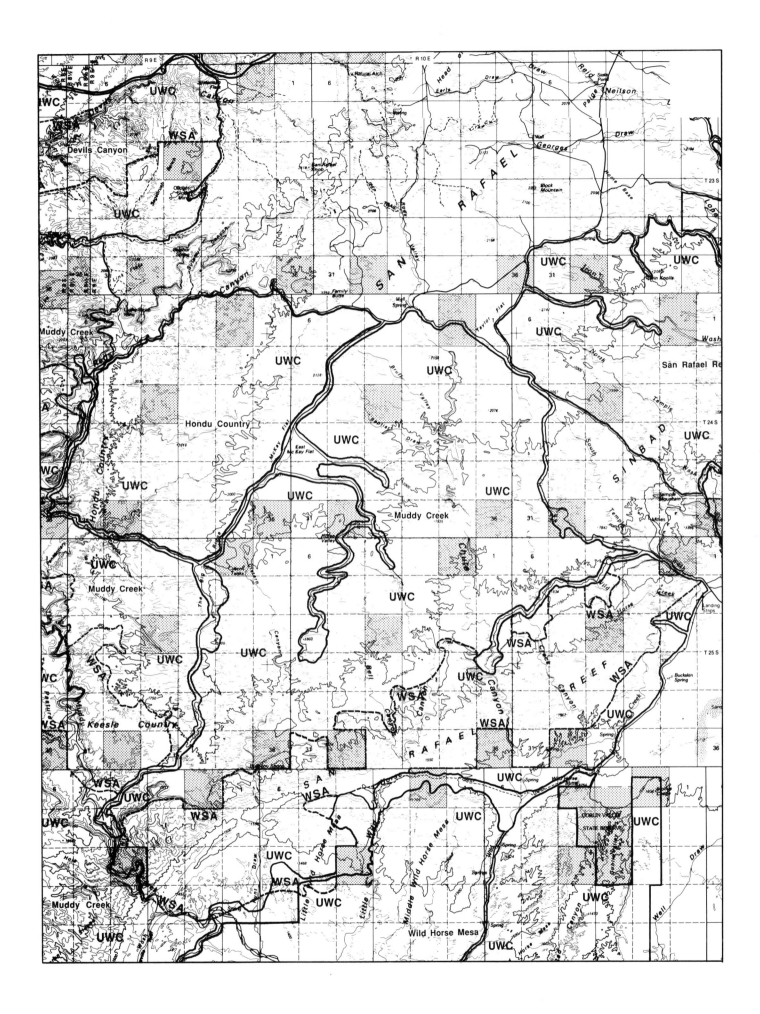

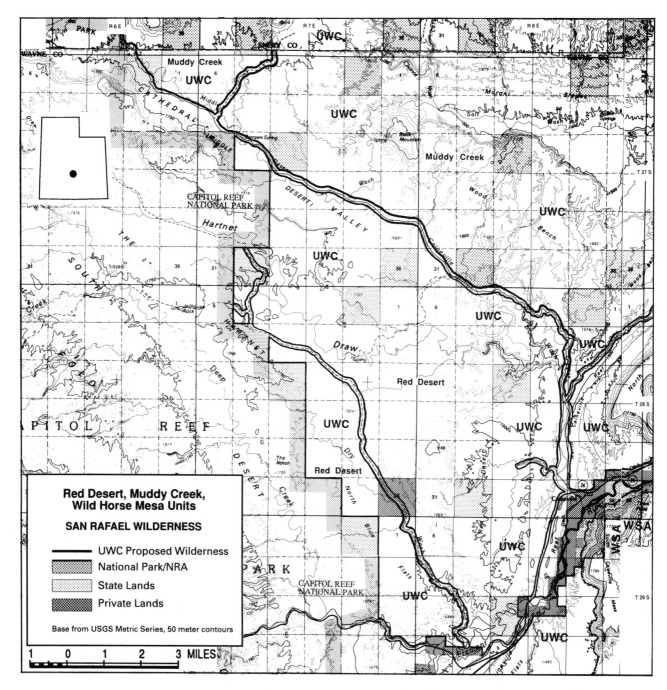

Red Desert, Muddy Creek, Wild Horse Mesa Units

SAN RAFAEL WILDERNESS

——— UWC Proposed Wilderness

National Park/NRA

State Lands

Private Lands

Base from USGS Metric Series, 50 meter contours

1 0 1 2 3 MILES

1979, and the last two were part of the Crack Canyon, Chute Canyon, and Cistern Canyon intensive inventory units that were released in 1980.

(1) *Muddy Creek Gorge* (1,000 acres)—Below the southern boundary of the BLM's Muddy Creek WSA, the stream enters the deepest canyon along its entire course where it cuts through the southern rim of the San Rafael Swell, winding between colorful, thousand-foot-high sandstone walls. During the wilderness inventory the BLM identified a "road" running up the bed of this canyon. On the east side of the canyon, the BLM recommends wilderness designation for its Crack Canyon WSA. Yet during the hasty accelerated inventory, the BLM cut the west side of the canyon, asserting that it lacked wilderness character. While visible in several places for short distances, the old jeep trail is neither a road nor a significant human impact. Indeed, for most of the canyon's length, the track either runs down the bed of the stream or, where located above the streambank, has been completely obliterated by erosion or so thoroughly revegetated that it is difficult to locate or recognize. The Crack Canyon

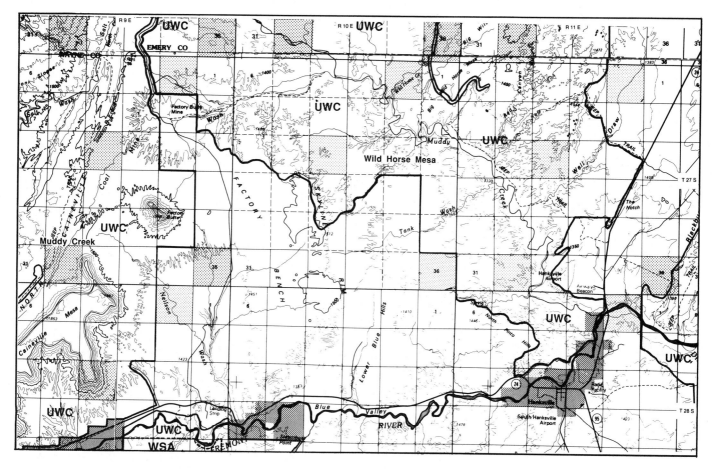

WSA should have included this insignificant impact and been extended west and south to include the lands described below.

(2) *Segers Hole* (7,000 acres)—Segers Hole is a 3,000-acre basin, bounded by Navajo slickrock walls, which drains through a deep, narrow slot canyon into lower Muddy Creek Gorge. Rugged slickrock fractured by the folding of the San Rafael Reef and Moroni Slopes extends north and south of the slot canyon. The BLM released Segers Hole in its 1979 inventory decision, citing mineral exploration impacts dating from 1974. The way which was used for access to Segers Hole is now badly eroded and probably will soon be completely impassable. It should be closed to protect scenic and wilderness values. The BLM has proposed a 7,120-acre ACEC "to protect the scenic values from irreparable damage that could occur from possible mineral exploration or ORV use" (BLM, 1988b, vol. 2, p. 97). However, the agency's proposal would not prohibit mineral entry or leasing or close the old ways to ORV use.

(3) *Moroni Slopes, Factory Butte, and Salt Wash* (101,000 acres)—This area—the entire southwest half of the Muddy Creek unit—was dropped by the BLM from wilderness review. It is studded with spectacular landforms, including the 400-foot-high, dark orange-colored cliffline at the northern edge of Wood Bench, the volcanic apparitions of Black Mountain and Little Black Mountain, the 2,000-foot-high monocline called the Moroni Slopes, the fin of steeply tilted sedimentary rocks known as North Caineville Reef, Factory Butte—a landmark visible for nearly 100 miles in every direction—and Salt Wash itself, a huge valley harboring a perennial stream and surrounded by these towering natural wonders.

(4) *Hebes Mountain and East Cedar Mountain* (16,000 acres)—These brooding basalt-capped mountains loom above the rim of the Muddy Creek canyon system in the northwest portion of the unit. They contain striking displays of volcanic intrusions, including radiating systems of

"dikes"—thin blades of dark volcanic rock that cut over the land like the Great Wall of China.

(5) *Cat Canyon and the Dike* (15,000 acres)—Cat Canyon: An extremely rugged and beautiful canyon bordering the unit on the north. The Dike is a steeply sloping plateau rising to an abrupt cliffline on the north side of the unit, offering spectacular views of the interior of the San Rafael Swell, Tomsich Butte, and Muddy Creek Canyon. The BLM (1979) noted that "Around Cat Canyon (both to the north and south) there are 13 miles of ways and one long seismograph line (four miles), but they are not obvious in the finely dissected tablelands."

(6) *Keesle Country* (12,000 acres)—Wildly shaped and colored terrain, yet more than half (including a portion of Muddy Creek itself near the mouth of Penitentiary Canyon) is omitted from the BLM's Muddy Creek WSA.

(7) *Cistern and Chute canyons* (33,000 acres)—These lands north of the Crack Canyon WSA were excluded from the WSA in violation of inventory policy. The BLM properly cherrystemmed a regularly used and maintained road from near Temple Mountain to Chute Canyon five miles to the southwest. However, it improperly excluded a vehicle way extending from the end of the maintained road at Chute Canyon west to Muddy Creek, forming the north boundary of the WSA. A vehicle way does exist but at the time of the wilderness inventory no grading had occurred in many years. Perennial shrubs (ephedra and shadscale) as well as grasses could be found in both the center and wheel paths of the route. At the mouth of an unnamed canyon west of Bell Canyon, the way was so badly eroded that all passage by standard highway vehicles ends. (The boundary between Chute and Crack canyons also follows a similar jeep trail that also does not qualify as a road.) The BLM claimed that the lands north of the way were natural but released them from study saying that they lacked outstanding opportunities for solitude or primitive recreation.

(8) *Wild Horse Creek* (3,000 acres)—These lands are along the southeast boundary of the Crack Canyon WSA. They are natural and should have been included in the WSA.

Coalition proposal—We recommend wilderness protection for 246,300 acres surrounding Muddy Creek, incorporating all of the major features of the unit, from Cat Canyon on the north to North Caineville Mesa on the south, while excluding all significant human impacts around the perimeter of this roadless area through boundary adjustments. The Coalition also urges the BLM to aggressively pursue a land exchange with the State of Utah to acquire state-owned sections T. 25 S., R. 8 E., no. 2 and T. 26 S., R. 9 E. no. 16—both of which lie along the path of Muddy Creek in the heart of the unit.

HONDU COUNTRY UNIT

Highlights—Hondu Country is a six-mile square of canyons and ridges without names. Little known and seldom visited, it provides habitat for a growing herd of desert bighorn sheep and range for a small band of wild horses. This unit is broken by ridges and canyons up to 400 feet deep. The BLM found Hondu Country to be roadless and natural, but refused to designate a study area. The Coalition recommends an 18,900-acre wilderness unit to protect this eminently wild area which complements the scenic and wildlife values of the Muddy Creek unit to the west and south.

Geology and landforms—The Moenkopi Formation outcrops which cover most of the unit are deep red and often lie in rippled layers reminiscent of the mudflats and tidelands in which they were formed. The uplands are broken with ridges and ravines. The four major drainages are between 300 and 400 feet deep, twisting their way through canyons at two miles to every mile in a straight line. They cut through the Kaibab Limestone into the slickrock Coconino Sandstone.

Plant communities—Pinyon-juniper woodlands are scattered throughout the unit. Sage and annual grasses characterize the plateau on the east. The proposed endangered San Rafael cactus, *Pediocactus despainii*, may also exist in this unit.

Wildlife—A wild horse herd inhabits the unit, and the UDWR classifies it as yearlong bighorn habitat.

Recreation—Hondu Country offers many challenging hikes. Campers can easily find solitude and isolation within the rippled redrock.

BLM recommendation—In its intensive inventory the BLM dropped the Hondu Country unit, claiming it lacked outstanding solitude and recreational values even while acknowledging the lack of human intrusion. The quality and diversity of recreational opportunities is at odds with BLM claims. The BLM claimed the configuration of the unit limited solitude due to three state inholdings. The state inholdings neither limit solitude nor were considered legitimate obstacles to wilderness designation by the IBLA. These inholdings are land of the same basic character as the federal land. The BLM also inappropriately equated screening with solitude. Clearly the broken nature of the land provides solitude.

Coalition proposal—The Coalition proposes an 18,900-acre Hondu Country wilderness unit to protect challenging recreation opportunities in a remote, little known setting as well as habitat for desert bighorn sheep.

DEVILS CANYON UNIT

Highlights—Devils Canyon begins in the heart of the San Rafael Swell just south of Interstate 70 and flows west into the broad valley of Salt Wash. The Coalition's 21,500-acre proposed wilderness would protect a rugged, colorful landscape that is nonetheless easily accessible for primitive recreation and scenic overlooks. Cutting deep into ancient layers of rock, the cliffs and narrow canyons in this unit offer a splendid view into the past. The unit also has important habitat for golden eagles and contains a number of endangered plant species.

Geology and landforms—Devils Canyon slices 1,000 feet into the crest of the Swell, providing spectacular views from overlooks on the south side of Interstate 70. Here, erosive forces have exposed layers of ancient rock formations (chiefly the Glen Canyon Group) in the narrow, twisting canyon. Away from the canyon, benches, knobs, mesas, and colorful badlands give character to the land.

Plant communities—Despite its relatively small size, this unit is a treasure trove of endangered and threatened flora. The BLM (1986, p. 8) notes that its WSA may harbor two species currently listed as endangered, one proposed endangered species, as well as five candidate species. The dominant vegetation type in this unit is pinyon-juniper in the higher parts of the unit, with desert shrubs in the lower parts.

Wildlife—Along with bats, bobcats, badgers, coyotes, kit and grey foxes and black-tail jack rabbits, there is a wide variety of rodents, and an equally wide variety of raptors to consume them. The latter include golden eagles, ferruginous hawks, prairie falcons, American kestrels, and red-tailed and rough-legged hawks. Mountain lions and mule deer include this area in their winter range. Of particular interest is a small wild horse herd on the natural benches.

Archeology and history—The unit contains one recorded pictograph site, according to the BLM. Many others may exist; however, no cultural inventory has yet been made of the area.

Recreation—The deep, winding canyon and its tributaries can be explored and enjoyed in solitude. The 10-mile-long canyon bottom, with its short but impressive narrows, is a superb hike. The benchlands provide ample space and terrain for those who really want to stretch their legs. See Kelsey (1986b) for route information. Backpackers, wild horse viewers, and hikers frequent the area.

BLM recommendation—The BLM claimed in its 1986 DEIS that none of the 9,610-acre Devils Canyon WSA was worthy of wilderness designation but offered no supporting rationale. The BLM also omitted nearly 12,000 acres suitable for wilderness designation, claiming that vehicle ways, mining scars, and ORV use compromised the entire unit's wilderness character. But the areas of greatest impacts (such as on Justensen Flats) are outside of the WSA (as well as our proposal). Between the WSA boundary and Interstate 70, BLM maps show some routes which have been closed since the freeway was constructed and are no longer noticeable on the ground. Similarly, a route through Link Flats (cited by the BLM) is completely overgrown. North of Kimball Draw and Cat Canyon, the BLM deleted nearly 2,500 acres because of a three-mile-long unmaintained jeep trail that does not receive regular use.

Coalition proposal—The Coalition proposes that 21,500 acres be designated wilderness to protect the canyon system as well as surrounding benchlands, the scenic Copper Globe area and part of Link Flats. Our proposal deletes an area of significant vehicle use and mining activity south and east of Copper Globe. Substantially unnoticeable ORV trails in the Kimball Draw and Sagebrush Bench areas on the south are included as is an overgrown landing strip on Sagebrush Bench.

UPPER MUDDY CREEK UNIT

Highlights—The 70-mile float trip from Interstate 70 to Hanksville begins in this unit and continues into the Muddy Creek and Wild Horse Mesa units. Designation of all three as wilderness would protect the course of the creek through the full geologic cross-section of the San Rafael Swell. The BLM, in its 1979 inventory decision, exaggerated the extent of human impacts and released the entire unit. The Coalition proposes 17,000 natural acres for designation to protect recreation, scenery, and sensitive soils.

Geology and landforms—Muddy Creek and several of its tributary washes twist through multi-colored badland clays and cliff-forming sandstones on the western slope of the San Rafael Swell. There are also fantastic volcanic fins, some almost six miles long. (See Wild Horse Mesa unit for discussion of badland formations, Cedar Mountain for igneous intrusions, and Mussentuchit Badlands unit for sensitive soils.)

Plant communities—The unit's sparse vegetation consists of desert shrubs and grasses. According to the U.S. Fish and Wildlife Service, the endangered Wright's fishhook cactus, *Sclerocactus wrightiae,* may exist in the unit. Riparian habitat is found along Muddy Creek.

Recreation—Nichols (1986) calls Muddy Creek "a truly outstanding desert river" for its "incredible scenery, isolation, and numerous rapids." The first 10 miles of this 70-mile trip lie in this unit. Of this stretch Nichols says, "The water is swift with many Class 1 to 3 rocky rapids that prove fairly tricky for an open canoe." The unit also offers outstanding opportunities for scenic and geologic sightseeing, photography, and hiking.

BLM recommendation—The BLM dropped the entire Upper Muddy Creek unit from the wilderness inventory, exaggerating the extent of impacts and claiming that it lacked outstanding opportunities for solitude or primitive recreation. Proposed power and rail lines to the now-defunct IPP power plant may have been the major reason for the agency's decision (see area overview).

Coalition proposal—The impressive scenery and opportunities for river recreation on Upper Muddy Creek make this unit an excellent wilderness candidate. Our proposal excludes an abandoned mining area near Interstate 70. The Bureau of Reclamation once proposed a desalinization plant in the area but has since abandoned the idea, removing the only real obstacle to wilderness designation.

CEDAR MOUNTAIN UNIT

Highlights—Cedar Mountain rises over a thousand feet above the surrounding Mussentuchit and Muddy Creek badlands giving a high view across more than a million acres with almost no evidence of human use. Despite these vistas and fascinating igneous intrusions the BLM could find no outstanding solitude or primitive recreation.

Geology and landforms—Cedar Mountain is at the center of a unique region of igneous intrusions which extends north into the Mussentuchit Badlands and Upper Muddy Creek units, and east, south, and west into the Muddy Creek unit and Capitol Reef National Park. The intrusions at Cedar Mountain are even more spectacular than those at Little Black Mountain in the Muddy Creek unit. Cedar Mountain, and East Cedar Mountain in the Muddy Creek unit, have angular shapes and isolated pinnacles more like the southern Arizona deserts than the nearby slickrock country. (See Mussentuchit Badlands unit for discussion of the sensitive soils which cover most of this unit.)

Plant communities—Sparse desert shrubs and grasses cover most of the unit. The endangered fishhook cactus *Sclerocactus wrightiae* may be found on the west edge, according to the U.S. Fish and Wildlife Service.

Wildlife—The eastern third is mapped as yearlong desert bighorn habitat by the UDWR.

Recreation—Sightseers, hikers, and photographers can reach Cedar Mountain by a two-wheel-drive, unpaved road from Fremont Junction on Interstate 70.

BLM recommendation—In the accelerated Intermountain Power Project inventory, the BLM found this unit to be natural, but claimed that it lacked outstanding opportunities for solitude or primitive recreation. Scenic vistas, igneous dikes, and the hiking on a rugged mountain were ignored in the evaluation.

Coalition proposal—The Coalition proposes a 14,500-acre wilderness unit to protect scenery, wildlife habitat, geologic values, and sensitive soils. With improvement of the road from Interstate 70 south to Cathedral Valley, off-road vehicle use will likely increase. Wilderness designation would limit ORV use to existing roads, thus sparing the badlands from more unsightly scars and erosion.

MUSSENTUCHIT BADLANDS UNIT

Highlights—These badlands are named after Mussentuchit Wash, a tributary of Muddy Creek. The name, pronounced "mustn't touch it," is appropriate because the unit is highly susceptible to erosion. The sensitive soil areas on the south and west sides of the San Rafael Swell also have high scenic and recreational values which should be protected by wilderness designation. The BLM eliminated this unit as a conflict with the once-proposed Intermountain Power Project by claiming it lacks wilderness characteristics, while the Coalition proposes 23,000 acres for designation.

Geology and landforms—This unit is one of the most colorful areas in the state. Glittering shards of selenite litter its maroon and cream-colored hills, and volcanic dikes cut across it. It has been identified by the BLM as a critical soil and watershed area. Surface disturbances such as off-road vehicle use, livestock grazing, and mineral exploration cause nearly as much soil loss across the San Rafael region as natural processes, significantly increasing the Colorado River's costly salinity load (BLM, 1988, vol. 1, p. 4-8). (See Wild Horse Mesa unit for discussion of badland formations and Cedar Mountain for igneous intrusions.)

Plant communities—Much of the unit is barren but desert shrubs and grasses predominate. The endangered Wright's fishhook cactus may be present, according to the USFWS.

Recreation—The Mussentuchit Badlands have outstanding opportunities for extended hiking, photography, and scenic and geologic sightseeing. They can be reached via the Last Chance road from Fremont on Interstate 70. The badlands are constantly changing in form and topography with hundreds of draws, ravines, and gullies. The challenge is finding your way through the maze of such complex topography.

BLM recommendation—The proposed coal railroad to Salt Wash, one of the alternative sites for the Intermountain Power Plant, would have crossed the eastern edge of this unit. The BLM claimed the unit was heavily impacted and lacked solitude, a finding which may have been influenced by a desire to promote coal development.

Coalition proposal—The Coalition proposes a 23,000-acre wilderness unit to protect scenery and recreation values. Clearly the area possesses outstanding solitude. Opportunities for recreation including scenic and geologic sightseeing, photography, and hiking are also outstanding. The major human imprints are excluded from our proposal. On the east, there is a regularly used vehicle way which leads to cattle facilities just north of Twin Peaks. This vehicle way is several miles long and, with the range improvement next to the route, affects a total of 40 acres. It is cherrystemmed from the Coalition proposal. In the west on the southern part of the Blue Flats, a vehicle way travels from the boundary road south and east for 1.7 miles to a regularly used stock area. An old jeep track, unused and impassable, continues for an additional 2.4 miles. This 2.4-mile section has not seen regular use and has not been maintained. The area possessing significant human impacts totals 60 acres and is outside our boundary. In the eastern part of the Last Chance Desert, several seismic lines are now used as vehicle routes, and maintenance ways created for fence lines. This area is also excluded from our proposal.

RED DESERT UNIT

Highlights—The Red Desert, located between the Muddy Creek unit on the east and Capitol Reef National Park on the west, forms the jigsaw piece linking the greater San Rafael to the park. Cliffs similar to those in the park's Cathedral Valley ring a large spectacular badland basin. The BLM dropped this unit from study, saying that impacts which occupy fewer than 50 acres destroyed the naturalness of tens of thousands of acres. The Coalition proposes a 36,800-acre wilderness unit to protect scenery, recreation, sensitive soils, and endangered plant and animal species.

Geology and landforms—In the south of the unit, a domed anticline has caused all but the harder rock layers to weather away. A circle of Entrada cliffs remains and surrounds phenomenal banded badlands of the Red

Desert. A canyon cuts the eastern portion of the dome. The north of the unit is also composed of badlands of softer strata.

Plant communities—Primarily badlands, the unit supports little vegetation. Some tamarisk grows along the intermittent stream in the southeast, while scattered grasses fill in the more fertile areas. The endangered Wright's fishhook cactus survives here as well.

Wildlife—The UDWR has identified an area used by the endangered peregrine falcon on the western edge of the unit.

Recreation—Excellent for hiking, backpacking, and photography, this large unit offers superb vistas and good camping. Solitude permeates the remote unit as it is nearly untouched by man. The striking colors and sculptured badlands coupled with the quiet vastness of the landscape fill the visitor with an unforgettable wilderness experience. An overlook of the Red Desert is described in the Park Service guide to northern reaches of the park.

BLM recommendation—The BLM concluded that the entire Red Desert unit lacked wilderness qualities, although human impacts were limited to a few acres which could have been deleted by making simple boundary changes.

Coalition proposal—We propose that 36,800 acres of the Red Desert be designated wilderness. Our field work confirms the area's wilderness characteristics, and simple boundary changes exclude impacts from the unit. A regularly used vehicle way into Hartnet Draw is cherrystemmed out of our proposal and divides the unit into eastern and western portions, both of which abut the National Park and with the park form a single roadless unit. The openness and remote solitude of the Red Desert deserve wilderness designation.

LIMESTONE CLIFFS UNIT

Highlights—This spectacular 1,000-foot-high escarpment links the alpine world of Thousand Lake Mountain and the Fishlake Plateau with the desert and canyon country below. It is an important corridor for elk, antelope, and large herds of deer migrating between winter and summer range. With the adjacent Forest Service roadless area, the unit features a remarkable range of habitat zones, from ponderosa forest to sagebrush flats, and provides magnificent views across the San Rafael Swell. In its accelerated inventory decision, the BLM exaggerated the impacts found in the unit and did not consider a boundary change to exclude significant impacts. The Coalition proposes a 21,300-acre wilderness unit to protect wildlife winter range, sensitive soils, and scenery.

Geology and landforms—Elevations vary from 6,000 to 7,800 feet; in the adjacent national forest roadless area they exceed 10,500 feet. The geologic formations in the Limestone Cliffs unit range from the Entrada Sandstone to the Mancos Shale. (See Wild Horse Mesa unit for discussion of formations and Mussentuchit Badlands unit for critical watershed areas, which also cover most of this unit.)

Plant communities—Pinyon-juniper forest predominates with desert grass and sagebrush communities at lower elevations. The endangered *Sclerocactus wrightiae* may be present, according to the USFWS.

Wildlife—The UDWR lists elk winter range on the southwest edge and in the central portion, and critical mule deer winter range in the southern third. Antelope also use the unit.

Recreation—Hikes are possible from the desert floor through the cliff wall and up onto the national forest. Vistas from the high cliffs out across the San Rafael Swell are breathtaking. Wildlife viewing is good.

The spectacular badland basin of the Red Desert.

Ray Wheeler

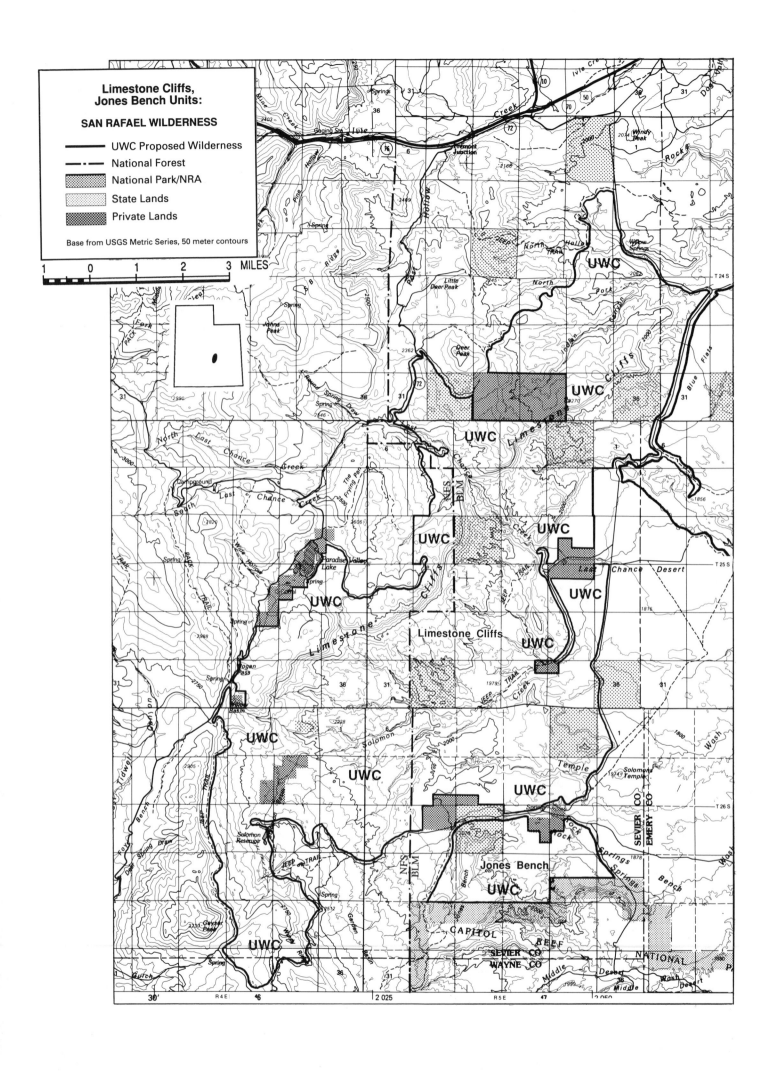

**Limestone Cliffs,
Jones Bench Units:**

SAN RAFAEL WILDERNESS

—— UWC Proposed Wilderness
—·—·— National Forest
National Park/NRA
State Lands
Private Lands

Base from USGS Metric Series, 50 meter contours

1   0   1   2   3   MILES

BLM recommendation and Coalition proposal—In the special IPP inventory the BLM stated that the unit had lost its naturalness. No specific information on the location or significance of the impacts was provided. Field inventory of the unit revealed that the impacts are associated primarily with a ranch located on Last Chance Flats. Excluding these impacts and an abandoned mining operation at the mouth of Last Chance Creek, the remaining area of 21,300 acres is substantially natural.

JONES BENCH UNIT

Highlights—The 2,800-acre Jones Bench unit abuts recommended wilderness within Capitol Reef National Park. The unit is a logical continuation of the geologic formations and scenic values found in the national park and is also a small, yet integral part of the San Rafael Swell area. The endangered *Sclerocactus wrightiae* may be present, according to the USFWS, and the UDWR identifies the west half of the unit as critical winter range for mule deer. The BLM dropped the entire unit from its initial wilderness inventory, claiming it was heavily impacted. Fewer than 600 acres on the west side actually have human impacts; they are deleted from the Coalition's proposal. The BLM also argued that adjacent ranch operations visible from Jones Bench interfere with wilderness opportunities. Such outside sights and sounds are not a valid criterion for excluding inventory areas from WSA status.

THE BOOK CLIFFS-DESOLATION CANYON WILDERNESS

Summary

North of Green River, Utah, the 2,000-foot-high escarpment of the Book and Roan cliffs marks the southern perimeter of a million-acre wilderness of exceptional geographic and biological diversity. Abundant wildlife and rugged beauty have made the Book Cliffs wilderness one of Utah's most popular backcountry destinations. Each year the region draws more than 6,000 hunters, and an equal number of river runners make the float trip through Desolation Canyon annually. But the BLM's wilderness proposals would leave half of those wild lands open for the development of coal, petroleum, and natural gas. The Utah Wilderness Coalition's 718,600-acre proposal would protect the region's nationally significant wildlife and recreational resources.

Cliff, Plateau, and River

Between Price, Utah and Grand Junction, Colorado, Highway 6 and Interstate 70 cross 170 miles of barren and windswept terrain. The drive would be lonely but for a constant companion: the thousand-foot-high wall of the Book Cliffs that parallels the highway just to the north. Winding for 250 miles across Utah and Colorado, it is the longest continuous escarpment in the world.

Near the town of Green River, Utah, a second escarpment, the Roan Cliffs, rises above the Book Cliffs, and together the two climb a vertical mile above the desert. From a distance the double rampart appears to be a smooth, unbroken wall, but on closer inspection it resolves into a complicated network of spurs, ridgelines, and canyons. The ridges climb steeply, collect, and finally join to form a long, unbroken crest called "The Divide."

The Divide is a seam between worlds, a shoreline where the earth meets the sky. To the north lies the vast, gently north-sloping surface of the Tavaputs Plateau. Hanging at elevations between 8,000 and 10,000

IN BRIEF

Index Map: Area No. 55

Highlights: One of the largest unprotected natural areas in the western U.S., this area includes the Book Cliffs escarpment, the high forests of the Tavaputs Plateau, and the mile-deep canyon system cut by the Green River. Abundant big game, superb white-water floating, and rugged beauty have made the area one of Utah's most popular backcountry destinations.

Guidebooks: Kelsey (1986), Hall (1982), Nichols (1986)

Maps: USGS 1:100,000 Price, Seep Ridge, Huntington, Westwater

Area of wilderness proposals in acres:

Unit	UWC	BLM
Desolation Canyon	527,100	247,990
Turtle Canyon	36,900	27,960
Eastern Book Cliffs	154,600	52,005
TOTAL	718,600	327,955

Adjacent wild lands: Book Cliffs State Roadless Area

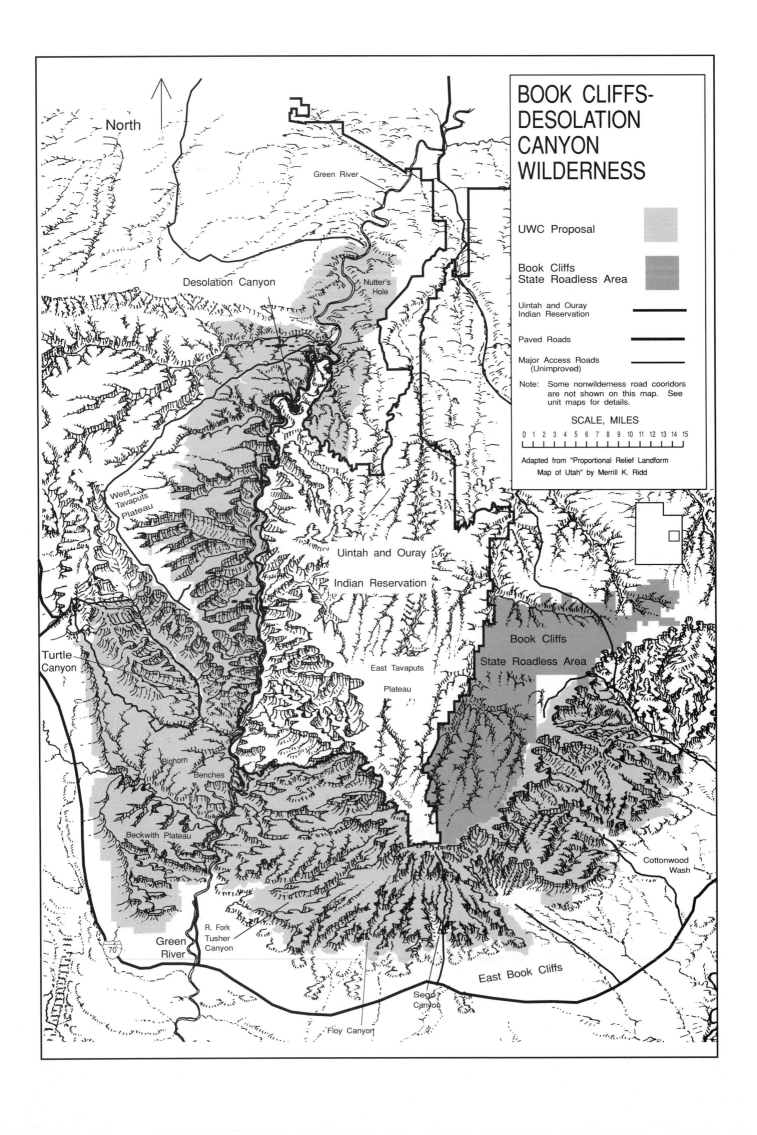

North

**BOOK CLIFFS-
DESOLATION
CANYON
WILDERNESS**

UWC Proposal

Book Cliffs
State Roadless Area

Uintah and Ouray
Indian Reservation

Paved Roads

Major Access Roads
(Unimproved)

Note: Some nonwilderness road cooridors
are not shown on this map. See
unit maps for details.

SCALE, MILES

0 1 2 3 4 5 6 7 8 9 10 11 12 13 14 15

Adapted from "Proportional Relief Landform
Map of Utah" by Merrill K. Ridd

Green River

Desolation Canyon

Nutter's
Hole

West
Tavaputs
Plateau

Uintah and Ouray

Indian Reservation

Turtle
Canyon

Book Cliffs

State Roadless Area

East Tavaputs

Plateau

Bighorn
Benches

The Divide

Beckwith Plateau

Cottonwood
Wash

R. Fork
Tusher
Canyon

Green
River

East Book Cliffs

Sego
Canyon

Floy Canyon

feet, the Tavaputs is as cool and moist as the Roan and Book cliffs are rugged and dry. Its ridgelines are covered with forests of spruce, aspen, and fir. Its narrow, north-trending valleys are carpeted with grass and watered by perennial streams.

The Tavaputs Plateau is a monument to the battle between uplift and erosion. This two-mile-thick block of sedimentary strata was uplifted directly in the path of the Green River; as the land rose the Green scoured its channel deeper, gradually cutting the Tavaputs Plateau in half.

Between those two halves—the East Tavaputs and West Tavaputs plateaus—the Green winds for 80 miles in a gorge nearly as deep as the Grand Canyon. " . . . the river is very rapid," wrote the explorer John Wesley Powell, "and many lateral canyons enter on either side . . . . crags and tower-shaped peaks are seen everywhere, and away above them, long lines of broken cliffs; and above and beyond the cliffs are pine forests, of which we obtain occasional glimpses as we look up through a vista of rocks . . . . We are minded to call this the Canyon of Desolation."

One-hundred and thirty years have passed since Powell made his voyage of discovery through Desolation Canyon—a century of development and progress. Yet the canyon and a large region surrounding it remain as wild as they were when Powell explored them.

In 1936, 67 years after Powell's voyage, Wilderness Society founder Bob Marshall identified the region surrounding Desolation Canyon as the fifth-largest desert wilderness in the nation. Marshall called it the "Book Cliffs Roadless Area" and estimated its size at 2.4 million acres. In the 50 years since Marshall's 1936 survey, mineral development and road construction have reduced the size of this roadless area by more than 60 percent. Even so, the core of the region—nearly a million acres of extremely rugged canyon country—remains today, one of the largest unprotected wilderness areas in the West.

Three Worlds

The Desolation Canyon-Book Cliffs wilderness is a merging of three different worlds: the great rampart of the Roan and Book cliffs, the high alpine forests and meadows of the Tavaputs Plateau, and the inner world of Desolation Canyon. Land ownership in the region is likewise tripartite. The East Tavaputs Plateau, a traditional hunting ground for the Ute Indians, lies within the Uintah and Ouray Indian Reservation. Reaching east from the Green River and north from the Roan Cliffs Divide, the Ute reservation encompasses over 200,000 acres of wild land. East of the reservation and north of The Divide lies a 48,000-acre tract of roadless land owned by the state of Utah. South of The Divide and west of the Green River, the remaining 720,000 acres of the Desolation Canyon-Book Cliffs wilderness are BLM land.

It is all marvelous wilderness. The region is one of Utah's most popular backcountry destinations. Each year some 6,000 visitors make the 6-day float trip through Desolation Canyon. The trip features 60 rapids and one of the most impressive river gorges in the country. Equally challenging, though less well known, are the hundreds of miles of pack trails that wind through the canyons. The Outlaw Trail, used by Butch Cassidy's gang, runs the entire length of Desolation Canyon, providing an 80-mile trip for adventurous riders or hikers. Four private lodges located around the perimeter of the wilderness offer starting points for guided horsepack trips.

Big Game Sanctuary

Because of its size, the lack of human intrusions, and the diversity and abundance of its habitat, the Desolation Canyon-Book Cliffs wilderness is

The thousands who float through Desolation Canyon each year bring nearly half a million dollars to local counties.

Tom Till

an important sanctuary for wildlife. The region between Interstate 70 on the south and the White River on the north harbors an estimated 375 vertebrate species of wildlife—half of the number found in Utah (UDWR, 1977, Appendix H). Wildlife inventories have identified 50 species of mammals on the East Tavaputs Plateau alone; as many as 14 threatened, endangered, or candidate species of wildlife may exist in the area (BLM, 1986). The Green River in Desolation Canyon is a major migration route for waterfowl and a favorite winter roosting site for the endangered bald eagle. As many as 38 bald eagles have been sighted on a winter day in the 15-mile stretch of river between Chandler Creek and Rock Creek (UDWR, 1977, p. 53).

The area provides a wide variety of habitat for big game. The quiet forests and lush meadows of the Tavaputs Plateau are ideal summer habitat for elk, deer, cougar, and bear. During the winter, deer and elk move away from the Roan Cliffs Divide, seeking forage at lower elevations both to the north and the south. The canyons that head just south of The Divide, within the Desolation, Floy, and Coal Canyon WSAs, all provide critical winter habitat for elk. Some elk remain year-round in Rattlesnake, Floy, Cottonwood, and Diamond canyons, which provide critical year-round elk habitat. Deer moving down off the Tavaputs Plateau follow these canyon bottoms like highways. Desolation Canyon and the lower elevations of the Book Cliffs also provide critical winter habitat for deer.

Though hunting and livestock grazing caused the virtual extirpation of elk and bighorn sheep from Utah by the turn of the century, both species have been reintroduced successfully in this large roadless region. Introduced on the Uintah and Ouray Indian Reservation in the 1930s, elk quickly repopulated their traditional summer range on the East Tavaputs Plateau. Today the Book Cliffs elk herd numbers well over 400 animals and continues to grow and to expand its range.

Rocky Mountain bighorn sheep, which were reintroduced on the Ute reservation in the early 1970s, have spread rapidly throughout the region, ranging east as far as the Utah-Colorado border and crossing the Green River on winter ice to roam south to the Beckwith Plateau and west into Range Creek Canyon. The bighorn population is estimated at nearly 100 animals, and the Utah Division of Wildlife Resources (UDWR) is planning additional transplants of desert bighorn sheep, with the hope of reestablishing a hardy desert and Rocky Mountain bighorn crossbreed once abundant in the region.

Utah's Serengeti

Superb habitat and wise stewardship have made the Desolation Canyon-Book Cliffs wilderness one of the few places in Utah where one can find wildlife in numbers approaching those described in history books. An evening walk on the Tavaputs Plateau is the Utah equivalent of an African big game safari. In summer herds of deer roam the long, grassy valleys like wildebeest, and in the fall the air is alive with the music of bugling bull elk.

The area offers excellent opportunities for hunting. In the state-owned Book Cliffs Roadless Area, where bull elk permits are limited to 30 per season, the hunter success ratio is 75 percent. The quality of the hunt is reflected in the heavy demand for permits. In 1986, there were 29 applications for every permit issued, according to the UDWR.

The Book Cliffs deer herd is one of the largest in Utah. It is also one of the most popular, drawing over 4,500 hunters each year. The large deer herd, in turn, supports a healthy population of cougar. During the past decade more cougar were taken by sportsmen in the adjacent Range Creek and Book Cliffs cougar management units (which together span the wilderness) than in any other single cougar management unit in Utah. Bear, too, are unusually abundant in the area. "The black bear in Utah is rapidly facing extermination," the UDWR reported (Ranck, 1961). "A few scattered populations still exist in . . . those areas that are inaccessible and rarely frequented by man. The boreal sectors of the East Tavaputs Plateau represent one of these last remaining sanctuaries. The unspoiled regions of upper Willow Creek and Hill Creek and the high escarpments of the Roan Cliffs . . . support what is probably the largest population of black bears in Utah."

Protection Incomplete

Recognizing these superb wildlife and recreational resources, both federal and state agencies have taken measures to prohibit development in the region. As early as 1974, BLM planning documents identified up to 250,000 acres of lands qualifying for primitive area designation and recommended the entire length of the Green River in Desolation Canyon for Wild and Scenic River designation. In 1975, the State of Utah took the unprecedented step of creating a 48,000-acre roadless area on state-owned land in the Book Cliffs, closing the entire area to development to preserve wildlife habitat. In 1978, the Secretary of the Interior established a 61,000-acre Desolation Canyon National Landmark, and in 1983 the BLM identified the 40,000-acre Beckwith Plateau as a second candidate for National Landmark designation.

Thus, when the BLM began its wilderness inventory of the Book Cliffs region in 1978, public expectations were high. Surely the agency would recognize the value of protecting one of the largest roadless areas in the intermountain West. Yet by November, 1980, when the inventory was complete, something had gone wrong. While the BLM had identified a total of 362,000 acres in five WSAs in the Desolation Canyon-Book Cliffs area, it had omitted nearly as much wild land from wilderness study. The lands dropped were among the most rugged and beautiful in the region. They included the Nutters Hole roadless area, a 61,000-acre tract spanning the wildlife-rich bottomlands of the Green River just upstream from Desolation Canyon; 18,500 acres at the headwaters of 900-foot-deep Jack Creek Canyon; 13,000 acres on Big Horn Mountain bordering the west rim of Desolation Canyon; the entire 40,000-acre Beckwith Plateau; and 150,000 acres in the rugged canyons and ridgelines of the Book Cliffs east of the Green River.

Eager To Develop

Each of these huge tracts of roadless land is an integral part of the Desolation Canyon-Book Cliffs wilderness. By dropping them from its wilderness inventory, the BLM dropped nearly 40 percent of the area's wild lands from further review. Why would the agency refuse even to study the wilderness character of lands with such outstanding recreational, scenic, and wildlife resources?

The answer can be found by looking at an energy resources map of Utah. The Desolation Canyon-Book Cliffs wilderness contains coal, oil, and natural gas. In 1979 and 1980, even as the BLM's wilderness inventory was under way, a half dozen major energy companies, including Tenneco, Gulf, and Getty Oil, were pushing new roads into the lands under study. Instead of blocking this development, as required by law, the BLM seemed to be encouraging it. Indeed, even *after* large portions of the area's wilderness were identified as WSAs, the BLM continued to allow oil and gas exploration on lands under study for wilderness designation. In 1980 and 1981, the BLM authorized the drilling of at least 17 exploratory wells and the construction of 14 miles of seismic drilling inside its Book Cliffs WSAs.

In its eagerness to open the wilderness to energy development, the Utah BLM had repeatedly violated its own wilderness inventory regulations. Utah conservationists challenged the agency's inventory decisions in a series of protests and appeals. In 1983, the U.S. Interior Board of Land Appeals (IBLA) ruled that the BLM's inventory omissions had been in error on 92 percent of the land under appeal, and directed the agency to conduct a second study of lands improperly omitted. By 1984 protests and appeals had forced the BLM to add nearly 180,000 acres to its Book Cliffs WSAs.

What it had failed to do during the inventory phase of its wilderness review, the BLM again recommended in its February 1986, draft wilderness recommendation for Utah. Claiming that the value of potential mineral development outweighs wilderness values, the BLM recommended against wilderness designation for nearly 400,000 acres in the Desolation Canyon-Book Cliffs area. The final recommendation is expected to be only 328,000 acres, with additions in the eastern Book Cliffs but further deletions in Desolation Canyon and Turtle Canyon.

The BLM's wilderness recommendations thus represent a highly development-oriented plan for the future. We are losing this wilderness, and we are losing it fast. In a single lifetime—the 50 years since Bob Marshall's 1936 roadless area inventory—we have lost more than half of the region to development. The BLM's recommendation would open to development half of the remaining wild area.

Although the energy resources of the entire Desolation Canyon-Book Cliffs area are marginal, and energy prices are temporarily depressed, it is likely that prices eventually will rise high enough to make some oil, gas, and coal production in the Book Cliffs economically viable. Should that happen, the consequences for recreation, scenery, and wildlife will be severe. Mineral development will require the construction of hundreds of miles of new roads, most of them following the canyon bottoms which have traditionally served as a migration corridor for deer and critical winter and year-round range for elk.

Elk are especially sensitive to such intrusion. "Elk use is primarily in the canyon bottoms where water is available," says UDWR Director Tim Provan. "Canyon bottoms would also be the easiest and most logical place to develop access roads. Research has demonstrated that elk will abandon habitat 0.6 mile on either side of a road. This could preclude elk from areas they now inhabit."

Deer, too, would be affected by energy development. Virtually all of the critical deer winter range in the Book Cliffs east of the Green River lies on roadless land omitted from the BLM's draft wilderness recommendation.

Robbed of Their Beauty

Today, the numerous canyons that cut deeply into the Book and Roan Cliffs are remote, solitary, and wild. But if energy development should once again boom, they will rapidly change from scenic pack-trails and wildlife migration corridors into heavily traveled haul routes bristling with pipelines, powerlines, and pumping plants. The new roads will do more than drive wildlife from the region. They will also rob the canyons of their silence and beauty.

Developers argue that the area contains mineral deposits that are important to Utah's economy. Yet wilderness, too, is a powerful economic asset. Commercial river running in Desolation Canyon generates direct sales of over a million dollars a year and accounts for $460,000 of earned income and 40 jobs in Carbon, Emery, and Grand Counties (BLM, 1986, p. 43).

Even by the BLM's generous estimates, the total recoverable resources of oil and natural gas in the area's seven WSAs would meet the nation's demand for less than one week. The total coal recoverable from the Sego Coal Field, the largest in the area, represents less than one-tenth of one percent of total U.S. proven recoverable reserves (BLM, 1986, p. 18). Even these figures, however, are generous, because of economic and environmental constraints on coal recovery.

While the BLM's wilderness recommendation is a mandate for such development, the Utah Wilderness Coalition's 718,600-acre Desolation Canyon-Book Cliffs wilderness proposal is based on a sharply different philosophy. While the mineral and energy resources of the area are of marginal importance, its wildlife, scenic, and recreational opportunities make it one of the most important blocks of public wild lands in the nation. Recognizing that the sheer size of the Desolation Canyon-Book Cliffs wilderness is one of its most important assets, the Coalition proposal would protect *all* BLM lands that today remain wild.

Ray Wheeler

DESOLATION CANYON UNIT

Highlights—At more than half a million acres this is the largest block of federal wild land in the Lower 48 states not designated as a park or wilderness area. Another 200,000 acres are managed as wilderness in the Uintah and Ouray Indian Reservation. The Green River twists through this 25- by 60-mile tract in a canyon that is up to 5,000 feet deep. Whitewater float trips (including day trips in Gray Canyon) draw 60,000 visitor-days of use annually. This is an outstanding wildlife area with growing herds of mountain bighorn sheep and elk, critical winter range for deer along the river and canyon bottoms, and excellent habitat for black bear and mountain lion. Five endangered species are present: bald eagle, peregrine falcon, and three species of fish. The BLM initially recommended 265,140 acres for designation while excluding a nearly equal acreage in 13 separate parcels including: Nutters Hole (an excellent canoeing section of the river), Bighorn Benches (leaving a protected corridor just one mile wide at the center of the unit), and most of the Floy Canyon area (important wildlife habitat with high scenic values). The final BLM recommendation is expected to omit an additional 17,150 acres. The Coalition proposes a 527,100-acre wilderness unit to protect the entire BLM portion of the wild area.

Geology and landforms—The Green River forms the eastern boundary of the unit through Desolation Canyon. Named by Powell during his 1869 journey, this canyon is cut into light-colored Tertiary sediments. The river then cuts directly through the unit in Gray Canyon, named on Powell's second trip, which is carved into darker Cretaceous sandstones and shales. The long, steep slopes of the canyons in these relatively soft formations present a different aspect from the vertical cliff-forming slickrock sandstones farther south in the Colorado Plateau, although arches, alcoves, fins, and spires are common here, too. Rising above the river to the isolated Beckwith Plateau and the huge expanse of the Tavaputs Plateau are the nearly impenetrable Book Cliffs and the intricately eroded, little known Roan Cliffs.

Plant communities—Diverse plant communities are found here, ranging from high desert shrubs to Douglas fir and aspen in the higher mountains. Thick pinyon-juniper forests cover the ridges and lower slopes. Riparian habitat is found along about 200 miles of perennial streams. The threatened Uinta Basin hookless cactus (*Sclerocactus glaucus*) is found on the north edge, and in the northeast is the endangered toadflax cress (*Glaucocarpum suffrutescens*). The BLM also lists Graham catseye (*Cryptantha grahamii*) and Graham beardtongue (*Penstemon grahamii*) in the Nutters Hole area (BLM, 1980). The Beckwith Plateau has been proposed as a National Natural Landmark area (Welsh and others, 1980). This mesa has several relict plant areas, as well as the rare Jones psorothamnus (*Psorothamnus polydenius* var. *jonesii*).

Wildlife—Because of its vast size and remote location, the unit has a number of sensitive species that benefit from a large area to roam in. Elk herds have been reestablished and are growing. Mule deer make use of critical winter habitat along the bottomlands; the eastern edge of the unit is critical deer summer range. Black bear, mountain lion, coyote, and bobcat are common predators in the unit. The BLM notes historic reports of the extremely rare black-footed ferret adjacent to its WSA; the Fish and Wildlife Service has identified potential ferret habitat within the unit. The FWS also lists three endangered fish residents in the Green River (bonytail chub, humpback chub, and Colorado squawfish). Rock and Chandler creeks support trout, and the Green has catfish. Due to the wealth of riparian habitat, a number of songbirds and migratory ducks and shorebirds inhabit or frequent the unit. Several birds that are candidates for threatened and endangered status are potentially in the unit, including the long-billed curlew, Southern spotted owl, Western yellow-billed cuckoo, ferruginous hawk, and white-faced ibis. The endangered bald eagle and peregrine falcon are known to inhabit the unit. The FWS has identified wintering bald eagle populations in the northern part of the unit along the Green River.

Archeology and history—The unit is rich in cultural resources of the Paleo-Indian, Archaic, Anasazi, Fremont, and Ute cultures, including rock art, rock shelters, campsites, and burial grounds. Castleton (1979) notes that there are "numerous rock art sites along the river . . . several are large and impressive." The French trapper Denis Julien carved his initials on a rock near Chandler Creek (Aitchison, 1987). Other remains include the historic Rock Creek cabin and ranch and the Outlaw Trail along the Price River and up the Green. The Green River corridor is a designated National Historic Landmark commemorating Powell's explorations. The Flat

Canyon Archeological District, located in the northern part of the unit, was established to protect significant Fremont cultural sites (BLM, 1986, p. 36).

Recreation—Desolation's superb recreation opportunities include boating the Green and Price Rivers, trophy deer and elk hunting in the high plateaus, and hiking the numerous drainages, including historic Rock Creek. Desolation Canyon is one of the premier whitewater rivers in Utah and helps support two dozen river outfitting businesses. Gray Canyon, above the town of Green River, is an enjoyable day outing for novice boaters trying their skills. Many horseback riders and hunters enter the unit from four guest lodges on the west boundary. Hiking the rugged drainages is made easier by excellent streamside campsites. Kelsey (1986a) and Hall (1982) list hikes along the Green River and in sidecanyons, and the BLM has noted more than 140 miles of trails. The Green River, Price River, and Range Creek were identified as candidates for wild and scenic river status in the Nationwide Rivers Inventory.

BLM recommendation—In 1986, the BLM recommended 265,140 acres as suitable for designation as wilderness—barely half of the qualifying wild lands. (The final recommendation is likely to omit an additional 17,150 acres). The BLM improperly excluded 280,000 acres from WSA status during the wilderness inventory, partly as a result of dividing the unit into three separate WSAs: Desolation Canyon, Floy Canyon, and Jack Canyon. The agency then omitted more than 100,000 acres from its 1986 wilderness recommendation for those WSAs. Most of the excluded lands are in less steep areas on the margins of the unit which are proposed for resource development. By allowing this development, the BLM would eliminate much of the topographic, ecological, and recreational diversity of the unit.

Lands excluded from wilderness study by the BLM:

Nutters Hole (60,700 acres)—Upstream from Sand Wash, at the northern end of the Desolation Canyon unit, the BLM omitted 11 miles of the wild Green River from its wilderness inventory. The agency claimed that 10 miles of vehicle ways on the ridges east of the river rendered the area unsuitable for wilderness. These vehicle ways are two-wheel tracks with mature shrubs growing between them; they occupy a total area of eight acres. Use is infrequent and serves no established need. A fence and oil facilities at the northeast edge are excluded from the Coalition proposal. The BLM claimed that lands west of the river, although natural, lacked outstanding opportunities for solitude or primitive recreation—despite herds of antelope and deer, numerous bird species, great scenery, and the wild and scenic Green River. New roads built in this area could have been excluded from the wilderness as the Coalition has done.

Nine Mile Canyon (22,700 acres)—The lower reach of this major drainage flows through wild land before entering the Green River. A well-used vehicle route forms the northern boundary and a pipeline along a ridge forms the southern boundary; it is connected to Nutters Hole and the main Desolation Canyon unit by undeveloped private lands along the Green River.

West Tabyago Canyon (26,000 acres)—The BLM failed to inventory these lands in the Naval Oil Shale Reserve, thereby isolating the Nutters Hole inventory unit from the main body of Desolation Canyon. Within this area are eight miles of the Green River, the first part of the Desolation Canyon trip thousands enjoy each year. Oil shale reserves managed by the BLM in Colorado were inventoried for wilderness; with oil shale development halted nationally by high economic and environmental costs, this reserve should not block wilderness designation.

Horse Bench (6,000 acres)—The BLM claimed that this area in the northwestern side of the unit lacked outstanding opportunities for solitude

Wildlife richness and diversity is directly correlated to this area's roadless condition . . . intrusion of roads and increased human activity will have a detrimental effect.

UDWR Director Tim Provan
[speaking of the Book Cliffs State Roadless Area]

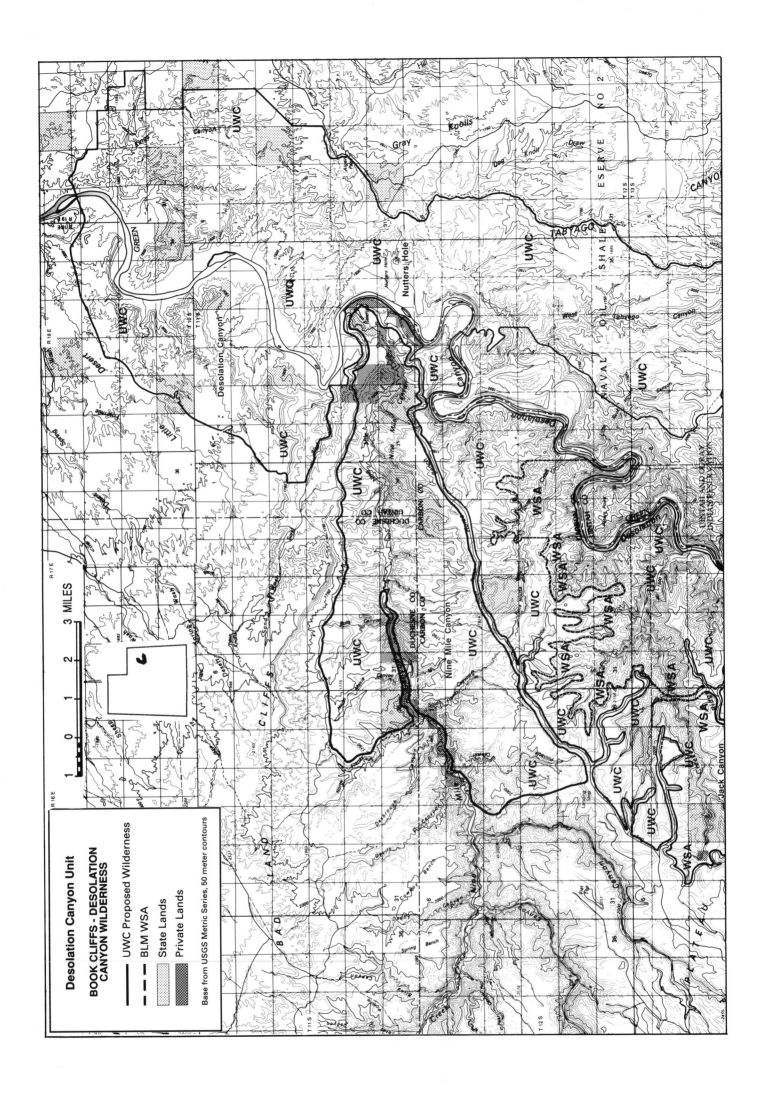

Desolation Canyon Unit

BOOK CLIFFS - DESOLATION CANYON WILDERNESS

UWC Proposed Wilderness

BLM WSA

State Lands

Private Lands

Base from USGS Metric Series, 50 meter contours

3 MILES

2

1

0

1

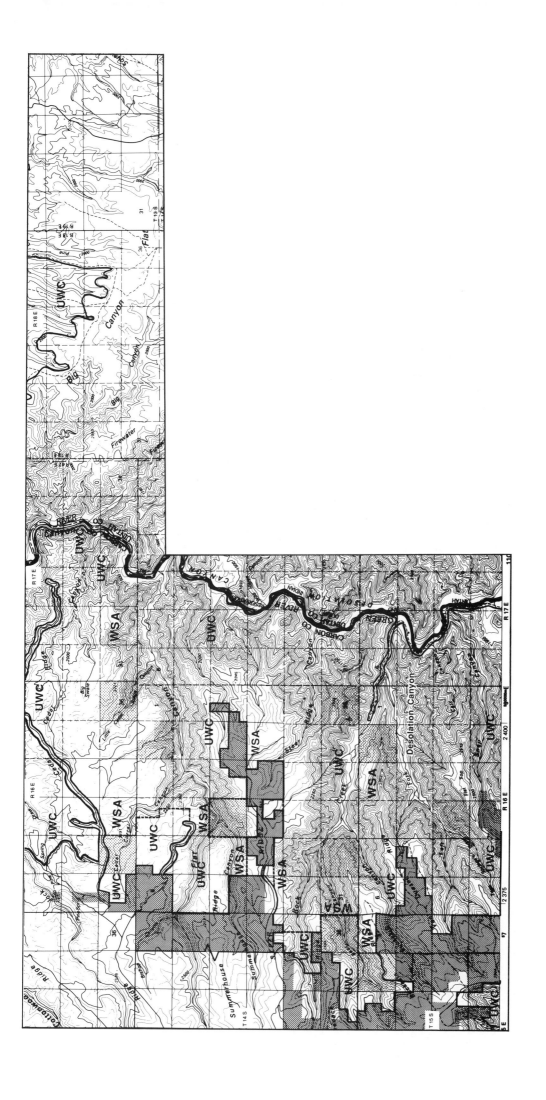

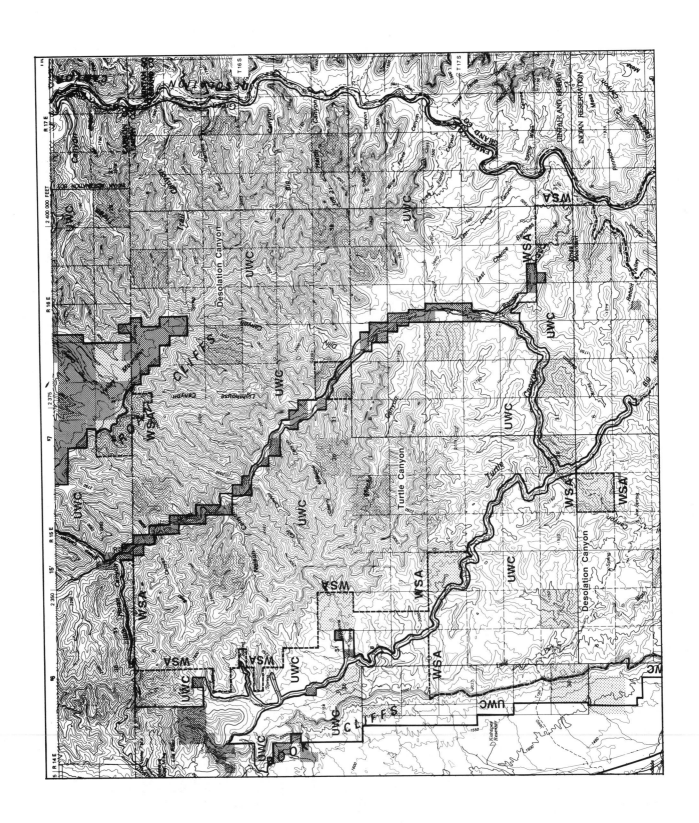

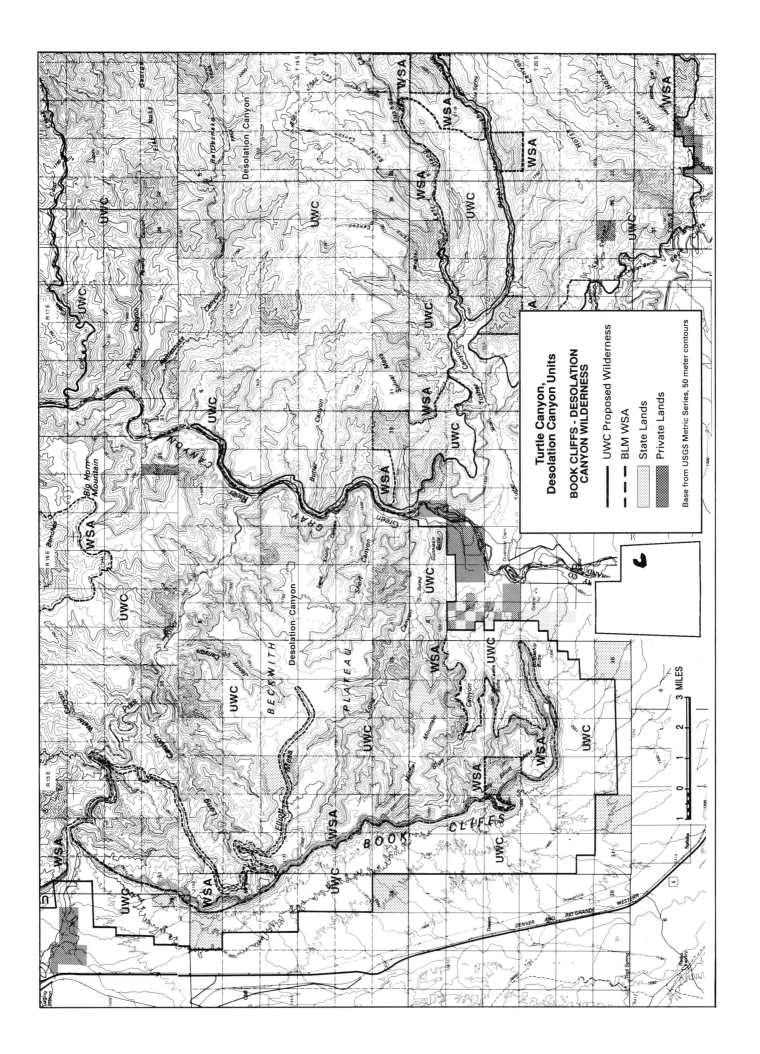

Turtle Canyon,
Desolation Canyon Units

BOOK CLIFFS - DESOLATION
CANYON WILDERNESS

UWC Proposed Wilderness	
BLM WSA	
State Lands	
Private Lands	

Base from USGS Metric Series, 50 meter contours

0   1   2   3 MILES

and primitive recreation, although it gives access to several canyons and has spectacular vistas of Maverick Canyon, Ninemile Canyon, and the Bad Land Cliffs. Horse Bench, high and relatively flat, adds recreational and ecological diversity to the unit.

Face of Book Cliffs (27,000 acres)—These lands on the southwestern side of the unit (around Beckwith Plateau) were dropped in the initial inventory for "lack of naturalness." They are badlands and cliffs free from significant human imprints. The BLM violated inventory policy by not drawing the WSA boundary to the edge of physical disturbance. The Mancos Shale badlands along the cliff face are a scenic backdrop for Interstate 70 and Highway 6.

Big Horn Benches and Xmas Canyon (13,000 acres)—This pocket of land in the southwestern part of the unit is surrounded by the Desolation Canyon WSA on three sides and by the Turtle Canyon WSA on the fourth side. The BLM exaggerated the impacts of old, inaccessible mineral exploration roads that are largely unnoticeable even from the air. The scenic, broken topography of the area should be closed to further mineral exploration to protect wildlife, scenery, and recreation.

West Suluar Mesa (3,000 acres)—The BLM (1980) claimed there is a five-mile-long way on the lower bench above Tusher Canyon. Our field work indicates no such way.

Tusher Canyon (6,000 acres)—The BLM (1980) separated a large natural mountain between Left and Right Hand Tusher canyons from its Desolation Canyon WSA along a "traveled way" to the head of Left Hand Tusher Canyon that "then follows a bench to the boundary road in Right Hand Tusher Canyon." Our fieldwork indicates that only the first few miles of this way are actively used; accordingly, we cherrystem that part and include the remainder in our proposal.

WSA lands not recommended suitable by the BLM:

Floy Canyon (49,465 acres)—The BLM designated the 72,605-acre Floy Canyon WSA only after conservationists filed an administrative appeal. It then divided Floy Canyon from the Desolation Canyon WSA to the north along a post-FLPMA road. Now the agency recommends only 23,140 acres as suitable for wilderness designation. The southern two-thirds of the WSA would be dropped because of coal, even though the BLM (1986) states that "It is questionable that coal development would occur in the WSA in the foreseeable future due to more favorable areas located in the region near the WSA." Outstanding wilderness qualities of the WSA, which the BLM recognized in its 1986 DEIS, include solitude, primitive recreation, and scenery. The BLM and the UDWR have identified 56,575 acres of the WSA as "crucial winter habitat for black bear, cougar, deer, and elk" (BLM, 1986, p. 18).

Head of Right Hand Tusher Canyon (430 acres)—Three oil exploration wells were drilled on this parcel and an adjacent state section to the east in 1981. One and a half miles of new road were built from the end of the existing road in Right Hand Tusher Canyon to reach the drill sites. Post-FLPMA impacts were not supposed to be considered in drawing WSA boundaries.

Suluar Mesa (23,250 acres)—This parcel in the southeastern part of the Desolation Canyon WSA was made part of the WSA after an appeal filed by conservationists. The BLM claimed a lack of outstanding opportunities for solitude and primitive recreation as a pretext for releasing these lands, which it considers to have relatively high potential for oil and gas. However, numerous wells adjacent to the unit in the Tusher canyons have failed to establish commercial production (BLM, 1986, p. 58). There is riparian habitat in Winter Camp, Bobby and Naylon canyons on the south

The Green River in Gray Canyon, part of the Desolation Canyon-Book Cliffs proposed wilderness.

Tom Miller

side of Suluar and outstanding opportunities for hiking, backpacking, hunting, photography, rock climbing, and cross country skiing throughout.

Cherrystemmed way on the Beckwith Plateau—The BLM excluded this impassable, 18-mile-long mineral exploration route along the Price River and on the Beckwith Plateau from the Desolation Canyon WSA. It does not meet the definition of a "road" since it is not maintained or regularly used. Except for a few cuts and the drill pad, the way is substantially unnoticeable from the ground. It should be designated wilderness with the rest of the Beckwith Plateau to protect important bighorn sheep range and a spectacular, isolated expanse of wilderness.

Little Park (13,400 acres)—The BLM excluded this area on the west tip of the Desolation Canyon WSA from its recommendation because of coal reserves and a proposed 350-acre chaining. But Little Park is critical winter range for deer and should not be sacrificed for possible coal development. A five-mile-long way which the BLM says is not noticeable is used for maintenance of small stock reservoirs; this use would be allowed to continue under wilderness designation.

Jack Canyon and Cedar Ridge (18,500 acres)—This parcel on the northwest side of the unit includes the 7,500-acre Jack Canyon WSA and 11,000 acres in the Desolation Canyon WSA. Jack Canyon is separated from the main WSA by a four-inch surface pipeline that is difficult to see and could be removed easily when production ceases. It should not have been used as a WSA boundary. This scenic area is important habitat for mountain lion, bighorn sheep, elk, deer, bear, sage grouse, peregrine falcon, bald eagle, golden eagle, prairie falcon, and wild horses. Although oil and gas are present, short cherrystemmed roads would permit their extraction. A proposed chaining of about 1,000 acres would harm naturalness and wildlife habitat in this parcel.

Coalition proposal—Our 527,100-acre wilderness proposal would include the wild lands listed above that the BLM omitted as well as those the BLM recommends for wilderness. Here is an opportunity to protect one of the nation's largest and most spectacular roadless areas intact, without the fragmentation and loss of wildness that characterizes so much of our treatment of the original frontier.

TURTLE CANYON UNIT

Highlights—The rugged, scenic terrain of the 36,900-acre Turtle Canyon unit supports diverse plant and animal communities and offers exceptional opportunities for solitude, hunting, and primitive recreation. The unit exemplifies the topography and ecology of the Roan Cliffs. Turtle Canyon is located about 30 miles southeast of Price.

Geology and landforms—Alternating soft and resistant layers of sedimentary rocks have been deeply dissected to form a rugged landscape with 4,500 feet of vertical relief. A high, notched ridge runs across most of the unit at elevations generally above 8,000 feet, reaching 9,300 feet in the north. From this ridge precipitous canyons drop into Range Creek and Turtle Canyon. The southern part is more gentle, but virtually all of the unit is sloping.

Plant communities—Pinyon pine, juniper, and Douglas fir cling to the slopes, while grasses and sagebrush line the drainages. Species more typical of mountains than desert are found here, including mountain mahogany, serviceberry, and snowberry. Several candidates for threatened and endangered status may grow in the unit, including yellow blanketflower (*Gaillardia flava*), canyon sweetvetch (*Hedysarum occidentale* var. *canone*) and Jones psorothamnus (*Psorothamnus polyadenius* var. *jonesii*), (BLM, 1986).

Wildlife—Dramatic variations in topography and the presence of springs and streams provide diverse habitat for wildlife. Large mammals include Rocky Mountain bighorn sheep, mule deer, elk, mountain lion, and black bear; the BLM (1986) lists significant summer and winter range for both deer and elk, and almost a third of the unit is bighorn habitat. Birds include blue grouse, ruffed grouse, golden eagle, and prairie falcon. Other nesting raptors thought to be present, according to the BLM, include the peregrine falcon, bald eagle, and ferruginous hawk. The BLM also lists the Western snowy plover, the white-faced ibis, and the long-billed curlew, all candidates for protection.

Archeology and history—Early settlers homesteaded along Range Creek at the edge of the unit; this drainage was also visited by people of the ancient Fremont culture, who left their rock art and other artifacts. The BLM notes that the Pillings Collection of Fremont figurines at the College of Eastern Utah was collected from along Range Creek, and that based on such occurrences, as many as 30 archeological or historical sites could be found within the unit.

Recreation—The ruggedness and remoteness of the unit provide excellent opportunities for solitude and primitive recreation. Few visitors get beyond the side drainages on the edge of the unit. Although the steep terrain borders on requiring technical rock climbing, views from the ridge crests are rewarding. Hunters make use of guest lodges along Range Creek, and the BLM notes that some hunting occurs in the lower, more accessible reaches of the unit. A light-duty road through Horse and Little

Horse canyons, which has a marked exit from Highway 6, passes along the northern boundary of the unit and connects with an unimproved dirt road along Range Creek, the unit's eastern boundary. Private lands along Range Creek may require permission for entry.

BLM recommendation—The BLM initially recommended designating all 33,690 acres of its Turtle Canyon WSA as wilderness, but is expected to reduce this to 27,960 acres in its final EIS, omitting wild lands in the northern part of the unit. Its final boundary would slice across hills and buttes, leaving land open to speculative oil and gas exploration. The BLM describes the terrain as the most rugged and scenic in the Roan Cliffs region and recognizes the varied topographic features and wildlife habitat as highly unusual for an area the size of the WSA. The BLM (1986) concluded that there are no substantial human intrusions in its WSA. Vehicle tracks run a short distance up the canyon bottoms adjacent to Range Creek, and the remains of two seismic tracks, covering fewer than 30 acres, are returning to nature. Wilderness values exceed mineral potential in the WSA. Commercial grade coal underlies a small portion of the unit on the northwest, but if it were mined the surface facilities would probably be outside the unit. About 80 percent of the WSA is under lease for oil and gas (BLM, 1986, p. 16). However, nearby exploration has not shown commercial quantities at current prices (BLM, 1986, p. 15).

Coalition proposal—The Coalition seconds the BLM's initial all-wilderness recommendation but recommends additions to the west of the WSA that would form the 36,900-acre Turtle Creek unit.

EASTERN BOOK CLIFFS UNIT

Highlights—The Eastern Book Cliffs, a 10- by 20-mile expanse of forested mountains and canyons, provide important habitat for elk, black bear, mountain lion, and other wilderness species. The unit is part of the larger Book Cliffs ecosystem, one of Utah's most important wildlife areas. Adjacent lands in the Book Cliffs State Forest form a combined roadless area of 190,000 acres that is separated from the main Desolation Canyon roadless area to the west only by the dirt road up Sego Canyon. The BLM initially recommended just 30,000 acres for wilderness designation, but following public review of the draft EIS it apparently will recommend 52,000 acres. The Utah Wilderness Coalition proposes a 154,600-acre wilderness unit to protect wildlife, watershed, and scenic values.

Geology and landforms—The intricately interlocking ridges and canyons of the Book Cliffs rise 3,000 feet in 10 miles from the Grand Valley of the Colorado River on the southeast to the 8,500-foot-high rim of the Tavaputs Plateau on the northwest. Cottonwood Canyon and its major side-canyons (including Coal, Spruce, and Flume) run through the central part of the unit; Nash and Sagers canyons through the southwest, and tributaries of Westwater Creek through the northeast. Cottonwood Point and Westwater Point are high ridges that extend from the plateau rim to divide the major drainages. Strata of the Mesaverde and Wasatch groups predominate: thin, cliff-forming sandstones alternate with sloping softer sediments. The Flagstaff Limestone of the Wasatch Group is found at higher elevations with colorful outcrops reminiscent of those in the same formation in Bryce Canyon National Park.

Plant communities—A fifth of the unit is covered by Douglas fir forest and three-fifths by pinyon-juniper, Douglas fir, aspen, and mountain shrubs, reflecting relatively high elevation and precipitation compared to most Utah BLM lands outside the Book Cliffs. The remaining fifth of the unit is covered by pinyon-juniper, mountain shrub-grassland, and riparian communities.

Wildlife—The mixture of productive plant communities and diverse topography provide excellent wildlife habitat. The BLM (1986) estimates that 160 elk inhabit the three WSAs in this unit during at least part of the year. That is nearly 40 percent of the estimated 425 elk in the South Book Cliffs herd (BLM, 1983a, p. 3-11). The northwest side of the unit is elk winter range, and the entire unit is yearlong habitat (BLM, 1983a, p. 1-9 and 1-16). Black bear and mountain lion find crucial habitat in the East Book Cliffs, and like elk, are sensitive to human activity and disturbance. Nearly the entire unit is winter range for deer (BLM, 1983a, p. 1-16). Four candidate endangered species may inhabit the unit: ferruginous hawk, long-billed curlew, Southern spotted owl, and Western yellow-billed cuckoo. Common species include coyote, bobcat, cottontail rabbits, other small mammals, lizards, snakes, blue and ruffed grouse, golden eagles, great horned owls, and many other birds.

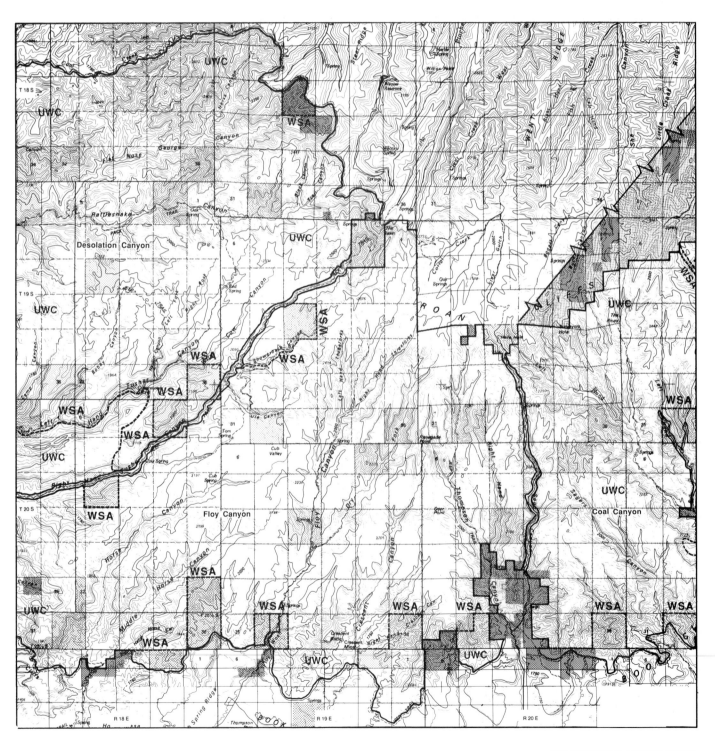

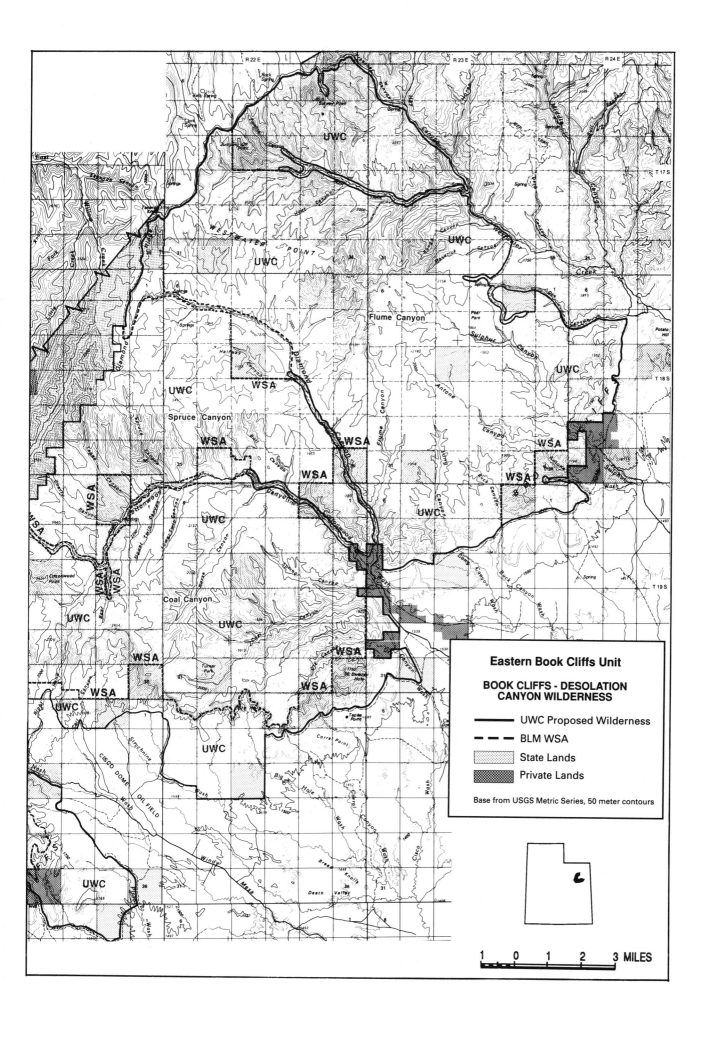

Eastern Book Cliffs Unit

BOOK CLIFFS - DESOLATION CANYON WILDERNESS

——————— UWC Proposed Wilderness

– – – – – BLM WSA

State Lands

Private Lands

Base from USGS Metric Series, 50 meter contours

1 0 1 2 3 MILES

Recreation—The Eastern Book Cliffs offer outstanding hunting, hiking, backpacking, and wildlife viewing in a highly scenic area. The unit is reached by the Sego Canyon road north from Thompson, the Cotton-wood Canyon road (north from I-70 at an exit 5 miles northeast of Cisco), and the Hay Canyon road on the northeast boundary.

BLM recommendation—In its 1986 DEIS, the BLM recommended wilderness designation for only 30,000 acres out of the 132,400 acres in three WSAs (Coal Canyon, Spruce Canyon, and Flume Canyon). The final recommendation is slated to include some wilderness in each WSA for a total of 52,000 acres, but would move the wilderness boundary to an average of six miles from the WSA's southern boundary, protecting only the highest area and omitting some of the most important wildlife habitat. In addition, more than 20,000 acres were improperly excluded from WSA status. A block of natural land at the north end around Preacher Canyon should have been included in wilderness study by placing the boundary at the Hay Canyon road and cherrystemming the Westwater Creek trail. Other small parcels at the base of the cliffs on the southeast side should have been included as well.

Coalition proposal—Our 154,600-acre wilderness unit would retain the natural integrity of these scenic, wildlife-rich lands. Unlike the BLM, which divided the unit into three WSAs, we would cherrystem roads in Cottonwood and Diamond canyons. The BLM drew its boundaries across natural terrain from the end of the roads to the northwest boundary. The Coalition proposal would block these roads where they become impass-able. In Diamond Canyon there is a gate a few hundred yards above the mouth of Halfway Canyon. Vegetation is growing waist-high beyond the gate, and the way is not negotiable. In Cottonwood Canyon, the road shrinks to a track too narrow for a four-wheel-drive vehicle just above the mouth of Horse Canyon. The road used to go another five miles to a gas well in Bear Canyon but is now completely washed out in the southeast corner of Section 32. The BLM did not recommend most of its WSAs for designation because of claimed oil and gas potential, although its consult-ants rated the likelihood of large deposits as low. Watershed rehabilitation structures are planned for the major drainages in the unit but if designed properly would be allowed within the wilderness.

THE WHITE RIVER WILDERNESS

Green Corridor in the Desert

The White River wilderness provides a wonderful opportunity for novice canoeists, including families with small children, to spend a com-fortable, relaxing, and moderately challenging time in a primitive area. One needn't be an expert canoeist or rafter to negotiate the White River. It has no hazardous rapids or treacherous water. There are areas of mild to moderate turbulence and what may be called "rapids," which vary with the season but may be negotiated easily by most canoeists.

The area is an easy one-hour drive from Vernal, Utah and can be reached in four to five hours from Salt Lake City or from Steamboat Springs, Colorado. The canyon of the White River begins about 15 river miles west of the new Bonanza Bridge, which is south of Vernal at the end of the new paved highway to Bonanza. The proposed wilderness area flanks the river for about 12 river miles downstream.

The White River canyon is a perfect example of how a river brings life, beauty, and diversity to the desert landscape. Climbing the ridges to the south of the river, one can appreciate the green corridor that the river makes possible and the variety of life it brings to an arid zone. Looking

IN BRIEF

Index Map: Area No. 56

Highlights: Canoe trips along this lovely, non-technical river offer wildlife and water-fowl viewing. Spring and fall are good times to bring the family to enjoy this wild river canyon.

Guidebooks: Nichols (1986)

Maps: USGS 1:100,000 Seep Ridge, Vernal

Area of wilderness proposal in acres

Area	UWC	BLM
White River	9,700	0

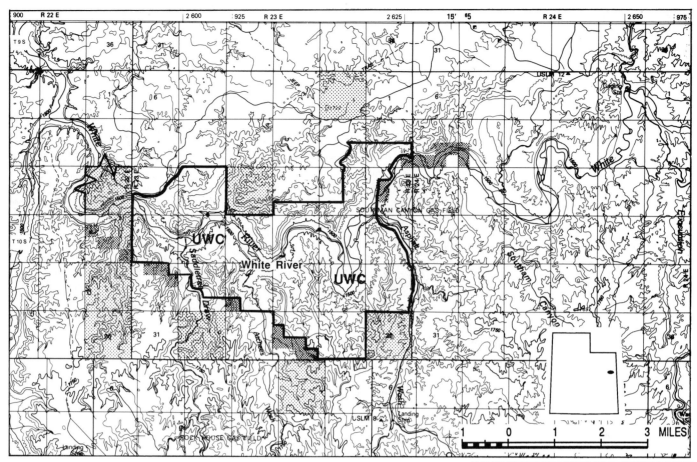

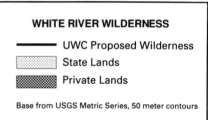

north of the canyon, one sees the browns and grays of the high desert. In the distance, the entire axis of the High Uinta Mountains stands snow-clad against the sky. The observer can get a feeling for the transitions in the topography of northeastern Utah and for the special significance of a desert river.

The river canyon consists of broad, sloping terraces that end at the river and sandstone walls that have been eroded into fascinating buttes, pinnacles, and towers. Shale outcroppings and sidewalls along the river help to define its course. The river meanders broadly along a mild gradient, producing a slow current and constantly changing banks and beaches. Flow and water clarity change with the seasons, ranging from a turbid, forceful, working river in the spring to a clear, gentle, often quite shallow stream in autumn.

Large, flat, grassy parks along the meanders and bends of the river are dominated by cottonwood groves, which are ablaze with bright yellow and gold in the fall. (One lovely 80-acre grove was literally set ablaze by unknown persons in April 1989, pointing out the need for protection of the area's botanic resources.) Wild rose, rabbitbrush, and sagebrush are the common shrubs. There are the usual thickets of willow, tamarisk, and reeds at the river's edge. These flat areas are bermed on the uphill side by hummocks, terraces, and outcrops—evidence of another time in the river's history. Excellent, protected campsites can be found in these flat or gently sloping parks. On the higher benches above the river the dominant vegetation is juniper, sagebrush, saltbush, and shadscale. In the spring, a profusion of wildflowers can be found over the rolling terrain and in the sidecanyons. The high, bare benches and ascending ridges feature cactus and desert primrose.

The entire canyon, with its benches, sidecanyons, and riverside groves, supports a variety of large and small mammals and birds. Beaver

The White River south of Vernal, Utah offers a fine 3-day family canoe trip. Waterfowl favor this scenic desert river.

Ray Wheeler

and deer are abundant. Geese nest along the river, and waterfowl are common depending on the season. Raptors, including golden eagles, are plentiful; the endangered peregrine falcon has been sighted in the area. Songbirds frequent the cottonwood groves and streamside thickets. Wild horses and, occasionally, elk have been sighted.

Boundary Killed Study

In 1979, the BLM inventoried about 27,000 acres along the White River for potential inclusion in a wilderness study area. The agency rejected this area from further study because of significant resource conflicts and "the many roads which approach the river." It is no wonder that the area, as circumscribed by BLM staffers, was rejected. The generous boundaries of the study proposal encompassed several roads, well sites, and pipelines, and brushed up against some gilsonite veins (an asphalt mineral used in paints and inks).

The Utah Wilderness Coalition Proposal

The boundary created by the BLM at the time was far too ambitious, and anyone who didn't know better would swear that the boundary lines had been drawn with an eye to *introducing* resource conflicts. The Uintah Mountain Club, a local recreational club based in Vernal, drew its own boundaries to exclude the significant conflicts yet maintain the integrity of the White River canyon. The Utah Wilderness Coalition adopts the Uintah Mountain Club's proposal, which includes 9,700 acres of BLM lands. The proposal calls for the agency to acquire state-owned inholdings, which would raise the total size of the proposal to about 10,600 acres and would protect three more miles of the wilderness river, including some of the most beautiful stretches of the canyon. Oil and gas production surrounds the area, but existing production would not be affected by protecting this river corridor as wilderness. Four surface-occupancy leases occur within the area on flat points above the river; one is currently proposed for development. We recommend that the BLM pursue exchanges, purchases, or other means of acquiring these leases so as to protect the river corridor. There are no significant impacts in the proposed wilderness. Old, currently unused vehicle routes would be closed to protect wildlife and backcountry recreational values. The vehicular approach to the river is via a sandy wash, and the road in Atchees Wash ends less than one mile from the river. Saddletree Draw is a dry wash until two and a half miles from the river, where a maintained road begins. In these sandy washes, all signs of vehicular travel are easily erased by the elements.

Currently, Uintah County has no designated wilderness. Growing support for designation in the county, and the absence of significant resource conflicts, make this overlooked area a high priority for wilderness designation.

Will Durant
Uintah Mountain Club

THE GREATER DINOSAUR WILDERNESS

Summary

The area including and surrounding Dinosaur National Monument is the northernmost extent of the Colorado Plateau region. At Echo Park, inside the national monument, two of the great rivers of the West come together, the Green and the Yampa. The canyons of these rivers and a mile or two on either side are protected within the monument. Many tens of thousands of acres of equally spectacular uplands, plateaus, canyons, and mountains encircle Dinosaur and are administered by the BLM. These unprotected wild lands encompass critical viewsheds of the monument or the upstream segments of the monument's watersheds.

The Greater Dinosaur wilderness consists of six units totalling more than 120,000 acres (of which 21,100 acres lie in Utah). When combined with recommended National Park Service wilderness within the national monument, upwards of 300,000 acres of *de facto* wilderness can be found in this outpost of the Colorado Plateau. The Greater Dinosaur wilderness includes four BLM WSAs—Bull Canyon, Cold Springs Mountain, Daniels Canyon, and Diamond Breaks—and two other roadless areas, Moonshine Draw and Wild Mountain. Daniels Canyon and Moonshine Draw are entirely within Utah; the rest straddle the Utah-Colorado border and were studied by the Colorado State Office of the BLM.

Dinosaur's Viewshed

The boundaries of Dinosaur National Monument were drawn to include only the primary features of the Green and Yampa River canyons. As a result, many of the spectacular vistas from the monument's many scenic overlooks are outside of the monument, on unprotected BLM roadless lands. For example, the skyline to the north from the Harpers Corner and Echo Park overlooks is dominated by Wild Mountain, a proposed wilderness on the monument's north boundary. The Park Service picnic area and scenic viewpoint at Plug Hat Rock, north of Dinosaur, Colorado, overlooks the Bull Canyon WSA. Beyond the Josie Morris Cabin at the end of the Cub Creek road, Daniels Canyon continues up onto the Yampa Plateau.

Approaching the northernmost end of the monument, at the Gates of Lodore, one confronts a rugged, dark mountain range that rises high above the Browns Park plain. These are the mountains of Diamond Breaks. They fill the western horizon from the Zenobia Peak lookout within the monument, and the low shield of Cold Springs Mountain rises to the north across Browns Park.

The BLM wild lands that ring the monument, blanketing every approach and filling every vista, are crucial to the experience of the visitors to Dinosaur. They create the wild context for Dinosaur and are magnificent wildernesses in their own right.

IN BRIEF

Index Map: Area No. 57

Highlights: The boundaries of Dinosaur National Monument exclude BLM wild lands that offer scenic vistas, good habitat for big game, and many ridges and canyons to explore. Wilderness protection is needed to protect these BLM lands in their own right, as well as protect the monument's larger ecosystem.

Maps: USGS 1:100,000 Vernal, Dutch John

Area of wilderness proposals in acres (Utah):

Unit	UWC	BLM
Bull Canyon	500	0
Daniels Canyon	5,300	0
Diamond Breaks	7,800	2,700
Moonshine Draw	3,500	0
Cold Springs Mtn.	3,400	3,400
Wild Mountain	600	0
TOTAL	21,100	3,400

Adjacent wild lands: Dinosaur National Monument; Colorado BLM

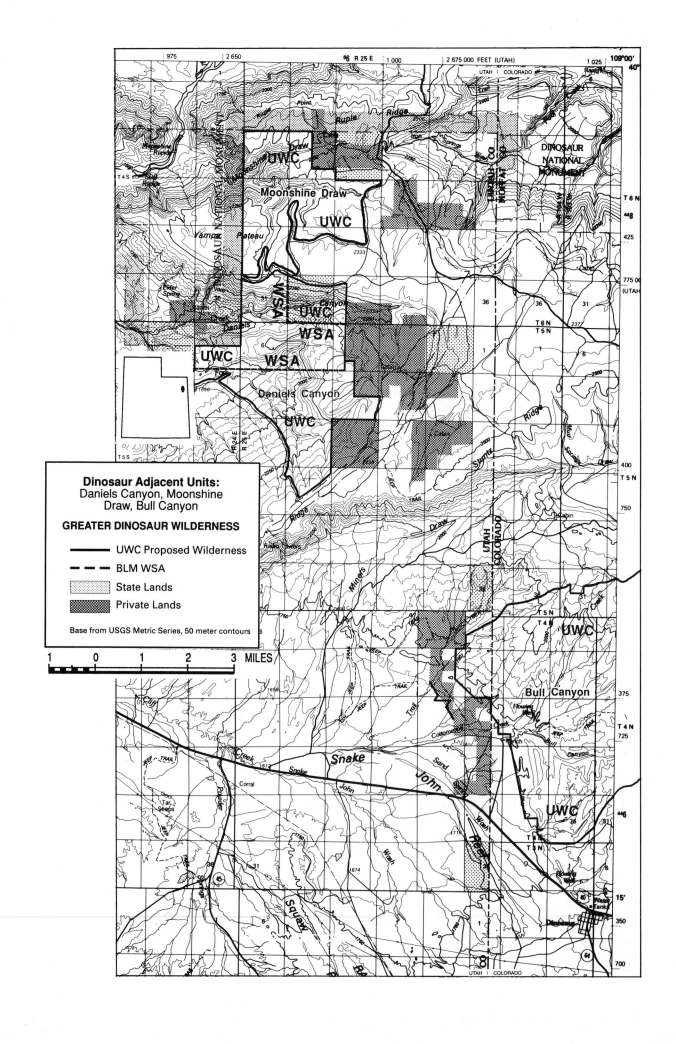

Dinosaur Adjacent Units:
Daniels Canyon, Moonshine
Draw, Bull Canyon

GREATER DINOSAUR WILDERNESS

——— UWC Proposed Wilderness

– – – BLM WSA

State Lands

Private Lands

Base from USGS Metric Series, 50 meter contours

Where the Deer and the Antelope Play

Whereas the wilderness within Dinosaur National Monument is rugged terrain with great vertical relief, the proposed BLM wildernesses such as Diamond Breaks and Cold Springs Mountain contain broad valleys more suitable for big game habitat. Much of Diamond Breaks is considered critical winter range for both deer and elk, while Beaver Creek within Cold Springs is home to 30 reintroduced bighorn sheep. The two areas have deer population densities ranging from 6 to 12 deer per square mile. In recognition of the outstanding big game hunting opportunities present, the Colorado Division of Wildlife intends to manage Cold Springs Mountain for trophy-quality hunting by limiting access and restricting licenses.

The Utah Wilderness Coalition Proposal

We propose 21,100 acres of wilderness in Utah's portion of the six units composing the Greater Dinosaur wilderness. Three small units are contiguous with the Dinosaur National Monument boundary, as is the larger Diamond Breaks unit. Cold Springs Mountain and Bull Canyon offer protection for representative landscapes to the north and south of Dinosaur, respectively. All six units enhance the wilderness setting of Dinosaur National Monument by protecting either the highlands above the rugged canyons of the monument or prominent vistas from the monument. Most of these units lie at least partly within Colorado, and two lie mostly within Colorado; they are described here with emphasis on their Utah portions. Designation of the Greater Dinosaur wilderness units will ensure that the wild nature of flagship units of the National Park System, such as Dinosaur, is not lost amidst clutter and development on their boundaries.

Mark Pearson

DINOSAUR ADJACENT UNITS

[Daniels Canyon, Moonshine Draw, and Bull Canyon]

Highlights—These units lie on the southern boundary of Dinosaur National Monument. They offer spectacular sandstone canyons and scenic high plateaus with views of the Green River. Daniels Canyon may be reached from either an existing trailhead within Dinosaur National Monument at the Josie Morris Cabin or from the monument's Harpers Corner access road atop Blue Mountain. Moonshine Draw can be reached via several dirt roads leading west from the Harpers Corner access road, nearly opposite the Echo Park road turnoff, or along Ruple Ridge, also starting from the access road. Bull Canyon can be reached from the Park Service's Plug Hat Rock picnic area on the rim of the upper canyon.

Geology and landforms—Daniels Canyon has cut near-vertical walls through the massive Weber Sandstone, dropping between 900 and 1600 feet below the rim of the canyon. There are dramatic panoramic views from the highest points of the unit atop Blue Mountain. Moonshine Draw contains a high plateau and steep canyons with scenic vistas of the Green River before it reaches Split Mountain. Bull Canyon is intricately carved through the spectacular geologic formations found in the adjacent monument, such as green and purple Morrison shales and deep vermillion Triassic shale and sandstone.

Plant communities—The units are largely covered by sagebrush, mountain mahogany, and serviceberry intermixed with pinyon-juniper forest. There are small stands of ponderosa pine at the highest elevations of the Daniels Canyon unit on Blue Mountain. The canyon bottoms contain

Exploring a slickrock watercourse in Daniels Canyon.

Jim Catlin

patches of riparian habitat such as box elder and, in shady places, Douglas fir. The lower flats of the Bull Canyon unit are covered with sage, saltbush, greasewood, and grasses. Ancient stands of pinyon pine in the Bull Canyon unit have been studied by researchers at the University of Arizona, who have applied the results of tree-ring chronology to studies of climatic variability in North America.

Wildlife—Mule deer and mountain lions frequent the units. Nearly all of Bull Canyon is critical winter range for mule deer. Some sage grouse are found at the higher elevations. Golden and bald eagles as well as peregrine falcons have been sighted in the area.

Archeology and history—Daniels Canyon contains numerous rock-shelters, cliff dwellings, and storage pit ruins. There are 82 recorded archeological sites in the vicinity of the unit, most of which date to the Fremont period. The historic Josie Morris Ranch in Dinosaur National Monument is at the trailhead to Daniels Canyon. A documented campsite of the 1776 Dominguez-Escalante expedition is located in Bull Canyon as well as a segment of the proposed National Historic Trail following the expedition's route.

Recreation—An existing trail runs from the Josie Morris Ranch to the head of Daniels Canyon. Day hikes are possible throughout the length of the canyon. Bull Canyon's easy accessibility along the Dinosaur National Monument entrance road makes it ideal for day hikes, birdwatching, and photography. Horseback riding and deer and grouse hunting are common uses of all three units.

BLM recommendation—The BLM designated a small 2,545-acre WSA in Daniels Canyon and a 12,297-acre WSA in Bull Canyon. The Colorado BLM recommended Bull Canyon as suitable for wilderness, whereas the Utah BLM, which studied Daniels Canyon, recommended against wilderness designation for that unit. Moonshine Draw was not designated a WSA and was not studied. During the wilderness inventory for Daniels Canyon, the BLM failed to draw boundaries that included all natural areas and excluded impacted areas. The WSA boundary bisected slickrock canyons and striking badlands cliffs, following mining claims that had small, largely reclaimed impacts. The resulting small size of the Daniels Canyon WSA, plus state-owned inholdings and private lands, led the BLM to recommend against wilderness.

Coalition proposal—We propose a total of 9,300 acres of wilderness for these three units (Utah portion), with an additional 12,500 acres in Colorado. Our boundaries, unlike some of the BLM's, follow the edges of man-made impacts. In Bull Canyon, our proposal conforms to natural, easily identifiable topographic features such as hogbacks and creek beds. Only 500 acres of Bull Canyon fall within Utah. In Daniels Canyon we recommend a 5,300-acre wilderness with boundaries that follow the edges of man-made impacts. All of this unit lies within Utah. Our 3,500-acre Moonshine Draw unit, also located entirely within Utah, excludes impacts associated with livestock grazing such as corrals and fences. We recommend exchange of state lands to consolidate public ownership. The contiguity of these units to a much larger surrounding wilderness in Dinosaur National Monument gives them added significance.

WILD MOUNTAIN

Highlights—Wild Mountain straddles the Colorado-Utah state line on the western boundary of Dinosaur National Monument. Wild Mountain is the ridge that rises high above the Jones Hole National Fish Hatchery and dominates the view from the Harpers Corner overlook within the national monument. In the context of the larger Dinosaur area wilderness, this unit

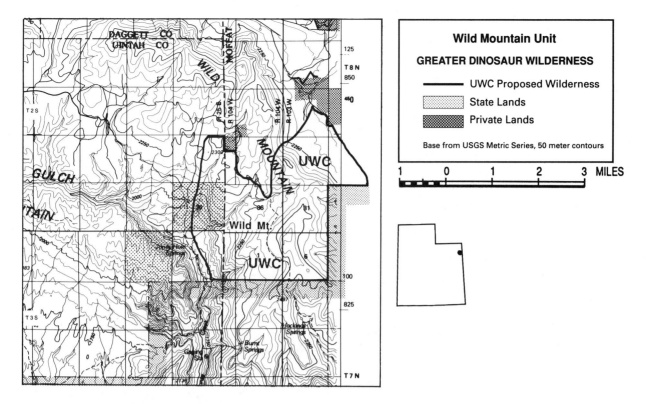

lies several miles south of Diamond Breaks. Any development or road construction on Wild Mountain, such as might occur given the BLM's support for oil and gas leasing of the area, would be highly visible to park visitors. The mountain is covered largely by grasses and sagebrush, with scattered stands of aspen along the base of its northern slopes. Deer and elk may be found here, and raptors grace the skies above. Our proposed boundary for Wild Mountain generally encompasses the BLM's roadless area as identified during the wilderness inventory and adjacent state lands. The unit covers about 5,700 acres, of which about 600 are in Utah. The Colorado BLM did not recommend the unit for wilderness designation.

DIAMOND BREAKS UNIT

Highlights—Diamond Breaks consists of the semiarid, dissected mountains on the western boundary of Dinosaur National Monument. The unit straddles the Colorado-Utah state line, with 7,800 acres located within Utah. The unit is adjacent to both the National Monument and to Browns Park National Wildlife Refuge, sharing a common boundary for over 20 miles. Diamond Breaks creates an extended, all-encompassing ecosystem when considered in conjunction with the canyons and floodplain of the Green River through Browns Park and Dinosaur National Monument, offering recreation ranging from whitewater boating deep within the canyons to rockclimbing and ridge hiking high above the canyon rims. The unit is easily accessible from Colorado Highway 318 as it traverses Browns Park National Wildlife Refuge. A wildlife refuge primitive campground along the Green River at the Swinging Bridge on the northern edge of Diamond Breaks provides an excellent starting point for hikes into the area.

Geology and landforms—Diamond Breaks gets its name from the breaks in Diamond Mountain carved by Hoy, Chokecherry, Davis, and other creeks as they drain into the Green River. Local lore has it that Diamond Mountain itself was named after the exploits of a shyster in the late 1800s who planted diamonds on the mountain and lured unsuspecting Eastern investors into parting with their money in a get-rich-quick diamond mining scheme. Of course, the con-man departed the region soon after, with

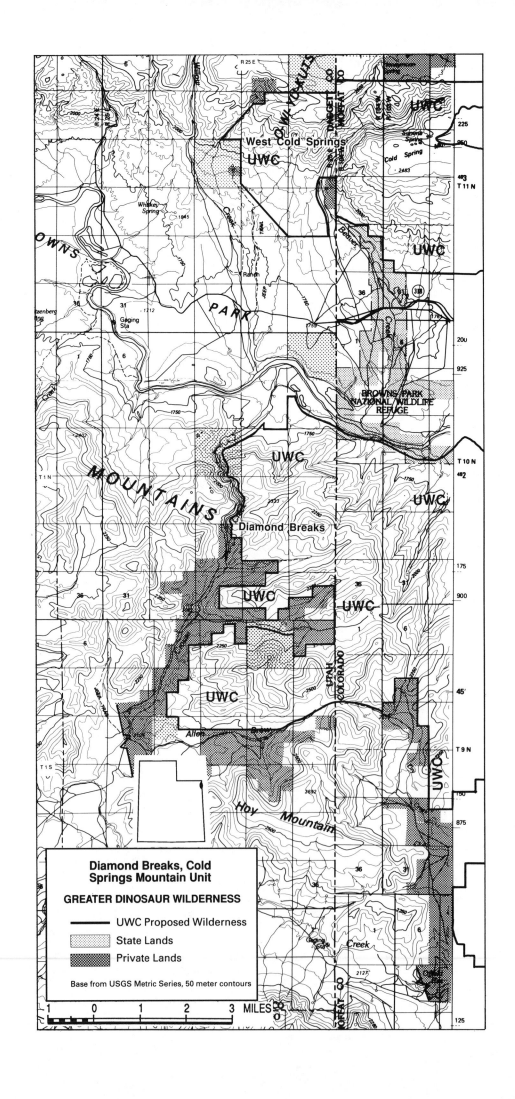

**Diamond Breaks, Cold
Springs Mountain Unit**

GREATER DINOSAUR WILDERNESS

——— UWC Proposed Wilderness

State Lands

Private Lands

Base from USGS Metric Series, 50 meter contours

1   0   1   2   3   MILES

money in hand and nary a diamond to be found on "Diamond Mountain." Diamond Breaks is distinctive for the variety of its topography. Ridges and peaks rise to 8,700 feet in abrupt contrast to the gentle plain of Brown's Park. The rugged mountains of Diamond Breaks are broken by open draws, complementing the Green River's mighty Canyon of Lodore in adjacent Dinosaur National Monument.

Plant communities—A majestic, gnarled ponderosa pine forest covers the southern edge of the area, growing out of bare rock in many places. The open draws and hillsides are a virtual rainbow of color in early spring as flowers of every shade burst forth among the sagebrush. Lovely stands of aspen also are found in the draws. The higher peaks and ridges are covered with pinyon and juniper.

Wildlife—The area is rich in wildlife such as mule deer, elk, black bear, and mountain lion. Diamond Breaks provides critical deer winter range and encompasses a major portion of the range for a herd of 250-300 elk. Antelope roam the lower valleys near the wildlife refuge.

Archeology and history—Diamond Breaks has a high potential for significant archeological finds. Granaries, petroglyphs, and widespread lithic scatters dating to the Fremont era have been recorded in the area. There are rumors of wickiups as well.

Recreation—Diamond Breaks provides a remote and rugged setting for outdoor activities, including hiking, hunting, and birding. Spectacular panoramic views are found from atop the ridges and peaks of Diamond Breaks, taking in the snow-capped peaks of the Uintas, Flat Tops, and Zirkel Range, the Green River plain, the Canyon of Lodore, and gentle Cold Springs Mountain.

BLM recommendation—The BLM has recommended 36,240 acres for wilderness designation (mostly in Colorado), an increase over its 35,380-acre WSA. The BLM proposes to add 1,500 acres on the north side of the unit in the vicinity of Chokecherry, Yellow Jacket, and Warren Draws. This addition adds low-elevation sagebrush plains along the breaks of Diamond Mountain, bringing the wilderness boundary up to the boundary of the National Wildlife Refuge. The agency recommends closure to ORV recreation use of one road along the river. Traditional use by livestock operators would be allowed to continue.

Coalition proposal—We propose wilderness designation for 7,800 acres within Utah. We include a major drainage between Allen and Marshall Draws that was left out of the BLM proposal. This 3.5-mile-long drainage consists of flower-covered meadows and dense thickets, surrounded with ridges capped by rock outcrops which afford unrestricted views of the three-state region. Douglas fir and aspen hug the northern slopes of the ridges, creating unexpected forest glens in the midst of this semi-arid region. Inclusion of this drainage would provide currently lacking easy access into Diamond Breaks from the west side.

COLD SPRINGS MOUNTAIN

Highlights—Cold Springs Mountain is located immediately north of Browns Park National Wildlife Refuge. Over 50,000 acres of wilderness lands (3,400 acres within Utah) straddle the state line along the east-west trending summit of Cold Springs Mountain. Cold Springs Mountain is directly across Browns Park from the Diamond Breaks WSA. The two areas together frame one of the region's most remote and undeveloped fertile valleys. Cold Springs Mountain is easily accessible from Colorado Highway 318 as it traverses Browns Park National Wildlife Refuge. The Matt Trail and the Beaver Creek drainage provide routes to the top of the mountain. Alternatively, dirt roads turning west off of Highway 430 through Irish Canyon can be used to reach the top of the mountain.

Geology and landforms—Cold Springs Mountain encompasses the southern flank of the 8,200-foot-high O-wi-yu-kuts Plateau as it drops to 5,800 feet in Brown's Park along the Green River. The mountain is the eastern extension of the Unita Mountain uplift. Numerous springs surface on top of the mountain amidst glades of aspen, giving the mountain its name. Multiple drainages and canyons cut through the distinctive horizontally bedded pink and dark red Precambrian rocks of Cold Springs Mountain.

Plant communities—The northern, or higher, side of Cold Springs Mountain has rolling grass and sagebrush covered hills with intermittent stands of pinyon-juniper and aspen.

Wildlife—The many springs in the unit support large numbers of elk, deer, and antelope. The unit harbors one of the largest mountain lion populations in the region and an array of smaller creatures including bobcats, foxes, golden eagles, peregrine falcons, grouse, and prairie chickens. Beaver Creek, a permanent stream that supports a population of threatened cutthroat trout, has cut a dramatic canyon in the western end of the mountain, creating a rich riparian habitat. A herd of 30 reintroduced bighorn sheep thrive along Beaver Creek. Just east of the Matt Trail are Big Joe and Little Joe Basins, open parks in the forest that support both wildlife and cattle grazing. Both parks have been identified as important big game winter range.

Archeology and history—Evidence of prehistoric cultures is scattered throughout the unit. Although this cultural resource has never been inventoried, there have been a number of significant amateur finds. The Matt Trail climbs from the valley floor, through dense pinyon-juniper forest, to the mountain crest. This trail traces its origins to the colorful days when cattle barons and rustlers dominated the region and is named after Matt Rash, a principal figure in those times.

Recreation—Cold Springs Mountain is understandably very popular with big game hunters given its abundant herds of deer, elk, and antelope. The Colorado Division of Wildlife owns a large amount of land on the crest of the mountain, along the boundary of the proposed wilderness. Hunting is a boon to the regional economy of northwest Colorado and northeast Utah.

BLM recommendation—The BLM has proposed that none of its 17,682-acre WSA be designated wilderness.

Coalition proposal—Our proposal covers 3,400 acres in Utah (the western part of the mountain). We add 700 acres to the WSA in the upper reaches of Beaver Creek canyon along the state line, including the steep upper canyon walls and valuable riparian habitat they enclose. This creates a logical topographic boundary as opposed to the WSA's boundary along section lines.

APPENDICES

ABBREVIATIONS USED IN TEXT

ACEC	Area of Critical Environmental Concern
BLM	Bureau of Land Management
DEIS	Draft environmental impact statement
EIS	Environmental impact statement
FEIS	Final environmental impact statement
FERC	Federal Energy Regulatory Commission
FLPMA	Federal Land Policy and Management Act of 1976
FWS	U.S. Fish and Wildlife Service
IBLA	Interior Board of Land Appeals
IPP	Intermountain Power Project
NEPA	National Environmental Policy Act
NPS	National Park Service
NRA	National Recreation Area
ORV	Off-road vehicle
RMP	Resource management plan
UDWR	Utah Division of Wildlife Resources
USFS	U.S. Forest Service
USGS	U.S. Geological Survey
UWC	Utah Wilderness Coalition
WSA	Wilderness study area

GLOSSARY

Candidate species—Under review for possible listing as threatened or endangered species under the Endangered Species Act.

Cherrystem—A wilderness boundary feature that excludes a narrow road or other human intrusion from an area.

Crucial or critical habitat—Areas needed by wildlife, perhaps during winter or reproductive seasons, to sustain a population.

Endangered species—In danger of extinction due to very low or declining numbers.

Endemic—Found nowhere else.

Kiva—A ceremonial chamber, typically a circular stone pit, found in some ancient Anasazi villages.

Lithic scatter—Site where prehistoric humans chipped or flaked stone projectiles or other tools.

National Register of Historic Places—A list of historical or archeological sites protected by federal law.

Petroglyph—Prehistoric rock art chipped into stone.

Pictograph—Prehistoric rock art created with natural pigments.

Sensitive species—Occurring in limited areas or numbers due to restricted habitat.

Threatened species—Likely to become endangered.

Unit—A subdivision of a Utah Wilderness Coalition proposed wilderness area. Generally separated by narrow road corridors from nearby units sharing similar topographical and ecological features.

Way or vehicle way—A path worn in the land by the passage of vehicles, without bulldozing or other improvement.

Wilderness Area—An area of federal land designated by the Congress under the Wilderness Act of 1964 for preservation of its natural qualities.

Wilderness area (proposed)—The Utah Wilderness Coalition's proposal for Congressional designation. Subdivided, in some cases, into individual wilderness units demarcated by roads or other development.

Wilderness inventory—The BLM's survey of potential wilderness areas required under FLPMA. The inventory was composed of an initial phase completed in August 1979 and an intensive phase completed in November, 1980. Led to selection of 83 wilderness study areas (WSAs).

Wilderness study area (WSA)—BLM land selected by the agency for detailed study of its potential for Congressional designation as a Wilderness Area and meant to be managed so as to protect its wilderness values until the Congress acts.

ACKNOWLEDGMENTS

Many people contributed to the preparation of this book, not all of whom are acknowledged with a byline or photo credit. Preparation of the maps, photographs, and individual unit descriptions involved painstaking research and effort on the part of the following individuals:

VOLUNTEERS

Text preparation and research

Charles Bagley	Miki Magyar
Joe Breddan	Mark McAllister
Bruce Chesler	Jean McIntyre
Nancy Christensen	Alan McKnight
Lance Christie	Julie McMahon
Valerie Cohen	Sally Miller
Scott DeLong	Steve Montgomery
Tom Fleishner	Tina Nielsen
Betsy Gordon	Tom Noble
John Gould	Christine Osborne
Carol Hall	Mark Pearson
Dave Hamilton	Janet Ross
Steve Harris	Michael Salamacha
Matthew Haun	Doug Stark
Suzanne Hecker	Deborah Threedy
Jan Holt	John Wahl
Jesse Johnston	Linda Wilburn
Laura Lockhart	Kate West

Area Maps

Eldon Byland	Rudy Lukez
Jim Catlin	Amy O'Connor
Bruce Gillars	Paul Rogers
Jim Highsmith	David Stoker
Susan Krushat	

Unit Maps
Jim Catlin
Cheryl Grantham

Text Editing
Pat Briggs
Ruth Frear
Jane Sheffield

Photo lab
Bob Bauer
David Stoker
Fred Wright

Photo library
Frandee and Dale Johnson

STAFF

Fran Crofts, Southern Utah Wilderness Alliance (SUWA)—research
Kris Dangerfield, SUWA—writing
Rodney Greeno, SUWA—research, writing, editing
Scott Groene, SUWA—writing
Darrell Knuffke, The Wilderness Society (TWS)—policy direction,
   editing, research
Lissa Leege, SUWA—research, writing, editing
Jane Leeson, TWS—coordination
Lawson LeGate, Sierra Club—writing
Mike Medberry, TWS—field research and writing
Amy O'Connor, SUWA—text coordination

CONSULTANTS

Fred Swanson, editing, writing, and layout
Ray Wheeler, research, writing, area maps
Brian Haslam, Steve Thomas, Patti Guest, and DIGIT lab, cartography

SPECIAL THANKS

Autodesk, Inc., donation of AutoCAD mapping software
Jim Catlin, use of computer and home office; field research
Dale and Frandee Johnson and Project Lighthawk, overflights
Amar Hanspal of Autodesk, Inc., for help with area maps
Shirley Hopkins of Whipple/White, typesetting help (maps and text)
Rudy Lukez, use of computer and home office; computer consulting
Merrill Ridd, use of Utah relief map
WordPerfect Corporation, donation of word processing software

UWC AREAS AND UNITS WITH THEIR BLM EQUIVALENTS

UWC Name	BLM Name	BLM Inventory No.	Other Names
Little Goose Creek	Little Goose Creek #1	UT-020-001/ NV-010-161/ID-22-1	
Newfoundland Mountains	Newfoundland Mountains	UT-020-037	
Silver Island Mountains	Silver Island Mountains	UT-020-040B/C	
Cedar Mountains	Cedar Mountains*	UT-020-094	
Stansbury Mountains			
North Stansbury	North Stansbury Mtns*	UT-020-089	
Big Hollow	Big Hollow	UT-020-105	
Deep Creek Mountains	Deep Creek Mountains*	UT-020-060/050-020	
Fish Springs Range	Fish Springs Range*	UT-050-127	
Dugway Mountains	Dugway Mountains/Range	UT-020-129	
Rockwell	Rockwell	UT-050-186	Rockwell-Little Sahara (UWC)
House Range			
Swasey Mountain	Swasey Mountain*	UT-050-061	
Notch Peak	Notch Peak*	UT-050-078	
Howell Peak	Howell Peak*	UT-050-077	
Conger Mountain	Conger Mountain*	UT-050-035	
King Top	King Top*	UT-050-070	
Wah Wah Mountains			
North Wah Wahs	Wah Wah Mountains*	UT-050-073	Wah Wah Mtns. North (UWC)
Central Wah Wahs	Central Wah Wah Range	UT-040-204B	Wah Wah Mtns. South (UWC)
Granite Peak	Granite Peak	UT-040-166	
White Rock Range	White Rock Range*	UT-040-216/ NV-040-202	
Cougar Canyon-Docs Pass	Cougar Canyon*	UT-040-123/ NV-050-166	
	Doc's Pass	UT-040-124	
Beaver Dam Slopes			
Joshua Tree	Joshua Tree	Instant Study Area	
Beaver Dam Wash	No name	UT-040-059/ NV-050-18 AZ-010-127	
Red Mountain	Red Mountain*	UT-040-132	
Cottonwood Canyon	Cottonwood Canyon*	UT-040-046	
Greater Zion			
Canaan Mountain	Canaan Mountain*	UT-040-143	
Parunuweap Canyon	Parunuweap Canyon*	UT-040-230	
The Watchman	The Watchman*	UT-040-149	
North Fork Virgin River	North Fork Virgin River*	UT-040-150	
Orderville Canyon	Orderville Canyon/Gulch*	UT-040-145	
Deep Creek	Deep Creek*	UT-040-146	
Goose Creek	Goose Creek Canyon*	UT-040-176	
Red Butte	Red Butte*	UT-040-147	
LaVerkin Creek Canyon	LaVerkin Creek Canyon*	UT-040-153	
Spring Creek Canyon	Spring Creek Canyon*	UT-040-148	Spring Cyn.,Quannarah (BLM)
Taylor Creek Canyon	Taylor Creek Canyon*	UT-040-154	
Beartrap Canyon	Beartrap Canyon*	UT-040-177	
Black Ridge	Black Ridge-LaVerkin Cr	UT-040-041B/C	
Moquith Mountain	Moquith Mountain*	UT-040-217	

UWC Name	BLM Name	BLM Inventory No.	Other Names
Upper Kanab Creek	Upper Kanab Creek	UT-040-255	
Grand Staircase			
Paria-Hackberry	Paria-Hackberry*	UT-040-247	
Squaw and Willis Creek	Squaw Creek	UT-040-222	
	No name	UT-040-236	
East of Bryce	East of Bryce	UT-040-266	
Box Canyon	Bulldog Canyon	UT-040-267	
The Blues	The Blues*	UT-040-265/268	
Mud Spring Canyon	Mud Spring Canyon*	UT-040-077	
The Cockscomb	The Cockscomb*	UT-040-275	
Kaiparowits Plateau			
Wahweap-Paradise Canyon	Wahweap*	UT-040-248	Wahweap & Death Ridge (UWC)
	Death Ridge*	UT-040-078	
	Coyote Creek	UT-040-249	
	No name	UT-040-250	
	No name	UT-040-254	
Nipple Bench	Nipple Bench	UT-040-253	
Warm Creek	Head of the Creeks	UT-040-256	
Squaw Cyn	No name	UT-040-258	Smoky Hollow (UWC)
Burning Hills	Burning Hills*	UT-040-079	
Fiftymile Mountain	Fifty Mile Mountain*	UT-040-080	
Fiftymile Bench	Fiftymile Bench	UT-040-086	
Cave Point	Cave Point	UT-040-090	
Carcass Canyon	Carcass Canyon*	UT-040-076	
Horse Spring Canyon	Horse Spring Canyon	UT-040-075	
Escalante Canyons			
North Escalante Canyons	N. Esca. Cyns/The Gulch*	Instant Study Area	
Little Egypt	Allen Dump	UT-040-081	
Scorpion	Scorpion*	UT-040-082	
Hurricane Wash	Escalante Cyns Tract 5*	Instant Study Area	
Fortymile Gulch	Dance Hall Rock	UT-040-085	
Phipps-Death Hollow	Phipps-Death Hollow*	Instant Study Area	
Steep Creek	Steep Creek*	UT-040-061	
Lampstand	No name	UT-040-060	
Studhorse Peaks	White Canyon	UT-040-069	White Canyon (UWC)
Colt Mesa	Colt Mesa	UT-040-074	
Long Canyon	Long Canyon	UT-050-253	
Notom Bench	Notom Bench	UT-050-257	
Dogwater Creek	No name	UT-050-257B	
Fremont Gorge	Fremont Gorge*	UT-050-221	
Henry Mountains			
Mt. Ellen-Blue Hills	Mt. Ellen-Blue Hills*	UT-050-238	Blue Hills-Mt. Ellen (UWC, BLM)
Bull Mountain	Bull Mountain*	UT-050-242	
Ragged Mountain	Ragged Mountain	UT-050-244	
Mt. Pennell	Mt. Pennell*	UT-050-248	
Bullfrog Creek	No name	UT-050-252	
Mt. Hillers	Mt. Hillers*	UT-050-249	
Dirty Devil			
Dirty Devil-French Spring	Dirty Devil*	UT-050-236A	
	French Spring-Happy Cyn*	UT-050-236B	
Fiddler Butte	Fiddler Butte*	UT-050-241A/B	
White Canyon			
Cheesebox Canyon	Cheesebox Canyon*	UT-060-191	Cheese Box & Hideout Cyn. (BLM)
	Burch and Deer Canyon	UT-060-241	
Harmony Flat	Harmony Flat	UT-060-194	
Gravel Canyon	Long and Gravel Canyons	UT-060-179	Gravel and Long Canyon (UWC)
Fortknocker Canyon	Fort Knocker	UT-060-178	

UWC Name	BLM Name	BLM Inventory No.	Other Names
Glen Canyon			
Mancos Mesa	Mancos Mesa*	UT-060-181	
Little Rockies	Little Rockies*	UT-050-247	
San Juan-Anasazi			
Nokai Dome	Lake Canyon	UT-060-183	
	No name (3 areas)	UT-060-184, 185, 186	
Grand Gulch	Grand Gulch*	Instant Study Area	
	Grand Flat	UT-060-187	
	Pine Canyon*	UT-060-188	
	Mormon Flat	UT-060-195	
	Bullet Canyon*	UT-060-196	
	Sheiks Cyn*	UT-060-224	Sheiks Flat (BLM)
	Slickhorn Canyon*	UT-060-197	
	John's Canyon	UT-060-198	
Fish and Owl Creek Cyns	Fish Creek Canyon*	UT-060-204	
Road Canyon	Road Canyon*	UT-060-201	
San Juan River	Sugar Loaf	UT-060-203	Sugarloaf (UWC)
Comb Ridge	Comb Ridge	UT-060-208	
Arch and Mule Canyons	Mule Canyon*	UT-060-205B	
	Arch Canyon	UT-060-205A	
Squaw-Cross Canyons			
Squaw-Papoose Canyons	Squaw and Papoose Canyon*	UT-060-227	
		CO-030-265A	
Cross Canyon	Cross Canyon*	UT-060-229	
		CO-030-265	
Dark Canyon			
Dark Canyon	Dark Canyon*	Instant Study Area	
	Middle Point*	UT-060-175	
	Sweet Alice Canyon	UT-060-171	
	Fable Valley Plateau	UT-060-173	
	No name (3 areas)	UT-060-174, 176, 242	
	Lower Horse Flats	UT-060-177	
Sheep Canyon	No name	UT-060-243	
Canyonlands Basin			
Shafer Canyon	Dead Horse Point	UT-060-086	
Gooseneck	North Goose Neck	UT-060-087	
	South Goose Neck	UT-060-088	
Indian Creek	Indian Creek*	UT-060-164	Lockhart Basin (BLM)
Harts Point	No name	UT-060-162	
Bridger Jack Mesa	Bridger Jack Mesa*	UT-060-167	Sixshooter Peaks (UWC)
	North Sixshooter Peak	UT-060-165	
	Little Bridger Jack	UT-060-166	
Butler Wash	Butler Wash*	UT-060-169	Ruin Park (BLM)
Behind the Rocks			
Goldbar Canyon	Gold Bar Canyon	UT-060-089	
Behind the Rocks	Behind the Rocks*	UT-060-140A/B	
Hunters Canyon	Behind the Rocks West	UT-060-141	
Hatch Wash	Hatch Point	UT-060-143	
La Sal Canyons			
Mill Creek	Mill Creek Canyon*	UT-060-139A	
Negro Bill Canyon	Negro Bill Canyon*	UT-060-138	
Mary Jane Canyon	Mary Jane Canyon	UT-060-137	
Fisher Towers	Fisher Towers	UT-060-136	
Sewemup Mesa	Sewemup Mesa*	Colorado	
Beaver Creek	No name	UT-060-123	Lower Dolores (UWC)
Granite Creek	Granite Creek	UT-060-122/CO-070-132A	
Westwater Canyon			
Westwater Canyon	Westwater Canyon*	UT-060-118	Star-Marble Cyn. (BLM)
Black Ridge Canyons	Black Ridge Canyons West*	UT-060-116/117	Wrigley Mesa/Jones Cyn. (BLM)
		CO-070-113A	

UWC Name	BLM Name	BLM Inventory No.	Other Names
Arches-Lost Spring Canyon	Lost Spring Canyon*	UT-060-131A/B	
	Dome Plateau	UT-060-132	
Labyrinth Canyon			
Labyrinth Canyon	Horseshoe Canyon (North)*	UT-060-045/050-237A	
	No name (2 areas)	UT-060-080, 081	
	Hell Roaring Canyon	UT-060-082	
Upper Horseshoe Canyon	Horseshoe Canyon (South)*	UT-050-237	
San Rafael Swell			
Sids Mountain	Sids Mountain*	UT-060-023	
Mexican Mountain	Mexican Mountain*	UT-060-054	
San Rafael Reef	San Rafael Reef*	UT-060-029A	
	East of San Rafael Reef	UT-060-029B	
Wild Horse Mesa	No name	UT-050-235	
Muddy Creek	Muddy Creek*	UT-060-007	
	Crack Canyon*	UT-060-028A	
	Cistern Canyon	UT-060-028B	
	Chute Canyon	UT-060-028C	
	No name	UT-050-233	
Hondu Country	North Big Ridge	UT-060-026	Tomsich Butte (UWC)
Devils Canyon	Devils Canyon*	UT-060-025	
Upper Muddy Creek	Upper Muddy Creek	UT-060-011	
Cedar Mountain	Cedar Mountain	UT-060-008	
Mussentuchit Badlands	Mussentuchit Badlands	UT-060-009B	
Red Desert	No name	UT-050-234	
Limestone Cliffs	No name	UT-050-225	
Jones Bench	Jones Bench	UT-050-256	
Book Cliffs-Desolation Canyon			
Desolation Canyon	Desolation Canyon*	UT-060-068A	Deso/Gray/Rattlesnake Cyns. (BLM)
	Jack Canyon*	UT-060-068C	
	Floy Canyon*	UT-060-068B	
	No name	UT-080-605	
	Nine-Mile Canyon	UT-080-612/060-069	
Turtle Canyon	Turtle Canyon*	UT-060-067	
Eastern Book Cliffs	Coal Canyon*	UT-060-100C2	Cottonwood Canyon (BLM)
	Spruce Canyon*	UT-060-100C1	Cottonwood Canyon (BLM)
	Flume Canyon*	UT-060-100B	Cottonwood Canyon (BLM)
White River	No name	UT-080-713	
Greater Dinosaur			
Daniels Canyon	Daniels Canyon*	UT-080-414	
Moonshine Draw	Moonshine Draw	UT-080-415	
Bull Canyon	Bull Canyon*	UT-080-419/CO-010-001	
Wild Mountain	Wild Mountain	UT-080-104	
Diamond Breaks	Diamond Breaks/Mtn*	UT-080-113/CO-010-214	
Cold Springs Mountain	West Cold Springs*	UT-080-103/CO-010-208	Cold Springs Mtn. (BLM)

Notes:

Asterisk (*) denotes WSA (Wilderness Study Area)
Letters at end of inventory numbers indicate subdivisions made by the BLM of its original inventory areas.
"Other Names" are those formerly used by the UWC or the BLM but no longer in use.

REFERENCES

[Note: frequent reference is made in this book to the seven-volume, 2,700-page draft environmental impact statement issued by the Utah State Office of the BLM in February 1986. To avoid long, cumbersome citations, the applicable volume number and WSA name are not given in text. Thus a citation "BLM, 1986, p. 12" under The Blues refers to The Blues WSA within volume III-A of the BLM's draft EIS.]

Abbey, Edward, 1968, Desert solitaire. New York, McGraw-Hill, 269 p.

Aikens, C. Melvin, and Madsen, David B., 1986, Prehistory of the eastern area. *In* Prehistory of the Eastern Great Basin, Washington, D.C., Smithsonian Institution.

Aitchison, Stewart, 1987, Utah wildlands. Salt Lake City, Utah Geographic Series, 112 p.

Austin, Mary, 1903, The land of little rain. Reprint by University of New Mexico Press, 1974, 171 p.

Baars, Donald L., and Stevenson, G., 1986, San Juan canyons, a river runners guide and natural history of the San Juan River canyons. Evergreen, Colo., Canon Publishers, 64 p.

Barnes, F.A., 1977, Canyon country hiking and natural history. Salt Lake City, Wasatch Publishers, 174 p.

_____1987, Canyon country arches and bridges, and other natural rock openings: an illustrated guide. Moab, Utah, Canyon Country Publications, 416 p.

_____1988, Canyonlands National Park, early history and first descriptions. Moab, Utah, Canyon Country Publications, 160 p.

Bauman, Joe, 1987, Stone house lands, the San Rafael Reef. Salt Lake City, University of Utah Press, 225 p.

Brereton, Thomas, and Dunaway, James, 1988, Exploring the backcountry of Zion National Park: off-trail routes. Springdale, Utah, Zion Natural History Association, 112 p.

Briggs, Kent, 1987, The high frontier—a discussion paper about creating a world-class tourism destination on the Colorado Plateau. Unpublished report prepared by the Center for the New West, Boulder, Colo., for the Western States Strategy Center, Denver, Colo., Nov. 6, 1987, 26 p.

Brower, David R. (ed.) and Porter, Eliot, 1963, The place no one knew: Glen Canyon on the Colorado. San Francisco, Sierra Club Books, 170 p. Reprinted in 1988 by Peregrine Smith Books, Layton, Utah.

Bureau of Land Management (BLM), 1976, Kaiparowits power project environmental impact statement. Denver, Colo., U.S. Department of the Interior, Government Printing Office.

_____1979a, BLM Utah initial wilderness inventory proposals, April 1979. Salt Lake City, Utah, U.S. Department of the Interior, 115 p.

_____1979b, BLM Utah final initial wilderness inventory, August 1979. Salt Lake City, Utah, U.S. Department of the Interior, 50 p.

_____1980a, Draft BLM intensive wilderness inventory, Utah, April 1980. Salt Lake City, U.S. Department of the Interior.

_____1980b, BLM intensive wilderness inventory, final decision on wilderness study areas, Utah, November 1980. Denver, Colo., U.S. Department of the Interior, 404 p.

_____1980c, Alton coal field unsuitability determination. Washington, D.C, U.S. Department of the Interior, Government Printing Office.

_____1980d, Allen-Warner Valley energy system final environmental impact statement, December 1980. Denver, Colo., U.S. Department of the Interior.

_____1983a, Grand Resource Area draft management plan and environmental impact statement, Moab District. U.S. Department of the Interior, 391 p.

_____1983b, Final Henry Mountains grazing environmental impact statement, Richfield District. U.S. Department of the Interior, 334 p.

_____1984, Utah combined hydrocarbon leasing regional final environmental impact statement. Denver, Colo., U.S. Department of the Interior.

_____1985, San Juan resource management plan, management situation analysis, September 1985. U.S. Department of the Interior, Bureau of Land Management, San Juan Resource Area and Moab District.

_____1985b, San Rafael Swell combined hydrocarbon lease conversion, draft environmental impact statement.

_____ 1986, Utah BLM statewide wilderness draft environmental impact statement, seven vols. (publication date listed as 1985, issued February, 1986).

_____ 1986a, San Juan resource management plan—draft resource management plan/environmental impact statement, May 1986. U.S. Department of the Interior, Bureau of Land Management, Moab District, 562 p.

_____1987a, Warm Springs resource area proposed management plan—final environmental impact statement. U.S. Department of the Interior, 162 p.

_____1987b, Proposed resource management plan and final EIS for the San Juan Resource Area, Moab District, Utah. U.S. Department of the Interior, September 1987, 2 vols.

_____1988a, Proposed Pony Express resource management plan and final environmental impact statement, September 1988. U.S. Department of the Interior, 144 p.

_____1988b, San Rafael draft resource management plan/environmental impact statement. U.S. Department of the Interior, 2 vols.

Castleton, Kenneth B., 1979, Petroglyphs and pictographs of Utah. Salt Lake City, Utah Museum of Natural History, 2 vols.

Dalton, Michael J., and Royer, Lawrence, 1972, Land use in the Utah canyon country: tourism, Interstate 70, and the San Rafael Swell. Logan, Utah, Utah State University, 133 p.

Deacon, J.E., 1988, The endangered woundfin and water management in the Virgin River, Utah, Arizona, Nevada. *Fisheries*, vol. 13, p. 18-24.

Doelling, H.H., and Graham, R.L., 1972. Southwestern Utah coal fields: Alton, Kaiparowits Plateau, and Kolob-Harmony. Salt Lake City, Utah Geological and Mineralogical Survey Monograph Series no. 1., 333 p.

Durrant, Stephen D., 1952, Mammals of Utah, taxonomy and distribution. Lawrence, Kansas, University of Kansas, 549 p.

Dutton, Clarence. E., 1880, Report on the geology of the High Plateaus of Utah, with atlas. U.S. Geographical and Geological Survey of the Rocky Mountain Region, Washington, D.C., Government Printing Office.

ERT, 1980, Kaiparowits coal development and transportation study, final report, August 1, 1980. Fort Collins, Colo., Environmental Research and Technology, Inc., 257 p.

Frost, Kent, 1971, My canyonlands; I had the freedom of it. New York, Abelard-Schuman, 160 p.

Geerlings, Paul F., 1980, Down the Grand Staircase. Salt Lake City, Utah, Grand Canyon Publications, Inc.

Gilbert, G. K., 1877, Report on the geology of the Henry Mountains. U.S. Geographical and Geological Survey of the Rocky Mountain Region, Washington, D.C., Government Printing Office, 160 p.

Goldwater, Barry M., 1941, Delightful journey down the Green and Colorado rivers. Tempe, Arizona Historical Foundation (1970 reprint).

Gottlieb, Robert, and Wiley, Peter, 1972, Empires in the sun: the rise of the new American West. New York, Putnam, 332 p.

Gregory, Herbert E., 1951, The geology and geography of the Paunsaugunt region. U.S. Geological Survey Professional Paper 226, Washington, D.C., Government Printing Office.

Gregory, Herbert E. and Moore, Raymond C., 1931, The Kaiparowits region, a geographic and geologic reconnaissance of parts of Utah and Arizona. U.S. Geological Survey Professional Paper 164, Washington, D.C., Government Printing Office, 161 p.

Grey, Zane, 1924, Wild Horse Mesa. Roslyn, N.Y., W.J. Black, 365 p. (1956 reprint).

Hall, Dave, 1982, The hiker's guide to Utah. Helena, Mont., Falcon Press, 212 p.

Hart, John, 1981, Hiking the Great Basin, the high desert country of California, Oregon, Nevada, and Utah. San Francisco, Sierra Club Books, 372 p.

Hedges, Steven, 1985, Utah birds—Beaver Dam Wash. *Journal of the Utah Ornithological Society*, vol. 1, no. 1, p. 5-10.

Hintze, Lehi, 1988, Geologic history of Utah. Provo, Utah, Brigham Young University Department of Geology.

Hunt, Charles B., Averitt, P., and Miller, R.L., 1953, Geology and geography of the Henry Mountains region, Utah. U.S. Geological Survey Professional Paper 228, 234 pp.

Huser, Verne, Canyon country paddles. Salt Lake City, Wasatch Publishers, 96 p.

Jennings, Jesse D., 1978, Prehistory of Utah and the eastern Great Basin. Salt Lake City, University of Utah Press, 263 p.

Kelsey, Michael R., 1983, Utah mountaineering guide and the best canyon hikes. Springville, Utah, Kelsey Publishing Co., 192 p.

_____1986a, Canyon hiking guide to the Colorado Plateau. Provo, Utah, Kelsey Publishing, 256 p.

_____1986b, Hiking Utah's San Rafael Swell, *with* A history of the San Rafael Swell by Dee Anne Finken. Springville, Utah, Kelsey Publishing Co., 144 p.

_____1987a Hiking and exploring Utah's Henry Mountains and Robbers Roost. Provo, Utah, Kelsey Publishing, 224 p.

_____1987b, Hiking and exploring the Paria River. Provo, Utah, Kelsey Publishing, 208 p.

Lambrechtse, Rudi, 1985, Hiking the Escalante. Salt Lake City, Wasatch Publishers, 192 p.

L'Amour, Louis, 1963, Dark Canyon. New York, Bantam Books, 133 p.

Lindsay, La Mar W., and Sargent, Kay, 1977, Prehistory of the Deep Creek Mountain area, western Utah. Division of State History, State of Utah: Antiquities section selected papers, vol. VI, no. 14.

Lister, Florence C., 1964, Kaiparowits Plateau and Glen Canyon prehistory, an interpretation based on ceramics. Salt Lake City, University of Utah Anthropological Papers No. 71.

Madsen, David B., 1979, 1986, volumes in Prehistory of the Eastern Great Basin, Washington D.C., Smithsonian Institution.

McClenahan, Owen, Utah's scenic San Rafael. Castle Dale, Utah, (author published), 128 p.

McMillan, Calvin, 1948, A taxonomic and ecological study of the flora of the Deep Creek Mountains of central western Utah. University of Utah, unpublished Masters thesis, 96 p.

Meinke, Robert J., 1975, A preliminary ecological and historical survey of North and South Caineville Mesas, Wayne County, Utah. Unpublished document, Richfield District, Bureau of Land Management, 127 p.

Millar, Rodney D. and Degiorgio, Joan, 1986, The Colorado Plateau: a proposed thematic World Heritage List nomination. Unpublished document submitted by the State of Utah, June 1986, to the Federal Interagency Panel for World Heritage, National Park Service.

National Park Service, 1979, Draft wild and scenic river study and draft environmental impact statement: Colorado and lower Dolores wild and scenic rivers. U.S. Department of the Interior, National Park Service, Denver Service Center, 292 p.

_____ and Bureau of Land Management, 1984, Draft environmental impact statement on conversion of oil and gas leases to combined hydrocarbon leases, Tar Sand Triangle, Utah, July 16, 1984. U.S. Department of the Interior, National Park Service, Rocky Mountain Regional Office, Denver, Colo., and BLM Utah State Office, Salt Lake City, Utah.

_____1982, The nationwide rivers inventory. Washington, D.C., U.S. Department of the Interior.

Newberry, J.S., 1876, Report of the exploring expedition from Santa Fe, New Mexico, to the junction of the Grand and Green rivers of the great Colorado of the West. Washington, D.C., Government Printing Office, 168 p.

Newmark, W. D., 1987, A land-bridge island perspective on mammalian extinctions in western North American parks. *Nature*, vol. 325, January 29, 1987, p. 430-2.

Nichols, Gary C., 1986, River runners' guide to Utah and adjacent areas. Salt Lake City, University of Utah Press, 168 p.

Pope, C. Arden III, and Jones, Jeffrey W., 1987, Non-market valuation of wilderness designation in Utah. Provo, Utah, Brigham Young University Agricultural Economics Department, May 1987, 36 p.

Powell, John Wesley, 1875, Report on the exploration of the Colorado River of the West and its tributaries. Washington, D.C., Government Printing Office.

_____1895. Canyons of the Colorado. Republished in 1961 as The exploration of the Colorado River and its canyons. New York, Dover, 400 p.

Ranck, Gary L., 1961, Mammals of the East Tavaputs Plateau. Salt Lake City, University of Utah Press.

Redford, Robert, 1978, The Outlaw Trail. New York, Grossett and Dunlap, 223 p.

Richardson, Elmo R., 1965, Federal park policy in Utah: the Escalante National Monument controversy of 1935-1940. *Utah State Historical Quarterly*, vol. 33, no. 2, p. 109-133.

Rogers, Garry, F., 1982, Then and now—a photographic history of vegetation changes in the central Great Basin Desert. Salt Lake City, University of Utah Press, 152 p.

Sargent, K.A., 1984, Environmental geologic studies of the Kaiparowits coal-basin area, Utah. U.S. Geological Survey Bulletin 1601, Washington, D.C., Government Printing Office.

Stegner, Wallace, 1980, The sound of mountain water. New York, E.P. Dutton, 286 p.

Stokes, William Lee, 1986, Geology of Utah. Salt Lake City, Utah Museum of Natural History and Utah Geological and Mineral Survey, Department of Natural Resources.

Tuhy, Joel S., and MacMahon, James A., 1988, Vegetation and relict communities of Glen Canyon National Recreation Area. Logan, Utah, Utah State University, final report for contract CX1200-6-B076.

U.S. Department of Agriculture, Forest Service, 1986, Land and resource management plan, Manti-La Sal National Forest. Moab, Utah.

_____1986, Dixie National Forest land and resource management plan. Cedar City, Utah.

U.S. Department of the Interior, Interior Board of Land Appeals, 1981, Sierra Club (IBLA 80-937) appeal decision. Arlington, Virg., Interior Board of Land Appeals, 7 p.

_____1982, Sierra Club (IBLA 80-308) appeal decision. Arlington, Virg., Interior Board of Land Appeals, vol. 61, p. 329-337.

_____1982b, Sierra Club, Utah Chapter (IBLA 81-655) appeal decision. Arlington, Virginia, Interior Board of Land Appeals, vol. 62, p. 263-73.

U.S. Department of the Interior, Heritage Conservation and Recreation Service, 1980, A survey of natural landmark areas of the north portion of the Colorado Plateau.

U.S. Geological Survey, 1989, Mineral resources of the Swasey Mountain and Howell Peak wilderness study areas, Millard County, Utah. USGS Bulletin 1749, ch. A.

Utah Department of Natural Resources, Division of Wildlife Resources, 1977, Wildlife inventory for Carbon and Emery counties and the Book Cliffs and Cisco Desert portions of Grand County. Prepared by the UDWR under contract no. YA-512-CT7-13 for the Bureau of Land Management, Moab, Utah.

Utah State Planning Board, 1936, Proposed Escalante National Monument. Preliminary report by Ray Benedict West to Governor Henry B. Blood.

Welsh, S. L., Rigby, J.K., and Hamblin, W.K., 1980, A survey of natural landmark areas of the north portion of the Colorado Plateau—biotic and geologic themes. Provo, Utah. Brigham Young University.

Wheeler, Ray, 1985, Last stand for the Colorado Plateau. *High Country News*, vol. 17, nos. 18-19.

Zwinger, Ann, 1978, Wind in the rock. New York, Harper and Row, 258 p.

_____1984, Run, river, run: a naturalist's journey down one of the great rivers of the American West. Tucson, Ariz., University of Arizona Press, 317 p.

INDEX TO WILDERNESS AREAS AND UNITS

Utah Wilderness

Sources: *BLM Wilderness Status Map, June 1986; Utah BLM Statewide Wilderness Environmental Impact Statement, Draft, BLM Proposed Action, 1986;* Utah Wilderness Coalition.

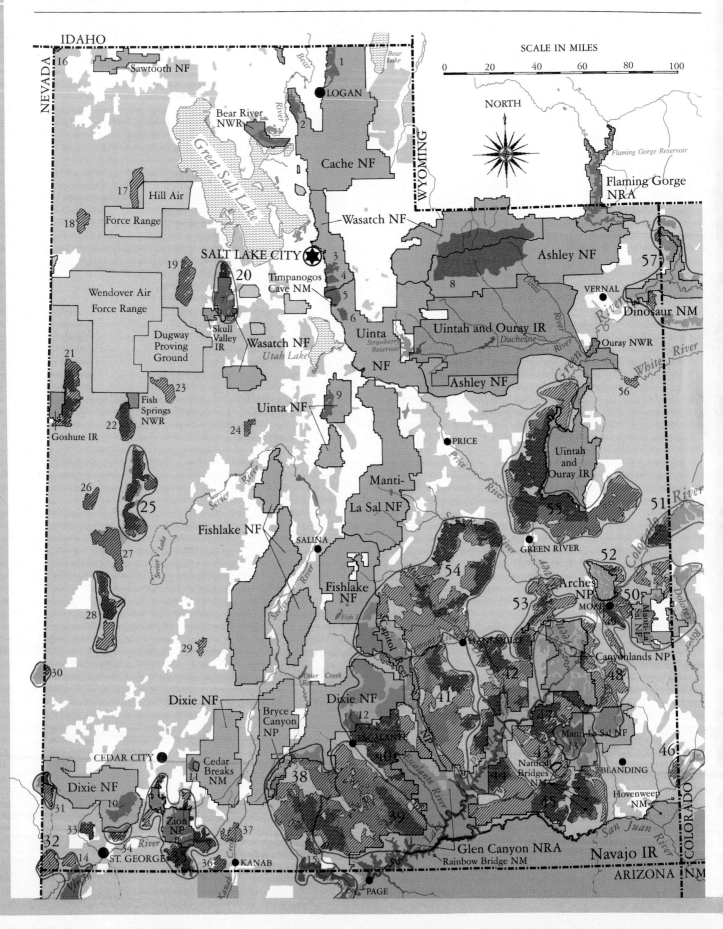